Return this book on or before the

Institute of Social and Religious Research

1000 CITY CHURCHES

H. PAUL DOUGLASS

1000
CITY CHURCHES

PHASES OF ADAPTATION TO
URBAN ENVIRONMENT

BY

H. PAUL DOUGLASS

NEW YORK
GEORGE H. DORAN COMPANY

1000 CITY CHURCHES
— B —
PRINTED IN THE UNITED STATES OF AMERICA

INTRODUCTION

THE PROJECT AND ITS OUTCOME

Origin and Development

In response to requests from religious leaders especially interested in the city church, two projects in the city field were provided for in the 1922 appropriations of the Committee on Social and Religious Surveys (now the Institute of Social and Religious Research). One was defined as the religious study of a representative industrial city of from 50,000 to 150,000 population; Springfield, Mass., being ultimately chosen for this purpose. It was urged by the Institute's advisors that concurrently with this survey of a particular city some more general study in the field of the city church be undertaken. The second project was therefore authorized under the loose designation, "City Church Handbook," with the assumption that it would be a source book of information about the work of many such churches, particularly in relation to their environments.

Those particularly interested in the second project held extended conferences on February 9th and 10th, 1922, at which time the character and objectives of the project were further sharpened and major decisions as to its conduct reached.[1] It was agreed (1) that the study should concern churches in cities of 100,000 population and over; (2) that it was statistically desirable to secure a 10 per cent. sample of such churches; and (3) that comparison with results of surveys of rural churches previously undertaken by the Institute might profitably be made.

Negatively, it was decided that the study should not be of any single type of city church nor of a single problem, and that, on the other hand, it should not undertake to cover the entire subject of the city church. Neither was it to be an attempt to give the working pastor direct help in meeting his immediate parish problems. Rather, it was to be a book of description and classification, a study of types of churches which should determine what kinds exist, characterizing them and pointing out their similarities and differences.

[1] Those present at these conferences were Rev. Thomas Burgess, Secretary for work among foreign-born Americans, Department of Missions, Protestant Episcopal Church; Rev. Ralph E. Diffendorfer, D.D., Methodist Episcopal Church; Mr. Kenneth Gould, American Hygiene Association; Rev. George Wales King, D.D., Pastor, Markham Memorial Church, St. Louis; Rev. William P. Shriver, D.D., Director, City and Immigrant work, Presbyterian Board of Home Missions, and Prof. Arthur L. Swift, Union Theological Seminary, together with Galen M. Fisher, Executive Secretary, and representatives of the staff of the Institute.

In reaching this decision, it was assumed that the study was the first of a series, and that the resulting book would "furnish the basis for the volumes which are to follow." The discussion repeatedly characterized it as a "first book." As such alone should it be judged.

The discussion of the conference left unsettled the question of whether ready-made categories for classifying churches already existed or whether they would have to emerge from statistical processes. It also failed to determine the fundamental issue: namely, what philosophy of the church and its functions should be assumed and what standards of judgment applied.

PHASES OF THE STUDY

The project, as thus initiated and partially defined, was then turned over to the survey staff for execution. In its hands, and partially incident to change in personnel, it underwent further significant developments. In its earlier phase it sought primarily to secure information from churches recommended by and usually approached through denominational departments dealing with city churches, by means of brief schedules describing the church and its community. A predetermined classification of churches in current use by these agencies was assumed to be valid and to constitute a proper basis for sorting into groups, the characteristics of which were then to be determined statistically.

This process was later modified and supplemented for the following reasons: (1) As time elapsed the number of schedules returned was not nearly sufficient to constitute a reasonable and convenient statistical sample. (2) It came to be questioned whether the churches recommended by the denominational departments were broadly representative. A strong bias was apparent in favor of the type of church in which a given department was particularly interested and with which it was officially concerned. Consequently, a new method of selection seemed desirable in order to assure a more genuinely cross-sectional view of the city church. (3) The denominational departments were found not to agree fully upon the classifications to be used, while the churches sometimes found it impossible to classify themselves under the categories offered. These facts rendered some of the resulting material statistically noncomparable.

In the second phase of the study, efforts were made to avoid these difficulties. The number of churches from which information was received was greatly increased in two ways: first, by the discovery of a considerable number of Interchurch World Movement surveys of city churches; and, secondly, by the employment of additional field workers who secured new schedules. The Interchurch surveys had attempted to cover all of the churches in their respective cities and thus tended strongly, so far as they went, to show complete cross-sections of the organizations under investigation. The field workers were forewarned against bias in their selection of churches for study. Finally, all predetermined classifications were abandoned and an attempt was made to find a principle of classification in statistical examinations of the actual data. Wide field contacts with churches and their leaders greatly illuminated the inquiry.

TIME AND WORKERS

The first phase of the field work occupied the spring, and the second the summer and early fall of 1922. During this entire period the time of the staff was divided between the present study and the Springfield survey.

From the early fall of 1922 to the beginning of 1925 the interpretative phase has been under way, involving the preparation of statistics and the writing and editing of the present manuscript. During this period, however, other projects have had the major share of time and attention from those concerned.

From the beginning of the project to the late summer of 1922, Miss Merle Higley, acting director of the then city survey department of the Committee on Social and Religious Surveys, had active executive responsibility, with H. Paul Douglass as Field Director. The major part of the field work was carried on by the Field Director, with the assistance of Prof. W. L. Bailey, Northwestern University, Evanston, Ill.; Rev. Victor G. Flinn, New York City, and Miss Helena M. Dickinson of the Institute staff.[2] Miss Dickinson was also statistician of the project in its interpretative phase. The principal responsibility for handling and interpreting material and for the preparation of manuscript was entrusted to the Field Director, with the collaboration of Prof. W. L. Bailey especially with respect to the environmental classification of churches and the interpretation of the church in the metropolitan city.

The Data

The primary data for this study are schedules of information for 1,044 churches in cities having 100,000 population or more.[3]

2 The number of cities visited and schedules secured by the field work assistants was as follows: Prof. Bailey, 6 cities, 159 schedules; Mr. Flinn, 8 cities, 96 schedules; Miss Dickinson, 3 cities, 56 schedules.

3 Twenty-seven schedules were admitted from cities with less than 100,000 population,

As already indicated, the schedules were obtained at different times and by different methods. Many already secured by the Interchurch World Movement in 1920 were known to exist here and there. A few of them had been gathered into the central office of the Movement, and at its lapse came into the custody of the Committee on Social and Religious Surveys. More had lodged in the files or storage rooms of city Church Federations or in the offices of local denominational executives. These had to be discovered and tabulated by field workers going from city to city. In a few cases there had been a hasty local interpretation and utilization of the survey results, but for the most part this material was pure salvage. One hundred eighty-one tabulable schedules were secured in this way from a much larger number that were examined. It is of some significance in the total history of the Interchurch World Movement that the present study could and did partially utilize much of these otherwise waste data.

NEW DATA

The major part of the basic data of the study was, however, new. It was secured during the spring and summer of 1922 by the two methods previously noted: namely, (1) through the city departments, or some analogous bureau, of most of the denominations whose administrative boards had such specialized agencies. These departments recommended the churches of their denomination for study and generally sent out the schedules to them. The denominations thus coöperating were the Baptist, Congregational, Methodist Episcopal, Methodist Episcopal South and Presbyterian. This coöperation yielded a total of 101 valuable schedules. (2) Six hundred sixteen schedules were secured by direct field investigation made specifically for the project.

SUMMARY OF SOURCES

Stated summarily, the sources of the primary data were as follows:

Old Schedules—Interchurch World Movement

On file in Central Office 146
Secured by field workers 181
                                                            ———
    Total 327

according to the 1920 Census, all but one of which were believed to have reached this mark by the date of the survey, or were already included by the United States Census in metropolitan districts of more than 100,000 people.

New Schedules
Secured coöperatively, through denominational boards...... 101
Secured directly by field workers 616
                                                            ___
Total 717
                                                            ___
Grand Total .... 1,044 [4]

CONTENTS OF SCHEDULES

Drawn from different sources as the material was, and secured under different auspices and with different objectives, its several strata naturally showed different contents. The Interchurch schedules covered several hundred items, most of which had to be ignored because there was nothing to correspond to them in the data secured through denominational coöperation. Obviously, full comparison and interpretation could be based only upon the particular items of information which were common to all the schedules as supplemented by correspondence and field work. Other information could be used only incidentally.

The thirty-five items common to all the schedules are listed in Appendix A. Practically, they constitute the content of the schedule for purposes of this study; that is to say, they were the only items on which information was available for the entire number of churches.[5]

ENVIRONMENTAL DATA

The second most important body of data used by the study concerned the parish environment of 314 churches. In seeking new schedules the study set itself to determine whether a church was in a "downtown" or a residential location and what the social quality of its immediate neighborhood was; also, how many members lived within one, two, three and four or more miles of it; and how many north, south, east, or west. The Interchurch World Movement material contained no such data. To answer such questions was difficult, since they went beyond matters ordinarily included in church records and involved the actual mapping of membership lists, or at least very systematic and painstaking estimates. The exact content of the environmental data is shown and the inferior statistical value of the more limited number of schedules on which it depends is recognized and discussed in later paragraphs.[6]

4 The distribution of churches covered by these schedules by cities and by denominations appears in Appendix Tables 1 and 45.
5 Twelve more items were included in about four-fifths of the schedules. See p. 229. and Appendix Table 36.
6 See p. 248.

Entering into the final interpretation of the data above described was a great mass of supplementary material not susceptible of comparable statistical treatment.

> Among the 1,044 churches studied were 121 included in exhaustive surveys of St. Louis and Springfield, Mass., made under the same field direction as the present study. Competent local tabulations and general summaries on the basis of the included Interchurch schedules had been made in the cities of Hartford and Los Angeles, and summaries of more limited scope were available in certain other cities. For almost every church studied first-hand, calendars, annual reports, photographs and, frequently, parish maps were secured, totaling many thousands of illustrative documents. Independent surveys made by individual churches and surveys and reports existing in denominational or Church Federation offices in cities visited were all drawn upon for collateral information.

The whole constitutes by far the largest body of first-hand information concerning American city churches of the Protestant communions ever assembled or investigated at one time.

Definition and Limitations

The assertion of the last paragraph implies two issues of definition. It raises the questions: (1) What is a church? and (2) What churches are Protestant? The former is so basic that it can have only preliminary discussion here, full consideration being reserved for the body of the text.[7] In principle every Protestant religious institution was accepted as a church which labeled itself such. The question, "What churches are Protestant?" was theoretically settled by the inclusion of everything except Roman Catholic, Greek Catholic and Hebrew churches and those of the historic non-Christian faiths.

Actually, however, the churches studied were drawn from a narrower range than is thus indicated. The limitation in practice was determined by the auspices under which the schedules were originally obtained and by the fact that the working contacts of the study were with the body of Protestant churches that sentimentally and practically recognize one another as such.

> The exact limits of this group are not capable of theoretical definition. It excludes certain churches which are neither Catholic, Jewish nor his-

7 See p. 42. It may be indicated here that one of the major emphases of the study is upon the fact that the churches lie within the field of a larger group of religious institutions and that the boundary line between the two is not perfectly defined. The study is particularly insistent upon the significance of the inchoate and embryonic forms of religious organization commonly ignored in religious thinking, not practically recognized nor belonging within the self-conscious church group. If everything was counted as a church which the social student will wish to recognize as such the distribution of sorts and varieties which the sample of 1,044 churches reveals might be far from accurate.

torically non-Christian. Practically, however, the grounds of distinction are well recognized by the Protestant bodies of every city and of the country at large. In any given situation it is easy to determine exactly who are included and who are excluded. Thus, the intensive survey of Springfield, Mass., showed that the Theosophical, Spiritualistic and more radical Pentecostal groups, although denominational status is accorded to them in the United States Census, were practically ignored by the main Protestant body, as were certain International Bible Student and "Russellite" groups not recognized as denominations by the Census. If these religious fringes are omitted for the simple reason that they are practically excluded (though from the strictly sociological standpoint they ought not to be), the major body of recognized and well-established Protestant churches is left as the subject of this study.

THE BROADLY REPRESENTATIVE SAMPLE

The sample is, therefore, broadly representative of the entire body of Protestant city churches which are practically recognized as such by the group at whose initiative and in whose immediate behalf the study was made. This group contains the recognized and better-established denominations those which are accustomed to count one another as part of the common Protestant forces and to coöperate practically as such.

It is within this "universe of discourse" that the study assumes to portray the "American city church." In other words, just as the limitation to Protestant churches is always assumed, so is the limitation to the group of Protestant churches which have definitely emerged into ecclesiastical status and which practically recognize one another as being Protestant.

Outline of Method

The discovery of types of churches is so preëminently a question of method that this phase of the subject has necessarily been expanded and constitutes the bulk of the material in Part I (Chapters I-IV).

The types were determined and classified on the basis of thirty-three items [8] of information regarding function derived from the schedules. Information had been secured for the entire 1,044 churches on thirty-five other items [9] concerning general church life and work; and on twelve additional items from 853 churches. The next major problem of method was to determine whether the churches previously grouped as types on the basis of part of the data would show similar and confirmatory characteristics and trends from the standpoint of these further units of information. Answers to these questions served as a check upon the basic method of classification.

8 See p. 56.
9 See pp. 208 f.

Other Phases of Method

This phase of the methodology falls into three stages: First, the types and subtypes were described in terms of the additional items of information, and their inner similarities and differences were noted and measured.

THE MODAL SUBTYPE

For example, the group that was found to contain the greatest number of churches showed the following characteristics:

> A unit of this group is most frequently a church of from one to two hundred members; of American rather than of foreign antecedents; but if foreign, Northern European rather than Southern or Eastern.
> It is a one-man enterprise. Eighty-two per cent. of the pastors have a conservative college and seminary education. They represent all ranges of experience. They usually stay less than five years and receive salaries of between $1,000 and $2,000.
> The median amount of operating cost of such a church is about $5,000, but the largest number cost less than $3,000 for operation. Benevolence in this kind of church amounts to ten dollars per capita. Its Sunday school equals in size about three-fourths of its membership and usually has an average attendance of 150, predominantly of children. Judged by the sample, it is the representative Protestant church of the larger American city.[10]
> It occurs more frequently in the South or East than in the less conservative Middle West or West. It is most characteristic of the very small denominations or of the southern denominations or of the Lutherans.

The characteristics of each type were drawn out in detail with reference to all the items under consideration, with results which appear in Chapters V-X. The exact difference between subtypes within each type is statistically measured in Appendix Tables 5-39 and the average church's characteristics are summarized in Chapter X.

THE PHASE OF COMPARISON

The second stage was to compare type with type and with all churches, item by item, with the results that appear in Chapter XI. On twenty-one out of the thirty-five items of general information, a direct and consistent quantitative increase appears throughout the successive types, corresponding to the enlargement of service program. This is true also of each of the twelve supplementary activities recorded for 853 churches.

On eight of the thirty-five items no direct correspondence of quantitative change is found to accompany increasing complexity of church program; but these cases are in large measure self-explana-

---

10 For a sample case, see p. 117.

tory and prove the rule rather than the exception. All told, the consistency of tendency which runs through the succession of types as determined by character of program also reveals itself in most of the related aspects of church life when quantitatively measured. The general statistical results are thus thoroughly congruent with the statistical analysis by which the types were discovered.

METHODS OF HANDLING ENVIRONMENTAL DATA

The final stage in technical method related the environmental data [11] to the classification of churches by types. The process was: (1) to calculate what per cent. of the churches of a given type were located in central or residential environments. (2) In the case of those centrally located to determine (a) what degree of importance had the center to which they were tributary? (b) how strategic was their location with respect to their non-local constituents? and, (c) what was the social quality of the immediate environment? (3) For churches in a residential environment to determine the per cent. of each type located in environments of a given social quality. The results of this study appear in detail in Chapter XII.

Little correlation was found between type and environment. The modal subtype B II, for example, is environmentally ubiquitous, occurring about two-fifths of the time in a down-town location and three-fifths of the time in residential areas. While there is a definite tendency for central location and more than average development of program to go together, it is rather slight. *On the whole all of the types occur in all environments, and none is so character-istic* of a given immediate environment as to justify one in using immediate environment as the major clew to its interpretation. This will be interpreted as showing how generally the principle of accessibility has triumphed over that of proximity in the structure of cities and the relations of their institutions to constituencies.

The other aspect of the environmental data, namely, that concerning the distribution of the homes of the members by distance and direction with respect to the church building, involved the setting up of statistical intervals determining what would be defined in terms of distance as "compact," "medium" and "scattered" parishes; and in terms of direction as "balanced," "unbalanced" and "very unbalanced" parishes. Forty-five per cent. of the churches studied were found to have "compact" parishes, in that 75 per cent. or more of the members of these churches lived within one mile of the church building. About one-third of all churches, however, had parishes

11 See pp. 248 f.

which were "unbalanced" to a greater or less extent, some of them having less than 9 per cent. and others more than 43 per cent. of their membership living in one of the four quadrants. The detailed results of this study also appear in Chapter XII.

Studied type by type, these parish characteristics were found to bear no direct relation to the increasing complexity of church program registered by the successive types. They did, however, show important relations to the size of the city in which the church was located.

As a final step in method, the relations between the whole group of larger environmental factors and the several types of churches were systematically studied. The trends of a given type toward a given size of city, or section of the country, or toward a given denomination or type of denomination, or toward constituencies of a given nationality, were systematically measured, with results appearing in Chapter XIII.

USE OF HYPOTHESES

The facts as discovered having been set against the general background of American religious history and of the present rural church, a group of hypotheses was arrived at which, to the author's mind, afforded the major explanation of the facts. These hypotheses are used as explanatory clews in Part II of the book in sections alternating with factual findings. The transition from a body of facts to their hypothetical explanation is clearly indicated in each context and should be kept in mind throughout the reading of the book.

Limitations and Values of the Study

The book has already introduced itself as a venture in pioneer exploration. In salvaging and utilizing much previously existing material, it increased the number of its cases but narrowed the content of its data, giving to that content a certain unevenness of texture. The method of classifying churches did not prove to have allowed statistically for all necessary factors,[12] and the supporting case studies were not intensively enough made to illuminate all the problems raised by the data.

Consequently the book will need supplementing by later studies as well as by criticism from the standpoint of other hypotheses.

In spite of these limitations the study has somewhat unusual values in the minds of those who made it. Among them are the following:

12 See p. 72.

the environmental data and their discussion uncover phenomena susceptible to treatment along the lines begun, and offer inducement to further study. The preliminary interpretation of the present book will, it is believed, have helped to clarify the meaning both of immediate environment and of the geographical factors determining church life that cannot be defined in terms of immediate environment.

(7) The author's interpretations of this or that detail will doubtless vary in value from item to item. They constitute first efforts at explanation for a highly important body of new data. They merely open the discussion.

(8) The provisional use of statistically discovered trends as norms for current judgment and future control of church life and work constitutes the final value of the study. By these norms specified areas of the city church field may easily be re-surveyed. They do not define the good or the bad in the absolute sense, but only the more or less—and thus the relatively better or worse—with respect to what is actually most frequent or most characteristic. By their use any pastor or layman may define and appraise his church in precise terms, with reference to the whole range of urban church development.

When such a one has located his church he may read off quite exactly the characteristic items of program, agencies and facilities which go with its position and note which of them his church has or has not. If he wants his church to develop to the full within the limits of its present type, he will know what is involved. If he wants it to expand into a different and more complex type, he can measure the cost in men, facilities and current budget. If unfortunately he has to conduct the backward steps of the waning church, he will understand how to retreat in good order. There is nothing holy about an inch or a foot. They are simply conventional units of measurement and as such are highly standardized and safeguarded. Neither is there anything holy about statistical types and subtypes. They merely help churches to find themselves and to measure their progress in terms of and partially by means of known and definable characters toward ineffable and imponderable values which transcend and escape definition.

Significance of the Study for Church Administration

The study addresses itself first of all to some of the problems of the group of church administrators at whose suggestion and for whose sake it was initially undertaken. In the guidance of city church policies and affairs, they have hitherto had to act upon experience and upon current generalizations, which were little more than guesses, as to the basic tendencies operating in the field. Certain averages had been discovered, based, however, on the indiscriminate grouping together of all city institutions called churches without regard to their inner differences. Only to a slight extent could the underlying trends be formulated, and no means of measuring them were at hand. The present study creates new, though only tentative, norms for the use of church administrators.

With this use of the study as an aid to practical church administration in mind, it may be worth while to indicate in some detail the kinds of persons for whom it should have value.

THE THEOLOGICAL STUDENT

The theological student no longer prepares for the ministry in general. Specialization in all professions is the modern note, and the prospective minister is likely to have some idea of the type of ministry in which he hopes to serve. Hitherto he has had little chance really to appreciate the urban church problem. The range of possibilities and the actual preponderance of prospects had not been formulated. He rarely guessed and was never told how small an affair the average city church is. Its variations and their reasons, its course of evolution and consequent limitations, were not clearly analyzed. Even in so narrow a realm as that of his vocational prospects, the theological student had no certain means of knowing what was before him. The relative numbers of workers in the several types of specialization, their functions, the types of churches which call for such workers to perform such functions, the varied preparation demanded, and the remuneration to be expected, were none of them precisely stated. From the present study the prospective minister should gain an idea as to the range of possibilities offered by the modern city church.

THE THEOLOGICAL PROFESSOR

The increased proportion of the theological curriculum given to practical theology and the multiplication of courses in this department are among the outstanding marks of modern theological training.[17] There are, however, few courses in city church administration, and still fewer based upon actual surveys and case studies of a sufficient number of samples to make possible the discernment of representative types. Such courses have been based mainly upon the professor's recollection of the pastorate as it was years ago,

17 Kelly, *Theological Education in America* (Institute of Social and Religious Research), pp. 84 f.

and with this has gone an almost certain over-emphasis upon the striking and successful, but non-representative, church. The theological seminary has had available little precise knowledge of the relative proportions in which phenomena existed even in the field for which it was attempting to give vocational preparation. Its large experience enabled it to tell some of the things which would be found there, but it had never made a count of how often they would be found, or determined which were numerically preponderant. If this study does nothing else, it is hoped that it may constitute a point of departure for a more critical and successful account of the city church problem as part of the material for educating its future leaders.

THE PASTOR

The active pastor is the man on the firing line of actual church experience. If he does not understand the city church in the vital aspects of its life no one can explain it to him. If he cannot direct it effectively no one else can. A sincere, spontaneous interest in his work, the zest of the job and its problems, ambition and the spur of competition, often combine to give him a keen and shrewd practical sense of the standing of his church in relation to others and an appreciation of actual differences. This is a beginning of the recognition of church types. But the scientific categories for thinking the matter through have not been available, and the pastor could not know enough churches accurately enough to compare one with another or to discern the trends which they express.

The results of this study may serve as a tool to the intellectual, alert minister who wants to do straight thinking and to make his work clear-cut and decisive rather than imitative. Any type of church is commendable in its place. By use of the methods outlined in the following pages the pastor can first locate his church in the evolutionary series and then compare it with the provisional norms. His church is not beyond the authority of the "divine average." A margin of opportunity for improvements is open to it in its present status, as is true for all churches. This margin being faithfully attempted, he is called upon to make honest and responsible decisions with respect to the next step. The destinies of the church are fixed by a series of such steps. Nothing that the minister does in his entire professional lifetime is of such strategic importance.

MINOR SUPERVISORY OFFICERS

The active advisor of the local churches and the man who has frequent face to face relations with them is the superintendent or local secretary of the various denominations. He is also the representative of the ecclesiastical boards and agencies of the denominations at large, and the one who most influences their decisions in local issues. It is hoped that the present study will illuminate the job of this key man, helping him to see what types of churches are actually present in the field for which he has the supervision and enabling him to make up his mind as to what types ought to exist and in what proportion. If a large number of such minor officials would actually undertake to use the analysis of this book as provisional norms, they would soon be able to work out a more precise technical procedure and method of evaluation and control than was ever before available to the church. Recommendations for appropriations and improvement of property, as well as the choice of ministers for particular types of churches, and determination of church locations, removal and progress, would all be immensely improved by a clear understanding of what actually exists in the city church field.

DENOMINATIONAL STATESMANSHIP

The ultimate thinking for the denominations is actually done by a relatively small number of executives and the committees, commissions or boards which they represent. These strategists of American Christianity have spent many hours of labor and risked many utterances upon the city church problem. It is a rather striking fact, however, that the literary output up to date is very inconspicuous compared with the importance of the field and with the exceedingly large number of crucial decisions which it involves. The list of titles even purporting to deal with the city church at large is very brief, and until the efforts of the Interchurch World Movement no conspicuous and far-reaching effort to get at the scientific roots of the matter had ever been made.[18] Occasional and fugitive surveys of individual churches or parishes were sometimes sound in method, but did not cover anything like the total area of the field and had never been gathered into a single result. There is no intention here to disparage the experience and thinking of the past. The present study is itself the product of that thinking and simply attempts to go one step further in a field of which the greater part still remains scientifically unexplored.

18 For example, Mode, *A Source Book of American Church History* (1920) cites no article on the city church later than 1895 and no book except Josiah Strong's *The Twentieth Century City* (undated) and Bishop Leete's *The Church in the City* (1915).

CHURCH FEDERATION LEADERS

One of the central features of the Federation movement is the attempt to secure comity between the coöperating denominations in the establishment and maintenance of churches. A common strategy is sought in contrast with the competitions and rivalries too often characteristic of the past. The discrimination of types of churches and the implied challenge as to their normal distribution in a city should be one of the main interests of such officials and committees as have comity problems in charge. Within a given territory, two churches which are not in the least alike do not present at all the same problem as two churches which are very much alike. There have been hitherto no categories in which to conceive and no language in which to express the difference between churches as a ground for judging whether or not they are rendering equivalent service, or whether one is fairly a substitute for or a rival of another. It is hoped that the present study may make a practical contribution to this problem of church comity.

THE SOCIOLOGIST

Though the influence of the practical sociologist upon church administration may be small, nevertheless the judgments and insights of those who include the church among the permanent and significant institutions of human society are gradually getting a hearing in religious circles, and their verdicts are in turn strengthening the church in its contacts and adjustments with the other institutions of the city. Social workers inclined to ignore the church or to criticize it harshly may find a corrective in this exposition of its evolution. Its limitations, as well as its normal tendencies, are revealed. The church has come to be what it is by a long process and cannot lightly or hurriedly turn itself into something else. Nevertheless the processes of social adaptation are well under way and the number and variety of original and promising experiments cannot escape recognition.

THE HARD-HEADED LAYMAN

Finally, it is hoped that even so technical a discussion of the city church may not altogether escape the attention of the more thoughtful and discriminating of its lay supporters. Men who are called upon to supply financial resources and to follow the recommendations of their experts in practical decisions may be aided in independent judgment if they take the time to trace in detail the evidence concerning the city church presented in this book. It is not a promotional document and does not hold that all churches in all places are important or even desirable. What it seeks to do is to put a broad foundation of ascertained fact under the total work of urban Christianity as ecclesiastically organized. It explains and partly extenuates that which seems weakest and least creditable. It demonstrates and on the whole defends what is the church's characteristic and average urban expression, even though it be not very conspicuous or commanding. It interprets the more highly developed forms of city church life, but without urging that they should be adopted wholesale or suddenly, without discrimination as to time or place, or without regard to other forms of religious organization and to the total constructive forces of the city's life. It is felt that on the basis of this study the ordinary churchman can take a sane and not unduly discouraged view of the urban church problem. At any rate, since the forces of control are actually operative, attempting to make the city church what they think it ought to be, it is well to understand what it already is and in some measure why it is, in order that such influence on the future as is possible shall be wise as well as courageous.

CONTENTS

INTRODUCTION

PART I

SUMMARY OF METHOD, RESULTS AND CONCLUSIONS

PART II

FINDINGS AND CONCLUSIONS IN DETAIL

APPENDICES

xxiii

LIST OF TABLES

LIST OF CHARTS

LIST OF ILLUSTRATIVE CASES

PART I

SUMMARY OF METHOD, RESULTS AND CONCLUSIONS

Is this Brotherhood of clean people a church? The largest of all Allegheny churches owns and has physically attached to it a magnificent community house. Its support, however, is independent of the church's budget, and it is not administered as an integral part of the church work. Is this settlement house part of a church or a separate institution—a non-church just as the Young Men's and Young Women's Christian Associations are non-churches?

What Is a Church?

The units of religious organization in American cities show the interesting variety thus illustrated. Their relationships are relatively complex. Just what then is a church? For the purposes of this study an answer has been adopted, originating, it is to be noted, not in theological definition, but through an actual handling of more than a thousand working models of organizations that call themselves churches. It summarizes the characters that fall under their own self-designations. If they had claimed something else as constituting the "church," then the definition would have been different. It stands merely as a record of agreement in practice at the following points:

(1) A church is a definable group of Christian people. It has a membership list in most cases, and at least some sort of mark of relatively permanent adherence. Mere occasional groups of believers do not call themselves churches. Continuing associates in religion define the fact of their association in some recognizable way.

(2) A church is a fellowship for religious worship and instruction—the latter invariably taking the form of preaching and generally also of organized Sunday-school work. If the study had found definite associations of Christians permanently omitting worship and preaching and limiting themselves to some other parts of the collective church program, yet calling themselves churches, it would have modified its definition so as not to require these limitations. But no such case has been met. Christians who want to work together, but who do not wish to worship together, simply do not call themselves churches.[1] They merely associate themselves under some of the numerous other forms of non-church religious organization. Worship and preaching, then, are invariable features in the 1,044 churches studied.

(3) A church is usually a complete cross-section of humanity with respect to its age-groups and sex-groups. It includes men and women, old and young. This is a magnificent general characteristic.

---

[1] In rare cases the name church was found surviving for a period in an institution which had discontinued stated worship and preaching. But the tendency in such cases to drop the name church is so strong as to prove the rule. See p. 125.

It is omitted sometimes in the case of exceptional populations such as age-groups or sex-groups segregated in schools, or in charitable and penal institutions. There may be churches of students all of a given age, or of penitentiary convicts all of a given sex. The usual way of ministering to such populations, however, is through a chaplaincy and not through a full church organization; and the 1,044 samples happen not to have included any such exceptional case.

(4) A church usually stands in recognized relationship with a body of churches like it in faith and government, called a denomination. This is not to deny church status to single groups of religious people that claim to be churches and that have the other characteristics of the class. Religious organizations that rise in opposition to established denominations are as truly churches in the logical sense as the most venerable examples. In point of fact all the non-denominational churches met with during the study had actual relationships—such as membership in organized groups of similar churches—that established the rule.

By the four characteristics above enumerated the 1,044 churches were separated from the twenty-seven non-churches included in the collected schedules.

Relations of Churches and Non-Churches

The process of separating the data not only excluded all organizations not strictly churches from statistical comparison and consideration, but compelled an analysis of the relations of churches and non-churches which had profound influence upon the method of the study.

Clearing the field and arranging the churches and non-churches in their respective positions resulted in four different classes of non-churches being discovered.

NOT-YET CHURCHES

Some of the non-churches are clearly churches in purpose and prospect. Such are the familiar mission Sunday schools and branch organizations. It is in such beginnings that the full-grown churches have generally originated. They are related to the churches as a tadpole is to the frog. One cannot yet call them churches, but they are churches in the making. Their disability is supposedly temporary. They are pre-churches.

Within this group, however, some will be found whose prospect of reaching church estate is not very good. They are composed of people too feeble, ignorant or unstable to have much prospect of arriving, institutionally speaking. Their religious group-life is on a lower level of stability than is required by a true church. Such is the case of the rescue mission made up of representatives of the transient and intermittent class, both physically and morally. One may call these sub-churches. These never-to-be churches belong with the pre-churches by position though not by practical prospect.

NO-LONGER CHURCHES

A small group of non-churches must be placed at or beyond the farther limit of the church field. Such are the community centers specializing in social service but retaining conventional church organization and activities. Ninety per cent. of the service of the Wesley Neighborhood House in St. Louis, for example, is in fields rarely occupied by a church and only 10 per cent. falls within the ordinary range of church activities. It would be easy to drop entirely the church program and to operate merely a Christian settlement, as has been done in certain cases.

> A good example is Furman House, built upon the foundations of the Ewing Street Congregational Church in Chicago. Here social and community work have been grafted on to historic church organization and have evolved into independence as changed conditions of population have caused the old church to dwindle and die. This is a no-longer church.

All institutions of this group which still call themselves churches and have activities on both sides of the line must be classified as churches. They have, however, more in common with the above type of non-churches, which are simply the churches of yesterday that have passed on into a more specialized class.[2]

NEVER-WERE CHURCHES

A great majority, however, of non-churches lie neither before nor beyond, but beside the broad field which the church occupies. They never have been churches and in the majority of cases probably never will be. One thinks first of the Young Men's and Young Women's Christian Associations in this connection; then of hospitals, orphanages, old people's homes and kindred philanthropies. These constitute a very important aspect of Protestant religious service, one of immense proportion and cost. Such organizations are clearly not churches, but their historic and present relations to the churches are well known and often confessed, and their range covers the entire breadth of the field of church activities.

2 For sample programs of churches and settlements showing these affinities, see p. 172.

NOT-MERELY CHURCHES

On the opposite side of the church field from the parallel not-churches just described, lies another non-church group smaller in number, but very similar in range. These are unit-institutions, companion to the churches and attached to individual churches, but so separate in function and generally in location and administration as to require separate recognition.

> Thus, the First and Westminster Presbyterian churches of Buffalo maintain settlement houses, as Plymouth Congregational church of Minneapolis did for many years. A church in Kansas City has its own children's home and Westminster Presbyterian church of Minneapolis its own hospital. Many Lutheran churches maintain individual old people's homes for their members. Branch churches are the traditional forms of this dual institutionalism, and kindergartens, clubs and fresh-air homes its minor phases.

While there is great difference in the degree and method of actual contact between the two parts of such related institutions, the part which is not merely a church (though under the auspices and administrative control of a single congregation) clearly adds a unique and distinctive aspect to the field of religious organization. Here is something which extends beyond the ordinary field of the church as a unit-organization and includes functions which are ordinarily performed by separate institutions, frequently supported by denominations.[3]

The diagram on page 46 summarizes the story of the field of religious organization as divided between churches and not-churches. It shows the pre-churches logically coming before the churches, the post-churches following them and the parallel institutions attached or unattached flanking them on either side.

How to Classify Churches?

Now a very striking difference appears between churches and non-churches in that the latter include a large number of kinds of institutions whose differences are not merely obvious but are separately labeled. The former are all covered by the common name "churches." It is very possible that important differences are thus concealed. As suggested by the names, a hospital is clearly different from a Young Men's Christian Association. If, however, one church differed from another as much as a hospital differs from a Young Men's Christian Association, both would still be called by

---

3 One of the shortcomings of the present study was its inability to deal statistically in any adequate fashion with these dual institutions and their inter-relationships. The importance of inquiries in this direction was foreseen neither by the Interchurch World Movement schedules nor by those subsequently provided.

the same name and no easy means would be at hand to distinguish them.

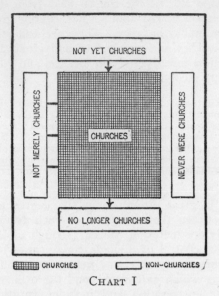

CHART I

THE FIELD OF RELIGIOUS ORGANIZATION
Relation of Churches and Other Agencies.

WIDE DIFFERENCES BETWEEN CHURCHES

The fact that churches differ but that their designations do not tell how much or in what respects they differ, provides the central problem of the present study. From its inception it was committed to the attempt to discover whether there were fundamental distinctions between churches and to define the resulting types if precise ground of distinction existed. It assured itself, therefore, first of all that there were such grounds of distinction.

This was accomplished in simple fashion merely by counting the number of organizations and activities, within a list of thirty-three items, reported by 362 churches in cities in which a large proportion of the total number of churches had been covered by the study. The results appear in Table I.

It was noted that the most frequent number of activities was six or seven and that two-thirds of these churches had not more than eight. One-fourth, in turn, had four or less activities, while only about 10 per cent. had thirteen or more. It was obvious that with such extreme variations churches were far from being alike.

TABLE I — DISTRIBUTION OF ORGANIZATIONS AND ACTIVITIES IN 362 CITY CHURCHES

No. of Organizations and Activities	Distribution of Churches Number		Per Cent.
1	7		
2	17	91	25.0
3	31		
4	36		
5	32		
6	43	156	42.8
7	52		
8	29		
9	31		
10	25	82	22.7
11	14		
12	12		
13	13		
14	8	27	7.9
15	4		
16	2		
17	3		
18	0	4	1.1
19	1		
20	0		
21	0		
22	2	2	0.5
Total	362	362	100.0

THE SEARCH FOR AN INTERPRETATIVE PRINCIPLE

Mere counting of organizations and activities without considering their functions was not, however, a satisfactory basis of classification, since it gave no suggestion as to how or wherein they differed. A more adequate means of measuring was therefore sought, one which should suggest a reason for the facts as well as the bare facts of difference.

In this search certain obvious clews were followed. Since the needs of different city neighborhoods and populations differ, it was assumed that churches would perhaps have come to differ in the process of adapting themselves to the service of these needs; but how far this might be true and what results it might have wrought no one knew.

THE FIRST CLEW

The present study got its first reliable clew from the process by which the churches were separated from the non-churches met in field investigation. That separation had been reached by excluding organizations below the minimum of what a religious organization could be and do and remain a church. No clear light was thrown on the question how much more than this minimum a church could be and do and still remain a church. Superficially examined the range of variations appeared to be very large. Thus, while virtually all churches had Sunday schools, less than half had boys' organizations and not one in twenty had a day nursery or clinic. Churches differed enormously in the number of paid workers, the plant and equipment with which they worked, and the cost of operation relative to the church membership. These variations were so wide as to suggest that one was probably dealing with diverse institutions having different sets of functions and not merely with one institution exercising more or less of the same functions. It was quite possible to imagine that the churches at the extreme edge of the ecclesiastical field might more closely resemble some of their cousins, the non-churches just over the fence, than they resembled their sister churches at the other extreme.

These considerations impelled the study to seek some clew to the classification of churches which should arise out of the data themselves and prove more profound and practically useful than any previously known.

THE FINAL SOLUTION

The solution of the problem of classification was found in the discovery that there were systematic relations between the churches and the parallel non-churches with respect to their functions. Examples suggesting the range and variety of the non-church group were first classified under conventional categories expressing major function or emphasis, with results shown in the following arrangement:

Major Functions	*Corresponding Non-Church Religious Organizations*
Worship and Evangelism	Gospel centers
Religious Instruction	Independent Bible Study organizations
Social Life	The Y. M. C. A. and Y. W. C. A.
Recreation	Boy and Girl Scouts
General Social Service	Social Settlements and Neighborhood Centers
Specialized and Technical Social Service	Clinics, employment offices, day nurseries, hospitals, children's homes, old people's homes, etc.

Now, the 1,071 schedules showed cases of non-churches performing all the major functions ever performed by churches and of churches performing all of the functions performed by any of the non-churches; also of churches stopping at all points on the list. Some had worship and evangelism, but no Sunday school. Some added a Sunday school, but made no provision for social life—and so on.

> For example, parallel with the religious worship and evangelism common to the many churches of the city of Rochester, N. Y., there was discovered a Gospel Center continuously carrying on services of worship and evangelism. This organization declined to have a permanent or formally recognized membership, or to admit that it was a church. It definitely desired to affect all recognized religious bodies equally by "boring from within" in behalf of ultra-evangelical aspects of faith, yet without itself becoming institutionalized.

Parallel with the Sunday school and the religious education activities of the church, inter-denominational Bible schools or Bible Students' organizations were frequently found not under church auspices.

It was obvious that the whole range of organization of age-, and sex-groups as expressed in the churches' young people's meetings and women's societies was parallel to the Young Men's and Young Women's Christian Associations with their senior and junior departments. The religious, cultural, recreational, educational and physical ministries which the more modern church program admits have been still more completely worked out in a group of familiar institutions which are permanent non-churches.

Certain churches in especially needy environments were found to include in their programs of service such activities as clinics, visiting nurses, employment offices, day nurseries and other child welfare agencies. As was previously noted, the usual thing has been for a church or churches which want to serve humanity in these ways, to contribute money and found a separate institution—a hospital, children's or old people's home, nursery or similar form of non-church. Yet virtually every phase of their work was included by some church somewhere in connection with a strictly ecclesiastical organization and program.

Theoretically, then, there is a complete set of options before any group of religious people who want to perform any function or group of functions or services in the name of their faith; namely, to do them through a church or through a non-church organization; for virtually all functions performed by either class are performed now by the one, now by the other.

THE DISCOVERY GENERALIZED

Obviously, however, these functions divide into (1) things usually left to the church; (2) things usually performed through non-church agencies; and (3) things performed by either one with about equal frequency.

Thus the permanent conduct of worship and preaching by a non-church group is rare. Such things are usually left to the church and custom makes people who want to foster them organize themselves into churches.

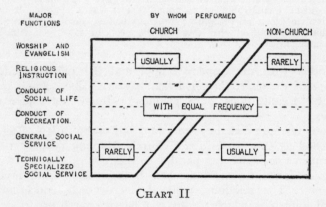

CHART II

Division of Functions Between Churches and Non-Churches.

Again, a certain amount of provision for the general social life of its members is commonly undertaken by the city church through women's and young people's societies; but the organization of special age-, and sex-groups for specialized group-programs is still generally left to such agencies as the Young Men's and Young Women's Christian Associations.

Finally, though in rare instances individual churches maintain settlements, hospitals, children's or old people's homes, such services are usually performed by special institutions often maintained by groups of churches or denominations but not organically attached to the individual church. So far a rough observation of the phenomena carries one; if worship is the object of religious people they *may* achieve it through a non-church agency, but a thousand chances to one they will take a church. If hospital treatment is the object, they *may* take a church to perform it, but a thousand chances to one they will take a hospital. If general social life is sought, the city church will generally think itself adequate, but if specialized age-, and sex-differentiation in social and recreational development is sought, it is more likely to call in a specializing agency or to let the matter go.

The frequencies of the actual decisions of religious groups in exercising their choice between churches and non-churches in the performance of functions attempted by either are suggested by the diagram on the preceding page.

TABLE II — CLASSIFICATION OF 1,044 CITY CHURCHES BY TYPES AND SUBTYPES

Statistical Designation	Types and Characteristics of Subtypes	Distribution of Churches			
		Number		Per Cent.	
		Sub-Types	Types	Sub-Types	Types
	I. *Slightly Adapted Churches.*		360		34.5
B II	Modal Subtype (Most Frequent)	161		15.4	
B III	Development of Program Toward Novelty	84		8.1	
C I	Development of Program Toward Conventionality	115		11.0	
	II. *Unadapted Churches*		253		24.2
A I	Smallest, Narrowest Program...	90		8.6	
B I	Small, Narrow Program	101		9.7	
A II ⎱ A III ⎰	Other Unadapted	62		5.9	
	III. *Internally Adapted Churches*		196		18.8
C II	Narrower Phase of Program ...	116		11.1	
D II	Fuller Phase of Program	80		7.7	
	IV. *Socially Adapted Churches*		110		10.5
D III	Narrower Phase of Program ...	43		4.1	
E II	Fuller Phase of Program	67		6.4	
	V. *Widely Variant Churches.*.		125		12.0
A IV ⎫ A V ⎪ B IV ⎬ C III ⎭	In Direction of Novelty	32 15 11 30		3.1 1.4 1.0 2.9	
D I ⎱ E I ⎰	In Direction of Conservatism ..	27 10		2.6 1.0	
	Total	1,044	1,044	100.0	100.0

DIFFICULTIES OF THE TRANSITION

How this apparently precise and accurately measured classification was derived from the principle crudely discerned through the introductory analysis is a long story. From the scientific standpoint it is the most important step taken in the study and its exact method and validity require careful scrutiny.

THE PARTING OF THE WAYS

Readers, however, will at this point probably wish to classify themselves into two groups: (1) those who will want immediately to pass on and get the results of the study now that its general approach has been made clear; and (2) those who want to know first exactly how its basic classification was reached.

The former should omit the remainder of this chapter and the one which follows and continue their reading with chapter iv, returning later to follow the somewhat complicated methodology of classification. The latter should read on and satisfy themselves of the validity of the process before submitting their minds to the consideration of its details.

Statistical Phase of Classification

The study attempted to meet the requirements for precise categories, exact measurements and a method allowing for all significant factors in the following ways:

I. *Substitution of Ultimate Units of Program for Loose Generalizations.*

The smallest functional unit of church life upon which the schedules furnished information was the specific activity or organization of the church or any of its organically related subsidiaries. The obvious way for a church to broaden or to contract its program was to organize or fail to organize some of the group of recognized subsidiaries whose names somewhat indicated their functions, or to take on or fail to take on some of the current activities of churches.

The schedules furnished information concerning thirty-three such organizations and activities which are listed in the next table. These specific factors of service were substituted for such loose generalizations as "social and recreational life" or "field of social service," exactly as "human nature" is now broken up by the psychologist into a series of unit-characters.

II. *Determination of Frequency.*

The frequency of occurrence of each of these items was then calculated for 357 churches which were known to have been chosen without bias and to represent an essentially complete cross section of churches in their respective cities.[1]

The results of this calculation appear in Table III.[2]

It is a striking fact that about one-half of the entire list of thirty-three organizations and activities occur in less than 20 per cent. of the churches, while certain others, namely, Sunday school, Ladies' Aid Society or Guild, Women's Missionary Society and

---

1 The location of these "cross-sectional" churches by cities appears in Appendix B.

2 For reasons for fearing bias in the selection of some part of the 1,044 churches studied, see p. vi. As a matter of fact the frequency of organizations and activities in the 357 "cross-sectional" churches varied but slightly from that found in the total number of churches. For exact comparison and discussion of the variations, see Appendix Table 2 and Chart LXVI.

TABLE III — FREQUENCY OF 33 ORGANIZATIONS AND ACTIVITIES IN 357 CITY CHURCHES

Order of Frequency	Organizations and Activities	Range of Frequency %
33	Civics and Economics Classes	
32	Dispensary or Clinic	
3i	Day Nursery	
30	Dramatic Classes	
29	English Classes	
28	Health Classes	1–10
27	Visiting Nurse	
26	Music Classes	
25	Employment Office	
24	Domestic Science Classes	
23	Kindergarten	
22	Sewing Classes	
21	Gymnasium Classes	
20	Dramatic Club	11–20
19	Young Women's Organization	
18	Mothers' or Parents' Organizations	
17	Girl Scouts or Equivalent	
16	Concerts	
15	Girls' Club (not Scouts)	
14	Library	21–40
13	Lectures	
12	Boys' Club (not Scouts)	
11	Orchestra or Band	
10	Organized Welcome	
9	Mission Study Classes	
8	Boy Scouts	41–60
7	Men's Organization	
6	General Social Events	
5	Chorus Choir	61–80
4	Young People's Society	
3	Women's Missionary Society	81–100
2	Ladies' Aid or Guild	
1	Preaching and Sunday School	

Young People's Society, are common to more than 80 per cent. of all city churches. These are the conventional elements of the Protestant program as contrasted with the exceptional ones which stand at the top of the list. The degree to which any given organization or activity is invariable, usual or exceptional appears from its position in the list. This is not an ideal list; it is simply an existing one representing items which were enumerated both by the Interchurch World Movement schedules and by all the others used in the present study. It was thus the best list available.[3]

[3] For the frequency of occurrence of twelve additional organizations and activities, see p. 229.

THE FREQUENCY LIST USED AS A SCALE

This classification of these thirty-three functional units of church work by frequency of occurrence in 357 churches was used as a preliminary yardstick for measuring the program of any church.[4]

Its use may be conveniently illustrated by the churches of a single city, Springfield, Mass.[5]

To classify a church, one begins by standing its program against the yardstick to see how high it measures. A church, for example, like the First Swedish Methodist in Springfield, reporting only a Sunday school, a ladies' aid and missionary society and a young people's organization, is doing only the most common and usual things which a city church can do. It has the narrowest and most traditional type of program. It falls short of the characteristic development of the American city church as revealed by the sample of 357 churches and also by the 1,044 cases. Indeed, it has more in common with the rural than with the urban type of church organization. Stand this program up against the yardstick and it proves to be a one-story affair.

Again, a church like North Congregational, with one exception, has no activity or organization which is not shared by at least 40 per cent. of the 357 Protestant city churches included in the sample. On the whole it is carrying on a very usual program. The one exception does not constitute a sufficient part of its total program to determine its classification. It is simply expanded a little beyond the program of the Swedish Methodist Church.

There are, as a later chapter will show, probably more churches of this than of any other sort in American cities. It shows traces of urban adaptation. One may call it a two-story church.

Still again, a church like the Park Memorial Baptist shows a program which measures as far as the eighteenth place on the frequency scale. In other words, in some part of its work it is doing what only about 15 per cent. of the 357 sample churches do. Furthermore, a very significant fraction of its program falls within this exceptional range of activity. It has elaborated its program until work exceptional for most city churches is usual and characteristic of it. Its internal organization reflects all-sided interests. One may call it a three-story church.

Two Springfield churches, namely, South Congregational, through its Olivet Community House, and St. John's Congregational (with its institutional activities) are undertaking types of work in the line of social adaptation and service which only 2 or 3 per cent. of the 357 sample churches have attempted. These thus fall in the very exceptional class and may be said to have sky-scraper programs.

Now, to classify all Springfield churches according to likeness and unlikeness, one will simply put the churches with the narrowest and most

[4] It should be noted that quantitative measurement does not imply evaluation. No presumption of superiority or inferiority attached to either the presence or the absence of any item. Should a church have Boy Scouts, or a Sunday school for that matter, or dances? As scientific process the study has had no judgment. It has simply recorded the frequency with which the total body of churches have or have not any specified activity. This determines statistically how far it is common; how far exceptional; how far rooted in the religious habit of American Christianity and how far sporadic. Religious history, however, is still in the making and the exceptional functions of to-day may be common to-morrow.

[5] No Springfield church performs all of the functions indicated by the thirty-three items of the frequency scale, but so far as the list of functions is comparable, the order of its items with respect to frequency is almost identical. Those which are rare elsewhere are rare in Springfield; those which are frequent elsewhere are frequent in Springfield.

traditional programs into one pile with the Swedish Methodist, those with programs that show slight urban adaptation into another with North Congregational, and those with elaborated programs into still another with Park Memorial Baptist. This will leave the South and St. John's Congregational churches which constitute the whole of the socially adapted group in Springfield.

FURTHER COMPLICATIONS OF PROCESS

The actual method of classifying the 1,044 churches is necessarily considerably more complicated than the foregoing illustration suggests, primarily for the reason that no single scale is adequate to express the variety of factors involved. Two factors have already

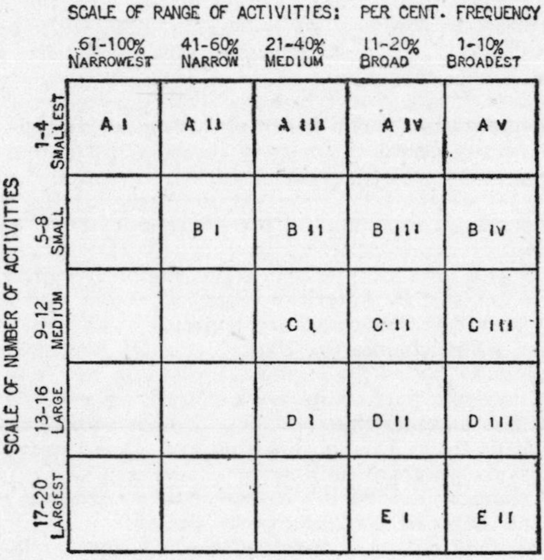

SCALE OF RANGE OF ACTIVITIES: PER CENT. FREQUENCY

	.61-100% NARROWEST	41-60% NARROW	21-40% MEDIUM	11-20% BROAD	1-10% BROADEST
1-4 SMALLEST	A I	A II	A III	A IV	A V
5-8 SMALL		B I	B II	B III	B IV
9-12 MEDIUM			C I	C II	C III
13-16 LARGE			D I	D II	D III
17-20 LARGEST				E I	E II

SCALE OF NUMBER OF ACTIVITIES

Chart III

Chart for Classification of Churches

emerged from previous analysis; namely, number and range of functions or activities. This calls for a scale in two dimensions. Such a scale appears in the above chart, which shows the exact process whereby these factors are combined into a single method of classification.

At the top of the chart from left to right are indicated the percentage frequencies with which the thirty-three organizations and stated activities appear on the frequency scale or general yardstick already presented. At the left of the chart from top to bottom is a scale for number of activities from one to twenty divided into groups of four—twenty being practically the maximum number of activities out of the combined list of thirty-three which were found in any single church.[6]

The 1,044 churches have now to be classified by a method noting the number and range of their organizations and stated activities with reference to the two scales; that is to say, each church must be placed in the proper square indicated by the intersecting lines drawn from the proper point on each. It may assist the reader's imagination to think of the diagram as set on edge and constituting a series of country post-office boxes, with himself as the postmaster with letters to each of the 1,044 churches which have to be distributed according to the method above indicated.

ILLUSTRATIVE CLASSIFICATION OF CHURCHES

In order to show the imaginary postmaster how to sort the letters correctly it will be wise to try a number of sample cases.

Table IV, on page 60, shows the number of activities of five churches and their distribution in terms of the frequency scale.

Number one of our sample churches has four activities and thus comes within the upper row of spaces as defined by the left-hand or number-of-activities scale. Its least frequent activity ranks as item six on the frequency scale and thus comes in the first column to the left as read on the upper or range-of-activities scale on Chart III. This fixes it in the space marked A I, which is the statistical designation given to the churches which fall in this space. Together they constitute Subtype A I with the smallest, narrowest program.

Church number two has seven activities. It, therefore, falls in the second row from the top on the number-of-activities scale. Its least frequent item is nine on the frequency scale. Reading across on the second row from the top and down from the space headed "41-60 per cent. frequency" one locates this church in space B I which serves as the designation of all other churches which fall in the same space. Relative to the total sample, these churches have small-narrow programs.

A similar process locates church number three in the C II space, showing that it has a medium-broad program.

So far the method of classification by scales combining two factors has worked perfectly, as it actually did with a great majority of the 1,044 churches.

---

[6] A very few churches (5 per cent. in the sample quoted on p. 62) did have slightly more than twenty activities. These, in accordance with statistical practice, were thrown with the group having from seventeen to twenty activities, in order to get an equal number of intervals on the two scales.

TABLE IV — ORGANIZATIONS AND ACTIVITIES OF FIVE CHURCHES

Range of Frequency	Organizations and Activities Ranked by Frequency	Churches				
		No. 1	No. 2	No. 3	No. 4	No. 5*
		Number of Activities				
		4	7	11	6	4
	1. Preaching and Sunday School	x	x	x	x	
	2. Ladies' Aid or Guild	x	x	x	x	x
81–100	3. Women's Missionary Society		x	x	x	
	4. Young People's Society		x	x	x	
61–80	5. Chorus Choir	x		x		
	6. General Social Events	x	x			
	7. Men's Organization		x	x	x	
41–60	8. Boy Scouts			x		
	9. Mission Study Classes	x				
	10. Organized Welcome					
	11. Orchestra or Band				x	
	12. Boys' Club (not Scouts)			x		x
	13. Lectures					
21–40	14. Library					
	15. Girls' Club (not Scouts)			x		
	16. Concerts					
	17. Girl Scouts or Equivalent					x
	18. Mothers' or Parents' Organization					
	19. Young Women's Organization		x			
11–20	20. Dramatic Club		x			
	21. Gymnasium Classes					x
	22. Sewing Classes					
	23. Kindergarten					
	24. Domestic Science Classes					
	25. Employment Office					
	26. Music Classes					
	27. Visiting Nurse					
1–10	28. Health Classes					
	29. English Classes					
	30. Dramatic Classes					
	31. Day Nursery					
	32. Dispensary or Clinic					
	33. Civics and Economics Classes					

* See p. 198 for a discussion of churches of this sort.

A THIRD FACTOR INVOLVED IN CLASSIFICATION

The case of church number four is introduced to show the modification of method occasionally found necessary owing to the presence of a third factor; namely, that of the particular distribution of any given number of activities within a given range. With a total of six activities this church includes Item eleven (Orchestra or Band), a manifest embellishment of church program indulged in by

only 21 to 40 per cent. of the 1,044 churches. The next least frequent item of its program is Item seven (Men's Organization). If
its program stopped with this item it would be within the range of
activities practiced by more than 40 per cent. of all churches. The
question is whether one item out of six which falls within the range
of lesser frequency, should be allowed to classify a church, most of
whose tendencies are clearly to a more conservative program.

The issue may be made clear by analogy. Suppose a house laps
over by a few inches on to its neighbor's lot. We practically ignore
this discrepancy and say that it is located upon its own lot. Suppose
one puts so little sugar into his tea that he cannot taste it. The tea
is not sweetened and we ignore the fact that some sugar was put in.
But if a house was halfway over on the wrong lot, or one spoonful
of sugar were put into a cup of tea where none was expected, we
could not ignore it. It would constitute too much of an invasion of
the realm in question. In the matter of churches we are dealing
with a working methodology which seeks practical results. Obviously the question is how much of an overlap or invasion charac-
terizes a situation as practically different.

Now, with a church which has but four activities in all, if one
falls in an infrequent range it clearly carries the classification of the
church. However conservative the rest, if a fourth part of its program is exceptional the church cannot be counted ordinary. But if
only one activity out of twenty is exceptional, one would scarcely
think of counting that as against the major trend of the church.

The question is where to draw the line methodologically and how
to apply the decision uniformly. At this point some arbitrary decision had to be made and the one chosen by the study was as
follows:

The average per cent. distribution of items of program between
the different spaces on the classificatory diagram (Chart III) was
calculated for the churches of each subtype. It was determined that
a church should not be classified by the least frequent range of activities of which it included any example unless it entered that range
to an average extent. If it failed to do this, it was classified by the
preceding space—exactly as a house which laps over onto the wrong
lot is identified by the lot on which it is mainly located. Churches
with from five to eight activities chose on the average 18 per cent.
of the total activities from those having a frequency of from 21 to
40 per cent. (items ten to seventeen). Church number four, with
only one item out of six within this range, falls a little short of the
average. It was accordingly set back in place and classified as belonging to Subtype B I rather than to Subtype B II.

This correcting of classification was systematically carried out for all churches requiring it, in accordance with the average incidence of the items of program in the churches of the respective subtypes in each frequency position. For Subtype C I, for example, the average incidence of items in the least frequent range was 36 per cent., for Subtype B II, 28 per cent. Each church was subjected to the test of its own subtype. This added the factor of specific distribution or emphasis of program to those of number and range of activities in the classificatory method.

Results of the Classification

The entire process described was exactly applied to each of the 1,044 churches. Their classification was in effect a sorting of their schedules as though a set of Noah's Ark working models were actually distributed into compartments corresponding to the rectangles shown in Chart III. The result was as follows:

TABLE V — 1,044 CITY CHURCHES CLASSIFIED BY SUBTYPES

Sub-type	Number of Activities	Range of Activities	Churches Number	Per Cent.
A I	Smallest	Narrowest	90	8.6
A II	Smallest	Narrow	35	3.3
A III	Smallest	Medium	27	2.6
A IV	Smallest	Broad	32	3.1
A V	Smallest	Broadest	15	1.4
B I	Small	Narrow	101	9.7
B II	Small	Medium	161	15.4
B III	Small	Broad	84	8.1
B IV	Small	Broadest	11	1.0
C I	Medium	Medium	115	11.0
C II	Medium	Broad	116	11.1
C III	Medium	Broadest	30	2.9
D I	Large	Medium	27	2.6
D II	Large	Broad	80	7.7
D III	Large	Broadest	43	4.1
E I	Largest	Broad	10	0.9
E II	Largest	Broadest	67	6.4
Total			1,044	100.0

THE SUBTYPES AS STATISTICAL UNITS

The method thus achieved what it set out to do. It derived from the number and frequency of unit-items in church programs a classification of churches by purely statistical methods. The classes could be accurately described in relation to the scales used and to the modifying process introduced to allow for the factor of emphasis. This is shown in the second and third columns of the table. The number of churches in each class and the per cent. distribution of all churches among the seventeen classes show considerable inequality, a fact which furnishes initial clews to interpretation.

The seventeen classes are the actual working units of the investigation. To be sure, they are combined with larger groupings and come to be considered as subtypes (as in Table II); but not until their own internal characteristics and their affinities have been further explored statistically. Data for the entire seventeen subtypes appear in detail in Appendix C and most of the refinements of interpretation are definitely based on direct study of them.

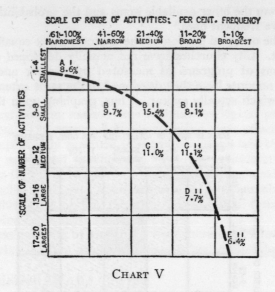

SCALE OF RANGE OF ACTIVITIES: PER CENT. FREQUENCY

| | .61-100%
NARROWEST | 41-60%
NARROW | 21-40%
MEDIUM | 11-20%
BROAD | 1-10%
BROADEST |

CHART V

THE MAJOR STATISTICAL GROUPS

Location and Per Cent. Distribution of Subtypes Which Constitute 5 Per Cent. or More of the Total.

LOGICAL POSSIBILITIES

With respect to the position of any given class of churches indicated upon the diagram, it was further observed that variations of three sorts are possible. There may be other churches which have increased or decreased the range and variety of their programs without increasing or decreasing the number of their activities. These will be located by moving along the horizontal lines in the chart in the plane of the range-of-activity scale. Other churches may have increased or decreased the number of their activities without increasing or decreasing their range. They will be found by moving along vertical lines on the chart in the plane of the number-of-activities scale. Still other churches may have increased or decreased both the range and the number of their activities. These will be found by looking along the diagonal line of the chart. No other variations are possible.

Since the preponderant historic movement of the churches was known to be toward larger and broader programs,[2] the logical possibility of recession as a basis for classification was ignored and de-

2 See pp. 76 f.

gree of change was reckoned only in the direction of ampler and
more complex activities.

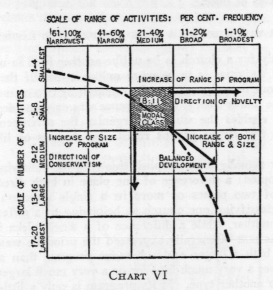

CHART VI

Possible Directions of Development Toward Complexity of Program.

SIGNIFICANCE OF VARIATION

Within the path of this forward movement these possible variations and what they indicate in terms of the relations of one class
to another are indicated on Chart VI. Thus, with respect to the
modal class, to increase the range of activities without increasing
their number is change in the direction of novelty. It goes beyond
the average practice of churches in the selection of infrequent elements for a program of a given size. Statistically it is a dilution
of program. Such churches tend to spread out abnormally, considering the number of activities. They are more adventurous than
the modal type. They tend toward the unusual.

On the other hand, to increase the number of activities without
increasing their range is simply to do more of the same sort of thing
that all of the churches of the type do. This is a further concentration of program along existing lines. Various motives may lead
churches to adopt this alternative, but it is likely to include the more
docile and traditional examples of the type. It expresses the trend
toward conservatism.[3]

3 For samples of actual programs of these contrasting types, see p. 97.

that it represents preëminently the characteristics of the city church. More than one-third of the 1,044 churches fall within this range. A later chapter will show reason for believing that it does represent the most frequent and statistically characteristic religious institution which the stronger and more completely organized denominations recognize as a "church" in the American city—the one which constitutes the central mass about which their urban church development varies. In order, however, not to anticipate this claim before its proof has been established, this type is designated simply as moderately developed and slightly adapted to urban environment.

II. CHURCHES WITH LESS EXTENSIVE AND DIVERSIFIED PROGRAMS

Working backward from the modal subtype to the next subtype which differs from it both in number and in range of activities, one comes to the one designated A II on the classification table. Its nearest variant in range of activities is A III with a smallest-medium

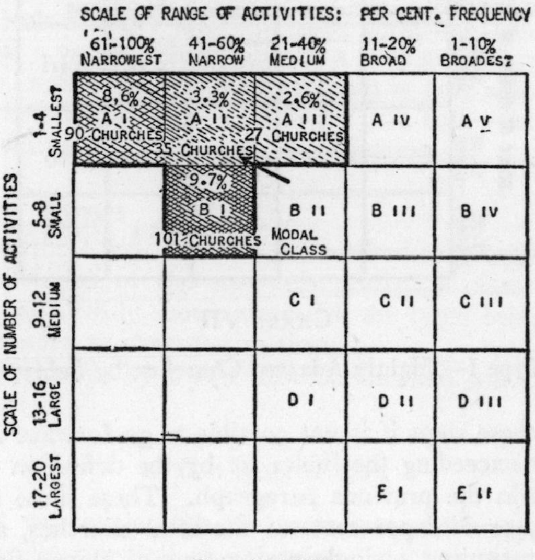

CHART VIII

Type II—Unadapted Churches, by Subtypes.

program, and in number of activities, B I with a small-narrow program. The relation of these three subtypes to one another and to the modal subtype and the number and per cent. of total churches included in each appear in Chart VIII. By strict definition they should stand as a complete major type. In order, however, to reduce the number of major types for purposes of discussion, Subtype A I, consisting of the ninety churches that have the narrowest and most limited program of all, is grouped with them. A single major type is thus constituted by combination of all the subtypes which are inferior to the modal subtype either in number or in range of program, or in both respects. Their combined total is 253 churches, or 24.2 per cent. of the 1,044.

Since the slightly adapted group is the largest and statistically most characteristic group within the sample, the group inferior with

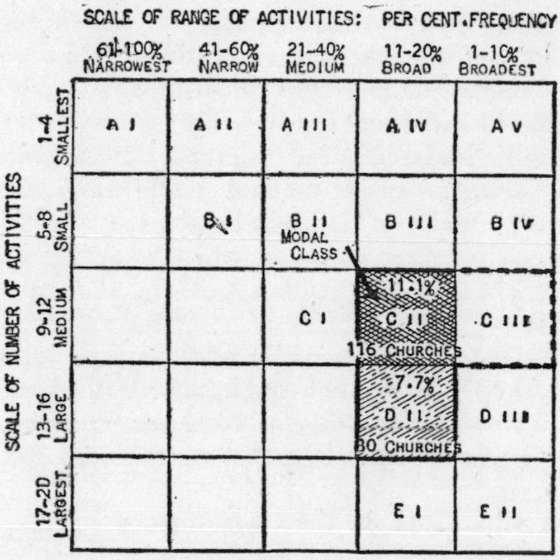

CHART IX

Type III—Internally Adapted Churches, by Subtypes.

respect to it may be called relatively undeveloped and from the standpoint of the city environment, unadapted.

This designation is merely quantitative. It does not imply inferior social or religious value. All it means is that measured by a common scale these 253 churches do not show the kind or degree of institutional development which most city churches of the recognized denominations have.

III. MORE DEVELOPED CHURCHES

The next major type is located by passing beyond the modal subtype both in number and in range of activities. This starts the new type with Subtype C II with a medium-broad program and consisting of 116 churches or 11.1 per cent. of the total. This is next to the most numerous subtype. Differing from it by only one degree in the direction of increased number of activities within the same range is Subtype D II with a large-broad program and including eighty churches.

Obviously the definition requires that Subtype C III also be added to complete the major type. Only an individual study of the small group of churches falling within this subtype discovered practical reasons why this should not be done. Such a study showed that the churches of C III were very unlike those of C II in spite of their statistical nearness.

Of course the entire statistical process of classifying churches as now being described was checked for validity by an objective study of many of the individual churches constituting the statistical groups. If on the whole it had been found not to group together churches which looked alike and felt alike in actual acquaintance when compared on this basis, the entire method would have been abandoned. In point of fact, intensive field study showed that to an amazing degree it grouped together churches which experience discovered to be alike. Evidence of this will appear in the exhibition of its detailed results.

The internal homogeneity of a subtype was in no case more fully demonstrated by intimate acquaintance with cases than in that of C III, which follows the medium-broad program of C II and from which one expects a medium-broadest program as the next step in development.

Its linkage with C II in the classificatory process is, however, evidence of weakness in that process at one point. Classification was based upon three factors,[4] namely, number of stated organizations and activities, the range of these and the proportion of them that fall within any interval on the frequency scale. In taking into account the proportion of activities falling within the varying intervals of the frequency scale, the mistake was made of reckoning only with those *of less than average* frequency of occurrence. In their case it was ascertained that a church which went into the realm of infrequent activities went far enough in and with sufficient emphasis to justify one in classifying it accordingly.[5]

It was not considered, however, that a church with a limited number of activities might occupy an infrequent range by the expedient of *cutting off most of the basic activities common to the churches as a group.* It might permit itself to drift far by the device of being attached to its original anchorage by a very long and slen-

4 See pp. 58-61.
5 See p. 61.

der rope. Church number five in Table IV is a good example. It has a women's organization, boys' and girls' clubs and gymnasium work, but no regular preaching. Yet it calls itself a church!

With most of the churches of Subtype C III this is what has happened—generally in less flagrant degree. Upon examination the majority of them were found to be neighborhood houses or Christian centers, or else churches which have evolved in a similar direction. All maintained the name "church" and some of the original functions of worship and systematic instruction. But they had largely dropped the conventional women's and young people's societies with other frequent marks of the "family church" in exchange for novel activities more suited to their peculiar constituencies. Consequently while they had the same number of activities as Subtype C II and increased by but one step their range of activities (namely, from broad to broadest), they actually varied greatly *by reason of the activities which they omitted*. This the basic method of the study failed to find out statistically. Consequently the boundaries of the major type, starting with Subtype C II, are not determined exclusively by systematic grouping of statistical classes according to a uniform method. Subtype C III is excluded contrary to the definition.[6] This appears in Chart IX.

As contrasted with the slightly adapted group the 196 churches left in this third major type have a larger and more varied program. The designation "elaborated" is therefore warranted on purely statistical grounds. By reason of the character and significance of the new elements admitted into the program it has been thought apt to call it the internally adapted type.[7]

IV. EXTREME COMPLEXITY OF CHURCH DEVELOPMENT

The first subtype of the next major type (identified as "socially adapted") is found by going a single step in both number and range of activities from the modal subtype of the preceding group.[8] This starts one with Subtype D III, as shown on Chart X, consisting of forty-three churches, which constitutes 4.1 per cent. of the total.

6 For representative programs showing the difference as explained above, see p. 148 and p. 193; for a sample case, see p. 198. The failure of the basic method—by a rigid statistical process—to classify this subtype in harmony with experience proves that it was not "one hundred per cent. perfect." The missing factor can easily be allowed for in the subsequent development of methodology simply by applying to all the ranges of program—including the most frequent activities—the method of determining the average number of items which fall in this range exactly as has already been done to the ranges including the least frequent activities explained on p. 61.

7 See p. 147.

8 The designation "socially adapted" chosen for this type does not rise out of statistical considerations. With respect to designations used for the preceding types it ought to have been called the "highly elaborated" or the "most fully developed." But the nature of the new elements entering into its program, as they appear from the items on the frequency scale, is self-interpretative. They include such items as employment agencies, visiting nurses, day nurseries, dispensaries or clinics, which are clearly attempts at adapting a church's service to the needs of socially deficient communities.

With respect to range of activities this brings one to the limits of the field. Subtype D III combines a significant number of activities from the entire gamut of the thirty-three enumerated on the frequency scale. Consequently no subtype can exceed it in this direction. In the direction, however, of more activities within this same range, Subtype E II, with sixty-seven churches, constituting 6.4 per cent. of the total, belongs with D III—the two completing a fourth major type. This is shown on Chart X. This type shows a

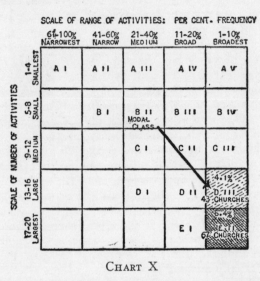

CHART X

Type IV—Socially Adapted Churches, by Subtypes.

combined total of 110 churches, or 10.5 per cent. of the 1,044 under classification.

V. VARIANTS

The four major types of churches thus far determined account for 88 per cent. of the total. Chart XI shows the location of the remaining 12 per cent. which are furthest from the dominant line of church development (indicated by the diagonal curve on the chart) and which are excluded from the preceding types by definition; with the addition of Subtype C III irregularly excluded from the major Type III on grounds previously explained.

This small remainder of churches does not constitute a homogeneous group. They are simply the wandering stars which shoot off from the main paths of development in the opposite directions of extreme novelty or extreme conservatism of program. The subtypes which lie in these two directions will have later description and interpretation.[9]

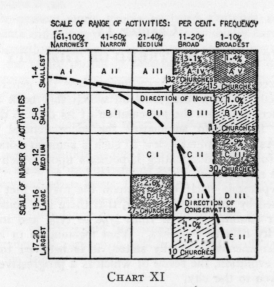

SCALE OF RANGE OF ACTIVITIES: PER CENT. FREQUENCY

CHART XI

Type V—Widely Variant Churches, by Subtypes.

That these widely variant churches are relatively few and that there is a main path along which the great majority of city churches are distributed is the chief discovery to which the long process above described has led. There is something of unity and consistency in the church-making process as going on in the American city. And whether one likes its results or not, to understand the process must surely be one of the first tasks of interpretation.

9 The discovery of their statistical position of course implies no criticism of these churches. When one comes to interpret their conduct he may decide that they are making radical and thoroughgoing adaptation to some specific element in the urban situation. This may be preëminently the thing for them to do.

"From the beginning of our churches," says Bacon, speaking of New England, "the Dorcas Society or charitable sewing circle was characteristic of them." Based on the New Testament example and the neighborly and social impulses of women of the frontier village, this type of organization—Ladies' Aid Society, association or guild —has become one of the fundamental agencies of the church.

WOMEN'S MISSIONARY SOCIETIES

Scarcely less frequent is the third item of the established subsidiaries of the church, namely, women's missionary organizations. At this point the economic interpretation of American religious history wavers. How could mere fragments of population, struggling desperately for a foothold in the wilderness, in constant danger of complete annihilation at the hand of the savage, write so early and so deeply into their religious story their concern for the heathen across the seas? It was chiefly in New England, whose soil was uncongenial to profitable agriculture, but whose ships sailed the farthest seas, that this vision of world-wide Christian relationships was natural. In this as in so many other respects the schoolmistress of the frontier, the New England influence wrote women's missionary organizations into the original program of the American church at a very early date. Mite societies of this type appear in the eighteenth century, while the "Boston Female Society for Missionary Purposes" (1800) and the "New Hampshire Female Cent Institution" (1804) mark the beginning of formal organization and were soon widely copied. In this single aspect of the American church what is now a most widely established feature cannot be regarded as the product of general American evolution, but rather of a provincial idealism propagated by its own strength and sincerity.

THE ERA OF YOUTH

From the beginning of the last century, when the woman's missionary societies were originating, it was eighty years before anything new happened in the realm of religious organization at all commensurate with the facts previously enumerated. In 1881, the first Young People's Society of Christian Endeavor was established, initiating the era of formal organization of young people for service under their own leadership and initiative. This story is part of contemporary experience and does not require further illustration, except to say that nothing has happened since which has really become generally characteristic of the American church.

The story of these first four items in the program of the American church in order of present frequency thus epitomizes its more general history. It makes plain the mild beginnings of that specialization of organization for the different age-, and sex-groups which has so greatly lengthened the list of activities to-day. So far evolution had provided societies only for children, for women, and

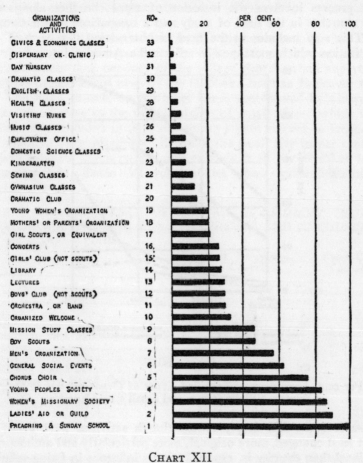

CHART XII

Per cent. Frequency of Church Organizations and Activities.

for young people in mixed organizations, but the tendency toward differentiation which these beginnings marked out is clear.

No set of organizations is so deeply embedded in American religious history as these which have been considered. It will not be questioned that this fact explains why they stand at the top of the list in the contemporary frequency scale.

in consequent complexity of social organization) and in complexity of church program. It also shows that the type of church prevalent in the small city begins slightly beyond where the town leaves off.

TOWN AND CITY CHURCH COMPARED

The comparisons of the above table involve the entire range of rural churches. It is more accurate to compare the most highly developed form of genuinely rural church, namely, that of the town, with the most frequent and representative church of the large city as described in a subsequent chapter.[2] The degree of their correspondence and difference appears in Table VII:

TABLE VII — FREQUENCY OF CERTAIN SUBSIDIARY CHURCH ORGANIZATIONS IN TOWN CHURCHES AND IN MODAL CHURCHES OF LARGE CITIES

Organization	Per Cent. Frequency	
	Town Church	Modal City Church
Some Subsidiary Organizations besides Sunday School	93	100
Women's Organization	87	99
More than one Women's Organization	44	81
Mixed Sex Organizations (usually young people's)	67	77
More than one Mixed Sex Organization	37	8
Men's Organization	10	53
Boys' Organization	15	52
Girls' Organization	20	34

ADVANCE AND OVERLAPPING

According to the showing of the above table, the most character istic city church is considerably ahead of the highest rural type in complexity of organization. The more general differences between the two are easily intelligible. In only one item, namely, mixed sex organization, is the town church ahead of the city church; but mixed sex organization is exactly what the city church is getting away from. It substitutes rather organizations specializing in service to a single age or sex, as illustrated by separate organizations for men, women, boys and girls.

In other words, the average development of the city church lies beyond the utmost point which the rural church has reached.[3]

Below the average city church, however, are numerous undeveloped city churches which overlap the higher reaches of the rural church. Roughly speaking, the 25 per cent. or more of city churches

2 See pp. 95 f.
3 For discussion of the competency of the evidence to determine "average" development, see pp. 95 f.

which are least developed, are no larger and no more completely organized than many average rural churches. So far as the criteria go, they register no response to urban environment. They are un-adapted.

At the other extreme come the highly developed city types which lie farthest from their country origins and indeed have gone far beyond the urban average. In them the precise marks of the city's influence are easy to trace.

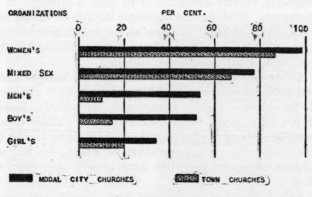

CHART XIV

Per Cent. Frequency of Specified Organizations in Town Churches and in Modal Churches of Large Cities.

An Evolved Rural Church

With the aid of history and the extension of the contemporary series of phenomena to include the rural church, it is at length possible to bring the dominating hypothesis of the study to its complete development. This hypothesis is that the city church is an evolved rural church. What it has come to be is the result of an evolution from a rural parent stock. Its immediate ancestor is the town church. This does not mean, of course, that every highly developed church has followed exactly the same steps, nor that all churches should evolve as far as the farthest in order to serve the city in the best way. On the other hand it is not a figure of speech. Specifically it means five things:

(1) Some city churches date back to the time when the city was still a village and have never grown out of their early village attitudes. City growth in America has shown unparalleled rapidity. Certain institutions have grown up along with the city; others have

(5) Finally, by common consent, the church as an institution is judged conservative. Since its roots are so deeply embedded in rural civilization it may be assumed to have brought over much of the past into ecclesiastical life. This is in contrast with other factors of modern life which have reached their most novel and dynamic form in the modern city.

Such is the rural inheritance of the city church.[6] It is this inheritance which the undeveloped types perpetuate and from which the modal type has departed but slightly.

Beyond the modal type begin those forms of church life which reflect the city in some conspicuous degree. There is no direct evidence to show whether they actually reflect populations that have lived for longer time in a city environment, or populations of mixed antecedents—rural and urban—in which the process of urbanization has been speeded up by some special pressure. In either case they are a minority bearing the special brand of the city.

In contrast with them, and by reason of the underlying rural inheritance, more than half of all urban churches must be regarded, in the light of the hypothesis of the study, as in the city rather than of it. The city church on the whole has not yet shaken the dust of the country from its feet.

The validity of the hypothesis that the city church is an essentially evolved rural church must stand or fall with the evidence of data to be presented in the following sections. All that is sought at this point is to maintain its inherent credibility.

Why the City Should Modify the Church

The virtual certainty that the city would impress its own forms and characteristics upon an institution would probably be taken for granted in any other case than that of the church. All the city's human institutions are involved in the urbanizing process. The former simplicity of human relationships is lost, and their elements are recombined in the more and more complex patterns.

Thus, one of the most frequent concerns of the church is with what the city has done to the family. It immensely reduces the traditional sphere of the home and substitutes numerous external social processes. The rural child is born in the home; the city child in a hospital. In the country, eyes, teeth and tonsils are the incidental care of the family physician; in the city, they have become the specific business of armies of specialists. Rural education is a narrow interest typically carried on by a single teacher for a handful of pupils; urban education is a vast and complicated set of affairs in

6 See Williams, *Our Rural Heritage* (New York, Knopf, 1925) for a much broader application of the theory to civilization in many aspects.

which even the small child is subjected to a wide variety of instructors. The youth who goes to a city high school finds a more specialized institution than was the college of yesterday, while the college has been drawn into the mazes of university interests and organizations. The majority of youth, however, pass early into industry or business. Here they find themselves subjected to highly organized systems in extreme contrast with rural working and exchanging of goods. A most flagrant difference is the presence in the city of a very high proportion of women workers, many of whom are married and many more of whom live as well as work away from home. Urban social pursuits and organizations take on a parallel degree of variety and intricacy. To a degree formerly unknown to village communities, for all epochs of life beginning with childhood, social satisfactions are found outside of the home by individuals going their several ways rather than by family groups. The family under such circumstances cannot be the closely knit unit that it formerly was. The city has urbanized the family.

Not a few of the characteristic organizations and activities undertaken by the city church are deliberate and confessed efforts to supply a substitute environment affording the same moral atmosphere that the home formerly was supposed to afford. It is, therefore, probably not amiss to regard the city church's wide range of new activities, organized by age-, and sex-groups, in the large, as a sign of urbanization and of the larger adaptation to city environment.

Under such conditions, that adaptation has not gone farther than it has is probably to be explained by the conservatism of ecclesiastically organized religion. From this standpoint, the modification of the family's functions appears as its disintegration. As a mere investigation of objective facts, it is no part of the business of this study to speculate how far this attitude may be justified. Very likely the very terms of present urban existence constitute an overshooting of the mark for humanity. Perhaps its stuff was not made for such extreme pressure or specialization.

Quite possibly the effort of man to live in cities like ours involves both organic and moral overstrain in certain phases. It is simply not yet known whether man is going to succeed in the great adventure of a highly urbanized civilization.

The bearing of these considerations upon the hypothesis of this study is this: Confronted with such alternatives, it is no wonder that emotions are stirred concerning the evolution of the city church, and that fears are aroused. Unquestionably the city breeds a different philosophy from the country's and threatens a changed morality. Such characteristics of the city will naturally be resisted by a transplanted rural church which instinctively senses shifting standards and looks upon emancipation from past conventions as a surrender of character.

Certain phenomena of the city church, therefore, are not to be explained as the result of the reasonable pressure of the city to make the church over into its own pattern and the natural resistance of conservatism. The city shows churches on the primitive as well as on the rural level. Later paragraphs will deal in detail with certain rural phases of the unadapted city church showing how strong an influence the extreme revulsion of the non-urban mind exerts in its origins and perpetuation. Many of the new sects and isms of the city are largely marks of an undermining of the rural tradition of certain immigrant populations, which are too feeble or too uncourageous to make genuinely urban adaptations, but are at the same time unable to stand still in the changeful city.

For the most part, however, the church does respond to the city. Greater complexity of organization and wider range of service are the most general symptoms of it. The most outstanding and obvious result is that some churches respond faster than others, so that they string out in a series registering differing degrees of urban adaptation.

As a result, the American city has a church that is gradually coming to reflect its general environment—but that does so very incompletely. In more than one-half of its area the city church is not urbanized in the sense of the preceding analysis. It reflects the newness of the city and the relative disinclination of ecclesiastical organization to change—also the relative total weakness of Protestantism and its extreme divisions and over-small local units. It expresses the attitudes of many city dwellers who have but recently come from the country or who came too late to change their minds— the permanently un-urbanized. It may suit such people; but it has not proved that it can serve them adequately in a city environment. Here they are literally demoralized. Their earlier manners of thought and conduct were the expression not necessarily of superior virtue, but of a simpler environment. They have lost this environment and cannot maintain the continuity of the new life with the old. They are uneasy victims of corresponding psychological changes. The unanswerable demonstration of this is the fact that they so frequently lose the younger generation. The church cannot stay with the backward-looking and unadventurous. It must go forward with youth to some version or other of urban adaptation.

How fast it has done this and how far it has gone can be discovered only by the study of the steps of adaptation in detail. How far it ought to go one will, in some measure, be in position to guess at the end of the study. What must first concern one is the process as a whole. It is a process of evolution and adaptation. This is its meaning and the meaning of its successive types as statistically determined.

The Possibility of Retrogression

Up to this point the discussion has proceeded as though city churches came to be as they are always and entirely through a process of evolution. This would be to imply institutional immortality—something which the nature of society by no means guarantees. While progressive development is a general tendency actually encountered in the study and while a fully adapted religious institution, like the church, has every prospect of living as long as the civilization of which it is a part, not all individual churches are thus adapted. There is, therefore, a backward secondary tendency to be reckoned with. Churches decay as well as develop. This no more denies the evolutionary process than the dissolution of man denies the story of his growth. An old man does not go to pieces "all at once and nothing first." Sometimes it is his eyes which go, again his ears. What is left of him is a fragment of his former powers. Similarly, churches decline gradually and irregularly.

Thus the downward course of a church in St. Louis was traced for ten years following a previous decade during which it stood still. It was the last survivor of a slow retreat which has swept a dozen of the strongest churches of the city out of a favored residential area of a quarter of a century ago, now teeming with sordid Negro tenements and the crowded homes of rural immigrants. During this period of decay it progressively lopped off one function after another until it had become practically a shell of its former self. Its actual constituency was so remote that when a new site was chosen, it was entirely beyond the city limits.

CHURCHES COMING AND GOING

This possibility must enter into the particular judgment passed on any individual church. One must know its ancestors and must also know its own life-history. Before asking how far it has gone, one must investigate the way it is coming and be sure that it is coming at all.

It is plain that a church may come to fall within any given type as a result of retrogression. Any present level, except the highest, may conceivably be a stranding by reason of a recessive movement. One finds it not at the highest point to which it has climbed but at the place where it has landed after a fall.

Usually abnormalities of program mark retrogressive churches. Many a dignified man becomes a temporary contortionist in an effort to save himself from a fall. Similarly, with churches on the down grade. There is a desperate snatching at this and that resulting in an ill-balanced and lopsided program.

At the very bottom, in the company of new and always unfortunate churches, the great church of yesterday may sometimes be found. This motley company of failures is like the tragical mixture of population in an almshouse where homeless children, feeble-minded and unfortunates in their second childhood are herded together.

Summary

The book has now presented the relationships between the churches included in its study from two points of view. The former was methodological, the present one is explanatory. In the previous chapters no clew to the meaning of the relationships of the church types had been presented. In considering them, one started, merely as an expedient, with the most frequent type, and measured backward and forward from it for degrees of difference. In the present chapter, on the contrary, the possession of an explanatory hypothesis makes it possible to begin at the beginning of the series and to view it as a continuous whole.

Including the additional possibility of a recessive movement as now recognized, the version of the facts to which the basic hypothesis leads may be restated as follows: City churches as a group are found distributed along a path leading from simplicity to complexity of program. The most general explanation of this phenomenon in the light of the host of ecclesiastical organizations and activities, is that they are increasingly getting away from a rural tradition and are moving toward urbanization. Individual churches, however, may sometimes have to move in an opposite direction and to retrace their own steps. The type of any given church is, therefore, to be determined primarily with reference to its degree of development beyond a rural parent stock in the effort to adapt itself to the city, or in terms of its retrogression from some previous peak of its own evolution.

Subordinate Hypotheses

It is not assumed, of course, that the hypothesis of rural tradition and partial urban adaptation can explain every phenomenon of the city church. Differences in numerical and financial strength obviously modify its working programs. One does not always have what he wants; sometimes one cannot afford it. Again, there are numerous particular ecclesiastical traditions, perpetuated in the various denominations, as well as a general rural tradition. What a given body of Christians believes to be the proper organization and sphere of church activity manifestly enters into the determination of the types of its churches. Then there are the numberless special circumstances that affect the institutional strategy and practice of the individual church.

The influence of these factors has not been segregated nor directly measured, but the study assumes that they function constantly either reënforcing or checking the general processes of urban adaptation. After the concrete situations in which they seem to appear have been considered and illustrated in the chapters that follow, these factors receive more formal recognition as subordinate hypotheses and principles of explanation.[7]

With this section the first major division of the book is completed. Following an historical preface, the method and its outcome in the determination of types of churches was explained in Chapters II and III. The present chapter introduced the dominant hypothesis which was implied earlier in the naming of the types.

According to this hypothesis, the "unadapted" type is to be regarded as essentially the hold over of a rural institution which has not begun to make distinctive urban adjustments. The "slightly adapted" type is the product of a struggle between traditional and novel forces resulting in a small degree of adaptation. The "internally adapted" type shows the church committed to urban attitudes and adaptation but limiting their organized expression primarily within its own institutional sphere and with respect to its own constituency. The "socially adapted" type, on the contrary, molds itself upon phases of service to the city beyond its original constituency and frequently adopts a special constituency on the grounds of its acute social need.

Subordinate hypotheses show why the evolution of individual churches, which classify statistically within these types, may have special principles of explanation, and warn against overworking the major hypothesis or depending upon it too exclusively as the clew to the facts.

7 See pp. 240 f. and 302 f.

PART II

FINDINGS AND CONCLUSIONS IN DETAIL

Chapter V

THE SLIGHTLY ADAPTED CHURCH

Part II presents the main body of statistical data and conclusions resulting from the method and leading to the explanatory hypothesis stated in Part I.

Findings and Conclusions in Detail

This part in turn falls into two divisions. In the first (Chapters V to X), the results of the study are exhibited and the data directly interpreted. In the second, the significance of the results as a working classification of churches is tested and reënforced from various points of view.

ADEQUACY OF THE DATA

The kind of validity which attaches to the data also differs in the two divisions. In the first, one is dealing with data entirely adequate to constitute a sound basis for determining the types of city churches, which is the fundamental problem that the study sets for itself. The 1,044 churches constitute a numerically adequate sample of the city church field.

The relative size of the sample is seen from the comparison in Table VIII.

TABLE VIII—ESTIMATED NUMBER OF PROTESTANT CHURCHES AND MEMBERS IN CITIES OF 100,000 POPULATION AND NUMBER OF PROTESTANT CHURCHES AND MEMBERS INCLUDED IN THE PRESENT STUDY

	Estimated Total, 1922	Number Included in Present Study	Ratio of Sample to Total
Churches	13,182	1,044	7.9
Members—Method 1	4,500,883	578,146	12.8
Method 2	4,297,591	578,146	13.5

The numbers in the column entitled "Estimated Total, 1922," are necessarily estimates because no one has counted city churches since the United States Religious Census in 1916. The last previous census was in 1906.

An obvious method of estimating the actual total number at the date of the survey was to project the same yearly amount of increase over the six years following 1916 as was known to have pertained in the previous ten years. There were 10,096 Protestant churches in cities of 100,000 and over in 1906, and 12,025 in 1916. This gives a probability of 13,182 in 1922.

In estimating the membership by the same method, one starts with 2,954,955 members in cities of the above-mentioned size in 1906, and 3,921,160 in 1916. At the same amount of increase, the 1922 membership should have been 4,500,883.

A second method starts with 3,921,160 known members of 1916 and adds an estimated increase for the six following years of 1.6 per cent. annually, which is the average increase revealed by the annual Protestant church membership statistics published by the Federal Council of the Churches of Christ in America. This estimated increase is for total membership and it is not known how accurately it applies to the churches in larger cities taken alone. On this basis, the estimated total membership in cities of more than 100,000 should have been 4,297,591 in 1922.

The results of both methods are presented because they are significantly close together considering the large number of the cases involved, and consequently tend strongly to confirm each other.

The numerical adequacy of so large a sample for comparing types of churches will not be questioned.[1] Unless broken up into types which include an excessively small number of churches it affords enough cases for the determination of trends through statistical processes. The likenesses and unlikenesses between resulting types, when accurately measured, will closely reflect the likenesses and unlikenesses of similar groups of Protestant city churches throughout the nation.

In the second division of Part II (which tests and reënforces as a working classification the major types as statistically and analytically determined) the adequacy of the underlying data is less perfect. It is valid for the uses made of it and its limitations are sufficiently discussed at the beginning of the chapters concerned.

The Slightly Adapted Church

In beginning the description in detail of the several types of churches which are identified by the study, one naturally starts with the modal type of the sample—the slightly adapted church. Each section of description is followed by one of explanation, applying and amplifying the explanatory hypothesis and adding supplemental explanations as suggested by the matter treated.

[1] The fact that the sample includes about 13 per cent. of the membership of city churches but only about 8 per cent. of the churches of course indicates that the churches included in the sample were beyond average size. In view of this, the problem of their competency to throw light upon the actual group-distribution of all city churches is raised by later uses of the data (see p. 301), but is not involved at this point.

The study of this type is based upon 360 cases, these constituting 34.5 per cent. of the total number of churches investigated.

The slightly adapted group includes the following subtypes:

Sub-types	Type of Program by Activities Number Range	Number of Churches	Per Cent. of All Churches
B II	Small Medium	161	15.4
B III	Small Broad	84	8.1
C I	Medium Medium	115	11.0

PROGRAMS AND THEIR VARIATIONS

The range of their respective programs and five sample programs for churches of each subtype appear in Table IX.

TABLE IX — SAMPLE PROGRAMS OF SLIGHTLY ADAPTED CHURCHES

Organizations and Activities	B II 1	2	3	4	5	B III 1	2	3	4	5	C I 1	2	3	4	5
1. Preaching and Sunday School	*	*	*	*	*	*		*		*	*	*	*	*	*
2. Ladies' Aid or Guild.	*	*	*			*	*	*	*	*	*	*	*	*	*
3. Women's Missionary Society	*	*	*			*					*	*	*	*	*
4. Young People's Society		*	*	*	*		*		*		*	*		*	*
5. Chorus Choir	*	*				*					*	*	*	*	*
6. General Social Events	*	*						*			*	*	*	*	*
7. Men's Organization		*	*			*	*	*	*		*	*		*	*
8. Boy Scouts								*	*	*	*	*	*	*	*
9. Mission Study Classes								*			*	*	*		
10. Organized Welcome					*						*	*			
11. Orchestra or Band	*		*					*				*			
12. Boys' Club (not Scouts)	*	*											*		*
13. Lectures	*		*									*	*		
14. Library	*											*	*		
15. Girls' Club (not Scouts)					*								*		
16. Concerts	*							*				*	*		*
17. Girl Scouts or Equivalent								*	*	*					*
18. Mothers' or Parents' Organization															
19. Young Women's Organization								*	*						
20. Dramatic Club								*	*	*					
21. Gymnasium Classes								*		*					
22. Sewing Classes															
	8	7	7	5	8	6	8	5	8	8	11	9	12	11	9

A still further analysis of the difference between the subtypes is presented in the following comparison:

Sub-types	Range of Program	Number of Activities	
		Range	Average
B II	Items 1–17	5–8	6.3
B III	Items 1–22	5–8	6.5
C I	Items 1–17	9–12	9.1

As compared with the modal Subtype B II, Subtype B III increases the range of its activities without increasing the number, while Subtype C I increases the number without increasing the range. These alternatives are graphically presented in Chart VII.

If, for example, a church of Subtype B II has only five items in its program, they are most likely to be preaching and Sunday school, ladies' aid and women's missionary societies, young people's organization and a chorus choir. If it has eight activities, it is most likely to add church receptions and dinners, a men's organization and Boy Scouts; but it at least chooses its activities somewhere within the first seventeen items of the list.

A church of Subtype B III may have as few as five activities, but enjoys a range of twenty-two items from which to select them, provided that one activity must come from items 18 to 22. Any one who will make the experiment of organizing a church program out of five to eight items within such limitations will be convinced that they afford opportunity only for an unbalanced, attenuated program. Yet that is the choice which 8.1 per cent. of the 1,044 sample churches make.

Contrast now a church of Subtype C I. It may have as many as twelve activities selected from the first seventeen on the list. A pastor may build an exceedingly compact program for an average church out of such elements. He perhaps does not need a boys' club if he has Boy Scouts, and may omit an orchestra as something of a refinement. Less than one-fourth of the 1,044 sample churches have any separate girls' organization, so he will round out an amply "typical" program though omitting one.

Eleven per cent. of the 1,044 sample churches have programs of from nine to twelve items approximating such a character.

SIMILARITIES OUTWEIGH DIFFERENCES

If it is objected that a program of five items chosen from a list of twenty-two is so different from one of twelve items chosen from a list of seventeen that they ought not to be classified as belonging to a common type, the answer, as previously indicated,[2] is that the

2 See p. 64.

types are constituted by a systematic grouping of the subtypes merely for convenience and economy of thinking. The three subtypes, B II, B III, and C I, are composed of churches more nearly like one another than they are like those of any of the other fourteen subtypes. There are really extraordinary differences within the total sample of city churches compared with the differences within the type. This justifies the inclusion within a single class of churches differing in program as widely as those above described, provided they show other common tendencies and trends. That they do so will appear from later paragraphs.

CONTENTS OF PROGRAMS

Without forcing any hard and fast classification upon the twenty-two items constituting the possible program of a slightly adapted church, it is at least possible to discuss the tendencies which they express. Beyond the four elementary activities common to more than 80 per cent. of the 1,044 sample churches, namely, preaching and Sunday school, two women's organizations and a young people's society, four tendencies are clear: (1) to embellish the church's services by the development of such organizations as a chorus choir or, less frequently, of an orchestra; (2) to enrich the church's social life; (3) to add organizations based upon the differentiations of age-, and sex-groups (men's, boys', girls', young men's), and (4) to add organizations reflecting more varied interests (missions, culture, recreation). These are the tendencies at work within the typical church program. To explain these tendencies and to interpret more fully the content and limits of the program is the task of the next chapter.

Other Aspects of the Slightly Adapted Church

Each type of city church has been separately studied on all the items of information by which the city churches as a whole have subsequently been characterized.[3] The results as regards the slightly adapted church appear in the following paragraphs.

MEMBERSHIP SIZE

The type is not narrowly limited by size of membership, as is evident from Table X.

The most frequent size of the slightly adapted church is between one and two hundred members, but the larger memberships up to 400 are nearly as frequent and the medium size is 408. In this

3 See p. 205.

TABLE X — MEMBERSHIP OF SLIGHTLY ADAPTED CHURCHES *

Number of Members	Per Cent. Distribution
Under 500	57.0
Under 100	6.7
100 to 200	15.6
200 to 300	13.4
300 to 400	13.7
400 to 500	7.6
500 to 1,000	25.6
1,000 and over	17.4

* 328 churches reporting.

type there are more churches of fewer than 200 members than there are of 1,000 members. A considerable number of relatively small churches may carry on a typical program of service, while a considerable number of very large ones evidently do not care to do more.[4]

AGE AND PERMANENCE

Somewhat fewer than one-third of the churches of the type are less than twenty-five years old; just about one-third are between twenty-five and fifty years old; while somewhat more than one-third are over fifty years old. Only 31.9 per cent. are still located on the spot where they were organized; consequently, a much larger proportion are young in present location than are young in years.

TABLE XI — AGE AND NUMBER OF YEARS IN PRESENT LOCATION OF SLIGHTLY ADAPTED CHURCHES

Years	Per Cent. Distribution	
	Age *	Years in Present Location †
Less than 25	30.4	50.0
25–49	32.2	33.3
50–74	21.3	12.2
75–99	11.5	3.6
100 and over	4.6	0.9

* 286 churches reporting.
† 222 churches reporting.

That nearly two-thirds of typical city churches are less than fifty years old reflects the fact that the American city is of relatively recent growth. That so few have stood on one spot as much as fifty years reflects the enormous mobility of city life as it affects church fortunes.[5] Few indeed are the churches of seventy-five years of age and over which have never moved.

4 Appendix Table 5.
5 Appendix Tables 6, 7 and 8.

In terms of its paid religious workers, the typical city church is characteristically a one-man enterprise, as shown by Table XII.

TABLE XII — PAID RELIGIOUS WORKERS IN SLIGHTLY ADAPTED CHURCHES *

Number Employed		Per Cent. Distribution of Churches
1	....	59.7
2	....	19.4
3	....	12.3
4	....	5.3
5 or more	....	3.3

* 340 churches reporting.

Of paid workers other than pastors there are about eight women to every five men.

The range of activities discovered in the program of the slightly adapted church convincingly explains the presence in 40 per cent. of them of multiple staffs. In a large church the parish work, the church office, the Sunday school or the finances may easily call for an additional worker to supplement the pastor. These are the most frequent types of paid assistance.[6]

It is significant that Subtype C I has a larger proportion of churches with multiple staffs than the average of the type. To add either to the range or to the number of a church's activities, it appears, tends to require more workers.[7]

THE PASTOR

The pastors of typical city churches show all degrees of experience in the ministry as evidenced by Table XIII.

While not many men of very brief experience can command city churches of even moderate development, about one-sixth of the pastors of this group are men of more than thirty years' experience. Assuming that they entered the ministry at an average age of twenty-eight, the men in this group must be fifty-eight and over. The employment of a considerable proportion of men of this age somewhat contradicts the prevailing impression that elderly men cannot hold average city pulpits. Discrimination against inexperience is far greater than against age.[8]

6 The nomenclature in use to describe the workers who perform these services is not sufficiently fixed to enable one to calculate the exact number of each type. The name does not tell exactly what an "assistant pastor" does or how a "pastor's assistant's" time is divided as between clerical and parish duties.

7 Appendix Table 9.

8 Appendix Table 12.

Almost always the pastor of the typical city church is well trained in the traditional sense, 83.5 per cent. having full college and seminary preparation or better, while 10.9 per cent. more are

TABLE XIII — LENGTH OF PASTORS' EXPERIENCE IN
SLIGHTLY ADAPTED CHURCHES *

Number of Years' Experience	Per Cent. Distribution of Pastors
Less than 10	28.9
Less than 5	11.4
5–9	17.5
10–19	26.5
20–29	28.4
30–39	11.9
40 and over	4.3

* 211 pastors reporting.

college graduates. As between the subtypes, B III, whose program inclines toward novelty, has a very high proportion of post-graduate pastors, constituting two-fifths of the total. It is an interesting question how far youth and advanced education on the part of leaders may go toward explaining the characteristics of the subtype.

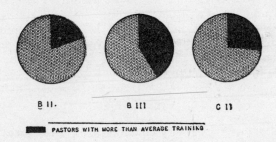

B II.   B III   C II

■■ PASTORS WITH MORE THAN AVERAGE TRAINING

CHART XVI

Proportion of Pastors of Slightly Adapted Churches Who Have More Than Average Theological Training, by Subtypes.

An inspection of the schedules reveals frequent cases in which some unusually enterprising pastor has pushed his church out beyond the natural boundaries of its type in the direction of his special interests or enthusiasms.

Forty-three and five-tenths per cent. of the pastors of slightly adapted churches have been in their present positions between two and five years, and comparatively few maintain themselves as long as ten years in one place. The distribution is as follows: [9]

9 Appendix Table 14.

TABLE XIV—LENGTH OF PASTORS' SERVICE IN PRESENT
POSITION IN SLIGHTLY ADAPTED CHURCHES*

Number of Years	Per Cent. Distribution of Pastors
Under 10	85.3
Under 2	24.9
2–4	43.5
5–9	16.9
10–19	10.7
20–29	1.8
30 and over	2.2

* 225 pastors reporting.

The most frequent salary that the slightly adapted church pays
its pastor is between one and two thousand dollars, apart from parsonage, concerning which no adequate information was received.[10]
Table XV shows the distribution by amount of cash salary. Less

TABLE XV—SALARIES OF PASTORS OF SLIGHTLY
ADAPTED CHURCHES*

Amount	Per Cent. Distribution of Pastors
Under $1,000	3.9
Under $500	0.7
$1,000 to $2,000	33.2
$2,000 to $3,000	24.5
$3,000 to $4,000	14.7
$4,000 to $5,000	8.0
$5,000 to $6,000	6.6
$6,000 to $7,000	4.5
$7,000 to $8,000	2.8
Over $8,000	1.8

* 286 pastors reporting.

than one-fourth of the entire number of pastors receive more than
$4,000.

THE MALE ASSISTANT

Compared with the pastor, the assistant male worker is naturally
younger and less experienced. At the other extreme, however, the
ranks of male assistants include a large proportion of men of over
thirty years' experience (constituting about one-fourth of the total),
which shows that elderly ministers continue as associates beyond
the age at which they can command pulpits.

10 Appendix Table 15. Of city churches reporting to the United States Census of Religious Bodies in 1916, 35.8 per cent. had parsonages. In expense budgets of city families
of moderate means rent averages from 15 to 20 per cent. of the total. The total value
of salaries should, therefore, be increased in about this proportion for those who have
parsonages in addition to cash remuneration.

The education of the male assistant varies strikingly from that of the pastor—there being a much larger proportion of college men without seminary training and a somewhat larger number of non-college men. As in the case of pastors, Subtype B III shows the largest proportion of assistants with post-graduate training. The male assistant's tenure is briefer than that of the pastor and his salary is smaller. Over one-half receive less than $2,000, while $4,000 is virtually the upper limit. Of approximately one-sixth receiving less than $1,000 a large proportion are doubtless unmarried men in their first apprenticeships.[11]

THE FEMALE ASSISTANT

More than half of the female assistants have had less than five years' experience in paid religious work, with fifteen years as the upward limit for churches of this type.

Somewhat less than one-half are college graduates, and nearly one-ninth of the total have had post-graduate or other advanced education; while the remainder are only high-school graduates. Half of them have been less than two years in their present positions and nineteen out of twenty less than five years. Four-fifths of their salaries are under $1,500, with from $1,000 to $1,500 strongly characteristic. In brief, the woman employed as a church worker in this type of city church has little experience, exceedingly brief tenure and small pay, in spite of a high average degree of education, but an education showing little professional specialization.[12]

CURRENT EXPENSES

The annual cost of current church support and operation in the slightly adapted city church averages about $10,000, but the amount most frequently falls between $2,000 and $3,000, and for two-thirds of the churches the annual cost is less than $10,000, as shown in Table XVI.

TABLE XVI — CURRENT EXPENSES OF SLIGHTLY ADAPTED CHURCHES *

Amount	Per Cent. Distribution of Churches
Under $5,000	43.8
Under $1,000	1.5
$1,000 to $2,000	11.4
$2,000 to $3,000	13.9
$3,000 to $4,000	10.2
$4,000 to $5,000	6.8
$5,000 to $10,000	22.5
$10,000 to $15,000	9.6
$15,000 to $20,000	9.6
$20,000 to $25,000	5.6
$25,000 to $50,000	7.4
$50,000 and over	1.5

* 324 churches reporting.

11 Appendix Tables 16-19.
12 Appendix Tables 20-23.

The per capita cost of the slightly adapted church averages $17.96, and the differences between the subtypes become exceedingly instructive. While Subtype C I, with its churches much larger on the average, tends to cost more per church, its per capita cost is only $17.06, or ninety cents below the average; while the per capita cost of churches in Subtype B III is $22.75, or $4.79 above the average, this making it one of the most expensive of the seventeen subtypes. This high per capita cost reflects the high cost of novelty of program coupled with institutional instability by which the subtype is strongly marked.[13]

BENEVOLENCES

Of the slightly adapted churches, 37.7 per cent. give less than $1,000 per year to benevolences, and 66.2 per cent. less than $5,000. Benevolences show no strong tendency to any particular amount, but nearly half of the churches of Subtype C I give in excess of $5,000 annually, whereas only a little more than one-fourth of the churches of the other types reach this level.

Benevolent gifts per capita also show striking contrasts. The average of the type is $12.14, but the churches of Subtype B III

TABLE XVII — EQUIPMENT FACILITIES OF SLIGHTLY
ADAPTED CHURCHES *

Number	Per Cent. Distribution of Churches
Under 5	16.6
5–9	17.1
10–14	29.1
15–19	7.2
20 and over	—

* 278 churches reporting.

give but $9.94 per capita as compared with $15.17 for those of Subtype C I. Novelty of program coupled with institutional instability registers in lack of resources to meet external and general needs, while conservatism of program with economy of per capita operating costs leaves more for such needs. Of the seventeen subtypes, C I and E I have the highest rate of benevolence.[14] This looks as though the best place to get money for Christian enterprises elsewhere is in the church which attempts nothing unusual at home.

13 Appendix Tables 24, 24a and 25.
14 Appendix Tables 25, 26 and 26a.

EQUIPMENT

Of twenty-five equipment facilities for administration, education, publicity and service as listed on the schedule, the slightly adapted church strongly tends to have only from five to nine. The distribution of equipment facilities is given in Table XVII.[15]

NUMBER OF ROOMS IN CHURCH BUILDINGS

The slightly adapted church is most likely to have from five to nine rooms. The distribution of number of rooms is given in Table XVIII.[16]

TABLE XVIII — NUMBER OF ROOMS IN SLIGHTLY
ADAPTED CHURCHES *

Number	Per Cent. Distribution of Churches
Under 10	46.3
Under 5	17.5
1	3.7
2	4.4
3	6.3
4	3.1
5–9	28.8
10–19	33.1
20–29	16.2
30 and over	4.4

* 160 churches reporting.

SEATING CAPACITY OF AUDITORIUMS

The returns on this point are given in Table XIX.

TABLE XIX — SEATING CAPACITY OF AUDITORIUMS OF
SLIGHTLY ADAPTED CHURCHES *

Type and Subtype	Number of Sittings	
	Average	Median
All Slightly Adapted	568	450
B II	466	400
B III	504	425
C I	730	600

* 257 churches reporting.

It will be noted that Subtype C I greatly exceeds the characteristic level of the type measured either by the average or by the median, while Subtype B III is considerably below it.[17]

15 Appendix Table 27.
16 Appendix Table 28.
17 Appendix Table 30.

VALUE OF CHURCH PLANT

This item also was measured both by the average and the median for the type and its subtypes.[18]

TABLE XX — VALUE OF CHURCH PLANT OF SLIGHTLY ADAPTED CHURCHES *

| | Value of Plant | |
Type and Subtype	Average	Median
All Slightly Adapted	$95,113	$39,000
B II	75,897	36,600
B III	116,393	33,000
C I	113,801	45,000

* 200 churches reporting.

The extreme costliness of a few buildings separates widely the average values of plant from the median values for the type and all its subtypes; while the unimpressive median indicates that the type has many very inexpensive structures.

SUNDAY-SCHOOL ENROLLMENT

The size-range and characteristic size of the Sunday school of the slightly adapted church is made apparent through a comparison with church membership. This is shown in Table XXI.[19]

TABLE XXI—PER CENT. DISTRIBUTION OF SLIGHTLY ADAPTED CHURCHES BY SIZE OF SUNDAY-SCHOOL ENROLLMENT AND CHURCH MEMBERSHIP

Number of Members or Pupils	Per Cent. Distribution of Churches*	Per Cent. Distribution of Sunday Schools †
Under 500	57.0	79.5
Under 100	6.7	10.1
100 to 200	15.6	23.8
200 to 300	13.4	21.1
300 to 400	13.7	14.4
400 to 500	7.6	10.1
500 to 1,000	25.6	13.4
1,000 and over	17.4	7.1

* 328 churches reporting.
† 298 churches reporting.

The table shows strikingly that there are many more small Sunday schools than there are small churches.

Attendance averages 59 per cent. of enrollment.[20]

18 Appendix Table 29.
19 Appendix Tables 31 and 32.
20 Appendix Tables 33 and 34.

AGE OF SUNDAY-SCHOOL PUPILS

The Sunday-school pupils of the slightly adapted church are divided among age-groups as shown in Table XXII.[21]

TABLE XXII — SUNDAY-SCHOOL PUPILS BY AGE-GROUPS IN SLIGHTLY ADAPTED CHURCHES

Age	Per Cent. Distribution of Pupils
Under 6	10.5
6–14	45.8
15–20	18.2
21 and over	25.5

The Sunday school of this type is more of a children's institution and has relatively fewer adolescents than has the average city church.

CRADLE ROLLS AND HOME DEPARTMENTS

About one-third of the slightly adapted churches report cradle rolls and about one-fifth report home departments. In both of these items Subtype B III is deficient, while Subtype C I stands above the average.

SLIGHTLY ADAPTED CHURCHES IN THEIR IMMEDIATE ENVIRONMENTS

Data concerning general environment were obtained from 124 out of the 360 slightly adapted churches. Of these, 43.5 per cent. were located at or immediately adjoining the central business section of the city, or at a sub-center commanding a population of 100,000 people or more; while 56.5 per cent. were in residential areas.[22]

THE CENTRAL CHURCHES

Of the fifty-four centrally located churches thirty-one were at the great downtown centers of cities, while eight were at, and fifteen near, minor centers. But a much larger proportion of the churches of Subtype B III—more than three-quarters—were at major centers, while the same proportion of C I churches were at minor centers. This squares with the fact discovered earlier, that the former churches have not moved so frequently as the latter. They tend rather to have stuck where they were—downtown.

21 Appendix Tables 35 and 35a.
22 Appendix Tables 37 and 38a.

Again, twenty-five of the centrally located churches were judged, upon first-hand study of the field, to be strategically located with respect to their more distant constituencies; as, for example, by reason of good street-car connections and attractive surroundings. Nine were non-strategically located and five doubtful. But more than three-quarters of the churches of Subtype C I were put in the strategic class and nearly three-fourths of the churches of Subtype B III in the non-strategic or doubtful. The churches of Subtype B III, in other words, have stuck to their old locations to their present disadvantage.

In quality of environment, the central churches were classified as follows: [23]

Quality	*Number*
High grade	11
Medium grade	20
Low grade	8
Transient	2
Industrial	4
Slum	2

Slightly adapted churches in residential areas were found located in middle-class neighborhoods in forty out of seventy cases. As judged by the surveyors, there were fourteen of them in high-class neighborhoods to sixteen in industrial or foreign neighborhoods. It is thus primarily a middle-class type.[24]

DISTANCE OF MEMBERS' HOMES FROM CHURCH BUILDING

For sixty-seven slightly adapted churches studied in this aspect the following situation was disclosed:

Per Cent. of Members Living Within One Mile	*Parish Designation*	*Number of Churches*
75 and over	Compact	37
50–74	Medium	17
25–49	Scattered	12
Less than 25	Very scattered	1

More than half of the churches of this type have three-fourths or more of their members living within one mile of the church. As defined by the study [25] such parishes are called "compact." Only twelve churches have scattered parishes and only one a very scattered parish. Thus, so far as the evidence goes, the slightly adapted church draws most of its constituency from near at hand.

23 Appendix Tables 38b and 38c.
24 Appendix Table 39a.
25 See p. 253.

There is a great difference in this respect between the centrally located churches of the type and the residential ones. Out of twenty-five of the former, only seven have compact parishes, while out of forty-two of the latter, thirty have compact parishes.[26]

DIRECTION OF MEMBERS' HOMES FROM THE CHURCH

Church members do not distribute themselves equally about their church. Forty-six slightly adapted churches were studied in this

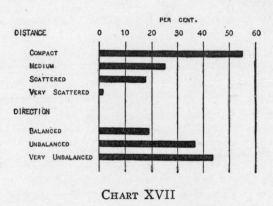

CHART XVII

Per Cent. Distribution of Types of Parishes of Slightly Adapted Churches, by Distance and Direction.

aspect of parish geography; the percentage of members living North, South, East and West, respectively, being measured and designated according to the method explained on page 255. The following results were found:

Designation	Number of Churches
Normally balanced parish	9
Unbalanced parish	17
Very unbalanced parish	20

It is a striking discovery that in most of the parishes of this type of city church the location of members with respect to the church building is so highly unbalanced. Their distribution probably reflects and follows either some general drift of population within a given city or one peculiar to a given racial or other parochial constituency.

All told, the slightly adapted church group does not show any exclusive tendency toward a particular type of environment. Only

26 Appendix Tables 41 and 42.

a few more are residentially located than centrally. They tend slightly to medium grade environments though showing a good many examples in both high-, and low-grade environments. They do, however, incline quite strongly to have compact parishes as measured by distance, but decidedly unbalanced ones measured by the direction of the members' homes from the church building.[27]

Larger Environments and Relationships

The most general aspects of the investigation of city churches concerned the regional, racial and denominational tendencies of the several types and their relation to the size of cities.

The evolution of the city church more frequently stops with the rather limited program implied by the slightly developed type in the South and West than in the North and East. The churches of this type constitute 34.5 per cent. of the 1,044 sample churches, but they constitute 39.2 per cent. of the sample from western cities and 40.4 per cent. of the sample from southern ones.[28]

As between the subtypes, the cities of the North Central states excel the rest of the country in the proportion of churches belonging to the adventurous Subtype B III, while the South has few churches of this type, but many of the conservative Subtype C I.

EFFECT OF SIZE OF CITY

In the 1,044 cases studied, slightly adapted churches are relatively more frequent in cities of 250,000 to 750,000 population than in smaller cities or in the very largest ones as shown by the comparison in Table XXIII.[29]

TABLE XXIII — RATIO OF SLIGHTLY ADAPTED CHURCHES TO TOTAL CHURCHES IN CITIES OF VARYING SIZE

Population of City	Ratio of Slightly Adapted Churches to all Churches
100,000 to 250,000	33.3
250,000 to 500,000	39.9
500,000 to 750,000	38.2
750,000 to 1,000,000	28.5
1,000,000 and over	27.6
All cities	34.5

An explanation of this phenomenon is attempted in a later connection.[30]

27 Appendix Tables 43 and 44.
28 Appendix Table 47.
29 See Appendix Table 46.
30 See p. 282.

RACIAL AND DENOMINATIONAL AFFINITIES

Since it is the most representative American church as judged by the sample, and builds most squarely upon the national tradition, the slightly adapted type naturally is not characteristic of foreign-speaking churches of recent urban immigrants. For example, it is notably deficient in churches of southern Europeans.

On the other hand, this type is well distributed denominationally. All the major denominations except one have approximately the same proportion of slightly adapted churches that they have of all churches, as is shown in the comparison in Table XXIV.

TABLE XXIV — DISTRIBUTION OF SLIGHTLY ADAPTED AND ALL CHURCHES BY DENOMINATIONS

| | *Per Cent.* | |
| | *Total Churches* | *Slightly Adapted* |
Denomination	*Studied*	*Churches*
Baptist	15.8	15.9
Congregational	10.5	12.5
Disciples	4.4	3.6
Methodist Episcopal	19.3	14.7
Methodist Episcopal South	3.7	3.9
Presbyterian, U. S. A.	17.3	19.7
Protestant Episcopal	10.5	10.3
Lutheran (all bodies)	4.4	5.8
All others	14.1	13.6

The Methodist Episcopal and Lutheran denominations constitute exceptions to the general tendency, the former having fewer slightly adapted churches and the latter more.[31]

Divergent Tendencies of Subtypes

Recalling that Subtype B III is a development of program in the direction of novelty, and that Subtype C I represents development in the direction of usual activities, the following list of their divergent tendencies from the average of the slightly adapted type proves significant:

Divergent Aspect	*Subtype B III*	*Subtype C I*
Size	Somewhat more very small churches	Many more very large churches
Age	Fewer young churches	More old churches
Permanence	Slightly more permanent	More permanent
Staff number	Slightly fewer multiple staffs	Many more multiple staffs
Staff functions	Narrow — variety in functions of assistants	More variety in functions of assistants
Pastor's experience	More young men, fewer elderly ones	Fewer young men, more elderly ones
Pastor's tenure in present position	Somewhat shorter	Appreciably longer

31 Appendix Table 45.

Divergent Aspect	Subtype B III	Subtype C I
Pastor's salary	More small salaries	More large salaries
Per capita current expenses	More than type-average	Slightly less than type-average
Per capita benevolences	Much less than type-average	Much more than type-average
Number of facilities	Many more with many facilities	Fewer with few facilities
Rooms in church	More small church buildings	More large church buildings
Seating capacity of auditorium	Slightly smaller than average	One-third larger than average
Value church plant	Slightly below median	Slightly above median
Sunday school enrollment	More smaller, fewer large, schools	Larger schools
Age of pupils	More children, fewer adolescents	Fewer children, more adults
Location	Fewer in central, more in residential, districts	More in central, fewer in residential, districts
Advantageous location of central churches	Fewer strategically located	More strategically located
Quality of neighborhood of residential church	Fewer middle-class, more industrial and foreign	More high class

The two subtypes agree in being on the whole older and more permanent in their present locations than the average of the type.

Summarizing separately for each: Subtype B III is slightly but somewhat definitely beyond the average on the following items: variety of staff functions, proportion of young pastors and tendency to location in residential and in foreign and industrial districts.

Subtype B III is considerably below the average on the following items: membership size, length of pastor's tenure, per capita gifts for benevolences, character of plant judged by the size of the building, capacity of the auditorium and the money value; also in Sunday-school enrollment and in the proportion of adolescents in the Sunday school. Its central churches decidedly lack strategic location.

The only factor in which it is decidedly beyond the average is the number of facilities with which it does its work. This suggests a tendency to try to substitute an advantage in small and incidental matters for great and fundamental deficiencies.

The pastors of this type receive about average salaries and their education is typical.

Most of the above characteristics suggest attenuation of effort, institutional instability and less than average success.

All told, however, the deficiencies of Subtype B III are not very great or radical.

Subtype C I is definitely beyond the average of the type in respect to length of tenure of its pastors, size and value of its church buildings, the number of facilities and the Sunday-school enrollment.

It is below average in proportion of young pastors and number of churches in residential location. In other words, it tends to choose men of long experience and its churches are more often found in central locations.

This subtype is decisively above the average on the following items: size of church membership, frequency of multiple staffs, variety of staff functions, proportion of large salaries, per capita expenditures for benevolences, capacity of the auditorium, proportion of adults in the Sunday school and frequency in high-class residential environment.

All told, the departures of Subtype C I from the average of the type are greater and more significant than those of Subtype B III. They concern very substantial qualities, the possession of which marks institutional success.

The general features of the slightly adapted church as above depicted bear a close resemblance to the generalized picture of the city church derived from the total number of churches studied.[32] This was obviously inevitable, since the modal average represented by the slightly adapted church must come somewhere near the arithmetical average of the total number of churches.

32 See p. 205.

Chapter VI

INTERPRETING THE SLIGHTLY ADAPTED CHURCH

It remains now to explain in terms of the dominating hypothesis why the largest and most representative group found within the sample of 1,044 city churches should be as it is.

The slightly adapted church is a slight departure from its rural prototype and a slight response to the challenge of the city. For the most part it drifts forward unconscious of any new principle. It feels that the urban civilization demands something more of it, but it does not know exactly what. It instinctively desires to live up to the requirements of the city, but it does not clearly see what these requirements are.

This church, however, is able to do a little more than its rural prototype. Its advantage is expressed in larger budgets, more extensive plants [1] and more full-time workers than the town church has. It has additional wealth which can be drawn upon for the expansion of its program.

The first form which this expansion takes is suggested in the following example.

Case I—Subtype B II

This case illustrates very fairly the changes which come to many a rural church located on the edges of a growing city. The main growth of this particular city has been in an opposite direction, but during forty years of moderate expansion it has finally built up solidly about the church until the whole contiguous area is urbanized.

Responding to this process, the church evolved normally out of the rural stage into the first stage of urban character. As at present developed, it corresponds somewhat closely to the modal church of the 1,044 samples. In addition to the range of purely conventional activities inherited from the past, it has a graded Sunday school, a Junior Christian Endeavor Society, a mission study class and Boy Scouts.

It has 211 members. Its college- and seminary-trained pastor receives a salary of $1,600. Its parish is strongly localized. Its Sunday school (of 319 pupils) is considerably larger than the church membership, and, there being no rival churches in the immediate vicinity, the Sunday school takes on a broadly neighborhood character. It is unusually strong in adolescent and adult members and has an excellent average attendance of 185.

The total operating budget in the recent past has been about $1,900, or a little more than $9 per capita, which is an exceedingly modest scale of operation and considerably below the average of the type. Benevo-

[1] Morse & Brunner, *The Town and Country Church in the United States*, p. 140.

115

The outreach of the church is of the conventional sort. For example, the pastor coöperates with the Young Men's Christian Association in holding shop meetings. Besides its denominational benevolence it contributes to a local orphanage, sends books to hospitals and is counted as one of the constructive forces of the city in all helpful movements.

At the end of more than thirty years as an ordinary church, Case II is now undertaking a definite movement to relocate and equip itself for a more fully developed type of service, commensurate with the spirit and growth of the city. It finds its present site no longer at the center of its parish and naturally proposes to move in the direction of its own membership and of the city growth. At the point of convergence of important thoroughfares about one-half mile to the southeast, it has secured a lot, and it hopes, with national and local denominational assistance, to erect a $100,000 church, furnishing facilities for an elaborated program. This removal, it is expected, will also enable the church to command a somewhat higher class constituency from an economic standpoint.

So far the story of this church has been that of a very typical evolution and it will be entirely natural if the stage of its Pilgrim's Progress, to which it is now looking forward, should bring it into a more complete version of urban adaptation and service.

Case I and Case II both substantiate the generalization of Chapter III. The urban church has received from its rural heritage a tendency to increase and differentiate subsidiary organizations for the age-, and sex-groups, somewhat in proportion to the complexity of the social community in which it exists. Open country, village, town and small city are successive steps in such development, and rather short steps at that. Naturally, then, the ordinary city church will be expected to show some little further advance in this direction, together with some reflection of more varied interests in the realms of culture and recreation. Thus, in slight beginnings, even the slightly adapted church manifestly begins to reflect the city.

THE AVERAGE CHURCH MILDLY ADVENTUROUS

As shown by Table V, Subtype B III substitutes a "small-broad" program for a "small-medium" one. This means that it departs from the modal type in the direction of novelty of program. Of course such a change might occur without any objective shifting of the elements of church structure, merely in response to a progressive idea. But dealing with subtypes as groups, rather than with individual cases, one learns to look for a concomitant change either in the strength of the church or in its environment which tends to explain the change in program. And since, in the case of this subtype, it is definitely known that it is not accompanied by any radical change in internal proportions, it is probably safe to presume that its newly outstanding characteristics are caused by special environmental pressure. As has been shown, these churches have largely stuck to their original locations. They are frequently located in industrial surroundings or disadvantageously at the downtown centers, but sometimes in "good" residential districts. In any case they have undoubtedly experienced special stress and difficulty.[3] These handicaps they have attempted to meet by means of broader programs commonly undertaken without adequate resources.

Case III—Subtype B III

An excellent example of such an over-extended church is found in a northwestern city. When the old rivalry between its east and west sides had definitely been settled against the original site of settlement and in favor of a new metropolitan center across the river, residential development began to occupy the highlands to the south, about a mile from the main business district. Here, intrenched behind a succession of parks, flourished the highest class residential development of the city for a quarter of a century; and the district still retains its quality and prestige. The choicest homes of the city now spread out beyond it, to "the Lakes."

During the years when the leading churches of the city were still prosperous on the edges of the downtown center, smaller neighborhood organizations sprang up in this newer part of the city. One of these was a Congregational church, with a middle-class constituency, which for twenty-one years now has occupied its present site slightly in rear of the mansions on the crest of the hill, but in the direct line of population movement.

But in a growing city nothing stands still. Within the last decade, expansion of business and industry at the heart of the downtown district has driven a group of the strongest churches to seek new locations. Several of them have naturally hit upon the slopes of the "Hill" section which now constitutes the aristocratic outpost of the residential area. Here these leading churches have made a second stand where they can still maintain their old prestige as central institutions. And, as in parallel cases in nearly every important city, their coming has greatly diminished the prospects of the group of weaker local churches which have grown up with the neighborhood.

The present status and work of Case III show what happens in many similar cases. Competitive pressure reduces the resources of the old church and, consequently, forces it to undertake novelties in an attempt to meet the competition. These influences have almost naïve expression in the prospectus recently issued by the church in question. Eight months ago, it states, its situation was regarded by many as hopeless. The present program is definitely experimental; essentially an effort to rescue the situation by intensified financial expenditure and high-pressure work. The pastor's report at the end of eight months narrates ten experiments which are under way. All told, they simply indicate the effort of a church with somewhat feeble resources to approximate the all-around program of the internally adapted type. Boys' and girls' and young people's work have all taken on specialized forms and the minister has received an allowance for automobile maintenance in order to carry on an intensive pastoral and financial campaign. The organization of a boys' radio club speaks eloquently of the trend toward up-to-date novelties; while the designation of a young people's society as the "Sky Rocket Society" strikes one as just a bit ominous in view of the fact that sky rockets come down as well as go up.

The Sunday school, of about eighty pupils, is not in keeping with the church membership of 328, most of which is actually resident in the parish. The announced objective of the church's proposed two years' campaign is to double the membership and to increase the Sunday school and

[3] See pp. 356 f.; Tables 38a, b and c, and 39a and b.

young people's groups tenfold. The pastor is a young and well-educated man with five years' experience. In the face of a large and impending deficit, his salary is to be increased from $3,000 to $4,500. The total budget reaches more than $11,000, two-fifths of which has to go toward a mortgage indebtedness. The church building, of rather crude colonial architecture, is valued at $35,000 and is modestly equipped.

Allowing for various expressions of individuality and for the locality of the particular church, this case fairly represents a large number of churches which, under some pressure or other, depart from the average of the city type in the direction of the unusual.

In contrast to pressure due to the invasion of an advantageous field by stronger churches is the far more usual case of the eviction of an American population by incoming foreigners. In the face of such adverse change churches which cannot adapt themselves fully to the situation tend to develop one-sided programs.

Case IV—Subtype B III

Thus, in the decade following 1880 no less than three denominations in a New England city started missions in what was then a promising area newly built up with American homes. One of the missions later moved out of the district; another died; while the third, which developed into full standing as a Baptist church in 1887, lives on at a "poor dying rate."

The radical changes in location of population which the city has experienced during the past forty years have nowhere been more violent than in this vicinity. They have left the church near the center of the most distinctly foreign area, close to the heart of the Ghetto and surrounded by the swarming habitations shared by Jews, Poles and Negroes, with the main Greek and Syrian colonies of the city in close proximity.

Although its Sunday school has slightly gained in the last years, the church has inevitably lost ground. Its present financial receipts are not more than two-thirds enough to maintain previous standards of church life. It is thus left to face a most depressing social environment with depleted resources. Its membership, now registered at 286, is about modal for its city; but its religious services have relatively small attendance and its total service-program is considerably below the natural level of its membership-size. Its Sunday school, with an attendance of about 125, is strong in adolescents. The pastor's salary and the budget of operating expenses are again below the normal level of a church of this sort; though its building, a rather unprepossessing frame structure of thirteen rooms (remodeled after a fire in 1904), has more varied facilities and is somewhat more valuable than the average house of worship in the city. Its equipment makes fair provision for simple educational work and for visual instruction, but has nothing specifically designed for community service. It is also distinctly deficient in facilities for publicity and popular appeal.

The work of the church remains mainly conventional, keyed to the remnant of rather humble Protestant families who occupy the fringes of the neighborhood.

It has a very compact parish, 77 per cent. of its following living within one-half mile of the church, though the remainder, including most of the competent leadership, is widely scattered throughout the city.

Its pastor, however, is actively and responsibly interested in community welfare, in touch with localized social problems and agencies and active in denominational and interdenominational work. He has conducted successive campaigns of street evangelization in the heart of the foreign quarter (in coöperation with the Young Men's Christian Association), maintains through the church an active employment service, and disburses a relatively large amount of charitable relief. The church is thus responding to its local situation just enough to attenuate its program, but not enough to transform it.

Its most promising adaptation is in the service of childhood. About two-thirds of the members of the "Junior Achievement" clubs held in this church are children of Roman Catholic parentage, while one-sixth are children of Jewish parentage. A small Russian congregation is denominationally fostered and shares the use of the church building.

More than any other in its city, Case IV illustrates a church maintaining Protestantism in an alien environment, though with manifestly inadequate resources and numerically declining strength. Herein it represents the fortunes of a large group of partially stranded, yet struggling, organizations, scattered throughout the cities of America.

REMNANTS OF FORMER GLORY

In certain churches of this group the factor of retrogression is still more spectacularly present. Churches decay as well as develop. Sometimes churches decline gradually and irregularly, till what is left is but a fragment of its former self. Their lopsided present program may be the remnant of a more complete one of the past. They show the raggedness of institutional decrepitude. Though the history of most of the cases under consideration has not been studied in detail, their present environment makes it virtually certain that they have had unstable and frequently changing constituencies. What one finds, when he suddenly steps into the situation and analyzes the current program of activities, is a group of remnants poorly fitted together and symptomatic of age and failure. "How are the mighty fallen!" Such a tragedy is illustrated by a church whose pulpit was made famous by one of the most original and outstanding religious leaders of the last generation.

Case V—Subtype B III

In comparison with its other activities no other church in the city so greatly over-emphasizes the preaching function as this church does. This is partly due to its downtown location and its historic tradition, but is also the mark of an unequal decline of functions. While the city has doubled its population in twenty years, the church has suffered a continuous decrease in membership, showing the highest ratio of losses to gains of any church for which local records were available. Because it is a downtown church as well as a declining one, it is relatively deficient in Sunday-school enrollment, the ratio of pupils to church membership being the third from the smallest in the city. Its small nominal increase in financial resources is not more than one-fifth enough to keep the church on its actual former economic level.

A present membership of 467 makes the church rank in size in the upper third of churches of the city. It is unusual, however, for so large a church to have no paid worker except the pastor. As a result the pastor's salary accounts for 58 per cent. of the total church budget, whereas, in other churches of comparable size, that item represents not more than one-third or even one-fifth or one-sixth of the budget. The benevolence of this church is very small. Its property, valued at $65,000, includes one of the most churchly and beautiful auditoriums of the city, but facilities for religious education and social life are relatively limited. The total program of service amounts to an average of seven and eight-tenths hours per month per member, which is below the city average of between ten and eleven hours.

This is all that is left of a church distinguished in its generation for broad vision and wide activity. The church is nevertheless strongly intrenched in the city. Only two others have more widely scattered memberships. It has large groups of adherents on the "south side" and on the "Hill" and nearly as many members in the downtown section as its more prosperous near neighbors. It has the backing of a small invested fund, and in its children's organizations is making some progress in increasing contacts with the newer populations of its neighborhood.

This would seem to be the point of most fruitful possibility for enlarged service. The church is surrounded by boarding houses occupied by transient Americans and overlooks the valley up which Italian settlement is rapidly moving. From the standpoint of an immediately surrounding American constituency its position is becoming less tenable. If, however, while maintaining its conspicuous pulpit ministries, it could bring itself to undertake whole-heartedly a program definitely adapted to the new foreign elements in the near vicinity, it might render a distinctive service to the community as well as discover a new motive for existence.

Considering the data in the light of these examples, one sees that the churches of Subtype B III are characteristically under extraordinary environmental pressure. They are forced thereby to extend themselves; yet are not strong enough to overcome adverse conditions entirely, nor to achieve fully the rounded development of the next higher type. Or else they are remnants of the past, churches which have fallen back from what they once were and did. Either going or coming, they are transitional. Their proved instability is not normal nor wholesome. Their response to the city is not complete enough to be strikingly significant. They should either muster enough resources to carry themselves over into a fully elaborated program or else should retain a more consistent and usual version of conventional development.

THE AVERAGE CHURCH TURNED CONSERVATIVE (C I)

Environmentally speaking, the churches of this subtype were found in the main to be fortunately located. When, in addition, the general advantages of larger size, staff, plant and resources are taken into consideration, one finds a very complete explanation of this subtype. It is primarily the more conventional variety of the typical church fallen upon easy circumstances.[4] Sometimes denomi-

4 See p. 112.

national conservatism tips the scales in the same direction, as with an occasional Scotch Presbyterian church in the liberal atmosphere of New England.

Again, the explanation of the tendencies of this type may be an abnormal distribution of constituents with respect to age. In Los Angeles, a city in which the disproportionate number of elderly people is plainly revealed by the Census, a church of this type found that 80 per cent. of its families had no children under nineteen years of age. Those that had young children averaged only one and six-tenths per family. It is not strange that a church so composed should have less "doing" than the average one of its size and strength.

Case VI—Subtype C I

This is a case of a church on "Easy Street" in a sheltered residential suburb of New York. It illustrates the favoring conditions that foster this subtype. The church's forty years of life have shown continuous and almost inevitable growth, as block after block of superior homes have built up about it. The present membership is nearly one thousand, worshiping in an edifice of rustic Norman architecture set in a spacious lawn and worth some $300,000. Its annual local budget is about $25,000 and it is accustomed to give perhaps $35,000 more to various benevolences.

Forty years ago the suburb developed out of the Dutch countryside as an intimate community where adventurous young families from the city crowded into school children's desks in a one-room battened school house for church services. It is now a "bosses'" suburb where four-fifths of the commuters are employed in some executive capacity. Its own children cannot afford to make homes there and have to move away when they marry. "It isn't etiquette to ask one's business here," a Western visitor explained with some dismay. "He might be a bootlegger." Men are anonymous in the creative and achieving half of their lives.

Under these circumstances ordinary community functions and relationships are much distorted. For example, it is not a good library town. The librarian complains that people are unwilling to use books to which others have access. If they want them they buy or rent them themselves. Even the movies do not flourish. As the disappointed theater manager explains, "It takes apartments to furnish movie audiences." This suburb of privileged people living in single-family houses, with the city easily accessible, asks for a full round of near-at-hand institutions, but does not ask much of them when it gets them. People go to the city for their larger satisfactions, except golf and motoring.

In such a "dormitory" community, used chiefly for play and sleep, what kind of a church will one find? Not exactly an ordinary one—people are too intelligent and well-to-do for that; yet not an original one. What they want is a magnified institution of a conventional sort—distinguished preaching, chorus choir in vestments, Tiffany windows—and this is what they get. The Sunday school is relatively small, but they hire a director of religious education. There are Boy Scouts. Missionary organizations flourish. The fortunes of the young people's work are, however, kaleidoscopic. Men's fellowship is expressed in outings and golf tournaments rather than in a sharing of serious outlooks upon life.

It would be a great mistake, however, to doubt the genuine religious uses of such a church or the sincerity of its people. They take religion seriously just as they take family life and recreation, largely divorcing all three from the more aggressive aspects of existence. Organized service to mankind is primarily something to be bought and paid for through benevolent contributions. The church genuinely functions as a guide to sane and constructive thinking and as a somewhat indirect interpreter of practice in the practical sphere. In a busy and crowded world with vast stretches of weariness and defeat at the bottom of it, it offers its indispensable ministries of consolation and quiet.

One generally can discern in such a church an exact working out of whatever minor elements distinguish its particular situation, within the limitations of the general tradition. As a type it is opulent; yet, on account of the large average memberships involved, is financially economical. Individual cases may reach the extremes of city bigness and wealth without involving more than that minimum of adaptation to urban conditions which is inherent in the type.

Such considerations as slight urban stimulus, imitation, docility, response to environmental pressure and conventional expansion on the basis of more than average resources, appear to explain satisfactorily most of the characteristics of the "average" church of the American city.

Chapter VII

THE UNADAPTED CHURCH

The 253 churches that have a smaller number or a narrower range of activities than the modal subtype, or both, have been grouped under this designation. They constitute 24.2 per cent. of the total churches studied and are thus the second largest type.

The unadapted type includes the following subtypes:

Subtype	Type of Program by Activities		Number of Churches	Per Cent. of All Churches
	Number	Range		
A I	Smallest	— Narrowest	90	8.6
A II	Smallest	— Narrow	35	3.3
A III	Smallest	— Medium	27	2.6
B I	Small	— Narrow	101	9.7

As a whole, the type confines its program to the first seventeen organizations and activities as previously listed, but only one of the four subtypes, containing about 11 per cent. of the churches of the type, goes beyond the ninth item.

This is made plain by sample programs for five churches of each of the four subtypes in Table XXV.

TABLE XXV — SAMPLE PROGRAMS OF UNADAPTED CHURCHES

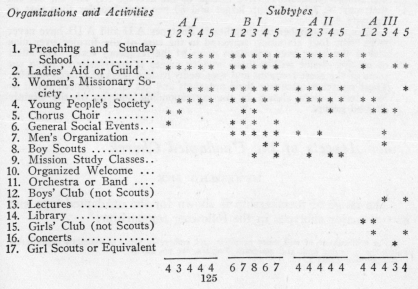

Organizations and Activities	A I					B I					A II					A III				
	1	2	3	4	5	1	2	3	4	5	1	2	3	4	5	1	2	3	4	5
1. Preaching and Sunday School	*		*	*	*	*	*	*	*	*	*	*	*	*	*	*				
2. Ladies' Aid or Guild	*	*	*	*	*	*	*	*	*	*						*	*	*		
3. Women's Missionary Society	*		*		*	*	*	*	*	*	*	*	*	*						*
4. Young People's Society	*	*	*	*		*	*	*	*	*	*	*	*	*	*	*	*			
5. Chorus Choir		*			*		*	*							*	*	*	*		
6. General Social Events				*		*		*	*	*										
7. Men's Organization						*	*	*	*	*	*				*				*	
8. Boy Scouts																			*	
9. Mission Study Classes							*	*		*		*	*	*						
10. Organized Welcome																				
11. Orchestra or Band																				
12. Boys' Club (not Scouts)																	*			*
13. Lectures																				
14. Library																				
15. Girls' Club (not Scouts)																		*		*
16. Concerts																		*		*
17. Girl Scouts or Equivalent																			*	
	4	3	4	4	4	6	7	8	6	7	4	4	4	4	4	4	4	4	3	4

CHARACTERISTICS AND VARIATIONS OF PROGRAM

How the churches of the unadapted type as a whole differ from the slightly adapted churches is shown in the following comparison:

Types	Range of Program	Per Cent. Range of Frequency of Least Frequent Group	Range of Number of Activities
Slightly Adapted	Items 1–22	11–20	5–12
Unadapted	Items 1–17	21–40	1–8

This comparison means that the unadapted churches have one-third fewer activities than slightly adapted churches and that there are five fewer items from which to select their activities.

As noted by the sample church programs, the churches of Subtype A I are most likely to carry on four out of the first six items of program, and most frequently they select the first four in order. Even an organization so characteristic of most churches as the young people's society is not characteristic with churches of this type. All told, more are without it than have it. Thus we find here the narrowest and smallest type of city church program that exists among the established denominations of white Christians.[1]

Subtype B I offers a possible eight items of program out of nine that constitute the limit of the subtype. It most frequently adds additional age-, and sex-group organizations for men or boys, with a further selection of activities suggesting the general embellishment and social development of the churches and institutions. It still keeps within a small and narrow program relative to that of the average city church, but one that may be 100 per cent. larger and 50 per cent. broader than that of Subtype A I.

The small number of churches in Subtypes A II and A III have never more than four activities, scattered in the case of the former over nine and of the latter over seventeen items of the frequency scale. The effect of making choice within these broader ranges is necessarily to leave out some of the most frequent and supposedly basic aspects of church activity. These churches attenuate their programs and get an unbalanced result as has already been shown in the corresponding subtype of the slightly adapted group.

Other Aspects of the Unadapted Church

MEMBERSHIP SIZE

The range of membership is shown for the unadapted type and its two major subtypes in the following comparison:[2]

[1] For a discussion of still more primitive and embryonic types of religious organization among the irregular sects and emigrant Negroes, see pp. 139 f.
[2] Appendix Table 5.

Number of Members	Per Cent. Distribution of Churches		
	Unadapted Type*	Subtypes	
		A I†	B I‡
Less than 500	83.5	97.4	70.1
500 to 1,000	10.4	1.3	17.5
1,000 and over	6.1	1.3	12.4

* 231 churches reporting.
† 78 churches reporting.
‡ 97 churches reporting.

It should be noted that almost all the churches of 500 members and more belong to Subtype B I, and that a significant fraction of them have more than 1,000 members.

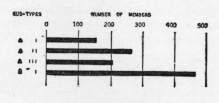

CHART XVIII

Average Size of Churches of Four Unadapted Subtypes.

There is no inherent reason why a narrow program should not go with a large church if the desires and convictions of the membership are thus limited. That large churches generally have broad programs is a point for later consideration and interpretation.

AGE AND TIME IN PRESENT LOCATION

About four out of ten unadapted churches are less than twenty-five years old, and nearly two-thirds have been located less than twenty-five years upon their present sites. One quarter of the churches of this type are fifty years old or more, and one in ten of them have occupied their present sites for that length of time.[3]

When this showing comes to be compared with that for the more fully developed types, it will be seen that time is a significant factor affecting the average degree of church evolution.

PAID RELIGIOUS WORKERS

More than four-fifths of all unadapted churches operate on the basis of one paid religious worker, namely, the pastor. Their distribution according to size of staff is shown in Table XXVI.[4]

[3] Appendix Tables 6 and 7.
[4] Appendix Table 9.

TABLE XXVI — PAID RELIGIOUS WORKERS IN
UNADAPTED CHURCHES *

Number Employed	Per Cent. Distribution of Churches
1	85.1
2	9.8
3	1.7
4	3.0
5	....
6	0.4

* 234 churches reporting.

Among the subtypes striking differences appear. While one-fourth of churches of Subtype B I have more than one paid worker, only one in fifteen of those of Subtype A I have multiple staffs. As previously remarked with respect to membership size, there is

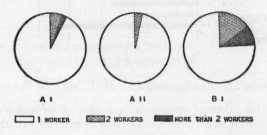

A I   A II   B I

☐ 1 WORKER   ▨ 2 WORKERS   ▧ MORE THAN 2 WORKERS

CHART XIX

Size of Staffs of Churches of Three Unadapted Subtypes.

no inherent necessity tying a narrow program to a small staff. The most meager church programs exemplified by the unadapted type include parish and Sunday-school work with the accompanying clerical and financial processes. Any church large enough to require, and wealthy enough to support, assistants for the performance of these functions may be expected to do so.[5] Since 6 per cent. of the churches of the type have 1,000 members or more it is not strange that 5 per cent. of them have three or more paid workers.

THE PASTOR

The pastors of unadapted churches have the poorest education, the shortest experience and the briefest tenure of any group of city ministers. They also get the lowest salaries—about 70 per cent. of the total receiving $2,000, or less, annually, while 11 per cent. receive less than $1,000. No type, however, uses so many old men in its ministry.

5 For the actual distribution of twenty-one male and thirty-two female parish assistants found in the churches of this subtype, see Appendix Tables 10 and 11.

In all of these respects, save the last, the churches of Subtype A I rank lower than those of Subtype B I—thus showing that the narrowest and feeblest program commands the poorest type of men to operate it.[6]

FINANCES

The general budget of the unadapted church averages about $3,000 annually.

The annual per capita cost of current support for the unadapted churches and their more important subtypes are as follows: unadapted, $14.75; Subtype A I, $16.98; Subtype B I, $14.13. The average per capita cost of operations of all city churches is $18.17. While, therefore, the type in general costs its individual member

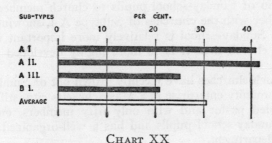

CHART XX

Per Cent. of Pastors Without Standard Theological Training in Churches of Four Unadapted Subtypes.

$3.42 less than the average and the churches of Subtype B I are even slightly more economical, the churches of Subtype A I cost only $1.19 less than all city churches, while their programs include not more than half as many activities and cover only one-third as broad a range, besides being administered by an inferior type of pastor. This makes the unadapted church the most expensive type of all, considering the quantity of service which this money buys. Its average benevolence is only about one-half that of city churches in general.[7]

PROPERTY

The median value of the property of the unadapted church is $20,000, or only about one-half that of the slightly adapted church, which is $39,000. Two-thirds of the churches of this type have fewer than ten rooms and one-third fewer than five rooms. The

6 Appendix Tables 12-15.
7 Appendix Tables 24-26a.

average number of items of service equipment is only five. The unadapted church is generally without an office, and its working facilities consist of a little Sunday-school material, a kitchen and toilets.[8]

THE SUNDAY SCHOOL

The average Sunday school of this type enrolls about 220 pupils. Ninety-one and eight-tenths per cent. of the Sunday schools have fewer than 500 pupils, while only 83.5 per cent. of the churches have fewer than 500 members. This indicates that the average Sunday school is even more feeble numerically than the average church of this type. Almost half of the Sunday schools of Subtype A I have fewer than one hundred pupils.

The ratio of Sunday-school pupils to church membership, however, is higher with the churches of Subtype A I, showing that even so feeble a Sunday school is relatively more important in the total life of the church than it is in more highly developed church organizations.

Many such churches have recently grown out of Sunday schools. Such a community enterprise in a Massachusetts city, still served by a non-salaried pastor and with only fifty members, enrolls more than 150 Sunday-school pupils and has a well-organized cradle roll and home department.

Sunday-school attendance averages about two-thirds of enrollment. The pupils are primarily children, the Sunday school of this type being distinctly weak in its appeal to adolescents and adults.[9]

NEIGHBORHOOD ENVIRONMENT

Only thirty-two unadapted churches were studied with respect to the character of the neighborhoods in which they were located. This number did not constitute a sufficiently large sample to permit of any reliable generalization as to the permanent environmental tendencies of the type. It is worth noting, however, that of the churches observed only one-half appeared to be strategically located with respect to the constituents which they were attempting to serve, and only two were found in high-grade neighborhoods.[10]

PARISH CHARACTERISTICS

Of twenty-six unadapted churches whose parishes were studied

8 Appendix Tables 27-29.
9 Appendix Tables 31-35a.
10 Appendix Tables 37-39a.

the following distribution of members according to the distance from their homes to the church building was found:

Per Cent. of Members. Living Within One Mile	Number of Churches
75 and over	9
50–74	10
25–49	6
Less than 25	1

Unadapted churches, on this showing, tend strongly to have compact parishes or parishes with medium dispersal of members, rather than scattered ones. Naturally the centrally located churches show a somewhat greater tendency to draw members from unusual distances than do the residentially located ones.

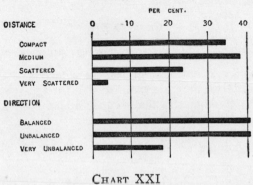

CHART XXI

Per Cent. Distribution of Types of Parishes of Unadapted Churches, by Distance and Direction.

Of twenty-two churches of this type studied with respect to the direction of their members' homes from the church building, nine were found to have a normal distribution, nine, an unbalanced distribution, and four, a very unbalanced distribution.[11]

The majority were thus not drawing people from all directions, but exhibited distinct preferences and aversions on the part of populations living within the same distance. The nature of the barriers and deflections which produced such results is considered in a later connection.[12]

LARGER RELATIONSHIPS

Unadapted churches are found more often in the small and medium-sized cities than in the larger, though this tendency is not

11 For method of measuring directional distribution, see p. 255.
12 See p. 256. Also Appendix Tables 40-44.

invariable.[13] They occur much more frequently in the West and in the South than in the North. While they constitute only 24.2 per cent. of the total churches, they constitute 42.1 per cent. of the foreign churches studied.[14]

Such churches are especially characteristic of the foreigner who has detached himself from the downtown colony of his nationality

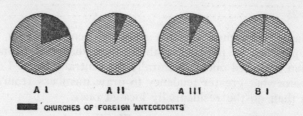

A I   A II   A III   B I

CHURCHES OF FOREIGN 'ANTECEDENTS

CHART XXII

Proportion of Unadapted Churches of Foreign Antecedents, by Subtypes.

to settle in small residential groups on the outskirts of cities. Under these circumstances the program of the foreign-speaking church frequently almost duplicates that of the feebler American churches. Thus, a tiny Mexican church on the edge of Los Angeles has all the outward aspects of the surrounding English-speaking family churches, maintaining an every-member canvass, using duplex col-

TABLE XXVII — DISTRIBUTION OF UNADAPTED CHURCHES
BY DENOMINATIONS

Denomination	Per Cent. Distribution	
	Total Churches Studied	Unadapted Churches
Baptist	15.8	14.2
Congregational	10.5	7.9
Disciples	4.4	6.3
Methodist Episcopal	19.3	17.0
Methodist Episcopal South	3.7	4.8
Presbyterian, U. S. A.	17.3	12.3
Protestant Episcopal	10.5	5.5
Lutheran (all bodies)	4.4	6.3
All others	14.1	25.7

lection envelopes, and otherwise imitating current denominational standards.

Only a single foreign church, however, is found in Subtype B I. This confines the unadapted foreign churches almost exclusively to

13 Appendix Table 47.
14 See p. 276.

the subtypes which have the smallest possible programs, and these frequently carried out in a very unbalanced manner.[15]

Though the number of Negro churches involved in the study was inadequate as a basis of generalization as to the racial tendencies of the types, a relatively large number of such churches were found in the unadapted group.

DENOMINATIONAL AFFINITIES

The denominational affinities of the unadapted churches are shown in Table XXVII.[16]

The Methodist Episcopal and Baptist denominations are seen to bear about the same proportion to the unadapted churches as they do to the total of all churches. The Congregational and Presbyterian

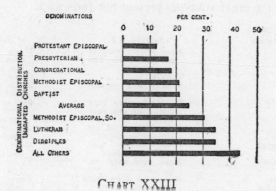

CHART XXIII

Ratio of Unadapted Churches to Total Churches in Specified Denominations.

denominations have a considerably smaller ratio, and the Protestant Episcopal denomination a very much smaller ratio of unadapted churches; while the Methodist Episcopal South denomination has a considerably larger ratio, and the Disciple and Lutheran denominations a very much larger ratio. Finally, the group of "all other" denominations shows a most excessive tendency toward churches of the unadapted type.[17]

> The group classed as "all other" denominations is non-homogeneous and includes numerous small denominations similar in faith and government to the major denominations of the nation. It also includes some denominations ordinarily regarded as non-evangelical or peculiar, a considerable proportion of which are of recent origins. The unadapted type thus manifests a certain affinity for the small, novel and young sects.

15 See pp. 275 f.
16 Appendix Table 45.
17 For list of denominations included in this category, see p. 277.

Within the subtypes, the Baptist and "all other" denominations are found to have the greatest tendency toward the smallest and feeblest group of churches as represented by Subtype A I, while the Congregational, Disciple and Methodist Episcopal South denominations tend somewhat strongly toward churches of Subtype B I. The Methodist Episcopal, Presbyterian, Protestant Episcopal and Lutheran denominations divide about equally between the two subtypes.

Divergent Tendencies of Subtypes

To illustrate more generally the range and character of divergencies within this type it will be sufficient to compare with the type-average the churches with the smallest, narrowest programs (Subtype A I) and those with small, narrow programs (Subtype B I), since the other subtypes present but few cases.

Divergent Aspect	Subtype A I	Subtype B I
Size	Much smaller (nearly one-half under 100 members)	Much larger (less than one-tenth under 100 members)
Age	Younger	Older
Permanence	Slightly less permanent	Much more permanent
Staff-number	7% of churches have more than one paid worker	25% of churches have more than one paid worker
Staff-functions	Only 3 types of assistants employed	13 types of assistants employed
Pastor's education	Fewer college and seminary trained	More college and seminary trained
Pastor's experience	More with brief experience	Fewer with brief experience
Pastor's tenure in present position	More with short tenure	Fewer with short tenure
Pastor's salary	86% under $2,000	53% under $2,000
Per capita current expenses	Much larger	Slightly smaller
Per capita benevolences	Very much smaller	Considerably larger
Number of facilities	Fewer	More
Rooms in church	Fewer	More
Seating capacity of auditorium	Much less	Much greater
Value church plant	Much less	Much greater
Sunday-school enrollment	44% under 100	8% under 100
Age of pupils	Fewer adolescents	More adolescents

These contrasts lie all in one direction. They show a clear-cut distinction between higher and lower degrees of development all along the line and would justify a strict statistical separation which, as previously explained, was ignored in grouping the two subtypes together.[18]

Subtype A I is much less developed than Subtype B I, and this distinction must be kept in mind in the later non-statistical interpretations of the type.

18 See p. 70.

The Ragged Edge

The preceding paragraphs have reviewed the characteristics of the city church on the lowest level of urban adaptation in which it occurs among the established denominations in America.

It is virtually certain, however, that the 1,044 cases under consideration did not actually include a proportionate number of the very smallest and feeblest examples of city churches. While the statistical count showed only one-fourth of city churches unadapted, this ratio would not hold if all organizations, however rudimentary, of obscure religious bodies that come within the sociological definition of a church, were properly counted. The study attempted to be all-inclusive, but previous experience in the intensive studies of cities has proved how difficult it is to get comparable information from Gospel Missions occupying rented halls, from transient Negro and other churches in their "store front" meeting places and from organized religious groups meeting in private homes.

Their development has scarcely reached the phase of ecclesiastical organization. Their church life is less definite and permanent than the smallest and narrowest type which can be statistically defined. Frequently they are positively opposed to institutionalism in religion.

Case VII

Opposite the peaceful public library in a western city, almost overlooking the deep gorge of the river whose falls at this point fixed the original location of the city, one hears on a summer Sunday afternoon a droning of gospel hymns. It proceeds from an inconspicuous store building. Drawing closer, one catches the strained and monotonous rise and fall of a woman's tones. Within one discovers a faded yellow-haired speaker of medium stature, younger than middle age, exhorting a congregation of some forty five believers. The group, as well as the preacher, show definite Scandinavian traits

This is the "Church of the Elect," the only one in all the world. It is ministered to by two women preachers.

The most outstanding peculiarity of the speaker is a slightly wry neck emphasized by a neurasthenic bobbing of the head in connection with an oft-recurring use of an unintelligible shibboleth. This is supposed to express the gift of tongues as experienced in the New Testament church. Sometimes it is accompanied by ejaculations of "Blessed Jesus!" and others intended to help the spirit in the enunciation of the word.

True to its phlegmatic temperament, the Norse audience makes only a moderate response. Waves of suppressed emotion, however, follow the ebb and flow of the speaker's feeling. The audience includes a fringe of people who are not Scandinavian, and all ages and sexes are well represented. It appears to be composed exclusively of laboring class people, and not, in the main, of residents of the vicinity.

Here is the propagandist movement that seeks central location, adjacent to public buildings and the great central institutions of the city, but brings adherents from all quarters.

The sermon is on the "Sword of the Lord." "Jehovah's sword," the preacher declares, "is always wielded constructively." It is far easier to preach the "love side," but today God's wrath must be emphasized. The sword only crushes the sinner when it is unable to sever him from his sin. This theme is illustrated by a series of detached, forceful scriptures beginning with Lot in Sodom. The myth of Paul and Thekla is elaborated at great length as though it were authentic scripture. The preacher manages to see with great clearness the white horse of Revelation, from his arched neck down to his polished hoofs. Of the rider she sees only his eyes—no more. She refrains from describing the second coming and is only sure that, as things go with God, it will be "soon." This, it is explained, does not mean necessarily very soon as man counts time.

"Preachers are all liars. Noah was called a calamity howler and scorned, as are prophets of today." Such is the defensive anti-climax of the rhapsody.

After the sermon, a motherly and fine-faced old lady, the co-pastor, gives out the notices, which include a very human announcement of a Sunday-school picnic. The collection follows upon the statement that they need "Just twenty-one dollars today in order to be able to say that we owe no man anything." It is soberly taken up by a man and a young girl.

Next follow testimonies as to healing, three cases being presented. The first, a middle-aged woman, tells how she fell off the lower step of a ladder yesterday, landing on the back of her head and lying unconscious part of the night. She "passed a terrible night," but today the pastor and some of her friends prayed with her, and "Now I am here."

Next came a boy of about eighteen who worked in a wholesale grocery establishment. "Mother was away," he says, "so I ate downtown." In the afternoon he was lifting heavy sacks of sugar and piling them in tiers four feet high. He felt sick and struggled home. "When I got there mother says I was purple." (One imagines a case of ptomaine poisoning.) The story ends to the effect that the mother put her hand on his stomach and he felt it relax instantly. He slept well and was back at work the next day.

As the final case, a neighbor tells graphically and not without humor how a heavy woman squeezed herself through a street-car window when the car was thought to be on fire and "came down on the pavement hard." She could walk ("Glory to God!") even before she was prayed for; but "Her husband would not let her come to church today."

Religion on this level is but partly tamed—an unregulated power not yet harnessed to ecclesiastical forms.

It is of course obvious that many such churches will be in a pre-statistical stage of development. They publish no official records, have indefinite terms of membership and are satisfied with loose business and administrative relationships. Consequently it is more than likely that the accountings of local Church Federations and the statistics of the United States Census of Religious Bodies both fail to do full justice to them.

Thus the failure of many months of field work to secure accurate data from certain theosophical, spiritualistic and Pentecostal and "Bible Student" groups has already been confessed. Statistics were manifestly far from the thought of the religious leader who figures in the following case.

Case VIII

The following paragraphs narrate the experience of a young theological student who investigated the "Bethel Pentecostal Association" in a Massachusetts city. He called at the mission hall at meeting time. What he found was eighty-five chairs arranged in rows—all empty. The hall was very neat, "a jewel," he says, "in that part of the city," and surrounded by fine old colonial dwellings in various stages of decay, now occupied by Jews and Negroes. The immediate district affords the largest number of licensed boarding-, and rooming-houses in this stirring industrial community and is the chief center for the rural newcomer.

The walls of the mission are decorated with vivid scriptural quotations. The leader approaches the investigator, who says that he supposes there is to be a meeting. "Praise the Lord!" replies the man, and explains that they have had difficulty during the last few months in keeping the meetings going. "He asked, 'Are you a Pentecostal member?' I said 'No.' He said, 'You have Christ in your heart?' I said, 'Yes, sir.' Then he talked about the difficulties they have had, and was continually praising God for my presence, even though there was no meeting. Then he said the Lord had been trying their faith very much lately and they had had much difficulty and many struggles. He said, 'If the Lord does not want me to do this I will stop, but I think He does want me to do it. I think that this lack of attendance at the meetings is the work of the devil.'"

The leader then goes on to explain how some oppose the work, calling it "of the devil," but that he is persuaded that the mission has the "only true baptism, that which takes control of the body and soul and gives it over to God." His main worry is about the finances. The rent has been raised and it is very difficult to get along. (It is interesting to discover that this familiar anxiety of the poor is also the anxiety of poor churches. Hundreds of little store-front enterprises, and others occupying rented property, actually do not know from month to month whether they can pay the rent and not infrequently are evicted.)

The investigator continues his narrative: "The leader asked whether I would pray with them [There seem to have been two men by this time.], and we got on our knees at the rear of the church and the leader prayed in a mournful tone. After the 'Amen' the leader used psychological means to make me feel that I ought to pray." (The student does not explain just what these psychological means were, but says that they were forced and artificial and most repulsive to him.) "After explaining that I did not feel at liberty to pray, I took his hand to bid him good-by when he drew my head down and kissed me on the forehead. He said that he would pray for me as I traveled from city to city and asked me to include him in my prayers."

AN EMBRYONIC PHASE

These are samples of some thousands of Protestant religious enterprises represented by a multitude of obscure denominations and evangelistic associations in the larger American cities. Statistically classified as somewhat less than simply developed churches, they are evidently better understood as peculiar states of mind—expressions of religion that are at the same time crude, chaotic and conventional. Yet there is something heroic in the spectacle of so feeble a church attempting the conquest of the mighty city thought of as the incarnation of the present evil world. With such poverty of resources and such richness of faith, without prestige or the advantage of denominational standing and wealth, such little fragments of religious enterprises play their part and sometimes put to shame the better organized ecclesiastical bodies by reason of devotion and fresh spiritual impulse.

The total number of adherents to such churches is not large but they are divided up into a large number of congregations.[19] These constitute an obscure but important phase of city religious life and may contain the germs of great denominations of the future. Christianity itself had such beginnings and many now venerable denominations have had similar origins within the last two centuries.

If, therefore, all these even more unadapted types were properly included it might turn out that the unadapted group as a whole was really the most numerous and representative in the larger American cities. If this were true the disparity between the feeble city church and the overpowering modern city would be even more striking.

SUMMARY

Summarizing the purely statistical characteristics of the unadapted type, one notes that only a small proportion of these churches adopt the alternative of increasing the range of activities without increasing the number. With so narrow a program to start with this is to be expected. If a church is to limit itself to four activities or less, it is likely to choose from those which the tradition of the city church has made most invariable. Novelty does not often occur, though its presence in Subtype A II and Subtype A III points to the fact that under sufficient pressure of other things even the narrowest program may become somewhat untraditional. The possible causes leading to such a tendency have later explanation.

As a matter of fact what the unadapted church generally does is to fill out the narrow program which its tradition permits before trying anything new. Much the largest subtype (B I) lies in the direction of conservatism. It doubles the number of organizations and activities without increasing their range.

Within such limits the group has primarily the unity of possessing less than average institutional development. Seventy-five per cent. of the 1,044 sample churches reach or surpass the modal stage. If their development is to be regarded as normal the development of this type is sub-normal. If the ways of the majority are good, its ways are not so good. One should repeat, however, that a narrow program is not necessarily a small one in moral and spiritual results. "This one thing I do" may sometimes be a good church motto. A broader program is not necessarily a greater one, religiously speaking. On the whole, however, the total impression of the study will

---

19 See Appendix Tables 52 and 57 which, while not directly measuring the number of such churches, throw strong light upon it.

probably be that the more highly developed types reflect broader incentives and a more inclusive vision of the possibilities of urban Christianity.

Interpreting the Unadapted Church

In terms of the basic hypothesis the unadapted church is the city church nearest the country; it is organized urban Christianity showing its rural side. It overlaps the higher ranges of rural development, thus clearly showing a transplanted and but slightly extended rural program. As has been statistically proved, such churches appear most frequently in the cities of the more rural sections of the country and in the more rural denominations.[20] They are also characteristic of the parts of cities frequented by rural immigrants.

VARYING RURAL LEVELS REFLECTED IN THE CHURCH

While the most general clew to the unadapted church would seem to be found in such rural origins, it must be recognized that they reflect not one but several levels of rural fortunes. There are rural heritages rather than one single heritage. Churches which carry over to the city the tradition of the successful rural classes—of home and community building farmers living on good land—will differ decidedly from the churches of the rural failures or handicapped country folk such as plantation Negroes. The country delivers up to the city both its best and its worst. On the one hand factory labor utilizes many men who are too unintelligent to farm, while, on the other, the city drains the country of its most ambitious and forceful personalities.

The passing over of the rural church into the city must, therefore, be looked for on different levels. They may be distinguished as the normal and the sub-normal. The resulting subtypes of unadapted city churches are clearly marked. The smallest and narrowest of all—Subtypes A I and A II—are largely made up of the churches of poor rural immigrants and recently come Negroes, of which the following is a fair example. It might be called "An Ecclesiastical Country Cousin."

Case IX—Subtype A I

Near the heart of the "blighted area" over which a metropolitan city has poured out her chief civic lamentations, between solidly massed populations of Negroes and Jews, one comes upon a sort of thicket of rural life in the midst of a great city. More than one-half of the school children of this district were not born in the city. This measures the recency with which the population has immigrated. It consists, in the main, of

20 See pp. 280 and 292.

rural recruits from the neighboring states of Missouri and Illinois. Waves and billows of rapid social change have broken over this district, driving out before them the formerly great and prosperous Protestant churches of the city and leaving in their place a nest of irregular organizations— Pentecostal, Spiritualist and Mormon—seven of which are near neighbors to Case IX.

The church belongs to a denomination which seceded from one of the great historic communions in the assertion of a more emotional type of religious expression. The denomination itself bears the brand of rural origin and recent migration, having ventured, up to 1916, into only twelve of the sixty-eight American cities of over 100,000 population.

Many of the immediate constituents of the church represent a very poor rural level. They are refugees from the thin soils of the Ozarks, economic failures which the farm has passed on to the city. Their exigencies are registered in the fact that Case IX, a small and highly conventional church (whose program otherwise consists of only two women's organizations besides preaching and Sunday school), has ventured on so unusual an enterprise as conducting an employment agency.

Forty-eight members constitute the nucleus of this enterprise. The pastor, with college and seminary education and seven years' experience, receives a salary of $1,200 a year. Fifty children are enrolled in the Sunday school. The total enterprise costs $1,650 a year. Yet these poor people are sustaining a financial burden of $34.37 per capita annually in the operating of this enterprise—well on toward twice the average of the internally adapted churches. Their church building is worth $12,000.

The churches of the neighborhood are accustomed to pitch tents in their side yards for summer service, or else to build tabernacles of boughs in testimony of their recent rural origin. The weird voices of their evangelists compete with the noise of roller-skating rinks, movie orchestras and the rattling of street cars. It is appropriate that Hick's Almanac, the meteorological Bible of the Southwest, is published in the immediate vicinity. When the church goes to the city on the poor rural level this is the manner of its behavior and such are the limits of its immediate outlook.

Similar cases of ecclesiastical "country cousins" may be found in eastern cities. In a New York city, for example, a little "Church of God," consisting of forty members, has been established within the last six years. It is one of the very few of its denomination to venture into a larger city. Its pastor, with fifteen years' experience, receives $780. Its Sunday school has an average attendance of thirty-five and its total budget of $1,000 costs each individual member $25.

With these petty resources, the church is giving $390, or $9.75 per capita, to missions and serves God after its own conscience and standards in a little meeting-house seating 150 people.

The beginnings of Negro churches are sometimes even more humble, as the following example shows:

Case X—Subtype A I

The decline of foreign immigration incident to the World War brought hundreds of thousands of southern plantation Negroes to northern cities. The story of how these strangers have struggled to strike root religiously in this new and distant environment has positive dramatic interest. Villagers in their native Africa, dwelling in little plantation clusters in the old South, largely inhabiting the undeveloped outskirts of the Southern cities today—cities which themselves are scarcely urbanized—the Negroes have remained the most completely rural of the American groups. Intensely sectarian as the Negro is and with strong tendencies toward social fragmentariness, it is not strange that his church beginnings in the North are frequently of the smallest and feeblest sort. Not infrequently, little groups of neighbors have undertaken the venture of northern migration together and have set up their transplanted church quite in the spirit of the older Pilgrims. Ninety-eight per cent. of all Negroes are either Methodist or Baptist, and it used to be a witty saying of Booker Washington that, if a Negro does not belong to one of these faiths, "some white man has been tampering with his religion." The Negro has, however, split up these denominational families into numerous sects, three of which appear in a single neighborhood of some 800 Negroes in a New England city.

The People's African Methodist Episcopal Zion Church consists of twelve members, six men and six women. It is one of seven churches for the 2,600 Negroes of the city. Organized in 1920, the church meets in a one-story "shack" of frame and sheet metal built as a storeroom. It holds some forty people. Two diminutive back rooms are rudely partitioned off. One, eight by ten feet, figures as a kitchen. With such a setting, six families have separated themselves into a church organization, their place of worship being within two blocks of two other Negro churches.

Within a month previous to the survey, an experienced and ambitious pastor had arrived upon the scene. He claimed one year of college education and proceeded to map out a campaign of expansion on the theory that an industrious minister can always beg money from a generous public on the score of sympathy for Negro religious enterprise. He agreed to accept a salary of $32 a month for the first six months while he was building up the enterprise.

Even at this rate, the smallest church in the city would be paying at the rate of $32 per capita annually or almost twice the average cost of all city churches covered in the survey, including the most elaborate and prosperous. This made the People's church easily one of the most expensive religious enterprises in its city.

Its average morning attendance is six, while the evening audience is eighteen. Prayer meeting is maintained for six attendants and there is a nominal young people's society of seven. This, with a woman's organization and a missionary society for children, called "Buds of Promise," constitutes the organization of the church. All, however, were reported in process of reorganization on the date of the survey. It would seem that they had been held intermittently, if at all, in the recent past. To a question as to the number of regular meetings a month the naïve answer was, "This is subject to change according to weather conditions." Roughly estimated, this church is rendering an aggregate monthly religious service of thirty-seven hours. No one would call such an enterprise commensurate with the problem of religion in the city. Its immediate adherents think of it only as a beginning, yet their utmost stretch of imagination pictures a building to cost $2,000 upon which they have set their hearts and for which they are attempting to raise money.

Another pioneer in the same city, St. Mark's Colored Methodist Episcopal church, started in 1918 in a similar store building; next moved to a schoolhouse, and then, in 1920, to a brick residence still undergoing the process of remodeling. Most of the carpenter work has been done by the pastor and the presiding elder. St. Mark's numbers forty-two members, but lost nineteen while gaining thirty-two members during the year before the survey. This 50 per cent. turnover of membership indicates how fluctuating and impermanent the constituency is. The pastor is classically educated, interested in Greek and regretting that he has never had time to master Hebrew. His salary is $1,000 out of a total operating budget of $1,387. The congregation has paid nearly $1,000 more on the building and is now spending a total per capita of about $55. It has a valuable adjunct in the colored man's dormitory administered by the church but supported by public benevolence through the Community Chest.

Should religion attempt to build itself into a city in this way and by such units? To classify these as unadapted churches is of course a mere abstraction; but to put the matter concretely, is it well for a few hundred Negroes to try to maintain three churches on this level in a progressive, northern industrial city? With their indomitable purpose to serve the Lord and help themselves one must have the sincerest sympathy, but one may fairly ask whether it is either necessary or socially wise for the general public to pay the bills.

OTHER LEVELS

Most rural people transplanted to the city naturally trickle into the existing churches by single families, mixing with the general population and not segregating their homes in particular neighborhoods nor establishing separate churches of rural colonists.

Hence it is not easy to identify individual churches as typical products of the rural heritage on such levels. But this is not to cast doubt upon its strong influence. Even in so urbanized a section as New England, a typical city (Springfield, Mass.) shows seven native-born Protestant church members of rural origin for every ten of urban origin. Further, it is known from the Census that not only is the interchange of population among cities of the South and some states of the Middle West practically negligible, but that cities in these regions receive only a small influx of native-born population from cities of other regions. In the West, the regions from which population is preëminently drawn are strongly rural. There is thus a continuous dilution of city attitudes and habits by rural immigration beyond anything which has yet been traced in objective investigations of the church. With so numerous and actively renewed rural sources, reëstablishment of essentially rural churches on more prosperous levels is highly probable. The dominance of people of rural antecedents (often including a strong element of retired farmers) is clearly manifest in the most typical churches of not a few cities of the sections indicated.[21] The following case serves as a fair example of such a situation. It may be described as "just an ordinary church."

Case XI—Subtype B I

About a mile and three-quarters from the business center of a far-western city, in one of the older residential sections, is a Baptist church.

21 For regional characteristics of churches throwing further light upon this point, see p. 293.

As population changes in the immediate downtown region drove the original central churches back upon the hills, the churches in this belt found their exclusive parishes seriously cut into by stronger rivals. The largest church of its denomination has, within a few years, relocated its commanding structure within three-quarters of a mile of the site of Case XI. Meanwhile, its own membership has been scattering to the newer parts of the city. Thus, in a residential area without any natural center of its own, too near the great central institutions to be free from their rivalry, this church, like many another in similar circumstances, has been left to deal with the less energetic and more commonplace people even of its immediate vicinity—primarily those of rural origins who have remained rurally minded. Adjoining it are many of the newer high-grade apartment houses and some of the finer residences of the city. By a sort of natural selection their people avoid the unattractive neighborhood church. This general condition leaves it, as its pastor explains, "just an ordinary church" after twenty-six years of life and in spite of its 271 members.

Its pastor confesses to no preparation for the ministry except that which his twenty-eight years of experience have given him. He receives a salary of $2,700. The Sunday school of 210 members consists largely of adults, an indication that the young people have gone elsewhere. There is, however, a small but enterprising young people's society. The church of fifteen rooms is a commonplace piece of architecture but affords a considerable range of equipment and comfortably seats 350 in a pleasant auditorium. The total operating budget is $5,500, and the church proves that it is not wholly ordinary in giving $3,200 for missions. Its limitations are shown by the fact that it has no Brotherhood, Scout organization or recreational program. It stresses strongly a conservative and individualistic type of theology, and personal evangelism. Its most successful feature is the prayer meeting at which the attendance is nearly one-fourth of the membership. Tracts are widely circulated and the bulletin board in front of the church exhibits in large type Bible texts of evangelical flavor. A certain sense of inferiority and inability to make progress seems to characterize the enterprise. It wonders at the thronged services of the Christian Science Church in the same vicinity.

FOREIGN ORIGINS

Until recently American urban growth has been more largely due to foreign immigration than to any other single external cause. This immigration has been, however, mainly non-Protestant, and its effect on types of Protestant churches has, therefore, not been dominant. Yet the church of foreign origin is an appreciable element within the unadapted types. Many of these immigrants bring a rural tradition of their own. They were peasants in the Old World and their transplanted rural characteristics are conservative. Frequently these become all the more pronounced in America as the foreign group, reacting against a strange land of undesired change, withdraws into a self-protective shell of clannishness. Its church life, in turn, reflects this ultra-conservatism, which is sometimes accompanied by institutional weakness, as in the following example, but not infrequently occurs also in spite of considerable financial strength and material prosperity.

Case XII—Subtype A I

This diminutive Swedish Baptist church has thirty-one members. There are only two smaller churches in the Northeastern city of 130,000 people in which it is located. It has no morning service. Its range of organizations and activities consists merely of an evening and a mid-week service, a Sunday school of twenty-eight members, a small young people's society and a ladies' aid organization to which the men of the church are attached as honorary members. Twenty-five people constitute its average congregation and its weekly total of service-hours is 126. The Sunday school is made up exclusively of children, and has no adolescent classes. The pastor is neither theologically trained nor ordained. The place of worship is a room twenty-eight by thirty-seven feet in dimensions, built as a one-story addition against the small residence in which the pastor lives. Under these circumstances it is natural that the salary and average expenditures of the church are far below normal, while the total value of its property is but $6,000.

For ten years a mission of the Swedish Baptist church in a neighboring city, this little group was recognized as a full church organization in 1905. But throughout the last two decades it has had losses relatively larger than those of any other church in the city that still survives. Like other little churches, the only terms on which it can live at all, even with so limited a program, is by demanding a very high number of hours per week from its members. In this respect its record is sixteen and three-tenths hours per member—more than 50 per cent. above the city average.

A very large number of American city churches of foreign antecedents are just like this example. They are particularly characteristic of semi-Americanized groups that have broken away from original, crowded, downtown foreign sections and begun to build little bungalow colonies on the outskirts of cities. The central problem of the foreign-speaking church, as of the American church, is, therefore, the urbanizing of a precious rural type, although the continuity of evolution is not so exact in detail.

REMNANTS AND FAILURES

Anything that makes a church fundamentally unsuccessful tends to pull it down into the unadapted type. For this reason there are more varieties of unadapted churches than of any other sort and greater contrasts between subtypes. In the slums of cities one finds swept together as companions in misfortune not only the foreigner, the new rural immigrant, Negro and white, but also representatives of decayed old families stranded in homes that were once mansions but which they are too poor to sacrifice or too old to leave. Naturally the religious institutions of such neighbors will mingle in one complex statistical class. Besides the very small foreign or Negro church will be found new and feeble American enterprises.

Within this type in considerable numbers will also be found churches whose development has been arrested because of poor location or failure of the constituency to grow. Frequently they represent very small denominations whose peculiarities are unacceptable to the majority and which are not fed by large natural constituencies. A denomination which, although strong in other sections of the country, is regionally weak because out of its natural habitat, will frequently contribute churches to this group. For example, Presbyterianism in New England and Congregationalism in the South find it hard to pull their churches up out of the unadapted type.

Again, there are the noble ruins of churches that have seen better days exhibiting a more advanced stage of recession than did similar churches in the slightly adapted group. In the retreat of the "nice people" before population changes, these churches were a little too slow or more stubborn than others, and were caught in the backwash of the social current. They cannot now move to advantage or are still held by a sense of obligation, only to dwindle and disintegrate.

Case XIII—Subtype C II

No better example could be found of a church that has seen better days than Christ Church on Salem Street, Boston, at the end of two hundred years. This, the famous "old North Church," sharing Revolutionary renown with Paul Revere, is now a symbolic candle flickering on an altar rather than a lofty beacon signifying a great cause. A total reversal of fortune lies between the church maintaining the élite academy in which Henry Ward Beecher as a boy was learning Latin, and the present Salem Street neighborhood identified in college doggerel as a Jewish quarter.

Copp's Hill, on which the church stands, still looks across to the "Charlestown Shore," where Bunker Hill rises. Paul Revere himself has left a sketch of the old North Church spire rising high above the low dwellings of 1723; but it does not rise above the many-story tenement houses of to-day.

The church is an historic shrine rather than a vital place of present service. It counts sixty-two members but has no Sunday school. The rector receives $1,200 salary and is assisted by a woman social worker. The budget of $8,700 is largely expended on the upkeep of the property. Though this building is valued at only $56,000, the interior of the church is a distinguished piece of architecture. Its ancient structural and decorative features have been piously restored in recent years under the leadership of Bishop Lawrence. Scarcely any church in America has more venerable memorials. These include the ancient chime of bells, a communion service of high artistic value and a copy of the "vinegar" Bible.

But the "old North Church" belongs to the ages much more than to the present day. It is more significant for the nation than for the neighborhood. Not a few such venerable churches exist within the feebler extremes of the unadapted group.

The unadapted type thus turns out to be the catch-all of the unsuccessful as well as the hold-over of the rural tradition. For this reason its interpretation is complicated. No one or two principles will explain all the facts. While, speaking broadly, the type represents the weakness of small resources, the poverty of the poor, the strangeness of the foreigner, the relatively poor standards of the farmer recently come to the city—all frequently superimposed upon a rural tradition—not all unadapted churches are numerically and financially weak. Some are unadapted because they want to be so. Thus a surveyor of a certain church was reminded rather tartly, "We have everything that a Southern Baptist church is supposed to have." [22]

Case XIV—Subtype B I

Urban conservatism rather than rural finds an example in a church of solid Teutonic virtues, though largely Americanized, located in a metropolitan city. Its relatively large and well-balanced Sunday school is a mark of the American rather than German tradition, and shows that the younger generation is ready to move on. For thirty-six years it has occupied the center of the middle-class residential district a little apart from the brewery industrial section, where the old-world flavor of the original German quarter is left behind and the tree-lined streets are fronted by houses showing the substantial and ugly American city architecture of a generation ago.

The present membership is just over 600. The pastor, a fully educated man with twenty years' experience, has been seven and one-half years in his present position and receives a salary of $1,650. The total budget of the church is $5,460 for current expenses—less than $10 per member—and nearly $1,200 for missions. With a well-equipped, though old-fashioned, building of ten rooms, seating 525 in the auditorium, and with thriving subsidiary organizations within a narrow range, the church is, nevertheless, unadapted from the standpoint of the average American city organization. It has no boys', girls' or young people's organizations. This reflects the pull-back of conservative tradition. In spite of its size and resources it stands a little to the rear of average American church progress.

This interpretation is justified by detailed comparison of the group of larger churches within the unadapted type. While inferior to the slightly adapted churches, they stand nearer to them in many respects—size, for example—than they do to the other subtypes of their own group. Their resources are demonstrably superior and they can have more of a varied program whenever they want to. They have what they regard as proper, but their development is below the average of the majority of American city churches.

22 Some of the reasons held by other churches for not wanting to be adapted are discussed on pp. 240 f.

Chapter VIII

THE INTERNALLY ADAPTED CHURCH

The 196 churches designated "internally adapted" are in development one statistical stage beyond the slightly adapted churches according to the methods of measurement explained in Chapter iii.

Concretely stated, their programs are larger and broader. They round out the set of subsidiary organizations within the church so that there is specialized provision for every age-, and sex-group. They develop the programs of these organizations, or else add still newer activities, until all the more outstanding human interests and aspects of life are ministered to under church auspices.

PROGRAM

These obvious tendencies are illustrated in Table XXVIII, showing sample programs of five churches each from the two subtypes included in the internally adapted type.

In these programs organizations and activities appear as frequent and characteristic that occur in only a few marginal churches of the slightly adapted type, and then in very unbalanced relation to other elements of the program.[1] These new activities are modal for the internally adapted type as a whole, although appearing more frequently in Subtype D II which shows the maximum elaboration that is normally found.

These activities include separate organizations for young women, clubs or classes for mothers, recreational activities like dramatics, organized athletics or gymnasium classes, together with the beginnings of practical instruction illustrated by sewing classes. From this range of activity Subtype C II selects from nine to twelve items for its program and Subtype D II from thirteen to seventeen items.

Other activities, rare in city churches as a whole, have become relatively frequent with churches of this type, though not of general occurrence even with them. They are frequently open daily for private religious devotion; they often use moving-pictures; they have Sunday afternoon sociables or teas; they tend to maintain daily vacation Bible schools and week-day classes for religious instruction.

[1] See Table IX for sample programs of Subtype B III.

TABLE XXVIII — SAMPLE PROGRAMS OF INTERNALLY ADAPTED CHURCHES

Organizations and Activities	C II					D II				
	1	2	3	4	5	1	2	3	4	5
1. Preaching and Sunday School	*	*	*	*		*	*	*	*	*
2. Ladies' Aid or Guild	*		*	*	*	*	*	*	*	
3. Women's Missionary Society	*	*	*	*	*	*	*	*	*	*
4. Young People's Society	*	*	*			*	*		*	*
5. Chorus Choir		*	*	*			*	*	*	*
6. General Social Events	*	*			*	*	*	*	*	
7. Men's Organization	*	*	*			*	*	*		
8. Boy Scouts		*	*	*		*	*	*		*
9. Mission Study Classes					*	*	*	*		
10. Organized Welcome					*	*	*	*		
11. Orchestra or Band	*						*		*	*
12. Boys' Club (not Scouts)				*	*		*		*	*
13. Lectures							*			*
14. Library	*	*		*		*	*		*	
15. Girls' Club (not Scouts)			*	*					*	*
16. Concerts										*
17. Girl Scouts or Equivalent	*						*		*	*
18. Mothers' or Parents' Organization	*						*	*	*	*
19. Young Women's Organization			*	*	*			*	*	*
20. Dramatic Club	*	*	*					*	*	*
21. Gymnasium Classes	*		*	*		*	*		*	*
22. Sewing Classes								*	*	
	10	11	11	10	11	14	14	15	16	16

Other Characteristics

SIZE

In popular judgments of the city church the most characteristic church of the internally adapted type would be called fairly large, having between 500 and 1,000 members; and over one-third of internally adapted churches have more than 1,000 members as shown in Table XXIX.[2]

TABLE XXIX — MEMBERSHIP OF INTERNALLY ADAPTED CHURCHES *

Number of Members	Per Cent. Distribution of Churches
Under 500	27.2
Under 100	....
100 to 200	3.8
200 to 300	9.2
300 to 400	8.2
400 to 500	6.0
500 to 1,000	38.6
1,000 and over	34.2

* 184 churches reporting.

2 Appendix Table 5.

AGE AND PERMANENCE

The internally adapted church is middle-aged or old rather than young, 14.6 per cent. of its examples having been organized for more than a century. It has moved more frequently than the church of any other type, its average age in a given location being only half its age in years. Only a little more than one-fourth of its examples are now located on their original sites.[3] How far mobility accounts for elaboration is a question for later discussion.[4]

STAFF

Nearly three-fourths of the internally adapted churches have more than one paid religious worker. The staff consists most frequently of one or of three workers, but quite often of four or five as shown in the following comparison:[5]

TABLE XXX — PAID RELIGIOUS WORKERS IN INTERNALLY ADAPTED CHURCHES *

Number Employed	Per Cent. Distribution of Churches
1	27.2
2	22.0
3	27.2
4	12.1
5	6.3
6	2.1
7	0.5
8	2.1
9	
10	0.5

* 191 churches reporting.

Among additional male workers relatively fewer are classified as assistant pastors than in the slightly adapted churches, and many more are designated as directors of religious education or of recreation or of boys' or young people's work. One finds also occasional business managers or full-time treasurers. Secretaries, deaconesses and visitors are the most frequently designated women workers, but women directors of social service or of women's, girls' or young people's work appear in significant numbers.

THE PASTOR

The internally adapted church has a highly educated ministry, 86.5 per cent. of its pastors having at least full college and semi-

3 Appendix Tables 6 and 7.
4 See p. 212, Chart XXXII.
5 Appendix Table 9.

nary training, and 33.6 per cent. having taken additional post-graduate work. They are predominantly in the prime of life, three-fourths of them having had from ten to thirty years' experience in

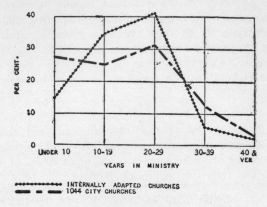

CHART XXIV

Experience of Pastors of Internally Adapted Churches Compared with Experience of Pastors of 1,044 City Churches.

the ministry. Few are very young or very old. They tend to stay in the same pastorate slightly longer than those of other types.[6]

The characteristic salaries for pastors of this type of church

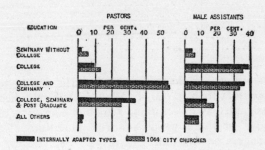

CHART XXV

Education of Pastors and Male Assistants in Internally Adapted Churches and in 1,044 City Churches.

range from $2,000 up, one-fourth being as high as from $5,000 to $7,000, and nearly one-tenth over $7,000. The salary range is shown in Table XXXI.[7]

6 Appendix Tables 12-14.
7 Appendix Table 15.

TABLE XXXI — SALARIES OF PASTORS OF INTERNALLY
ADAPTED CHURCHES *

Salary	Per Cent. Distribution of Pastors
Less than $1,000	....
$1,000 to $2,000	11.0
$2,000 to $3,000	20.6
$3,000 to $4,000	19.9
$4,000 to $5,000	13.2
$5,000 to $6,000	12.5
$6,000 to $7,000	13.2
$7,000 to $8,000	6.6
$8,000 and over	3.0

* 136 pastors reporting.

These larger salaries go with larger average size and more
elaborate program. The men who receive them are administering a
bigger business than that of the average church, one that involves
larger plants, heavier current expense budgets and benevolences,
more fellow workers and wider constituencies.

FINANCES

Characteristic budgets of the internally adapted churches range
from $5,000 to $10,000, but in over one-fifth of the cases they exceed
$25,000.[8]

TABLE XXXII — CURRENT EXPENSES OF INTERNALLY
ADAPTED CHURCHES *

Amount	Per Cent. Distribution of Churches*
Under $5,000	15.5
Under $1,000	0.6
$1,000 to $2,000	2.3
$2,000 to $3,000	4.6
$3,000 to $4,000	3.4
$4,000 to $5,000	4.6
$5,000 to $10,000	25.8
$10,000 to $15,000	13.8
$15,000 to $20,000	14.4
$20,000 to $25,000	9.2
$25,000 to $50,000	19.6
$50,000 and over	1.7

* 174 churches reporting.

The per capita cost of internally adapted churches is only slightly
above the average for the 1,044 city churches; namely, $19.12 as
compared with the average of $18.17. The subtypes are close to-

8 Appendix Tables 24-25.

gether in this respect. This would seem to indicate that the program of the average city church can be greatly enlarged as to both number and range of activities without appreciable additional expense to the individuals participating.

Over one-half of the internally adapted churches give more than $5,000 annually to benevolences, and 10.9 per cent. give more than $25,000. In this respect again the two subtypes are close together. The per capita benevolence of the type is $12.03 as compared with the average for 1,044 city churches of $11.52.[9]

PROPERTY

The median value of the church building of the internally adapted type is $120,400, but the subtypes differ strikingly, the churches of Subtype C II showing a median value of $86,570, as compared with one of $150,000 for Subtype D II. The representative church of the type has from ten to twenty rooms and seats 700 people in the auditorium. It has a much larger working equipment than the less developed types. In respect to value, the subtypes show well-defined differences on every point relating to property.[10]

SUNDAY SCHOOL

Sunday-school enrollment of the internally adapted church reaches the characteristic mode of from 300 to 400 pupils, but considerably over one-third of them have more than 500 pupils, and over one-tenth have more than 1,000.

Sunday-school attendance is about average compared with enrollment, but relative to church membership the Sunday-school enrollment is smaller than in the less developed types.

The Sunday school of the internally adapted church is, however, especially strong in adolescent and adult membership. Of the seventeen subtypes only one other has so high a proportion of adolescents in its enrollment as Subtype D II.[11] Whether or not the fuller and wider program of the churches of this type is the cause of its superior ability to hold adolescents in Sunday school, it is at least a striking fact that the two phenomena coincide.

ENVIRONMENT

On the basis of eighty-four cases studied the internally adapted type has the largest proportion of centrally located churches, most

9 Appendix Table 25.
10 Appendix Table 29.
11 Appendix Tables 31-35a.

of which are found at the business heart of the city. This type also shows more churches in high-class neighborhoods than any other, and more residential churches strategically related to neighborhood centers.[12]

PARISH CHARACTERISTICS

Because it has so many downtown churches, the internally adapted type naturally has a large proportion of parishes with scattered memberships brought from long distances and from all directions. The evidence for the sixty-two cases studied is shown in the following comparison:

Per Cent. of Members Living Within One Mile	Parish Designation	Distribution of Internally Adapted Churches		
		Total	Central	Residential
75 and over	Compact	27	4	23
50–74	Medium	17	8	9
25–49	Scattered	12	5	7
Less than 25	Very Scattered	6	5	1

In view of the average distance from which churches succeed in drawing members, most of the centrally located churches of this type would seem to be no longer strategically located. If they are succeeding, it is under difficulties. Perhaps the development of their

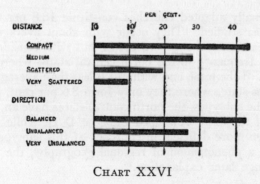

CHART XXVI

Per Cent. Distribution of Types of Parishes of Internally Adapted Churches, by Distance and Direction.

programs is partly a reflection of the effort to meet these difficulties.

The residential churches of the type, on the contrary, have an unusual proportion of compact parishes whose elaboration must be due to some other cause.[13]

12 Appendix Tables 37–38c.
13 Appendix Tables 40–42.

With respect to the direction of members' homes from the church building, the showing of the internally adapted type is most interesting, especially in connection with the facts as to the distance of the constituents from the church. As shown in the following comparison, the parish of the internally adapted church tends to be normally balanced.[14]

Designation	Number of Churches
Normally balanced parish	21
Unbalanced parish	13
Very unbalanced parish	15

If the small number of cases under examination is at all typical, this indicates a much larger proportion of balanced parishes than any other type has. It suggests a sort of church which is able to draw constituents from all directions as well as from great distances. This is in striking contrast with churches having more limited programs.[15]

Larger Environments and Relations

The internally adapted type shows definite geographical, racial and denominational affinities.

REGION

The internally adapted churches constitute 18.8 per cent. of the 1,044 churches studied. They occur with about average frequency in the northeastern and southern states, but with considerably more than average frequency in the north central states where they form 25.2 per cent. of the total, and with much less than average frequency in the western states where they only form 8.6 per cent. of the total. As between the subtypes, the north central states have an even higher proportion of the more developed Subtype D II, while the western states are even more deficient in churches of this subtype. Elaboration, then, is a phenomenon of regional geography, the reasons for which challenge later explanation.[16]

SIZE OF CITY

Although the internally adapted churches constitute 18.8 per cent. of the 1,044 churches, they only make 10.5 per cent. of those churches which are in cities of from one-half to three-quarters of a million. On the other hand, they constitute 25.7 per cent. of the

14 For explanation of the categories used in this comparison, see p. 255.
15 Appendix Tables 43 and 44.
16 See pp. 294 f. Also Appendix Table 47.

churches found in cities of more than one million, and almost as high a proportion in cities of from a quarter to a half a million population. This comparison appears in detail in Table XXXIII.[17]

TABLE XXXIII — RATIO OF INTERNALLY ADAPTED CHURCHES TO TOTAL CHURCHES, IN CITIES OF VARYING SIZE

Population of City	Ratio
100,000 to 250,000	19.5
250,000 to 500,000	23.9
500,000 to 750,000	10.5
750,000 to 1,000,000	17.2
1,000,000 and over	25.7
All cities	18.8

An explanation of this phenomenon is attempted in a later connection.[18]

RACIAL AFFINITY

Out of fifty-seven "foreign churches" as defined for the purposes of this study [19] only one belongs to the internally adapted type. This degree of ecclesiastical development is distinctly beyond the reach of Protestants of the more recent immigrant races.

DENOMINATIONAL TENDENCIES

The denominations generally share in the churches of the internally adapted type in approximately their due proportion on the basis of the 1,044 churches studied. There are two striking exceptions, namely, the Methodist Episcopal, whose churches constitute 19.9 per cent. of the sample, but reach 27 per cent. of the internally adapted type; and the Methodist Episcopal South, whose churches make up 3.7 per cent. of the sample but only 2 per cent. of the internally adapted type. "All other denominations" and the Lutherans are also proportionately below their ranks in per cent. of internally adapted churches while the Disciples are considerably above it. On the whole, however, the tendency to elaboration is well distributed throughout the major denominations, though reaching more than one-fourth of the total in only one denomination.[20]

Divergent Tendencies

As previously noted [21] the internally adapted type exhibits only one of the two logical tendencies involved in the general evolution

17 Appendix Table 46.
18 See p. 282.
19 See p. 276.
20 Appendix Table 45.
21 See p. 72.

TABLE XXXIV — DISTRIBUTION OF INTERNALLY ADAPTED
CHURCHES BY DENOMINATIONS

| | Per Cent. | |
Denomination	Total Churches Studied	Internally Adapted Churches
Baptist	15.8	13.3
Congregational	10.5	11.7
Disciples	4.4	5.6
Methodist Episcopal	19.3	27.0
Methodist Episcopal South	3.7	2.0
Presbyterian U. S. A.	17.3	16.3
Protestant Episcopal	10.5	12.3
Lutheran (all bodies)	4.4	3.1
All others	14.1	8.7

of the subtypes. Subtype D II has more activities than Subtype
C II; but there is no adventurous subtype, corresponding to those
found in the types previously considered, that increases the range
of its activities without increasing their number and that still keeps
a due proportion of the more frequent activities.

On a considerable number of counts there is little difference
between the subtypes. Their pastors have equal experience. The
proportion of salaries in the higher ranges is about the same, as is
the proportion of budgets beyond $25,000. Per capita current ex-
penses and benevolences are close together, as are also the average
capacity of auditoriums and the distribution of Sunday-school enrollment. The following divergences, however, appear:

Divergent Aspect	Subtype C II	Subtype D II
Size	Approximately 13% more churches of under 500 members	Approximately 12% more churches of 500–1,000 members
Age	Average younger	Average older
Permanence	Less permanent	More permanent
Staff-number	20% have 4 or more workers	29% have 4 or more workers
Staff-functions	Fewer with unusual functions	More with unusual functions
Pastor's education	More without semi-nary training	More with seminary training
Pastor's tenure in present position	Trend to shorter ten-ure	Trend to longer ten-ure
Pastor's salary	More under $3,000	Fewer under $3,000
Current expense budgets	More under $10,000	More $15,000–$25,000
Facilities	Trend to smaller number	Trend to larger num-ber
Rooms in church building	Trend to smaller number	Trend to larger num-ber
Value church plant	Average much smaller	Average much greater
Age of Sunday-school pupils	More adults	More adolescents
Location	Many more residen-tial	Many more central
Advantageous location of central churches	More strategically lo-cated	More doubtfully lo-cated
Quality of neighbor-hood of residential churches	More high class	More middle class

Reading down the list, one notes a clear-cut distinction between the lower and higher phase of general development. Subtype D II has more of everything generally accounted good than the less developed Subtype C II. With respect to environmental factors, however, this is not true. The churches of the less developed subtype appear to be more frequently located in high-class residential neighborhoods and better located if downtown. This difference will have weight in the environmental interpretation.[22]

The variations within the type are thus limited to a leaner and fuller phase of elaboration. One subtype simply has more of the same sort of program than has the other.

ADVANCE BEYOND THE SLIGHTLY ADAPTED TYPE

The four tendencies found in the expansion of the program of the slightly adapted type are all simply carried farther in that of the internally adapted church. Church services are further enriched; the general social life of the parish becomes more complex; additional organizations based upon age-, and sex-differentiation are included, and still more varied expressions of cultural and recreational interests appear. The internally adapted church has thus moved beyond the slightly adapted church but in the same general direction. An attempt to interpret its peculiar stage of development follows.

Interpreting the Internally Adapted Type

FUNDAMENTAL CHARACTERISTICS

The basic hypothesis of this study is that city churches represent various phases in the adaptation of the rural church to an urban environment. Viewed in the light of this hypothesis, the unadapted church, as has been seen, is in the city but not of it, while the slightly adapted church has driven forward with no clear notion of where it is going. The internally adapted church, on the other hand, represents a definite step forward in the process of urban adaptation; it possesses an urban outlook and spirit and tends to have a distinctly urbanized program.

ELEMENTS OF THE NEW URBAN OUTLOOK

Among other things the internally adapted church senses the presence in the city of enlarging numbers of people not living in

22 See p. 264.

family groups. All cities are young men's and young women's towns. About 10 per cent. more of city populations are found in the group twenty to forty-four years of age than in rural communities. This gives a distinct spirit of energy and adventure to the city. Not only do multitudes of youths flock there to seek independent fortunes but marriage is often deferred or avoided altogether. Seven per cent. fewer of the urban than of the rural females above fifteen years of age are married. In consequence the non-family population of the city becomes a larger, maturer and more controlling factor than in any other type of community.

Even to those who are members of it, the family ceases to mean exactly what it did in rural society. Instead of living in its own separate home it shares a multi-family dwelling with strangers who are served collectively by one agency for heat, light, water and sanitation. Space is so scarce that infancy is crowded out on the streets for air, childhood for play, and youth for its inevitable activities and curiosities. Life is public rather than private.

EFFECT OF CHANGED ECONOMIC STATUS

The tendency away from the home is reënforced by economic changes. There are 5 per cent. fewer of the city's young people in school than there are of the country's. Thus while country boys and girls are still in school, their city contemporaries have often gone to work. Independent wages and an earlier contact with the world make youth increasingly independent of parental authority and critical of the ideas of the older generation. Similarly the married woman who works away from home inevitably shifts her attitude toward marriage and the family. Thus family ties are forced to adjust themselves to the new set of relationships under urban conditions.

THE PART OF THE CHURCH

A distinguished Detroit minister who left the city some fifteen years ago and returned to the same pastorate after seven years' absence—during which Detroit grew two and one-half times as fast as any other American city of its class except Los Angeles—is in a unique position to sense what has happened in the meantime. Leaving a localized constituency in a residential neighborhood and coming back to a downtown church with an ever-scattering following, he epitomizes the change by saying: "We used to gain members by families; now it is by individuals." The city, he goes on to say, has developed a type of religious "seekers" who go about hunting for churches with which they have spiritual affinity. Their sense of need is untraditional, individual, sometimes more and sometimes less steady or profound. But they are especially available material for the ministries of the more alert and adaptable city church.

In brief, city life needs, and is ripe for, new social and ethical interpretation. Here are found the raw materials of new loyalties, urging upon the imagination and will the holiness of human perplexity and the experimental spirit of the gang, of the social class, of the city itself. Here is opportunity for new moral leadership based on the fact that the city is a new method of human association capable of full idealistic rendering. Consequently any institution that has followed the people from country to city is under the necessity of finding a new appeal and program, or else of losing the people.

ELABORATION WITHOUT ENTHUSIASM

Not a few internally adapted churches appear, however, to have drifted somewhat unconsciously into their present positions. They have followed instinct rather than conviction. Having to live up to their official positions or their historic reputations, they accept the examples of other successful churches without understanding the principles involved. Or they do somewhat grudgingly what their own younger generation expects.

Case XV—Subtype C II

A good example of such a situation is the "Old First" Church in a New England city

The mother church of the entire region and the fourteenth to be founded in the state, for 285 years it has occupied the focal point of the city, always standing adjacent to the public square. Now, with its fourth meeting house, it occupies the very center of the square, facing the great municipal buildings. The street-car system—at once the best friend and, by reason of its noise, the worst enemy of the church—also focuses at this point. The church stands where paths have always met, and an unrivaled degree of prestige attaches both to the spot and to the organization.

For 170 years First Church was the only church in the city. The individualistic habit of mind fixed during this period is still strong upon it. Its membership of some 1,500 covers the entire area of the city and is frequently stronger in a given locality than the strongest of the neighborhood churches. Indeed in nine out of the eleven districts into which the city was divided for purposes of survey, the membership of the First Church constitutes one of the major religious groups.

Many of its local parish organizations are older than the usual agencies through which similar work is now currently done in the majority of churches, and their distinctions without a difference are cherished piously. Enormous civic authority is attached to the utterances of the First Church pulpit. Its building is the natural geographical center for interdenominational and other general gatherings.

All this has given the church a unique character with respect to the total religious movements of the city. Churches of greater financial ability, however (some of them children of First Church), tend to dispute its ascendancy in the community. As a reaction from this situation, the First Church has developed the habit of going it alone in the strength of its members and historic standing. It does not therefore exercise in fact the leadership that it sometimes assumes.

Its main instincts are conservative; but by reason of its position and central location, there has gradually grown up within it a range of activities which have now reached something like all-around elaboration of program.

The city grew more in the last two decades than in the previous 200 years. It is not strange therefore that the First Church should be 50 per cent. larger than it was twenty years ago. Its religious leadership consists of the services of an enormously industrious pastor with a single woman secretary to assist him. The pastor's salary is $6,000 and the secretary's $1,500. The total operating budget of the church is about $20,000 and the annual benevolence nearly $10,000. This is about one-third less than the average per capita rate of support of the churches of its denomination in the city—reflecting the rather modest average of the present economic standing of its constituency. The per capita rate has increased 50 per cent. over a period of twenty years, but has remained practically stationary for the last ten. The present per capita expenditure for current support approximates very closely the average for the 1,044 city churches included in the study.

The rate of per capita benevolence approximates closely that of the church's denomination in the city, but is considerably below the average for the 1,044 city churches.

The Sunday school enrolls nearly 800 pupils and has an average attendance of 73 per cent. of the enrollment, which exactly agrees with the city average. Its age-distribution, however, shows striking variations, reflecting the central location of the church. This appears in the following comparison:

Age Period	Per Cent. Distribution	
	City	First Church
Infants	9	3
Children	49	24
Adolescents	20	27
Adults	22	46

This showing reflects a tendency common to centrally located churches. Adults and adolescents can naturally go longer distances than small children. It suggests also that the degree to which an elaborated program serves all elements in the church constituency necessarily varies with the character and balance of that constituency. The church that has an elaborated program for adolescents and adults may still be in a position to offer only a narrow program for young children on account of its location. In other words, the location most strategic with respect to the total constituency may be disadvantageous with respect to some part of it.

The outstanding merit of the present work in the First Church is its careful parish organization and the active and intensive cultivation of its constituents. The parish is divided into twenty districts in which there are weekly neighborhood programs of social and religious character. The church thus makes good its elaborated program by taking it home to the dispersed membership in their own neighborhoods. How much the central character of the church is a matter of prestige and general sentiment and how little a matter of everyday use, is evidenced by the fact that it is not felt necessary to have the church office open throughout the day. Central facilities for parish work are ample, though old-fashioned.

The pulpit ministries of the church, however, constitute its central services. Cultural responsibility is recognized in preaching as well as the evangelistic message. There is a conservative use of literary subjects in the pulpit. The church does little formal advertising, being universally known in its relatively small city and continuously in the public eye.

Churches like this constitute the first distinctively urban type. They are brought to elaboration of program less by the realization and acceptance of any specific urban viewpoint than by the unconscious addition of one feature after another—frequently to meet the competition of churches whose positions compel them to be more aggressive. One gets the impression that First Church would be just as willing not to do some of the things it is doing if it did not have to live up to its position in the city. Its real interests are in the evangelistic pulpit and in an elaborate system of careful, old-fashioned parish ministrations.

CONSTRUCTIVE ADAPTATION

In contrast with the hesitancy with which a church like the Old First approaches the urban situation certain churches are more deliberately aggressive. Churches of the former type feel the disorganization of old attitudes by the urban spirit more definitely than they do its creative and constructive aspects. Churches of the latter type are warm-hearted, self-confident, opportunistic. They feel responsible for meeting changing conditions and are not slaves to any limiting theory. They do not see, therefore, why the church should not move along with the city in the lines of its distinctive characteristics. They have acted experimentally more often than from any fully thought-out policy. The result is the internally adapted church program developed by about one-fifth of the 1,044 city churches being studied.

Case XVI—Subtype D II

A Congregational church in one of the large cities of the Middle West presents a characteristic example of an old-time city enterprise meeting a crisis due to changed environment and solving it by a deliberate right-about-face.

In 1920 this church decided to take stock of its changed situation. A large proportion of its members were supposed to have moved to the suburbs, though actual count showed three-fourths still living in reasonable proximity to the church. The church was, therefore, really more scared than hurt. Half of its Sunday school, however, had come to represent families not otherwise connected with the church. Sixty per cent. of the population of the community was new, and the neighborhood had gradually changed from a place of homes to a rather congested district of multi-family dwellings.

Three choices appeared to be before the church: namely, to continue the former program while the church progressively dwindled away; to remove to the suburbs in order to perpetuate an average church of the family type; or to make a new adjustment. The last course was decided upon, and the church attempted to think its way through an effective program for the next ten years.

Without designating its new program as an elaborated one, the church actually did what corresponds exactly with the characteristic procedure of the type. It added extensively to its cultural and recreational activities. It established a full round of subsidiary organizations for all the age-, and sex-groups and supplied them with a week-day, as well as a religious, program. It changed its Sunday evening services into a platform for the discussion of current problems and gave two nights per week to organized recreation. It established a choral society which gave monthly musical entertainments.

The resources of the church were smaller than formerly. The staff necessary to operate so elaborate a program had therefore to be secured by the employment of part-time workers at nominal salaries. Four such workers were added, namely, two recreational directors, a parish visitor and a secretary.

The spacious old stone building (worth $90,000), with its enormous auditorium but few rooms for other purposes, did not easily lend itself to the demands of the new program. Rather makeshift devices were resorted to in order to accommodate a more exactly graded Sunday school and the various recreational activities. The total budget of the church is now about $15,000, and the new order has had several years of successful operation.

An important factor in the church's transformation has been publicity. Its printed matter has been plentiful, varied and clever. Still more important, however, has been the reëducation of spirit to which the church set itself. Characterizing its tradition as that of a "secluded family church," it recognized that the achievement of wider community influence would be a gradual process in which the church would have to change its traditional attitude and make good in the minds of its new neighbors. The resolution of the church on this point is worth quoting: "It will require conscious and consistent effort on the part of the members of the church at all times to interest others in church activities and to welcome them to church activities in the friendly, democratic spirit of service. No church can possibly become great without that spirit. Men and women, of whatever degree or station, generally do not fully appreciate the power, as well as the duty, of affable democratic manners, and friendly association with their fellows. Human nature craves friendship. These things are absolutely imperative to the growth of a community church. What is more, they are a personal Christian duty."

Besides reinserting itself into the original neighborhood in which it had ceased to be fully at home, the church has maintained active touch with its suburban members by organizing special group activities for them. Whether this is wiser than to help them to active identification with churches nearer their homes is a question. Their services and support, however, have been an important factor in enabling the church to stay where it was and to face about instead of retreating from its difficulties.

The next case is that of a preponderately young people's church that has adopted an elaborated program without preconception, as a sort of natural birthright of urban youth in this stage of the world's history.

Case XVII—Subtype D II

"The best church of foreign origins in its denomination," is the verdict of a prominent church official upon this Methodist Episcopal enterprise. It is a shining example, well beyond the average, of a broadly developed church in a working-class neighborhood of foreign antecedents. The membership of about 775 is mainly of Bohemian extraction, and separate services in the Bohemian tongue are still maintained. But English is the language of most of the church's manifold activities, and its spirit is distinctly American.

The church has a staff of eight workers and a budget of over $21,000 in round figures, about $4,000 of which comes from its denominational board of missions. It worships in a recently erected church structure of exceptionally dignified design and complete appointment. The building, constructed of stone, has thirty rooms, including the most up-to-date equipment for administration, religious education and recreational life.

It is a church rich in young people, as indeed it should be, with three special directors, one for boys' activities, one for girls' activities, and one for general social interests. It has an especially well-equipped gymnasium. The Sunday school enrolls over a thousand and includes an unusual proportion of adolescents. Its pupils represent the following nationalities:

Nationality	Per Cent. Distribution
Bohemian	45.0
German	26.0
American	25.0
All other	4.0

The last item includes a considerable minority of pupils from Irish and Polish families.

The Sunday-school membership is more widely distributed in the city than that of the church, 57 per cent. of its pupils living within a mile of the church.

Half of the boys' activities are classified under the head of "general community interests" (social gatherings, etc.); 33 per cent. as gymnasium work; 14 per cent. as games; 3 per cent. as formal devotional services. Sixty per cent. of the boys participating are from the church's own Sunday school, 30 per cent. are Catholics, and 10 per cent. are from families of no faith.

These items are taken from the very complete statistical records of the church. It has analyzed its work and knows its field. Seventy-five per cent. of its church members live within a mile of the church, mainly within a well-defined sector, including a minor trade center and joining a factory section. The church is one of three of its neighborhood rated by the city Church Federation as doing special community work for foreigners. Near by is located a well-known training school for foreign Protestant workers, mainly Slavs.

The church carries on an unusual number of up-to-date features. It has a weekly "all Broadway night" combining a supper, a social and a prayer service, and then breaking up into groups for a forum, teacher-training classes, a story hour and a Girls' Circle. It maintains a Daily Vacation Bible School of over 400 members and a boys' camp. Its weekday Bible class started off last year with an attendance of 159 pupils.

With all this variety the church is emphatically not setting itself to serve sub-normal populations. It has no health work, no special emphasis on charity, and maintains no employment agency, dormitory or home. Its pastor is influential in denominational circles in the city at large, and the church actively participates in denominational affairs.

Perhaps its most unique distinction is a considerable endowment for church music, which assures a varied ministry in this department of service. This perpetuates the best traditions of the church's Bohemian ancestry. It adds the touch of an honestly inherited special genius to an institution thoroughly adapted to the service of a progressive and forward-looking urban population. All told, the church expresses a dynamic group teaming with young energies, contributing to as well as receiving from America, courageously accepting new responsibilities and hopefully sharing the destinies of a great city.

THE ELABORATED SUBTYPES

In the evidence as presented, two variations worthy of illustration are discovered: namely, a less highly elaborated type tending toward a residential environment and a more highly elaborated one found characteristically in central environments.

Case XVIII—Subtype C II

Just at the point where the zoning ordinance limits the westward expansion of retail business on the main boulevard of a Californian city is a cluster of high-class hotels and exclusive clubs. Among them is located a Congregational church. All the area beyond, rising gradually to the foothills crowned with splendid residences, is reserved for high-class single family dwellings. The location is most strategic for a family church of upper-class people.

The church has grown up with this section of the city. Its recently erected plant, a memorial chapel, is merely a first unit, designed essentially for religious education and social activities, which will later be supplemented by a great auditorium. It is one of the best pieces of church architecture in the city and, with perhaps no exception, the best in the details of its construction and equipment. When this study was made, the church had 434 members, thirty-four of whom were absent. It had 106 accessions during the year and twelve removals.

Its program is a typical elaborated program of a family church, with the leading stress on religious education, including directed activities. It uses moving-pictures for its evening service. It announces that it appeals to the high-grade transient population of the vicinity—which is somewhat of the semi-permanent type.

The staff consists of a pastor, a woman assistant to the pastor doing both clerical and parish work, and a "director of Christian education."

The present unit of the plant is worth $125,000 and is carefully designed for efficient and fully departmentalized work in religious education as well as for the refined social life of a well-to-do parish. The vacant corner lot designed for the future auditorium is occupied by tennis and basketball courts.

The budget for current expenses in recent years has been about $12,500. Besides this, $7,500 was paid during the year preceding the case study on the building indebtedness.

A printed list of the boundaries of the "circles" into which the parish is divided for social purposes indicates that above a half, and probably two-thirds, of the members' families live in the western half of this section of the city within a half mile of the church, the remainder being scattered throughout the section.

A church operating on such a scale and with such tastes as are expressed in its appointments and publicity inevitably draws people by selection. Its program seems to bring its adherents into many and close human relationships. In this respect its program is as different as possible from one that deals with transient crowds in the downtown section.

It is a social center for a select group to which it furnishes religious inspiration and social and clubhouse facilities. Everything about the church is cultured, business-like, and popular in a restrained way. The leadership is competent and congenial with the ways of its constituency.

In brief the church is an upper middle-class family institution with an elaborated program that it is carrying out in a way technically very superior.

Such a church is a characteristic expression of the religious faith of its constituency. It enables the social group which it represents to realize itself in a more Christian manner than it would otherwise do and probably more humbly and thoughtfully, but it is far from being a revolutionary institution.

In time the church will complete a great plant. Its community will be much larger in population. The business center will be more important and will gather around it a rim of less desirable people. The zoning ordinance and the topography of the district will probably hold it to a superior quality of residential occupancy for many years. As the reflection of such an environment the church ought to have a great future. But whether its present version of adaptation to the city will fit it for leadership as inevitable changes come remains to be seen.

A not infrequent aspect of the internally adapted church in such residential surroundings is its service to a wider circle than is identified with it religiously. Thus, a church in one of the best sections of a Californian city is a regular meeting place of the neighborhood Merchants Association, the headquarters of a community athletic club and of a great variety of group organizations only remotely attached to the church. The aggregate monthly attendance at the activities of its center is about 4,000, fully one-half of whom, it is believed, are not connected with the church on its religious side.

TWO PROBLEMS OF ELABORATION

The difference between elaboration in residential areas and elaboration "downtown" requires explanation. The full round of age-, and sex-groups, for whose service the elaboration of program is presumed to occur, are normally present in churches of the former environment but not in downtown constituencies. Thus, the deficiency of the downtown church in younger Sunday-school pupils has already had notice.[23]

The downtown church, in other words, has actually fewer different age-, and sex-groups accessible to its ministries than the average church. Why then is an elaborated program adopted and how does it register adaptation?

Prof. W. L. Bailey points out that there are really two problems of elaboration: first, to meet the needs of the age-, and sex-groups centering in the family; and secondly, to provide for the particular conditions which distinguish the larger cities; namely, a large excess of employed adolescents, a preponderance of male population in nearly all downtown sections, and disproportionate numbers of the unmarried.

While, therefore, the internally adapted churches in the residential section may develop the outlines of an all-sided program and become the church homes of near-by people on a varied and somewhat ample scale, when the centrally located church elaborates its

23 See p. 160.

program it must put on a more complete and extended set of activities to meet the needs of these distinctive urban classes so largely detached from the family setting.

Many of them it finds living in rooming-houses or in furnished apartments for transients adjoining the central business sections of cities, or in its downtown hotels. Others it attracts from long distances.

THE "DOWNTOWN-MINDED"

The internally adapted downtown church is able to give the service it does because of the habitual attachment that young people without family ties acquire for the city center. This center is the focus of their work and of their pleasure and is more "home" to them than any other place in the city. A centrally located church with an elaborated program meets their habits and their needs as the ultra-mobile and wide-ranging elements of the population. They are, however, generally without financial strength enough to sustain a great downtown enterprise. Such an enterprise can rarely succeed, therefore, unless it has a nucleus of old and well-to-do members, established in the community, who give the enterprise its standing and largely pay the bills.

DUAL CONSTITUENCIES

In this subtype (D II) accordingly, one finds the most frequent traces of dual constituencies. The church consists of two sets of people, representing older and newer strata of the constituency respectively. The two do not always agree perfectly; but the church has to have both, one to furnish the numbers, the other to furnish the money. Between the two the most highly elaborated programs are worked out. The downtown internally adapted church is typically a little larger and more expensive an enterprise than the residential one. Its Sunday school is stronger in young people than that of any other type, thus confirming the diagnosis which identifies this church with detached city youth rallying to a downtown center. All the additional activities, movies, Sunday evening socials, forums, etc., are most developed with churches of this variety.

Case XIX—Subtype D II

This is very definitely a church of the downtown-minded showing a dual constituency. Eighty per cent. of its membership comes from within a mile of the church site, but 99 per cent. of the leadership is said to reside in remote parts of the city.

Its story is as follows: For a quarter of a century the leading churches of a Missouri city occupied the brow of the hill east from the central business section. The growth of the city was toward the northeast and prestige and advantage lay this way. Later one of those dramatic and sudden turns of the tide of population left this area completely encircled by movements of foreign and Negro populations, and swept church after church from its old site with the new current of growth and prestige toward the south.

The destruction of its building by fire in 1917 gave opportunity for this leading church of the Disciples of Christ to join the general procession.

The immediate vicinity of the building was occupied by cheaply built wooden apartment hotels characteristic of the city. They present some of the most unsatisfactory traits of multi-family dwellings. Business was steadily encroaching upon the district and the desirable residences of a former decade were now occupied by Negroes and transient population. The main physical improvements, including the new civic center and Union Station, had moved farther south.

Nevertheless, the church decided to stay, deliberately accepting the rôle of a downtown church. It erected a plain but commodious church building designed to house numerous activities and especially to afford an enriched social life for the community. It provides the standard facilities of a modernly organized Sunday school, full-size gymnasium, and unusually well-designed provision for general social life and meetings of small groups. The architecture and appointments carry out the downtown atmosphere.

What has come of the decision to stay may be judged from the following sample program which unquestionably merits the designation "elaborated."

Sunday. Class breakfast; Bible school; two church services; four Christian Endeavor services; baptismal service; choral club rehearsal; two junior choir rehearsals; one junior orchestra rehearsal; one Dynamo orchestra rehearsal; one committee meeting.

Monday. Ministerial Alliance; gymnasium; Christian Endeavor social.

Tuesday. Graded Sunday-school union; religious school of education; music teachers' association musical; gymnasium.

Wednesday. Buxton School of Music; gymnasium; play rehearsal; dinner; finance meeting.

Thursday. Sewing circle; committee meeting; parliamentary law class; gymnasium; play rehearsal; dinner; prayer meeting; choir practice.

Friday. Girl's club; picture show.

Saturday. Blue Birds; Camp Fire Girls; boys' class picnic; Boston School of Music; junior choir; junior orchestra; gymnasium.

There are from three to seven meetings of subsidiary groups per day resulting in a total of 588 for the four months for which the records were examined, or an average of 147 per month. Besides the ordinary religious service, a type of Sunday evening preaching is offered which may fairly be characterized as sensational. Illustrative topics were: "The picture Fatty Arbuckle did not intend to release." "The Ku Klux Klan— blessing or menace?" "William J. Bryan says universities are hot beds of infidelity and irreligion. Is he right?" "A sermon to Satan."

In the summer, evening services are held in a neighboring auto park following a band concert.

Such a program has been accompanied by an intensive culture for five years of a parish area about a mile in diameter.

The church undertakes no slum activities or other program indicating that its constituents are under special social handicap. It exists rather for the transient and unplaced multitudes largely living in temporary quarters and without permanent homes. It is a place of resort for the downtown-minded, a place, for example, where students "drop in." Many students from neighboring schools are brought into church activities

largely in connection with the various choirs, three of which sing an-
tiphonally in the evening service. This phase of the work is in charge of
a special musical director. The other staff consists of a pastor and a
woman assistant.

The atmosphere and central location of the church make it a natural
place for union religious effort seeking a downtown center. It has housed
a school of week-day religious education for all the denominations and is
frequently the place of other interdenominational meetings.

All told, it is a fair example of a downtown church with an elaborated
program serving the more transient elements of the community.

In such cases the older element of the constituency usually sticks
to its downtown church home from a sense of loyalty or because it
finds its prestige renewed by the incoming of downtown-minded
people. Some of the most popular and successful churches of the
American city are of this type, especially in cities that have failed
to develop influential sub-centers to rival the original center.

LARGER URBAN-MINDEDNESS

A further qualification needs to be added; namely, that some of
the older and better established populations themselves experience
their own version of downtown-mindedness. The strongest and
most rewarding ties of many Americans are found where they work
and with their working associates rather than where they are said
to "live." This minority of people have the urban impulse not because they are immature but because they are mature. They think
in terms of the city as a whole and wish to join in religious fellowship with fellow-workers with whom they have common interests.
These often contribute to the success of the downtown internally
adapted church and sometimes dominate it. In rare cases they have
reiterated the civic and social notes in religion till these have become
the major clew to the church's life.

ELABORATION OF PROGRAM BY SMALL CHURCHES

A study of cases shows that genuine elaboration of program is
possible under exceptional conditions without exceptional plant,
budget or multiple staff. Over one-fourth of the churches of the
type are served by a single pastor each. Under such circumstances
success usually depends upon a semi-detached and homogeneous
community of at least ordinarily well-circumstanced people, sometimes a neighborhood of high-grade workingmen. A definite idea
of the kind of service the church proposes to enter, a specially
planned, though modest, building, or even the utilization of the
homes of the community, together with a specially trained pastor
and a set of neighbors who want to do much of their living together,

make this possible. The key to the situation is the minister, but the situation itself must not be too set by tradition. Consequently, small internally adapted churches are commonly new ones that started out with a real urban version of service and put it into execution on a modest scale without having to live down an obstructionist past. It goes without saying that most of the labor of such a church will be the ordinary services of unpaid people skillfully organized. It means the intensive cultivation of the neighborhood spirit and the practice of many aspects of life in common.

Case XX—Subtype C II

This case furnishes an example of such a situation. It is the youngest Methodist church in a New England city and has primary Protestant responsibility for a great sector of its industrial frontier that has been largely neglected by organized Protestantism. It occupies the center of the district shown by a recent survey to have the largest percentage of unchurched Protestants but is strong enough to cultivate intensively only its immediate neighborhood. Its parish is very compact. The church originated as a Sunday school, and its present Sunday school of 151 pupils is still the only one in the city that is larger than the church membership. The Sunday school is thus the most outstanding feature in the church's program. With a church membership of 150, the church is the twenty-ninth in size among the forty-three churches of the city. In attendance at morning service it ranks twenty-fourth, but in total aggregate hours of service, twenty-second. It is thus a large church in service, considering its membership size. Its average monthly program involves sixteen and four-tenths hours of service per member. This contrasts strikingly with the average for the city of from ten to eleven hours.

But while ranking high in activity, the church shows immaturity and instability on the financial side. The pastor's salary of $1,800 is below the modal average, and the contributions from within the church for operating expenses have not held their own in relation to the decreasing value of the dollar.

The church possesses a small plant—worth $50,000—but one of the most artistic and modern ones in the city, including among its total of fourteen rooms a community hall and gymnasium. The excellent landscaping of the grounds is a feature unique among the churches of its city. The church is still, however, very deficient in furnishing and facilities for carrying on an adequate program.

This case shows how a small church may still have an elaborated program. It must appeal to the community beyond sectarian lines; it must create the habit of using the church as a center; it must have competent leadership; and it must have adequate equipment. This church lacks some of the accepted ecclesiastical organizations of its denomination. For example, it has no women's home missionary society. It shows financial weakness and its ladies' aid society has to help largely to meet the current running expenses—just as it might in a country church. It has specially selected leadership, however, and with denominational encouragement is able to undertake numerous unique services. It maintains three orchestras, a choral organization, several "Achievement Clubs" and a radio class. It reports exceptional recreational development and facilities, including a "circus equipment."

Enough examples like the above exist to make it a question whether any more unadapted or average churches should be started by people who believe in elaborated programs. A city church need not pass through all the preliminary rural stages. It may be founded definitely on the city level and after the city pattern. Denominations that count success in these terms would be much stronger if, before establishing new enterprises, they would wait until they could command enough following and resources to begin at least on the minimum elaborated scale. The extension work of the Methodist Episcopal church in the use of some of its "Centenary" funds amply demonstrates this conclusion.

SUMMARY

The broadened and rounded program of the internally adapted church is thus seen to be an adaptation to urban psychology and to the essentials of the urban situation. It intends to reflect and to serve life as city people more and more live it. Within the scope of this general purpose differences in environmental demands serve to give the downtown internally adapted church a more extensive program. It brings its constituents—largely young people—from farther off; while the internally adapted church in the residential districts serves neighborhoods whose families require an elaborate set of age-, and sex-organizations to care for the specialized needs of their members, and who make the church a sort of local clubhouse as well as a religious center.

Chapter IX

THE SOCIALLY ADAPTED CHURCH

This chapter presents the results of the study of 110 churches whose programs go beyond those of the internally adapted churches in both number and range of activities and include items that seem to show on their face adaptation of program and method to the service of peculiar constituencies, frequently those laboring under social handicaps.

Individual study of the churches of this group proved that this generalization was not absolutely true in every case and that frequently socially adapted churches had two constituencies, only one of which was peculiar or in need of specialized ministries. These facts require and receive further comment.[1] The general character of the type, however, is accurately suggested by the designation "socially adapted." Churches of this type constitute 10.5 per cent. of the 1,044 churches studied. In Subtype D III are forty-three churches, or 4.1 per cent. of the total 1,044, and in Subtype E II are sixty-seven churches, or 6.4 per cent. of the total.

PROGRAM

The program of the socially adapted churches covers the entire range of organizations and activities measured by the frequency list which was the basis of the total classification and interpretative of the types. Subtype D III, however, is limited to thirteen to seventeen activities, while Subtype E II has from seventeen to twenty.[2]

The content of the program and typical distribution of activities are shown and illustrated by sample programs for each of the subtypes in Table XXXV, which also compares their programs with those of seven church centers and settlements (selected from cases incidentally included in the survey) so as to show examples both of relatively small and relatively large programs.

The contrast in the above sample programs between the thinly developed social service functions in Subtype D III and the much more complete development in Subtype E II is striking. Minor

1 See p. 189.
2 A small number of churches actually reported more than twenty activities, but they were too few to constitute a group for separate statistical handling and were therefore classified with those having from seventeen to twenty.

TABLE XXV — SAMPLE PROGRAMS OF SOCIALLY ADAPTED CHURCHES AND OF CHURCH CENTERS AND SETTLEMENTS

Organizations and Activities	Socially Adapted Type Subtype D III					Subtype E II					Church Centers and Settlements						
	1	2	3	4	5	1	2	3	4	5	1	2	3	4	5	6	7
1. Preaching and Sunday School	*	*	*	*	*	*	*	*	*	*							*
2. Ladies' Aid or Guild	*		*	*		*	*	*	*	*	*						
3. Women's Missionary Society	*	*	*	*	*	*	*	*	*	*							
4. Young People's Society	*		*	*		*		*	*							*	*
5. Chorus Choir	*		*	*		*	*	*	*		*	*	*				
6. General Social Events	*		*	*	*	*	*	*	*	*							
7. Men's Organization	*	*	*	*	*	*		*		*						*	*
8. Boy Scouts	*	*		*				*	*		*	*		*			*
9. Mission Study Classes	*					*	*	*	*	*							
10. Organized Welcome	*					*	*	*	*		*						
11. Orchestra or Band	*		*						*				*				
12. Boys' Club (not Scouts)		*		*	*	*	*	*	*				*				*
13. Lectures	*		*		*		*	*	*	*							
14. Library	*	*		*	*	*		*	*	*	*	*	*	*			
15. Girls' Club (not Scouts)	*					*	*	*	*	*							
16. Concerts							*	*	*	*			*				
17. Girl Scouts or Equivalent	*	*	*			*	*	*	*	*			*				*
18. Mothers' or Parents' Organization	*		*	*		*	*	*	*		*	*	*	*			*
19. Young Women's Organization	*					*		*	*								*
20. Dramatic Club						*	*	*	*		*	*	*				*
21. Gymnasium Classes			*			*	*	*	*	*		*	*	*			
22. Sewing Classes	*		*	*		*	*	*	*	*		*	*	*			*
23. Kindergarten						*	*	*			*	*	*				
24. Domestic Science Classes	*	*	*	*					*		*	*		*	*		*
25. Employment Office	*	*				*	*	*					*				
26. Music Classes							*		*				*				*
27. Visiting Nurse	*	*	*	*							*						*
28. Health Classes	*										*						*
29. English Classes						*		*			*						*
30. Dramatic Classes		*	*					*			*						
31. Day Nursery	*	*	*			*	*	*					*	*			*
32. Dispensary or Clinic								*	*					*			
33. Civics and Economic Classes	*																
	15	16	15	16	14	20	20	22	24	20	5	6	17	9	11	7	11

differences also appear; for example, the Boy Scout type of organization is the most frequent general form of boys' work with churches in general. With socially adapted churches, however, this is less frequent than other types of boys' clubs, a fact quite probably reflecting a difference in the type of constituency.

The outstanding difference between the socially adapted churches and the centers and settlements is unmistakable. Whether the programs of the latter are larger or smaller, they differ from those of the churches in omitting many of the most frequent and conventional of church functions. On the other hand, however many social service activities the churches may add they are still attached to old ecclesiastical roots.

DISTINCTIVE ELEMENTS OF PROGRAM

Roughly summarized, the new elements of program characteristics of the socially adapted churches are:

(1) Child welfare—kindergarten, day nurseries.
(2) Health—clinics and dispensaries.
(3) Education—English and civics classes; "Americanization"; domestic science and art.
(4) Culture—music, dramatics and fine arts.
(5) Vocational—vocational advice; employment agencies.

This list includes a range of activities exceeding that of any other type of church in its variety of organization and lines of work by 50 per cent. Only 10.5 per cent. of the city churches included in the 1,044 cases attempt anything in this new realm, and the frequency of some of the activities is only 3 or 4 per cent. in the entire sample.

Certain additional activities are characteristic of the socially adapted churches and of no other type; for example, separate children's congregations; the use of visual means of instruction, especially motion-pictures; daily vacation Bible schools; Sunday afternoon socials or teas.

A church with such a program is naturally open seven days in the week. Various items of recreation are nearly always organized into many-sided programs. Often the socially adapted church attempts to direct popular thought through the maintenance of a church forum. A considerable number of them provide dormitories or make other efforts to secure proper housing for their constituencies.[3]

Other Aspects of the Socially Adapted Church

To carry on this greatly enlarged program naturally requires enlarged staffs of paid workers, larger buildings and more numerous

3 Appendix Table 36.

facilities than the other church types have. The average membership of the socially adapted church is larger, as is the value of the
church property. The average current expenses are not so great
as those of the internally adapted church. The evidence of these
points appears in the following paragraphs.

NUMBER OF MEMBERS

Nearly one-half of the socially adapted churches have more than
one thousand members. Distribution according to membership size
is shown in Table XXXVI:[4]

TABLE XXXVI — MEMBERSHIP OF SOCIALLY ADAPTED CHURCHES *

Number of Members	Per Cent. Distribution
Under 500	26.2
Under 100	2.9
100 to 200	2.9
200 to 300	7.8
300 to 400	3.9
400 to 500	8.7
500 to 1,000	28.2
1,000 and over	45.6

* 103 churches reporting.

AGE AND PERMANENCE

Fourteen out of the eighty-three churches of the type reporting
as to age are more than one hundred years old, and only twelve, or
about one-seventh, are less than twenty-five years old.

While the median age of all churches of the type is fifty-five
years, the median length of time that the church has been located
on its present site is only thirty-six years. Nevertheless, more
churches of this type than of any other—31.8 per cent. in all—have
never moved but are still located where they were first founded. It
is preëminently the type which stays and adapts its program to
changed conditions.

PAID RELIGIOUS WORKERS

The most frequent number of paid workers is two; yet only 34
per cent. of the socially adapted churches have one or two workers,
while 37.7 per cent. have three or four, and 28.3 per cent. have five
or more. Detailed figures are shown in Table XXXVII.

Subtype D III, however, rarely goes beyond six workers, leaving
nearly all the very large staffs to Subtype E II.[5]

4 Appendix Table 5.
5 Appendix Table 9.

TABLE XXXVII — PAID RELIGIOUS WORKERS IN
SOCIALLY ADAPTED CHURCHES *

Number Employed	Per Cent. Distribution of Churches
1	11.3
2	22.6
3	17.9
4	19.8
5	12.3
6	7.6
7	1.9
8	3.8
9	0.9
10 and over	1.9

* 106 churches reporting.

The following comparison shows the designations used for men and women assistants, together with the number falling under each designation:

Men		Women	
Total male assistants	97	Total female assistants	165
Assistant pastor	48	Secretary	59
Director men's and boys' work	16	Director social service	25
Director recreation or athletics	14	Deaconess	23
Director religious education	9	Visitor	16
Secretary	6	Director women's and girls' work	13
Director social service	4	Matron or housekeeper	13
		Pastor's assistant	9
		Director religious education	7

Both with men and women assistants, the conventional and non-specialized positions designated respectively "assistant pastor" and "secretary" are the most frequent. The other designations used suggest the range of functions performed, though, as already explained, only exact job analysis could tell exactly what functions are performed under each of them.

THE PASTOR

The education of the city pastor is so highly standardized that there is little difference between the types in the number of conventionally prepared men. One-third of the pastors of socially adapted churches, however, have had more than conventional preparation (including some form of post-graduate work), this being conspicuously the case with pastors of churches with the most varied programs.[6]

6 Appendix Table 13.

TABLE XLI — AVERAGE CAPACITY OF CHURCH AUDITORIUM
   AND VALUE OF CHURCH PLANT OF SOCIALLY ADAPTED
   CHURCHES

	Socially Adapted Churches	Subtype D III	Subtype E II
Seating Capacity of Auditorium ..	880	821	959
Value of Property	$242,194	$208,111	$266,811

In socially adapted churches a total of from fifteen to nineteen
equipment facilities (within a total list of twenty-five such facilities) is most frequently found. One-third of the churches of the
type, however, have only from ten to fourteen facilities, though not
many have fewer than ten. There are more churches with many
rooms and many facilities in Subtype E II than in Subtype D III.[12]

TABLE XLII — NUMBER OF ROOMS IN SOCIALLY
ADAPTED CHURCHES *

No. of Rooms	Per Cent. Distribution of Churches
Less than 5	2.9
5–9	19.1
10–19	47.1
20–29	13.2
30 and over	17.7

   * 68 churches reporting.

SUNDAY SCHOOL

More than one-half of the Sunday schools of socially adapted
churches have fewer than 500 members, but over one-third have
from 500 to 1,000 members, and about one-twelfth have more than
1,000 members. When it is recalled that almost 46 per cent. of the
churches of the type have more than 1,000 members, a great discrepancy between the size of the church and of the Sunday school
becomes apparent. This is more marked with churches of Subtype
E II than with those of Subtype D III. In the ratio of attendance
to enrollment, the churches of the type closely approximate the
average. No other type has so large a proportion of adolescents in
Sunday-school enrollment.[13]

Environments and Parishes

Of the seventy-three socially adapted churches studied in their
environments, just about one-half are centrally located. Although

12 Appendix Table 27.
13 Appendix Tables 31-34.

the type constitutes but one-tenth of the total sample of 1,044 churches, of all centrally located churches whose environments were studied, one-fourth were found to be socially adapted.

Of the thirty-eight centrally located churches of this type that were studied, twenty-five stood at the center of the downtown section of their respective cities. In view of the average distance that church members are willing to come to attend church and the character of the neighborhoods, more than one-half of these were judged not to be strategically located with reference to their constituencies. Of eighteen whose neighborhoods were intensively studied, five were in high-class neighborhoods, two in middle-class and eleven in low-class, the last being chiefly in industrial neighborhoods, but with some examples in slum territory. In the majority of cases, though not always, the programs of these centrally located churches definitely reflect the immediate environment in some degree.

Of thirty-four churches of the type located in residential neighborhoods, ten were found in high-class neighborhoods, nineteen in middle-class and five in industrial neighborhoods. In brief, residential examples of the type were found in all sorts of environments and reflecting all social levels.[14] This fact concerning a type which has frequently been assumed to require a sub-normal constituency to justify its work needs further explanation.[15]

DISTANCE AND DIRECTION

With half of its churches centrally located, the socially adapted type naturally has a relatively large number of scattered and very scattered parishes in which more than 50 per cent. of the members

TABLE XLIII — TYPES OF PARISHES OF SOCIALLY ADAPTED CHURCHES

| Per Cent. of Members Living Within One Mile | Parish Designation | Distribution of Churches All | | |
		Socially Adapted	Centrally Located	Residentially Located
75 and over	Compact	14	5	9
50–74	Medium	16	12	4
25–49	Scattered	6	3	3
Less than 25	Very Scattered	3	3	0

come a mile or more to church. This appears in Table XLIII, based upon thirty-nine cases studied from this point of view.[16] Only the unadapted type has so few compact parishes.

14 Appendix Tables 37-39a.
15 See pp. 265 f.
16 Appendix Tables 41 and 42.

For twenty churches studied with respect to the direction of their members' homes from the church building, the following distribution was discovered.[17]

Destination	No. of Churches
Normally balanced parish	5
Unbalanced	2
Very unbalanced	13

So far as the evidence goes, the churches of this type manifest a strong trend toward constituencies massed in narrow sectors

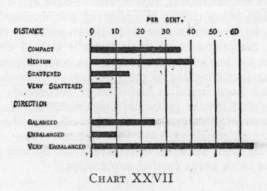

CHART XXVII

Per Cent. Distribution of Types of Parishes of Socially Adapted Churches, by Distance and Direction.

rather than distributed widely around the church building. This would be but natural in so far as their services are specialized in meeting the needs of peculiar populations.

Larger Environments and Relations

REGION

No other type of city church shows such sharp regional variations. Constituting 10.5 per cent. of the sample of 1,044 churches, the socially adapted churches number 8.7 per cent. in the northeastern states, 7.3 per cent. in the southern, but 20.1 per cent. in the north central and only 1.6 per cent. in the western states. More than anywhere else, apparently, certain cities of the north central states have evolved the phase of adaptation of service-functions which this type of church expresses.[18]

17 Appendix Table 43.
18 Appendix Table 47.

SIZE OF CITY

The above statement must immediately be related to the data concerning relation of the types to cities of different sizes as shown in Table XLIV.[19]

TABLE XLIV — RATIO OF SOCIALLY ADAPTED CHURCHES TO TOTAL CHURCHES, IN CITIES OF VARYING SIZE

Population of City	Ratio
100,000 to 250,000	7.2
250,000 to 500,000	9.6
500,000 to 750,000	7.9
750,000 to 1,000,000	12.9
1,000,000 and over	23.0
All cities	10.5

The affinity of the socially adapted type for the largest cities is strongly suggestive. Inasmuch as Chicago is the only city of the north central states with more than one million population, it is manifest that the superiority of these states in number of socially adapted churches may largely rest with this single city. Some bias in the selection of Chicago churches for study in favor of the more interesting types of social adaptation is probable. The fact, however, that cities of 750,000 to 1,000,000 population also show more than an average number of socially adapted churches makes the generalization highly reliable that the larger the city the more churches it will have of the highest degree of development and adaptation.

RACE

Of the fifty-seven "foreign churches" studied, only two belong to the socially adapted type. This showing may occasion some surprise in view of the natural supposition that social adaptation follows social needs. Why not, then, the exceptional needs of the foreign-speaking Protestants of the American cities? An answer to this question will be found in a following section, in which it will be shown that foreign-speaking churches that are not slightly adapted or unadapted chiefly fall within the widely variant type, which may represent exact and original, but nevertheless partial and unbalanced, efforts at social adaptation. The fully developed church program exhibited in the socially adapted type has not often been developed exclusively in the service of the foreign-born.

19 Appendix Table 46.

DENOMINATION

Table XLV shows the per cent. of the churches of the several denominations that are socially adapted compared with their proportion in the total number of churches studied.[20]

TABLE XLV — DISTRIBUTION OF SOCIALLY ADAPTED CHURCHES, BY DENOMINATIONS

Denomination	Per Cent. Total Churches Studied	Distribution Socially Adapted Churches
Baptist	15.8	20.0
Congregational	10.5	9.1
Disciples	4.4	1.8
Methodist Episcopal	19.3	21.8
Methodist Episcopal South	3.7	4.5
Presbyterian U. S. A.	17.3	20.0
Protestant Episcopal	10.5	16.4
Lutheran (all bodies)	4.4	0.9
All others	14.1	5.5

In proportion of socially adapted churches three denominations, namely, Congregational, Methodist Episcopal, and Presbyterian, U. S. A., somewhat closely approximate their proportion in the total number of churches. The Disciples and "all other" denominations have considerably fewer, and the Lutheran very many fewer socially adapted churches; while the Methodist Episcopal, South, Baptist and Protestant Episcopal denominations have proportionately very many more. Variations between the denominations in this field are of genuine interest and may constitute a challenge to denominational policy.

Divergent Tendencies Within the Socially Adapted Type

Between the subtypes D III and E II no great difference appears with respect to permanence, range of staff functions, pastor's experience, proportion of salaries in the higher salary range, per capita cost of current expenses, Sunday-school enrollment in the higher range, age-distribution of Sunday-school pupils or environmental location.

The points at which divergence appears and its direction and approximate degree are shown by the tabulation on page 183.

The contrast between the subtypes is definitely that between smaller general development going with a narrower program and larger general development going with a broader one. Environmental tendencies, however, are somewhat contradictory.

20 Appendix Table 45.

Divergent Aspect	Subtype D III	Subtype E II
Size	More under 500 members	More over 1,000 members
Age	More younger churches	More older churches
Staff-number	Fewer staffs with 6 workers and over	More staffs with 6 workers and over
Pastor's education	Fewer with post-graduate education	More with post-graduate education
Pastor's tenure in present position	Trend to briefer tenure	Trend to longer tenure
Pastor's salary	More under $3,000	Fewer under $3,000
Per capita benevolences	Larger	Smaller
Number of facilities	Average fewer	Average greater
Rooms in church	Average fewer	Average more
Seating capacity auditorium	Average smaller	Average much greater
Value church plant	Average smaller	Average much greater
Sunday-school enrollment	More schools under 300 pupils	More schools over 300 pupils
Advantageous location of central churches	More strategic	More non-strategic
Quality of neighborhood of residential church	More industrial and foreign	More middle-class

NON-STATISTICAL DISTINCTIONS

The most significant differences within the socially adapted type are not revealed statistically, but are thoroughly substantiated by observation, and could have been statistically demonstrated had a sufficient number of cases of each variant been secured. Thus it is obvious that social adaptation to the needs of a community of native American wage-earners will not work out in identical ways with adaptation to the needs of foreign groups. Again, solid communities of a single nationality or race present different practical problems from those found in polyglot neighborhoods. Nor is social adaptation necessarily limited to communities on low economic levels. It is practiced with variations by a few churches of people in upper middle-class circumstances. Finally, the historic background of any attempt at adaptation makes a difference. If it is made by an old and traditional church the results may contrast strikingly with those obtained by a young and plastic church.

There are too many variations to permit each to be illustrated separately; but the following cases cover the three most fundamental distinctions: namely, (1) those between churches in which social adaptation is the result of local initiative; (2) those in which it is imported by forces external to the organization and neighborhood; and finally (3) those in which a dual constituency is included within the church itself—the one rendering and the other benefiting by the particular services implied in the adapted program. With churches of the first kind the members themselves constitute a self-conscious social group who have directed their church in response to a sense of their own needs. With churches of the second kind somebody else from a philanthropic or denominational organization is attempting to provide for the needs of a poor and dependent constituency.

Case XXI—Subtype E II

This church took time by the forelock and worked out its own salvation. Impending change was sensed before it came on destructively, and when it came the church was adequately prepared to meet it.

Back in 1894 when the present church edifice was erected, the church had a large and thriving constituency in a growing part of the city. Most of its people would have described themselves as belonging to the middle class. But even then broad-minded leadership foresaw the need of a popular and varied ministry and began to prepare for it by the introduction of so-called institutional features. As the older constituency scattered throughout the city, the church had unusual success in assimilating newcomers, many of whom were of foreign extraction. More diverse foreign elements have since occupied the margins of the neighborhood, Polish, Russian, Ukranian and Syrian people coming in increasing numbers.

In the face of these changes, the church which realized its problem from the beginning has quite naturally grown into a socially adapted ministry.

Its regular religious services gather about 300 for morning worship and 700 in the evening. The church has everything that an active and normally developed family church could have and takes an active, though not a conspicuous, share in the affairs of its denomination.

In addition to these typical activities, it maintains the "Institute" housed in a special adjunct building attached to the church, but of more recent construction. This building consists primarily of a modern gymnasium and facilities for club work.

The program of the Institute includes an entertainment course, kindergarten, mothers' club, visiting nurse service and welfare work among boys and girls. It also serves as a community center, providing organized recreation for all ages and sexes.

In addition to some $22,000 for the church budget (including the support of a pastor receiving $4,500, and an assistant pastor receiving $3,000, a secretary and a visitor receiving $1,200 and $800 respectively), there is an Institute budget of more than $6,000 divided as follows:

Kindergartner, Welfare Worker	$2,000
Visiting Nurse	600
Recreational Director	600
Entertainment Series	400
Vacation School	450
Printing	200
Supplies	200
Uniforms	175
Caretaker	780
Light and Heat	700
	$6,105

The Sunday-school budget is also counted separately. It amounts to $1,200, of which $800 comes from the school itself. The gross budget is thus about $30,000, besides some $4,500 for benevolences.

The nursing service is associated with the city Visiting Nurse Association, which partially supports it.

In its week-day program the church serves an average of 150 persons per day. The professional staff numbers six, besides those in charge of the plant and the music.

This adapted program is the product of the church's own initiative and is under its exclusive support and control. Endowment furnishes a total annual income of $9,000 for the regular church budget, in addition to which fees bring in about $2,000 for the Institute budget. These have greatly aided the church in meeting changed conditions. It stoutly resists the implication that there is anything unusual in its course. It dislikes the term "Americanization" in connection with its successful efforts to assimilate successive waves of population. It is unwilling to concede that its program grows out of any special handicap in its constituencies. They are self-respecting people ably meeting their own problems.

The mobilizing of resident strength exhibited by Case XXI is often more important than institutions specially devised. This case and the following are excellent examples of social adaptation originating with and carried out by the resident forces themselves.

Case XXII—Subtype E II

This is another church whose "own arm wrought salvation," though it has been increasingly backed by community appreciation and assistance.

The Negro population of a northern city has remained at about 2 per cent. of the total for the last fifty years. Mission work for it was carried on from an early time, and in the oldest Negro church John Brown worshiped during his residence in the city. The present church resulted from the union of two older ones in 1890, at which time its location was fixed in the secondary Negro center on "the Hill." The original membership consisted of twenty-three members.

The development of St. John's Church since that time is covered by the pastoral leadership of a remarkable man, and to a very large measure is an expression of his personal ability and consecration. For twenty-three years he has grown into really distinguished civic and religious leadership in the city, while his persistence, calmness, balanced judgment and organizing ability have made St. John's Church what it is. Its gains have not only been among the largest but among the most consistent of any in the city. It now has 468 members, which is about the median membership of its denomination, and which puts it in the upper third of the churches of the city in respect to size. By reason of its broad program of activities its total influence is proportionately much more far-reaching than mere membership.

It is a young people's church, the average age of its members being much lower than that of the characteristic Protestant constituencies and its Sunday school particularly strong in the adolescent group. It is also one of the most highly organized churches of the city. The membership is divided into eighteen "Circles for Service" each with an objective definitely fixed annually. Partly as a result of this method the church gets an average of 15.8 hours of service per member each month, which is more than 50 per cent. above the city average.

Besides the stated activities of a church, St. John's has developed through the years a notable addition to the social institutions of the city called St. John's Institutional Activities. The staff, plant and budget are shared by the two branches of the enterprise in ways impossible to distinguish clearly. The church reports an assistant pastor in charge of religious education and a church visitor. Its annual budget of expenditures is about $6,000 and the church plant is worth about $40,000. The interior has distinct ecclesiastical dignity and there is an excellent pipe organ.

The total enterprise has a staff of eight full-time paid workers, together with five additional ones giving part-time, and represents an annual expenditure of about $20,000. In addition to the church building, the plant includes a specially designed working girls' home of twenty-eight rooms and eight dwelling-houses for rent. Of the latter two are one-tenement houses, five have three tenements and one has eight tenements. These house a total of twenty-eight families as well as various phases of the church's social work.

The institutional activities are organized in seven departments:

(1) Two rooms in the church are open daily as a headquarters for women and there are classes in cooking, arts and domestic science. Classes in gymnasium work are held three nights a week in the basement of a near-by public school. A social hour for both sexes is held in these rooms each Sunday.

(2) A home for working girls includes living quarters at nominal cost for both transient and resident guests and is designed to furnish a suitable and comfortable home for colored girls attempting self-support among the unaccustomed surroundings of a northern city. The home was erected at a cost of $15,000.

(3) A boys' and young men's club occupies a nine-room dwelling-house and is a meeting place for recreation for the young men of the vicinity. They are afforded excellent athletic opportunities in the use of the near-by college gymnasium which is made freely available to Negro young men.

(4) The housing facilities already enumerated constitute a notable aspect of the St. John's Institutional Activities. As a movement it grew out of the difficulty that colored people found in securing suitable living quarters during the war-shortage of houses.

(5) A fifty-four-acre outing farm in a near-by rural town is successfully administered by the church both as a summer recreation center and as a means of summer employment. During the mornings a farm manager uses boys sent by the church for work, while afternoons are spent in recreation and sociability.

(6) The department of music organizes the unusual musical gift of Negro people and has been a considerable source of financial support as well as of publicity for the enterprise. It conducts a vested choir, glee club, band and a Saturday morning music school for children.

(7) A free employment bureau places an average of twelve persons per month in response to an average of thirty calls. Girls living in the home and others are trained by the church for domestic and other opportunities of service.

The primary relationships of St. John's Church and Institutional Activities are with the Negro community on "the Hill." Its parish is very compact, though its superior facilities, standards and program naturally give it city-wide appeal to the better element of the Negro community. More than three-fourths of its constituency come from areas of medium social quality. It has a large development of charitable relief for the very poor, but its particular success is in organizing the initiative and moral tone of the Negro community for the support of normal and worthy social life.

The Institutional Activities are separately incorporated and are controlled by an able board of directors which includes representative citizens both white and colored. Their general value and the non-sectarian character of the work has secured them recognition and aid from the Community Chest.

The difference between socially adapted churches that have initiated their own programs and those whose adaptation has been projected from outside is of fundamental practical importance. Though outside of the categories statistically developed by the study, this difference in practice involves an exact discrimination between the socially adapted churches of industrial populations of American or Americanized stock and those of more recently arrived foreign and polyglot neighborhoods. These latter remain to be illustrated.

Case XXIII—Subtype E II

The "Institutional Church" of the Methodist Episcopal Church, South in a Missouri city is essentially a church made to order—a creation rather than a spontaneous growth. The usual story of social adaptation tells of changing conditions that have challenged an existing local church to adapt itself to the new order. The present case, on the other hand, exemplifies the deliberate attempt of a denomination to devise a specialized urban type of ministry in a rapidly growing city.

The church is located on an edge of the bluffs overlooking the original site of the city in the Missouri River bottoms. It is on a margin of the present business section at the exact point where the foreign and Negro population from the lowlands first broke over the bluffs and invaded the better residential section, scattering its people and driving out its churches. At this strategic point of redistribution of population and of social need the church has stood for fourteen years.

The church explicitly proclaims its theory of service in its publication of announcements. It exists "to overcome bad heredity and to create a better environment." It seeks to strengthen the demoralized home. It lays chief stress on service to child life.

Its constituency is principally composed of Americans of the transient and boarding-house type, but also, in increasing numbers, of Italians, Hebrews and Syrians. Negroes also are included to some extent in the social ministries. In other words, the church has a typically polyglot constituency.

Its relationships are unusually complicated. First of all, it is a dual organization consisting (1) of a weak church drawing membership from a total of twenty-one families and standing in the usual ecclesiastical relationships and (2) of an institutional or settlement department separately supported and administered by the women's board of city missions of the denomination. This board is a large body with numerous representatives from each Southern Methodist church of the city, and from these churches large numbers of volunteer workers are obtained.

The health activities are primarily financed by the Community Chest, which aids the institution to an amount of about $8,000 annually. The clinic and nursing service thus have primary relations to social agencies outside of denominational control.

Besides a pastor, the staff of workers primarily concerned with the institutional work consists of a head resident, a secretary, two deaconesses working for American and Italian families respectively, a matron and eight or nine part-time paid workers for handcraft, music and recreation, besides a nurse in charge of infant welfare work.

The annual budget aggregates from $18,000 to $20,000, about $13,500 of which is directly spent in institutional ministries.

Besides a wide variety of children's welfare activities, the chief work is for women, the greatest response coming from foreign mothers and employed girls. There are successful clubs for younger boys, but the work is a relative failure with older boys and men.

Specific activities are reported as follows:

Daily Vacation Bible School
Saturday Afternoon Bible School
Day Nursery
Kindergarten (Saturday afternoon)
Reading-room
Story Hour
Kitchen garden
Camp Fire
Blue Birds
Boy Scouts
Knights of the Silver Shield
Choral Club
Philathea Club
Dramatic Class
Piano Lessons
Italian Mothers' Club

Junior Italian Boys' Club
Young Matrons' Knitting Club
Gymnasium for Italian Boys, Four Teams
Gymnasium for American Boys
Gymnasium for Jewish Boys, One Team
Gymnasium for Young Women, Two Teams
Gymnasium for Girls, Two Teams
Gymnasium for Italian Women, One Team
Home Economics Class, Italian Women
Supper Club for Young Women
Industrial Classes
Community Social Evenings
Senior Italian Girls' Club
Junior Italian Girls' Club

As will be noted, Americans and Italians are ordinarily organized into separate groups.

Besides the institutional ministries, the deaconesses' work involves a large amount of family relief. The entire body of Southern Methodist churches of the Southwestern Missouri Conference are annually solicited for food supplies and old clothes which are distributed to the needy, Thanksgiving and Christmas dinners being a special feature.

Week-day religious education is carried on throughout the year in a Saturday evening Bible school having an average attendance of more than 150 Italian children. The church has received interested coöperation from the Camp Fire Girls and Boy Scouts in adapting their programs to its special constituencies.

The relative service of the church to the various racial elements of its community is interestingly shown in the following table:

Activity	Total	Italian	American	Hebrew	Syrian	German	Irish	Greek	Negro
Day Nursery	85	21	40	3	18	3	0	0	0
Baby Clinic	667	420	135	67	17	1	3	1	23
Clubs and Group Organizations—									
Junior	490	416	51	13	10	0	0	0	0
Intermediate	46	1	41	4	0	0	0	0	0
Senior	131	25	83	23	0	0	0	0	0
Adult	166	164	2	0	0	0	0	0	0
Sunday School	263	52	201	1	6	3	0	0	0
Daily Vacation Bible School	448	406	28	9	5	0	0	0	0

As is the universal experience of similar churches, the health and recreational opportunities are used by populations whose religious antecedents make them inaccessible to Sunday school and church services. The strong preponderance of Italians in the daily vacation Bible school is interesting, and a very definite religious element runs throughout the activities of the institution.

A very useful adjunct institution is a children's home in another part of the city.

The Institutional Church is an example of a definitely paternalistic type of social adaptation. Its motive and resources are almost wholly external to the community, although the forms of a small self-governing church afford opportunity for the more forceful and independent of its constituents to express themselves through organization. In the main, the superior advantages offered by the church are imported from the more successful populations of the city, and the forms of activity thought desirable are imposed upon the plastic life of childhood.

This is all in most glaring contrast to the type of social adaptation illustrated by Case XXI that resulted wholly from the self-transformation of a local self-supporting church. Between these two extremes stands the Methodist Episcopal church, Case XXX, described in a later chapter.[21] This church has been greatly assisted in its social adaptation by its denomination and by community funds, but is still essentially self-determining, having experienced a new birth in the discovery and mobilization of the sound elements remaining in a deteriorating community. These three churches illustrate radically diverse ways in which exceptional churches deliberately enlarge their sphere of service and transform previous traditional ministries in response to the needs of the changing city.

SOCIAL ADAPTATION THROUGH DUAL CONSTITUENCIES

A final variation in the socially adapted type is presented by the case of the historic church which by reason of unusual prestige or the loyalty to principles of an "old guard" has been able to maintain itself in a downtown location although surrounded by a new and undesirable class of population. Such churches are sometimes able to hold dual constituencies by means of a socially adapted program added to the original one. When the two constituencies are socially distinct, attending services at different hours and belonging in the main to separate organizations, the actual result is not very different from what occurs in the case of a church having a branch church or a settlement carried on in another locality. The work indeed is under one roof, is carried on through the same staff and is administratively one, yet the right hand of such a church frequently does not know what the left hand is doing. While statistically classified as socially adapted, such churches often carry on only a narrow round of work as a basic program for their older membership. If their second constituency were served through a branch organization a mile away they would unhesitatingly be classified as merely slightly adapted churches. The social separation of the two constituencies is sometimes painfully extreme and complete. On the other hand, it is scarcely possible that the atmosphere of such a church will not be affected by its enlarged social program, and frequently with the years the two constituencies tend to fuse and to develop a new and broader basis of fellowship showing real social adaptation. This issue is present in the following case.

Case XXIV—Subtype E II

Located at the very center of a manufacturing city in the East, this great historic church is in the full height of its prestige and success—a splendid example of ecclesiastical power and opulence.

Its nearly 3,000 members are scattered in a widening arc across the

21 See p. 266.

city toward the east and into the suburbs beyond. They are also numerous in the desirable suburbs in the northwest and south. Few live in the vicinity of the church.

One reason for the church's continued success under these circumstances—unusual as it is in so large a city—is that it could find no better place. This city has pushed out its more residential sections far from the center, but in all directions. The business center is thus about equally distant from all. Under these circumstances, in spite of numerous migrations, an unusual number of downtown churches remain.

An equally pertinent consideration is that the church is tied to the spot by the terms of the original gift of land, and gets a large income from its land rentals.

Parallel with the ample, though conventional, services and organizations of a typical family church, there goes on a varied and aggressive social ministry, which includes in its reach both the poorer populations of the central city and its business transients. This work is conducted under the same roof as the ordinary service, but with little social contact between the constituencies.

The major part of the week-day social work consists of club activities, sample programs of which follow:

MEN AND BOYS

Tuesday —4: 30 to 6: 15 Older Boys' Club Rooms open
  6: 15 to 6: 45 Supper served, 25 cents
  6: 45 to 7: 30 Club Meetings and Devotions
  7: 30 to 10: 00 Basketball Games, Bowling, Gymnasium Work

Wednesday—4: 30 to 6: 15 Younger Boys' Club Rooms open
  6: 15 to 6: 45 Supper served, 15 cents
  6: 45 to 7: 15 Devotional Period
  7: 15 to 7: 45 Club Meetings
  7: 45 to 10: 00 Basketball, Bowling and Gymnasium Work

WOMEN AND GIRLS

Thursday —11: 30 to 1: 30 Business Women's Meeting and Lunch
  5: 45 Cafeteria Supper
  6: 30 Singing
  7: 00 Devotional Meeting
  7: 15 Classes in Bible Study, Gymnasium, Cooking, China Painting, Ukelele, Current Events, Dramatics, Basketry, Christmas Gifts and Novelties, Girl Scouts, Dressmaking, Fancy Work, Millinery

Friday —5: 45 to 9: 00 Clubs for Girls. Cafeteria and schedule same as Thursday evening

Boys' groups divide along age lines, while the girls represent the segregation of the more highly paid women workers from the more poorly paid and more local constituencies.

A most useful additional activity is the business women's noon service and cafeteria.

Saturday morning a sewing class of over one hundred members meets. On Sunday evening there is a men's meeting ranging in attendance from seventy-five to 300 and closing with a dinner. Very extensive fresh-air and outing ministries are conducted during the summer, both for boys and girls, the camp costing $10,000 for the season.

There are very active ministries of old-fashioned family visitation and charity which have brought considerable numbers of foreign-speaking children into the Sunday school.

The paid staff more particularly related to the ordinary church work consists of a pastor, associate and assistant pastors, a secretary and a clerk, and also a Sunday-school secretary. Those more exclusively concerned with the social work are a girls' club secretary, a church missionary and a church nurse, each receiving a salary of $2,000, and also a directress of the cafeteria. There are also part-time physical directors.

The current operations of the church cost about $50,000 annually, in addition to which it contributes some $60,000 to benevolences. Its total activities reach 10,000 people per week during the busiest months of the year.

The social work of the church is insistently related to its religious work. All clubs and social meetings begin or end with devotions and those who will not attend the devotions cannot belong to the clubs. In other words, religious conformity is made the price of participation in the social benefits of the church. Its groups are not self-governing clubs. This is of course in striking contrast with the current ideals of club work as conducted by social settlements and with the policies of some churches of the same type. The club is regarded by these organizations as a spontaneous and largely self-directed expression of group life, a school of coöperation and of democracy. The policy of Case xxiv, however, is to make its clubs the occasion for the religious indoctrination of passive groups. They are encouraged to participate in a large amount of recreational activity, which, nevertheless, is always regarded as a means to the end of formal religious influence.

This is an extreme case of social adaptation involving dual constituencies. On the one hand, there is the rich and embellished but essentially unchanged life of the traditional church with somewhat reactionary tendencies; and on the other, a well-sustained group of separate activities for a poorer type of people. Numerous individuals doubtless overlap the line of demarcation, but the total situation is as described. The church's right hand does not know what its left hand does, except in terms of financial accounting.

Chapter X

WIDELY VARIANT TYPES AND THE AVERAGE

The classification of 1,044 city churches by types discovered that 88 per cent. of the total register a consistent tendency of development, while 12 per cent. depart from the main path of evolution of city churches. This 12 per cent. remainder does not constitute a homogeneous group. Eighty-eight churches, comprising 8.4 per cent. of the total, shoot off from the main path in the direction of extreme novelty of program, while thirty-seven churches, or 3.6 per cent. of the total, vary in the contrary direction of extreme conservatism.

The Adventurous Variants

The former group comprises the following subtypes:

Subtypes	Number of Churches
A IV	32
A V	15
B IV	11
C III	30

These spread out all along the path of adventure with programs varying in range from medium to broadest, but with their variety always achieved at the expense of balance and usually by dropping out a considerable proportion of the more frequent elements of a city church program.

This is shown in five sample programs for widely variant subtypes in Table XLVI.

The number of cases included in most of the subtypes showing wide variations is relatively small and generally insufficient to yield very reliable statistical conclusions. Subtype A IV appears simply as a church with not more than four functions that for some reason selects one of them from a relatively infrequent range of church activity, such as the Mothers' Club or Dramatic Organization. On the whole its tendency is to consistency rather than to an erratic behavior.

Compared with Subtype A III, which also exercises four func-

TABLE XLVI—SAMPLE PROGRAMS OF WIDELY VARIANT CHURCHES

Organizations and Activities	Subtypes																			
	AIV					AV					BIV					CIII				
	1	2	3	4	5	1	2	3	4	5	1	2	3	4	5	1	2	3	4	5
1. Preaching and Sunday School	*	*	*	*	*	*	*	*	*	*	*	*	*	*	*	*	*	*	*	*
2. Ladies' Aid or Guild	*	*	*	*	*	*	*	*	*	*	*	*	*	*	*	*	*	*	*	*
3. Women's Missionary Society	*		*	*	*	*	*	*	*	*	*	*	*	*	*	*	*	*	*	*
4. Young People's Society		*	*		*	*	*		*	*		*	*		*	*	*	*	*	*
5. Chorus Choir											*	*		*		*	*	*	*	*
6. General Social Events				*												*	*	*		*
7. Men's Organization																*	*		*	*
8. Boy Scouts		*		*	*											*	*	*	*	*
9. Mission Study Classes																*		*		
10. Organized Welcome																	*			*
11. Orchestra or Band								*								*		*	*	
12. Boys' Club (not Scouts)																	*			
13. Lectures																*	*	*	*	*
14. Library	*	*	*				*			*		*	*		*	*	*	*	*	*
15. Girls' Club (not Scouts)																			*	
16. Concerts																*	*	*		*
17. Girl Scouts or Equivalent	*	*	*			*					*	*								*
18. Mothers' or Parents' Organization						*	*													
19. Young Women's Organization																*	*			
20. Dramatic Club									*		*			*				*		
21. Gymnasium Classes																*		*		
22. Sewing Classes																	*		*	
23. Kindergarten																*	*			
24. Domestic Science Classes																	*		*	
25. Employment Office																*	*			
26. Music Classes																			*	
27. Visiting Nurse																*		*		*
28. Health Classes																			*	
29. English Classes																*				*
30. Dramatic Classes																			*	
31. Day Nursery																		*		*
32. Dispensary or Clinic									*						*					
33. Civics and Economics Classes																				
	4	4	4	4	4	4	4	3	4	4	7	5	8	5	7	10	12	10	9	12

tions, but which classifies merely as a normal variant within the unadapted group, A IV's specific difference consists in this choice of a less frequent fourth activity.[1]

With two of the erratic subtypes, however, the case is different. The small number of churches involved enables one to see at a glance the source of common characteristics in which they vary widely from the modal tendency.

SUBTYPE B IV

This subtype consists of only eleven churches, eight of which are those of foreign-speaking people, four being churches of southern and eastern Europeans.

In age they are the youngest of all the types, more than half being less than twenty-five years old. The median age is only fourteen years. This suggests that they are churches of newer immigrants. Foreign-speaking churches of the northern European races also have a disproportionate tendency toward the erratic types, but to no such degree as have those of the southern and eastern Europeans. Perhaps this is because their constituencies have been longer in America and had a tradition nearer to that of the American churches to start with.

This subtype, dominated as it is by little foreign churches, has the smallest churches of any of the groups, only one of them having more than 300 members.

In spite of its unimpressive size, the little foreign church has generally more than one paid worker. The distribution of staffs for ten cases reported is as follows:

Size of Staff	Number of Cases
1	2
2	3
3	2
4	1
5	1
7	1

This striking combination of a multiple staff with small memberships is the distinctive mark of the subtype.

The pastors of these foreign churches have an average degree of education but the shortest experience of any group of ministers. Their salaries are usually from $1,000 to $3,000. They have relatively long tenures, possibly reflecting the fact that they are less dependent upon their congregations and more upon supporting missionary agencies than others, or that there is little competition.

[1] For sample programs of Subtype A III, see Table XXV.

Possibly, also, the foreign church has not yet acquired the American habit of frequently changing its minister.

BUDGETS AND PROPERTY

With so many multiple staffs the budget of small foreign churches is necessarily beyond that of the average of the unadapted type. Three-fourths of the budgets, however, are of less than $10,000. The cost per capita is more than twice the average, being $42.21. This makes the type the most costly of all. Frequently, however, membership is a very poor reflection of the size of the work. Members recruited from a foreign population, especially one originally Catholic, are almost invariably few compared with the number of

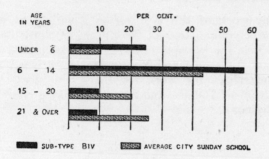

CHART XXVIII

Age Distribution of Sunday-School Pupils in Subtype B IV and in Average City Sunday School.

people served by social ministries and by religious instruction. Only one subtype has a larger ratio of Sunday-school pupils to church membership.[2]

Benevolence is in striking contrast with current expenses, being only about two-thirds of the average.

The average value of the church property used by this type is approximately $48,000 (median $30,000) against the average of about $98,000 for all city churches studied. The auditorium seats on the average 372 people (median 275) and the varied program is reflected by the fact that the building has more than an average number of rooms. On the other hand, it has usually very little equipment.

No Sunday school of these foreign churches enrolls as many as 300, and the highest average attendance is less than 200.

2 Appendix Table 32.

Case XXV—Subtype B IV

Most of these characteristics are reflected in a little Italian Baptist church in a city in New York State.

The enterprise is only twelve years old. It is located in the heart of the Italian sector which squeezes between the Lake and the main thoroughfare leading out from the business center. It has some thirty members, most of whom, however, have removed from the immediate vicinity. For so diminutive a work, measured in terms of membership, there is a staff of four workers—an Italian pastor with some seminary training but not college educated, receiving $1,400 salary, and three lady missionaries, each receiving $90 a month. There is a Sunday school of 144 pupils, only eight of whom are over fourteen years of age. The work is housed in a three-story frame building generally resembling the cheap tenements by which it is surrounded. It has ten rooms and is valued at $8,000. Special features of the work are numerous children's clubs, a daily vacation Bible school, gymnasium classes, a kindergarten (operated at public expense), English classes and moving-pictures. Charitable aid is an important factor, as are medical and legal advice.

Frequently work of this type serves a variety of nationalities mingling in a polyglot quarter of the city. The North Beach Center in San Francisco, for example (since 1920 under joint Presbyterian, Congregational, Episcopal and Young Men's Christian Association auspices), centralizes the work for the Latin races. There are separately organized Italian-, and Spanish-speaking churches besides clubs for Filipinos.

ACTIVITIES

Most of the exceptional features of these little churches directly reflect the particular problems and vicissitudes of their constituencies in a strange country. They are identical with some of the things that churches of new rural immigrants or Negroes newly come to the North have felt driven to undertake. Among them are employment agencies, dormitories, kindergartens, day nurseries and clinics. In other words, in order to meet some of the crying needs of its group, and in spite of its numerical weakness, the little church (usually, of course, with mission board help) gallantly undertakes one or two items of a service program carried out in a completer and more balanced way by socially adapted churches.

Daily vacation Bible schools and the use of moving-pictures are also characteristic of the type.

The churches of Subtype B IV are distributed among the denominiations as shown on the following page.

This showing undoubtedly reflects to some degree the development of foreign-speaking work in the several denominations, but it must not be assumed to reflect accurately the relative importance of that work.

Most of these churches have compact parishes. This was to be expected since a primary characteristic of the type is that they are related to some particular foreign colony.

Denomination	Number of Churches
Baptist	2
Congregational	1
Disciples	1
Methodist Episcopal	2
Presbyterian, U. S. A.	2
Protestant Episcopal	3

OTHER REASONS FOR UNUSUAL PROGRAMS

While the particular needs of racial and nationality groups are the most general factors entering into the development of the extremely one-sided program shown by Subtype B IV, they are not the only ones. Extreme poverty in American populations may require similar special treatment. Abnormal conditions in a church's founding may cause malformation from the beginning, or a decaying church may limp into an exceptionally erratic position through the uneven loss of its functions.

Case XXVI—Subtype A IV

This case strikingly illustrates the "uses of adversity." It is that of an historic and once wealthy church which has dwindled to a mere shadow of its former self. Its present one-sided program has been arrived at through the loss of one after another of its former functions as a result of the changed character of the neighborhood. The church is a victim of the expanding business section of the city, which has meant the deterioration of its environment as a place of homes.

Possessing one of the most beautiful church plants of the city from the architectural standpoint, and still retaining a nominal membership of about 400, with a budget of some $20,000, its Sunday school is practically zero and its total program consists of a poorly attended preaching service, a remnant of women's organizations and an interesting exceptional group of ministries for transient constituents, chiefly students. For them it maintains an open church, a special student pastorate, a Sunday afternoon social hour and forum, as well as varied social attractions.

In this work it is sustained by the loyalty of an "old guard" of well-to-do people who also contribute generously to denominational missions. The staff consists of a pastor, an assistant pastor specializing in student work, and a secretary.

Thus, in the face of radical change of circumstances and relative institutional failure, the church has found a distinctive ministry of contemporary importance. It is not a mere decrepit survivor of a former generation, but is striving to serve in a unique and original way—one, however, which does not quite fall in naturally with the tradition of the church. One questions whether this particular service might not be done as well or better by other institutions with the same money and staff.

An old family church (the second oldest of its denomination in a Pacific Coast city) somewhat similarly maintains an active week-day program, although its religious work has reached a very low ebb. Representatives of the central Young Men's Christian Association conduct a boys' club and the city playgrounds commission makes it a center of recreational work. In addition to this, the public library has made it a branch, sending a librarian one day per week. The balance of the resulting program is extremely unusual for an institution calling itself a church.

More cases of such special adaptations would undoubtedly be encountered now and then in a wider survey. So far as the sample goes, however, this group of erratic types is most closely identified with Protestant effort for foreign-speaking people.

SUBTYPE C III

The exceptional position of this subtype has already been discussed.[3] It belongs statistically with the internally adapted churches, but a comparison of the five sample programs of churches of this subtype with five similar programs of the internally adapted type[4] shows conclusively why it cannot practically be so regarded. It not only spreads over a wider range of activities—thus creating an unbalanced program from the standpoint of usual evolution—but the basic ecclesiastical character of the enterprise is more and more attenuated. Thus, while it has a program like that of the socially adapted churches with respect to many of its activities, it is unlike these churches in that it sacrifices (or has never developed) a large proportion of habitual church functions in order to carry on unusual social ministries.

Case XXVII—Subtype C III

This example chosen from a Californian city deliberately calls itself a "Christian Center" for Mexicans. It is located on First Avenue in the heart of the Mexican district and consists of three branches of work: namely, a Mexican church, a theological seminary for the training of Mexican native ministers, and social-center work. The theological seminary is a new venture, but the social center has been largely developed in connection with a new building occupied a year and a half ago. The social-center work largely takes the place of the conventional activities of an American parish, except as to the Sunday services and Sunday school. There are adult classes in English for men and women (rather poorly attended); a woman's society; cultural and recreational clubs for young men and for young women; manual training classes and clubs for younger boys and girls, and a daily kindergarten, besides Saturday classes for religious and manual instruction and a daily vacation Bible school. A second building will furnish excellent facilities for a clinic. It provides living apartments for the social workers on the second floor. The staff, other than that of the theological seminary, consists of a Mexican pastor and two lady community workers. The plant is modern and excellent in con-

3 See p. 72.
4 See pp. 143 and 198.

struction and design. Besides the two recent buildings, the old chapel stands in the rear of the lot and has been made over into a boys' manual training shop.

The institution is doing a localized neighborhood social work, characterized by many community gatherings and an attempt to establish social relations on a Christian basis. The workers in charge of community service appear to be well qualified and interested, and the head of the theological work is a man of strong personality and constructive spirit.

The Center is an unusually interesting and well-supported example of a many-sided mission to a single foreign nationality, with a local social program supplementing religious work. A Japanese group meets in the building for religious services only, but this is incidental.

Except for its theological adjunct, such a church is really first cousin to the social center or settlement that has never claimed to be a church at all.[5]

OTHER CHARACTERISTICS

While the most characteristic size for churches of Subtype C III is less than one hundred members, five out of the twenty-two have more than 500 members and two more than 1,000 members. Their median age is about the median for all churches studied, but the proportion of churches now occupying their original locations is only one-half that of the city churches in general, showing that the churches of this subtype have been subject to exceptional vicissitudes. In a word, they are somewhat larger enterprises than the average church of the other erratic types and, whatever their present variations, are generally built upon older American foundations.

Multiple staffs are characteristic of this subtype, the distribution being as follows:

Size of Staff	No. of Cases
1	8
2	10
3	5
4	1
5	1
8	2

Of thirteen male assistants employed, four are called assistant pastors, three directors of religious education, while the balance are gymnasium directors and social workers of various sorts. Of the twenty-two women workers six are called directors of social service, while eleven are deaconesses and visitors, two secretaries and two matrons.

The experience of the pastors of these churches is shorter even than of those in the smaller foreign churches. Their pastorates

5 Compare sample programs of socially adapted churches and Christian centers and settlements, p. 172.

The Conservative Variants

The subtypes that exaggerate the conservative tendency are Subtype D I, with twenty-seven churches, and Subtype E I, with ten churches. The former is an extreme variant of the slightly adapted church and the latter of the internally adapted church, both varying too widely to be included statistically in the types to which they naturally belong. They do not accordingly require special comment except to note again the surprising fact that the sample does not show more of them. They have and do nearly everything that churches at their stages of development can have and do, but their fortunes are so exceptional that they have little company.

Case XXVIII—Subtype E I

Such a super-elaborated church (not the most extreme case) is found in a prosperous Chicago suburb which for many years has attracted the choicest elements of a metropolitan denominational constituency. It has some 1,600 members, and a Sunday school less than one-half as large. It pays its pastor a salary of $7,200, while its director of religious education gets only $1,800. A church secretary completes the staff. Its building, worth $320,000, has forty rooms and seats 1,400 people in the auditorium. Its annual operating budget is $40,000, and the church is accustomed to contribute $63,000, or more, annually for benevolences.

The church's program includes almost everything one can think of for active all-around service to prosperous people; to which it adds a strong civic influence. Its pastor has been many years in this position. He has a highly original style, is a clever advertiser and a notable administrator.

ADDITIONAL EVIDENCE AND MINOR CHARACTERISTICS

The general characteristics of this subtype may be confirmed in detail by an examination of Appendix Table 35,[8] which shows the relative frequency of a small group of newer church activities by church types. In this table, the churches that show extreme variance in the direction of conservatism from the general trend of ecclesiastical development as judged by the general frequency scale, nevertheless definitely reveal a strong tendency to go in for all of what one may call the "recognized novelties." In other words, they go in for the up-to-date features that round out the characteristics of the internally adapted church but do not go beyond them. In the frequency of these activities such churches rank just beyond the internally adapted, as their statistical position would lead one to expect.

It is of further interest that, in the exceedingly brief list of these churches, one may note two whose pastors have recently held the titular leadership of their respective denominations. They are, in

8 See also Table LIII.

short, quite the sort of churches of which moderators of a General Assembly or Synod might be expected to have charge.

Additional comment on their stand-pat characteristics is found in the fact that they have moved their locations less frequently than any other type.

Since the group of churches classified as widely variant is not homogeneous, no common or consistent explanation for them is to be expected. In the case of the more significant subtypes, the specific causes of their departures from the average have been suggested. They are the results of extraordinary pressure or else of extraordinary lack of pressure, coupled with institutional easy circumstances.

The affinities of the former group for the various "non-churches" that parallel or go beyond the most extreme church type were sensed even at the outset of the investigation, as illustrated by Pittsburgh and Chicago. Writing of the latter city, Professor W. L. Bailey says: "A noticeable number in Chicago have developed unique churches in which the traditional functions are distinctly secondary; some have gone over into institutions that are no longer regular churches: several notable cases occur where they have definitely espoused the Settlement idea, or created a Christian neighborhood house of the same essential type: a number have dropped the name 'Church' and substituted 'Institute' or other such title. But many have practiced a difference of emphasis in the carrying on of activities which amounts to an eccentricity of a certain degree, and is scarcely less significant, being the more widespread."

It will be shown in a later connection that extreme variations are more frequent among the churches of the larger cities. Although relatively few anywhere, their prophetic significance may be very great, especially if the dominant hypothesis of the entire study is right, namely, that the urban church is in a process of adaptation. These more extreme, exceptional, original and adventurous churches may thus well be the vanguard of a procession which will be considerably enlarged in the future.

A General Study of the City Churches

The announced objective of the present study was to break up the total body of city churches into significant types.

This precluded emphasis upon any interpretation of the results of the study of the group as a whole by means of the average. Such a study is, however, recognized as one of the minor values of the book. To insert it into the discussion of the several types would, however, have interrupted the progress of their interpretation. It appears here, therefore, as a sort of appendix to their description and furnishes a generalization which may have value for those who are not particularly interested in their separate determination.

Before proceeding with this composite picture of all city churches, it will be helpful to recall exactly how it comes to exist. Somebody had gone to see and to study each of the 1,044 churches. Identical information concerning them on sixty-eight items had been recorded on sets of schedule cards. To this were added supplementary data and statements of personal impressions.

What the first-hand observer had done was in effect this: he had provided for the imagination of the interpreter not a collection of dull statistical records, but rather little working models of 1,044 individual churches, each a diminutive Noah's Ark with a steeple— 1,044 localized units of organized urban Christianity, each drawn to scale. Inside each imaginary model might be seen all the people with all their organizations and activities. Everything was accurately constructed so that not only the church as a whole but the various elements that make it up might be compared statistically for the 1,044 cases. Thirty-one such highly individual samples have been described in the text of this volume. Would anything be gained by the attempt to make a composite picture of so varied a group as they suggest?

THE STATISTICAL COMPOSITE

The statistical processes employed in determining the types made such a generalization possible. Returns from the schedules had been tabulated and totaled under their respective items for all comparable data. The results were then arranged in quantitative sequences from smaller to greater and the range noted. The series was thus broken up into convenient statistical intervals and the proportions of churches falling within the groups defined by these intervals were noted. This made it possible to discover the central tendency of the series as evidenced by frequency; or the median case was separately calculated.

Such a process, utilized in the successive studies of the types, is equally applicable to the entire 1,044 churches. Thus in the matter of membership (on which only 952 churches reported) the distribution shown in Table XLVII was found.

Judged by this sample, more than one-half of all city churches have fewer than 500 members, while one-fifth have more than 1,000 members; but the most frequent single size-group is one with from one to two hundred members.

A similar process was carried out with respect to each of the items covered by the schedules, and the more obviously important ratios calculated, such as that between church membership and Sunday-school enrollment and between Sunday-school enrollment and average attendance.

GENERALIZED PICTURE OF THE CITY CHURCH

The results of these elementary processes appear in the totals of Appendix Tables 5-58. Together they yield a picture of "the city church" much more complete than that commonly available, and startlingly at variance with it at certain points. "The city

TABLE XLVII — MEMBERSHIP OF 952 CITY CHURCHES

Number of Members	Distribution of Churches Number	Per Cent.
Under 100	111	11.7
Under 50	37	3.9
100 to 200	143	15.0
200 to 300	114	12.0
300 to 400	93	9.8
400 to 500	67	7.0
Under 500	528	55.5
500 to 1,000	226	23.7
1,000 and over	198	20.8
Total	952	100.0

church" is characteristically a small organization, most often of from one to two hundred members. Somewhat fewer than one-third of the churches are less than twenty-five years old, and considerably more than one-third are over fifty years old. Nearly one-half have been in their present locations less than twenty-five years, and 71 per cent. have moved at least once since organization. Nearly one-half have more than one paid worker, and in the combined total of the paid staff there are more assistant workers than there are pastors. Women constitute about one-third of the total of paid workers. Male assistants fall into seven fairly distinct types. Just one-half are assistant pastors and other half workers in specialized lines. Women religious workers employed by city churches fall into nine types. About half are clerical or general assistants and the other half engaged in specialized services. The most representative city pastor is a college and theological seminary graduate who has been from twenty to thirty years in the ministry, though 28 per cent. have served less than ten years. Only 15 per cent., however, have served over thirty years. By far the larger number— over 40 per cent.—have been in their present fields from two to three years, and only 16 per cent. have stayed as long as ten years.

The most frequent salary, enjoyed by slightly over one-third of city pastors, is from $1,000 to $2,000 (exclusive of parsonage), though nearly one-sixth get over $5,000.

FINANCES AND PROPERTY

As represented by the sample, 43 per cent. of city churches have current expenses of less than $5,000 annually, the most frequent sum being between $2,000 and $3,000. Twelve per cent., however, spend annually more than $25,000. The average expenditure per member is $18.17. Nearly two-thirds of these churches give more than $1,000 a year to benevolences, yet the most frequent amount is between $100 and $200. The average benevolent gift per member is $11.52. On a sample of 507 cases reporting, the average value of the Protestant church building in large American cities is $97,645, but there are as many churches worth less than $35,000 as there are worth more. The average seating capacity of the auditorium is 591, but the median only 450. The representative city church, comprising more than two-fifths of the total, has fewer than ten rooms, but 36 per cent. have between ten and twenty rooms and 8 per cent. have more than thirty. Out of the list of equipment facilities enumerated in the schedules, from five to nine is the number most frequently found.

THE SUNDAY SCHOOL AND OTHER ACTIVITIES

While approximately half of the churches have fewer than 500 members, three-fourths of the Sunday schools have fewer than 500 enrolled pupils, and 87 per cent. of the Sunday schools fewer than 500 in average attendance. From one to two hundred is the most frequent number both for enrollment and for attendance. Attendance averages 61 per cent. of enrollment. The pupils are distributed by ages as follows:

Ages	Per Cent.
Under 5	10
6–14	43
15–20	20
21 and over	27

Thirty per cent. of the schools have cradle rolls and 17 per cent. home departments. About one-fifth of the city churches are open daily for devotions and about two-fifths have an office open daily for business. One-third have organized athletics; 18 per cent. have Sunday evening socials or teas, and 17 per cent. use motion-pictures; about one-fifth maintain daily vacation Bible schools; 14 per cent.

have some form of week-day religious education, while 13 per cent. have children's congregations or children's sermons. About 8 per cent. have forums, and 2 per cent. maintain homes, dormitories or other forms of housing facilities.

PARISHES AND CONSTITUENTS

In 222 cases reported 45 per cent. of the churches had more than three-quarters of their membership living within one mile of the church building, but 23 per cent. had less than one-half of their membership within the same radius. Nearly one-third reported unbalanced distribution of members as to the direction of their homes from the church, and an additional third very unbalanced distribution. In other words, the church building is not usually anywhere near the geographical center of its constituency.

In 1916 there was one Protestant church to every 1,731 of the native-born population of large cities. Their total membership equaled nearly one-fifth of the total native-born population, men comprising 38 per cent. of the membership. Protestant churches constituted three-fourths of all church organizations. There was an average of twenty-four Protestant denominations per city, the irregular and not fully recognized denominations constituting 7.5 per cent. of the total. Twelve per cent. of all city churches owned no property but worshiped in rented halls.

These generalized results cover a much wider range of statistical information than previously existed for the city church. They do not, however, discover types of churches nor do they yield any explanatory hypothesis; and consequently, whatever their values, they figure merely as a by-product of the larger study.

Chapter XI

GENERAL DEVELOPMENT ACCOMPANYING DEVELOPING PROGRAMS

In the five preceding chapters the several major types of churches have been systematically described and explained in accordance with the general hypothesis that they express successive stages of adaptation to the city.

The present chapter considers the general development of the city church under topics derived directly from the basic and supplemental schedules used in the field investigation. Under these as headings it compares the major types and, where significant variations appear, the subtypes. This comparison constitutes a virtual restatement and summary of the concrete data of the study in the aspects that are internal to the organization and activities of the local church. It is followed by chapters which carry the comparison into the field of external relationships.

The outstanding result of the comparison, as one would naturally expect, is that when a city church enlarges its service program it also enlarges nearly every aspect of its life and work. But just how many factors would show enlargement corresponding to the increased scope of program and to what degree in each case could only be discovered by actual statistical enumeration and measurement. The result of such processes applied to the items of the schedules for 1,044 sample churches appears in the following paragraphs.

Naturally not every factor of church life responds to the stimulus of an increased service program in the same way. Accordingly the consideration of those factors that run parallel with the development of service program will be followed by a section devoted to those that run counter to it or are not affected at all.

Changes Accompanying Enlarged Programs

SIZE

Size is directly correlated with complexity of program and registers an increase corresponding with the enlargement of program in every stage of development as measured either in the types or in the subtypes.

The unadapted churches with their narrow programs are relatively small, more than four-fifths having fewer than 500 members, one-fourth fewer than one hundred, and nearly one-twelfth fewer than fifty members.[1]

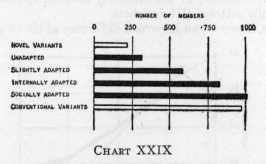

CHART XXIX

Average Size of Church, by Types.

The slightly adapted churches whose programs are a little ampler and more varied than those of the unadapted type are also relatively small, 57 per cent. having fewer than 500 members.

The internally adapted churches divide as follows as to size: under 500 members, 27 per cent.; 500 to 1,000 members, 39 per cent.; over 1,000 members, 34 per cent. This type has only one-half

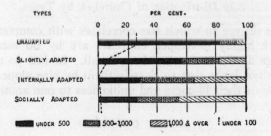

CHART XXX

Per Cent. Distribution of Size of Membership in Four Major Types of Churches.

as many churches of fewer than 500 members as the moderately developed type has.

The socially adapted churches tend to be large but are not always so. More than 25 per cent. of them have fewer than 500 members, while, on the other hand, 46 per cent. have more than 1,000 members.

1 Appendix Table 5.

It is only the extremely undeveloped church that is never large. Churches with limited programs are sometimes large in membership.

The general trend of increase is measured by the fact that the median size of the unadapted church is 187 members, of the slightly adapted 408 members, of the internally adapted 796 members, and of the socially adapted 921 members.

There is, however, an important difference at the two ends of the

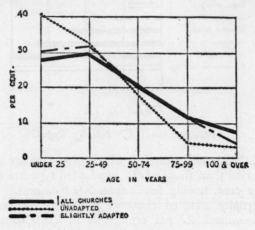

CHART XXXI

Age Distribution of Churches, by Types.

scale in the degree to which size correlates with complexity of program. The highly developed churches are by no means as uniformly large as the undeveloped are small. In fact so many of the former are not large that to classify them by size alone would give a false view of their likeness and unlikeness to one another.

AGE OF CHURCHES

The 820 churches reporting on this item were divided as shown in Table XLVIII.[2]

TABLE XLVIII — NUMBER AND AGE OF 820 CITY CHURCHES

Age	Distribution of Churches	
	Number	Per Cent.
Under 25	231	28.2
25–49	252	30.7
50–74	171	20.9
75–99	101	12.3
100 and over	65	7.9

2 Appendix Table 6.

Of the total number of churches reporting as to age, 3.4 per cent. are less than five years old and 8.8 per cent. are less than ten years old. The average age of all churches approximates forty years.

The more highly developed churches are on the whole older than the less developed ones. Thus the unadapted type has a much larger per cent. of churches less than twenty-five years old and considerably fewer more than seventy-five years.

The slightly adapted churches approximate the general average, as is their characteristic.

The internally adapted type is strikingly below the average in

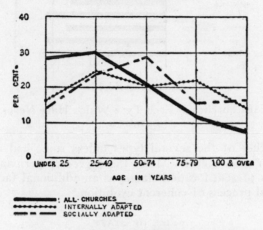

: ALL-CHURCHES
INTERNALLY ADAPTED
SOCIALLY ADAPTED

CHART XXXIa

Age Distribution of Churches, by Types.

the proportion of young churches and above it in the proportion of old ones. This type has the largest number of very old churches, while the socially adapted type has more middle-aged ones.

Within each general type the less developed subtype has more of the younger churches than the more developed have.

The age of the church, then, is reflected in its type as defined by complexity of service program. The less developed churches tend to be the younger, and the more developed the older.[3]

YEARS IN PRESENT LOCATION

While the median age of the churches studied is forty-two years, the median length of time which they have occupied their present

---

3 The age of churches of course depends somewhat upon the age of the city in which they are located, but also upon the rate of its recent growth. Thus, Springfield, Mass., an old city, grew more in the last twenty years than in the previous two hundred. Accordingly, just about one-half of its churches are less than twenty-five years of age.

sites is only twenty-five years. This means that many of them have moved at some time during their histories.

As among churches of the major types, the length of occupancy of their present sites corresponds directly to the degree of development of their service program. The unadapted churches have been the shortest time in their present locations, and the socially adapted the longest. This was to be expected in view of the relative ages

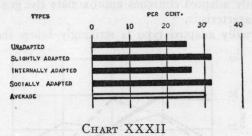

CHART XXXII

Per Cent. of Churches in Each Type Which Have Never Changed Location.

of the churches of the several types unless some had moved very much oftener than others.[4] Thus the degree of permanence of the church in its present location stands as an additional factor relating to the general process of coherent evolution.[5]

SIZE OF STAFF

Of the 988 churches reporting on this item, 47 per cent. have more than one paid worker. Almost three-quarters, however, have

TABLE XLIX — NUMBER OF CHURCHES EMPLOYING STAFFS OF SPECIFIED SIZE AND NUMBER OF WORKERS EMPLOYED

Number of Churches	Size of Staff	Workers Employed
523	1	523
185	2	370
131	3	393
76	4	304
37	5	185
16	6	96
4	7	28
12	8	96
1	9	9
3	10 and over	38
988		2,042

4 Considerable difference on this point was found, but not enough to affect the general tendency as stated.
5 Appendix Table 7.

not more than two. This indicates the present tendency of the city church toward a multiple staff.[6]

The distribution of staffs according to the number of religious workers employed is shown in Table XLIX.

The unadapted churches rarely have more than one paid worker.

Sixty per cent. of the slightly adapted churches have a pastor only, and 80 per cent. have not more than two workers.

The internally adapted type has about the same number of staffs of one, two and three workers respectively, a staff of three workers being slightly the most characteristic. This combination typically provides a pastor, a male assistant functioning often as a special

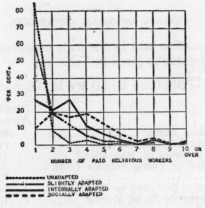

CHART XXXIII

Per Cent. Distribution of Size of Staffs of Four Major Types.

director of religious education and a woman worker, generally combining clerical and pastoral work.[7]

Staffs of two or more workers are strongly characteristic of the socially adapted churches. This is the obvious corollary of their more specialized program. Recreational, educational and health experts constitute the most usual additions to such staffs.

There is an absolutely consistent increase in staff from subtype to subtype after the very earliest stages of development have been reached. Each and every appreciable addition to program is accompanied by additions to the size of staff. This correlation is more absolute than on any other item, as obviously it should be if the program to be carried out determines the employed personnel of a

6 Appendix Table 9.
7 Explanation of how an elaborated program can be carried out by a one-man staff is suggested on p. 168.

church organization. Size of staff is thus directly proportionate to the scope and complexity of the service program. The more complex it is the larger the staff and the more varied the specialized functions of its members.

The total body of workers represented by reports on this point from 988 churches is 2,042, an average of somewhat more than two per church. If it is assumed that each church has a pastor, 1,054 other workers are left, of whom 653 are women and 401 men.[8] In other words, the combined staff in the modern city churches already includes more persons belonging to other types of paid religious work than it does pastors. Women constitute just about one-third of the total body of workers.

VARIETY OF MALE ASSISTANTS

The particular office held by the male assistants was specified in 372 cases with the results given in Table L.[9]

TABLE L—OFFICES HELD BY MALE ASSISTANTS

Office	Distribution of Assistants Number	Per Cent.
Assistant or Associate Pastor	186	50.0
Director of Religious Education	71	19.1
Superintendent of Athletics or Recreation *	34	9.1
Director Men's, Boys' or Young People's Work	30	8.1
Secretary	18	4.8
Financial or Executive Secretary or Treasurer	14	3.8
Director Social Service or Social Worker	12	3.2
Pastor Emeritus, etc.	7	1.9

* Includes Scout Masters, Superintendents of Camps and Outing Farms, etc.

It is recognized that less difference exists in actual function than the difference in names suggests; yet the following general tendencies are apparently indicated: The more highly developed types of churches employ proportionately the larger number of specialists such as directors of men's, boys' or young people's work, social service supervisors, gymnasium directors and scoutmasters; while the less developed types maintain more of the conventional offices represented by assistant pastors and directors of religious education. Male assistants of any sort are so rare in the unadapted type as to be statistically negligible, but it is a striking discovery that this type has more male "financial" and "executive" secretaries than any other. This directly indicates the presence of large but institutionally undeveloped churches whose pastors give themselves pri-

8 The sex of the workers was not always reported in connection with the staff. The proportion of women and men is therefore assumed to be the same as in the sample reporting as to sex under "functional distribution of staff." See Appendix Tables 10 and 11.
9 Appendix Table 10.

marily to pulpit ministries while male executives are employed for business management—a condition that pertains in no other type.[10] An analogous position would be that of manager to the musical or dramatic star.

VARIETY OF WOMEN ASSISTANTS

The offices held by women assistants were named in 608 cases with the results given in Table LI.[11]

TABLE LI — OFFICES HELD BY FEMALE ASSISTANTS

Office	Distribution of Assistants Number	Per Cent.
Secretary	265	43.6
(Deaconess or Visitor combined)	*137*	*22.5*
Director Social Service or Social Worker	70	11.5
Visitor	69	11.3
Deaconess	68	11.2
Pastor's Assistant	41	6.7
Director Women's, Girls' or Young People's Work	38	6.2
Matron, etc.	29	4.8
Director Religious Education	21	3.5
Financial Secretary	7	1.2

In the matter of frequency secretaries greatly exceed all other types of women church workers. The functions of deaconesses and visitors are so nearly, if not wholly, identical that they are reported together in the second item of the list as well as separately. This type of service is next to the most frequent.

As among the types, the following tendencies prevail: The more highly developed naturally employ the larger number of specialized workers, such as social service directors, directors of women's and girls' work, whereas the older types of women's service represented by deaconess or visitor are more frequent with the less developed churches. Clerical work, however, is the most characteristic form of women's service with all types.

PASTOR'S EXPERIENCE

Most young ministers serve their apprenticeships in the country or else as a pastor's assistant in the city. Pastorates of city churches are generally not open to the young. On the other hand, the city church properly requires and gets the maturest powers of a minister before the inevitable letting down of age.

Twenty to twenty-nine years is the most characteristic term of experience for city pastors, 31 per cent. having been in the ministry

10 See p. 128.
11 Appendix Table 11.

for this period of time. Fifteen and four-tenths per cent. have had
more than thirty years' experience and very few go beyond forty

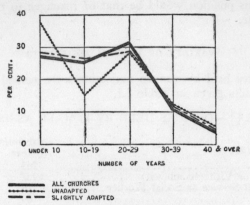

CHART XXXIV

Per Cent. Distribution of Pastors with Specified Number of Years'
Experience, by Types.

years. On the other hand, only 12.5 per cent. have had less than
five years' experience.

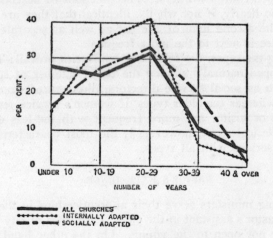

CHART XXXIVa

Per Cent. Distribution of Pastors with Specified Number of Years'
Experience, by Types.

Each added stage of the development of the church program in
complexity requires additional experience on the part of the minister.

The unadapted church has twice as many pastors of less than five years' experience as the average. On the other hand, it also has more men of more than forty years than any other. Naturally its financial weakness compels it to take more of the very young and of the very old.

The slightly adapted type is characteristically close to the average in the experience of its ministers.

The internally adapted type has a very strong tendency toward middle-aged pastors. It selects in the main men of proved success, but discriminates definitely against old men. The qualities that it demands perhaps diminish with approaching age.

The socially adapted type, with the most complex and varied program of all, uses more old men than any other. Executive capacity, maturity of judgment and sympathetic experience, which are the primal qualifications in such pastorates, perhaps last longer than the brilliant qualities of leadership demanded by polite congregations.[12]

Over 15 per cent. of the pastors of the entire number of churches studied were found to have had more than thirty years' experience in the ministry. If they entered the ministry at the usual age, these pastors were fifty-eight years old or more.

But, according to actuarial tables for the Presbyterian and Congregational denominations, out of every one hundred men who enter the ministry only a few more than seventy will remain available for service beyond thirty years—death and disability accounting for the remainder. In other words, while the employed pastors with this length of experience constitute only about 15 per cent. of the total number of pastors, they include more than 30 per cent. of the available pastors of the age-group in question. This does not show such a degree of discrimination in the pastorate against elderly men as is usually assumed. Besides this, assistant's positions are available to a higher proportion of elderly men than are sought for the pastorate.

If both ends of the minister's career be taken into consideration, a fair summary of the data is that the young minister has less chance at a city church than an old one. Apprenticeship is generally found in the country, but the city utilizes the experienced man in considerable numbers beyond the age of greatest physical vigor.

PASTOR'S TENURE

The length of the pastor's service in his present place was reported by 628 churches.

12 Appendix Table 12.

From two to four years' tenure is strongly characteristic for the entire body of city churches examined, 40 per cent. of the cases falling in this period. Eighty-four per cent. of all ministers were found to have been in their present place less than ten years, and about 25 per cent. less than two years.

The unadapted type has the largest per cent. of short-stay men; the slightly adapted is closest to the average, while ministers of the internally adapted and socially adapted types tend to stay much longer.

A direct relation is thus established between the type of church and the tenure of the pastor. The higher the development, the longer the stay; though the difference between the types is not marked. Something in the better organization, the better remuneration and the more adequate assistance makes this difference in favor of the more highly developed churches. One confesses, however, that the impression made by this slight difference is almost lost in the contemplation of the brief tenure for all and the terrific turn-

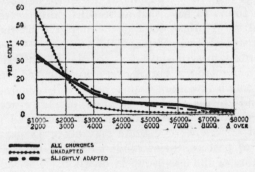

CHART XXXV

Per Cent. Distribution of Pastors Receiving Specified Salaries, by Types.

over. Whether starved out, worn out or thrown out, most ministers go after a very limited period of service in a given place.[13] One may fairly ask what chance there is under these circumstances for continuity and constructive leadership.

SALARY

Cash salaries of from $1,000 to $2,000 are strongly modal for the 774 churches reporting on this item, one-third of all falling within these limits. Sixty-two per cent. of all city ministers reporting have less than $3,000 salary, while 5 per cent. have less than

13 Appendix Table 14.

$1,000. On the other hand, almost 18 per cent. have more than $5,000.[14]

The pastor of the unadapted church is very likely to get less than $2,000 salary and has scarcely any chance of getting more than $3,000.

Similarly, the pastor of the slightly adapted church is more likely than not to get less than $2,000 salary.

The pastor of the internally adapted church, on the other hand, is almost certain to get more than $2,000, salaries of from $2,000 to $3,000 and from $3,000 to $4,000 being equally characteristic. Thirty-five per cent. of the pastors of this type receive more than $5,000.

From $3,000 to $4,000 salaries are strongly characteristic of the

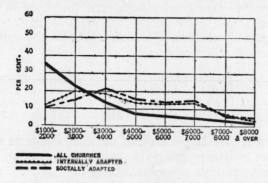

CHART XXXVa

Per Cent. Distribution of Pastors Receiving Specified Salaries, by Types.

socially adapted churches and a larger proportion of the pastors of these churches get more than $5,000 than do those of any other type. The socially adapted type also have the largest number of very high salaries, three cases going above $8,000.

There is thus a definite increase of salary with each increase of complexity of program as expressed by church types.[15]

Part of the higher pay in the more complex types is for the administration of a more varied organization. Doubtless the ministers of these churches have a higher general grade of ability for things that all ministers have to do, but job analysis would also show them doing additional and different things corresponding with the general increase in the rate of pay. The pastor of the more highly

14 Parsonages in addition to salary were reported inadequately and appear to be about equally distributed among the types. They are ignored in the figures because of the striking differences in rental value in various parts of the country, in various cities, and in various parts of the same cities.
15 Appendix Table 15.

organized church, in other words, has a greater range of administrative functions.

The characteristic salary of the city minister is extremely low; and when the difference in cost of living is considered, appears to be no better than that paid by many town churches. The range of salary is also narrow compared with that in other professions. The highest paid city doctor or lawyer receives a much larger emolument than the most highly paid minister.

SALARIES OF MALE ASSISTANT WORKERS

On the basis of 181 cases reporting, the male assistant worker receives on the average just about one-half of the salary of the pastor in churches that employ both, and the range in salary for male assistants is just about one-half as great as that of the pastor.

The per cent. distribution of pastors' and male assistants' salaries by amount received is as follows:

	Under $1,000	$1,000 to $2,000	$2,000 to $3,000	$3,000 to $4,000	$4,000 to $5,000	Over $5,000
Pastor	4.7	34.6	22.4	12.9	7.6	17.8
Assistant	17.1	32.0	31.5	17.1	1.7	0.5

The fact that over 17 per cent. of the male assistants receive less than $1,000, of course, must signify that most of them are unmarried men, frequently students in apprenticeship.

The salary of the male assistant rises with each type of church from the slightly adapted to the socially adapted. The unadapted churches are left out of the count because they so rarely have assistants. In the socially adapted churches only does the range of assistants' salaries go beyond $4,000, reaching as high as $8,000 in one case.[16]

EDUCATION, EXPERIENCE AND SALARY OF FEMALE WORKER

In strong contrast with the prevalence of higher education for all male church workers, 55 per cent. of all female paid assistants do not have education of college grade. Sixteen per cent. of this group, however, have some special vocational training. This leaves 39 per cent. who are neither college graduates nor specially trained; whereas but 8 per cent. of pastors and 16 per cent. of other male assistants are without specific professional preparation.

The proportion of college-trained female assistants increases directly but slowly with the complexity of the church types. In

16 Appendix Table 19.

other words, higher education is definitely associated with the more permanent and better paid jobs.[17]

The more highly developed the types of churches the longer the average experience of the woman workers, but the socially adapted are practically the only churches that secure female assistants of really long experience. In other words, church work has not yet become a career for women except in connection with the specialized and semi-professional service included in the work of the internally adapted and socially adapted churches. Like the American school-teacher, the woman assistant in the city church is generally very young and her stay in her religious calling very brief.

The salary of the female assistant, based on 321 cases reported, is almost always under $2,000 and one-third of the salaries are less than $1,000. Nearly one fourth are in the group of from $1,500 to $2,000, the latter sum being virtually the maximum.

The salary increases somewhat with each development of type, but the difference is slight.[18]

CURRENT OPERATING EXPENSES

The 917 churches reporting on annual current expenses represented a total of 539,233 members and a combined annual current expenditure of $9,798,920, an average of $18.17 per capita. The range of current expense budgets is shown in Table LII.

TABLE LII — CURRENT EXPENSES OF 917 CITY CHURCHES

Amount	Distribution of Churches Number	Per Cent
Under $5,000	391	42.7
$5,000 to $10,000	191	20.8
$10,000 to $15,000	93	10.1
$15,000 to $20,000	72	7.9
$20,000 to $25,000	57	6.2
$25,000 to $50,000	95	10.4
$50,000 to $75,000	15	1.6
$75,000 and over	3	0.3

The vast difference between the highest and the lowest rates of expenditure shown in this table is impressive. In the "under $5,000" group are thirty-one churches that spend less than $1,000 as contrasted with the three churches in the highest group that spend more than $75,000 annually. The most characteristic group (constituting 43 per cent. of the total) spends less than $5,000. Eighty-eight per cent. spend less than $25,000.

17 In conflict with this general tendency, it is the internally adapted church that has the lowest proportion of trained women. This is doubtless due to the fact that their large staff requires more purely clerical specialists. Such positions can be held by women of proper business training but without higher education.
18 Appendix Tables 20, 21 and 23.

The per cent. of churches spending more than $5,000 increases directly with the complexity of the types as based on program. This is merely the reflection in terms of finance of the concomitant increase in all aspects which has been traced in detail.

Thus, the modal expenditure of the unadapted church is from $2,000 to $3,000 a year, although there are nearly as many of this group that spend from $1,000 to $2,000, and 10 per cent. of them even less than $1,000.

The most frequent budget of the slightly adapted church is also from $2,000 to $3,000. The range, however, is greater; more than one-fifth of such churches spending from $5,000 to $10,000, while some budgets in this type run as high as from $50,000 to $75,000. Such large, conventional churches which spend great sums without broadening their program may be spending extravagantly and ostentatiously. Others, probably, are maintaining missions and philanthropies whose cost is covered in the church budget but could not be disentangled statistically.

The most representative budgets of the internally adapted type are from $5,000 to $10,000, while one-fifth of the churches of this type cost over $25,000.

The modal expenditure of the socially adapted church is from $10,000 to $15,000, while nearly one-third cost over $25,000, and 3 per cent. over $75,000. The last named, of course, constitute groups of social institutions under the administration of a church rather than single church enterprises.

Although, in view of the broad variation in current expense budgets that characterize all the types and virtually all the subtypes,[19] averages on this point are less revealing than the modal tendencies already commented upon, the striking reflection of general development in terms of finance can best be shown by their use in Chart XXXVI.

Each and every regular increase in program, either novel or conventional, is accompanied by an enlarged budget. The ascending scale is unbroken. More work inevitably means greater cost.

When per capita current expenditures are substituted for absolute costs, the only considerable difference between the types turns out to be between the unadapted group and all the others, as shown in the following tabulation:

Type	Per Capita Current Expense
Unadapted	$14.75
Slightly adapted	$17.96
Internally adapted	$19.12
Socially adapted	$19.95

19 Appendix Table 24.

While the unadapted church costs approximately one-fourth less per member to operate than the other three types, these last differ but little among themselves. Decidedly the most economical type is the socially adapted. With four times as broad a program and three times as large an average staff as the unadapted, it costs only one-fourth more per capita. The slightly adapted type, with a program

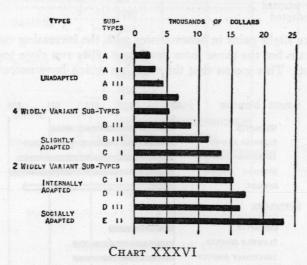

CHART XXXVI

Average Current Expense Budgets of Churches, by Types and Subtypes.

twice as broad, and the internally adapted type, with a program three times as broad and a staff twice as large, are also more economical, in terms of service rendered, than is the unadapted type.[20]

ANNUAL BENEVOLENCES

A total annual benevolence of $5,917,540, or an average of $11.52 per capita, was reported by 842 churches, with 513,511 members.

There is an enormous range in benevolence between the 4.5 per cent. of churches giving less than $100 and the 8.1 per cent. giving more than $25,000. However, benevolences of less than $1,000 are strongly characteristic, more than one-third (35 per cent.) of all cases falling within this limit. Two-thirds of the churches give less than $5,000 in annual benevolence.

The proportion of churches contributing less than $1,000 decreases and the proportion contributing more than $5,000 increases directly with the complexity of the types.[21]

20 Appendix Table 25.
21 Appendix Tables 26 and 26a.

rooms being the median for this type. At the other extreme, about one-third of the socially adapted churches have more than twenty rooms.

In other words, there is a close correlation between the complexity of church program and the number of rooms in the church building.

The church structure is relatively permanent, while the church program is flexible and easily changed from year to year. While, therefore, it is only natural that the church building should reflect

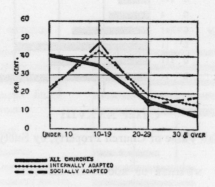

ALL CHURCHES
INTERNALLY ADAPTED
SOCIALLY ADAPTED

CHART XXXIXa

Per Cent. Distribution of Number of Rooms in Church Buildings, by Types.

the program for the sake of which it is built, it is somewhat of a surprise that the correspondence is so close. It had been supposed that many churches, especially those that had "seen better days," would show buildings far too large for them. This does not appear to be the case so far as the maximum needs of their programs are concerned. On the other hand, it is easy to see that size and character of the building would necessarily limit the church's program. All in all, the city church in general seems to fit very definitely the building in which it is housed.

EQUIPMENT FACILITIES

From five to ten out of the following classified list of twenty-eight equipment facilities were the most frequent number reported for the 1,044 city churches:

Administration

Typewriter
Addressograph
Mimeograph
Office
Study
Card index, members
Card index, constituency

Education

Stereopticon
Blackboards
Printing Plant
Library
Movies
Maps

Publicity

Electric Sign
Letterhead
Bulletin Board
Church Paper

Service

Kitchen
Dining-room
Baths
Toilets
Drinking Fountains

Community Service

Gymnasium
Swimming Pool
Day Nursery
Kindergarten
Bowling
Billiards

The more highly developed types naturally show a larger number of such facilities, from ten to fifteen being characteristic of the internally adapted type and from fifteen to twenty of the socially adapted. In movable equipment for work, then, as well as in fixed plant, increasing complexity is directly registered.

SUNDAY-SCHOOL ENROLLMENT

The most frequent city Sunday school has from one to two hundred enrolled pupils. Over three-fourths have fewer than 500, while about 7 per cent, have more than 1,000 pupils.

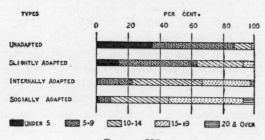

CHART XL

Per Cent. Distribution of Number of Equipment Facilities of Four Major Types.

The rule is that the more developed the type the larger Sunday school it has, both in enrollment and in average attendance, but the internally adapted type has more very large schools than has the socially adapted. The correspondence between complexity of program and increasing Sunday-school enrollment runs with great exactness from subtype to subtype. Thus the Sunday school, although frequently administered with relatively little connection with the church and seemingly loosely attached to it, turns out to respond very minutely to the general development of the parent organization.

ADDITIONAL CHURCH ACTIVITIES

The original determination of church types was upon the basis of number and frequency of specified organizations and activities within a list of thirty-three which occurred on all the schedules by

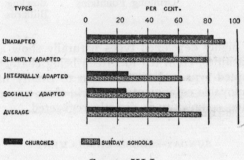

CHART XLI

Per Cent. of Churches and Sunday Schools with Fewer Than 500 Members, by Types.

means of which the 1,044 cases were studied. Twelve additional items of information were available for 853 churches. Their relative frequency in the churches reporting is given in Table LIII.[23]

The frequency of these items almost invariably increases with the complexity of church program. All are far more characteristic of the highly developed types than of the less developed ones.

The frequency of these twelve items was calculated independently. It confirms absolutely the principle established by the original thirty-three items included in the general frequency scale; namely, that churches may be divided into types according to the number and range of their activities. The briefer and arbitrarily chosen list has been proved a good yardstick. If the twelve supplemental items had been incorporated into it the results in the determination of types would have been substantially the same.

23 Appendix Table 36.

TIME GIVEN TO THE CHURCH

The use of any mere check list of organizations and activities for the determination of church types would have been open to question had its validity not had such ample confirmation from so many standpoints. An interesting final demonstration of its validity

TABLE LIII — PER CENT. OF CHURCHES REPORTING CERTAIN SPECIFIED ACTIVITES, IN EACH TYPE *

Activities	Un-adapted	Slightly Adapted	Internally Adapted	Types Socially Adapted	Widely Variant Adven-turous	Conserva-tive	Total
Coöperation with social agencies..	26.7	43.4	61.6	84.4	41.3	77.1	49.2
Church office open daily	16.8	34.1	64.4	72.9	18.7	65.7	40.8
Organized Athletics	13.1	27.2	52.0	69.8	20.0	54.3	34.5
Church open daily for devotion ...	8.4	14.7	26.0	41.7	10.7	25.7	18.8
Daily vacation Bible school	8.9	15.1	26.6	47.9	22.7	37.1	21.3
Motion-pictures ..	3.7	10.8	22.6	40.6	20.0	40.0	17.0
Children's congregations	5.2	9.0	16.9	32.3	2.7	20.0	12.7
Week-day school of religious education	7.9	9.0	20.3	28.1	14.7	20.0	14.2
Children's sermons	4.2	9.7	14.7	32.3	....	28.6	12.0
Sunday evening tea	2.6	13.6	28.8	43.8	8.0	34.3	18.1
Forum	2.1	4.7	10.7	26.0	2.7	8.6	7.7
Room and board..	1.0	1.1	1.1	9.4	1.3	2.9	2.1

* See Appendix Table 35 for number of churches reporting under each type.

is found when, instead of counting each organization and activity as one and merely considering the frequency of their occurrence, the actual hours of attendance on church activities which the differ-

TABLE LIV — AGGREGATE HOURS OF MONTHLY ATTENDANCE ON CHURCH ACTIVITIES AND HOURS PER MEMBER, BY TYPES

Type	Number of Churches	Average Hours Per Church	Average Hours Per Member
Unadapted	12	1,173	9.5
Slightly adapted	15	2,645	7.5
Internally adapted	19	7,493	8.9
Socially adapted	4	12,559	14.6

ent items of the check list imply are calculated. This has been done for a limited number of churches (chiefly in Springfield, Mass.) for which information was available, with the results given in Table LIV.

As appears in this table the more highly developed types not only have more activities, but greatly excel the less developed in the average aggregate of monthly attendance-hours by which their total activities have been measured. They also tend to show a larger average number of hours per member spent in church activities. There is, however, one striking exception: the smaller average membership of the unadapted church compels it to spend a large amount of time even to operate the very limited kind of activities which its type affords. This type, therefore, shows more average hours per member than the two succeeding types. Its high cost in time goes with its relatively high per capita cost in money, as previously demonstrated. It is also to be noted that the slightly adapted church spends nearly as many hours per member on the average in church activities as does the internally adapted church, in spite of the less extended program. This is also probably due to the larger average memberships of the internally adapted churches. In many respects this broader participation in church life by the average member of the less developed types is a striking advantage over the more developed ones.

Twenty-one factors have now been enumerated that show concomitant change corresponding to the increasing complexity of church programs. A few factors varying from the main tendency will be next considered.

Changes Not Accompanying Enlarged Programs

RATIO OF SUNDAY-SCHOOL ENROLLMENT TO CHURCH MEMBERSHIP

This factor shows a tendency exactly the reverse of that which was demonstrated in the previous section. Enrollment in all city churches combined averages 63 per cent. of church membership, or slightly less than two-thirds. This shows the relative size of the Sunday school as a factor in the general church program. It is usually a larger factor with the less developed than with the more highly developed types and diminishes directly with the degree of complexity of program as follows: [24]

Type	Ratio
Unadapted	69
Slightly adapted	68
Internally adapted	61
Socially adapted	52

This tendency appears perfectly natural when it is considered that in the smallest and narrowest programs the Sunday school is

[24] Appendix Table 32.

one-third or one-fourth of the total area of church activity, while it becomes only one item out of twenty or more in the highly developed churches.

The frequency of the cradle roll also fails to increase with the development of the types. The home department, indeed, is less characteristic of the more highly developed than of the traditional church. Highly developed churches, however, more frequently have teacher-training classes, daily vacation Bible schools, week-day re-

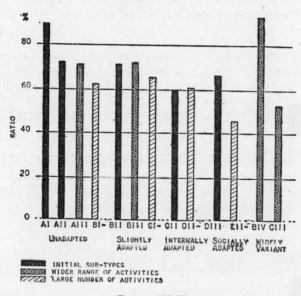

CHART XLII

Ratio of Sunday-School Enrollment to Church Membership, by Subtypes.

ligious instruction (though this is infrequent in any case), and separate children's congregations on Sunday.

The relative importance of these several items cannot be determined, but it is at least questionable whether the combined agencies of religious education have proportionately expanded to match other aspects of the church's development of program.

PASTOR'S EDUCATION

The tradition that the city pastor should be fully educated, in the sense of having both college and seminary training, has authority among all types of churches, with the result that there is less variation among the types in this respect than in any other. Nearly 80 per cent. of all city pastors have the degree of education above indicated.[25]

RATIO OF SUNDAY-SCHOOL ATTENDANCE TO ENROLLMENT

The average attendance of the city Sunday school is 61 per cent. of its enrollment and there is very slight difference among the types on this point. No one of them is doing appreciably better or worse in getting its enrolled pupils into actual attendance.

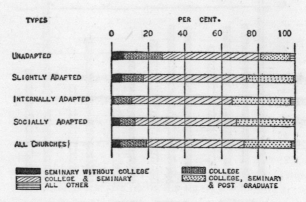

CHART XLIII

Per Cent. Distribution of Pastors Having Specified Degree of Education, by Types.

A few factors show a number of significant variations from type to type, but no regular tendencies. They introduce minor discords into the close harmony which has been discovered between development of programs and other factors.[26]

FREQUENCY OF REMOVAL

The median age of city churches has been discovered to be forty-two years, while the median length of occupancy of their present site is only twenty-five years. The relative frequency with which any type has moved has been determined by comparing the ratio of occupancy to age, as shown on the opposite page.[27]

25 Appendix Table 13.
26 Appendix Table 34.
27 Appendix Table 8.

Of course the higher the ratio of occupancy to age the less frequently have the churches of the type moved.

The results show no uniform tendency as among the types. The slightly adapted have been most permanent relatively to their average age and the internally developed least so. The unadapted have had

Type	Ratio of Occupancy to Age	Rank by Degree of Permanence
Unadapted	53	3
Slightly adapted	70	1
Internally adapted	49	4
Socially adapted	55	2

the next to the most frequent removals, while the socially adapted have been next to the most permanent. Explanations of these phenomena are attempted in a later connection.

EDUCATION, EXPERIENCE AND TENURE OF ASSISTANT MALE WORKER

On these points again there is no regular tendency as among the types. Assistant workers are so rare in the unadapted churches that they may be ignored. When the slightly adapted church has a male assistant he is usually traditionally trained and functions as a pastor's understudy, whereas with the internally adapted and socially adapted churches he is more likely to be a specialist in some form of recreational or educational leadership without full ministerial training. Here again, however, variations appear. The socially adapted type, with its ultra-specialization, has the largest number of such people in its employ, while the internally adapted church takes more men of the Young Men's Christian Association type, presumably with specialized ability as leaders of boys or as athletic coaches, but without higher education of any sort.

The slightly adapted type is the only one employing men of long experience as male assistants. The tenure of the male assistant also shows erratic variations, being shortest with the internally adapted type.[28]

SUNDAY-SCHOOL AGE DISTRIBUTION

One of the most significant variations from the prevailing tendency is at this point. The distribution of the nearly 150,000 Sunday-school pupils enrolled in the 841 city churches reporting on this item is given on the next page.[29]

28 Appendix Tables 16-18.
29 Appendix Table 35.

It will be observed that over one-half of the enrollment consists of pupils in infancy and childhood, one-fifth of young people and one-fourth of adults.

Age Groups	Per Cent. Distribution
Under 6 (infancy)	10.2
6–14 (childhood)	43.3
15–20 (adolescence)	20.2
21 and over (adulthood)	26.3

Variations are discovered among the several types as follows: Compared with the average, the slightly adapted is deficient in adolescence; the unadapted strong in childhood but deficient in adolescence and maturity; the internally adapted deficient in childhood but exceptionally strong with adolescence and maturity; while the

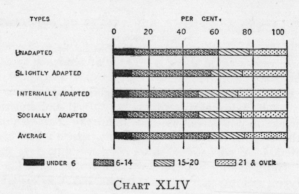

CHART XLIV

Age Distribution of Sunday-School Pupils, by Types.

socially adapted is deficient with infancy and childhood and especially strong with youth. In other words, the Sunday school of the unadapted churches is chiefly a children's institution, while the slightly adapted churches have somewhat more children but fewer adolescents. The two more highly developed types, on the contrary, have the largest number of young people and adults, the internally adapted holding both of these groups while the socially adapted succeeds mainly with adolescents.

The general tendencies revealed by the types run pretty steadily throughout the subtypes also.

In other words, the more varied and extensive program of the more highly developed types tends to success in holding young people and adults in the allegiance of the Sunday school. Holding young people has been the particular difficulty of all churches and the discovery that churches with a more complex program succeed better in this respect is an important contribution to religious knowledge in an important realm.

While there is a definite tendency for developed church programs to go with centrally located churches, most of the environmental factors influence the types irregularly. If they are centrally located, their average character and the quality of local environment varies without apparent relationship to the ascending or descending scale based upon scope of program. If they are residential, the quality of residential territory and the compactness or dispersion of members in the parish show no regular tendency. These factors have special discussion in a later connection.[30]

Minor Variations

Beyond the study of general tendencies, the main purpose of breaking up the total body of city churches into statistical types registering degrees of likeness and unlikeness, was, first, to discover the more detailed course of urban adaptation, and secondly, to find its limits. While to a remarkable degree the general tendencies illustrated in the above discussion of the related factors of church life are followed by the statistical subtypes as well as by the general types, it was not to be expected that there would be no variations. The more significant ones are discussed in connection with the several types and appear in detail in the statistical tables of the appendix.

Certain interesting tendencies appear, however, which show that variations of the subtypes from the general types have a certain orderliness and follow implicit laws.

NUMBER OF ACTIVITIES VS. RANGE OF ACTIVITIES

An increase in the number of church activities tends to be accompanied by greater variation in other aspects of development than an increase in their range. It was not known in advance what effect one degree of development in either direction would register. Would a single step in one or the other coincide with equal degrees of change? This proved not to be the case. Almost invariably, adding more activities of the same kind was associated with greater change than an increase of activities involving wider range but no greater number. Chart XLV shows this tendency in terms of church mem-

30 Appendix Table 37.

bership. The adventurous subtypes A III and B III have a broader program than the subtypes A I and B II, but they average but little larger in membership, while the conservative subtypes B I, C I and E II (which represent a fuller program without increase of range) are much larger than the initial subtypes of their respective types.[31] Subtype D II, which is only slightly larger than Subtype C II, proves something of an exception.

Apparently a church of a given membership finds it easier to

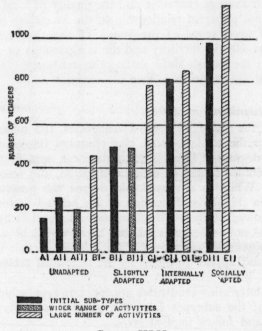

CHART XLV

Average Size of Church Membership, by Subtypes.

operate selectively, dropping out some elements of the traditional program in order to take on novelties, than it does to add to the total number of its activities. In other words, the tendency toward novelty and adventuresomeness requires less all-around change and development than an equal tendency to conservatism.

The same tendency is shown by the average size of church auditorium. Within each type the subtypes that imply novel development (A III and B III) have but slightly larger average facilities for preaching than the initial subtype of their respective types, while

31 See pp. 327 and 65 f.

those that imply conservative development (B I, C I and E II) tend
to have considerably larger facilities as shown in Chart XLVI. If
widely variant types are also considered, those expressing novel
tendencies do not have larger auditoriums than the average of the

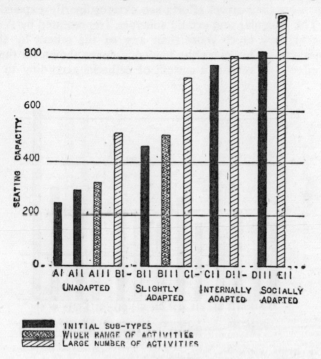

INITIAL SUB-TYPES
WIDER RANGE OF ACTIVITIES
LARGE NUMBER OF ACTIVITIES

CHART XLVI

Average Seating Capacity of Auditoriums, by Subtypes.

unadapted type, while those expressing conservative tendencies almost equal the socially adapted type in average size.

RESULTS FROM ANOTHER ANGLE

Translated, however, into terms of per capita averages and
ratios, certain phases of church life show a contrary tendency.
Measured on this basis, a smaller degree of concomitant change
accompanies increase in number of activities than accompanies increase in range. One of these aspects is illustrated in Chart XLVII,
which graphs per capita current expenses by subtypes.

Three phenomena are outstanding in this chart.

(1) The less developed of the regular types—the unadapted and

slightly adapted—include subtypes whose churches cost as much as or more per capita than those of the most highly developed types.

(2) The subtypes of which this is true are those with adventurous programs (A III and B III). In terms of cost *to the individual member* their novel efforts are extraordinarily expensive.

(3) The irregular and erratic subtypes (represented by A V and B IV) cost very much more than any of the others by the per capita measure. This gives the tendency curve shown on the chart a wavy effect. It reveals a system of setbacks according to which

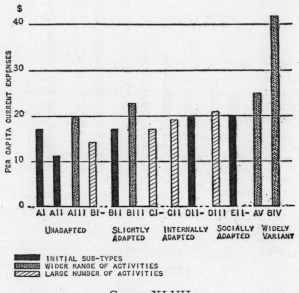

CHART XLVII

Annual Per Capita Current Expenses, by Subtypes.

the costliest subtype within a given type tends to be ahead of the least costly of the succeeding type and frequently ahead of its average. Economy lies in the performance of a larger number of functions of a usual sort while costliness is associated with attempts at novelty.

Somewhat oddly, the tendency to an increased number of more traditional activities is accompanied by a decreased ratio of Sunday-school enrollment to church membership, while change in the direction of novelty of program makes little difference in this point. This appears in Chart XLII. Within the major types, the conservative subtypes B I, C I and E II register a declining importance of the Sunday school relative to church membership, while the adventurous subtypes A III and B III differ little from the ones preceding them. For purposes of comparison two widely variant subtypes also are shown on the chart. One, composed almost exclusively of churches for foreigners (B IV), has a higher ratio of Sunday-school enrollment to church membership than any other subtype except its equally erratic neighbor, Subtype A V. This reveals the relative inaccessibility of the adult foreigner to the approach of the church compared with the familiar ease of reaching the foreign child. In Subtype C III, however (which is largely identified with the church center or Christian settlement type of institution), the Sunday school is of smaller relative importance than in the regular types. Of the regular types, it is a striking fact that the Sunday school has its smallest relative importance in connection with the highly developed social ministries of Subtype E II.

Such phenomena suggest a general trend of church evolution which has produced a definite and highly coördinated structural result. Extreme dilution of church program is evidence of lack of external resources (expressed in members and money) and is connected with other lesions and displacements requiring further studies for their systematic explanation. The probable general order of cause and consequence is this: When a church gets larger and more wealthy than the average of its type, it adds to its program along lines of conventionality and imitation with virtually no increase of the per capita cost. If it attempts expansion with no increase of size, but at greater gross cost, increased per capita cost is inevitable. This symptom would necessarily be found in all churches of a type that are trying to keep up with others in better circumstances. When, as frequently, this effort takes the form of a broadened range of program, it generally signifies, as the next chapter will demonstrate, that the church involved is suffering from adverse environmental pressure.

CONCLUSIONS BASED UPON COMPARISON

The consideration of general development as accompanying the development of church programs from simplicity to complexity, strikingly confirms the hypothesis that the series of church types reflects stages of urban adaptation. The church suggests an organism in that it exhibits an exceedingly complex and delicately balanced character and life-principle. The general trends, as statistically determined, apply not only to the 88 per cent. of the 1,044 sample churches that walk in a single pathway, but just as significantly to the few variant churches. One can almost always isolate the phenomenon that makes their behavior statistically erratic. The general agreement covers nearly all of the phenomena investigated. Since this is true, if the study had begun at some other end of the problem, and with other factors than those concerning program, it would undoubtedly have reached the same fundamental conclusions— though it is hard to see how an approach through any other aspect should have resulted in so extensive and harmonious a formulation of major clews to the life of the church in the American city.

Unmeasured Forces

Even the most consistent and pervasive trends do not cover quite the entire body of facts. The present study has never deluded itself into thinking that it was measuring nor that its major hypothesis comprehended all the forces involved in the making of the city church. Exceptions remain and these exceptions are data needing explanation. Thus, for example, a few large and practically important churches have been found within the less developed types. Their position is somewhat of a surprise and raises natural questions. To explain these and similar exceptions three supplemental principles are necessary: (1) Greater or smaller resources determine and limit the adaptations that churches can make. (2) Varying religious convictions influence the ways in which churches express urban adaptation. (3) Specialization also modifies the usual course of urban adaptation.

The first of these principles is too obvious to require elaboration, and is well illustrated by the characteristics of Subtype B III.[32] Of course the church is not merely a mechanically constructed organism in which equal resources, numerical or financial, are necessarily reflected in program, and vice versa. It is fundamentally the expression of a large number of diverse social groups called sects or denominations, each possessing a considerable degree of working harmony within itself, and each attempting to express distinctive religious convictions which are generally formulated into a more or less explicit religious philosophy. It would be strange indeed if these varying convictions did not register as modifying influences in the general process of adaptation. That they have not been more decisively present tends to show the essential homogeneity of Protestantism.

EFFECT OF VARYING RELIGIOUS CONVICTIONS

The following paragraphs attempt to show how differences in religious convictions explain such exceptions as (1) failure to

32 See p. 112.

evolve; (2) satisfaction with programs more limited than a given stage of general development seems to warrant; and equally (3) a degree of development beyond that which concomitant factors are ordinarily able to support.   (4) Finally they show how religious convictions sometimes challenge the entire trend of urban church development and compel one to face even larger and more radical considerations than those utilized in the present inquiry.

(1) The church confronted by the city may do nothing different from the tradition of its rural prototype because this wicked world is past saving and is soon to end.   This is the answer of the pre-millenarian; essentially also of other deliberately narrow churches. Religion is apart from the rest of life, and modern social tendencies, especially as expressed by the city, are essentially irreligious or evil. Such considerations enter into the lack of development of such movements as were illustrated in Cases VII and VIII.[33]

The premillenarian has the unassailable logic of his position; if it is true he is right.   The traditionalist on the contrary has no logical leg to stand on.   It is historically proven that even his present meager program of church activity once had an evolution and was the result of an attempted adaptation of the church to the needs of a bygone age and social order.   If the traditionalist would follow his own history he would again try to adapt his program to the living present.   Instead he will only preserve on ice what his fathers got cold from grandfathers who wrought it in hot blood.

(2) The second course open is to let some other agency than the church do anything new that needs to be done.

This is essentially the choice of the typical church.   It supports the Young Men's Christian Association and the Young Women's Christian Association, conventional city missions and non-sectarian charities.   Often it carries on quite adventurous programs of work, through branch churches or settlements and for another grade of people.   Meanwhile its program for people of its own sort is un-original and merely average.   It does not act as though its con-stituents were city people with modern urban characteristics; and probably the controlling group is not composed of such people. They are most likely people whose habits were fixed before the city became as complex as it is now.   If prosperous they have intrenched themselves in outlying or suburban single-family dwell-ings where they live in the past.   Their children went away from home so long ago that they do not realize how changed are the conditions of bringing up a family in the city.   If poor and beyond middle age they may have little homes out of the main currents of life, perhaps in one of the less changed sections of the older city;

33 See pp. 135 and 137.

or else they have so recently come to the city that they do not understand its characteristics.

All these conditions make it possible for conventional churches to continue in large numbers even when not hopelessly chained by ironbound traditions and in spite of the immense pressure of the city in new directions. The most frequent type has very little true urban adaptation, as shown, for example, in Case I.[34]

From a totally different standpoint, a small minority of churches, controlled by people radically critical of fundamental aspects of the existing social order, are for letting some one else than the organized church meet the new needs of the city. They are anything but drifters. Their program, if anything, is too precise. They would have the public carry on most of the new functions proposed for the church. Public school and recreational centers would furnish the plant and highly organized neighborhood activities would contrive programs of helpful and uplifting life suited to the downtown city. Neighborhood organization would associate people without regard to creed or race.

The theory of such a church is that to project the personalities of its members into public and non-sectarian idealistic activities is better than to attempt to organize them primarily through the activities of the church as an institution. The theory works sometimes, at least to the extent of a very wide enlistment of members in civic and social responsibilities in which such a church may go far beyond that of any other in the city.

Such a result, it is felt, is more truly Christian than anything that can be accomplished through the denominational church and under the professed Christian label. The church remains as the inspirer and interpreter of life. It should adapt itself by understanding and sympathizing with life on all sides rather than by elaborating its service-program. It must subordinate itself institutionally and literally lose itself in the larger collective activities of the community.

By thus limiting the development of church programs, this position in practice comes to much the same ground as that of the slightly adapted church. It would not carry the church as such any farther. Positively, however, it would go much farther than any church program yet projected through socialized public and voluntary activities under Christian ideals and the Christian impulse.

(3) A third option is implicit in the position of the internally adapted church.

It feels the distinctive life and atmosphere of the city and desires to serve it. It does not see why the church should not go ahead

34 See p. 115.

and supply any activity that may be necessary to meet the demand of additional age-, and sex-organizations or why it should not directly do what Christian activity and finance have long done through the Young Men's Christian Association, etc. It is entirely opportunistic as to the limits of its program and, in general, quite satisfied when it has added a few additional recreational and educational features under specialized leadership, so as to give a fairly rounded outline to the older traditional elements.

In general, however, the church does not attempt to elaborate its program except under favorable conditions, the chief of which is homogeneity of constituency. This was strikingly true of Case XX.[35] Its following must be, on the whole, of the same social level. As will later be seen, a church generally achieves this condition either by moving away from mixed neighborhoods or by bringing its own people from long distances, neglecting the immediate neighborhood if its inhabitants are radically different from the church's own clientele. The church thus dodges the deeper issue of adaptation, namely, how all sorts and conditions of men can be thrown together and still live as Christian brethren.

(4) Exceptional internally adapted churches, as illustrated by Case XIX, and the socially adapted type generally meet this issue squarely. The special genius of the latter is, first, inclusion, and, second, localization. It tries to get down to the level of the lowest man and to assist all who are physical neighbors to achieve a fraternity in the bonds of Christian fellowship. It undoubtedly shows the completest phase of urban adaptation. In this type, the church has begun, at least, not only to be adapted to the city as a whole but to all aspects of the city as they are localized, including all the varieties of its people and their manifold social needs.

The novelty of the programs of socially adapted churches, rather than their number, has given the type so large a place in the imagination. As a matter of fact, the socially adapted churches make up less than one-tenth of the sample of 1,044 churches and probably a considerably smaller fraction of all city churches. This proportion is large enough to show that the church is conscious of the city's challenge to it to undertake radical experiments in the direction of adaptation. At the same time the relative infrequency of such experiments emphasizes the caution and perhaps the wisdom of the city church, which are obviously based in large measure on religious conservatism. The church's instinct may be right. Is it really within the power of any sectarian version of life to solve the more serious social problems of city communities? The answer supplied by common practice is that the church shall not attempt social service

35 See p. 169.

of a general kind. And that answer, based perhaps upon the church's knowledge of its own limitations, may be wise, provided, however, that Christian initiative and leadership must not rest until they have found and used interdenominational and civic organizations better suited to the task.

A FURTHER QUESTION

Increasing complexity is the genius of institutionalism. No other major tendency appears more likely to lead to larger service and the final Christian conquest of the city. Yet it is by no means sure that the greatest power of Christianity is ever to be expressed through ecclesiastical development. The church is the discoverer and inspirer of motives, a mighty creator of group-ideals of men and a leader of human capacity for fellowship. Its ultimate values, of course, go beyond any possibility that is measured or even prophesied by the mere study of the city church in its present functions and tendencies. Perhaps the main contribution of this investigation is therefore properly negative—a demonstration of how few churches on the whole have really adjusted themselves to the more radical needs of the city and at least a query as to the bearing of religious conservatism upon the fact. Can the church as a denominational organization and with its present average outlook hope to do better?

The Influence of Specialization

Unusual success in some one aspect of church life or unquestionable failure frequently leads to further deliberate limitations within any given type of program. The first experience magnifies some particular part of the possible program and inhibits the will to evolve further, tempting the church to specialize on some one thing that it can do easily and well. The other proves that some lines of effort are impossible and leaves the church doing at least passably what it is still able to do in spite of many aspects of failure. Churches that yield to specialization from either of these causes often stand out as exceptions to the general tendencies of the types to which they belong. They occur often enough to compel one to recognize the principle of specialization as operating somewhat independently of the main trend of ecclesiastical development.

The most frequent form of specialization in conservative directions is found to be specialized emphasis upon preaching. This is in line with the oldest traditions of the church and is frequently the direction of greatest advantage. Where, by specializing on pulpit ministries, the church affords a platform from which a prophet may speak or on which a great popular expositor of life may exercise distinguished gifts, it may well afford to minimize the rest of its program. No other function can match that of giving splendid utterance to a life-giving word. A considerable number of churches, therefore, will be found in the unadapted groups whose pulpits are filled by influential men, but whose programs are extremely limited measured by general practice.

Case XXIX—Subtype C I

A church that is nationally known on account of the distinction of one of its members falls in the slightly adapted class. In this case it is quite obviously the principle of specialization that has halted further development. Some of the things that fall without the range of the ordinary church, this church can do easily and naturally under its peculiar circumstances, and these things it has chosen to do superlatively. It is, in brief, not only a church but a public platform.

Centrally located downtown on a site occupied since 1866 and adjoining the present heart of the shopping district, with over 1,500 members, its Sunday school numbers less than 200 and has an average attendance of about 125. Its children's departments are amazingly weak, reporting enrollment in a recent year as follows.

Department	Pupils
Primary	33
Junior	24
Intermediate	33

On the other hand, public worship draws vast congregations, the sign "Standing room only" being usual on Sunday mornings. A large proportion of those at the morning service and the great majority attending the evening service are strangers, many of them visitors to the city. At the monthly evening communion service, however, during a recent year, it was noted that most of this unknown audience joined in the sacrament. This showed that those who came were in the main publicly confessed Christians, using the church as a place to enjoy services, but bound to it by no other tie and accepting no responsibility.

In addition to being a great public platform on Sundays, the church conducts "preaching missions," lasting a week at a time and held at intervals throughout the winter, at which are heard some of the great religious leaders of the country. Nearly $5,000 a year is expended on this feature alone.

Finally, the church gathers great Sunday afternoon audiences for organ recitals, for which the foremost organists of the country play upon one of the most notable instruments possessed by any church.

In each of these functions the church ministers to listeners; and this is by far the greatest part of all that it does. Obviously, if it did nothing else, it would be performing a great religious ministry.

It does, as a matter of fact, also carry on the more ordinary work of a city-wide parish. About one-third of the members live within one mile of the church, another third within the second mile, and the remainder farther out in the direction of the city's main growth. Further than this, there are the ordinary organizations of a slightly adapted church for women and young people. An assistant pastor is employed, and a church office is open part of each day. The church takes a worthy, though not a conspicuous, part in denominational enterprises, but it is singularly lacking in breadth of enterprise. In the large it specializes in conventional ministries which it can do best, showing no notable originality of program.

This specialization appears definitely in the finances of the church. It largely supports itself, for example, out of its floating congregations, taking in as much money from loose collections as it does from all stated contributions and pew rents. Furthermore, income from these sources is increasing faster than that from any other source. This is the direction in which the church is striving. In order to secure this income it spends more than $5,000 annually on publicity and printing, over three-fifths of which amount goes outright to newspaper advertising.

Somewhat similar in its exceptional character is a church in the downtown part of a far western city which is locally said to have "more attendance than all other Protestant churches in the city put together." Despite this fact, its program, from the standpoint of the ordinary church, is very undeveloped. The pastor cheerfully admits that his whole policy is sensational. He advertises extensively and handles the attractive features of his service exactly as if it were high-class vaudeville. The so-called sermons are rather bits of contemporary journalism than of ordinary preaching. The church, in other words, is primarily the reflection of a unique personality who understands urban psychology and how to cater to transient people. His theory is that when folks go to church at night they wish to fill the entire evening exactly as they would at an entertainment. Consequently his services are two hours long, whereas in an ordinary church people complain if the service exceeds one hour. As a result of this policy the preacher "plays to standing room only" on both Sunday and Wednesday nights. It is, of course, impossible to identify such a performance with any standard type of church.

The existence of such churches as the two described under Case XXIX modifies, but does not nullify, the principle that urban adaptation is generally reflected in development of program. There are exceptions but they do not disprove the rule.

SPECIALIZATION ON THE SUNDAY SCHOOL

The biggest thing about some churches is the Sunday school. This may be either the old-fashioned mass school strongly promoted and ably administered but innocent of modern educational ideals, or less frequently, an elaborate course of instruction not, however, carrying over into varying week-day activities. A few churches may and do specialize thus on religious education as the type of service that constitutes for them the greatest and most useful contribution to the community.

OTHER SPECIALIZATIONS

Still other churches specialize on philanthropy. Their programs are conservative and their preaching and religious education undistinguished; but they are great missionary enterprises to the exclusion of normal development. Still others specialize on the maintenance of tradition. They are historic churches whose basic motive is to keep up with the past instead of with the present. They, too, fail to respond normally to urban adaptation.

One is tempted to say that still other churches specialize merely on self-complacency. Usually they are wholly without other distinction. They are so well pleased with themselves that they do not evolve normally. Their dominant purpose is to be "leading churches."

In comparison with the forms of conservative specialization, certain other churches specialize on practical phases of social service to an extent which takes them out of the general trend of adaptation. Plentiful examples of this tendency have been found in the chapter on "Widely Variant Types."

Equal strength and resources being assumed, it is believed that the three supplemental principles above described, namely, strength and resources, distinctive religious convictions and specialization, account for practically all exceptions to the rule that the city church types follow successive stages of urban adaptation and that substantially all significant aspects of church life increase quantitatively in harmony with development of program.

Tentative Conclusions

Of course, strictly speaking, none of the data of the present study bears upon the question whether the city church is evolving in the right direction. Since the data were not gathered over a period of time, the conception of evolution itself had to be derived from very general historical knowledge and comparison with the rural church. There is, however, virtually unchallenged agreement among religious observers that more and more city churches are undertaking more functions. This is in the face of all the restraints of ecclesiastical conviction, and in spite of all the not infrequent advantages of specialization and of the several courses open to radicalism for affecting religious adaptation to the city in other ways than through the evolution of the church as an institution.

Evolution that has taken place against such forces must have some strong inner sanction; and it will not be an extreme assumption to hold that probably, on the whole, the city church is moving in the right direction. When, however, the question is raised, "How far should the movement go?", or "Under what circumstances should the individual church yield to it?", the facts as described can do no more than suggest caution in answering. One may feel quite certain that a larger number of city churches are likely to try the experiment of elaborating their programs in attempted urban adaptation and at the same time quite unsure as to what the final evolution of the urban church will or should be, further than to suspect that it will include more variations than in the past.

Chapter XII

LOCAL ENVIRONMENT AND THE CHURCH TYPES

This chapter begins the second logical division of Part II. In the six preceding chapters the major church types have been described and directly compared in terms of factors internal to the individual church. But individual churches have also many external relationships. The results as exhibited may have been accepted by the reader as an interesting and accurate account of facts reflecting programs and organization, but not therefore as working categories for thought or action upon general church problems in the American city. The following chapters enlarge the point of view and give the data a broader setting. They test the classification of churches by five major types from various external standpoints, showing its value as supplementing other angles of approach to the urban church problem, and its probable superiority as a basic classification.

The first of these other angles of approach is that of local or neighborhood environment.[1]

It raises the question of how the classification of churches by types on grounds which have so far ignored particular environment fits in with previous efforts to classify directly by means of local environment.

Adaptation and Local Environment

Does the adaptation of the church to the city (as progressively illustrated in the series of types) mean, in the case of each church, adaptation to some particular geographical area of the city as its local environment? Obviously the city is not all of one social texture. The character of population and the social conditions surrounding one church location will differ greatly from those surrounding another. Will a church generally reflect these differences so that it can be characterized in terms of the local environment?

[1] The adequacy of the environmental data requires special consideration. These data were secured for 313 churches only. Not only, therefore, is the basic material more limited than the main data, but there was no means of judging whether the churches studied constituted a fully balanced sample. The entirely random selection of cases renders it extremely probable, however, that they suggest something of the actual distribution of churches among the environments recognized. But the study makes no pretense of proving, for example, how many city churches are "downtown" and how many residential, or of finally settling any environmental principle. The most it attempts to do is to define certain important problems, as the basis of trends shown by its limited number of cases, and to make a beginning in the methodology of the study of the parish environment.

POPULAR VOGUE OF ENVIRONMENTAL CLASSIFICATION
OF CHURCHES

It is widely assumed that such is the case. A popular way of putting the matter is as follows: Starting with the center of a typical American city, one finds the downtown church. Working out from this center, one comes upon an ugly belt of territory characterized by less desirable habitations, especially boarding-, and rooming-houses, and frequently representing an old residential neighborhood that has seen better days. Here, crowded upon by industry and second-rate business, one finds the "near-downtown" church. Passing this zone by way of the avenues, one comes upon the high-class residential districts with their family churches. Off the side streets, one glimpses the working-class churches. Down in the hollow by the railroad tracks are the foreign and Negro churches. Just beyond the edge of the city are the suburban churches, and still farther out the rural churches.

This principle of classification governed the various lists of church types furnished by denominational executives as a basis for this study in the first steps of its development. Its most brilliant expression has been made by Dr. William P. Shriver.[2] He distinguishes ten urban types of Protestant churches resulting from city evolution, which, he says, "tend largely to reflect the economic neighborhoods to which they minister."

Following this implied logic, the current popular classification of city churches is environmental. That is to say, the explanation of the *why* of the church is sought by discovering its *where*.[3]

ACTUAL INFLUENCE OF LOCAL ENVIRONMENT

The degree to which particular immediate environments are actually associated with particular types of city churches is shown for 313 cases in Table LV in terms of the most familiar environmental contrast between "central" and "residential" sections of cities.[4]

---

2 *Interchurch World Survey, American Volume,* p. 31.

3 In Chapter VI of *The St. Louis Church Survey* dealing with the kinds of churches found in that city, the present author attempted by analysis to show that a greater variety of factors than are usually recognized, including historic and psychological ones, would have to enter into a proper classification of city church types. The present statistical classification had not at that time been devised.

4 Centrally located churches are defined as (1) those located within the central business district of a city; or (2) located within the wholesale and manufacturing zone immediately surrounding the central business district; or (3) located at a secondary business center serving 100,000 people or more. The churches around Harvard Square in Cambridge are clearly central, even though Cambridge is a satellite of Boston. But so are the churches at the heart of the Wilson Avenue district of Chicago, which has a larger tributary population than Cambridge, though this district is within the city limits. The distribution of 145 churches among these three types of centers appears in Appendix Table 38a.

TABLE LV—TYPES OF CHURCHES LOCATED ACCORDING
TO ENVIRONMENT *

	Environment	
	Per Cent.	Per Cent.
Types of Churches	*Central*	*Residential*
Unadapted	28.1	71.9
Slightly adapted	43.5	56.5
Internally adapted	52.4	47.6
Socially adapted	49.3	50.7

* See Appendix Table 36 for number of churches reporting under each type.

This table shows in general that the more complex types show slightly greater affinity for central location and, indeed, as the detailed statistics indicate,[5] for location at the heart of the downtown center. Yet the extremest case of reaction from the downtown center shown by the unadapted type still leaves more than one-fourth of the churches of the sample in this non-characteristic en-

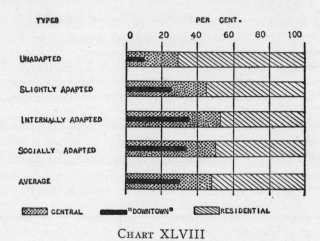

CHART XLVIII

Per Cent. of Central and Residential Churches in Each Type.

vironment, while, as between the two environments, the tendency is almost half and half with the internally adapted and socially adapted churches.

INFLUENCE OF SOCIAL QUALITY OF NEIGHBORHOODS UPON
CHURCHES

Table LVI shows for 167 cases the affinity between different church types and the quality of neighborhood in which the resi-

5 Appendix Tables 37 and 38a.

dential portion of their churches are located.[6] It describes immediate environment in the somewhat loose, yet significant, categories "high-class" neighborhood, "middle-class" neighborhood and "industrial or foreign" neighborhood, as determined by first-hand exploration of individual parishes. The unadapted and socially adapted types show a slightly greater affinity and the internally adapted a slightly smaller affinity for middle-class neighborhoods. In turn, the internally adapted churches are most frequent in high-class

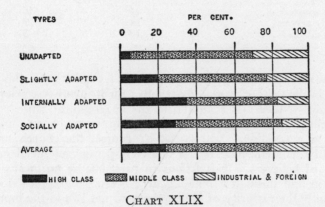

CHART XLIX

Quality of Environment of Residential Churches, by Types.

neighborhoods and the unadapted in industrial and foreign ones. All types, however, are found in fair proportion in all environments (with the exception that the unadapted type is rare in high-class neighborhoods) and none could be fairly characterized as belonging especially to one neighborhood rather than to another.[7]

Light from Parish Geography

In some minds the lack of close correspondence between the types and local environment will not serve to commend the five major types for use as a working classification of city churches. It at least constitutes a legitimate challenge to the major hypothesis of the study: namely, that the types as discovered show different de-

6 Of course many churches in residential neighborhoods are visibly attached to such tertiary centers as a group of neighborhood stores, a bank, branch post office and moving-picture house; or to still smaller clusters of business and other institutions or to axial streets lined with retail business establishments. Naturally such points or lines of differentiation accompany the growth of cities. Residential districts expect to have them, and frequently locate churches with reference to them. This does not challenge the essentially residential character of the areas in question. Appendix Table 39 reports sixty-one out of 170 residential churches as tributary to such groupings of neighborhood institutions.

7 Appendix Table 39a.

grees of the church's adaptation to the city. If the hypothesis does not mean adaptation to local environment, then what sort of urban adaptation does it mean?

TABLE LVI — CHURCHES IN RESIDENTIAL NEIGHBORHOODS LOCATED ACCORDING TO QUALITY OF NEIGHBORHOOD

| Types | Quality of Neighborhood | | | |
	High-class	Middle-class	Industrial or Foreign	Total
Unadapted	1	15	7	23
Slightly adapted	14	40	16	70
Internally adapted	14	19	7	40
Socially adapted	10	19	5	34
	39	93	35	167

It would be making a false start to try to answer this query except in the light of parish geography; for it involves a prior question, namely, *where* is a church in the geographical sense?

A church is surely not a building, nor even the activities that go on in a building. Ultimately, of course, the church must be defined by its members. It is a relatively permanent social group— a body of believers. It functions in part, but by no means exclusively, in and through a building at a given geographical location. Frequently the majority of its members do not live in the immediate vicinity. Furthermore, its pastoral ministries, as well as certain organized group meetings, are scattered over the parish. The "Old First" Church of Springfield, Mass., for example, divides its people into twenty districts, each maintaining social and religious gatherings of its own. The practice of religion by the people, which has its distinctive expression through Christian service, must surely be regarded as diffused wherever the people work or live. It will not do, therefore, to assume to express the environmental relations of any church merely by the location of its plant, nor even to settle the question of its local adaptation without asking, first, how far the homes of its members actually occupy a concentrated geographical area around it; and secondly, how it is related or adapted to the actual area in which most of them live. There is a third obvious question: namely, how completely the parish area is occupied by the members; in other words, the degree to which the influence of the church actually fills any geographic district which it may purport to serve.

DISTANCE OF MEMBERS' RESIDENCES FROM CHURCH BUILDING

Distribution of parish membership was studied accurately and measured as to distance for 222 churches and as to direction for

154. To express the results the following designations of types of parish were adopted based on the percentage of members living within one mile:

Geographical Type of Parish	Per Cent. of Members Living Within One Mile
Compact	75 and over
Medium	50–74
Scattered	25–49
Very scattered	Less than 25

The distribution of the churches of the several types among the types of parishes as thus defined was found to be as given in Table LVII.[8]

TABLE LVII — TYPES OF CHURCHES BY TYPES OF GEOGRAPHICAL PARISHES *

Types	Per. Cent Distribution of Parishes				
	Compact	Medium	Scattered	Very Scattered	Total
Unadapted	34.6	38.5	23.1	3.8	100.0
Slightly adapted	55.2	25.4	17.9	1.5	100.0
Internally adapted ...	43.5	27.4	19.4	9.7	100.0
Socially adapted	35.9	41.0	15.4	7.7	100.0
Widely variant	50.0	32.2	7.1	10.7	100.0
Total	45.5	31.1	17.1	6.3	100.0

* See Appendix Table 40 for number of churches reporting under each type.

Forty-five per cent. of all churches have "compact" parishes, that is to say, parishes in which more than 75 per cent. of the members live within a mile of the church building. The rest are dispersed

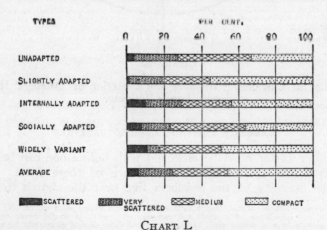

CHART L

Per Cent. Distribution of Parishes According to Distance in Each Type.

8 Appendix Tables 40–42.

as shown in Table LVII.[9] The ranking of the major types with respect to the proportion of compact parishes is (1) slightly adapted, (2) internally adapted, (3) socially adapted, and (4) unadapted.

Centrally located churches naturally have far fewer compact parishes than residential ones.

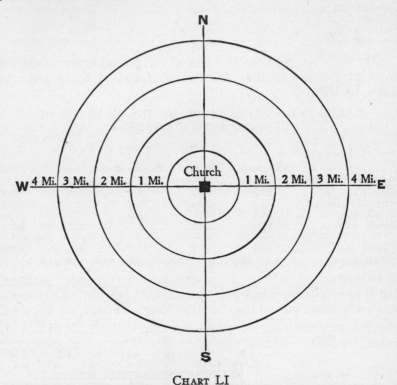

CHART LI

Diagram for Calculating Distance and Direction of Members' Homes from Church Building.

TENDENCY TOWARD LOPSIDED PARISHES

Another factor must be reckoned with before one can begin to understand the environmental significance of these facts. Even when the majority of the members live near the church they are

9 It is recognized, of course, that a mile radius from a given point might take in most of the area and population of a small and compact city, while it would cover very little of either in a large and roomy city. Of course, too, there should ultimately be a sliding scale for measuring dispersion of members in various sizes of cities. Since, however, the sample of churches whose parishes were studied is well distributed among cities of various sizes and in all parts of such cities, it is assumed that the arbitrary definition chosen will serve sufficiently to differentiate the tendencies of the types.

rarely distributed evenly. They rather tend to scatter out in sectors in one or two directions.

In order to compare churches on this point, the following scheme for expressing the differences in the directional distribution of members was devised. The parish maps of 154 churches were copied and the per cent. of members living in the four sectors corresponding to the directions North, South, East and West, was calculated by means of a figure shown on Chart LI. The cases were then thrown

TABLE LVIII — RANGE OF DIRECTIONAL DISTRIBUTION OF CHURCH MEMBERS USED IN DEFINING TYPES OF PARISHES

Type of Parish	A Per Cent. of Members Living Within One-Quarter of the Parish Area		B Per Cent. of Members Living Within One-Half of the Parish Area	
	Least Populous	Most Populous	Least Populous	Most Populous
Balanced	17 or more	34 or less	40 or more	60 or less
Unbalanced	10–16	35–42	26–39	61–74
Very unbalanced.	9 or less	43 or more	25 or less	75 or more

into three groups of approximately equal size, consisting of (1) those with the most nearly equal distribution on all sides of the church building, (2) those with the least equal distribution, and (3) those

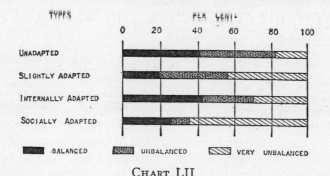

CHART LII

Per Cent. Distribution of Parishes According to Direction in Four Major Types.

falling between. The range of variation between the least fully occupied quadrant and the most fully occupied was calculated for each group, with results shown in Table LVIII.

It will be observed that a "balanced" parish has been interpreted generously as permitting a population running from as low as one-sixth to as high as one-third of its members to live in a single quadrant—this being the range of variation exhibited by the most symmetrical third of the parishes studied. On this basis the two-thirds which are still more one-sided must be called "unbalanced" or "very unbalanced." The second part of the Table (Section B) was arrived at by adding the per cent. of members living in the next least populous and next most populous quadrants to that already calculated for a single quadrant in Section A. The result thus shows the degree of balance or unbalance in a parish distribution of members in terms of two quadrants—not necessarily adjacent—covering half the area of a circle including the total parish. In the very unbalanced parish, for example, 75 per cent. or more of a church's constituents will be found in half of the area surrounding it and not more than 25 per cent. in the other half. The distribution of the types of churches as represented by the sample according to types of parishes as thus defined in terms of direction, is shown in Table LIX.[10]

TABLE LIX — TYPES OF CHURCHES DISTRIBUTED ACCORDING TO "DIRECTIONAL" TYPES OF PARISHES *

A — *As Defined by the Per Cent. of Members Living in the Least Populous and Most Populous Quarters of the Parish Area*

Type of Parish	Unadapted	Per Cent. Distribution			All Types
		Slightly Adapted	*Internally Adapted*	*Socially Adapted*	
Balanced	40.9	19.6	42.9	25.0	33.1
Unbalanced	40.9	36.9	26.5	10.0	31.8
Very unbalanced ..	18.2	43.5	30.6	65.0	35.1

B — *As Defined by the Per Cent. of Members Living in the Least Populous and Most Populous Halves of the Parish Area*

Balanced	45.5	23.9	46.9	20.0	37.0
Unbalanced	40.9	41.3	22.5	30.0	33.1
Very unbalanced ..	13.6	34.8	30.6	50.0	29.9

* See Appendix Tables 43 and 44 for number of churches reporting under each type.

It is of still further significance that in about one-seventh of the cases studied the largest number of members were located in opposite quadrants. Thus the parish took an hour-glass shape. This sometimes reveals physical barriers, but generally a definite avoidance of parts of contiguous areas as undesirable or untenable for church work, and the habitual seeking of members in opposite directions. Thus a great Minneapolis church, located at the edge of the business section, reaches inward to the people of the large apart-

10 For a more intensive study of lopsided parishes using a similar method for a single city, see the author's *St. Louis Church Survey*, p. 242.

ment hotels and outward to the polite residential section, but keeps clear of the Swedes on one side and the Jews on the other. It has practically no dealings with people in two of the four directions from the church as center.

In brief, even when the membership of a church occupies a contiguous area it rarely occupies it evenly. The Protestant genius is to pick and choose a church's field minutely and to direct all its developments according to the instincts of affinity and repulsion. It operates selectively rather than geographically. Even when it reflects a local environment it rarely reflects it exactly or totally.

SUMMARY

The combined influence of environmental and geographical factors operates as among the various types somewhat as follows:

The unadapted churches have the slightest tendency toward localized membership, though this tendency is somewhat more frequent in the residential churches of the type than in the centrally located ones. Their constituencies are often remote, but rather tend to come from all directions.

The slightly adapted churches are most frequently residential and show considerable tendency toward compact parishes. They are, however, most lopsided of all in the distribution of their parishes.

The internally adapted churches are about evenly divided between residential and central location and have the highest proportion of scattered and very scattered parishes. They have, however, a higher rate of normally balanced parishes drawing constituents from all directions as well as from long distances.

The socially adapted type, whether central or residential, has the smallest portion of compact parishes. This seems strange in view of the peculiar genius of the type, which ordinarily identifies itself with some particular neighborhood or class of people.

But the genuinely environmental character of this type is revealed by the study of the directional distribution of its members. Sixty-five per cent. of all socially adapted churches have very unbalanced parishes. That is to say, that 75 per cent. or more of the people live in one direction from the church building. The explanation of this phenomenon is scarcely open to question. Such churches are frequently old downtown enterprises largely abandoned by their former constituents. The poor population, foreign, Negro or rural, is apt to locate in a solid colony occupying a sector abutting on the old downtown business section. This explains the original lopsidedness of the parish. Later, as the foreign elements move farther into the city, they follow definite paths of dispersion away from their original seats. The socially adapted church identifies itself with their fortunes and thus reflects in its exaggerated degree the one-sided parish development.

RANK BY TYPES, BY DISTANCE AND DIRECTION

If the major types be compared as to distribution of members by distance and direction, as shown in the two preceding paragraphs, the following differences appear:

Types	Rank in Average Degree of Compactness	Rank in Average Degree of Balance
Slightly adapted	1	4
Internally adapted	2	1
Unadapted	3	2
Socially adapted	4	3

It will be observed that the divergence of the two tendencies is greatest in the case of the slightly adapted type, which ranks first in compactness but last in balance.

DEGREE OF OCCUPANCY

Even after the area covered by the distribution of church membership has been carefully defined, the question of completeness of occupancy of any given area still remains. This question takes two forms; the one absolute, the second comparative. In other words, one must consider how large the church membership and constituency is relative to population, or at least to population available to Protestant influence; one must also consider how large it is relative to other and possibly rival churches.

There was no statistical investigation on this point, but the issue is worth while formulating in the light of geographic data for the parish. Of course the membership must bear some significant ratio to the population in order to constitute the church a local force. It is useless to call upon a church of only two or three hundred members to "adapt itself" to a city neighborhood of 50,000 people, even if all the members living within the area should agree to do so. There are too few compared with the total population to be able to do so in any important sense.

On this point Prof. W. L. Bailey writes of Chicago:

"But within a given area and among any given portion of the city's people the number of homes or individuals related to the church was insignificant, and still so relatively if all the Protestant churches well within it were taken into account. For the Protestant churches tend strongly to appear in clusters at certain points and thus to have their parishes a great deal in common. The number of people in the above artificial area of say 3-4 sq. miles would be about 75,000 in the average district in Chicago. The average Protestant church membership in Chicago is about 500, and in very few cases above 1,000. With a very liberal provision of denominational plants in the area, the number of persons attached to the churches by even so loose and non-vital a tie as formal membership is very small. The district is not really a parish but might rather be called in a sense a 'sphere of interest.' "

Churches studied in certain cities intensively surveyed throw light upon the problem of comparative occupancy. Thus the membership of the First Congregational and Trinity Methodist Episcopal churches in Springfield, Mass. (a city of 130,000), covers the entire city. The former, located in the heart of the city, has the third largest membership in the South-side residential district in which there are seven local churches. In all, in six out of the eleven districts of the city, its membership constitutes one of the major religious groups resident within the district. It is thus far more localized, as well as more centralized, than many of the smaller churches. A big church, in other words, may fill up the entire area of a moderate-sized city fuller than the small church can fill even its contiguous neighborhood.

DISTRIBUTION OF MEMBERS OF SUBSIDIARY ORGANIZATIONS

Again, the various functional services performed by subsidiary organizations within the church may show a distribution of constituents different from that of the church membership, thereby complicating the problem of adaptation. Thus, the Kingshighway Christian Church in St. Louis has a parish greatly distorted in a southeasterly direction. The Sunday-school distribution is more evenly balanced than that of the church membership, reflecting the well-known fact that children are easily gathered from the neighborhood and from homes not connected with the church. Curiously, while the Young People's Society shows the most exaggerated one-sidedness compared with church membership, the membership of the Ladies' Aid Society is distributed most symmetrically, while that of the Boy Scouts again is strongest in a different direction.

In 1919 the First Baptist Church of Rochester, N. Y., had the largest group of its members (40 per cent.) to the southeast of its site, from which direction it drew seven out of eleven deacons, eight out of twelve trustees and 74 per cent. of its financial support; but 48 per cent. of the girls and boys of its Sunday school came from a single sector to the southwest! In other words, different aspects of the work of a church appeal to different constituencies which may occupy very different sectors of the parish field.

A new conception of the meaning of adaptation to locality is thus demanded. To be adequate, adaptation must be carried throughout the work of the church and must particularly apply to subsidiary organizations, since it is their total activity that makes up the church's program. In other words, the whole matter is more complicated than ordinarily imagined and needs further study.

Summarizing the environmental findings, one concludes that all types of churches exist in all environments. There are some environmental affinities—some slight, others fairly significant—but not such as to govern the main categories of classification. Environmental influence, however, helps greatly to explain the differences between the statistical subtypes and to connect them with the practical variations found between churches with similar programs.

EXPLAINING THE INFLUENCE OF LOCAL ENVIRONMENT

The facts being determined, it is next necessary to ask three questions: (1) why the types do not more completely reflect immediate environment; (2) why each type has the slight environmental trend previously discovered; and (3) how the inadequacy of immediate environment to explain the types harmonizes with the fact that total urban environment is the dominant principle explaining adaptation in general.

Why Types Do Not Reflect Immediate Environment

It is popularly assumed not only that urban adaptation has gone forward a good deal faster than is actually the case, but that it must have become thoroughly localized. At least the implication is that it ought to be localized; that a church should be fitted to the needs of its particular and immediate neighborhood. The logic of the thought seems to be: if the church should be adapted to the city, why not also to its parts? If it is to change when it becomes urban, why ought it not to change to match each inner variation of the urban community?

The answer is to be found in the complex structure of the modern city, in consequence of which geographic position does not necessarily imply local relationship. The corner grocery or drugstore, for example, may appeal for local trade on the plea of neighborliness, but often it is but one of a chain of similar stores, with capital, control and even immediate management located far from the spot where the store is said to "be." When it comes to the central institutions of the city one may find almost no relationship to immediate environment. The site of a great railroad station is usually determined, not by the needs of the people who live nearest to it, but with reference to the convenience and patronage of those who live at a distance. Similarly a great department store does not often depend for its trade upon the people who live near to it. In general, the larger the city, the less desirable are the residential areas lying immediately around the main center. Moreover, population is being progressively crowded out of these areas by the expansion of business and industry. Yet the focal points of such cities become increasingly important and valuable exactly in proportion as near-by population dwindles. In other words, their location has reference to the entire population, and scarcely any relation to the immediate surrounding one.[11]

ACCESSIBILITY VS. PROXIMITY

One may regard the modern city, then, as an attempt to combat the overcrowding of the center by facilities of rapid transit. Their use tends to equalize distant and near-by populations in the matter of accessibility to the most necessary central institutions. Thus, as has already been shown, the chief users of a utility are frequently able to live far from it. Such a triumph of accessibility over proximity generally removes the more prosperous elements of a city community to the remoter and less crowded sections, and thus creates the outlying wards and residential suburbs. Here the commuting population begins afresh to build social relationships based upon proximity, expressed in the neighborhood schools, churches and clubs. But even here the centralizing tendency does not leave them alone. In a generalized description of "The Growth of the City" Prof. Ernest W. Burgess cites Chicago as a case in point:

> The relation of centralization to the other processes of city life may be roughly gauged by the fact that over half a million people daily enter and leave Chicago's "loop." More recently sub-business centers have grown up in outlying zones. These "satellite loops" do not, it seems, represent the "hoped-for" revival of the neighborhood, but rather a telescoping of several local communities into a larger economic unity. The Chicago of yesterday, an agglomeration of country towns and foreign colonies, is undergoing a process of reorganization into a centralized decentralized system of local communities coalescing into sub-business areas visibly or invisibly dominated by the central business district.[12]

Within these "centralized decentralized" areas people come relatively long distances to accessible institutions located at focal points. Prof. W. L. Bailey found most of the Chicago churches with widely

---

[11] The fact that in certain cities there is a partial return of population to the center as a place of living does not contradict this general principle.
[12] *Publications of the American Sociological Society*, Vol. XVIII, p. 89.

scattered parishes thus located. Transit facilities are the clew to the situation. Centers and subcenters dominate the entire metropolitan area and fix the structure. Relatively little of vital functions or relations is left on a purely neighborhood basis, at least for adult populations, and what seems to be left is much less simple and localized than it appears.

In other words the attempt to classify city churches generally on the basis of their immediate environments proceeds from what is really the holdover of a rural idea. It takes a criterion applicable to a simple society and tries to apply it to a complex urban situation.

Environmental Trends of the Major Types

The above discussion has demonstrated the faultiness of an environmental classification of churches. Nevertheless, as previously indicated, each of the five major types may be said to have a slight environmental trend. What these trends are and how they are related to the facts of parish geography and of the general structure of the city will now be examined in more detail.

THE UNADAPTED CHURCH

While unadapted churches occur most frequently in the residential sections of cities, they show the smallest tendency toward localized memberships. As a group they cannot easily adapt their work to the characteristics of any given parish area because so often the homes of their members are not related to any church area.

For example, unadapted churches frequently have special racial or nationalistic constituencies or else they belong to unusual denominations or to denominations of rare occurrence in a given region. Such conditions mean that a church is not blessed with a near-by natural constituency out of which to build itself up. It must therefore hunt everywhere for the few dyed-in-the-wool adherents who naturally turn to it. People of one blood or language or of peculiar faith flock together to such churches with little reference to the location of their homes. For this reason few parishes of this type are lopsided. They draw from all quarters.

Again, a considerable fraction of unadapted churches are institutionally failures which have lapsed from their former prestige and are forced to accept a diminished type of organization. Very frequently the cause of their bad fortunes is some sudden movement of population which takes away an old constituency and brings in new neighbors with whom it is difficult to deal. It is characteristic of such churches to hang on desperately to their old members as they scatter throughout the city. They are virtually stranded churches with little vital relationship to the immediate environment in which they are found. If they have any business to continue along their historic lines, they must obviously do so by cultivating a remote population rather than a near-by one.

Still again, if an unadapted church drawing its peculiar constituency from all quarters has strength to relocate—say by reason of the sale of a downtown property—where will it go? Its financial weakness generally precludes the purchase of another expensive downtown site. Nevertheless, drawing members from all quarters, it desires to keep some of the advantages of central accessibility though escaping central costs. It is likely to seek out a location in a near-in residential section. Its major constituency may, however, continue to be scattered and its relations to its new environment may be relatively slight.

Thus we have at least a partial explanation of why the considerable tendency of the unadapted church toward location in residential sections fails to tie it in any complete sense to the fortunes of its immediate vicinity or to cause its program of work to reflect its immediate environment. The very nature of the type makes it fallacious to attempt its interpretation through such environment.

THE SLIGHTLY ADAPTED CHURCH

This type shows the next greatest tendency to location in residential districts. It also shows the largest percentage of churches with compact and medium-compact parishes both in its central and in its residential locations. Recalling the major characteristics of the type, one expects only a slight deviation from the rural prototype. Its churches have adapted themselves only a little. Probably, therefore, the residential churches of this type may to a considerable degree be interpreted by their environment. Their genius is really localized in the original sense. They tend to be parochial and, so far as the city will let them, to reflect their neighborhoods.

At the same time, it is not the total environment which is thus reflected. No type has so many unbalanced and very unbalanced parishes and so few with normal distribution of constituency. The probable reason is that so many of its churches lie in clusters adjacent to minor centers or along axial streets. The overlapping parishes of the clustered churches tend to spread out in sectors away from such focal points or limitations. They are without strength to reach over such artificial boundaries or to draw from wide fields. In the location of elementary schools or neighborhood parks, city planning authorities lay down the principle that their users must not be asked to cross a broad street devoted to heavy traffic. Similarly, as a family institution largely limited to serving the needs of women and children, the slightly adapted church tends to be confined between major streets.

These considerations harmonize the fact of the compact character of its parishes with the fact that they are, at the same time, characteristically lopsided.

The centrally located churches of this type, as judged by the field surveyors, were more strategically located than those of any other; that is to say, they appeared to be accessible to non-local attendants.[13] This tendency contrasts with that of the unadapted type which, while needing to be central in order to accommodate its scattered constituency, is generally too weak to afford a central site. The probable explanation is that the limited area of the average small city, in which the unadapted type is most frequent,[14] makes it still possible for typical "family" churches to survive at the center with little modification of program and at the same time with slight relation to the immediate vicinity. Under some such conditions a minority of the churches of the slightly adapted type maintain their very scattered parishes.

On the whole, however, the slightly adapted churches more than those of any other type, draw members from near by. This seems like a definite environmental trend; yet 44 per cent. of them are centrally located while 56 per cent. are residential. This division between the major environments makes it impossible to apply the current classification. As a type they are neither central nor residential, but sometimes one and sometimes the other.

THE INTERNALLY ADAPTED CHURCH

The internally adapted type is about equally divided between residential and central locations. Its relation to environment is as follows: It has the highest proportion of scattered and very scattered parishes, but at the same time has also the highest proportion of normally balanced parishes with respect to directional distribution of members. Thus it draws members from long distances but from all quarters.

In location the central churches of the type appear to be least strategic.[15] They show a high proportion of cases of churches with dual constituencies—one local, the other coming from a distance. It would naturally be expected that a downtown church disadvantageously located would attempt to overcome the disadvantage by holding forth the attractions of a novel and varied program. When

13 Appendix Table 38b.
14 Appendix Table 46.
15 Appendix Table 38b.

it has two constituencies to please it must almost inevitably strive for unusual variety. Such considerations help to explain the environmental characteristics of the type.

But almost one-half of the sample of internally adapted churches is not centrally located. That so high a proportion is found in residential locations is congruous with the fact that churches of this type have moved more frequently than any other except the unadapted. Churches generally move in order to escape undesirable conditions, the most frequent of which is the dwindling of a local constituency. Naturally they relocate nearer to their members. This would tend to give them both a higher proportion of residential churches and also a larger proportion of compact parishes, although the type as a whole has the smallest proportion. But residential location and compact parishes constitute no evidence that the migrating churches sought intimate environmental adaptations on their new sites. What they were seeking was strategic location in exchange for former locations which had become non-strategic.[16] But this is very different from a church's settling down to identify itself with a highly localized neighborhood. To characterize, therefore, even the residential churches of the internally adapted type in terms of immediate environment is certainly fallacious.

THE SOCIALLY ADAPTED CHURCH

While, on the face of it, this type is a confessed attempt to match a religious program to the needs of the people of its immediate environment, and while it often carries to great length its practical identification with the neighborhood fortunes, it actually shows a very small proportion of compact or medium-compact parishes and a more than average proportion of scattered and very scattered ones. In this respect there is little difference between its central and residential churches except that the former naturally have more extremely scattered memberships.

The probable explanation is that the socially adapted church is not very adequately judged by location of the homes of its members. It is often built upon the historic foundations of the "family church" which, as such, has failed. The original members are widely dispersed, though some of them continue their connections with the church in its new venture. The alien groups for whom the community work of such a church is primarily carried on are often not of Protestant stock and are not readily brought into full membership. Under these circumstances the bulk of the work may be highly localized while membership is scattered.

16 See p. 257. For an extensive study of the facts and motives of migrating churches, see the author's *St. Louis Church Survey*, pp. 61 f.

Few of such churches could man their activities or finance themselves without the leadership and support of these holdover members. With such origins, a goodly number of socially adapted churches have built up such dual constituencies, one local, the other consisting of old elements coming from a distance. The combination of these two elements enters successfully into the work of the church next illustrated.

Case XXX—Subtype D III:

Between the original central business section of a northwestern city and the extensive grounds of the state capitol was once a desirable residential district in which many central churches clustered. With the expansion of business, it has now become an area of depreciated property and handicapped human fortunes. While the cities of the Northwest lack the overwhelming foreign populations of the eastern seaboard, their poorer districts contrive to gather most motley elements. In this case they include the poorer types of Irish and Swedes, with considerable numbers of Italians, Hebrews and some Negroes, who now occupy this once aristocratic quarter.

Here stood the old Central Church of the Methodist Episcopal denomination, and here it still stands with the aid of its denominational mission board and the city's Community Chest, which share in its financial support.

The story of the transformation of this declining church of the family type into a fully adapted social ministry is a commentary upon the broad strategy of the Methodist Centenary movement. Its central achievement was that it enabled the church to minister to a definite parish neighborhood from which the supporting elements had largely moved away. The church still has a thousand members, scattered widely, but the pastor says frankly that what he wants most from the distant ones is that they help to pay the bills. The church primarily exists for and proposes to build itself up out of the people of the immediate vicinity.

A careful inventory has been taken of the sound elements of present population. First, there are young professional and business people, frequently unmarried. They are well educated and in every way promising, though their present income is small and they have to live in inexpensive surroundings. Secondly, there are stranded families of culture and good stock, many of them clinging to their depreciated property. Among them are many widows. Then there are incoming rural elements. The farmer in the Northwest has never paid carfare and he never proposes to. When, therefore, he moves to the city, he very frequently establishes himself within walking distance of the business center and puts up with poor living accommodations that come within his scale of expenditure. All these classes are promising materials for the church except from the financial standpoint.

The present service of the church is designed first of all to mold these diverse elements into a fellowship by creating a community consciousness. There is a weekly community evening, including spirited community singing, moving-pictures and a social hour. Transients coming into the neighborhood are helped to find homes through a rooming-house bureau. There are classes in industrial and craft work. The church systematically coöperates with the Juvenile Court. The Goodwill Industries and day nursery are located immediately across the street and the church is closely associated with their work. Americanization classes are maintained. Its active daily vacation Bible school in a recent period enrolled eighty Italians and ninety Jewish children. Athletics are carefully organized and the church actively participates in an interchurch athletic league. All this is in addition to the work of a well-organized traditional family church.

The staff consists of a pastor, an assistant pastor, a director of religious education and a visitor, and the operating budget approximates $12,000. This is apart from the workers and finances of the Goodwill Industries.

The church occupies a somewhat commodious but old-fashioned building of thirty-four rooms. They are, however, crude and in many respects unsuitable for its expanded program. Some of the crafts work was found in basement rooms without outside windows. Fortunately a spacious lot adjoins the building and the church lives in hope of securing a specially designed community building with further aid of denominational funds.

This is an excellent example of coöperation between a church that, in spite of its weakened condition, has residual ability and leadership of its own and socially minded forces both within and outside of the city. Together they are effectively meeting a changing urban situation by a clear-cut policy and suitably adapted program; but the scattered membership does not truly suggest the highly localized stress of the church's work.

It thus comes to pass that the type theoretically most nearly definable in terms of adaptation to immediate locality frequently turns out to have the most complex working relations with the city at large. Its characterization through local environment is significant, but fails to tell the whole truth.

Another example of the failure of local adaptation to tell the whole truth about a socially adapted church is Case XXXI. The reason in this case is that a church may enter into the problems of special groups or populations by attaching itself to the institutions of their organized life—which are themselves non-localized—in addition to dealing with them in their immediate environments.

Case XXXI—Subtype E II:

This church, occupying at present two ordinary frame dwelling houses, is located in the boarding-house and industrial neighborhood between the main retail business center of the city and the railroad yards and depots. A representative of the Methodist Episcopal board of missions who came to study it complained, "But this doesn't look like a slum district." It is not; it is, however, a district in which industrial labor congregates, the one in which the Central Labor Temple is located. The district was definitely chosen for this reason, though the work of the church is also highly localized in an area within a half-mile radius of its plant.

The church has for its historic background a Methodist mission previously operating in that district. Its present phase of work and constituency is, however, essentially new, the product of the vision and industry of the present pastor.

It is carrying on a seven-day program penetrated throughout by the religious spirit, but one in which religious services of the conventional sort are secondary as to time and interest. Besides a Sunday school and general Young People's Society, the most characteristic feature of the work is a series of group organizations, a large number of which are developed as fraternities, with special rituals. There is also a well-equipped clinic and a playground for group games on a vacant lot on which the church expects to build, as well as a second playground for small children. The church has made a strong contact with organized labor and is conducting

a "labor college" under the endorsement of the Central Labor Council.
The staff includes a pastor, assistant pastor, nurse, deaconess, and play-ground director, together with part-time workers attached to various clubs.

The present total attendance upon all activities is about 1,800 per week, 80 per cent. of whom at least are estimated to come from within half a mile of the church. The field allocated to the church as a Methodist parish by its denomination is somewhat larger than the area chosen by the church itself for intensive cultivation.

The two primary objectives of the church under its present adminis-tration are to mold the neighborhood feeling and community life under Christian impulse out of the diverse elements of the immediate vicinity, and to maintain a contact with organized labor in this, its city-wide, center. The pastor's influence is very much broader than this "Church of All Na-tions," and his ability to make influential contacts, especially in the indus-trial field, is due to his larger relationships and experience. He is much thought of as a speaker on industrial relationships throughout the state.

The enterprise is hard to characterize, because social adaptation may be very much more than geographical localization. By environment it is related to a transient residential section adjoining a central business and transportation section of a great city. On the one hand, it is doing a localized community work under strong Christian impulse in connection with a small church enterprise, but it is also seeking to exercise a city-wide influence in the industrial realm through its proximity to the central institutions of organized labor. It is a unique and inspiring piece of Christian work, which can be greatly improved technically and probably increased greatly in size when it secures a new and specially adapted plant.

SUMMARY

To summarize the environmental evidence: adaptation is to the city as a whole, as well as, and often more than, to any of its geographical divisions. There are great central metropolitan in-stitutions performing general functions; and, at the other extreme, local institutions performing neighborhood functions. There are many degrees and shades of adaptation between the two extremes. All these phases of adaptation, both the extreme and the mixed, should be expected in connection with the evolution of the city church. They afford many varieties and incomplete results. All progressive churches show adaptation, but some in one way and some in another. The clew of local environment is, therefore, not generally valid as a basis for church classification. Classification by the nature and content of program, on the contrary, has proved highly serviceable in unraveling the problems of general urban adaptation.

Chapter XIII

SPECIAL HEREDITIES AND LARGER ENVIRONMENT

At the outset of the study a sample was taken of 1,044 Protestant churches, of the recognized and well-established denominations that practically recognize one another as Protestant. This has been used as a basis for a discrimination of internal differences, by means of which a working classification by types has been reached. The sample was judged entirely adequate for this purpose. The next step involving the adequacy of the data was reached in the environmental discussions in Chapter XII. Here the data were more limited in amount and distinctly less adequate as a basis for generalization. The material was, however, used for what it was worth for determining trends, and yielded an intelligible version of the environmental relationships of city churches.

ADEQUACY OF THE DATA FOR FURTHER USE

The next step involving the adequacy of the data is now reached. There are four other pertinent approaches to the problem of the city church on which the study secured somewhat extensive information and which have already been included in the studies of the several types. With reference to these the utility of the classification by types may be still further checked and illustrated, provided the sample of 1,044 churches is fairly representative of the actual distribution by types of the Protestant city churches of America.

These approaches involve the attempt to determine in terms of the types (1) the racial characteristics of American city churches and (2) their denominational characteristics; also (3) their general characteristics as affected by different sizes of cities and (4) by geographical regions.

Thus in the sample of churches studied, certain types were found to contain an exceptional proportion of churches of foreign origin. Can one now turn the evidence around and say that in the United States churches of foreign origins as a group have affinities with such and such types? The same question may be asked of denominations. If the sample shows a disproportionate number of internally adapted Methodist Episcopal churches may one safely conclude that the

Methodist Episcopal denomination as a whole tends in that direction? Or, again, one may ask, Is the distribution of types for all cities of 100,000 population and over valid for those of a more limited size-range, say, from 100,000 to 250,000? And is the composite picture of city churches equally true for all sections, North, South, East and West?

The answer, as already indicated, depends first upon the competency of the sample to show how the city churches of the American Protestant denominations are distributed. If it can show this it be-

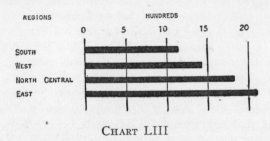

CHART LIII

Number of Native-born Per Protestant Church, by Regions.

comes a secondary question whether each of the above particular uses of the data which it is desired to make is also valid.

In answer to the first question, it is believed that the distribution by types in the 1,044 sample churches is a reasonable approximation to the actual distribution of American Protestant churches, except that the proportion of socially adapted churches is somewhat overstated.

The evidence for this assertion is briefly as follows: Some bias in the selection of the sample was suspected, growing primarily out of the sources from which schedules were secured.[1] It was recognized that in recommending "representative" churches for study each denomination would inevitably tend to put its best foot forward and to include more than a due proportion of interesting and successful cases.

Again, in securing new schedules there was chance of bias on the part of the field workers on account of the unequal accessibility of churches and the one-sidedness of local advisors on whom they had to depend for selection. Though they were urgently instructed to avoid favoritism in behalf of large and important churches, there was no absolute means of determining just how far their samples constituted a true cross-section of the churches of an entire city.

1 See p. vi.

THE "CROSS-SECTIONAL" SAMPLE

An important check upon the degree and location of the results of such bias (if any existed) was at hand in the shape of 418 schedules from seven cities that were known to have been secured without bias in the attempt of the Interchurch World Movement to make a 100 per cent. church survey in the cities in question and in a subsequent intensive and complete survey of the Protestant churches of Springfield, Mass., by the Institute of Social and Religious Research. These surveys covered about 40 per cent. of the total number of churches in the cities studied, whereas the general sample was but 8 per cent. Since, then, the surveys of the 418 churches were five times as complete as the total sample, and since their genuine cross-sectional character as representing the churches of the respective cities has a high degree of certainty, the correspondence or non-correspondence of the distribution of the 418 churches with that of the 1,044 would go far to prove or disprove the validity of the latter as a fair sample.

The "cross-sectional" sample was unfortunately very greatly overweighted by the larger number of churches from the far western cities. Nearly one-half of the cases came from them, while the Mountain and Pacific Coast states include less than one-tenth of the population of the major cities of the nation. The "cross-sectional" schedules from cities of these states were therefore weighted proportionately to the urban population represented by them and the weighted cross-sectional sample compared with the total sample for distribution by types, with the results shown in Table LX.

TABLE LX—PER CENT. DISTRIBUTION OF 1,044 CITY CHURCHES AND THE WEIGHTED PER CENT. DISTRIBUTION OF 418 "CROSS-SECTIONAL" CITY CHURCHES IN SEVEN CITIES, BY TYPES

Churches	Unadapted	Slightly Adapted	Internally Adapted	Socially Adapted	Widely Variant	Total
1,044 churches	24.2	34.5	18.8	10.5	12.0	100.0
418 churches	25.5	39.8	18.3	3.6	12.8	100.0

CONCLUSIONS FROM THE TWO SAMPLES

This method of comparison brings the two distributions remarkably close together except with respect to the slightly adapted and socially adapted types. The weighted cross-sectional sample shows the modal type (slightly adapted) still more strongly modal than in the general sample, but a wide discrepancy between the two results is still left in the case of the socially adapted.

American cities. In other words, the distribution of churches by denominations reflects a very good *urban* sample.

DATA BY SIZE OF CITIES AND BY REGIONS

With respect to size of cities, the sample of churches was relatively greater than the number of churches in cities from 500,000 to 1,000,000 population, and relatively smaller than the number of churches in cities of more than 1,000,000. Within each size-group, however, the number of cases studied was ample to determine the more general tendencies with respect to types.

The same assurance may be had with respect to the regional sample. No effort was made to make it exactly proportionate to the number of churches North, South, East and West, and some sections were actually better represented than others. The number of cases for each section was, however, ample to determine trends in that section.

> The influence of the factor of bias leading to a disproportionate number of "socially adapted" churches in the sample cannot be precisely located in the data last discussed. Whether it affects one size of city or region or one denomination more than another is not known. The probability is that they are all affected in some degree; and the fact that the limits of possible bias are rather narrow makes it legitimate to use the distribution of the sample as approximating that of the actual body of city churches, though one cannot prove exactly how close the approximation is.

With this reservation, the remainder of the chapter undertakes to show in terms of the types the influence upon city churches of special heredities like racial and denominational traits or traditions, and of larger environments such as the classes of cities and geographical sections to which they belong.

Distribution of Types of Churches by Nationality

Native rural stock is not the only population element that has built up American cities. Their growth until recently has been more largely due to foreign immigration than to any other external cause. On the other hand, relatively little of the foreign immigration has been Protestant in recent years; consequently the effect of the foreign church upon the development of urban types is not numerically considerable. Churches of foreign origin, however, constitute an appreciable element in the unadapted type.

Since the church of foreign antecedents does not start with American rural beginnings, it cannot be interpreted directly as a further evolution of the general national tendency. Foreign immigrants are, however, in many ways distinctly rural. They were

largely peasants in the Old World and their transplanted characteristics are rural and conservative.

These qualities often become exceedingly pronounced when a
foreign group constitutes a solid colony within a city. Under these
circumstances, a self-protective crust of clannishness is formed
about it.

Thus, as in the case of the American church, the central problem
of the foreign church is to urbanize a previously rural type, although
continuity is not so exact in detail.

THE FOREIGN CHURCHES

In the study of the 1,044 churches no effort was made to get an
exactly proportionate sample from the various nationalities represented. No clear-cut distinction can be made or ought to be attempted between churches of American and non-American origin
and characteristics. Many churches of foreign origin have become thoroughly Americanized. As a sign of this complete naturali-
zation some of them have dropped their original foreign label.
Ecclesiastical organization is, however, conservative. Consequently
not all have dropped such labels. Some that have dropped a foreign
label have not fully abandoned foreign-language preaching nor come
over entirely to the native point of view.

The only distinction that this study ventures to make, therefore,
is to take fifty-seven churches apparently definitely fixed as a foreign
group by reason of distinct self-designations. They represent the
following nationalities and denominations: Norwegian, Swedish,
Danish and German in branches or congregations of the Lutheran,
Baptist or Methodist Episcopal denominations; also Italian, French,
Hungarian, Slovac, Polish, Mexican, Chinese and Japanese churches
of various denominations.[4]

This sample of fifty-seven churches is regarded as sufficient to
demonstrate tendencies but not of course exact proportions.

Compared with the total group of city churches, the foreign
churches show the following striking variations: They have many
more unadapted churches, somewhat fewer slightly adapted ones
and almost no internally adapted or socially adapted ones. Still
more striking is the fact that they have two and one-half times as
many churches of the widely variant type as the average of the
sample. Examination shows indeed that with this erratic group it
is often a case simply of a foreign church driven, on the one hand,

4 No Lutheran churches are included in the "foreign" list except those branches that
continue to name themselves by a designation of nationality. The great body of German
Lutherans, therefore, escape this classification though a high per cent. of them still keep
up partial foreign-language preaching and maintain many nationality traits.

TABLE LXII—RANK OF DENOMINATIONS, BY FREQUENCY OF TYPES *

Unadapted	Per Cent.	Slightly Adapted	Per Cent.	Internally Adapted	Per Cent.	Socially Adapted	Per Cent.	Widely Variant	Per Cent.
Denomination		Denomination		Denomination		Denomination		Denomination	
All other	44.2	Lutheran	45.7	Methodist Episcopal	26.4	Protestant Episcopal	16.4	Protestant Episcopal	15.5
Disciples	34.8	Congregational	40.9	Disciples	23.9	Baptist	13.3	Baptist	14.5
Lutheran	34.8	Presbyterian	39.5	Protestant Episcopal	21.8	M. E., South	12.8	Methodist Episcopal	13.9
M. E., South	30.8	M. E. South	35.9	Congregational	20.9	Presbyterian	12.2	Presbyterian	13.3
Total	24.2	Baptist	34.6	Total	18.8	Methodist Episcopal	11.9	Total	12.0
Baptist	21.8	Total	34.5	Presbyterian	17.8	Total	10.5	Congregational	10.9
Methodist Episcopal	21.4	Protestant Episcopal	33.6	Baptist	15.8	Congregational	9.1	M. E., South	10.2
Congregational	18.2	All other	33.3	Lutheran	13.0	Disciples	4.3	Disciples	8.7
Presbyterian	17.2	Disciples	28.3	All other	11.6	All other	4.1	All other	6.8
Protestant Episcopal	12.7	Methodist Episcopal	26.4	M. E., South	10.3	Lutheran	2.2	Lutheran	4.3

* See Appendix Table 45 for number of churches reporting under each type.

(2) If the unadapted types alone be considered, the numerous small denominations grouped in the "other" column have a very much larger percentage of them and the Protestant Episcopal a very much smaller percentage.

(3) The Lutheran denomination has much the largest percentage of slightly adapted churches and the Methodist Episcopal much the smallest.

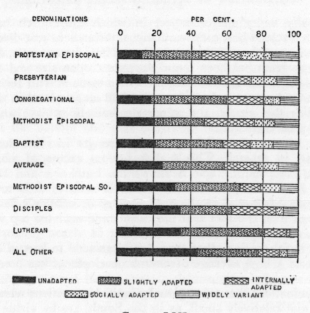

CHART LVI

Per Cent. Distribution of Types of Churches in Each Denomination.

(4) While the Methodist Episcopal has shown great superiority in the number of internally adapted churches, its sister denomination, the Methodist Episcopal, South, has the smallest number.

(5) While the Protestant Episcopal communion has the fewest unadapted and the most socially adapted churches, it is followed in this latter respect by the Baptist. On the other hand, the Lutheran, Disciples and smaller denominations have the largest proportion of unadapted churches.

(6) The distribution of the widely variant types follows in general the same denominational order as that of the socially adapted. It is most frequent with denominations that have the largest bulk of foreign work. Indeed, in this type the motive of social adaptation

tionally small in the cities of over one million population, while approximating the average in cities of the other sizes.

While the sample for largest cities is smaller than could be desired, there is no reason to doubt that, with such a distribution, a fair statement of the church situation in cities of all sizes is possible. Such a statement is attempted in the following paragraphs.

SIZE OF CITIES AND DEGREE OF CHURCH DEVELOPMENT

As a general principle the larger the city the larger the per cent. of highly developed churches that will be found in it, while the smaller the city the more less developed churches it will have, as shown in Table LXIV.

TABLE LXIV — DISTRIBUTION OF TYPES OF CHURCHES IN CITIES OF VARYING SIZE *

| | | Per Cent. Distribution | | | | |
Population	Unadapted	Slightly Adapted	Internally Adapted	Socially Adapted	Widely Variant	Total
Under 100,000	37.0	44.5	11.1	....	7.4	100.0
100,000–250,000 ...	30.6	33.4	19.5	7.2	9.3	100.0
250,000–500,000 ...	13.3	39.9	23.9	9.6	13.3	100.0
500,000–750,000 ...	32.0	38.2	10.5	7.9	11.4	100.0
750,000–1,000,000 ..	28.5	28.5	17.2	12.9	12.9	100.0
1,000,000 and over.	6.6	27.6	25.7	23.0	17.1	100.0
Total	24.2	34.5	18.8	10.5	12.0	100.0

* See Appendix Table 47 for number of churches reporting under each type.

While cities of over three-quarters of a million population have a slightly larger percentage of internally adapted churches and a much larger percentage of socially adapted churches than those of any other two groups, it will be noted that the narrower size-groups of Table LXIV show no exact sequence running from the smaller to the larger such as would be necessary to prove their exact correspondence between complexity of church types and size of cities. Indeed, none should be expected; first, because, considering the nature of the data, over-exact correspondence would be unnatural. Nothing more than a trend is assumed and the trend is clear.

The chief irregularity relates to cities of from 500,000 to 750,000 population which show a smaller proportion of highly developed churches than the two preceding size-groups. But there are only six cities in this group of which two—San Francisco-Oakland and Los Angeles—were extensively studied. They represent one-third of the total. This is a far larger proportion of cities than were extensively surveyed in any other size-group. But these two cities have actually a higher proportion of fragmentary churches than smaller ones that have been equally well surveyed.[7] The erratic showing of the cities of this size-group is therefore due to a statistical bias reflecting an actual fact.

7 Appendix Table 46.

Bias is demonstrably present in the case of the very largest cities. The samples for them are the least adequate and the limitations of the survey most pronounced. In other words, it was so impossible to reach any proper fraction of the thousands of churches in these cities that on the whole only outstanding ones were investigated. While undoubtedly the metropolitan cities have a large proportion of highly developed churches, the difference is probably not so great as the statistics show. These various cities have also the largest proportion of churches worshiping in halls, a situation that is elsewhere the mark of instability and lack of complete development. They also have a larger proportion of widely variant churches.

While, therefore, the tendency is undoubted, it is impossible to establish the exact degree of difference shown by the figures. What

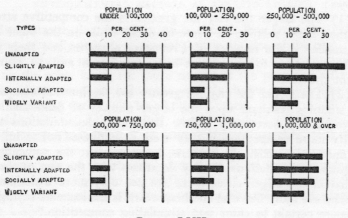

CHART LVII

Per Cent. Distribution of Types of Churches in Cities of Varying Size.

one can say is that large cities tend to have more highly developed churches and small cities tend to have more simply developed ones.

The fact that the proportion of erratic churches rises steadily with the size of the city is worth separate attention. It indicates perhaps the increased adventuresomeness of the metropolis; but also unquestionably the sort and kind of social pressure to which churches have to adapt themselves. If one considers types of churches as forms of such urban adaptation, it is a striking fact that one million people living in four cities of 250,000 population or in eight cities of 125,000 population will have fewer urbanized churches to serve them than if all lived in a single city of equal size. The needs of the lesser cities may not be so immediately exigent; but if the general conception of the urban version of religious organization is accepted as normal the lesser cities must be set down

INTERPRETATION

The probable explanation of the above phenomenon is that in the city of fewer than 250,000 people it is still possible, in spite of the large measure of social differentiation and the rapid changes of population, for many members to live conveniently within one mile of the church building. On the other hand, the entire area of the city is so small that there will be few "scattered" parishes according to the arbitrary definition that they have less than 50 per cent. of their people within a mile. At the same time, such cities generally have many churches with widely dispersed memberships living in all directions from the church and not localized in single neighborhoods.[16]

When a city passes beyond a quarter of a million in population, it becomes less and less likely that a large proportion of members will live within a mile of the church. By virtue of its increased geographical size parishes tend to thin out. A blighted zone or district, previously residential but now increasingly given over to industry and tenement houses, almost always intrudes between the downtown center and the better-class residential sections. This zone is probably not yet so large as to be uncrossable. Religious strategy, however, being conservative, clings to the idea of numerous central churches when it has ceased to fit the facts of the growing city. It still needs central institutions but not so many of them as previously. Too many such churches struggle heroically to maintain themselves by bringing their adherents from long distances. Thus it is that in the cities of this size, the very scattered parish, having less than 25 per cent. of its members within one mile, is more frequent than in cities of any other size, reaching 16.2 per cent. of the total.

In cities of between 500,000 and 750,000 population, the impossibility of maintaining compact parishes of the old sort increases, although a portion of the churches still make the attempt. There is, therefore, a return to the localized or partly localized parish, made possible by the removal of central churches and the building up of minor centers adjacent to residential neighborhoods. Churches in cities of this size are, therefore, divided about equally between scattered and compact parishes.

When the city passes the one million population mark the old order has been almost obliterated. There is a very marked return to the localization of membership. Distances are so great, social differences between classes so fixed, transportation so expensive and time-consuming that most of the churches give up the idea of

16 Appendix Tables 43 and 44.

bringing adherents from long distances. This appears to be the fact in spite of rapid transit and private automobiles. It is in striking variance with popular imagination. One sees the vast outstanding central churches of such a city as New York or Chicago and forgets to realize that probably in no city do so few people, relative to the total number of churchgoers, attend central churches. The majority are geographically related to neighborhoods, and although actual social identification with a neighborhood is in many cases very slight, there is a more hopeful basis for some sort of general decentralization in the largest cities of all than in any other kind.[17]

PARISH GEOGRAPHY OF CENTRAL AND RESIDENTIAL CHURCHES

The characteristics just described may be traced further to their sources by a comparison between the centrally and residentially located churches.[18] These characteristics are actually due most largely to the residential churches which constitute about 60 per cent. of the total and thus tend to dominate the result.

The variations between the central and residential churches are as follows. While in cities of all sizes centrally located churches naturally have much less compact parishes than the residential ones, the parish geography of the residentially located churches substantially agrees with that discovered for all churches. This is to say, they are most often compact in the largest cities and next in the smaller. Their exact agreement does not extend, however, to the cities in the middle-size groups.

The centrally located churches, on the other hand, have a tendency to compact parishes exactly corresponding to the increased size of cities. Thus, in the cases investigated, there were no centrally located churches with compact parishes in cities of less than 250,000. Here, it is obvious, central location generally means an effort at city-wide influence, which actually distributes membership at considerable distance from the center. With each successive size group the proportion of compact central parishes increases until it is two-fifths in cities of over 1,000,000 population. This means of course that many churches in such cities located at secondary centers do not attempt a city-wide ministry. Prof. W. L. Bailey writes with special reference to Chicago, "The church of the neighborhood on a relatively large scale is the successful church of the present under large city, and especially under metropolitan, conditions." The facts also correspond with the tendencies of the socially adapted and widely variant churches which are especially numerous

17 See p. 250.
18 Appendix Tables 41 and 42.

GENERALIZATION

The total significance of the size of cities with respect to the type of their churches and the degree of adaptation signified thereby, may be summarized somewhat as follows: Urbanization, both as general adaptation of church to city and in its special phases of program development, increases as cities grow larger. There are, however, exceptions to this tendency. Cities of from 250,000 to 500,000 population are irregular with respect both to development of program and to related size factors. This irregularity probably has been partly due to their retaining an outworn and unsuccessful policy as to membership distribution. There is thus registered a sort of hiatus between the smaller "large cities" and the really large ones. The former hesitate in development and stand "with reluctant feet" before stepping out into real metropolitan character.

The degree of local adaptation on the part of the churches seems to decrease with the size of the city until it reaches the group having populations of 500,000 or more. Then it increases again in churches in very large cities distinctly tending to have compact parishes.

These results amply justify breaking up the large-city group into its component size-groups as a means of the more accurate interpretation of the data. While all large cities make the same generic demands upon the church, its exact adaptation to its task is to be worked out through special policies fitting the different grades of urban communities. Subsequent studies will do well to carry on further investigation on this point.

Regional Distribution of Types of Churches

How far is the distribution of the major types equally characteristic of North, South, East and West?

Of course, since size of city makes the considerable difference that the last section shows, the regional distribution of types of churches will not be expected to correspond to that of the country as a whole.

No premeditated effort was made to secure balance in the distribution by types of the 1,044 churches studied as among the various sections of the country relative to their respective city populations. The sections differ greatly in this respect as shown by Table LXVII.

The northern sector is of course the urbanized area of the United States. Nearly 80 per cent. of all people living in cities of over 100,000 inhabitants live in this sector, in an area constituting only about 31 per cent. of the total area of the nation. Here are the three metropolitan cities whose combined population equals that of the twenty-two next largest cities having populations of between 250,000 and 1,000,000.

The two size-groups falling within these limits are distributed in about the same proportion among the sections. The north central section has

the largest proportion of urban people in cities of this size and the South
the smallest. Cities of from 100,000 to 250,000 people are relatively more
important in the Northeast, where they constitute the great group of
smaller manufacturing cities depending upon and largely suburban to the
great centers; and in the South, where they are the most characteristic
size. Thus the Northeast excels both in the smallest and the largest of

TABLE LXVII — DISTRIBUTION OF LARGE CITIES AND THEIR POPULATIONS BY SIZE IN EACH REGION

| | | | Per Cent. Distribution by Sections | | | |
Size of City	No. of Cities	Combined Population	North-east (26 cities)	North-Central (19 cities)	South (15 cities)	West (8 cities)
1,000,000 and over ...	3	10,145,532	73.4	26.6	0	0
500,000 to 1,000,000..	9	6,223,769	29.6	41.2	11.8	17.4
250,000 to 500,000 ..	13	4,540,838	22.2	41.3	18.2	18.3
100,000 to 250,000 ..	43	6,519,187	37.7	27.1	28.5	6.7
Total	68	27,429,326	46.4	32.5	12.4	8.7

the large-city group, while the north central division has more cities of
middle size.

It accidentally turns out that there is considerable correspondence between the distribution of Protestant churches by regions and the distribution of churches studied, as shown in Table LXVIII.

TABLE LXVIII — DISTRIBUTION OF POPULATION IN CITIES OF 100,000 AND OVER AND DISTRIBUTION OF PROTESTANT CHURCHES AND OF 1,044 CHURCHES STUDIED, BY REGIONS

| Population and Churches | | Per Cent. by Region | | |
	Northeast	North Central	South	West
Population	46.4	32.5	12.4	8.7
Protestant churches	35.1	31.3	23.1	10.5
Churches studied	34.2	31.9	10.4	23.5

The explanation of this showing is as follows: Protestant churches are
relatively more frequent in the South and West and relatively less frequent in the Northeast relative to total population, primarily because of
the preponderance of foreign-born and consequently of non-Protestants in
the last area.

If the percentage distribution of churches studied be compared with
that of all Protestant churches, it will be seen that the Northeast and North
Central cities are adequately represented in the 1,044 cases, the South decidedly under-represented, and the West greatly over-represented.

The discrepancy is not sufficient, however, to defeat an approximately correct sectional interpretation of urban church evolution.
In all sections the sample was adequate to demonstrate the general
tendencies of the churches therein although the distribution was
better in some sections than others.

VARIATION IN TYPES

The following tendencies, therefore, probably reflect the facts
somewhat closely.

(1) The Northeast corresponds most closely to the general average of the country in the distribution of its church types.

(2) The North Central has more internally adapted and many more socially adapted churches than the average. Church development has gone further here than in any other section.

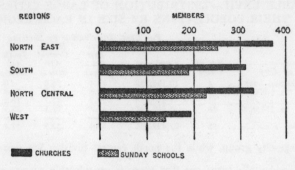

CHART LVIII

Average Membership of Protestant City Churches and Sunday Schools, by Regions.

(3) The South has more slightly adapted churches, an average number of unadapted and internally adapted ones and fewer socially adapted ones.

(4) The West has more unadapted and slightly adapted churches and far fewer of the more highly developed types. It has scarcely any of the socially adapted type.

These distinctions appear in the ranking of the sections according to types of churches in Table LXIX.

More refined distinctions among the sections begin to appear with the examination of the subtypes.[20]

(1) Within the unadapted group the West has far the largest proportion of the smallest and narrowest kind of church. The South also has an excess of unadapted churches, but they are one stage above those of the West.

(2) Within the slightly adapted group are found variations in two directions: first, toward increasing range or novelty of program, secondly, toward an increasing number of activities without wider range. As between these alternatives the South takes the conservative tack and the North Central section the adventurous one. The Northeast is also adventurous to a lesser degree, while the West stays close to the average.

(3) Within the internally adapted group the Northeast and

20 Appendix Table 47.

TABLE LXIX—RANK OF GEOGRAPHICAL REGIONS, BY FREQUENCY OF CHURCHES OF SPECIFIED TYPES

Rank	Unadapted		Slightly Adapted		Internally Adapted		Socially Adapted		Widely Variant	
	Region	Per Cent.	Region	Per Cent.	Region	Per Cent.	Region	Per Cent.	Region	Per Cent.
1	West	38.4	South	40.4	North Central	25.2	North Central	20.1	North Central	13.2
2	Total	24.2	West	39.2	South	20.2	Total	10.5	West	12.2
3	Northeast	23.5	Northeast	37.0	Northeast	19.3	Northeast	8.7	Total	12.0
4	South	22.9	Total	34.5	Total	18.8	South	7.3	Northeast	11.5
5	North Central	15.0	North Central	26.5	West	8.6	West	1.6	South	9.2

South approximate the average, while the North Central section tends to an exceptional degree of elaboration and the West to less than an average degree.

(4) Within the socially adapted group the Northeast and West

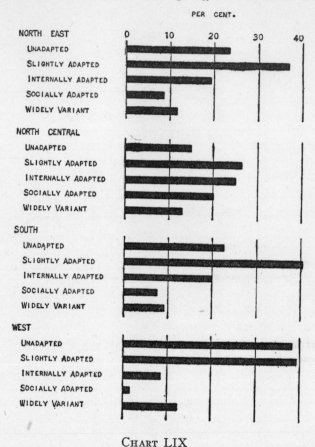

CHART LIX

Per Cent. Distribution of Types of Churches in Each Region.

agree in having more incompletely adapted churches, while the South has many more incompletely adapted ones, and the North Central section many more fully adapted ones.

GENERALIZATION

The Northeast is the section most representative of the national average. It is the oldest and most urban with the greatest variety of cities. This makes it natural that it should have the most balanced distribution of churches. It has a slight tendency toward novelty and experimentation.

The South, on the other hand, has distinctly the narrowest range of church development. It does not start so low nor rise so high. It is characteristically conservative.

The North Central section shows two strong tendencies, one toward novelty and experimentation; the other toward a higher degree of development of its more complex church types.

The West has the least balanced church development. Only 10 per cent. of its churches have evolved beyond the typical stage, and they are generally the less complete phases of such higher development.

Thus, in degree of development of their church types, the North Central section stands first, the Northeast second, while the South is below and the West very much below the average.

AGREEMENT WITH OTHER REGIONAL CHARACTERISTICS

This regional result of the 1,044 samples of city churches may be compared with still more general characteristics of church life in the various regions of the United States as revealed by the Census of Religious Bodies and summarized in Appendix Table 57. It is to be remembered that the census showing is based upon practically a 100 per cent. sample. Its large agreement with the present study is therefore important.

The standing of the regions in degree of general development of their churches is revealed by the present study as generally the same as their development measured by the average size of church membership, Sunday-school enrollment, annual expenditures and value of property, except that the Northeastern and the North Central sections exchange places. The comparative rank of the regions (A) by degree of development measured by types and (B) by degree of development measured by average number of members per church and related factors, is as follows:

	Rank	
Region	A	B
North Central	1	2
Northeast	2	1
South	3	3
West	4	4

Without attempting to pursue the explanation too far into the realms of sectional temperament as rooted in history and affected by the general type of civilization (including the relative numerical importance of urban populations), one may conclude that probably the most influential general factor in creating regional difference is degree of competition. Competition is both external as between Protestantism and other faiths and internal as between the Protestant denominations.[21]

The north central section, with the highest degree of development of the more complex church types, has next to the largest church units both absolute (as measured by average size of church membership, Sunday-school enrollment, annual expenditures and value of property) and relative, as measured by the number of churches per thousand native-born population. Competition with other faiths is considerably less acute than in the northeastern section.

On the other hand, not only are there the largest number of Protestant denominations in the North Central section, but these denominations tend to represent a common tendency, with somewhat fewer irregular and sporadic developments. This generally high degree of competition, both external and internal, combined with—and perhaps to some degree causing—the tendency of Protestantism to organize itself into units of more than average size and strength, permits and probably tends to result in the higher complexity of organization and range of service program.

The Northeastern section has also a high development measured by complexity of church types, though not the highest in spite of its largest church units. This, the oldest section, naturally had the largest degree of historic conservatism to overcome. Here the churches have experienced extreme competition from non-Protestant faiths; but this has not resulted in as full a development of the Protestant service program as is found in the Middle West. There is a narrower range of Protestant denominations so that the stimulating influence of variety is less present. Again, a relatively larger proportion of the northeastern denominations are of the irregular sort, not belonging to the main line of Protestant development nor likely to influence greatly the more settled churches. The combination of these factors may explain why the oldest section, with the largest Protestant units, stands, nevertheless, in the second place in respect to general development.

The case of the South is simple. It has less than average development as measured by the types, coupled with small church units. It has little competition either of other faiths or of numerous Protestant denominations. Its temper is reputed to be conservative and its cities are small. Its comparatively slight development in city church types is thus only logical.

21 Appendix Tables 48-55.

The West has the smallest degree of development measured by types of churches, coupled with the smallest church units in size and financial strength. It has less than average competition from other faiths because religion is weak all around, but any advantage which might accrue from this fact is frittered away by subdivisions of Protestantism and the largest number of unreported denominations, an excessive portion of which are of the irregular and unstandardized varieties. Of these, there are so many as to influence the standard denominations in the direction of erratic rather than of consistent programs.

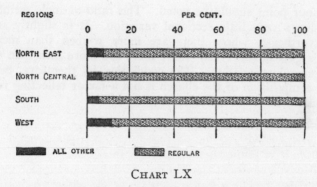

CHART LX

Proportion of "All Other" and Regular Protestant Churches in Total Protestant Churches of Each Region.

In terms of erratic or freakish development the West ranks first, the Northeast second, the North Central section third and the South last. This is demonstrated by three criteria in Table LXX.

TABLE LXX — PER CENT. OF CHURCHES WHICH HAVE SPECIFIED CHARACTERISTICS, BY REGIONS

| | | Region | | |
Characteristics	North-east	North Central	South	West
Churches of types widely variant in the direction of novelty	8.4	7.2	6.4	11.1
Rank	2	3	4	1
Churches of irregular denominations.	7.6	7.3	5.7	11.6
Rank	2	3	4	1
Churches worshiping in halls	17.5	8.4	7.1	9.8
Rank	1	3	4	2

While there is no inherent necessity why the local church of an exceptional and poorly established denomination should either show an erratic program or worship in a hall rather than in a church, these three characteristics actually tend to be associated from region to region. Except that the Northeast outranks the West in proportion of churches worshiping in halls—a result partly attributable to high real estate values—the regions rank in exactly the same order on all three criteria.

The findings of the present study and of the census thus make a consistent story accurately corresponding to the general reputation of the various regions with respect to church life.

RATIO OF MALE TO FEMALE CHURCH MEMBERS

A minor point should be noted. The ratio of male members to female shows very little sectional variation. It is slightly smallest in the Northeast, where there are more women than men, and slightly largest in the West, where there are more men than women in the general population. The conclusion is, therefore, negative. The sex composition of the church is not a factor reflecting regional variations.

Chapter XIV

THE PROVISIONAL USE OF TRENDS AS NORMS

In general, there are three ways of determining what the church ought to be and to do.

(1) The first is the way of authority. The matter is either presumed to be settled by the ultimate religious authority recognized by the particular church, or by some subsequent or contemporary authority resident in the church itself. This may vary from the ex cathedra utterances of a Pope to a majority vote of an ecclesiastical assembly or even the administrative decisions of a competent official.

From this point of view the prescription for a good church is found in official manuals and denominational standards promulgated by authority of an entire communion, or by special commissions or boards.

(2) The second way of discovering a good church is by consensus of experts. A good illustration of a judgment arrived at in this way is found in the original "par standard" for rural churches used by the Town and Country studies of the Institute of Social and Religious Research. It was essentially a score-card covering thirty-three points, worked out and adopted by the Town and Country Committee of the Home Missions Council on the basis of the best wisdom of denominational experts in charge of rural church affairs. It was defined as "not an ideal, but as a measurable example of what the church may, in all reasonableness, expect to attain."

Nearer to the field of the present study is the standard for the City Church Plants developed by the Interchurch World Movement. This norm for church buildings and equipment was also based upon the consensus of experts, who rated the different items on a total scale of 1,000, distributed under special classifications according to the average judgment of 200 "competent judges in the field of religious education." Somewhat curiously, it assigned 17.5 per cent. of the total score to "community service facilities" to be used in the performance of functions that fewer than one-tenth of city churches covered by this study have at all and that a considerable number of people believe to be a misdirection of the energies of the church, if not a definite departure from the proper field of religion.

Evidently the church that these experts had in mind was not the actual city church as the present study has found it.

pushed it back during the last century and hopes to do so still more. The wages of street-car conductors are very far from being permanently fixed. Indeed so little are the statistically "typical" wages accepted as a satisfactory standard that a labor union will compare them with the cost of living and argue that just in so far as they are typical they ought to be higher!

It is, of course, manifest that the status of church programs is more like street-car wages than it is like human stature. Not only can church programs be changed, but they are rapidly being changed. The central hypothesis of the present study implies that church development reflects a relatively recent and rapid adaptation to urban conditions. The most frequent type now may not be such in ten or twenty-five years. Here is simply the central tendency of the church program as now current. One may use it as a statistical norm, but by no means as a standard by which churches ought permanently to be judged.

WHAT AUTHORITY HAVE ACTUAL PRESENT TENDENCIES

Is the present frequency of church types, then, merely a point of departure for the understanding, a scale by which a church may locate its position with reference to the total number of churches, but no criterion of where it ought to be located?

A church that has located itself with reference to the scale can hardly escape asking itself, "Does my position indicate anything as to where I ought to be?" The answer is that the presumption of being practically wise or right is on the side of the average church. Variations are the things to be explained.

This is the sole authority that the study asks to have accorded to the present distribution of city churches by types. It furnishes a point of departure for interpreting the actual variations and tends to show within what limits variations are ordinarily profitable. It helps to make what has actually happened appear more or less desirable. The study shows many justifiable grounds for deviating from the average and has no reason to doubt that the actual deviations measured by the relative size of the types have been proper and right on the whole.

To make this position intelligible it will be wise to summarize the chief factors discovered in the course of the study that may qualify or modify the tendency of churches to develop in keeping with the central tendency. These may be classified under the heads of resources, presuppositions, strategy and relationships to other agencies.

(1) *Resources:* What *is* by no means reflects what *would be* if

all churches had equal strength in money and constituencies. The present programs of decrepit churches do not reveal what they will to do, but only their limited ability. This is often equally true of young churches. There are no universally applicable human standards that one would think of applying equally to the children and aged and the sub-normal, as to the normal adult. The present study has had reason to identify the unadapted type of church largely with institutional infancy or else with decrepitude.[3] It therefore declines to apply to it, directly and without qualification, standards derived from the whole body of city churches; and it does not believe that standards so derived can ever have universal applicability.

(2) *Presuppositions:* Again, the study has noted the influence upon church development and adaptation of varying theories of the function of the church in the world and of its relation to human society. It is not willing to mark a church down for not having what it does not believe in, in spite of the practice of majorities.[4]

(3) *Strategy:* Still further, the study has noted that some churches wish to specialize in a limited field in which they can serve with peculiar facility and success. It does not presume to rate these churches merely as above or below the average without giving the right to decide for themselves whether they are wiser to follow the general trend or to turn aside to such specialization. They may serve their ultimate objectives more successfully by the latter course.

(4) *Relationships:* Very early in the book it was pointed out that churches are only one element in larger groups of religious agencies such as hospitals, homes, the Young Men's and Young Women's Christian Associations, etc., which generally perform certain specialized functions that churches only occasionally undertake. In some of their functions the entire group of religious agencies supplement and are supplemented by other constructive agencies of the community. City governments, for example, foster healthful recreation; Boy Scouts and Camp Fire Girls try to build character. Obviously what a given church ought to do in these realms depends partly upon the number and effectiveness of other agencies in the field. This, in turn, implies that it ought to study its field.

Any church that desires to depart from the average for these or any other valid reasons is perfectly at liberty to do so. The average is not a norm in any such sense as to deny or abridge the right, and the results of a scientific study of the particular field must obviously supplement any and every general standard.

3 Chapter VII, pp. 139 f. and 144 f.
4 See p. 146.

churches and no more. Even for the future, it is not proved that the typical church will have a highly adapted program of its own. Perhaps the more conscious and carefully adapted program of the future will be carried on by a coöperating group of Christian agencies, rather than by individual churches with many activities. But this is beyond the present point of discussion.

OPTIONS BEFORE A SLIGHTLY ADAPTED CHURCH

If a slightly adapted church finds itself deficient in the characteristics belonging to its group, as statistically determined, it will naturally summon its utmost resources and attempt to bring itself up to the standard. Intimate studies show that the most general method of securing this result is to demand more time and money from members. Churches actually differ greatly in the average number of hours per week and in the average per capita contributions received.

However, the ability to improve by the pressure of such appeals is strictly limited. It is most unlikely that a church will have so exceptional a constituency that it can do work quantitatively equal to that of another church of larger size, more adequate staff and plant and greater financial resources. "Not all your piety nor all your wit" can normally escape the law of the average, though striking exceptions are and will be found, and happy is the church which can make much out of little.

If, on the other hand, a slightly adapted church finds itself fully equaling the average performance of the type, it is called upon to make a decision between further qualitative development without expansion of program and attempting a broader program.

The ordinary options to be considered are those broadly written upon the statistics of the type: thus, (1) with numerical growth and more than average resources in plant and current support, such a church may either follow conservative lines, making itself a superlative example of the type, or (2) it may venture upon a somewhat exceptional program without greatly changing the total character and emphasis of its work.[7] If it is under special environmental pressure, or if its immediate neighborhood presents exceptional opportunities or challenges to unique types of service, it will be in keeping with its type if it responds in moderate degree.

(3) Or, finally, if such a church can serve conspicuously by specializing, say, upon pulpit ministers or a highly effective Sunday school, it may be warranted in taking this quite exceptional course to the neglect of a balanced program.[8] Very good reason, however,

[7] See p. 98 and p. 112.
[8] See pp. 244 f.

should be given for departing from the general trend of church development. The brilliant preacher who tempts the church to turn itself into a platform for him will not always stay, and the last end of that church may be worse than the first.

SUMMARY

The case of the slightly adapted church may be summarized as follows: Since an ascending and descending scale of size and resources does, in large measure, characterize the church types, and since the great majority of city churches are not beyond the characteristics of the slightly adapted type in these respects and are growing but slowly if at all, it is probably not to be expected that the majority of them can or should plan at present to adapt themselves to the city beyond the performance of the typical services of "average" churches. They cannot lift themselves by their own boot straps into a higher institutional class.

Putting the matter in still another way: until the people who make up the constituencies of the slightly adapted churches are more radically transformed by the city than they now are, there is no reason for expecting very radical transformation in the majority of churches. For, after all, except in the very largest cities, the bulk of the urban area occupied by Protestant people is devoted to families living in one-, or two-family houses, a situation that does not vitally challenge or modify the continuity, privacy and independence of the family group. It is this little-modified manner of living that the modestly developed church reflects, under really average city conditions.

All told, however, it must be admitted that this, the most characteristic church of the American city, does not obviously display distinctive urban qualities of religious adaptation and strategy. This fact may not require apology, but it almost inevitably occurs to the observer to ask the reason for it. The typical church of the city is by no means a commanding institution. It is rather a one-story affair in a sky-scraper environment. One must remember, of course, that, besides being largely rural in origins or tradition, the masses of the city's Protestant population are poor people living under narrow limitations. Is it their humble level which explains the inconspicuous character of the average city church? Does the church represent the real average of the city?

It is not, to say the least, the vast building and thronging congregation which country people are likely to imagine as typical of the city. If they knew the average city church as it really is, they would be sorry for it and say, "Poor little city church!"

of the nation should be ashamed to begin or ordinarily to perpetuate church organization in large cities.

To this verdict a further qualification is necessary. In the smaller and "slower" cities the most frequent stage of church development falls within the boundaries of this type. Although in a comparison that includes New York and Chicago only slight urban adaptations are shown, from the standpoint of the cities in question, the response of the churches may be even notable. This forbids one to treat them as though the development reached was not *for them* creditable and important.

Norms for Internally Adapted Churches

The section on the internally adapted church indicates the various quantitative factors that tend to accompany this type of program. Its essential characteristic is a multiple staff carrying on a varied specialized ministry; this in turn requiring a more extensive and technically standardized plant and the larger funds necessary to support the entire process.[11]

But not in such quantitatively measured characteristics alone are the norms of the internally adapted church to be found. As interpreted in the body of the study, its clew lies in a certain urbanization of experience and spirit.[12] This may or may not go with any distinct type of external environment. The people whose minds and hearts create the internally adapted church are attuned to the city in a special degree and with special sympathy. Whether or not it is consciously defined, urbanization of program is an implicit objective. Though possibly living in one-family houses, they find that they cannot be re-living the experiences of the isolated family group. Frequently such churches have been found actually associated with apartment-house neighborhoods. They stand for the relative waning of the home environment and influence and the introduction of novel types of urban experience.

As shown in the body of the study, they frequently minister to downtown-minded people who use the center of the city and its interests for the peculiar congregate life centering in the non-family groups that characterize city population.[13]

The range of program possible and actual in the internally adapted church leaves room for considerable margins of difference. These churches are much less alike than those limited to the common core of conventional church organization. There is no one hard and fast program, nor is one desirable. They are still in the plastic and experimental stage. The only standard requirement is that

11 Chapter VIII.
12 See p. 157.
13 See p. 165.

there shall be an all-round ministry to human life with a corresponding variety of age-, and sex-group organizations.

Indeed many internally adapted churches show a strong tendency to internal reorganization in the interests of simplicity just in order to carry out the broader conception of religion with a more varied program. They are being compelled to reintegrate their too-numerous subsidiaries into a smaller number of groups; as, for example, by gathering up the total ministry of the church for men, women, boys and girls respectively, into departments which organize the expressional as well as the passive religious life, and attempt the control of leisure time, besides trying to relate the constituents more broadly to the life of the community.

STARTING NEW CHURCHES ON THE INTERNALLY ADAPTED LEVEL

In the section on the slightly adapted church it was argued that churches of average size could not ordinarily carry out more than an average program. This judgment is not contradicted by the increasing number of examples of new enterprises starting with elaborated programs. As pointed out in the body of the study,[14] these usually imply a highly urbanized point of view and the presence of powerful forces constituting a bond between the people and creating a neighborhood solidarity. With these exceptional conditions and a very definite ideal of broad religious ministries for normal group life, elaborated programs may be operated through voluntary group action and with rather simple facilities. "Community churches" making such an attempt are rapidly increasing in numbers, though a considerable number of those borrowing the label "community church" are palpable fakes. There is, however, an unexplored wealth of possibilities for the city church in the neighborhood spirit, which all the cross currents of urban life have not been able entirely to overwhelm, and which comes to the surface in most unexpected places. Internally adapted churches built on such foundations are still exceptions, but enough of them may serve to challenge the trend within a few years.

Norms for the Socially Adapted Church

The specifications based on the average experience of the socially adapted churches, as indicated in the body of the study, cover the staff, plant, finances and general lines of adaptation that constitute the point of departure for an individual church of the type.[15] They do not, however, closely determine its program. As already noted,

14 See p. 168.
15 Chapter IX.

of program is most needed. The church will, of course, next compare the specifications of the new type (which simply express the mode or average of the experience and achievement of a group of actual churches in somewhat similar circumstances) with its own present standards and resources. It will measure the consequences to itself of entering a new type of service in terms of the necessary staff, buildings, facilities and total cost of operation, and with specific reference to the particular programs and methods that it proposes to adopt.

It should then set for itself a time limit for a transitional phase of development, since it usually cannot make so radical a change all at once. This is most important as a check upon itself, since the transitional process leaves a church in a peculiarly vulnerable position, one in which it lacks definite character, and, in the vernacular, is "neither flesh, fish nor fowl."

The time limit in which transition is to be accomplished should be an imperative requirement of denominational or other agencies upon which the church calls for help. Thus, in assisting in a development or building program a church extension society or mission board should enforce upon a church an exact statement of its new objectives, a demonstration that it will reach standard practice in carrying out its proposed program, together with clear evidence that really normal results can probably be reached within a reasonable and definitely measured length of time.

When the standards of the new phase of development are fully reached, a church may continue with quantitative improvement and the more precise meeting of local needs (which is the main method by which the subtypes differentiate themselves), or it may undertake intelligent experiments, corresponding to the sending out of scouts by an army, to determine how far and in what precise directions it should evolve further. In so doing it should always keep in touch with the major trends as determined by the vaster experience of the total body of churches.

The above paragraphs have attempted to sketch a scientific formula for the institutional progress of organized religion. Its working norms are based upon actual experience stated with statistical exactitude and set up as practical guides and measures of progress at every stage. It was not forgotten that needs may be so urgent as to call for sudden and radical transformation of institutions, or that pioneers found empires by doing unusual things. It is merely urged that even a pioneer may well measure the distance from the old world to the new and plan in the light of experience by what methods and resources he hopes to establish himself in the new country.

Trends Present and Future

VALIDITY OF TRENDS AS NORMS

Those who think the trends of the modern church are all wrong will, of course, not be impressed by their use as norms, even in the guarded sense in which the study has used them.

The only answer to this attitude is to plead that one does not know enough to go outside of the facts and does not believe that any one else does. As between the attitude which would scrap the present trend of the church in favor of some theory of its radical re-ordering and that which would work along with it, using it as a provisional standard and point of departure, the study definitely sides with the latter. It is against single-track versions of adaptation holding that all urban church problems can be solved on one principle, as, for example, the sociological or environmental. What ought to be should at least be as varied as what is. It ought to do justice to the limitations as well as to the propulsions that inhere in urban situations and give freedom to the forces that pull back as well as to those that press forward. No deep-seated tendency ought to be entirely obliterated, no matter how much it is modified. It is a sincere conviction, therefore, that the demonstrated trends are, and of right ought to be, points of departure for urban church development. One may strike out legitimately from any point in the series of types or may go beyond them all into the realm of most radical and adventurous experimentation so long as he keeps his head and realizes that it is experimentation and not a coercive demonstration of the true and better way which every one else must accept.

A DIP INTO THE FUTURE

As to the rate of future evolution relative to that of the past, the present study has no data, since it was based upon a contemporary survey. It is considerably impressed, however, with Prof. W. L. Bailey's argument that it will probably be much more rapid, for the reason that the majority of American cities are now past the period of pioneer experimentation in which the church was merely covering the situation in temporary fashion and had had neither time really to adapt itself, nor opportunity—because the city itself had not fully found itself.

For the church to get foothold and survive at all under these conditions Professor Bailey calls both remarkable and creditable. Now that foreign immigration is checked and cities are to be re-populated more largely from native sources—probably also more largely from elements of urban origin—much of the social confusion of urban growth may be abated. On the physical side, the era of city planning means that the situation will be much more stable. In other words, just in proportion as the city settles down so that the church knows what to count on, the church will find it possible to make accurate adaptations. It will still, however, have to decide whether to make its most radical social adaptations through church forms or, as in the past, chiefly through non-church organizations under Christian impulse and support.

APPENDICES

Appendix A

ITEMS COVERED BY GENERAL SCHEDULES

1. Name and denomination of church
2. Location (city, by size and region)
3. Number of members
4. Age
5. Years on present site
6. Race or nationality
7. Staff: Number and designation of paid religious workers
8. Pastor: Education
9. Pastor: Experience
10. Pastor: Tenure in this position
11. Pastor: Salary
12. Other male worker: Education
13. Other male worker: Experience
14. Other male worker: Tenure in this position
15. Other male worker: Salary
16. Other female worker: Education
17. Other female worker: Experience
18. Other female worker: Tenure in this position
19. Other female worker: Salary
20. Current expenses of church
21. Benevolence
22. Equipment: Administrative
23. Equipment: Educational
24. Equipment: Publicity
25. Equipment: Convenience
26. Equipment: Community service
27. Seating capacity of auditorium
28. Number rooms in church
29. Value church property
30. Sunday School: Enrollment
31. Sunday School: Average attendance
32. Sunday School: Cradle Roll
33. Sunday School: Home Department
34. Sunday School: Teachers' training class
35. Sunday School: Age distribution

Appendix B

THE "CROSS-SECTIONAL" SCHEDULES

The seven cities from which "cross-sectional" schedules were secured are listed in the following table, which also shows how many regular Protestant churches each had in 1916 and how many churches in each were included in the 1,044 studied.

Cities	No. Regular Protestant Churches, 1916	No. Churches Studied
Springfield, Mass.	44	50
Hartford, Conn.	50	34
Providence, R. I.	85	47
Rochester, N. Y.	96	81
Los Angeles, Calif.	295	91
San Francisco, Calif.	150	54
Oakland, Calif.	129	61
Total	849	418

Of this total of 418 "cross-sectional" schedules, 357 from the same cities were used to determine the frequency of church organizations and activities.[1] The balance were secured subsequently to that calculation.

At the rate of increase of churches in all large cities between 1906 and 1916 about 11 per cent. should be added to the 1916 figures to get the probable number of churches at the date of the study, making the total between 900 and 950. Even so the ratio of the sample to the total in the individual cities ranges from a little less than one-third to 100 per cent. and the total sample is probably somewhat more than 40 per cent. of the present number of churches. In other words, the "cross-sectional" sample, so far as it goes, is more than four times as complete as the general sample.

These 418 schedules were originally secured under the Interchurch World Movement by the coöperation of local Protestant churches (in the majority of cases permanently organized into Church Federations) in an effort to get religious data which should be 100 per cent. complete. The securing of schedules sometimes stopped in its tracks when the Interchurch movement ceased to function financially and was sometimes carried further by the local Federations. In the first case the selection was accidental—churches of all sorts and descriptions and of all denominations being included

1 See p. 57.

so far as the work went—in the other it approached 100 per cent. completion. Springfield, Mass., was studied intensively at a later date. The size of the sample, the motive and auspices under which the data were secured and the circumstances that limited the completion of the process all conspired to make it balanced and without bias in its selections.

TABLE 1—DISTRIBUTION OF 1,044 CHURCH SCHEDULES OBTAINED FROM 56 CITIES, BY REGION AND SIZE OF CITY

Size of City	Northeast City	No. of Schedules	North Central City	No. of Schedules	South City	No. of Schedules	West City	No. of Schedules	Total
Under 100,000	New Britain ..	4	Duluth	2	Mobile	1	Tacoma	6	
	Utica	3 7	Flint	10 12	Oklahoma City.	1 2		6	27
100,000 to 250,000	Worcester	1	Kansas City,		Birmingham ..	1	Spokane	5	
	Springfield ..	57	Kan.	1	Louisville ...	36	Oakland	61	
	Fall River ...	6	Omaha	5	Memphis	10			
	New Haven ...	1	St. Paul	2	Nashville	10			
	Hartford	34	Akron	1	Wilmington ..	5			
	Bridgeport ...	1	Toledo	12	Richmond	12			
	Providence ..	47	Columbus	11					
	Paterson	5	Dayton	1					
	Trenton	2	Grand Rapids..	2					
	Scranton	4 158		35		74		66	333
250,000 to 500,000	Rochester	81	Kansas City,		Washington ...	15	Portland	10	
	Newark	8	Mo.	11			Seattle	12	
			Minneapolis ..	13			Denver	6	
			Indianapolis ..	9					
			Milwaukee ...	14					
		89	Cincinnati	9 56		15		28	188
500,000 to 1,000,000.	Boston	20	St. Louis	64	Baltimore	18	Los Angeles ..	91	
	Buffalo	14	Cleveland	19			San Francisco.	54	
	Pittsburgh	31 65	Detroit	33 116		18		145	344
1,000,000 and over ..	Philadelphia ..	29	Chicago	114 114					
	New York ...	9 38							152
Total		357		333		109		245	1,044

TABLE 2 — ORGANIZATIONS AND ACTIVITIES AS FOUND IN 357
CROSS-SECTIONAL SCHEDULES COMPARED WITH TOTAL
NUMBER OF SCHEDULES *

Organizations and Activities	Cross-Sectional Schedules		Total Schedules	
	No.	%	No.	%
1. Preaching and Sunday School ...	357	100	1,044	100
2. Ladies' Aid or Guild	318	89	909	87
3. Women's Missionary Society	306	86	873	84
4. Young People's Society	296	83	803	77
5. Chorus Choir	271	76	603	58
6. General Social Events	221	62	600	57
7. Men's Organization	203	57	597	57
8. Boy Scouts	168	47	481	46
9. Mission Study Classes	164	46	459	44
10. Organized Welcome	111	31	368	35
11. Orchestra or Band	105	29	260	25
12. Boys' Club (not Scouts)	105	29	343	33
13. Lectures	105	29	291	28
14. Library	96	27	286	27
15. Girls' Club (not Scouts)	92	26	373	36
16. Concerts	92	26	288	28
17. Girl Scouts or Equivalent	75	21	248	24
18. Mothers' or Parents' Organization	71	20	214	20
19. Young Women's Organization ...	71	20	385	37
20. Dramatic Club	50	14	137	13
21. Gymnasium Classes	46	13	242	23
22. Sewing Classes	43	12	131	13
23. Kindergarten	29	8	98	9
24. Domestic Science Classes	29	8	70	7
25. Employment Office	29	8	95	9
26. Music Classes	18	5	80	8
27. Visiting Nurse	18	5	46	4
28. Health Classes	14	4	58	6
29. English Classes	14	4	60	6
30. Dramatic Classes	10	3	46	4
31. Day Nursery	10	3	29	3
32. Dispensary or Clinic	7	2	49	5
33. Civics and Economics Classes	4	1	38	4

* The "cross-sectional" schedules were secured by the Interchurch World Movement
from the following cities and are known to represent a true and adequate cross section
of their churches: Hartford, Providence, Springfield, Rochester, Los Angeles, San Francisco, Oakland and Berkeley. The Providence and Springfield schedules included some
suburban churches within the metropolitan area.

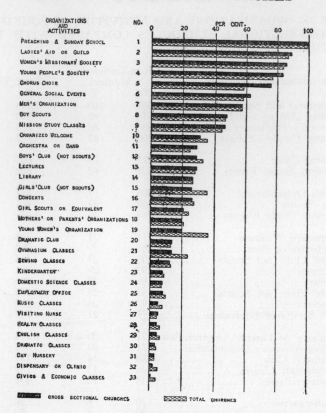

CHART LXI

Per Cent. Frequency of 33 Specified Organizations and Activities in 1,044 City Churches and in 418 Cross-sectional Churches.

TABLE 3— PROPORTION OF CHURCH MEMBERSHIP IN THE UNITED STATES LIVING IN PLACES SMALLER THAN 25,000 POPULATION IN 1910, BY DENOMINATIONS *

Denomination	Per Cent.
Churches of Christ	95.5
Christian Church (Christian Convention)	95.1
Lutheran (United Norwegian)	92.7
Baptist—Southern Convention	92.4
Church of the Brethren (Conservative)	90.4
Methodist Protestant	90.1
Methodist Episcopal, South	89.8
Colored Methodist Episcopal	89.6
Lutheran—Norwegian Synod	89.0
United Brethren in Christ	87.2
Lutheran—Synod of Iowa	86.9

TABLE 3 — PROPORTION OF CHURCH MEMBERSHIP IN THE UNITED STATES LIVING IN PLACES SMALLER THAN 25,000 POPULATION IN 1910, BY DENOMINATIONS * — (*Continued*)

Denomination	Per Cent.
Baptists—National Convention	84.3
Disciples of Christ	83.1
Church of Jesus Christ of Latter-Day Saints	81.3
Methodist Episcopal Church	77.4
African Methodist Episcopal Zion	77.1
African Methodist Episcopal	77.1
Presbyterian Church in the U. S.	77.0
Evangelical Association	75.1
Lutheran—Joint Synod of Ohio	75.0
Reformed Church in the U. S.	72.4
Lutheran—Synodical Conference	68.0
United Presbyterian	68.0
Lutheran—General Synod	66.9
Congregational Churches	64.3
Presbyterian Church in the U. S. A.	63.0
Baptist—Northern Convention	62.7
Lutheran—General Council	59.0
German Evangelical Synod	58.8
Reformed Church in America	55.7
Protestant Episcopal Church	44.4
Roman Catholic Church	43.5
Greek Orthodox (Hellenic)	15.8
Jewish Congregations	9.3

* *Census of Religious Bodies* (1916), Part I, p. 121.

TABLE 4 — RANK OF PROTESTANT DENOMINATIONS BY FREQUENCY OF OCCURRENCE IN THE 68 CITIES OF 100,000 POPULATION AND OVER IN 1920 *

Denomination	Number of Cities in which Denomination is Present
Protestant Episcopal	68
Baptist (Northern and Southern Conventions combined)	68
Methodist Episcopal	68
Lutheran (denominations not separately reported)	66
Presbyterian, U. S. A.	65
Congregational	60
African Methodist Episcopal	56
Disciples of Christ	53
Seventh-Day Adventist	51
Unitarian	47
National Baptist	45
African Methodist Episcopal Zion	42
Evangelical Synod	41
United Presbyterian	33
Evangelical Association	31
Reformed in U. S.	28
Universalist	28
Salvation Army	28
Independent churches	26
Methodist Episcopal South	23
Presbyterian, U. S.	22

TABLE 4—RANK OF PROTESTANT DENOMINATIONS BY FRE-
QUENCY OF OCCURRENCE IN THE 68 CITIES OF 100,000 POPU-
LATION AND OVER IN 1920 * —(*Continued*)

Denomination	*Number of Cities in which Denomination is Present*
Friends	22
Pentecostal Church of Nazarene	21
Colored Methodist Episcopal	21
United Brethren	20
Reformed in America (and Hungarian)	19
Church of Christ	17
Methodist Protestant	17
Brethren—Plymouth	14
Brethren—German Baptist	14
Advent Christian	13
Church of New Jerusalem	13
Free Methodist	12
Welsh Calvinistic Methodist Presbyterian	12
Armenian	11
United Evangelical	11
Swedish Evangelical Mission Covenant	11
Christian and Missionary Alliance	9
Volunteers of America	9
Primitive Methodist	8
Reformed Episcopal	8
Christian Church	7
Church of Living God	7
New Apostolic	6
Christian Reformed	6
Swedish Evangelical, Free	6
Cumberland Presbyterian	5
Reformed Presbyterian	5
Free Baptist	4
Assemblies of God	4
Christadelphians	4
Church of God and Saints of Christ	4
Evangelistic Association	4
Evangelical Protestant	4
African Union Methodist Protestant	4
Primitive Baptist	3
Mennonite	3
Union American Methodist Episcopal	3
Moravian	3
African American Methodist Episcopal	3
Pentacostal Holiness	2
Associate Reformed Presbyterian	2
Colored Methodist Protestant	2
Schwenkfelders	1
American Rescue Workers	1
Churches of God in North America	1
Reformed Zion Union Apostolic Methodist	1

* Based on *Census of Religious Bodies* (1916), Part I, p. 354.

TABLE 5 — CHURCH MEMBERSHIP, BY TYPES

Type and Subtype		Number of Members Under 500							500–1,000	1,000 and over	Total
		Under 50	Under 100	100–200	200–300	300–400	400–500	Total			
A I		13	37	23	9	4	3	76	1	1	78
A II		2	5	11	5	3	1	25	4	1	30
A III		3	9	8	4	2	1	24	2	0	26
B I		1	9	22	12	16	9	68	17	12	97
Unadapted	No.	19	60	64	30	25	14	193	24	14	231
	%	8.2	25.9	27.7	13.0	10.8	6.1	83.5	10.4	6.1	100.0
B II		3	15	32	18	19	12	96	36	17	149
B III		1	7	11	12	13	5	48	16	9	73
C I		0	0	8	14	13	8	43	32	31	106
Slightly Adapted	No.	4	22	51	44	45	25	187	84	57	328
	%	1.2	6.7	15.6	13.4	13.7	7.6	57.0	25.6	17.4	100.0
C II		0	0	7	11	9	8	35	36	36	107
D II		0	0	0	6	6	3	15	35	27	77
Internally Adapted	No.	0	0	7	17	15	11	50	71	63	184
	%	..	..	3.8	9.2	8.2	6.0	27.2	38.6	34.2	100.0
D III		1	3	2	3	2	4	14	11	15	40
E II		0	0	1	5	2	5	13	18	32	63
Socially Adapted	No.	1	3	3	8	4	9	27	29	47	103
	%	1.0	?.9	2.9	7.8	3.9	8.7	26.2	28.2	45.6	100.0
Total of 4 Types	No.	24	85	125	99	89	59	457	208	181	846
	%	3.8	10.0	14.8	11.7	10.5	7.0	54.0	24.6	21.4	100.0
A IV		5	7	9	5	3	1	25	3	1	29
A V		3	5	5	2	0	0	12	0	0	12
B IV		1	6	0	1	0	0	7	1	0	8
C III		4	8	3	3	0	3	17	3	2	22
D I		0	0	0	3	1	2	6	9	10	25
E I		0	0	1	1	0	2	4	2	4	10
Widely Variant	No.	13	26	18	15	4	8	71	18	17	106
	%	12.3	24.5	17.0	14.2	3.8	7.5	67.0	17.0	16.0	100.0
Grand Total ..	No.	37	111	143	114	93	67	528	226	198	952
	%	3.9	11.7	15.0	12.0	9.8	7.0	55.5	23.7	20.8	100.0

TABLE 6 — AGE OF CHURCH ORGANIZATION, BY TYPES

Type and Subtype		Number of Years Under 25						25–49	50–74	75–99	100 and over	Total
		Under 5	5–9	10–14	15–19	20–24	Total					
A I		6	7	7	7	3	30	19	8	1	2	60
A II		2	1	5	3	2	13	13	2	0	0	28
A III		1	3	2	2	1	9	7	4	5	0	25
B I		2	4	9	3	7	25	24	21	2	4	76
Unadapted	No.	11	15	23	15	13	77	63	35	8	6	189
	%	5.8	7.9	12.2	7.9	6.9	40.8	33.3	18.5	4.2	3.2	100.0

TABLE 8 — PROPORTION OF CHURCHES WHICH HAVE NOT CHANGED LOCATION OF CHURCH BUILDING SINCE ORGANIZATION, BY TYPES — (*Continued*)

Type and Subtype	No. of Churches Reporting	Per Cent. Remaining in Original Location
Total of Four Types	515	29.3
A IV	18	22.2 *
A V	10	20.0 *
B IV	3	..
C III	15	13.3 *
D I	19	42.1 *
E I	10	20.0 *
Widely Variant	75	24.0 *
Grand Total	590	28.6

* Base less than 100.

TABLE 9 — SIZE OF STAFF, BY TYPES

Number of Paid Religious Workers

Type and Subtype		1	2	3	4	5	6	7	8	9	10 and Over	Total Churches
A I		71	4	1	0	0	0	0	0	0	0	76
A II		33	1	0	0	0	0	0	0	0	0	34
A III		22	4	0	1	0	0	0	0	0	0	27
B I		73	14	3	6	0	1	0	0	0	0	97
Unadapted	No.	199	23	4	7	0	1	0	0	0	0	234
	%	85.1	9.8	1.7	3.0	..	0.4	..	..	..	..	100.0
B II		106	21	14	10	3	0	0	0	0	0	154
B III		48	17	9	3	1	0	0	0	0	0	78
C I		49	28	19	5	3	2	0	2	0	0	108
Slightly Adapted	No.	203	66	42	18	7	2	0	2	0	0	340
	%	59.7	19.4	12.3	5.3	2.1	0.6	..	0.6	..	..	100.0
C II		35	22	33	11	6	2	1	1	0	1	112
D II		17	20	19	12	6	2	0	3	0	0	79
Internally Adapted	No.	52	42	52	23	12	4	1	4	0	1	191
	%	27.2	22.0	27.2	12.1	6.3	2.1	0.5	2.1	..	0.5	100.0
D III		8	9	9	8	4	3	0	0	0	1	42
E II		4	15	10	13	9	5	2	4	1	1	64
Socially Adapted	No.	12	24	19	21	13	8	2	4	1	2	106
	%	11.3	22.6	17.9	19.8	12.3	7.6	1.9	3.8	0.9	1.9	100.0
Total of 4 Types	No.	466	155	117	69	32	15	3	10	1	3	871
	%	53.5	17.8	13.5	7.9	3.7	1.7	0.3	1.2	0.1	0.3	100.0
A IV		26	2	3	0	0	0	0	0	0	0	31
A V		9	2	0	1	0	0	0	0	0	0	12
B IV		2	3	2	1	1	0	1	0	0	0	10
C III		8	10	5	1	1	0	0	2	0	0	27
D I		11	9	2	2	2	1	0	0	0	0	27
E I		1	4	2	2	1	0	0	0	0	0	10
Widely Variant	No.	57	30	14	7	5	1	1	2	0	0	117
	%	48.7	25.6	11.9	6.0	4.3	0.9	0.9	1.7	..	..	100.0
Grand Total	No.	523	185	131	76	37	16	4	12	1	3	988
	%	52.9	18.7	13.3	7.7	3.8	1.6	0.4	1.2	0.1	0.3	100.0

TABLE 10 — MALE STAFF WORKERS OTHER THAN PASTOR, BY TYPES

Type and Subtype		Assistant or Associate Pastor	Director Religious Education	Director Social Service and Social Worker	Director Men's, Boys' or Young People's Work	Secretary	Financial or Executive Secretary or Treasurer	Director of Gymnasium or Boy Scouts, Superintendent, etc.	Total
A I		0	1	0	0	0	0	0	1
A II		0	0	0	0	1	0	0	1
A III		2	1	0	0	0	0	0	3
B I		6	5	0	0	2	3	0	16
Unadapted	No.	8	7	0	0	3	3	0	21
	%	*	*	*	*	*	*	*	*
B II		22	8	0	0	0	3	4	37
B III		12	0	0	1	0	0	1	14
C I		18	15	0	0	4	3	2	42
Slightly Adapted	No.	52	23	0	1	4	6	7	93
	%	*	*	*	*	*	*	*	*
C II		36	13	2	5	1	2	6	65
D II		26	12	4	4	1	3	7	57
Internally Adapted	No.	62	25	6	9	2	5	13	122
	%	50.8	20.5	4.9	7.4	1.6	4.1	10.7	100.0
D III		14	1	2	7	2	0	6	32
E II		34	8	2	9	4	0	8	65
Socially Adapted	No.	48	9	4	16	6	0	14	97
	%	*	*	*	*	*	*	*	*
Total of 4 Types	No.	170	64	10	26	15	14	34	333
	%	51.1	19.2	3.0	7.8	4.5	4.2	10.2	100.0
A IV		2	1	0	0	0	0	0	3
A V		1	0	0	1	0	0	0	2
B IV		3	0	2	0	0	0	0	5
C III		4	3	0	0	0	0	6	13
D I		4	1	0	3	3	0	1	12
E I		2	2	0	0	0	0	0	4
Widely Variant	No.	16	7	2	4	3	0	7	39
	%	*	*	*	*	*	*	*	*
Grand Total	No.	186	71	12	30	18	14	41	372
	%	50.0	19.1	3.2	8.1	4.8	3.8	11.0	100.0

* Base less than 100.

TABLE 11—FEMALE STAFF WORKERS OTHER THAN PASTOR, BY TYPES

Type and Subtype		Pastor's Assistant	Director Religious Education	Director Social Service and Social Worker	Director Women's, Girls' or Young People's Work	Secretary	Financial Secretary	Deaconess	Visitor	Matron, etc.	Total
A I		0	0	1	0	0	0	2	0	0	3
A II		0	0	0	0	1	0	0	0	0	1
A III		0	0	0	0	0	0	1	2	0	3
B I		2	1	5	1	8	1	3	3	1	25
Unadapted	No.	2	1	6	1	9	1	6	5	1	32
	%	*	*	*	*	*	*	*	*	*	*
B II		4	2	2	1	28	0	4	8	1	50
B III		4	2	0	2	13	0	2	6	1	30
C I		6	4	7	2	37	1	5	5	2	69
Slightly Adapted	No.	14	8	9	5	78	1	11	19	4	149
	%	9.4	5.4	6.0	3.4	52.3	0.7	7.4	12.8	2.7	100.0
C II		9	5	9	8	52	2	5	13	5	108
D II		3	0	7	8	45	1	11	7	3	85
Internally Adapted	No.	12	5	16	16	97	3	16	20	8	193
	%	6.2	2.6	8.3	8.3	50.3	1.5	8.3	10.4	4.1	100.0
D III		3	5	9	6	17	0	7	6	4	57
E II		6	2	16	7	42	0	16	10	9	108
Socially Adapted	No.	9	7	25	13	59	0	23	16	13	165
	%	5.5	4.2	15.2	7.9	35.8	..	13.9	9.7	7.9	100.0
Total of 4 Types	No.	37	21	56	35	243	5	56	60	26	539
	%	6.9	3.9	10.4	6.5	45.1	0.9	10.4	11.1	4.8	100.0
A IV		0	0	2	0	2	0	0	1	0	5
A V		0	0	0	1	0	0	1	0	1	3
B IV		1	0	4	0	1	0	2	0	0	8
C III		0	0	6	1	2	0	5	6	2	22
D I		1	0	0	1	12	2	2	1	0	19
E I		2	0	2	0	5	0	2	1	0	12
Widely Variant	No.	4	0	14	3	22	2	12	9	3	69
	%	*	*	*	*	*	*	*	*	*	*
Grand Total	No.	41	21	70	38	265	7	68	69	29	608
	%	6.7	3.5	11.5	6.2	43.6	1.2	11.2	11.3	4.8	100.0

* Base less than 100.

TABLE 12—PASTOR'S EXPERIENCE IN MINISTRY, BY TYPES

Type and Subtype		Under 10 years Under 5	5–9	Total	10–19	20–29	30–39	40 and over	Total
A I		12	8	20	6	8	5	2	41
A II		9	5	14	2	6	3	1	26
A III		7	0	7	1	5	3	0	16
B I		9	8	17	15	23	8	5	68
Unadapted	No.	37	21	58	24	42	19	8	151
	%	24.5	13.9	38.4	15.9	27.8	12.6	5.3	100.0

TABLE 12 — PASTOR'S EXPERIENCE IN MINISTRY, BY TYPES
(Continued)

Type and Subtype		Under 5	10 years 5–9	Total	10–19	20–29	30–39	40 and over	Total
B II		14	14	28	25	29	11	5	98
B III		5	12	17	13	13	4	1	48
C I		5	11	16	18	18	10	3	65
Slightly Adapted	No.	24	37	61	56	60	25	9	211
	%	11.4	17.5	28.9	26.5	28.4	11.9	4.3	100.0
C II		1	8	9	18	24	3	1	55
D II		1	5	6	16	16	3	1	42
Internally Adapted	No.	2	13	15	34	40	6	2	97
	%	*	*	*	*	*	*	*	*
D III		2	2	4	3	11	4	0	22
E II		0	5	5	12	7	7	1	32
Socially Adapted	No.	2	7	9	15	18	11	1	54
	%	*	*	*	*	*	*	*	*
Total of 4 Types	No.	65	78	143	129	160	61	20	513
	%	12.7	15.2	27.9	25.1	31.2	11.9	3.9	100.0
A IV		2	4	6	3	5	0	0	14
A V		3	0	3	1	2	2	0	8
B IV		0	3	3	1	1	1	0	6
C III		2	7	9	4	4	0	0	17
D I		1	1	2	6	6	5	0	19
E I		0	0	0	2	2	1	0	5
Widely Variant	No.	8	15	23	17	20	9	0	69
	%	*	*	*	*	*	*	*	*
Grand Total	No.	73	93	166	146	180	70	20	582
	%	12.5	16.0	28.5	25.1	30.9	12.0	3.4	100.0

Header note: Number of Years above columns.

* Base less than 100.

TABLE 13 — EDUCATION OF PASTOR, BY TYPES

Type and Subtype		Theological Seminary	College	College and Theological Seminary	College, Theological Seminary and Post Graduate	All others	Total
A I		3	12	22	5	4	46
A II		3	8	12	3	0	26
A III		2	3	11	4	0	20
B I		3	12	41	15	0	71
Unadapted	No.	11	35	86	27	4	163
	%	6.7	21.5	52.7	16.6	2.5	100.0
B II		5	12	65	18	1	101
B III		4	4	21	20	0	49
C I		3	9	47	21	0	80
Slightly Adapted	No.	12	25	133	59	1	230
	%	5.2	10.9	57.8	25.7	0.4	100.0
C II		2	8	32	23	1	66
D II		0	3	31	17	2	53
Internally Adapted	No.	2	11	63	40	3	119
	%	1.7	9.3	52.9	33.6	2.5	100.0
D III		0	3	17	5	0	25
E II		3	2	16	16	0	37
Socially Adapted	No.	3	5	33	21	0	62
	%	*	*	*	*	*	*
Total of 4 Types	No.	28	76	315	147	8	574
	%	4.9	13.2	54.9	25.6	1.4	100.0

TABLE 13 — EDUCATION OF PASTOR, BY TYPES — (Continued)

Type and Subtype		Theological Seminary	College	College and Theological Seminary	College, Theological Seminary and Post Graduate	All others	Total
A IV		4	2	11	1	0	18
A V		0	3	1	0	4	8
B IV		0	2	4	0	1	7
C III		5	3	9	7	0	24
D I		1	0	11	10	0	22
E I		2	1	3	3	0	9
Widely Variant	No.	12	11	39	21	5	88
	%	*	*	*	*	*	*
Grand Total	No.	40	87	354	168	13	662
	%	6.0	13.1	53.5	25.4	2.0	100.0

* Base less than 100.

TABLE 14 — PASTOR'S TENURE IN PRESENT POSITION, BY TYPES

Type and Subtype			Under 10		Number of Years			30 and	
		Under 2	2–4	5–9	Total	10–19	20–29	over	Total
A I		19	22	5	46	3	0	0	49
A II		13	5	4	22	2	0	1	25
A III		5	9	1	15	2	2	0	19
B I		17	32	14	63	7	2	0	72
Unadapted	No.	54	68	24	146	14	4	1	165
	%	32.7	41.2	14.6	88.5	8.5	2.4	0.6	100.0
B II		30	38	19	87	11	1	1	100
B III		11	27	7	45	3	1	1	50
C I		15	33	12	60	10	2	3	75
Slightly Adapted	No.	56	98	38	192	24	4	5	225
	%	24.9	43.5	16.9	85.3	10.7	1.8	2.2	100.0
C II		9	21	15	45	7	3	2	57
D II		8	23	7	38	8	5	2	53
Internally Adapted	No.	17	44	22	83	15	8	4	110
	%	15.5	40.0	20.0	75.5	13.6	7.3	3.6	100.0
D III		2	10	6	18	2	1	1	22
D II		4	12	6	22	6	2	1	31
Socially Adapted	No.	6	22	12	40	8	3	2	53
	%	*	*	*	*	*	*	*	*
Total of 4 Types	No.	133	232	96	461	61	19	12	553
	%	24.1	41.9	17.4	83.4	11.0	3.4	2.2	100.0
A IV		8	7	4	19	0	0	0	19
A V		2	2	2	6	0	0	0	6
B IV		2	1	1	4	1	1	0	6
C III		5	3	5	13	1	1	0	15
D I		4	7	7	18	1	1	1	21
E I		0	2	3	5	2	1	0	8
Widely Variant	No.	21	22	22	65	5	4	1	75
	%	*	*	*	*	*	*	*	*
Grand Total	No.	154	254	118	526	66	23	13	628
	%	24.5	40.4	18.8	83.7	10.5	3.7	2.1	100.0

* Base less than 100.

TABLE 15 — SALARY OF PASTOR, BY TYPES

Type and Subtype		Under $500	Under $1,000	$1,000 to $2,000	$2,000 to $3,000	$3,000 to $4,000	$4,000 to $5,000	$5,000 to $6,000	$6,000 to $7,000	$7,000 to $8,000	$8,000 and over	Total Reporting
A I		3	10	45	9	0	0	0	0	0	0	64
A II		1	4	20	7	0	0	0	0	0	0	31
A III		1	3	11	7	1	0	0	0	0	0	22
B I		0	4	37	20	7	4	2	1	1	2	78
Unadapted	No.	5	21	113	43	8	4	2	1	1	2	195
	%	2.6	10.8	58.0	22.0	4.1	2.1	1.0	0.5	0.5	1.0	100.0
B II		2	7	52	32	19	7	11	1	2	1	132
B III		0	4	26	13	11	4	3	3	1	1	66
C I		0	0	17	25	12	12	5	9	5	3	88
Slightly Adapted	No.	2	11	95	70	42	23	19	13	8	5	286
	%	0.7	3.9	33.2	24.5	14.7	8.0	6.6	4.5	2.8	1.8	100.0
C II		0	0	11	22	13	6	12	9	6	3	82
D II		0	0	4	6	14	12	5	9	3	1	54
Internally Adapted	No.	0	0	15	28	27	18	17	18	9	4	136
	%	..	..	11.0	20.6	19.9	13.2	12.5	13.2	6.6	3.0	100.0
D III		0	0	6	5	4	4	1	5	2	0	27
E II		0	0	1	5	10	6	8	5	2	3	40
Socially Adapted	No.	0	0	7	10	14	10	9	10	4	3	67
	%	*	*	*	*	*	*	*	*	*	*	*
Total of 4 Types	No.	7	32	230	151	91	55	47	42	22	14	684
	%	1.0	4.7	33.6	22.1	13.3	8.1	6.9	6.1	3.2	2.0	100.0
A IV		0	1	18	7	1	0	0	0	0	0	27
A V		1	3	3	1	0	0	0	0	0	0	7
B IV		0	0	3	3	1	0	0	0	0	0	7
C III		0	0	9	7	2	0	1	0	0	0	19
D I		0	0	3	2	4	3	6	3	2	0	23
E I		0	0	2	2	1	1	0	0	1	0	7
Widely Variant	No.	1	4	38	22	9	4	7	3	3	0	90
	%	*	*	*	*	*	*	*	*	*	*	*
Grand Total	No.	8	36	268	173	100	59	54	45	23	14	771
	%	1.0	4.7	24.6	22.4	12.9	7.6	7.0	5.8	3.2	1.8	100.0

* Base less than 100.

TABLE 18 — MALE WORKER'S TENURE IN PRESENT POSITION, BY TYPES — (*Continued*)

Type and Subtype	Under 2	Under 5	5–9	10–14	15 and Over	Total
			Number of Years			
Internally Adapted	11	23	3	1	0	27
D III	1	3	0	0	0	3
E II	8	14	1	2	1	18
Socially Adapted	9	17	1	2	1	21
Total of 4 Types	27	54	5	4	4	67
A IV	0	0	0	0	0	0
A V	1	1	1	0	0	2
B IV	0	0	0	0	0	0
C III	1	1	0	0	0	1
D I	3	3	1	0	0	4
E I	1	1	0	0	0	1
Widely Variant	6	6	2	0	0	8
Grand Total	33	60	7	4	4	75

TABLE 19 — MALE WORKER'S SALARY, BY TYPES

Type and Subtype	Under $500	$500 to $1,000	Total	$1,000 to $2,000	$2,000 to $3,000	$3,000 to $4,000	$4,000 to $5,000	$5,000 and Over	Total
	Under $1,000								
A I	0	0	0	0	0	0	0	0	0
A II	0	0	0	0	0	0	0	0	0
A III	0	0	0	0	0	0	0	0	0
B I	1	0	1	3	1	3	0	0	8
Unadapted	1	0	1	3	1	3	0	0	8
B II	0	2	2	4	3	3	0	0	12
B III	0	1	1	4	2	1	0	0	8
C I	1	4	5	8	7	4	1	0	25
Slightly Adapted	1	7	8	16	12	8	1	0	45
C II	2	5	7	4	12	5	0	0	28
D II	1	3	4	9	9	7	0	0	29
Internally Adapted	3	8	11	13	21	12	0	0	57
D III	2	0	2	5	4	1	0	0	12
E II	1	4	5	10	12	7	2	1	37

TABLE 19—MALE WORKER'S SALARY, BY TYPES—(*Continued*)

Under $1,000

Type and Subtype	Under $500	$500 to $1,000	Total	$1,000 to $2,000	$2,000 to $3,000	$3,000 to $4,000	$4,000 to $5,000	$5,000 and Over	Total
Socially Adapted	3	4	7	15	16	8	2	1	49
Total of 4 Types	8	19	27	47	50	31	3	1	159
A IV	0	1	1	0	0	0	0	0	1
A V	0	0	0	0	0	0	0	0	0
B IV	0	1	1	0	1	0	0	0	2
C III	0	1	1	5	1	0	0	0	7
D I	0	1	1	4	3	0	0	0	8
E I	0	0	0	2	2	0	0	0	4
Widely Variant	0	4	4	11	7	0	0	0	22
Grand Total	8	23	31	58	57	31	3	1	181

TABLE 20—FEMALE WORKER'S EDUCATION, BY TYPES

Type and Subtype	High School Only	College	College, Post Grad. or Other	Special Vocational	Total
A I	0	0	0	0	0
A II	0	0	0	0	0
A III	0	0	0	1	1
B I	4	2	1	1	8
Unadapted	4	2	1	2	9
B II	6	2	1	2	11
B III	7	5	1	0	13
C I	3	5	2	3	13
Slightly Adapted	16	12	4	5	37
C II	10	9	4	1	24
D II	17	12	0	3	32
Internally Adapted	27	21	4	4	56
D III	1	9	0	0	10
E II	16	13	1	7	37
Socially Adapted	17	22	1	7	47
Total of 4 Types	64	57	10	18	149
A IV	0	0	0	1	1
A V	0	2	0	1	3
B IV	0	0	0	1	1

TABLE 20 — FEMALE WORKER'S EDUCATION, BY TYPES
(Continued)

Type and Subtype	High School Only	College	College, Post Grad. or Other	Special Vocational	Total
C III	2	4	0	4	10
D I	3	2	0	0	5
E II	0	3	0	3	6
Widely Variant	5	11	0	10	26
Grand Total	69	68	10	28	175

TABLE 21 — FEMALE WORKER'S EXPERIENCE IN PAID RELIGIOUS WORK, BY TYPES

Type and Subtype	Under 2	Under 5	5-9	10-14	15-19	20-24	25 and Over	Total
A I	0	0	0	0	0	0	0	0
A II	0	0	0	0	0	0	0	0
A III	0	0	0	0	0	0	0	0
B I	0	1	0	0	0	0	0	1
Unadapted	0	1	0	0	0	0	0	1
B II	1	5	1	0	0	0	0	6
B III	0	1	2	1	0	0	0	4
C I	1	1	1	1	0	0	0	3
Slightly Adapted	2	7	4	2	0	0	0	13
C II	2	9	4	3	2	3	0	21
D II	0	7	2	2	1	0	0	12
Internally Adapted ..	2	16	6	5	3	3	0	33
D III	0	1	2	0	0	0	0	3
E II	2	5	3	3	0	3	1	15
Socially Adapted	2	6	5	3	0	3	1	18
Total of 4 Types	6	30	15	10	3	6	1	65
A IV	0	1	1	0	0	0	0	2
A V	0	1	0	0	0	0	0	1
B IV	0	1	1	1	0	0	0	3
C III	0	3	1	0	0	1	0	5
D I	0	0	2	2	0	0	0	4
E I	0	0	1	0	0	0	0	1
Widely Variant	0	6	6	3	0	1	0	16
Grand Total	6	36	21	13	3	7	1	81

TABLE 22 — FEMALE WORKER'S TENURE IN PRESENT POSITION, BY TYPES

Type and Subtype	Under 2	Under 5	5–9	10–14	15–19	Total
A I	0	0	0	0	0	0
A II	0	0	0	0	0	0
A III	0	0	0	0	0	0
B I	0	1	0	0	0	1
Unadapted	0	1	0	0	0	1
B II	4	6	0	0	0	6
B III	2	3	0	0	0	3
C I	4	10	1	0	0	11
Slightly Adapted	10	19	1	0	0	20
C II	2	12	0	2	0	14
D II	7	14	3	1	0	18
Internally Adapted	9	26	3	3	0	32
D III	1	1	0	0	0	1
E II	3	10	3	4	0	17
Socially Adapted	4	11	3	4	0	18
Total of 4 Types	23	57	7	7	0	71
A IV	0	0	0	0	0	0
A V	1	3	0	0	0	3
B IV	0	0	0	0	0	0
C III	2	2	0	0	0	2
D I	2	3	1	1	1	6
E I	0	0	0	0	0	0
Widely Variant	5	8	1	1	1	11
Grand Total	28	65	8	8	1	82

TABLE 23 — FEMALE WORKER'S SALARY, BY TYPES

Type and Subtype		Under $500	$500 to $1,000	$1,000 to $1,500	$1,500 to $2,000	$2,000 to $2,500	$2,500 and Over	Total
A I		0	1	0	0	0	0	1
A II		0	1	0	0	0	0	1
A III		0	0	0	0	0	0	0
B I		2	2	2	5	0	0	11
Unadapted	No.	2	4	2	5	0	0	13
	%	*	*	*	*	*	*	*
B II		3	5	6	1	0	0	15
B III		1	5	7	3	0	0	16
C I		2	10	15	8	1	0	36

TABLE 23 — FEMALE WORKER'S SALARY, BY TYPES — (Continued)

Type and Subtype		Under $500	$500 to $1,000	$1,000 to $1,500	$1,500 to $2,000	$2,000 to $2,500	$2,500 and Over	Total
Slightly Adapted	No.	6	20	28	12	1	0	67
	%	*	*	*	*	*	*	*
C II		2	18	28	15	0	1	64
D II		8	13	23	12	0	0	56
Internally Adapted	No.	10	31	51	27	0	1	120
	%	9.3	25.9	42.5	22.5	..	0.8	100.0
D III		1	4	11	6	0	0	22
E II		1	14	23	21	4	1	64
Socially Adapted	No.	2	18	34	27	4	1	86
	%	*	*	*	*	*	*	*
Total of 4 Types	No.	20	73	115	71	5	2	286
	%	7.0	25.6	40.2	24.8	1.7	0.7	100.0
A IV		0	0	1	0	0	0	1
A V		1	0	2	0	0	0	3
B IV		0	1	4	0	0	0	5
C III		0	4	1	2	0	0	7
D I		1	4	5	0	0	0	10
E I		0	6	2	1	0	0	9
Widely Variant	No.	2	15	15	3	0	0	35
	%	*	*	*	*	*	*	*
Grand Total	No.	22	88	130	74	5	2	321
	%	6.8	27.4	40.5	23.1	1.6	0.6	100.0

* Base less than 100.

TABLE 24 — ANNUAL CURRENT EXPENSES, BY TYPES

Type and Subtype		Under $5,000	Under $25,000					$25,000 to $50,000	$50,000 to $75,000	$75,000 and over	Total
			$5,000 to $10,000	$10,000 to $15,000	$15,000 to $20,000	$20,000 to $25,000	Total				
A I		63	8	0	0	0	71	0	0	0	71
A II		22	6	0	0	0	28	0	0	0	28
A III		20	3	0	0	0	23	1	0	0	24
B I		58	14	7	2	1	82	7	0	0	89
Unadapted	No.	163	31	7	2	1	204	8	0	0	212
	%	76.9	14.6	3.3	0.9	0.5	96.2	3.8	..	..	100.0
B II		73	33	11	16	5	138	6	2	0	146
B III		35	18	6	6	3	68	6	2	0	76
C I		34	22	14	9	10	89	12	1	0	102
Slightly Adapted	No.	142	73	31	31	18	295	24	5	0	324
	%	43.8	22.5	9.6	9.6	5.6	91.1	7.4	1.5	..	100.0
C II		22	28	13	13	7	83	19	2	0	104
D II		5	17	11	12	9	54	15	1	0	70
Internally Adapted	No.	27	45	24	25	16	137	34	3	0	174
	%	15.5	25.8	13.8	14.4	9.2	78.7	19.6	1.7	..	100.0

TABLE 24 — ANNUAL CURRENT EXPENSES, BY TYPES
(Continued)

		Under $5,000	$5,000 to $10,000	$10,000 to $15,000	$15,000 to $20,000	$20,000 to $25,000	Total	$25,000 to $50,000	$50,000 to $75,000	$75,000 and over	Total
Type and Subtype											
D III		5	9	10	2	4	30	7	1	0	38
E II		4	7	14	5	9	39	15	5	3	62
Socially Adapted	No.	9	16	24	7	13	69	22	6	3	100
	%	9.0	16.0	24.0	7.0	13.0	69.0	22.0	6.0	3.0	100.0
Total of 4 Types	No.	341	165	86	65	48	705	88	14	3	810
	%	42.1	20.4	10.6	8.0	5.9	87.0	10.9	1.7	0.4	100.0
A IV		21	7	0	0	1	29	0	0	0	29
A V		8	3	0	0	0	11	0	0	0	11
B IV		4	2	0	2	0	8	0	0	0	8
C III		12	5	3	1	1	22	1	0	0	23
D I		4	5	4	2	6	21	4	1	0	26
E I		1	5	4	0	2	8	2	0	0	10
Widely Variant	No.	50	26	7	7	9	99	7	1	0	107
	%	46.7	24.3	6.6	6.5	8.4	92.5	6.6	0.9	..	100.0
Grand Total	No.	391	191	93	72	57	804	95	15	3	917
	%	42.6	20.8	10.2	7.9	6.2	87.7	10.4	1.6	0.3	100.0

TABLE 24a — ANNUAL CURRENT EXPENSES UNDER $5,000, BY TYPES

Type and Subtype		Under $1,000	$1,000 to $2,000	$2,000 to $3,000	$3,000 to $4,000	$4,000 to $5,000	Total Under $5,000
A I		15	20	17	8	3	63
A II		3	5	9	2	3	22
A III		2	5	6	4	3	20
B I		1	15	15	14	13	58
Unadapted	No.	21	45	47	28	22	163
	%	9.9	21.2	22.2	13.2	10.4	76.9
B II		4	20	24	18	7	73
B III		1	11	12	3	8	35
C I		0	6	9	12	7	34
Slightly Adapted	No.	5	37	45	33	22	142
	%	1.5	11.4	13.9	10.2	6.8	43.8
C II		0	3	8	4	7	22
D II		1	1	0	2	1	5
Internally Adapted	No.	1	4	8	6	8	27
	%	*	*	*	*	*	*
D III		0	1	0	3	1	5
E II		0	0	1	2	1	4

TABLE 24a — ANNUAL CURRENT EXPENSES UNDER $5,000, BY TYPES — (Continued)

Type and Subtype		Under $1,000	$1,000 to $2,000	$2,000 to $3,000	$3,000 to $4,000	$4,000 to $5,000	Total Under $5,000
Socially Adapted	No.	0	1	1	5	2	9
	%	*	*	*	*	*	*
Total of 4 Types	No.	27	87	101	72	54	341
	%	3.3	10.7	12.5	8.9	6.7	42.1
A IV		1	9	4	4	3	21
A V		1	5	1	0	1	8
B IV		1	0	1	2	0	4
C III		1	1	5	3	2	12
D I		0	0	1	2	1	4
E I		0	0	0	1	0	1
Widely Variant	No.	4	15	12	12	7	50
	%	*	*	*	*	*	*
Grand Total	No.	31	102	113	84	61	391
	%	3.4	11.1	12.3	9.2	6.7	42.7

* Base less than 100.

TABLE 25 — PER CAPITA ANNUAL CURRENT EXPENSES AND CURRENT BENEVOLENCES, BY TYPES

Type and Subtype	Per Capita Current Expense	Per Capita Benevolence
A I	$16.98	$4.34
A II	10.50	4.11
A III	19.57	7.22
B I	14.13	9.24
Unadapted	14.75	7.79
B II	16.78	10.02
B III	22.75	9.94
C I	17.06	15.17
Slightly Adapted	17.96	12.14
C II	18.79	11.63
D II	19.55	12.64
Internally Adapted	19.12	12.03
D III	20.94	15.08
E II	19.57	11.57
Socially Adapted	19.95	12.55
Average of 4 Types	18.27	11.65

TABLE 25 — PER CAPITA ANNUAL CURRENT EXPENSES AND CURRENT BENEVOLENCES, BY TYPES — (Continued)

Type and Subtype	Per Capita Current Expense	Per Capita Benevolence
A IV	$18.83	$9.77
A V	25.48	7.00
B IV	42.21	8.16
C III	14.60	3.83
D I	16.37	11.40
E I	16.63	16.23
Widely Variant	17.23	10.33
Average of Total	18.17	11.52

TABLE 26 — ANNUAL BENEVOLENCES, BY TYPES

Type and Subtype		Under $1,000	$1,000 to $2,000	$2,000 to $3,000	$3,000 to $4,300	$4,300 to $5,000	Total	$5,000 to $10,000	$10,000 to $15,000	$15,000 to $20,000	$20,000 to $25,000	$25,000 and over	Total
A I		44	8	3	1	0	56	0	0	0	0	0	56
A II		17	6	1	1	0	25	1	0	0	0	0	26
A III		10	6	1	1	0	18	3	0	0	0	0	21
B I		32	17	8	5	3	65	3	2	2	1	5	78
Unadapted	No.	103	37	13	8	3	164	7	2	2	1	5	181
	%	56.9	20.4	7.2	4.4	1.7	90.6	3.9	1.1	1.1	0.5	2.8	100.0
B II		60	18	10	7	5	100	18	3	7	2	7	137
B III		33	6	4	4	5	52	11	2	0	2	4	71
C I		21	8	11	4	4	48	15	9	9	2	11	94
Slightly Adapted	No.	114	32	25	15	14	200	44	14	16	6	22	302
	%	37.7	10.6	8.3	5.0	4.6	66.2	14.6	4.6	5.3	2.0	7.3	100.0
C II		18	12	5	6	8	49	24	4	10	2	10	99
D II		4	6	6	8	5	29	13	8	4	4	8	66
Internally Adapted	No.	22	18	11	14	13	78	37	12	14	6	18	165
	%	13.3	10.9	6.7	8.5	7.9	47.3	22.4	7.3	8.5	3.6	10.9	100.0
D III		5	5	3	5	2	20	5	2	2	2	5	36
E II		3	3	7	4	2	19	11	7	5	5	10	57
Socially Adapted	No.	8	8	10	9	4	39	16	9	7	7	15	93
	%	*	*	*	*	*	*	*	*	*	*	*	*
Total of 4 Types	No.	247	95	59	46	34	481	104	37	39	20	60	741
	%	33.3	12.8	8.0	6.2	4.6	64.9	14.0	5.0	5.3	2.7	8.1	100.0
A IV		18	4	3	0	1	26	2	0	1	0	0	29
A V		5	1	2	0	0	8	0	0	0	0	0	8
B IV		7	0	1	0	0	8	0	0	0	0	0	8
C III		14	3	0	1	1	19	0	0	0	0	1	20
D I		2	1	4	3	2	12	5	3	2	0	4	26
E I		2	2	1	0	0	5	1	0	1	0	3	10
Widely Variant	No.	48	11	11	4	4	78	8	3	4	0	8	101
	%	47.5	10.9	10.9	4.0	4.0	77.2	7.9	3.0	4.0	..	7.9	100.0
Grand Total	No.	295	106	70	50	38	559	112	40	43	20	68	842
	%	35.0	12.6	8.3	6.0	4.5	66.4	13.3	4.7	5.1	2.4	8.1	100.0

* Base less than 100.

TABLE 26a — ANNUAL BENEVOLENCES UNDER $1,000, BY TYPES

Type and Subtype		Under $100	$100 to $200	$200 to $300	$300 to $400	$400 to $500	$500 to $600	$600 to $700	$700 to $800	$800 to $900	$900 to $1,000	Under $1,000
A I		11	9	3	5	5	2	2	4	2	1	44
A II		2	5	2	1	1	1	0	2	1	2	17
A III		3	0	0	2	0	0	2	1	0	2	10
B I		2	5	5	3	7	4	2	1	2	1	32
Unadapted	No.	18	19	10	11	13	7	6	8	5	6	103
	%	9.9	10.5	5.5	6.1	7.2	3.9	3.3	4.4	2.8	3.3	56.9
B II		7	10	5	9	8	6	8	3	2	2	60
B III		3	9	8	3	1	3	3	1	1	1	33
C I		1	2	3	4	2	4	1	2	1	1	21
Slightly Adapted	No.	11	21	16	16	11	13	12	6	4	4	114
	%	3.6	7.0	5.3	5.3	3.6	4.3	4.0	2.0	1.3	1.3	37.7
C II		1	0	1	0	4	4	3	2	0	3	18
D II		0	0	2	0	0	0	0	1	0	1	4
Internally Adapted	No.	1	0	3	0	4	4	3	3	0	4	22
	%	0.6	..	1.8	..	2.4	2.4	1.8	1.8	..	2.4	13.3
D III		0	0	1	0	0	1	1	2	0	0	5
E II		0	0	0	0	1	1	0	1	0	0	3
Socially Adapted	No.	0	0	1	0	1	2	1	3	0	0	8
	%	*	*	*	*	*	*	*	*	*	*	*
Total of 4 Types	No.	30	40	30	27	29	26	22	20	9	14	247
	%	4.0	5.4	4.0	3.7	3.9	3.5	3.0	2.7	1.2	1.9	33.3
A IV		5	1	1	2	0	4	1	1	3	0	18
A V		1	1	0	0	1	0	1	1	0	0	5
B IV		1	2	2	1	0	0	0	1	0	0	7
C III		1	3	1	3	4	1	1	0	0	0	14
D I		0	0	0	0	0	0	0	0	1	1	2
D I		0	0	0	0	2	0	0	0	0	0	2
Widely Variant	No.	8	7	4	6	7	5	3	3	4	1	48
	%	7.8	6.9	4.0	5.9	6.9	5.0	3.0	3.0	4.0	1.0	47.5
Grand Total	No.	38	47	34	33	36	31	25	23	13	15	295
	%	4.5	5.6	4.0	3.9	4.3	3.7	3.0	2.7	1.5	1.8	35.0

* Base less than 100.

TABLE 27 — NUMBER OF EQUIPMENT FACILITIES, BY TYPES

Type and Subtype		Number of Facilities					Total Reporting
		Under 5	5–9	10–14	15–19	20 and Over	
A I		31	24	2	0	0	57
A II		11	13	2	0	0	26
A III		5	15	2	0	0	22
B I		18	43	15	2	0	78
Unadapted	No.	65	95	21	2	0	183
	%	35.5	51.9	11.5	1.1	..	100.0

TABLE 27 — NUMBER OF EQUIPMENT FACILITIES, BY TYPES
(*Continued*)

Number of Facilities

Type and Subtype		Under 5	5–9	10–14	15–19	20 and Over	Total Reporting
B II		26	60	32	3	0	121
B III		15	25	16	8	0	64
C I		5	46	33	9	0	93
Slightly Adapted	No.	46	131	81	20	0	278
	%	16.6	47.1	29.1	7.2	..	100.0
C II		1	25	39	21	2	88
D II		0	10	29	28	2	69
Internally Adapted	No.	1	35	68	49	4	157
	%	0.6	22.3	43.4	31.2	2.5	100.0
D III		1	3	17	9	0	30
E II		0	4	13	32	7	56
Socially Adapted	No.	1	7	30	41	7	86
	%	*	*	*	*	*	*
Total of 4 Types	No.	113	268	200	112	11	704
	%	16.0	38.1	28.4	16.0	1.5	100.0
A IV		6	12	5	0	0	23
A V		1	5	3	1	0	10
B IV		3	2	1	2	0	8
C III		3	10	8	5	0	26
D I		2	3	9	11	0	25
E I		0	0	5	4	0	9
Widely Variant	No.	15	32	31	23	0	101
	%	14.8	31.7	30.7	22.8	..	100.0
Grand Total	No.	128	300	231	135	11	805
	%	15.9	37.3	28.7	16.8	1.3	100.0

* Base less than 100.

TABLE 28 — NUMBER OF ROOMS IN CHURCH BUILDING,
BY TYPES

Type and Subtype		1	2	Under 5 3	4	Total	Under 10 5–9	Total	10–19	30 and 20–29	Over	Total
A I		1	5	2	2	10	10	20	4	1	0	25
A II		0	2	0	0	2	3	5	4	2	0	11
A III		3	1	1	0	5	3	8	1	1	0	10
B I		4	3	3	5	15	13	28	17	3	0	48
Unadapted	No.	8	11	6	7	32	29	61	26	7	0	94
	%	*	*	*	*	*	*	*	*	*	*	*
B II		4	3	4	1	12	18	30	19	8	2	59
B III		1	2	4	1	8	13	21	12	4	3	40
C I		1	2	2	3	8	15	23	22	14	2	61
Slightly Adapted	No.	6	7	10	5	28	46	74	53	26	7	160
	%	3.7	4.4	6.3	3.1	17.5	28.8	46.3	33.1	16.2	4.4	100.0

TABLE 28 — NUMBER OF ROOMS IN CHURCH BUILDING, BY TYPES — (*Continued*)

Type and Subtype		1	2	Under 5 3	4	Total	5–9	Under 10 Total	10–19	20–29	30 and Over	Total
C II		0	1	0	1	2	14	16	21	8	6	51
D II		0	0	0	2	2	7	9	25	12	8	54
Internally Adapted	No.	0	1	0	3	4	21	25	46	20	14	105
	%	..	1.0	..	2.9	3.8	20.0	23.8	43.8	19.1	13.3	100.0
D III		0	0	0	0	0	5	5	13	4	2	24
E II		0	0	1	1	2	8	10	19	5	10	44
Socially Adapted	No.	0	0	1	1	2	13	15	32	9	12	68
	%	*	*	*	*	*	*	*	*	*	*	*
Total of 4 Types	No.	14	19	17	16	66	109	175	157	62	33	427
	%	3.3	4.5	4.0	3.7	15.5	25.5	41.0	35.8	14.5	7.7	100.0
A IV		0	0	2	0	2	4	6	3	0	1	10
A V		0	0	1	1	2	2	4	0	1	0	5
B IV		0	0	0	0	0	2	2	1	0	1	4
C III		0	0	2	1	3	3	6	4	3	0	13
D I		0	0	0	0	0	5	5	8	5	1	19
E I		0	0	0	0	0	2	2	1	1	3	7
Widely Variant	No.	0	0	5	2	7	18	25	17	10	6	58
	%	*	*	*	*	*	*	*	*	*	*	*
Grand Total	No.	14	19	22	18	73	127	200	174	72	39	485
	%	2.9	3.9	4.5	3.7	15.0	26.2	41.2	35.9	14.9	8.0	100.0

* Base less than 100.

TABLE 29 — VALUE OF CHURCH PROPERTY, BY TYPES

Type and Subtype	No. Reporting	Total	Average	Median
A I	46	$999,772	$21,719	$10,900
A II	20	444,525	22,226	20,050
A III	21	798,012	38,000	20,000
B I	64	4,141,068	64,704	28,350
Unadapted	151	6,383,377	42,274	20,000
B II	101	7,665,583	75,897	36,600
B III	35	4,073,750	116,393	33,000
C I	64	7,283,281	113,801	45,000
Slightly Adapted	200	19,022,614	95,113	39,000
C II	45	7,523,778	167,195	86,570
D II	23	4,172,819	181,426	150,000
Internally Adapted	68	11,696,597	172,009	120,400
D III	13.	2,705,438	208,111	111,500
E II	18	4,802,591	266,811	175,000
Socially Adapted	31	7,508,029	242,194	142,938
Total of 4 Types	450	44,610,617	99,135	35,000

TABLE 29—VALUE OF CHURCH PROPERTY, BY TYPES
(Continued)

Type and Subtype	No. Reporting	Total	Average	Median
A IV	17	$1,094,575	$64,387	$19,500
A V	5	152,341	30,468	12,000
B IV	5	241,125	48,225	30,000
C III	15	886,336	59,089	30,000
D I	12	1,789,626	149,135	105,750
E I	3	731,359	243,786	286,359
Widely Variant	57	4,895,362	85,884	30,000
Grand Total	507	49,505,979	97,645	35,000

TABLE 30—SEATING CAPACITY OF AUDITORIUM, BY TYPES

Type and Subtype	No. Reporting	Number of Sittings		
		Total	Average	Median
A I	56	13,889	248	200
A II	27	7,998	296	250
A III	23	7,526	327	250
B I	79	40,651	515	350
Unadapted	185	70,064	379	250
B II	110	51,260	466	400
B III	56	28,223	504	425
C I	91	66,386	730	600
Slightly Adapted	257	145,869	568	450
C II	74	57,260	774	700
D II	62	49,731	802	800
Internally Adapted	136	106,991	787	700
D III	27	19,475	821	600
E II	55	52,719	959	900
Socially Adapted	82	72,194	880	825
Total of 4 Types	660	395,118	599	500
A IV	26	9,377	360	312
A V	7	2,500	357	350
B IV	10	3,717	372	275
C III	20	8,210	410	300
D I	21	19,100	909	900
E I	9	7,170	797	800
Widely Variant	93	50,074	538	400
Grand Total	753	445,192	591	450

TABLE 31 — SUNDAY-SCHOOL ENROLLMENT, BY TYPES

Type and Subtype		Number of Pupils Under 500						Total	500 to 1,000	1,000 and Over	Total
		Under 50	Under 100	100 to 200	200 to 300	300 to 400	400 to 500				
A I		8	27	17	15	2	0	61	0	0	61
A II		0	5	9	8	2	0	24	1	0	25
A III		5	10	8	1	0	1	20	1	0	21
B I		2	6	21	19	13	4	63	11	2	76
Unadapted	No.	15	48	55	43	17	5	168	13	2	183
	%	8.2	26.2	30.1	23.5	9.3	2.7	91.8	7.1	1.1	100.0
B II		2	18	41	25	21	7	112	14	9	135
B III		1	8	21	15	5	8	57	6	3	66
C I		2	4	9	23	17	15	68	20	9	97
Slightly Adapted	No.	5	30	71	63	43	30	237	40	21	298
	%	1.7	10.1	23.8	21.1	14.4	10.1	79.5	13.4	7.1	100.0
C II		0	1	18	12	18	11	60	23	10	93
D II		0	1	7	11	9	13	41	19	9	69
Internally Adapted	No.	0	2	25	23	27	24	101	42	19	162
	%	..	1.2	15.4	14.2	16.7	14.8	62.3	26.0	11.7	100.0
D III		0	0	6	7	3	3	19	13	1	33
E II		0	1	3	7	13	8	32	20	7	59
Socially Adapted	No.	0	1	9	14	16	11	51	33	8	92
	%	*	*	*	*	*	*	*	*	*	*
Total of 4 Types	No.	20	81	160	143	103	70	557	128	50	735
	%	2.7	11.0	21.8	19.5	14.0	9.5	75.8	17.4	6.8	100.0
A IV		3	7	7	8	1	1	24	0	0	24
A V		1	3	5	1	1	0	10	0	0	10
B IV		2	5	3	2	0	0	10	0	0	10
C III		0	7	8	4	4	1	24	2	1	27
D I		0	0	1	3	3	6	13	8	5	26
E I		0	0	3	1	0	1	5	3	1	9
Widely Variant	No.	6	22	27	19	9	9	86	13	7	106
	%	5.7	20.7	25.5	17.9	8.5	8.5	81.1	12.3	6.6	100.0
Grand Total	No.	26	103	187	162	112	79	643	141	57	841
	%	3.1	12.2	22.2	19.3	13.3	9.4	76.4	16.8	6.8	100.0

* Base less than 100.

TABLE 32 — RATIO OF AVERAGE SUNDAY-SCHOOL ENROLL-MENT TO AVERAGE CHURCH MEMBERSHIP, BY TYPES

Type and Subtype	Per Cent.
A I	89
A II	73
A III	72
B I	63
Unadapted	69
B II	72
B III	73
C I	66

TABLE 32 — RATIO OF AVERAGE SUNDAY-SCHOOL ENROLL-
MENT TO AVERAGE CHURCH MEMBERSHIP, BY TYPES
(Continued)

Type and Subtype	*Per Cent.*
Slightly Adapted	68
C II	60
D II	61
Internally Adapted	61
D III	67
E II	47
Socially Adapted	52
Total of 4 Types	63
A IV	56
A V	101
B IV	94
C III	54
D I	67
E I	54
Widely Variant	62
Grand Total	63

TABLE 33 — AVERAGE SUNDAY-SCHOOL ATTENDANCE,
BY TYPES

Type and Subtype		*Under 50*	*Under 100*	*130 to 200*	*200 to 300*	*300 to 400*	*400 to 500*	*Total*	*500 to 1,000*	*1,000 and Over*	*Total*
A I		8	11	6	2	0	0	19	0	0	19
A II		0	4	6	0	0	0	10	0	0	10
A III		1	5	3	0	0	0	8	0	0	8
B I		0	9	21	8	2	1	41	0	1	42
Unadapted	No.	9	29	36	10	2	1	78	0	1	79
	%	*	*	*	*	*	*	*	*	*	*
B II		1	16	31	11	3	1	62	7	1	70
B III		3	7	13	6	1	0	27	3	0	30
C I		1	4	17	13	11	4	49	8	2	59
Slightly Adapted	No.	5	27	61	30	15	5	138	18	3	159
	%	3.1	17.0	38.4	18.9	9.4	3.1	86.8	11.3	1.9	100.0
C II		0	4	14	13	2	5	38	9	0	47
D II		0	0	14	13	12	1	40	4	2	46
Internally Adapted	No.	0	4	28	26	14	6	78	13	2	93
	%	*	*	*	*	*	*	*	*	*	*
D III		0	0	6	4	3	3	16	2	0	18
E II		0	0	4	8	11	1	24	8	1	33

TABLE 33 — AVERAGE SUNDAY-SCHOOL ATTENDANCE, BY TYPES — (*Continued*)

Type and Subtype		*Under 50*	*Under 100*	*100 to 200*	*200 to 300*	*300 to 400*	*400 to 500*	*Total*	*500 to 1,000*	*1,000 and Over*	*Total*
					Number of Pupils Under 500						
Socially Adapted	No.	0	0	10	12	14	4	40	10	1	51
	%	*	*	*	*	*	*	*	*	*	*
Total of 4 Types	No.	14	60	135	78	45	16	334	41	7	382
	%	3.7	15.7	35.4	20.4	11.8	4.2	87.5	10.7	1.8	100.0
A IV		2	4	6	0	0	0	10	0	0	10
A V		3	6	0	1	0	0	7	0	0	7
B IV		3	4	1	0	0	0	5	0	0	5
C III		0	5	4	2	0	2	13	1	0	14
D I		0	0	3	3	2	4	12	6	0	18
E I		0	0	1	0	1	0	2	2	0	4
Widely Variant	No.	8	19	15	6	3	6	49	9	0	58
	%	*	*	*	*	*	*	*	*	*	*
Grand Total	No.	22	79	150	84	48	22	383	50	7	440
	%	5.0	17.9	34.1	19.1	10.9	5.0	87.0	11.4	1.6	100.0

* Base less than 100.

TABLE 34 — RATIO OF SUNDAY-SCHOOL ATTENDANCE TO ENROLLMENT, BY TYPES

Type and Subtype	Per Cent.
A I	58
A II	66
A III	73
B I	63
Unadapted	63
B II	58
B III	52
C I	63
Slightly Adapted	59
C II	61
D II	64
Internally Adapted	62
D III	59
E II	65
Socially Adapted	63
Total of 4 Types	61

TABLE 34 — RATIO OF SUNDAY-SCHOOL ATTENDANCE TO ENROLLMENT, BY TYPES — (*Continued*)

Type and Subtype	Per Cent.
A IV	61
A V	58
B IV	62
C III	64
D I	59
E I	64
Widely Variant	61
Grand Total	61

TABLE 35 — SUNDAY-SCHOOL AGE DISTRIBUTION, BY TYPES

Type and Subtype	Under 6	6–14	15–20	21 and Over	Total
A I	655	2,643	815	1,031	5,144
A II	262	1,182	409	579	2,432
A III	216	1,109	275	341	1,941
B I	1,515	5,731	2,652	2,988	12,886
Unadapted	2,648	10,665	4,151	4,939	22,403
B II	2,207	9,736	3,955	4,681	20,579
B III	1,227	5,665	1,650	2,886	11,428
C I	2,002	8,253	3,790	5,582	19,627
Slightly Adapted	5,436	23,654	9,395	13,149	51,634
C II	2,415	10,227	5,316	7,851	25,809
D II	1,209	5,714	3,857	3,414	14,194
Internally Adapted	3,624	15,941	9,173	11,265	40,003
D III	546	1,918	1,305	1,361	5,130
E II	924	4,882	2,876	3,217	11,899
Socially Adapted	1,470	6,800	4,181	4,578	17,029
Total of 4 Types	13,178	57,060	26,900	33,931	131,069
A IV	281	951	201	255	1,688
A V	150	518	111	156	156
B IV	203	462	81	75	821
C III	319	1,206	336	631	2,492
D I	786	3,530	1,523	3,709	9,548
E I	264	843	888	552	2,547
Widely Variant	2,003	7,510	3,140	5,378	18,031
Grand Total	15,181	64,570	30,040	39,309	149,100

TABLE 35a — PER CENT. DISTRIBUTION BY AGE GROUPS OF
SUNDAY-SCHOOL ENROLLMENT, BY TYPES

Type and Subtype	Under 6	6–14	15–20	21 and Over	Total
A I	12.7	51.5	15.8	20.0	100.0
A II	10.8	48.6	16.8	23.8	100.0
A III	11.1	57.1	14.2	17.6	100.0
B I	11.8	44.4	20.6	23.2	100.0
Unadapted	11.8	47.7	18.5	22.0	100.0
B II	10.7	47.3	19.2	22.8	100.0
B III	10.7	49.6	14.4	25.3	100.0
C I	10.2	42.1	19.3	28.4	100.0
Slightly Adapted	10.5	45.8	18.2	25.5	100.0
C II	9.3	39.7	20.6	30.4	100.0
D II	8.5	40.2	27.2	24.1	100.0
Internally Adapted	9.1	39.8	22.9	28.2	100.0
D III	10.7	37.4	25.4	26.5	100.0
E II	7.8	41.1	24.1	27.0	100.0
Socially Adapted	8.6	39.9	24.6	26.9	100.0
Total of 4 Types	10.0	43.6	20.5	25.9	100.0
A IV	16.7	56.3	11.9	15.1	100.0
A V	16.0	55.4	11.9	16.7	100.0
B IV	24.7	56.3	9.9	9.1	100.0
C III	12.8	48.4	13.5	25.3	100.0
D I	8.2	37.0	15.9	38.9	100.0
E I	10.4	33.1	34.8	21.7	100.0
Widely Variant	11.1	41.7	17.4	29.8	100.0
Grand Total	10.2	43.3	20.2	26.3	100.0

TABLE 36—FREQUENCY OF CERTAIN CHURCH ACTIVITIES, BY TYPES

Type and Subtype	Number Cooperating with Organized Charities	Church Office Open Daily	Organized Athletics	Church Open Daily for Devotions	Daily Vacation Bible School	Motion-pictures	Children's Congregations	Week-day School of Religious Education	Children's Sermons	Sunday Evening Tea	Forum	Rooming and Board	Number Reporting
A I	10	6	3	2	9	2	2	3	1	3	0	2	74
A II	5	5	2	2	3	0	2	4	1	0	0	0	30
A III	5	6	2	5	2	0	0	4	0	0	0	0	19
B I	31	15	18	7	3	5	6	4	6	2	4	0	68
Unadapted	51	32	25	16	17	7	10	15	8	5	4	2	191
B II	40	29	29	13	20	12	6	8	6	13	5	1	119
B III	21	19	15	13	10	10	6	10	4	4	2	2	68
C I	60	47	32	15	12	8	13	7	17	21	6	0	92
Slightly Adapted	121	95	76	41	42	30	25	25	27	38	13	3	279
C II	51	50	47	18	18	18	12	14	8	22	8	2	104
D II	58	64	45	28	29	22	18	22	18	29	11	0	73
Internally Adapted	109	114	92	46	47	40	30	36	26	51	19	2	177
D III	27	20	18	10	15	14	6	6	8	9	4	2	37
E I	54	50	49	30	31	25	25	21	23	33	21	7	59
Socially Adapted	81	70	67	40	46	39	31	27	31	42	25	9	96
Total of 4 Types	362	311	260	143	152	116	96	103	92	136	61	16	743
A IV	9	4	2	2	1	2	1	3	0	1	1	1	23
A V	4	2	0	1	5	3	0	2	0	1	0	0	12
B IV	3	5	3	2	4	3	0	2	0	0	0	1	11
C III	15	16	10	3	7	7	1	4	0	4	1	0	29
D I	19	7	14	6	8	9	4	4	5	7	3	0	25
E I	8	3	5	3	5	5	3	3	5	5	0	0	10
Widely Variant	58	37	34	17	30	29	9	18	10	18	5	2	110
Grand Total	420	343	294	160	182	145	108	121	102	154	66	18	853

TABLE 37 — CENTRAL AND RESIDENTIAL LOCATION OF
CHURCHES, BY TYPES

Type and Subtype		Central	Residential	Total
A I		4	11	15
A II		1	5	6
A III		2	2	4
B I		2	5	7
Unadapted	No.	9	23	32
	%	*	*	*
B II		24	32	56
B III		14	22	36
C I		16	16	32
Slightly Adapted	No.	54	70	124
	%	43.5	56.5	100.0
C II		25	33	58
D II		19	7	26
Internally Adapted	No.	44	40	84
	%	*	*	*
D III		12	12	24
E II		26	25	51
Socially Adapted	No.	38	37	75
	%	*	*	*
Total of 4 Groups	No.	145	170	315
	%	46.0	54.0	100.0

* Base less than 100.

TABLE 38a — CENTRALLY LOCATED CHURCHES — CHARACTER
OF CENTER, BY TYPES

	Character of Center			
Type and Subtype	Major Center	Minor Center	Near Center	Total Reporting
A I	0	3	1	4
A II	1	0	0	1
A III	2	0	0	2
B I	0	0	2	2
Unadapted	3	3	3	9
B II	13	3	8	24
B III	11	1	2	14
C I	7	4	5	16
Slightly Adapted	31	8	15	54
C II	16	3	6	25
C II	13	3	3	19

TABLE 38a — CENTRALLY LOCATED CHURCHES — CHARACTER
OF CENTER, BY TYPES — (*Continued*)

	Character of Center			
Type and Subtype	*Major* *Center*	*Minor* *Center*	*Near* *Center*	*Total* *Reporting*
Internally Adapted	29	6	9	44
D III	7	3	2	12
E II	18	4	4	26
Socially Adapted	25	7	6	38
Total	88	24	33	145

TABLE 38b — CENTRALLY LOCATED CHURCHES — CHARACTER
OF LOCATION, BY TYPES

	Character of Location			
Type and Subtype	*Strategic*	*Non-* *Strategic*	*Doubtful* *or Mixed*	*No.* *Reporting*
A I	3	0	1	4
A II	0	0	0	0
A III	0	2	0	2
B I	0	0	0	0
Unadapted	3	2	1	6
B II	13	3	3	19
B III	2	3	2	7
C I	10	3	0	13
Slightly Adapted	25	9	5	39
C II	14	5	3	22
D II	2	4	11	17
Internally Adapted	16	9	14	39
D III	6	4	0	10
E II	2	3	0	5
Socially Adapted	8	7	0	15
Total	52	27	20	99

TABLE 38c — CENTRALLY LOCATED CHURCHES — QUALITY OF
LOCAL NEIGHBORHOOD, BY TYPES

	Character of Neighborhood					
	High	*Medium*	*Low*			*No.*
Type and Subtype			*Transient*	*Industrial*	*Slum*	*Reporting*
A I	0	2	1	2	0	5
A II	0	1	0	0	0	1
A III	1	0	1	0	0	2
B I	0	0	0	0	0	0
Unadapted	1	3	2	2	0	8

TABLE 38c — CENTRALLY LOCATED CHURCHES — QUALITY OF LOCAL NEIGHBORHOOD, BY TYPES — (*Continued*)

| Type and Subtype | High | Character of Neighborhood | | | | No. |
		Medium	Low Transient	Low Industrial	Slum	Reporting
B II	3	11	0	3	0	17
B III	3	4	2	0	2	11
C I	5	5	0	1	0	11
Slightly Adapted	11	20	2	4	2	39
C II	4	7	1	1	2	15
D II	0	2	2	0	0	4
Internally Adapted ..	4	9	3	1	2	19
D III	5	2	1	4	0	12
E II	0	0	1	3	2	6
Socially Adapted	5	2	2	7	2	18
Total	21	34	9	14	6	84

TABLE 39a — RESIDENTIALLY LOCATED CHURCHES ATTACHED TO SPECIFIED CENTERS, BY TYPES

Type and Subtype	Tertiary Centers	Institutional Clusters or Major Axes	Total Number	No. Reporting
A I	1	2	3	11
A II	3	0	3	5
A III	0	1	1	2
B I	0	0	0	5
Unadapted	4	3	7	23
B II	5	5	10	32
B III	5	4	9	22
C I	7	4	11	16
Slightly Adapted	17	13	30	70
C II	4	5	9	33
D II	3	3	6	7
Internally Adapted	7	8	15	40
D III	3	0	3	12
E II	4	2	6	25
Socially Adapted	7	2	9	37
Total	35	26	61	170

TABLE 39b — RESIDENTIALLY LOCATED CHURCHES — QUALITY OF ENVIRONMENT, BY TYPES

	Quality of Environment			
Type and Subtype	High Class	Middle Class	Industrial or Foreign	Number Reporting
A I	0	5	6	11
A II	0	5	0	5
A III	1	0	1	2
B I	0	5	0	5
Unadapted	1	15	7	23
B II	4	20	8	32
B III	3	12	7	22
C I	7	8	1	16
Slightly Adapted	14	40	16	70
C II	13	15	5	33
D II	1	4	2	7
Internally Adapted	14	19	7	40
D III	2	4	2	8
E II	8	15	3	26
Socially Adapted	10	19	5	34
Total	39	93	35	167

TABLE 40 — CHURCHES HAVING SPECIFIED PER CENT. OF MEMBERS LIVING WITHIN ONE MILE OF CHURCH BUILDING, BY TYPES AND SIZE OF CITY

	Per Cent. of Members				
Type of Church	Under 25	25–49	50–74	75 and Over	Total
Unadapted	1	6	10	9	26
Slightly Adapted	1	12	17	37	67
Internally Adapted	6	12	17	27	62
Socially Adapted	3	6	16	14	39
Widely Variant	3	2	9	14	28
Total	14	38	69	101	222
Size of City					
Under 250,000	3	10	20	37	70
250,000 to 500,000	6	14	5	12	37
500,000 to 1,000,000	5	11	18	17	51
1,000,000 and over	0	3	26	35	64
Total	14	38	69	101	222

TABLE 46—DISTRIBUTION OF TYPES OF CHURCHES, BY SIZE OF CITY

Size of City	Un-adapted	Slightly Adapted	Internally Adapted	Socially Adapted	Widely Variant	Total
Under 100,000	10	12	3	0	2	27
100,000 to 250,000 .	102	111	65	24	31	333
250,000 to 500,000 .	25	75	45	18	25	188
500,000 to 750,000 .	73	87	24	18	26	228
750,000 to 1,000,000	33	33	20	15	15	116
1,000,000 and over.	10	42	39	35	26	152
Total	253	360	196	110	125	1,044

TABLE 47—DISTRIBUTION OF TYPES OF CHURCHES, BY REGIONS

Type and Subtype		North-east	North Central	South	West	Total
A I		31	19	4	36	90
A II		11	6	5	13	35
A III		7	6	0	14	27
B I		35	19	16	31	101
Unadapted	No.	84	50	25	94	253
	%	33.2	19.7	9.9	37.2	100.0
B II		64	31	23	43	161
B III		33	25	3	23	84
C I		35	32	18	30	115
Slightly Adapted	No.	132	88	44	96	360
	%	36.7	24.4	12.2	26.7	100.0
C II		44	46	9	17	116
D II		25	38	13	4	80
Internally Adapted	No.	69	84	22	21	196
	%	35.2	42.9	11.2	10.7	100.0
D III		15	18	6	4	43
E II		12	24	2	0	38
Socially Adapted	No.	31	67	8	4	110
	%	27.3	61.8	7.3	3.6	100.0
Total of 4 Types	No.	316	289	99	215	919
	%	34.3	31.5	10.8	23.4	100.0
A IV		16	2	3	11	32
A V		4	6	0	5	15
B IV		4	4	2	1	11
C III		6	12	2	10	30
D I		7	14	3	3	27
E I		4	6	0	0	10
Widely Variant	No.	41	44	10	30	125
	%	32.8	35.2	8.0	24.0	100.0
Grand Total	No.	357	333	109	245	1,044
	%	34.2	31.9	10.4	23.5	100.0

TABLE 48 — AVERAGE NUMBER OF NATIVE-BORN POPULA-
TION PER PROTESTANT CHURCH ("TOTAL" AND "REGU-
LAR") AND RATIO OF PROTESTANT MEMBERS TO
NATIVE-BORN POPULATION IN CITIES OF 100,000 POPU-
LATION AND OVER, BY REGION AND SIZE OF CITY (1916)

| Region and Size of City | *Average Native-born Population* | | *Per Cent. Ratio of Total Church Members to Total Native-born Population* |
	Number per Protestant Church	*Number per "Regular" Protestant Church*	
Northeast			
100,000 to 250,000	1,552	1,792	22.0
250,000 to 500,000	2,100	2,346	17.4
500,000 to 1,000,000	1,726	1,826	21.9
1,000,000 and over	2,626	2,746	14.8
Total	2,119	2,293	17.5
South			
100,000 to 250,000	932	993	33.1
250,000 to 500,000	1,526	1,602	19.9
500,000 to 1,000,000	1,554	1,632	22.4
Total	1,133	1,201	27.7
North Central			
100,000 to 250,000	1,357	1,517	22.9
250,000 to 500,000	1,581	1,721	20.1
500,000 to 1,000,000	2,427	2,590	15.6
1,000,000 and over	2,194	2,262	14.5
Total	1,835	1,979	17.9
West			
100,000 to 250,000	1,335	1,527	12.4
250,000 to 500,000	1,240	1,428	16.9
500,000 to 1,000,000	1,719	1,893	11.4
Total	1,437	1,626	13.6
Total, 100,000 to 250,000	1,226	1,356	25.2
250,000 to 500,000	1,573	1,733	18.9
500,000 to 1,000,000	1,922	2,051	17.7
1,000,000 and over	2,495	2,595	14.7
Grand Total	1,731	1,870	18.8

TABLE 49 — NUMBER OF ALL CHURCH ORGANIZATIONS AND
PROTESTANT ORGANIZATIONS IN CITIES OF 100,000
POPULATION AND OVER, BY REGION AND SIZE OF CITY
(1920)

From Census of Religious Bodies, 1916

Region and Size of City	No. of Church Organizations, 1916	No. of Protestant Organizations, 1916	Per Cent.
Northeast			
100,000 to 250,000	1,587	1,159	73.0
250,000 to 500,000	492	354	71.9
500,000 to 1,000,000	1,099	788	71.8
1,000,000 and over	3,336	1,921	57.6
Total	6,514	4,222	64.7
South			
100,000 to 250,000	2,041	1,861	91.2
250,000 to 500,000	594	504	84.9
500,000 to 1,000,000	494	418	84.8
Total	3,129	2,783	89.0
North Central			
100,000 to 250,000	1,331	1,096	82.3
250,000 to 500,000	1,234	1,007	81.5
500,000 to 1,000,000	1,075	795	74.0
1,000,000 and over	1,226	863	70.4
Total	4,866	3,761	77.2
West			
100,000 to 250,000	357	262	73.4
250,000 to 500,000	633	530	83.7
500,000 to 1,000,000	589	467	79.3
Total	1,579	1,259	79.7
Total U. S.			
100,000 to 250,000	5,316	4,378	82.4
250,000 to 500,000	2,953	2,395	81.1
500,000 to 1,000,000	3,257	2,468	75.8
1,000,000 and over	4,562	2,784	61.0
Grand Total	16,088	12,025	74.7

TABLE 50 — MEMBERSHIP OF PROTESTANT CHURCHES IN CITIES OF 100,000 POPULATION AND OVER, BY REGION AND SIZE OF CITY

Region and Size of City	Number of Organizations	Number of Members	Average Members Per Church
Northeast			
100,000 to 250,000	1,158	395,627	342
250,000 to 500,000	354	129,162	365
500,000 to 1,000,000	785	298,125	380
1,000,000 and over	1,913	744,024	389
Total	4,210	1,566,938	372
South			
100,000 to 250,000	1,857	573,521	309
250,000 to 500,000	504	153,141	304
500,000 to 1,000,000	415	145,676	351
Total	2,776	872,338	314
North Central			
100,000 to 250,000	1,092	340,629	312
250,000 to 500,000	1,003	319,485	319
500,000 to 1,000,000	793	301,580	380
1,000,000 and over	862	274,731	319
Total	3,750	1,236,425	330
West			
100,000 to 250,000	252	43,289	172
250,000 to 500,000	530	110,849	209
500,000 to 1,000,000	466	91,321	196
Total	1,248	245,459	197
Total U. S.			
100,000 to 250,000	4,359	1,353,066	310
250,000 to 500,000	2,391	712,637	298
500,000 to 1,000,000	2,459	836,702	341
1,000,000 and over	2,775	1,018,755	367
Grand Total	11,984	3,921,160	327

TABLE 51 — AVERAGE NUMBER OF PROTESTANT DENOMINATIONS PER CITY, BY REGION AND SIZE OF CITY, IN CITIES OF 100,000 POPULATION AND OVER

Size of City	Northeast	South	North Central	West	Total U. S.
100,000 to 250,000	15	19	24	25	19
250,000 to 500,000	31	26	28	30	26
500,000 to 1,000,000	31	39	34	34	33
1,000,000 and over	47	..	53	..	49
Total	20	21	28	29	24

TABLE 54—AVERAGE ANNUAL CURRENT EXPENSES OF
PROTESTANT CHURCHES IN CITIES OF 100,000 POPULA-
TION AND OVER, BY REGION AND SIZE OF CITY (1916)

Region and Size of City	Average Current Expense
Northeast	
100,000 to 250,000	$5,650
250,000 to 500,000	6,442
500,000 to 1,000,000	7,769
1,000,000 and over	8,742
Total	7,536
South	
100,000 to 250,000	3,797
250,000 to 500,000	4,517
500,000 to 1,000,000	4,776
Total	4,083
North Central	
100,000 to 250,000	5,017
250,000 to 500,000	4,509
500,000 to 1,000,000	6,578
1,000,000 and over	5,254
Total	5,240
West	
100,000 to 250,000	2,881
250,000 to 500,000	3,241
500,000 to 1,000,000	3,729
Total	3,339
Total U. S.	
100,000 to 250,000	4,538
250,000 to 500,000	4,516
500,000 to 1,000,000	6,112
1,000,000 and over	7,672
Grand Total	5,592

TABLE 55 — VALUE OF PROTESTANT CHURCH PROPERTY IN
CITIES OF 100,000 POPULATION AND OVER, BY REGION
AND SIZE OF CITY

Region and Size of City	Number of Organizations	Total Property Value	Average Property Value
Northeast			
100,000 to 250,000	1,020	$41,859,116	$41,038
250,000 to 500,000	305	14,664,803	48,245
500,000 to 1,000,000	706	29,666,175	42,020
1,000,000 and over	1,708	152,507,758	89,290
Total	3,739	238,697,852	64,378
South			
100,000 to 250,000	1,663	33,179,170	19,951
250,000 to 500,000	359	14,625,783	40,740
500,000 to 1,000,000	378	12,060,818	31,907
Total	2,400	60,471,128	25,196
North Central			
100,000 to 250,000	995	23,723,216	23,842
250,000 to 500,000	801	24,808,939	30,972
500,000 to 1,000,000	713	26,581,983	37,282
1,000,000 and over	756	21,776,869	28,805
Total	3,265	96,891,007	29,673
West			
100,000 to 250,000	216	4,656,870	21,560
250,000 to 500,000	460	9,099,052	19,781
500,000 to 1,000,000	393	10,729,138	27,301
Total	1,069	24,485,060	22,905
Total U. S.			
100,000 to 250,000	3,894	103,418,372	26,558
250,000 to 500,000	1,925	63,198,577	32,778
500,000 to 1,000,000	2,190	79,038,114	36,090
1,000,000 and over	2,464	174,284,627	70,732
Grand Total	10,473	419,939,690	40,097

TABLE 56—RANKING OF CITY CHURCHES ON 12 SPECIFIC ITEMS, BY REGION AND SIZE OF CITY

	North-east	North Central	South	West	United States	100,000 to 250,000	250,000 to 500,000	500,000 to 1,000,000	1,000,000 and over	Total
Degree of Development of City Churches										
RANK	2	1	3	4	....	4	2	3	1	....
Native-born Population per Protestant Church										
NUMBER	2,119	1,835	1,133	1,437	1,731	1,226	1,573	1,922	2,495	1,731
RANK	4	3	1	2	....	1	2	3	4	....
Ratio of Protestant Members to Native-born Population										
PER CENT	17.5	17.9	27.7	13.6	18.8	25.2	18.9	17.7	14.7	18.8
RANK	3	2	1	4	....	1	2	3	4	....
Ratio Protestant Church Organizations to All Churches										
PER CENT	64.7	77.2	89.0	79.7	74.7	82.4	81.1	75.8	61.0	74.7
RANK	4	3	1	2	....	1	2	3	4	....
Ratio "Other" Protestant to Total Protestant Churches										
PER CENT	7.6	7.3	5.7	11.6	7.5	9.6	8.9	6.3	4.0	7.5
RANK	3	2	1	4	....	4	3	2	1	....
Average Number Protestant Denominations per City										
NUMBER	20	28	21	29	24	19	26	33	49	24
RANK	4	2	3	1	....	4	3	2	1	....
Average Membership per Protestant Church										
NUMBER	372	330	314	197	327	310	298	340	367	327
RANK	1	2	3	4	....	3	4	2	1	....
Ratio of Male to Total Membership										
PER CENT	36.9	40.1	38.4	39.4	38.3	39.5	38.6	40.0	35.6	38.3
RANK	4	1	3	2	....	2	3	1	4	....
Average Current Expense per Church										
AMOUNT	$7,536	$5,240	$4,083	$3,339	$5,592	$4,538	$4,516	$6,112	$7,672	$5,592
RANK	1	2	3	4	....	3	4	2	1	....
Average Sunday School Enrollment per Church										
NUMBER	253	227	193	141	211	206	196	225	253	211
RANK	1	2	3	4	....	3	4	2	1	....
Average Value of Property per Church										
AMOUNT	$64,378	$29,673	$25,196	$22,905	$40,097	$26,558	$32,778	$36,090	$70,732	$40,097
RANK	1	2	3	4	....	4	3	2	1	....
Ratio of Halls to Church Edifices										
PER CENT	17.5	8.3	7.1	9.8	12.0	7.8	8.6	9.1	21.1	12.0
RANK	4	2	1	3	....	1	2	3	4	....

TABLE 57 — HALLS AND ALL PLACES OF WORSHIP, BY REGION AND SIZE OF CITY

Population	Northeast			South			North Central			West			Total U. S.		
	Places of Worship	Halls	% Ratio	Places of Worship	Halls	% Ratio	Places of Worship	Halls	% Ratio	Places of Worship	Halls	% Ratio	Places of Worship	Halls	% Ratio
100,000 to 250,000..	1,528	148	9.7	1,968	130	6.6	1,289	91	7.1	340	31	9.1	5,125	400	7.8
250,000 to 500,000..	478	61	12.8	580	49	8.5	1,185	83	7.0	592	50	8.5	2,835	243	8.6
500,000 to 1,000,000	1,039	99	9.5	477	37	7.3	1,046	82	7.8	548	64	11.7	3,110	282	9.1
1,000,000 and over..	3,215	787	24.5	....	....	....	1,158	135	11.7	....	....	....	4,373	922	21.1
Total	6,260	1,095	17.5	3,025	216	7.1	4,678	391	8.3	1,480	145	9.8	15,443	1,847	12.0 *

* Omitting New York City the ratio is 9.4.

Contents

WOMEN WHO WRITE PLAYS

Published by
Smith and Kraus, Inc.
177 Lyme Road, Hanover, NH 03755
www.SmithKraus.com

Copyright © 2001 by Alexis Greene

Cover and Text Design by Julia Hill Gignoux, Freedom Hill Design

Cover Painting: Elisabeth Fiebig Writing
Lescar, France 1926
By Frédéric Fiebig (1885–1953)
Private Collection
Reproduit avec l'aimable autorisation
de Mlle. Raya Fiebig
Sélestat, France 2001
Cover photo by Sarah S. Lewis

First edition: July 2001
9 8 7 6 5 4 3 2 1

Library of Congress Cataloging In Publication Information
Women who write plays : interviews with American dramatists /
edited and with a foreword by Alexis Greene. —1st ed.
p. cm. — (An art of theater book)
Includes bibliographical references.
ISBN 1-57525-262-7
1. Dramatists, American—20th century—Interviews.
2. American drama—Women authors—History and criticism—Theory, etc.
3. Americn drama—20th century—History and criticism—Theory, etc.
4. Women and literature—United States—History—20th century.
5. Women dramatists, American—Interviews. 6. Playwriting.
I. Greene, Alexis. II. Series.

PS352.W66 2001
812'.54099287—dc21

Library of Congress Control Number: 2001032200

Women Who Write Plays

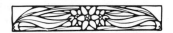

Interviews with American Dramatists

Edited and with a Foreword
by Alexis Greene

AN ART OF THEATER BOOK

Smith and Kraus, Inc.

For Janet S. Greene

Foreword

In 1997, I was teaching a graduate course at New York University about images of women in Western theater, and I found that there was little criticism or information about many of the contemporary playwrights whom we were studying. Even when there was the occasional critical essay, it often omitted discussing a playwright's cultural background and personal beliefs — context that was essential for grappling with the questions of gender, race, and class that were fundamental to the course. A collection called *Interviews with Contemporary Women Playwrights*, edited by Kathleen Betsko and Rachel Koenig, became our bible. But that had been published in 1987, and in the ten years since, the number of American women writing plays had grown enormously, even if their numbers were still not represented on the stages of American theaters.

Women Who Write Plays is a spiritual daughter of Betsko and Koenig's pioneering volume. Its intention is to find out what women writing plays at the beginning of the twenty-first century are thinking about, angry about, proud of, and desirous of. The book's aim is to find out what these playwrights experienced while they were growing up, why they write, how they write, what their artistic intentions are in their plays, and the connections between their lives and their art. The goal is to give these writers room to give themselves context.

Almost organically, diversity became the theme. The American women who speak in these interviews range in age — the youngest is in her early thirties, the oldest in her seventies. They work in many theatrical styles and have taken different professional paths. They come from diverse ethnic backgrounds and hold varying political beliefs. Some write overtly political plays, others do not. In their diversity is their strength. Each woman talks with a special voice, from her special culture and personal creative world. At the same time, possibly unbeknownst to them, the women in this volume have opinions and experiences in common: as artists; as writers making careers in the American theater; as daughters and mothers, friends and lovers; as human beings coping with our complex American society.

The seeds of the current surge were planted during the Women's Movement of the 1960s and 1970s, and watered by play-development programs at not-for-profit theaters during the 1980s. Like the mentors and teachers they often praise — Maria Irene Fornes, Ntozake Shange, Adrienne Kennedy, Lois Weaver and Peggy Shaw, and Megan Terry — the women in this volume affirm that all subjects, all styles, all modes of language are available to them. And like their predecessors, they want producers, audiences, and critics to recognize their art before their gender.

Ironically, the ongoing inability of the American theater to do that has resulted in an uneasiness about being associated with the group "women." In the so-called postfeminist era, many women are wary of solidarity. As Theresa Rebeck says succinctly in her interview, "The power structure ghettoizes you." Women who write plays in the twenty-first century are in the exciting position of freeing themselves from labels. But their personal struggles with professional inequities caused by their gender, and with how that tension affects their art and their identities, continue.

Just as disturbingly, the interviews suggest that the American theater divides racially. Many of the playwrights in this volume experience a split between mainstream regional theaters, which they believe tend to be run with white audiences in mind, and theaters that produce work for audiences of color.

The playwrights respond to this situation in a variety of ways. For some, crossing borders is essential to their career, their political outlook, and their art. "Can a writer cross cultural boundaries?" Lynn Nottage asks pointedly in her interview. "I certainly hope that I am permitted to source the different aspects of myself. And those aspects may come across as a white male or an Asian woman or a Latina . . ." Others, out of artistic need or political allegiance, choose to dramatize worlds dedicated to the ethnicity and culture to which they belong.

Both approaches reflect the cultural divides, the anger and confusion about race and ethnicity, that exist in the United States. Both approaches, as the plays by these writers testify, generate rich work. Still, the divisions to which these writers often refer are deeply troubling, not just in relation to women who write plays but also in terms of the future well-being of the American theater.

I have tried to bring together women who began to write in the 1970s and the 1980s with women who are just beginning to be heard, so that readers and students of theater can receive an historical range. I hope that these interviews will also provide a basis on which to build understanding and analysis of these women's art. To assemble a collection of interviews with American women who write plays is, in one sense, a foolhardy task. Every year, women begin to write plays. Every year, new voices tremble to be heard by artistic directors and producers, dramaturgs and critics. This book could easily have contained a hundred interviews. It is not complete. It is one more step.

Alexis Greene

Acknowledgments

This book could not have happened without the art and generosity of the playwrights themselves, who in each case spent hours of their valuable time talking with me. I particularly thank two outstanding women of the theater, Eve Ensler and Emily Mann, who courageously agreed to be interviewed at the start of this project. And I thank Wendy Kesselman for her artistry, encouragement, and dedication to excellence.

In addition, I am grateful for the patience and support of Smith and Kraus: Marisa Smith, Eric Kraus, and Elizabeth Monteleone, and for the keen-eyed skill of Julia Hill Gignoux of Freedom Hill Design. I am indebted to Raya Fiebig and Joseph Logel for allowing Smith and Kraus to use Frédéric Fiebig's exquisite painting, and to Robert Kashey and Joseph Gibbon of The Shepherd Gallery in New York City, and Myra Dorrell of the Kendall Art Gallery in Wellfleet, Massachusetts, for their advice and generosity. To my hard-working transcriber, Alison Stair Neet — untold appreciation. Encouraging friends: Cindy Cooper, Bob Fairbanks, Cathy Hemming, Ellen Herzog, Holly Hill, Susan Jonas, Gus Kaikkonen, Michael Sommers, and Elizabeth Swain. And others who offered invaluable suggestions, phone numbers, or simply a living room in which to meet: Jim Baldassare, Chris Burney, Michael Bigelow Dixon, Professor Jill Dolan, East West Players, Erin Dunn, Morgan Jenness, Rachel Koenig, Ron Lasko, Greg Leaming, Todd London and New Dramatists, Julia Miles and Women's Project and Productions, New York Theatre Workshop, Rosalind Pace, Michael Rogers, Carole Rothman, Sam Rudy, Helen Sheehy, Betsy Shevey, Don Summa, Gary Sunshine, and Peregrine Whittlesey.

And most importantly, my forthright and loving husband, Gordon R. Hough.

Preface

The playwright has always been at the center of the theater — shaping the world, prodding us on, invigorating us with ideas, stories, and passions.

For the last two thousand and some years, the playwright has been almost exclusively male — until the twentieth and twenty-first centuries, the centuries of women. Today, theater audiences are treated to stories told through the eyes of females, the senses of females, and the minds of females. As more women take over the reins of theater companies and as more women move into directing, women who write plays will be produced and celebrated.

Women are writing prolifically, and as a result, audiences are seeing plays from decidedly new angles. Are women writing differently than men? Of course they are. Women are stretching and experimenting with form and structure in ways not imagined before. Some of the subject matter could only be fully explored by women. And, oh the voices! As you will read in this wonderful book of interviews, the voices are distinct, driven, ardent, prickly, thoughtful, and emboldened. The kind of woman you'd like to spend time with around the dinner table — or nights with in the theater.

As a director, I read these women's words and savor the extraordinary range of temperaments and intellects. Some are young and comparatively untried in the theater, some are well-known. Each has her unique style. There is Paula Vogel, funny, edgy, and unafraid. Tina Howe, elegant and slyly humorous. Defiance and compassion emanate from the gutsy words of Cherríe Moraga, a gentle determination lives within the thoughts voiced by Cheryl West. How marvelous it would be to put all these women's work on every stage in

America; to see the art into which they have poured dreams, sweat, and commitment made manifest.

Let nobody be fooled; as these interviews demonstrate so acutely, writing a play is hard, as heart-breaking as it is rewarding. I have wrestled with new plays, listened and probed while writers expressed their aims and frustrations. I have waited while a writer retreated into her private world to solve a problem, seen a dramatist's grief and joy when a play leaves her embrace, to go forth into the scary but miraculous public world of the theater. Because the stage is where these women's plays must finally live. After the writer's imagination roams, after the words are written, comes that astoundingly truthful and demanding realm, a theater.

So don't stop with these interviews, rich though they are. After reading about these women's work, go out and buy their plays and get a taste of what they invent. And when you see their plays being produced, support them by going to experience the worlds they've created.

Molly Smith
Artistic Director, Arena Stage
Washington, D.C.
June 2001

Lynne Alvarez

Lynne Alvarez was born in Portland, Oregon, although she spent what she calls her growing-up time in Michigan, around Detroit and Ann Arbor. She went to the University of Michigan, where she focused on romance languages and majored in Italian. She did graduate work in Latin American history at the Universidad de las Americas in Mexico.

A poet first, Alvarez has published two books of verse: *The Dreaming Man* and *Living with Numbers* (Waterfront Press, 1984 and 1987). Her strongly imagist plays, which often evoke the heightened style of Lorca, include *The Guitarrón* (1981), an exploration of the relationship between love, violence, and art; *Hidden Parts* (1983), a blackly comic melodrama about a dysfunctional family living in America's heartland; *The Wonderful Tower of Humbert Lavoignet* (1984), in which a man's artistic obsession wars with his family's happiness; and *Eddie Mundo Edmundo* (1994), which dramatizes the conflicts of a young American of Mexican descent. Alvarez writes about the painful results of political rebellion in *Thin Air: Tales from a Revolution* (1987) and about a woman's personal rebellion in *The Reincarnation of Jaime Brown* (1988). Her play *Analiese* (1996) is a contemporary retelling of Hans Christian Andersen's fairy tale *The Snow Queen*.

In addition to writing her own plays, Alvarez translates the works of others, notably *Don Juan of Seville*, a translation of Tirso de Molina's *The Trickster of Seville*; Fernando Arrabal's *The Red Madonna: A Damsel for a Gorilla*; and the political satires of the contemporary Mexican dramatist Felipe Santander.

She is an alumna of New Dramatists, and her numerous awards include the LeCompte de Noüy Award (1984) for *The Wonderful Tower of Humbert Lavoignet.*

Alvarez and her husband, Barry Gould, live in Cherry Valley, New York, for part of each year, and in Savannah, Georgia. This interview took place at her home in upstate New York on September 9, 2000.

• • •

1

AG: WHEN DID YOU START WRITING POETRY?

LA: Oh, as far back as I can remember. I was going to be this famous, wild poet and die young. I was going to be Rimbaud, whom I idealized. Except I didn't know that he ran guns and lived for quite a while.

Poetry to me felt visceral. Things that weren't visceral, I was too impatient, too driven, too frenetic to concentrate on. Poetry and music were the big inspirational forces in my life. Never thought about drama. Didn't know anything about drama. I studied dance along the way, but I was never a dancer, because I didn't have the discipline. I was going to be a musician — I adore music, and I played flute, cello, and the piano. But I felt that I wasn't talented enough. I was a good, workmanlike musician. My brother was a genius as a musician; he could hear anything once and play it. I didn't have that kind of ability, so when I was a teenager I stopped.

AG: WHICH INSTRUMENT DID YOU LIKE THE BEST?

LA: Probably the cello. But I've never been a performer on any level. Poetry, which is such an introverted art form, is the only time I've performed publicly, because I had to read it out loud.

AG: DID YOUR BROTHER PURSUE MUSIC?

LA: No. I think my father would have loved him to be an artist, but my father pushed too hard. My brother is more a scientist than an artist.

AG: WHERE ARE YOUR PARENTS FROM?

LA: Argentina. Córdoba.

AG: WHY DID THEY COME TO THE UNITED STATES?

LA: I think it was because of political persecution. They went to Buenos Aires, and then my father came up here to study medicine, and my mother followed. This was in the late 1930s. They were engaged and then they got married up here. They went first to Detroit, because my father was accepted at medical school there, but also because it was the automobile capital of the world, where people could have jobs. Then my dad was in the army — he got drafted — and they went out to Portland and stayed there for a while, and he did a residency there. He was a general practitioner — the old kind of country doctor who made house calls. They stayed in Portland until I was born and then moved back to Michigan. Then we moved down to Mexico when I was eight or nine and spent a couple of years there, then back to Michigan, then I went down to Mexico. We had a house in Puerto Rico for a while, along the coast. We moved around a lot.

AG: DID YOUR PARENTS TALK AT ALL ABOUT ARGENTINA?

LA: No. In Michigan we were way out in the country — I don't think there were many Hispanic families around — and it was a time when everybody was busy assimilating. And since my family is fairly light-skinned — well, my father isn't so light — it didn't come up until later. I was very sheltered. In my late teenage years, a cousin came up from Buenos Aires, and she was terribly sophisticated. I was the country bumpkin. I got around more Latin Americans in college, but it wasn't like discovering my roots, because I had been to Mexico and down to Puerto Rico. But I floated on the surface. It wasn't a barrio kind of existence, it wasn't big, boisterous, family gatherings. My family are all rather reserved.

AG: WHY DID YOU GO TO MEXICO?

LA: I actually ran away with a boyfriend who was a published poet. He was doing a translation of *The Frogs* that was going to appear off Broadway, and I was overcome. He said, 'Where shall we go?' And I said, 'Oh, I have some relatives in Mexico.' He had a grant; we took off and went down to Mexico in 1966.

AG: 1966 WAS ALREADY A POLITICALLY ALIVE TIME IN THE UNITED STATES, AT LEAST IN SOME QUARTERS. WERE YOU PART OF ANY OF THE ANTI-ESTABLISHMENT MOVEMENTS?

LA: No. I was with people who were political, but I was much too confused and provincial. Very innocent and closed in a way. My father had always talked about adventures, but he always talked about that to my brother. Later, when I did go out and have adventures, he said, 'Why did you do that?' And I said, 'Well, I remember you always said to do something — be active and make your mark.' He said, 'But I was talking to your brother, I never meant it for you.' And I said, 'Well, I heard it.' Very chauvinistic family. But anyway, at the end of 1966, I went down to Mexico.

AG: WERE YOU FLUENT IN SPANISH THEN?

LA: No, but I understood it very well. In our family we spoke English at the table. In the early 1950s, you wanted to blend in. My parents spoke Spanish, and relatives spoke it, so I understood it. But it had no resonance for me. We were isolated.

AG: IN WHAT WAY?

LA: Geographically. Not a lot of people around. I was an introverted person, so that played into the isolation as well. My father knew so much about opera and music, and my mother did, too, but I grew up in a rural environment where there were mostly farms. I didn't know there was any awareness of us being different until years later, when I went back to find where our house had been. I was asking around, and someone said, 'Well, where did you live?' And I told them, and they said, 'Oh, next to the spic doctor.' That was such a shock, because I had always thought of myself as part of the community. I'm sure we were in a way.

AG: DO YOU STILL WRITE POETRY?

LA: I haven't for a while, because if I'm writing plays, so much goes into that. When I'm older and retire, I will go back to poetry. Even though I hope there's poetry in my plays, and even an occasional poem — lyrics for songs — I don't write poetry actively now. It's such a different way of thinking. It's more controlled. Poetry is short and intense, so that suited me; I had a short attention span. But a poem is such a tiny medium, you have to think in an extremely condensed way, which I don't feel like doing. I love the space and the movement and dimensions of theater. I'm not in the mood to be compacted.

AG: BUT THERE ARE THE POEMS THAT JAIME WRITES IN *THE REINCARNATION OF JAIME BROWN.*

LA: I used some poems that I never liked in *Jaime*, because she's a beginning poet and writes the intense, obscure poems that one does as a young poet. And in *Eddie Mundo Edmundo.* I figured, 'Nobody will read these anywhere else, so I'll put them in the play.'

AG: IN *JAIME*, THE POEM SHE INVENTS WHEN SHE'S HANGING OUT IN PORT AUTHORITY BUS TERMINAL IS LIKE A RAP. IT'S LOOSE AND FUNKY.

LA: Langston Hughes was a big influence. Poets were much more of an influence on me than any other kind of writer. It was only later, when I discovered more poetic playwrights like Tennessee Williams and Federico García Lorca, that I came to playwriting. I had to learn a whole new way of movement and thinking and action, which are quite different in a play. Even though there's movement in a poem, it's of a different sort.

AG: WHY WAS LANGSTON HUGHES AN INFLUENCE ON YOU?

LA: His poetry is funky. The dialogue, the sharp insights into character. The irreverence and the reverence at the same time. He treats some people with great reverence, yet at the same time they can be irreverent people. And he isn't stuck on form. He can do anything he wants — there are a variety of forms that he uses — and he is so much fun. That's what it is: he is great fun to read, because of that looseness. You never know what he will come up with. He isn't inward. A lot of the WASP poets are very inward and take themselves very seriously, and a lot of the women poets ended up killing themselves. When you think of the poets we were all reading in the sixties and seventies and eighties — they were inward. And I loved that, but there was a freedom and lightheartedness to Langston. Lorca was gorgeous. Neruda. And the French poets: Verlaine and Rimbaud, of course, and Malarmé. Those were my gods. The flow of the language, the imagery, the spirit. Rimbaud was luscious. Once in a while I steal a line. To me the poet outlaws are *it*. They drank and smoked opium and did all this stuff.

AG: ARE THERE OUTLAW CHARACTERS IN YOUR PLAYS?

LA: Not so much. I hope later on there will be. But I am an outlaw underneath. Ostensibly, I'm not at all. Ostensibly, also, I'm very outgoing.

AG: YOU'RE AN OUTLAW UNDERNEATH?

LA: I think I lived my early life fairly much as one. But ignorant in the way that outlaws can be, too. And probably as selfish.

AG: HOW DO YOU TAKE THOSE POETS INTO YOUR WRITING?

LA: With Langston, it would be through character, because he has characters in his poems who speak. My poems about Mexico, some of them are dialogue. It was my way of bearing witness to certain people or situations and getting inside them. Some of Langston's humor, his irreverence.

What I take from poetry are the images. The way I wrote poetry was through a striking image, and when I start a play, it will usually come as strong, dramatic, images. I will first see a visual image that's very key. Before I write, I usually know the ending, too, because then I have a sense of where the play is going — I don't know anything in between — and there's usually a visual image at the end, also. I think I carry that from poetry. That's why I like those French poets — they have such precise imagery.

AG: THE DESCRIPTIONS OF YOUR SETTINGS ARE ALMOST PAINTERLY.

LA: That's how I visualize. Once a play is onstage, I don't care if people change what I visualize. I feel once the play is done and out there, it's out there — like those little paper boats with candles that you send out on the water. But for me to write it, to be in the world of the play, the visual has to be there. I can immediately inhabit the world of any play that I've ever written if I think of the central image. It doesn't fade.

AG: WHAT WAS YOUR FIRST PLAY?

LA: The first play was *Graciela*, which I wrote at the Puerto Rican Traveling Theatre. I love it. It's about a real situation in a small Mexican town where I spent much of my time — you can tell, because I write about it a lot. I only knew the story after the fact, but I met the people. It's about a young girl who grew up in this town of five hundred people and took revenge for the killing of her father by dressing as a man and killing the cacique — the big guy — the local lord, who was very cruel. Walked down into town and shot him. Caused her brothers, who had been studying law and didn't want any part of this, to have to go out and kill all the people who were then after the boys for revenge. When the father was murdered, the family had wanted to get away from machismo, from this endless round of killing, so they had sent the boys away. But they kept the girls in Nautla. Graciela, whom I met, couldn't stand seeing this man who had killed her father and she shot him and inadvertently ended up pulling the family back into the cycle of revenge. The brothers not only went to jail for all the killings but they became drug lords, although I was so innocent, I didn't know that until after I left Nautla.

AG: READING *THE GUITARRÓN* AND *EDDIE MUNDO EDMUNDO* I THINK THAT ONE OF YOUR SUBJECTS IS MACHISMO AND WHAT IT MEANS TO BE A MAN.

LA: Very much. It's even in American culture. The buttons you push are maybe different, but if you tell a guy, 'Oh, you're just a pussy,' it's an insult, and you can get a man to do a lot of things, even a man that's intellectual, by saying something is unmanly. You could never do that to a woman. If I said, 'You're a coward,' you'd say, 'Oh, I don't know. I don't care.' But with men, there's this loss of stature. Different things in different cultures are called into play, but sometimes I feel men are pulled back to a very primitive level.

AG: IS MACHISMO RELATED TO CLASS DIFFERENCES IN MEXICO?

LA: No. It's active throughout the culture, but at different levels of violence. It has to do with power and with physical power. Being able to subdue your environment, be in control of your environment, whether your environment is women, land, or death.

AG: WHY DID YOU WRITE *THE GUITARRÓN*?

LA: That's a very special play, because it was probably, besides *Graciela*, the first one I really believed was a play. It was written because of three things. One was a physical experience I had. I was in my house in Veracruz, and there was a workman who was singing in an empty house nearby. And he was singing what they call a 'son huasteco,' which is a certain kind of country song, a cappella, and it sounds, believe it or not, sometimes like Bach. And he was in this empty house, working away. And the song was so gorgeous that it woke me up, and I literally went running around the neighborhood, going, 'What is that? What is that?' I had to know what it was. It was like magic. Totally unexpected. But I didn't know how to portray that: 'Oh, my God, this is the most beautiful thing I've ever heard in my life.' So that became Guicho, playing the cello.

The other thing was that we did have a master builder. My husband at the time decided to go into the fishing business, and we had a master builder who lived out back, who was an alcoholic. We gave him work, and he was fixing fishing boats. But not with wood, like the Master Builder does in *Guitarrón*, but with fiberglass. And he died there. So he is the Master Builder in the play.

I worked for a newspaper in Veracruz, and I went to interview this doctor, an older man who had his own private auditorium, and he was dying of cancer, and I was sent to interview him for a special article. And he lived right on the beach. And he'd studied in Paris and knew Pablo Casals from that time, so when Casals would come to Mexico, he would stay with the doctor and give private cello concerts, and he would practice on the beach. Now I knew, because of the fishermen, that the beach was probably one of the most dangerous places you could go, because it was a federal zone, and criminals would go there to avoid the local police. So just picturing this older man out there playing these priceless cellos on the beach — that was the image of the Maestro. It was Casals, although I never met Casals. That was *The Guitarrón*. It was my love of all those things.

AG: THERE ARE SEVERAL LOVE RELATIONSHIPS AMONG MEN IN THAT PLAY. THE TWO GAY MEN . . .

LA: They are not exactly gay. They wouldn't call themselves gay. To them it's a power relationship. I'm sure it was sexual. Some of the fishermen were homosexual, but they would be the last to admit it. They were very brutal. For instance, the character Antonio, the street beggar, was someone I knew, and he was just like that. He was a real wheeler-dealer. Beautiful face. Very crippled body. And he had his little cart, that he pushed himself around in. I found out later that the fishermen got drunk and threw him in the water and watched him drown. That's what these men were like. Casual brutality.

AG: WHY DO YOU THINK IT HAS INTERESTED YOU TO WRITE ABOUT MACHISMO?

LA: Two things. The idea of power and weakness: the interplay of the need for power and the weakness of the inner self. And also the idea that character is destiny, that you form your destiny by how you wend your way through life. What things are out of your control, what things are in your control? The idea of bravery. Machismo isn't just a bad term. It is when you use it in the chauvinistic sense, but it has a light part and a dark part. As Lorca would say, one half full of sun, one half full of shadow. In machismo there is also the nobility of spirit, the ability to face dangerous situations. Not in ignorance, but knowing the situations are dangerous and still taking on whatever challenge comes. Viewing women as a weaker sex in the sense of protecting them because they are physically weak. Machismo has its root in physical power. Physically facing death, physically facing your enemy, confronting things, mastering things.

As a woman living in the sixties, in order to go out in the world — because I was also a runaway and I would go out in the world in some very peculiar situations — I would think of myself as a young boy. Not consciously, and not even sexually. But that would be the front I would put on to feel impervious and safe. It took me a while to be able to feel vulnerable enough to think of myself as a woman in the world, because I felt there was so much danger around me.

AG: CERTAINLY IN *THE GUITARRÓN*, MICAELA, GUICHO'S GIRLFRIEND, DISAPPEARS FROM THE STORY. INDEED THE WOMEN IN SEVERAL OF YOUR PLAYS GET LEFT BEHIND BY THE MEN OR TAKE THEMSELVES OUT OF THE PICTURE. THEY ARE JUST NOT AS IMPORTANT IN THE PLAYS AS THE MEN. THEY ARE NOT THE PROTAGONISTS, FOR ONE THING.

LA: I know. I saw women as powerless. In many experiences of my childhood, growing up, I saw women as powerless. So when I thought of a protagonist, I couldn't think of a woman. It's been one of my struggles, to become acquainted with women. I think I see the world as a very dangerous place, especially for women, and so I would become the protector by becoming the man in the play. I don't know how to put it. I probably also didn't understand myself and didn't understand women very well. Because my family was so chauvinistic, what women thought and did was extremely secondary.

AG: DID YOUR MOTHER WORK?

LA: She had been an English teacher. But when she had three kids, she stopped working.

AG: GOING BACK TO MACHISMO, IF I UNDERSTAND WHAT YOU'RE SAYING, THERE'S A POSITIVE SIDE TO MACHISMO AS WELL AS A NEGATIVE.

LA: It's double-edged. In the pejorative sense, you use the word in connection with freezing out someone and killing them in the street. You use it in connection with gangs. But the roots of machismo are really in the medieval knight errant, the person who saves the damsel in distress, who takes on death and faces down the enemy. It's a romantic concept. It has certain aspirations toward mastery and nobility and bravery that are worthy. But the downside, the flip side of that, are dominance, aggression, violence, and negating the values of others — seeing yourself as more important than others.

AG: HOW DOES GUICHO FIT INTO THAT?

LA: He is neither. He is in the middle. He is driven by the world around him to be more violent than his nature. His nature is very peaceable. He doesn't want to fight Calorías. He doesn't want to kill. And yet he feels he has to stand up for something. He's forced to become violent. He has to come to the level of physical dominance that his world demands or he will be killed or stepped on. But he's also a poet, or he could be. But he probably won't be. He's had to cut himself off from his friends, and he's had to descend almost to the level of Calorías to get what he wants. His spirit has been roughened. And with the Maestro dead, Guicho doesn't know how to play the cello. He knows one note, an open-key note that he can get and that he plays over and over. But that may be all he ever gets.

AG: YOU DON'T HAVE CLOSED ENDINGS IN YOUR PLAYS.

LA: But I want things resolved in effect. I want things resolved in that you know what's happened this far and you know what the potentials are, that this is a certain corner in people's lives which has been turned, which then perhaps leaves them open.

AG: HOW DID YOU COME TO WRITE *THE GUITARRÓN* IN ITS PARTICULAR FORM?

LA: I couldn't fit Guicho into a poem, even though I had written poems on a lot of the other characters, so I tried a short story, and that wasn't quite right. And then I stumbled into a workshop at Puerto Rican Traveling Theatre. I had no intention of staying, but I decided to try. *Guitarrón* was the second play I tried. The first was *Graciela*.

The form I just found. I learned it in the workshop. I never took a playwriting class; I learned basically through the content determining the form. I kind of intuited it and shaped it.

AG: HOW DID YOU DISCOVER THEATER?

LA:. By accident. Out of frustration with the poetry world. I mean, I knew I was going to die of starvation as a poet; no one reads poets, no one pays them. Plus it's a very academic male world — or at least it was at the time. So I heard about a workshop at the Puerto Rican Traveling Theatre, for Hispanic writers who weren't playwrights. I gruous than it would have been in the States, because the materials are so different from adobe.

I remembered the image and translated it to Michigan, because I was trying to make my transition to writing about the States. I was having a crisis — one of the continual ones we all have as writers: 'Well, I'm not Mexican, but I'm writing these plays that take place in Mexico. I didn't grow up in the barrio, and everyone's very interested in the urban American situation, about which I'm completely ignorant. And I want to speak for the culture where I am . . . ' I translated the Mexican characters and that world into American characters and an American world.

AG: BUT SOON AFTER WRITING BOTH *HIDDEN PARTS* AND *WONDERFUL TOWER* YOU WENT BACK TO THE LATIN-AMERICAN ENVIRONMENT WITH *THIN AIR*, WHICH IS ABOUT A REVOLUTION IN A LATIN-AMERICAN COUNTRY.

LA: The plays set in America weren't getting produced either, because I wasn't writing in an urban vein. Those plays are done more now than they were in the 1980s. And I thought, 'Well, the hell with that. I guess I can't write American plays anyway.' I wanted to write some of my memories and my folks' memories. My husband had been thrown in jail down in Mexico, and I'd been threatened. I had been living in a volatile political situation, and relatives in Argentina would write about political events happening down there.

AG: IT'S NOT CLEAR IN THE SCRIPT WHERE *THIN AIR* TAKES PLACE.

LA: No. I didn't want it to be. As soon as you put it in a place, people say, 'That's not the way it was.' *Thin Air* actually incorporates a lot of revolutions through my ideas about revolution, but the experiences, the people, and the songs are really Mexican, because there wasn't a revolution there, at least not yet. I didn't set it in any particular country, because people are proprietary about their politics and their history, and I don't blame them. And for me, this was my statement about politics and violence in general. I feel that systems fail, that it's people who make them work or not, and people do terrible things for very human reasons or very idealistic reasons, and it's hard to find the good guys and the bad guys, except in broad strokes.

AG: CERTAINLY DEATH IS ALWAYS PRESENT IN *THIN AIR*. ANYA, THE MUSICOLOGIST'S DAUGHTER, DIES, AND THROUGHOUT THE PLAY THERE IS AN IMAGE OF A HOMELESS GIRL, A STREET URCHIN, BURYING HER BROTHER. NOT HAVING SEEN THE PLAY STAGED, IT'S HARD FOR ME TO VISUALIZE HOW YOU WANT THAT IMAGE TO RESONATE.

LA: You're going to laugh, but the play is laid out the way *Mad Magazine* is laid out, where you have the main image or story, and then you have these other things in the corners. Well, the homeless girl is one of the things in a corner. All of a sudden you notice her, but not all the time. If *Thin Air* were on a proscenium stage, she'd be over at the side. She's really a sideline, but she's a motif, like a musical motif. To me, that play is written very much like a piece of music. It's in three acts, like the three movements in a concerto.

AG: OFTEN YOUR PLAYS CONTAIN MANY BRIEF SCENES, BUT YOU BUILD *THIN AIR* IN LONG, CONTINUOUS SCENES.

LA: The full title is *Thin Air: Tales from a Revolution*. It would be like seeing Picasso's painting, *Guernica*. Boom — you notice certain things right away, and you don't notice other things until maybe the fifth time you see the picture. That's the effect I want. There is a picture of disaster, and the girl is a motif within it. She has one line of action: trying to find her brother, trying to bury him.

AG: DO YOU WANT US TO SEE A CONNECTION BETWEEN HER AND ANYA?

LA: The connection is that you follow this little girl in the present and intuit Anya's death because this little girl dies. It's like Roman Polanski's movie *Repulsion*, where the girl kills a man in the bathtub, and he is left there for days — weeks. You don't see him rotting in the bathtub, but you see other things slowly rotting in the house, and from that you extrapolate. There's the same approach in *Thin Air*. The girl's search doesn't parallel Anya's story, but gives it another dimension.

as you said, is a political writer. He writes very human stories, but he has certain political statements he wants to make. My statements are not as clearly formulated. I discover them as I write the play.

AG: WHY IS IT INTERESTING FOR YOU TO WRITE ABOUT SEXUALITY?

LA: Probably I have my own explorations. You can pick money, you can pick politics — in both of those areas, there are issues of power. Coming from my particular environment, there were issues of power involved in the relationships between men and women. What is the unspoken power, what is the spoken power? What is the bottom-line power? In the game of relationships is where I see the microcosm of power being played out, and I guess that's the focus for me.

It's where I see the stories. I can look at an urban environment and not see one story. There may be ten billion stories pulsating around me, and I can't really see them. Yet I can go out in a cornfield and say, 'There's a story here.' It's where the stories awaken for you, and for me, they awaken through images that are powerful yet not necessarily political. That isn't the lens, or what first attracts me. It's a color, it's a shape, it's emotion.

AG: ABOUT FOURTEEN YEARS AGO YOU MOVED TO COOPERSTOWN FROM NEW YORK CITY. WHY DID YOU MAKE THAT CHANGE?

LA: There's a very important reason, and it's connected with money and theater. The money aspect was that I wanted my daughter to go to a public high school, because I had and I thought it would be a good idea. But also I found that as time went on in New York, I associated more and more with artists, which was a first in my life. I had never been in a community of artists. That just wasn't what I was exposed to or put myself into. After I came to New York in 1977, I found myself for years relating only to artists, and I thought, 'I'm going to have nothing to write about. I'll start writing about other artists, because that's all I know.' I thought that I should get myself in an environment where art is a stranger again. Being the stranger, the outsider, is the usual posture for a writer, and I guess I've done that over and over in my life. So I came to a place where there are no artists around, no one around of my background, certainly no ethnic qualities. I did again what had always happened in one way or another — I was totally out of it. But I did not want to be with people who thought the way I did and lived the way I did. I thought, 'If I do that, I'll have nothing to say.' I find that only by getting away from something can I write about it. I need to externalize things to be able to see them. That's why I came so far. I wanted the environment to be really different, so I'd have to rub up against things and keep looking at them. I wanted a place where truly, politically, I would have to listen to other people and listen to myself.

AG: CAN YOU ORCHESTRATE A CAREER FROM WHERE YOU LIVE NOW?

LA: I travel a lot. Travel all over the country all the time. Cooperstown and Savannah, which I also like because it's quiet, are near airports.

AG: HAVE YOU BEEN ABLE TO MAKE A LIVING AS A PLAYWRIGHT?

LA: Filling in with grants, filling in with teaching. I wouldn't grace it with the term 'making a living.' But I've never done anything else full-time since I decided to do this. It's why I refuse to take any full-time job or job that has any other pulls on my life. I've done everything. Recently, too — not just when I was first starting out. I have been a chauffeur. I was a chambermaid this past summer. I want to do things that do not require thinking, because I'm not that cohesive a personality. Some people can do all kinds of things and write. I can't. It takes a lot for me to be able to concentrate in very profound isolation. I only have so much energy.

AG: WHAT WAS IT LIKE FOR YOU TO BE A PLAYWRIGHT AND A MOTHER?

LA: It focused me enormously. Not having any money, being a single mother — that was hard but uncomplicated. At a certain age, Nancy, my daughter, went to school, and I worked like a fiend. She would come home, I'd be with her; she'd go to bed, I'd work like a fiend. That was a wonderful balance, and I learned a lot of discipline, actually. There weren't distractions. Relationships with men were much more distracting.

AG: HAS BEING A WOMAN HELPED, HURT, OR NOT FIGURED AT ALL IN RELATION TO YOUR CAREER IN THE THEATER?

LA: I don't believe in victimization, but, yes, I think being a woman hinders. I think that when you are on a beginning level as a playwright, people may look at your work. But when it comes to a theater taking a chance, when it comes to seeing that a new play is a leap instead of a stumble, I think that, with women, theaters tend to see it as a stumble. Theaters are not as willing to go with the flow and take a chance. I feel that if a guy says, 'Look, I know this play works,' he'll get the money and the go-ahead. There is no woman playwright, I think, who is as successful as the most successful man playwright. I see women in theater more than before, and that has a lot to do with women being more prominent, but they're not more successful than men and not as successful.

AG: YOU ALSO TRANSLATE PLAYS.

LA: Yes, although I started by translating poetry. But when I was at INTAR, Fernando Arrabal was coming in with a play — *The Red Madonna* — and they asked me to translate. He came in and directed, and I could watch him create. On a shoestring budget, he made the most amazingly gorgeous, surreal production of his work. Then Classic Stage Company in New York asked me to do something, and I looked at the original Don Juan play, *The Trickster of Seville* by Tirso de Molina. I'm very lazy. I only like to do translations which are easy, and that period of Spanish literature actually is easy; it's only in the Romantic and Baroque periods that you get twisted metaphors and metaphors within metaphors, and translating becomes tedious. Before then, the writing is very direct, very hard-hitting, very delightful. Felipe's plays are full of humor and poignancy and also very direct.

I love translating. I think in my old age, it'll be like doing a cross-word puzzle. It's easy and it's fun, it's a great way to inhabit a work. Translating is like putting on a glove. You get inside a work in a way you don't when you're just reading it. Because it's not a literal translation — it's not only the letter of the law, it's the spirit. You can have a play on words in Spanish in one place, where you can't quite do it in English, but then three beats later, you find how to do it in English, even though you can't do the same play on words at the same time with the same meaning. I'm lucky in that I'm basically bilingual, especially when reading and listening, so I can get the flavor of a piece very easily. It's fun to find equivalents, especially when working with cultures where there are class differences which you cannot parallel in the United States. You can transpose a work — you can make Don Juan a gang leader, for instance — but that's an adaptation. If you're translating, you want to find the equivalents in another language. There are a lot of wonderful problems.

AG: I'D LIKE TO TALK ABOUT PLAYS THAT YOU ARE WORKING ON NOW, FOR INSTANCE *DEUX MARIAGES: ROMOLA AND NIJINSKY*. IS ROMOLA NIJINSKY A MORE DEFINED FEMALE CHARACTER THAN THE WOMEN YOU'VE WRITTEN BEFORE?

LA: Yes, but because I'm still working on the play. I always loved Nijinsky and the art deco period, and what happened is that his diaries were published in unabridged form, and I read them and I got very excited. The image of him in that time period, the wonderful costumes, the Ballets Russes — oh, gorgeous, the colors they used.

But whenever anyone talked or wrote about Romola, Nijinsky's wife, it was very disparagingly. You got no picture of her whatsoever, because the books were all written by balletomanes who didn't like her because they figured she destroyed him.

AG: SHE DIDN'T?

LA: No, she didn't. It was Diaghilev who destroyed him. That's what gets me. She didn't destroy him; she married him. Diaghilev told him, 'Well, fuck you.' It was Diaghilev who stopped him from doing anything. Nijinsky went to Diaghilev and said, 'Okay, here I am,' and Diaghilev shut him out. Romola was there for him when nobody else was. The line is, 'She ruined his life.' Bullshit. He was repulsed by Diaghilev anyway. He went out with prostitutes. His fantasies were women. The line is that she was this groupie. She was not. So that got me pissed off. I thought, 'Wait a minute.' She was twenty years old. Here is this woman, it's 1913, she travels all over, she studies ballet well enough to become part of the corps, she goes to South America. She is madly in love with him in this innocent way, thinking, 'He's a great artist, ergo he must be a great person.' She takes care of him for thirty years after he becomes psychotic, and even then they blame her? They complain that she used his name. What the hell else was she supposed to do? She had to keep him in a sanatorium — he tried to kill her a couple of times when he had psychotic episodes. She was basically a person with an artistic bent who wasn't a driven artist, but very talented, and so she would lecture about him and about ballet. And they said she used him? Give me a break.

So I said, 'Let me take a closer look at her.' Very difficult to get any material on her. All negative. Her mother was negative. She said Romola was a bad mother. But you see between the lines that Romola sacrificed everything to support Nijinsky. She gave up her children. She went through two world wars. They were in Hungary and couldn't leave, so she had to leave him to tour, to get money.

Anyway, I said, 'Her side hasn't been told.' I said, 'Okay, this is someone who's unexplored.' I'm just getting a grip on her, and it's been very difficult for me. It's not that she's totally sympathetic, and he wasn't totally sympathetic either. But there was kind of a bravura about her. She took a chance on someone. She said, 'I think he's a great man. I want to devote my life to love.' In a funny way, she was brave. I thought she was quite unusual. These books describe her as sitting on top of costume trunks smoking a cigarette. This was before the roaring twenties; we hadn't gotten to bobbed hair yet. Very beautiful. Could speak all these languages. I wanted to get away from this myth that she ruined Nijinsky. And he was never entirely honest with her. He wrote in his diaries that he told her she was the first woman he'd ever slept with, to make it special. He was so enamored of her. He would send her dozens of roses every day.

AG: SHE SOUNDS LIKE A COHERENT FEMALE CHARACTER.

LA: She is, but I want to know her better. Perhaps the fullest female characters are in my play *Analiese*, which is very loosely based on the fairy tale *The Snow Queen*, but set at the end of the nineteenth century. The fairy tale describes the picaresque journey of a young girl who goes to find her childhood friend, who has run off with the Snow

Queen; in my version they are teenagers, and the young man has run off with an actress from Henrik Ibsen's theater company. So the play focuses almost entirely on women — Analiese, who looks for her first love, and the seductive, rather brave actress. In *Dancing with the Devil*, a new play that I'm revising, I'm trying to hone in on women by reducing the characters from eight to four, two of whom are women. So I'm really throwing myself a challenge to write women. But it still isn't easy for me to write women protagonists. It's hard for me to see the other, to step outside. I'm so subjective when it comes to women that I can't externalize and make them characters, except in roles that aren't central. Because it's always me. When I visualize a play, I can see the male characters running around and doing things, but often the female character, if she's central, has her back to me, so all I see is the back of her head. And I keep trying to turn her around.

This probably stems from the way I saw society treating women as I was growing up — certainly not as people who were center stage. Women were the helpmeets and the picturesque characters. As I said, I used to run away from home, so the early women in my plays reflect me, as a teenager, running into predatory people and being in precarious situations where the issues were violence and sexuality. It's hard for me to step out of that and see women as other kinds of people. It's taken a lot to be braver in the world.

But I think I'm falling into an apologetic, defensive mode in talking about writing women, when what I truly feel is that neither as a woman nor as an Hispanic am I required to focus on any particular character. I love being a playwright because I feel totally free, and I resent it when I feel that old PC pressing in. I want to be anybody and everybody — no holds barred. ▽

Pearl
Cleage

Pearl Cleage is an Atlanta-based
activist and writer, whose plays
include *Flyin' West* (1992), about pioneering black women who settle the
town of Nicodemus, Kansas, during
the nineteenth century; *Blues for an
Alabama Sky* (1995), which dramatizes the loves and hates of a group
of friends in Harlem in 1930; and
Bourbon at the Border (1997), a
drama about a marriage that has been
irretrievably damaged by the racist violence of the 1960s.

She is also the author of poems, short stories, and essays, including the
collections *Mad at Miles: A Black Woman's Guide to Truth* (1990) and *Deals
with the Devil and Other Reasons to Riot* (1993). In 1998, her novel, *What
Looks Like Crazy on an Ordinary Day* (Avon Books, 1997), was an Oprah
Book Club Pick and also appeared on *The New York Times* bestseller list.

Cleage is the mother of one daughter, Deignan, and the wife of Zaron
W. Burnett, Jr. This interview took place at Spelman College in Atlanta, on
July 28, 1999.

• • •

AG: I WONDER IF WE CAN TALK FIRST ABOUT YOUR FAM-
ILY, BECAUSE YOU FREQUENTLY WEAVE THEM INTO YOUR
ESSAYS, AND PERHAPS INTO YOUR PLAYS.

PC: Sure.

AG: WHO WERE YOUR FATHER'S PEOPLE AND WHO WERE
YOUR MOTHER'S PEOPLE?

PC: My parents are both from Detroit families. Been in Detroit for a
long time.

AG: WERE YOU BORN IN DETROIT?

PC: I was born in Springfield, Massachusetts. My father had a church
in Springfield, so I lived there for two years. Then my father was too
radical for St. John's Presbyterian Church, so we went back to Detroit.
He has an African name now — Jaramogi Abebe Agyman — because
he's very much a Black Nationalist, but at that time he was Reverend
Albert Cleage.

My mother's people are from Alabama. My grandmother was from
Montgomery, and my grandfather was from Cousada Station, a little tiny town. He came north to work at Ford's factory during World
War II, back when Ford's was recruiting in Alabama. They said to
the black men, 'Come down to the railroad station and we'll give you
a ticket. You can go to Detroit, you've got a job waiting for you, we'll
help you get settled.' My grandfather was ecstatic. He was very ready
to get out of Alabama. So he told my grandmother that he would come
back for her — they weren't married yet — and went to Detroit. Moved
in with someone he knew, cousins who were there — traditional migration path. Went back and married my grandmother. My grandmother
came up and then she brought her mother and sisters. My grandfather worked at Ford's for forty years. My mother, Doris Graham Cleage,
was born in Detroit. Grew up there and lived there most of her life.
My father had churches in Los Angeles, Springfield, and Lexington,
Kentucky, so they lived where the churches were. But mostly those
were brief stays, and they came back to Detroit.

My father was actually born in Indianapolis, Indiana. His father
was a doctor. His mother lived in Indianapolis, and his father was taken

to church by a friend and saw my grandmother singing in the church choir, a story that I've always wanted to work in somewhere. They married, had my father, came back to Detroit, and my grandfather practiced medicine in Detroit all his life. My father is the oldest of seven children.

AG: WERE YOU NAMED AFTER SOMEBODY IN YOUR FAMILY?

PC: My father's mother is Pearl. I met a very old woman when they did *Blues for an Alabama Sky* at Hartford Stage Company. Her granddaughter brought her; she had to be in her nineties. She had known my grandmother in Indiana and saw in the paper that there was a play by Pearl Cleage, and she said, 'This can't be the Pearl Cleage that I know.' She came just to be sure. I said, 'No, I'm her granddaughter.' It was wonderful, because she was an ancient lady.

AG: WHAT DO YOU REMEMBER ABOUT GROWING UP?

PC: The only thing I remember about Springfield is snow. Lots of snow. Other than that, Detroit is what I remember. My family on both sides are very loyal to each other, very tight-knit group of people. Not very gregarious in the sense of having parties and going to nightclubs; they like to sit around and talk. Always very politically active. Especially my father and his side of the family. My mother's side, their activism translated more into church kinds of things — if the minister thought it was important for them to be involved in voting, then they would. But my father organized political parties, ran for office, marched on the police station. His father was one of the founders of the first black hospital fund and brought black doctors to Detroit, was outspoken about politics. So my father inherited that and became a very activist minister, which is why those church appointments didn't last too long. This was the mid-to-late 1940s and early 1950s, and people were nervous about the kinds of things my father was saying.

AG: WHAT KINDS OF THINGS?

PC: Registering people to vote. Boycotting for economic reasons, for jobs. Picketing. Very much in the Adam Clayton Powell mode. Activist gospel: Jesus was about people going out into the street and helping each other. Many churches did not want to draw that kind of attention. Which is why my father became Congregational, because in the Congregational Church, there is no board. The congregation gets to say who the pastor is and who stays. The congregations always loved him; it was the boards that he made nervous.

We were Congregational for a long time, and then he did a lot of thinking and reading and research, and reinterpreted his ideas about Christianity. Based on where Jesus was born, what people were there, he started talking about Jesus as a black Messiah who was involved in trying to free His people from imperialist Rome. Which lends itself to the politics of the 1960s, that we're black folks in America trying to free ourselves from imperialism. It gave people a way to embrace a Christianity that allowed them to be activist and do the kind of work that needed to be done politically. Out of that change in the church, my father founded the Freedom Now Party, which ran a full slate of candidates. He ran for governor of Michigan. Another time he ran for City Council. School Board. He used to run for office all the time, which was great, because our family used to pass out flyers and get petitions signed. Every Saturday there'd be a caravan of people to go some place and do something. It was a very rich environment.

My father also was very involved in supporting the young writers and artists who were part of the Black Arts Movement. He had done a lot of writing himself and probably would have liked to be a film director, but it wasn't a time when that was a real feasible thing. When he and my mother were in Los Angeles, he took film classes. He had done a lot of work in theater, directed community plays.

AG: WHILE YOU WERE GROWING UP?

PC: Really before. He directed a couple of plays when I was younger, and once I tried to be in one. But I'm so intimidated by my father, it was just horrible.

AG: ARE YOU LIKE YOUR FATHER?

PC: In some ways I'm very like my father. I have a real belief that people are good underneath, and that if they can hear the truth, they will change. Even as I say that, I know how idealistic and naïve it sounds, especially the way the world tends to be at this moment. But I always feel that people are more confused than evil, that they're angry about things they don't understand. They're violent because they can't figure out what's happening and it drives them crazy. I do believe that if you talk to people long and hard enough, and they hear you, they can change their lives and then change the communities we live in. That's very much like my father.

In the sense that my father made real sacrifices in terms of his personal life to do the work he did, I'm very different. I'm more like my mother. My mother was active in the political work and taught school for all of her working life, but her family was always really important to her. I have an older sister and a stepfather, and all of us were a critical part of my mother's life and way of approaching the world. My father approaches the world through groups of people, which is great for a minister but makes it harder to be a regular guy. My father never tended to be the regular guy. He was the oldest in his family, his mother just adored him. He was always allowed to be the king. Then when he got to be a minister, the minister is always the king. So it was difficult for him to have a smaller persona that would be amenable to reading stories to the kids. I wanted to be able to balance all of this change-the-world impetus with being able to have love affairs and family life and all of that.

AG: DID YOU HEAR HIM IN CHURCH EVERY SUNDAY?

PC: Oh, God, every Sunday, every Sunday. My father's a great preacher. He's eighty-eight years old now, so he doesn't preach much, but he was a very charismatic speaker. My parents got divorced when I was six, but they were very cordial to each other, and I used to spend every weekend with my father. I used to watch him prepare his sermons on Saturday nights and Sunday mornings — much later than he should have been preparing. Since I would be the only person there, he used to talk to me about what he was thinking and going to say. I'd be eight, ten, years old, but I'm like, 'Okay, I can pretend. He obviously thinks I understand this, so I want to understand this. I want my father to love me and take me around.'

The thing that stayed with me is that he was able to take what he was reading and thinking and talking about and translate it into a sermon that regular working people could understand. People who were never going to look at these books that my father was reading were able to get the ideas, because he tied them to something they already believed, which was Jesus. He could take a very radical, sophisticated idea and get people to go with it, because they didn't realize how radical and sophisticated it was. It was presented in a manner that gave them a way in. I want to be able to talk about complicated ideas in a way that gives people a way in. If audiences know about the Harlem Renaissance, they get more from a play like *Blues for an Alabama Sky*. But it's real important to me that people who never heard of the Harlem Renaissance also get something from the play, because they like the story or the characters.

AG: YOUR FATHER SOUNDS DIFFERENT FROM THE ULTRA-RIGHTEOUS REVEREND IN YOUR NOVEL AND FROM RIGHTEOUS, INFLEXIBLE LELAND IN *BLUES*.

PC: I have a very clear understanding of how powerful a minister is, and how powerful religion is, because my father was very popular and could move people to do things. 'Okay, now after church we're all going to go downtown and picket the police station.' And after church everybody would put their little gloves on, get on the bus, go downtown, and I mean these little old ladies would be picketing the police station.

My father used that power for good things. But what struck me when I started working with the character of the Reverend was, 'What if the minister isn't a good guy? What if the minister is not looking out for the best interests?' He still would have that power. He still would have that charisma that makes people want to throw themselves into his arms. But if he is a bad guy, it could be disastrous.

Leland. I've been in so many discussions about religion where people make Jesus a mean, judgmental guy. So I'm conscious of religion being a force that can help people do good things but can also make them rigid, like Leland.

AG: I SUSPECT THERE WERE RIGIDITIES AND PREJUDICES DURING THE HARLEM RENAISSANCE, AS WELL AS CREATIVITY.

PC: There was a huge homophobia. Which was interesting, because there were a lot of gay men involved in the Harlem Renaissance.

Langston Hughes. Countee Cullen. Some of the senior statesmen, like Alain Locke and that group, were nervous that if gay men were flamboyant and out, that would take away from being the respectable young Negroes Locke wanted them to be. Some of the gay men were extraordinarily flamboyant; all of that in *Blues* about the drag balls, that was real stuff. The conservative people in the Harlem Renaissance wanted that to be in the closet. And then of course there was sexism, the patting on the head of the women writers and saying, 'Step to the rear, because now the men are going to talk.' But that's the same old thing.

AG: ASIDE FROM THE MOTHER IN *HOSPICE*, THERE ARE NO ACTUAL MOTHERS IN YOUR PLAYS, OR IN YOUR NOVEL, ALTHOUGH SEVERAL CHARACTERS FUNCTION AS MOTHERS.

PC: That's interesting — I hadn't gone specifically to the mothers. But there's always people trying to put families together. *Flyin' West*, the characters were certainly trying to make a family, and the people in *Blues* have a little family. In *Late Bus to Mecca*, Ava, the prostitute, is trying to kind of mother this homeless woman in the bus station.

AG: ALICE, THE MOTHER IN *HOSPICE* RETURNS TO THE HOME OF HER DAUGHTER, JENNY, AFTER LIVING FOR YEARS IN PARIS. IS SHE BASED ON YOUR MOTHER AT ALL?

PC: No, not at all. The mother in *Hospice* is more like me. This is why my daughter was nervous when she saw the play. My daughter is twenty-four now, but she was much younger at that time, and she said, 'Did you ever think about leaving me?' And I said, 'I thought about leaving the life that I had here, but I never really felt I could leave you. I would have had to drag you to Paris with me.' She was very relieved.

AG: WHAT INSPIRED THIS PLAY?

PC: The play comes out of trying to look at a father like mine, because that father in *Hospice* is very much like my father. The father in *Hospice* is dead by the time of the play, but he was a Civil Rights leader. He told the mother she couldn't write these personal, erotic poems. She was enamored of the father and writing these sexy poems, and he was like, 'Please, I can't have that.' The woman gives him a poem she's written, and he eats it, so that no one else will see it. My father read this play and was like, 'Do you have to make everything so personal?' And I said, 'What are you talking about?' I'm sure he saw himself.

My mother did not like being a minister's wife, was not good at the roles that she was expected to play, so I'm sure some of that is in there in terms of the mother who's frustrated. But I was married to a politician — an excellent politician and a great guy — and the demands of being the wife of someone in public life were completely unexpected. A lot of that is in *Hospice*.

AG: I'M INTERESTED TO HEAR HOW PRODUCTIONS ENVISION THE CHARACTER OF THE DAUGHTER. ON THE PAGE, SHE BEHAVES WITH SO MUCH EQUANIMITY; IS SHE EVER HURT OR ANGRY ABOUT HER MOTHER'S REJECTION?

PC: In most of the productions I've seen, the daughter does get angry sometime. But she's trying to swallow the anger, because she still thinks there are secrets that the mother can tell her. More than anger, what comes across is the longing to break through to the mother. Several times they seem like they're going to have a nice moment, and then the mother's just a snake, just attacks her. I always feel very protective of the daughter when watching the play, because the mother says such cruel things. That's why I like the end, when she sends the daughter out to have the baby and says something kind of semi-nice to her, then says to herself, 'Don't fool yourself, Miss Alice. Just don't fool yourself.' In essence, 'You're getting ready to die and you're in pain and you're not going to have that moment either.' But she would kind of like it, too.

AG: IN PREPARING FOR THIS INTERVIEW, I CAME ACROSS MANY ESSAYS, POEMS, AND STORIES ABOUT THE FIERCE CONNECTION BETWEEN AFRICAN-AMERICAN MOTHERS AND DAUGHTERS.

PC: As most of our things do, it starts in slavery, because the child would often be with the mother, and the father would be gone. They would separate people. They would mate them, and then the father would be sent back to his plantation. So the child was often with the mother, at least until it was old enough for somebody to sell it somewhere else. The mother became the parent who had to interpret that world. For the girl child, it was like being raised in a war zone. The mother had to describe everything that was going to happen to her daughter, and the things that mothers in slavery had to describe, you can imagine. 'Not only are you going to work hard, but you're going to get raped and have those children.' The mother became the one who would tell the hard truth.

There's a father in *Bourbon at the Border* who can't deal with the terrible rape that happens to his daughter when she's in Mississippi, during the 1960s. She was raped by a white sheriff. The father can't talk to her, because he knows there's nothing he can do about it. He can't go to Mississippi and walk into the sheriff's office and say, 'What did you do to my child?' anymore than the slave father could go into the master's house and say, 'Let my wife and daughter alone.' He can't do it, unless he's prepared to kill them and be killed maybe in the process. My husband always says, 'Yes, the slaves could have, but they didn't.' His question as a man is always, 'Why didn't we go to the house and say, "You can't do this?"'

AG: AND THE ANSWER?

PC: Well, we don't know the answer. We know there was physical intimidation and fear of death, but deep down we still want to say, 'How could we let that happen?' It's a question that men think about a lot more than women do. Women are trying to figure out how to work within that horror. Men, because they are raised to defend, ask themselves, 'Why didn't we defend? Why didn't we, when the slave ships started coming, kill them all and send the boat home?'

AG: TURN THE SHIP AROUND.

PC: Exactly. My husband used to argue with his mother, because she would be protective about black men. He would say, 'You're going to defend black men to me? I am a black man. I get to be critical. I get to ask those terrible questions.' We don't want *him* to ask those questions because *we* don't want to ask those questions. We're already mad; if we ask the question that goes all the way back to Africa —

Where were you all when the boat came? — there's not going to be any peace in the house.

But for the mother and daughter relationship — to be growing up in an environment like slavery, like Reconstruction, like the post-Civil War South. Even today, the dangers of being a little black girl child in a white, male-dominated, racist country are tremendous. There has to be someone who can tell the truth about what it's going to be like, and what you need to do, and the mother is usually the one. Especially about the dangers of rape. Especially about white men and their role in the abuse of black women. Especially about the relationship between black women and white women. All of those things that your mother will tell you that your father doesn't talk to you about. That's why the mother is so revered by her daughters, and by her sons.

AG: DOES THAT ENTER INTO THE RELATIONSHIP BETWEEN JENNY AND ALICE IN *HOSPICE*?

PC: Absolutely. 'Tell me what you know. My dad told me everything he knew, but tell me what you know.' And Alice is not able to do that. She just is not able to give the lessons that we want the mother to give. Now, the lessons that she does have are also valuable: the world is open to you; Paris is different, it's not all the West Side of Detroit. You can go to Paris and wrap a silver ribbon around your head, date Frenchmen, and drink champagne.

AG: BUT THE PLAY'S ULTIMATE LESSON IS THAT PARIS IS NOT WORTH MUCH. ALICE COMES HOME WHEN SHE BECOMES ILL AND BROKE.

PC: Exactly. When she stopped being able to run up and down the streets with silver ribbons in her hair, they weren't interested. To them, she was just an exotic. The mother didn't really have anything to teach the daughter, but there's never a moment where the daughter realizes that. I never thought I knew more than my mother about anything, but I would imagine that's a pretty strange moment, to realize that she doesn't have anything to tell you.

AG: DO YOU REMEMBER THE FIRST THING YOU EVER WROTE?

PC: The first thing I ever wrote. I remember the first story I ever told. I don't remember the first actual piece of writing. I used to tell stories to my sister. My sister's two years older. I remember being in a crib and telling her stories. My mother must have been talking to us about Tecumseh, the Native-American chief. Why she would have been talking to me at that age about Tecumseh, I don't know, but I remember leaning over the crib, telling my sister these stories. We had wallpaper, and there was a little tear in the wallpaper that looked like a little eagle thing to me, and I took that as a sign, that this was why I was supposed to be telling this story. It was a little Indian symbol to me.

That's the first story I remember. The story was in parts, and every night before bed I would tell her some, and she listened to it, which was wonderful, because she made me think it was something I could do. Then she taught me to read, so I started keeping notebooks. But I don't remember the first thing that I wrote, knowing that it was a piece of writing, because I'd always written. I wrote little stories and diaries. I don't remember a time when I couldn't.

AG: YOUR SISTER TAUGHT YOU TO READ?

PC: My mother had always read to us, and then I realized my sister could read. I had assumed that older people could read, but nobody around my size could read, and my sister started, and I was outdone. I just was outraged that she could do it and I couldn't. So she sat me at a little table and taught me. We slept in the same room, and we had a street light that came in the window, and we would get up and sit at the table, and she would teach me how to read and write. I owe her a lot for that.

AG: YOU WENT TO HOWARD UNIVERSITY; DID YOU GO INTENDING TO MAJOR IN PLAYWRITING?

PC: I sure did. I wrote plays in high school and did some acting. I went to an all-black high school in an all-black neighborhood and — it was amazing to me — we used to do stuff like *Auntie Mame* and *Arsenic and Old Lace*. I played the southern belle in *Auntie Mame*. My parents were so ashamed. It was bizarre, but that was what the auditorium teacher liked. She was black. We were all black. But then I got cast in *Arsenic and Old Lace*, and the first day of rehearsal we're on the stage reading through the thing, and it was as if a voice spoke to me and said, 'This is really absurd. You need to stop this right now.' I had to drop out of the play. Nothing in *Arsenic and Old Lace* had anything to do with a sixteen-year-old black girl in Detroit.

But all that was past, and I wanted to write plays. Howard had a B.F.A. program with a drama component, and you could major in playwriting. You basically took courses where you read and wrote plays; none of that stuff that used to drive me crazy — science, math. My first year I had Owen Dodson, who was maybe in his sixties at the time. A great teacher — a real writer. My second year I had Ted Shine, who was also a working playwright, and the first person I'd seen who wore jackets with suede patches on the elbows. So he was suave. Then my third year, I had Paul Carter Harrison, who had just come back from eighteen years in Amsterdam and had European suits and an accent. We were just in heaven.

AG: WERE THERE OTHER WOMEN MAJORING IN PLAY-WRITING?

PC: There was another woman who was a senior, who didn't keep writing plays. Richard Wesley was also a senior, and the two of them were very nice to me. There weren't many playwriting majors; I was the only one in my class.

Then I came to Atlanta and finished at Spelman College, where I also had working playwrights for teachers. Which was great, because they not only talked about your writing, they also talked about the universe of black theaters and how to work with it.

AG: WHAT WERE THE INFLUENCES ON YOUR STYLE?

PC: I like Ibsen. I love Lorraine Hansberry. I like old-fashioned, well made plays, where there's a lot of talk. I'm not an avant-garde kind of a person. I wrote one play with a big puppet in it, and that was probably the most avant-garde thing I ever did. I tend to have an old-fashioned structure.

AG: THERE'S A REALISTIC TRADITION AMONG AFRICAN-AMERICAN WOMEN WHO WROTE PLAYS DURING THE TWENTIETH CENTURY: MAY MILLER, EULALIE SPENCE, ZORA

NEALE HURSTON, ALICE CHILDRESS, HANSBERRY. ARE YOU
CONSCIOUS OF BEING PART OF A CONTINUUM?

PC: I'm very conscious of being part of a tradition, not just of black
women playwrights, but of black American writers. I love Langston
Hughes because he exemplifies everything that I think is important
about being a black writer. He was absolutely grounded in Harlem,
in his own black community. Obviously loved black people. Wrote
the most loving things about a range of black people, working-class
characters who had wise things to say. He was also able to travel to
places where they'd never seen a black person before. As grounded
and loving and accurate about black people as he was, he could also
embrace other cultures. I'm very conscious of being a part of that tradition, and that the tradition is tied to social action, to wanting the
work to have impact on people thinking about freedom, thinking about
struggle, thinking about revolution.

AG: WHY DO YOU WRITE?

PC: There's all kinds of political reasons. Movement reasons. Wanting
to help black people. But the real thing — because there's a lot of different ways I could do that — is I love it. I love the process. I don't
think that I would be able to survive if I didn't write. I can't understand things if I don't write them down. I don't even understand what
the questions are that are driving me crazy until I'm writing. There
is no other way to figure out what I'm thinking, what I'm scared of.
When it's not going well, it's very difficult. But I've been writing long
enough to know that if I stick with it, there's a point where it's pleasure. Where I know who these people are, and where I'm writing the
story that I'm concerned about and I've gotten rid of the dreck.

Those are personal positives. The my-father's-child part of it is
that I'm able to take important ideas to a group of people, especially
to oppressed people. And since I'm black and female, I've got two groups
that I can talk to about that. That ability helps the people in those
primary groups take more control of their lives, in ways that they probably couldn't or wouldn't if they were presented with these ideas in
a more straightforward way. I saw lots of productions of *Flyin' West*,
some wonderful and some bad, and the audience always liked it. They
never came up to me afterwards and said, 'Don't you think that's kind

of rough, for her to poison this guy?' Nobody ever objected, because they hated him; he was beating a woman. Now in real life, if I said, 'Women should feed poison to guys who abuse them and bury them on the prairie and go to a dance and dance on their grave,' people would think that I was a terrible person. I know feminists who have said less radical stuff than that and been branded everything terrible that you can think of. Alice Walker has had to take a lot of abuse for *The Color Purple*, for saying these things happen. Ntozake Shange has taken horrible, horrible abuse that she still is suffering from for writing *For Colored Girls* . . . . The work that they did made a place for me to do the work that I do. But for whatever reason, my style doesn't engender the same kind of vehement anti-response. The most negative things I've had to deal with resulted from *Mad at Miles*.

AG: YOUR PERFORMANCE PIECE ABOUT HOW JAZZ MUSICIAN MILES DAVIS BEAT UP HIS WOMEN.

PC: Black men who were Miles Davis fans were very nervous about that piece. They would come to the show and sit in front, arms folded and looking very stern, to intimidate me so I wouldn't talk bad about Miles. I loved that. Then I would really get into it.

But once I got to the part at the end, about, 'What if Kenny G was kicking you all's ass, what would you do?' they'd laugh. They'd come up to me afterwards and say, 'Okay, you got me, that's really true. But I'm not breaking my Miles records.' I'd say, 'That's okay. I just want you to think about this guy, so that next time you can say that the music is great but the life was really not exemplary. That's all I'm saying. That you have to make the distinction.' It's a huge step, because talking about Miles Davis is like talking about God. But they could understand it. The way it was presented allowed them a way in.

Flyin' West is the same thing. I absolutely do believe that self-defense for women is critical in situations like that. If someone is going to beat you and your children to death, that you have the right to defend yourself shouldn't even be a radical idea. It wouldn't be a radical idea in any setting outside of people's homes. So I can write a play and at least have the idea flicker by.

Same thing with *Blues*. Guy, the costume designer, is flamboyantly, joyously homosexual; the black American community is very, very homophobic. But I've never seen a production where people did not embrace Guy. Where black men did not like him, where people did not applaud when he stands up to Leland for calling homosexuality an 'abomination.' That these straight black men in the audience, who I know are homophobic in their real lives, would applaud and say, 'Go on, brother,' and all of that, is wonderful, because my hope is always — and this is back to the idealistic thing — that if they can do it in the theater, perhaps when they pass somebody like Guy on the street, there'll be a bit left of what they liked about him. Not that they'll embrace him and invite him home for dinner, but they'll leave him alone. They'll feel he has a life, they've got a life. It's okay for him to be part of the community that we call our own family.

AG: DO YOU WANT WOMEN TO EMBRACE THE MOTHER IN *HOSPICE*?

PC: I don't want necessarily for them to embrace her. She is not a mother I would want to be. Definitely wouldn't want to have a mother like Alice. But I'm often annoyed by the image that black women have of being all-knowing, all-patient, all-hardworking.

AG: SHE IS THE OPPOSITE OF THAT.

PC: Exactly. And we have the right to say that. We're not all Miss Lena in *A Raisin in the Sun*. She's a wonderful woman, and we wouldn't have survived, and all that is true. But there are also women like Alice, and Angel in *Blues*. They are us too.

   The problem, when you are presented to yourself all the time as a woman who is so strong you can take anything — crazy children and sour men and racism and lynching — is that you start thinking that's supposed to be true. Even though you know that you have all of the frailties and craziness everybody else has. But when your own culture keeps feeding that back to you, then you start thinking that if you're like Alice and don't want to be the minister's wife, if you want to go to Paris, shave your head, and write poems, that you're a bad person. That you're not a black woman, that you're not a black mother. And that's wrong. Because we get to be the range. We get to have great mothers and we get to have really selfish mothers.

AG: IN AN ESSAY, YOU ONCE CALLED YOURSELF ONE OF THE 'AFRICAN AMERICAN URBAN NATIONALIST FEMINIST WARRIOR WOMEN.'

PC: I definitely still claim that. But I don't think that means flawless and perfect. I am definitely a feminist, but I also know there are contradictions in my life. I'm definitely a Black Nationalist, but I'm also an internationalist. I'm looking for the right to be a fully complex human being and the right to create characters who are fully complex. I define myself as a feminist because I think it's foolish not to. I don't know how you can be a sane woman and not define yourself as a feminist. As a black person who's always lived in black communities, I define myself as a Nationalist, not because I'm trying to keep anybody out but because the settings that I choose to live in are always all black. I'm trying to make that black environment whole, solid, and ready to negotiate with other communities, so we can say, 'Here's the Native Americans and here's the Chinese Americans and here's the European Americans, and we're all going to go down and talk to these people at the nuclear power plant.'

AG: BUT DESPITE NOT WANTING TO PORTRAY PERFECT WOMEN, YOU DO WRITE WARRIOR WOMEN FIGURES: JOYCE IN YOUR NOVEL; MISS LEAH IN *FLYIN' WEST*; DELIA, EVEN, IN *BLUES*. HOW CONSCIOUS IS THAT?

PC: It's conscious in that I don't often encounter women onstage like the women that I know and love and see every day. Regular women. They do admirable things within the context of ordinary lives: send people to school and support families, plant gardens and grow flowers. I don't see enough of that in what we write, in the movies and on the stage. We're either the strong one, the one totally focused on finding men, or the one destroyed by men and race. A number of us fit those categories, but there are also the ones who work hard, don't go crazy, are not found by the side of the road killed in a terrible way. Their stories are interesting to me. Their voices are interesting. I want women like that in the things I write. But I'm not consciously saying, 'Okay, this is the role model,' because as an artist, the whole idea of role models is restrictive. It's restrictive to say, 'Okay, I've got to make a good strong woman, because my people are oppressed, and if we don't have role models we won't know how to act.' We know how to act.

AG: BUT AREN'T THE CHARACTERS THAT I MENTIONED ROLE MODELS?

PC: Their behavior is worthy of emulation, but they're not role models in the sense that I'm creating them to say, 'This is how you should act.' I'm trying to make sure that the character is a real person.

I'm not sure why 'role model' is a problem for me. The implication is that if we as black people could just see somebody do it right, then we wouldn't be doing the things that we do. We wouldn't be smoking crack. We wouldn't be killing our grandmothers. We wouldn't be not working. We wouldn't be destroying our neighborhoods. For all kinds of reasons, we are not doing the things we need to do, but not because we don't see people who can. It's like, later for the role models. Let's get black people some jobs. Let's put a factory here. Seeing Thurgood Marshall doesn't help if your school doesn't teach you to read and you can't go to law school.

AG: IN YOUR BRIEF INTRODUCTION TO *CHAIN* AND *LATE BUS TO MECCA*, YOU CALL THESE TWO ONE-ACTS 'MORALITY PLAYS.' IS THERE CLEAR-CUT RIGHT AND WRONG IN YOUR PLAYS, IN *BLUES* FOR INSTANCE?

PC: I do want the audience to be clear about what I think the desirable behavior is and the undesirable. The problem with *Blues* was that Angel would not be redeemed at the end of the play. She wouldn't apologize. I had created this character who wasn't sorry about what she had done. I'm used to writing black women characters who, even when they do something wrong, it's because of oppression or something that's happened to them. Angel has those reasons, but is also prepared to use them to manipulate people, to say to Doc, 'You've got to do this abortion for me,' and to Guy, 'You've got to take me in.' That character was interesting because she was a black woman and she was not the person you needed to emulate as a black woman in the audience. You needed to say, 'Okay, this behavior is dangerous.' She hurt all who loved her. It's growth for me as a writer not to make all the black women exemplary, to say, 'Alice is not a great mother,

Angel is not a great friend, but it's okay, we've got Delia and Doc, so that you can see the positive.'

AG: DOC, TOO, IS A MORALLY AMBIGUOUS CHARACTER.

PC: Because Doc is doing illegal abortions. People have asked me did I do that on purpose, because there's such a question about abortion in this country. It's wonderful when the truth of something historical lends itself to what's happening now. I was doing it because I was looking at Harlem in 1930, and abortion was a big question.

AG: HOW DO PLAYS START IN YOU?

PC: With the character. I don't know where they come from. I wish I knew, because when they weren't here I could go find them. It's often a voice. I'm not really visual; I hear the people talking, but I don't see costumes and business. I was driving on the freeway and heard what ended up being Miss Leah's voice saying almost exactly the speech at the end to Minnie, 'We can't let nobody take our babies. We've given up all the babies we can afford to lose. Do you understand what I'm sayin' . . . ?' I pulled off and wrote it down and said, 'Who in the hell is this? What is this?' I love that, because then you know it's organic. You aren't saying, 'Okay, I need a play about women, because they've contracted with me to write a play about women.' The characters are already talking; the task becomes finding the story that they're in. That's the part I like. And you can't make that happen.

AG: WHY DID YOU SET *FLYIN' WEST* IN A HISTORICAL PERIOD?

PC: Well, the voice that I heard talking was a woman who had been born in slavery, so I was trying to make her the oldest possible living person that she could be — one hundred and something. But she refused to be involved in that. So I started thinking, 'Where would she be and what was she talking about?' And I realized she was a homesteader. I went and read the Homestead Act of 1860 and then went and read diaries and journals and tried to look at movies about women on the frontier. There's a great movie, a semi-documentary, called *Heartland*. Great movie. They're way out in the middle of Wyoming, and the older woman is talking to the younger woman, who says, 'Oh, I just can't stand . . . the Rip Torn character. I just don't know how to talk to him.' And the older one says, 'Well, you better learn before winter.' They're going to be in that room by themselves for the whole winter. That movie made me realize how isolated these people were. How isolated as women, trying to have babies and do all the stuff that we do. The harshness of the environment.

Once I got this character placed in the all-black town of Nicodemus, Kansas, I had to figure out where she came from, because it wasn't like she was born in Kansas. I'd read excerpts of Ida B. Wells' journals, where she talked about how two of her friends had gotten lynched and she said, 'Sometimes I wish I could just gather my people up in my arms and fly away West. Because we need to leave a place where they don't respect us and our lives aren't worth anything.' Which is exactly what I put in Miss Leah's mouth. And the image of people flying is a big part of African-American folklore. There's all these stories about Africans being brought here on the slave ships and landing and looking around and saying, 'Oh, hell no,' and just flying back across the ocean.

That's the part that's wonderful about writing: all the stuff that you know, that you read and see and experience, is going to filter through and come out to be Miss Leah or Guy or whoever. You can access it. It's there. Because you've experienced it, seen it, thought about it. Which is why I finally have gotten to the place, in the last ten years maybe, where I trust whatever I'm interested in. I just go with it. Because I know it's going to come back around in something that I'm writing. There's some part of me that knows the story already.

AG: YOU SENT ME A MARVELOUS REMINISCENCE ABOUT SEEING *A RAISIN IN THE SUN* FOR THE FIRST TIME. WHY DOES THAT PLAY STILL SPEAK TO AUDIENCES?

PC: The people are real. The things the play is talking about are still true. Ruth working so hard, and her husband with these unrealistic ideas about what he's going to do. He's going to invest with these people whom Ruth knows are fools and charlatans. That's a constant story. That's why people groan watching that play, because we know that Walter's friends are going to steal the money. No way is he going to be a successful liquor store owner. Beneatha trying to move from one class to the other, because she's smart. All of those absolutely contemporary things. Plus the language. The anger. The complete rage and powerlessness of Walter. He has a job, but he can't abide being a servant for all of his life. That this woman would have an abortion just because she can't imagine having another baby in that house.

It's not like everybody's okay now. It's not like we can move anywhere we want and figure there are not going to be problems if it's a neighborhood where there haven't been people of color.

AG: DO YOU WRITE FOR BLACK AUDIENCES IN YOUR HEAD?

PC: I do. Always. It's too confusing otherwise. I don't know what white people want from a black writer. I know exactly what black people want from a black writer. They want an interesting story where we win at the end. And sometimes that's what I'll write, and everybody's all happy, and sometimes it's *Bourbon at the Border*.

Audiences felt betrayed when they saw it; they wanted *Flyin' West*. People always want you to write the thing they like. But in *Bourbon at the Border*, May and Charlie don't get over what happened to them in the South in the 1960s. He was horribly injured, abused, and violated, and so was she. Now, it's Detroit 1997, but the guy has been in and out of mental institutions, and he finally figures that he needs to pay back the sheriff and the other two guys in Mississippi who raped his wife and beat him. He figures he'll be well again if he kills three white men. So he slits their throats over the period of the play, and of course it leads to him. At the end, the police start knocking on the door.

Nobody in the audience wants that. They want these people to cross the Ambassador Bridge from Detroit to Canada and go to a safe place. But these people have been destroyed by American racism. The audience wants a happy ending, but nothing good's going to happen once the police come.

The pull of what the audience wants is always a danger. I have to answer the questions that I have and not reassure the audience about the questions they have. There's always a temptation to lean toward what people want, and a black audience always wants the black person to win.

AG: WHAT INSPIRED THIS PLAY?

the way this community works.' There isn't that kind of group effort. The black writers who were writing as part of the Black Arts Movement did not agree on everything, but they agreed that their responsibility was to write about and for black people. There is no agreement that that's true anymore.

AG: WHAT DO YOU THINK ABOUT THAT CHANGE?

PC: It reflects where my community is. It's sad that we're no longer tied to working for our liberation, because we're doomed if we don't liberate ourselves from the madness around us. But writers can't be expected to also be the movement leaders, the strategists. You have to have community organizers. You have to have speechmakers. You got to have pamphleteers. And you have to have playwrights.

Since there isn't a movement, we're not putting forward movement kinds of writers. The plays are much more individualistic, which for me as a group-oriented person is sad. Because we as black people need all of the things that a good play can do. But almost none of us go to the theater.

AG: EVEN IN ATLANTA?

PC: Tiny, tiny percentage. I used to wring my hands, and Kenny Leon, artistic director of the Alliance, would kind of put a cold towel on my head, because I'd be saying, 'For the first three weeks of the production it's going to be all your season ticket holders.'

AG: WHO ARE WHITE?

PC: Oh, yeah. Well, since he's been there, a percentage are black, but most of them are well-to-do white people. Which is fine. I want them to go to the theater. But I also know that their reactions to what I'm writing are going to be very different than the reactions of black audiences. For me, that's dangerous, because if I'm standing in the back of the theater, pacing as we all do, I can't help but listen to the response. The response to *Bourbon at the Border*, because it made white people nervous too, was quiet. The black audiences, because there's a lot of humor in the first part of the play, do what black audiences usually do, which is respond very vocally to what's going on. We didn't get to them until the play had been running awhile, but it was a great relief to realize, 'Okay, that part of the play is working.'

It's a danger to be a playwright and not be able to work at the early stages in front of your own group. Not because other people shouldn't see it, and not because it's being mean about other people, but because it skews your ear. You're listening to the reactions of people who don't bring the cultural information that you have.

The cross-cultural exchange is wonderful, but it's difficult when you're not secure about what you know, either as audience or writer. In my novel, Ava Johnson owns a hair salon in Atlanta until she learns she is H.I.V. positive, then she goes to live with her sister, Joyce, in North Michigan. One day, she does her sister's hair and rubs 'a little oil in the kitchen, where the hair is always so soft.' My editor, a very nice white woman in New York, wrote me back and said, 'What is the kitchen? What does that mean?' Do you know what the kitchen is?

AG: NO.

PC: It's like the back of the hair. If you have straightened hair, the kitchen is usually the first part that will go home, which means go back to the regular hair that it really is. If you are wearing your hair down, you can get away with the kitchen being a little raggedy, because your straightened hair will cover it. But if you're going to put your hair up, then you got to get your straightening comb and touch up the edges, and get the kitchen together. I had to figure out another way to say that, because it didn't occur to me that she wouldn't know what the kitchen was.

I love that kind of stuff. But if my editor were the main voice in my head, there would be a problem, because I would always be writing for her understanding, as opposed to assuming that she'll ask me a question, and I can either say, 'No, this has to stay, because all the black women who are going to read it know this,' or, 'I can say what this means in a way that leaves a space for everybody to come in.'

As a playwright, I had worked almost exclusively in black theater since I was in college. Once I started working at the Alliance, with *Flyin' West*, I realized that my characters, my people, were going to be talking around people who were not like them at all, who were going to be looking at them through completely different eyes. Which is fine, but a playwright has to be really careful not to begin writing for that audience. The idea of audiences is something that I want to be very careful about, because I don't want to write to please anyone other than myself. I don't want to say, 'Okay, now I'm writing for the Alliance, and their audience is going to be upper-middle-class white people, so I need to make sure that I don't offend anybody.' There's no way that I would consciously say that, but if you sit in a room full of that audience for five nights a week and listen to where they laugh and where they don't, where they sigh and where they don't sigh, when they start looking at their watches and coughing — it's in there. It would be like trying to guess what the audience wants, and you can't guess. You can only try to stay alive in the world, so that you are probably moved by what moves other people whom you know.

AG: SHOULD AFRICAN-AMERICAN WRITERS ONLY WRITE FOR AFRICAN-AMERICAN THEATERS, WHITE-EUROPEAN WRITERS ONLY FOR WHITE-EUROPEAN THEATERS, AND SO FORTH?

PC: They all get to choose. You have to make sure that you stay in touch with the community of theaters where your audience is. After the Alliance did *Bourbon at the Border*, I said to myself, 'This is not going to be picked up on the white theater circuit that picked up *Flyin' West* or *Blues*.' Those other pieces have a historic context, which maybe blunts their accusatory nature. It's difficult to find a black play without an accusation at the heart, which is, 'Y'all see what racism did.' But my heart is not broken if my plays don't get to the Kennedy Center if they get to St. Louis Black Repertory. My heart is not broken if they don't get to the Goodman as long as they get to Bushfire Theatre Company in Philadelphia.

My politics are helpful to me in looking at that, because they help me not get distracted and say, 'Oh, my God, how come these big white theaters don't like this one, maybe I'd better go back and write what I wrote before,' rather than saying, 'I know there are theaters that are interested in every play I write and I hope they will be until I stop writing plays.' But I have to be careful that I don't forget about those theaters, that I don't do what we sometimes do, which is say, 'Oh, thank God I don't have to work that hard and sweep the stage anymore. I can just be up here and be the one black play in the season. The one black playwright who is produced at lots of white theaters.' I don't want to be that. That's like being the only black person at the dinner party, the only black person at the conference. It would drive me crazy.

AG: WOULD YOU LIKE TO WRITE FILMS?

PC: I'm curious more than burning to do it, since I'm not visual. I'm intimidated in that sense. But I love movies. Watch a lot of movies. I also know that, in terms of my community, nobody goes to the theater. No one in my neighborhood has ever seen one of my plays. There'll be a big piece in the paper, with a picture — this is a playwright, she's got a new play at the Alliance — and they all will come and tell me how wonderful the picture was, and how proud they are of me, but they never will go see the play.

AG: WHY NOT?

PC: The environment is not an environment that they're used to going into, and if they do go, they're usually not comfortable. Kenny Leon works real hard to make sure that the Alliance is a welcoming environment, but if you're my neighbors across the street and you go down to the Alliance on a night where there's no other black people in the audience, you're not going to have a good time. You're going to be too conscious of it the whole time. They want me to do well, and they love that I'm working at the Alliance, because I made these white people take me and put my play on the stage. They love it in that defiant way. But they won't go see it. That drives me crazy, because I write it for them. I sit in my little house and look at them all day, and I want them to see it.

AG: YOU AND YOUR HUSBAND RAN THE JUST US THEATER COMPANY IN ATLANTA FOR A WHILE. DID YOU GET AN AUDIENCE?

PC: We got an audience for the first chunk of what we were doing because we had other people to help us get the word out. Once we had to do everything ourselves — publicize *and* do the shows — it was difficult. But when we were able to get the radio ads and stuff, we used to sell out. We were doing performance art. Audiences were very open to it.

Pearl Cleage 49

My husband is a novelist, but he wasn't getting published. So I said, 'Why don't you think about doing something with theater?' And he was like, 'Oh, I hate proscenium, I'm really not about that.' So I said, 'Well, what kind of environment would you like to work in?' He said, 'I've always liked clubs.' I said, 'Okay, let's make a performance environment where you can feel comfortable.'

He created a wonderful thing called Club Zebra, which was set up like a nightclub. We had a bar — we had to give away the stuff because you can't sell it without a license. We had a jazz band. We had tables with zebra tablecloths. We let people talk. People thought it was a club that also did interesting stuff. Black people are not intimidated by nightclubs.

That's where I did *Mad at Miles* and *Good Brother Blues* for the first time, and it was wonderful, because it was an intimate environment. It made a space for me to do the feminist work I was doing, and I also had a comrade and a collaborator who was a conscious man. I don't think the problem with women telling their stories is that we're afraid of what other women will do. From my community, the response we're frightened of is black men saying, 'Negative images of black men.' I didn't have to deal with that, because my husband and the guys who worked with us were all schooled in feminism before they started. He would talk to them about, 'Now when you're working with us, you can't say "bitches," you can't say "hos," you can't hit on the young women who come here to act.' Which is like defining the new man that we love. If they were going to talk to these women, they had to elevate what the rap was. So we created a group of guys that had a really good superficial understanding of what feminism required of them, if they were going to be new men. And as long as they were in that environment they did great. Back in the world they haven't always been as exemplary, but the basics they hold onto.

But even a black theater audience is tiny compared to how many black folks go to the movies or own a TV. You can go in the poorest-of-the-poor house, and people will have a TV. Almost always VCRs now. All of these cable channels, we're watching all of those movies. My audience looks at TV more than any other group of people in this country. Little kids, everybody. So I'm interested in it for that. But it's a form that I haven't worked in, so I'm not real comfortable. Plus I know that in movies and TV, the writer is absolutely the non-person in the group. That would be an adjustment.

AG: TALKING ABOUT NEGATIVE IMAGES, THE WAY *CHAIN* BEGINS IS CHILLING. THE STAGE IS IN DARKNESS, WE HEAR A FEMALE VOICE SCREAMING 'NO! STOP IT! DON'T, DADDY! PLEASE DON'T!' I HAD THIS STEREOTYPICAL REACTION: HER FATHER'S RAPING HER. WHY DID YOU DO THAT?

PC: So that you would have that reaction. So that the reaction would be based on what we know happens to many girl children, but try not to think about. When you hear her scream 'Daddy' like that, you think that's what's happening. Then you realize that it's the opposite: he's trying to protect her. He's a good guy. He was absolutely trying to take care of her, do the best he could. It makes you let go of the preconceived idea about the black father. He's someone specific, just like those guys who are abusing their children sexually are specific. We can't assume anything. The girl's problem doesn't have to do with parents who are not protective of her. Her problem has to do with their not being able to stand up against what the culture has become, where she is.

AG: HOW DID THAT PLAY START?

PC: I saw a clipping in *The New York Times*. There was a case in the Bronx, I think — a Puerto Rican family where the girl was a crack addict. Her parents chained her in the house, and the social service people came and arrested the parents, and everybody in the family went down and said, 'We've been trying to work with her, and the parents are great parents, and maybe we shouldn't have chained her, but what would you suggest?' They had been through every possible social service agency trying to get some help with the child. But the child was a crack addict. It was a little article, but there was a picture — the Puerto Rican family outside the courthouse, and the girl was there too. She was fifteen, I think. She was crying, and the parents were crying, and they were all hugging, and it was tragic. She didn't want to be a crack addict. They didn't want her to be a crack addict. She lived in a neighborhood where it was very difficult not to be involved with drugs. It struck me as such a terrible thing, for parents to come from Puerto Rico to the United States, because they think they're going to do something wonderful for their kid, and then this happens.

I transferred it to somebody coming to New York from rural Alabama, saying, 'Okay, we're going to give our kids the advantages that we didn't have,' and it turns out to be the worst of the worst. People have a real hard time with that play. The things that the little girl says are awful. She talks about the drug dealer teaching her how to masturbate in front of people. People really don't want to think about the degree to which sexual abuse is present in the lives of young women — of every race. And when people hear it in the theater, they get nervous.

AG: PERHAPS SOME OF THE NERVOUSNESS HAS TO DO WITH THE NATURE OF LIVE THEATER.

PC: It's immediate. And you're hearing things out loud. If you're reading it, you can close the book, you can look up, you can take a breath. In *Chain*, once this girl starts talking, and once Ava, in *Late Bus,* starts talking about men wanting her to do it with dogs — they're talking. They are just telling everything. It doesn't seem strange to them, because they're used to talking to prostitutes or crack addicts, but the audience is middle class. It's like being in a room full of junkies, where all of the stories have to do with scoring and getting high. If you're not a dope fiend, it's scary to be in a group where everyone is talking about that, and it's the same for people who haven't allowed themselves to think about sexual abuse to be at a play about it. It's like, 'I don't want to know this, because then I have to start thinking about it. I have to stop assuming that everything is okay.'

AG: DO YOU THINK IT'S IMPORTANT FOR WOMEN TO TELL THESE STORIES TO EACH OTHER?

PC: Oh, it's critical. Sometimes women are also the ones preying on these girls, or cognizant of what's going on and not doing anything about it. But often women don't know what's happening. We are not present to protect the child, and she doesn't tell us. So we have to tell these stories, to let each other say the truth of our experience. If we don't know that sexual abuse is rampant in families and in the world, we can't say to the daughter, 'This is the stuff you have to look out for.'

We have to give each other the right to talk about all of the horror that happens, so that those of us who are not broken can stand between the next group and the abusers, who are overwhelmingly men. A lot of my work is committed to saying out loud what people have said to me, so that the ones who have been abused can say, 'Thank God. I thought I was the only person who this had happened to.' As much as people have talked about this, women still feel there's something that *they* did which made it happen. I was in an abusive relationship, and I felt I must have done something to make this guy start hitting me, so let me just stay here and figure it out, and then he'll go back to the way he was. Which never happens. Never happens.

AG: WHERE IN YOUR MIND OR ART DOES BEING AN AFRICAN-AMERICAN WOMAN INTERSECT WITH THE EXPERIENCE OF OTHER WOMEN OF COLOR, OR WHITE WOMEN?

PC: It intersects in what I know about the world. In my work, there isn't much of that, because I tend not to have characters who are not black. I don't feel like I know white women, Latina women, well enough to know that what I'm writing is true. I've always lived in black environments. I've had lots of interaction with other people, but I don't have one Asian person in my life. I don't have any close relationships now with white women. During my feminist-awakening years I had more, because none of the black women I knew were talking about feminism, and I was desperate to talk about it.

I would love to be able to write about black women from other places. But I have a dread of assuming that I know something about Afro-Cuban women because I'm African American. So I tend only to work with black characters, because I have a real good idea about black women and a pretty good idea about black men.

AG: DO YOU THINK BEING A BLACK WOMAN HAS HELPED OR HURT YOUR CAREER AS A WRITER, YOUR CAREER IN THE THEATER?

PC: I never have any regret about being black and female. I love being a black woman. I tease my male friends sometimes and say, 'You know, as a black man, you all are guiltless when you talk about race, because you're the oppressed. But when we talk about sexism, you're all the oppressors. When I would talk to my white women friends, they're guiltless when it comes to sexism, but when it comes to race, they've got to wear it, because they're still privileged whites. I don't have to wear any of that because I'm oppressed across the board.' As a person whose work is fed by reacting to oppression and looking at how we act when we're oppressed, there has never been a problem of, 'Oh, my God, I'm stymied, I'm blocked, I can't write because I'm oppressed.' It's like, 'I got to write fast, because we got to get free.'

In terms of being able to work, I've always found that black institutions, black schools, black theaters, black publishers, black newspapers have always been extraordinarily receptive to what I do. Many times, black people that write well leave the black environment, because the pay is usually better. But I never felt it was a disadvantage to make a life in a black community and do work within black institutions. When I'm at the Goodman Theatre and intimidated because it's the Goodman and a white male institution, I can say, 'Yeah, but I'm carrying a whole bunch of people with me who are really supportive of what I do, love what I do and understand what I do.' When I have a difference of opinion with a white male artistic director, I don't have the problem that some black people have, which is thinking, 'God, he's in charge of this multimillion-dollar institution. He must know best.' I always feel he can't possibly know best. He's a rich white male. His interests are completely different than mine. The reason I'm here is not because they think I'm wonderful, not because they like having lunch with me, but because they're trying to expand their audience base and keep their theater alive. And I don't have a problem with that, because I want their theater to stay alive too. That the Goodman did really well with *Blues*, had lots of audience and good response did not escape their attention. They know there's a huge audience of people who haven't seen some of my stuff, and if they can figure out how to get them into the theater, it's another shot in the arm for them.

But it's hard to keep those things in mind if you don't have a group that you're a part of, if you can't continuously remind yourself of why you're writing. Why you started, what you're trying to do. If you don't have that, it's much easier to be seduced into trying to write for the people who are in charge of the grants.

I get to sit on a lot of grant panels and go up to the beautiful offices at AT&T. They've given lots of money to my plays. I love AT&T. But as you ride up to the fortieth floor to this beautiful conference room, you have to remind yourself that you're taking your neighbors. My neighbor next door is a great guy. He's probably about seventy now.

He cannot read. I wanted to teach him. Not interested. So I always think about him when I'm riding up to these big offices or talking to the artistic director who intimidates everybody. I don't care about the artistic director because I'm thinking about my neighbor and I know that these people in the offices don't know him at all and don't love him either. But my neighbors are the people who make it possible for me to feel like I'm doing the work that I'm supposed to do. They make me feel like I'm Langston Hughes sitting on the steps of the brownstone, talking to the people who pass you while walking by.

AG: HE WAS CONFLICTED TOO.

PC: Because of the pull to leave that and be the exotic.

AG: AND MAKE MONEY.

PC: Well, to make money certainly, and also just to be petted in the way the big white institutions will pet a person of color. But in your own community, you never go out of vogue.

AG: PEARL'S MANIFESTO FOR THE TWENTY-FIRST CENTURY, FOR AFRICAN-AMERICAN WOMEN . . .

PC: And men. I wish people would tell the truth and not pretend that they don't know what they know. The popular culture encourages people to pretend that they don't know truth when they see it. People don't have to embrace my politics, just say, 'Okay, as a man, I'm not going to hit anybody.' And don't lie. Don't hit anybody and don't lie. I'd be amazed at what the neighborhood would be like. Because once you stop lying, and once the violence is no longer a problem, then you can begin to address the questions of, 'Why don't we own these stores in our neighborhoods? Why don't we pick up the trash in this vacant lot?' But we're caught up in all the lies and material stuff, all the wanting to be whatever we think it is that white people are.

I don't think we're going to make it if we don't change. I'm a writer so I'm going to keep writing, but I don't feel optimistic about the wider black community. I'm hollering as loud as I can, and those of us doing real creative work are hollering as loud as we can, but it's difficult to holler louder than Puff Daddy. ▼

Constance Congdon

Constance Congdon was born in
Rock Rapids, Iowa, and grew up in
a variety of places, among them Des
Moines, Iowa; Colorado Springs,
Colorado; and Garden City, Kansas.
These western and midwestern
locales imbue a number of her plays,
particularly *Native American* (1984);
No Mercy (1986), simultaneously set
in New Mexico in 1945, on the morning of the first test of the atomic bomb,
and in 1985, in the lives of ordinary Americans; and *Tales of the Lost Formicans*
(1989), which depicts an American family touched by aliens who cannot fathom
American culture. Her comic edge sharpens *Losing Father's Body* (1994), which
involves a missing corpse and the family awaiting its arrival, and *Lips* (1999),
a political satire about the sexual strategies of the first female president of
the United States. She has explored sexism and sexuality in *Casanova* (1991)
and the ravages of AIDS in *Dog Opera* (1997).

Congdon has also written for young audiences, notably *Raggedy Ann &
Andy* (1987), an adaptation of the books by Johnny Guelle; *Rembrandt Takes
a Walk,* from the book by Mark Strand and Red Grooms (1989); an adaptation of Ludwig Bemelmans' classic, *Madeline's Rescue* (1990); and her own
adaptations of *Mother Goose* (1989) and *Beauty and the Beast* (1992). *The
Automata Pieta* (1999), a realistic fantasy involving a teenage fashion doll,
and *Two Chairs* (2000), were written for young actors but for a general audience.

Congdon has received playwriting fellowships from the National
Endowment for the Arts, the Rockefeller Foundation, and the Guggenheim
Foundation. She is an alumna of New Dramatists and a member of PEN. She
teaches playwriting at Amherst College in Massachusetts.

This interview took place in Hamden, Connecticut, on August 27, 1999.

• • •

AG: WHAT DECADE HAS INFLUENCED YOU THE MOST?

CC: If I had to choose one, it would be the 1960s. In 1963, John F. Kennedy was shot, and things happened to me personally that were similar to what happened in the nation. I was in some ways completely orphaned: my father started exhibiting the characteristics of Alzheimer's disease; I had a huge break with my stepmother. With the murder of John F. Kennedy, there was the realization that this world I had been living in was a construct, not reality. It was as though someone took the earth and flung it over, and I was living on the other side. Yeats calls it 'ripping the veil.' But I always felt as though it was more than a rip. Someone took a knife and tore through a curtain in one stroke.

AG: WHERE WERE YOU LIVING IN 1963?

CC: I was in my first semester at Fort Hays State University in Kansas. I'd been on my own emotionally and to some extent economically since I was fifteen or sixteen. I got my first job when I was fourteen and contributed that money to the family to keep things going. So when I escaped to college, it was escape. When my father got ill about two years later, I attempted to go home — my father and stepmother had moved back to Colorado from Kansas — and I worked for a year in a library, again giving all my money to the family. I lasted in that sit uation about three months before I couldn't stand it anymore and bailed. I always felt guilty about leaving my father, who was really losing it, but I could not stay in the house.

So that threw me into the culture of the sixties. In 1966 I was living with my boyfriend in Colorado, and my family wasn't speaking to me. We had an underground magazine called *The Camp Primer*, based on a gay superhero named Captain Camp. It wasn't terribly sophisticated but — this was 1966. It had a beautiful silkscreen cover — a different cover every issue. We'd run it off on mimeo, then collate, staple, and sell it for a nickel. We went up to twenty-five cents. I was in the Antiwar Movement and worked in the draft resistance. I had a home in the political and cultural life of the sixties.

When I finally got my B.A., after six years in and out of school and huge bills, someone put up money and I opened a leather/head shop called Some Rough Beast, a version of Yeats' line, 'And what rough beast, its hour come round at last, slouches towards Bethlehem to be born?' I made leather clothes. Bought the leather, cut it, sewed it, glued it. Made pants, jackets, vests. I had made clothes for bands when I was in college, to get extra money.

One of my most horrifying memories is of being in a car on Nevada Street in Colorado Springs, on my way to a remnant shop to buy velvet, to make a pair of pants for my childhood friend, Jim Davis. He was driving, we had the radio on, and we heard that Martin Luther King had been shot. We were in traffic and we just sat there, and then we had somehow to go forward. We numbly drove to the fabric store and walked around, and then we got back into the car. We went to our friends. We all gathered.

The death of Bobby Kennedy. I was on a bus in the middle of Kansas, on the way home — my idea of home — to visit my high school English teacher, Max Goldsberry. We had stopped in the middle of the prairie, those high plains that identify my home. The bus driver stopped to pick up mail, and we were sitting on the dark, dark bus, and he came back on and said, 'Bobby Kennedy's been shot.' And we drove off.

I get into Garden City, and it's Republicanville, and people are saying, 'Oh, some guy shot Bobby Kennedy. I'm sure he was high on drugs.' Lame excusemaking. At least I was in the home of a surrogate parent of mine, who was a Republican and had no sympathy for Bobby Kennedy but a lot of sympathy for me. But I felt orphaned again. I had managed to build up hope until the death of King. Then I just lost hope. So when Bobby Kennedy was shot . . .

In some ways I'm still living in that era. Not that I'm back in the sixties, but in terms of the pain I feel — that *weltschmerz* which I live with all the time. I feel that was the decade in which, as an American, I became a member of the world. Started living in a world that people in other countries have lived in for generations, in which great leaders are murdered, and the power structure is overwhelming. In which evil doesn't come from heaven or hell but is earthbound and earthreal. That's the world that I live in now. I see the sixties as the time when I became an adult in the saddest sense of the word.

AG: HOW HAVE THE 1960S FILTERED INTO YOUR PLAYS?

CC: It's hard to know. I originally set *Tales of the Lost Formicans* in the sixties. Then I realized that I was more concerned about what was happening when I was writing the play, in the eighties, because I was raising a child in a vacuum of values. My concern about my son and what the world was going to be like for him was more alive to me than the sixties.

When I think of the traumas in my life . . . my mother died suddenly the day after my ninth birthday, and my father couldn't tell me; he had the neighbors tell me. In his mind the neighbors were his best friends, but to me, they were just the neighbors. He couldn't take care of me. He sent me off to live with relatives. And the relatives . . . in my family, there's a lot of alcoholism and a lot of crazy, wild, and at times funny behavior. I think that's when my 'observer' self developed. I started living in a movie of my life.

But the sixties got me back inside *me* again. My life wasn't a movie; I was living my life. Martin Luther King was inside me in a way — he'd become a surrogate father figure. So when he was killed, it was a loss all over again. Nationally and internationally his death was a huge tragedy, but it was always a personal tragedy to me, because I had identified so strongly with his values. And still do. I have been trying to resolve that attitude with what's happened to me in the last decades. My feelings about nonviolence are in complete disarray. I see some mass murderer on television, and I go, 'Kill him, kill him.' I can't imagine that I'm saying those words, yet that's what I've come to. It's irresolvable with what I believe.

AG: I ASKED WHAT DECADE INFLUENCED YOU BECAUSE I FEEL THAT IN *NO MERCY, TALES OF THE LOST FORMICANS,* AND *LOSING FATHER'S BODY* YOU ARE AN OBSERVER OF AMERICA AND HOW IT FUNCTIONS, OR DOESN'T FUNCTION.

CC: I'm glad you brought that up, because when people sit around — particularly in the age of identity politics — and say, 'Well, how do you define yourself?' — I say, 'I'm American.' Even before I say I'm female. I'm an American female. I'm an unhyphenated American.

It's confusing to be American, but it's a profound thing to be. And whether it's profound or confusing, it is who I am. My son, Sam, is even more American, because of my husband's pre-Revolution genes.

AG: HOW OLD IS YOUR SON?

CC: He's twenty-nine. I had a conversation with him recently where he told me that he feels like an alien in his own country, because of the distancing he feels from his friends who are first-generation Americans with immigrant parents. They go to Greece or India and can claim those countries as home. He can't. He's an American, and that includes the Native-American genes that are in me as well.

AG: WHERE DOES THAT COME IN?

CC: A lot of this is steeped in alcoholism — one of the things alcohol does is steal family history. But my father's grandmother evidently was a full-blood Native American, we think Dakota Sioux. We're not sure, because her son, Jim Congdon — my father's father — who was half Native American and half Welsh — was a terrible alcoholic. Big surprise. He was genetically predisposed, probably, to that affliction.

He basically went away after fathering five children, but through some research, my cousin Sheri and I found his grave in Glendale, California, and drove out there. The grave says 'James Congdon,' and next to the grave lies 'Elizabeth Congdon.' We're standing there going, 'Who is Elizabeth?' We found out that Jim had remarried and that Elizabeth had outlived him by twenty years. We have no idea who she was. There may have been other kids.

Jim was also in the Oklahoma land rush. The family was living in Iowa, and he was on his second horse by the time he got to Oklahoma and claimed land, but there were squatters on it, and these squatters were white and had buried their people on the property. So Emmet Dalton, a member of the Dalton gang, took my grandfather to another plot that had squatters but no people buried, strong-armed them out of there, and my grandfather claimed it. He came home to fill out the papers, but his father died, so he never settled on the land. However, Emmet Dalton bonded with the family, used to keep track of them and come visit. It was real Wild West stuff, but true. My grandfather also killed a man, and ordered the hanging of another in the oil fields of Oklahoma.

My life is intertwined with this country and its terrible, terrifying history. And its promise to be a great humanitarian nation. Now being revealed as a nation like any other.

AG: HAVE YOU WRITTEN ABOUT ANY OF THIS?

CC: In *Native American* I touch on it. But most of it is so unbelievably arch that I don't even know what to say about it.

AG: IT SOUNDS LIKE MATERIAL FOR SEVERAL MOVIES.

CC: Every time I watch a western, I think, 'Well, the story of *Cimarron* could be the story of my grandfather.' I wish I'd known him.

AG: WHY DO YOU WRITE PLAYS?

CC: I wrote poetry first. I wrote one piece of fiction, when I was in junior high school, but it was actually a retelling of a family story. I think I never wrote fiction because the stories I heard when I was growing up were more incredible than anything I could make up. But I wrote poetry. Why I ended up in the theater, I don't know. It's not as if I saw plays; I probably was in a play before I saw one, a hillbilly play in junior high.

But I was drawn to the theater. I saw my first play when I was fourteen: *Cyrano de Bergerac*, at the Fine Arts Center in Colorado Springs. My choir director played Cyrano, and he entered from the back of the house. It was fabulous. The next thing I saw was *The Music Man* with Forrest Tucker, in Chicago. It's a musical I still love.

When I was a freshman in college, I went to a Unitarian conference in Des Moines, where we had been living when my mother died. I contacted the neighbors who had been the ones to tell me she was dead, and they said, 'What do you want to do with your life?' And I said, 'I want to be in the theater.' I still remember that. I have no idea why I said that. No, maybe I do have an idea: a lot of it comes because my family performs a lot. They're great storytellers, and there's a performing aspect to it. Their storytelling is like *So Far. . .* , where people shift into a heightened language. People in the theater were like the people in my family.

AG: YOUR PLAYS ARE FINELY CRAFTED, BUT NOT CONVENTIONALLY CRAFTED. IF I WERE TO ASK YOU, FOR INSTANCE, WHOSE PLAY *FORMICANS* IS, WE COULD FIGURE THAT OUT, BUT IT DOESN'T REALLY APPLY.

CC: No, and I would probably hate that anyway. Three things happened in relation to my writing. I was deeply affected by the plays of Chekhov; in Chekhov's plays — even in *Uncle Vanya* — you can't say whose play it is. And that is my view of the world, in the sense that I don't see single characters, I see groups of people. I was also affected by how Chekhov interweaves ordinary speech in a poetic way, and I was deeply affected by Shakespeare.

I wrote my first play, *Gilgamesh*, because my friend Betty Osborn and I were teaching at St. Mary's College, in Maryland, and I wanted to write something that had a strong story, so that I could create a world out of it, and she wanted to produce it. I had gotten hooked on Joseph Campbell's writings about mythology around 1969 or 1970 — which is interesting, because that's the time of my big loss — and found the myth of Gilgamesh. Betty thought we were going to do story theater, but I wrote a play. I had scenes, characters, music and dance, huge puppet figures. It was three and a half hours long. I was horrified, but Betty didn't cut a word, bless her. Then I was hooked. But that problem of the end product being so different from the beginning — I still struggle with that.

AG: WHAT DO YOU MEAN?

CC: The way I envisioned the play at the start was very different from the way it was finally done. Yet I ended up bonding completely with the way it was done, so that now, if I read the script, I think of the production. That growth entails a certain amount of trauma. I write and create this trembling thing, and then the production connects with it, and the play becomes this other thing. Which is the whole point of production. *Gilgamesh* was the first time I experienced that. Now I write knowing that will happen.

AG: WAS *GILGAMESH* WRITTEN IN A FRACTURED STYLE?

CC: Not fractured, but constructed of many scenes.

AG: WHY DID YOU GRAVITATE TOWARD THAT APPROACH?

CC: Three reasons: Shakespeare (my idea of a play was small scenes); movies (small scenes); and life.

AG: DID YOU INHALE MOVIES WHEN YOU WERE GROWING UP?

CC: We actually went to a movie a year. I know it's incredible to imagine, but back in the long-ago days, movies were an event. At least where I lived. There wasn't a neighborhood movie theater; we went downtown. I saw *Them* and all the Disney stuff and big movie musicals. But what really happened was television and seeing old black-and-white movies, which I still have a tremendous fondness for. The wonderful thing is that a lot of the movies I loved as a kid turned out to have been written by playwrights.

Also, life isn't one big, long scene. That form of play where you're in the same place for so long is foreign to me. When the curtain rises, and I'm in an interior, my heart sinks. I think, 'I'm stuck here.' It's like being at a bad party. With Chekhov, there's always the sense of the outdoors: other rooms, other voices, other things happening. And I was affected by the movie musicals. They're never set in the same place. They take you on location.

AG: HOW DO YOU TALK ABOUT FORM AND STRUCTURE WITH YOUR PLAYWRITING STUDENTS?

CC: I only talk about those things in context. The way I teach playwriting is that on the first day, you write a small play. We do in-class writing — timed writing — using verbal prompts from me. I have a scenario that I've already constructed, and I'll give them a setting and two voices. I identify the voices for them, they're to listen to what the voices say, write it down. 'Go.' I make them write for ten minutes and then I say, 'Scene Two,' and I put the two characters someplace else. Again, very brief given circumstances. 'Listen to what the voices are saying. Go.' They write longhand, and then, because it's Amherst College, and they're all very anal, I ask them not to revise but to type the work up and bring in enough copies for each actor to read, and we read the plays in class.

So whenever I talk about structure, I'm talking about what has happened already in a classmate's play. I'm never prescriptive; I'm descriptive. I give them the vocabulary to describe what is there. And I make them believe in what they've written, rather than what they might write if only they were Edward Albee, or themselves on a better day. I have them treat a script that they've written as a code that they must decode, so that they can continue to work on it. I ask them to believe in what they have on the page, rather than what they have in their heads. I tell them that all they have is what they've written.

It works very well for my students. They have been trained to analyze and explicate works of literature, and I derail that and get them to accept what they've written instead. They have to recognize the value of what's there before they can criticize it, and then they look at what they've written in a kind way. I talk about the difference between a characteristic of the work and a problem. I bring in examples from the so-called canon, so that they respect what I'm saying. Some people would say that the problem with Shakespeare's *Antony and Cleopatra* is too many locales. Is that a problem or a characteristic of the work? If the story that you're telling is about two people who are trying to conquer the world, then showing that world is important, and having that world be fractured and unsettled is important. That becomes a characteristic of the work. My aesthetic has always been to write whatever I want, rather than latch on to a formal aesthetic. I think form and content are inextricably connected and need to be, so that plays will arrive in their own shape, their own vessel. A play needs to happen the way it happens.

At the end of the workshop, they've written lots of different things. I have exercises that make them explore different ways of writing a play, and that's not only about form, but about their imaginations.

AG: WHERE DO PLAYS BEGIN IN YOU?

CC: I used to say that I have to have an opening image or I don't feel like I have a play. I have to have a physical image, and when I don't, it's bothersome to me. But lately, sometimes I don't have an image, so I've taken the Mac Wellman approach and just start writing words.

I'm interested in language and ideas, and that's why I'm in the theater and not in Hollywood writing for the movies. The movies are not interested in language and they're really not interested in ideas. Of course I'm interested in visual image, but I'm lucky in that I live in an era when stage design is incredible, and I've had the honor to work with some of the best designers in the American theater.

AG: GOING BACK TO FRAGMENTED STYLE, WHAT DOES

THAT MODE LET YOU DO THAT A LINEAR APPROACH DOES NOT?

CC: *No Mercy* was the first time I went way out. The story of the first test of the atom bomb is immense, and I had many feelings and impressions. I wanted to write something through which I could express my emotions, rather than just tell the linear story. But it was hell. I had never seen a play like *No Mercy* before. Now I look back and can see traces of other plays, but those other plays have narrators in them. Mine didn't. To me, what I was doing was new. Jackson Phippen, who directed the first production at Actors Theatre of Louisville, called it 'shamanic,' which was the greatest compliment I've ever had. I was trying to make the play a closed system that opened out to the cosmos. If I can be completely out there, I wanted to make it like a poem. A good poem works through images and takes you on an emotional and intellectual journey. I wanted to construct the play so that everything resonated with everything else.

I had no idea what I was doing. I kept working through and working through. I wanted to put together disparate elements, even though I wasn't sure how they related. But I knew they belonged in the same work. And then in one particular draft, they were there, and the play told a complete story.

AG: BY THE TIME YOU WROTE *FORMICANS*, DID YOU FEEL MORE IN CONTROL OF THIS APPROACH?

CC: Yes. I used a lot of what I learned in *No Mercy* in the making of *Formicans*. But as the director Gordon Edelstein would tell you, initially *Formicans* was more incoherent. I had just come off a huge project, an adaptation of Mark Twain's *The Gilded Age* for the Acting Company, and I had had to cut so much for the good of the play, that I thought, 'All right, the next one is going to be for me.' Completely selfishly, I wasn't going to cut anything. Whatever came to me during that period of cooking *Formicans* was going to be in it. As it turned out, everything wasn't in it, but as an overall aesthetic approach, I decided to do what I think all artists must do, which is indulge themselves. Indulge the best of themselves. What do I want to see? That's what I wrote.

I decided to write about the death of my father. But I did not want the lights to go up and have the audience say, 'Oh, my God, he's got Alzheimer's, and I'm stuck here for two hours.' And it would not be fair to my father, who was a very funny, alive man before he got sick. To an extent I was using things that I couldn't stand to look at. The nursing home scene is absolutely literal. It was unbelievably painful to go back there, but I just started writing.

I've told this story many times, but it's the truth. I had to get my muffler fixed, so I dropped the car off and went to sit at a mall, at a deserted pizza place. I sat there thinking about mall culture. At this time I was extremely worried about my son, and I was thinking, 'What is my culture, what am I passing down to him? What is his legacy?' I started thinking about the beginning of the play and imagined a little kitchen chair on the enormous stage at Hartford Stage Company, and some light on it. That's when I wrote, 'First item. A situpon.' I imagined it being said in a John Cleese voice.

AG: AND THE ALIENS, ONE OF WHOM EVENTUALLY SPEAKS THAT DESCRIPTION OF A CHAIR — HOW DID THEY EVOLVE?

CC: The idea of aliens hadn't even appeared. When I finished the speech, I thought, 'Okay, this is in the play. I love it. It's funny. Who the hell is saying it?' I sent it to my friend, the director Greg Leaming, and on the phone we tossed this back and forth. 'Well, this sounds like an anthropologist.' 'Could it be aliens?' 'Well, maybe it's aliens.' 'I think it's aliens.' This idea was born. I asked Gordon Edelstein to work on it, and we arrived at Woodstock with fifty little scenes, put them in a sequence, and began working.

AG: ONE OF THE PASSAGES THAT I FIND MOST AFFECTING IS THE FATHER'S SPEECH ABOUT BUILDING HOUSES, WHICH BECOMES A WAY OF DESCRIBING THE DISINTEGRATION OF AMERICA. IT'S A VERY WORKING-CLASS, OR BLUE-COLLAR, METAPHOR.

CC: It's a very blue-collar metaphor. It's interesting how that came to be. I was at the workshop in Woodstock, and I had lunch with the playwright Mary Gallagher and her husband, Michael Swift, who is a carpenter. Michael was talking about lath and plaster houses and modular homes, because I wanted a description of sheet rock and how it is constructed.

But the speech is based emotionally on one of my father's last jobs, which was as a finish carpenter. Colorado Springs was having a housing boom, so a lot of prefabricated houses were going up. He'd put this great crown molding in, but he wasn't working quickly enough, and they fired him. He came home with all his tools. It was awful. And it wasn't only that he couldn't keep up, but that the work they expected was shoddy. It was the end of something for him.

My father was originally going to be a cabinetmaker. He had those skills. And if you think about the arc of coming out of zero economically, working hard and thinking you are going to be part of a field that's going to make something wonderful, then realizing that no one is going to be building it — that was horrible. Part of the reason he couldn't keep up was because his illness was starting to interfere. But the work people wanted was so cheap, that even if he had been able to keep up, I don't know what it would have taken from him.

I wanted to write about how that felt. What came out is how I feel about what has happened to America. Another thing that I love in that piece, which I got from Michael Swift, is that he said, 'Why would anyone want a house that will last one hundred years?' I thought, 'Of course. Everything now is about change.'

AG: DO YOU REFERENCE OTHER AMERICAN PLAYS IN *FORMICANS*?

CC: I quote *Death of a Salesman*, because *Formicans* is about respect and love and that play I can't get through because it's so devastating.

AG: EVELYN, THE MOTHER'S NAME, IS THE NAME OF HICKEY'S DEAD WIFE IN O'NEILL'S *THE ICEMAN COMETH*.

CC: That is a coincidence. Evelyn is my stepmother's first name, and I wanted to exploit my stepmother and her impossibleness. I wanted to key into that toughness. As it turns out, the character is more sympathetic than my stepmother.

AG: HOW DO YOU KNOW WHETHER A PLAY IS WORKING OR NOT?

ACTERS LEADING THEIR DAILY LIVES. DO YOU FEEL MORE
GROUNDED IN THAT TERRITORY THAN IN THE HISTORICAL
REALM OF *CASANOVA*, FOR INSTANCE?

CC: No, I don't. One of the things that is consistently true is that I
don't have the characters first. I have the voices. I sit at the computer
and think, 'Who is this?' I'm affected by what I've been reading, and
voices start to appear. *Casanova* came from reading his journals. The
next thing I know, that is what's appearing. *So Far. . .* happened because
I was reading Russell Hoban's *Riddley Walker* for the second or third
time, and all of a sudden, extreme language started to burst out. I'm
saying, 'What the heck is this?' But it was so much fun, I thought,
'Okay, I'm going with it.' I formulate who the people are based on
how they speak. Their names come later, and I frequently use letters
of the alphabet until I can create actual names. But naming a character is very important. I use family names and names of friends for
my characters; they are emotional or creative buttons for me, so I spend
some time on them.

AG: AT SOME POINT IN YOUR COLLECTED WORK, ISSUES OF
GENDER AND SEXUALITY START TO COME TO THE FORE.
HOW AND WHEN DID THAT HAPPEN?

CC: Gender is a huge issue that I became conscious of because of the
Women's Movement and just living in the world. I see traces of it in
my early work and my poetry and certainly in my life. When I was
growing up, before my breasts developed, people would sometimes
think I was a boy. I had short hair, I was very butch, and I did a lot
of so-called boy things, which were not unusual for my family. We
were farm people, so I had a gun and could shoot, and I could use
tools. If you met my female cousins, you would see a lot of the same
characteristics. It's the way we were raised.

But I had a difficult time with becoming heterosexual. I didn't fit
in with the heterosexual world. I didn't behave like other women. I
found a safe haven among gay men and women, but my coming out
has been about trying to come out as a heterosexual woman and being
comfortable with that. It's been a really long process and I suspect it
will continue. Luckily, the Women's Movement gave me language for
what I was going through, although I think a lot of our so-called spokes-

women are completely nuts. But on the day-to-day level of talking to other women about our lives, the Women's Movement has given me a vocabulary for understanding my own life. But unlike a lot of girlie girls trying to find a way in a man's world, I was a boyish girl trying to come to terms with being female. I still struggle with it.

AG: I THINK ANYBODY WHO SAYS THEY DON'T STRUGGLE WITH IT IS . . .

CC: Lying. Absolutely. Big denial.

AG: WHICH PLAY DO YOU CONSIDER YOUR MOST INTEN-SIVE EXPLORATION OF SEXUALITY?

CC: It would have to be *Casanova*. Interestingly, his journals reveal that, for his time, he was pretty humane when it came to women. But he didn't understand how they lived or what made them tick. He writes, 'Why are they so sweet and loving, and we so horrible?' But then it's, 'Oh, well, never mind.'

AG: ON TO THE NEXT.

CC: Exactly. It's frustrating, because he was a writer and he was also intelligent. His intelligence allows him to ask these questions, but his culture, and who he is as a Venetian man, shuts the door on it.

I read a fat, picturesque compilation that Erica Jong wrote the introduction to, and she says that Casanova liked women. But then I read his unexpurgated journals and was horrified. I was also horrified about the stories from his childhood. He was persecuted. There was a lot of violence. He was sent away. It probably wasn't an atypical childhood — the idea of the child as something to be protected is fairly new — but it was horrifying to read about.

There's political anger in my play, but my writing is always personal, so there's personal anger with Casanova and with the general unawareness of women's history. Because this play is about our history. Certainly I'm Sophie, Casanova's daughter — I used myself blatantly for Sophie. But Therese Imer, Sophie's young mother, is me trying to resolve this part of my history, which is that Casanova was a man of the Enlightenment. So was Rousseau, who had a fourteen-year-old love slave. We know that Benjamin Franklin behaved badly in France — visited whorehouses and generally was a lothario. Here are all these guys from the Enlightenment — father figures in a way and cultural icons — behaving horribly.

AG: THE POLITICAL FREEDOM THEY DEFENDED DIDN'T EXTEND TO WOMEN.

CC: Definitely not. So there's a lot of rage in the play. But the key moment for me is at the end, when Casanova says to Therese Imer, 'Can you forgive me?' And she says, 'No.' And he says, 'Is that why you've been in hell?' And she says, 'Yes.' That is the key moment, because it's double-layered. She's in hell in a literal sense, because Therese and Casanova were Roman Catholics, so not forgiving would be a sin. It's also true as a question between any woman and a man who is profligate. She's in hell — agony — because she can't forgive him for it.

I didn't find those four lines until after the production at the Public Theater. Margaret Gibson, the actress who played Therese, kept asking me, 'Why am I in hell? What have I done that put me in hell?' (Therese comes from hell to fetch him.) Margaret said, 'I think it's because of my abandonment of Sophie.' And I said, 'I think that's true.' And that's what we worked on, and it worked fine. But what I found is that Therese is in hell because she can't forgive him. Can you forgive the patriarchy? No. I can't. I can't forgive it.

AG: STILL, CASANOVA'S WOMEN ARE COMPLICIT IN HIS SEXISM.

CC: That's also true. I was thinking of my own complicity and women's complicity. After a long evening discussing this, most women eventually say, 'I don't really like women.' Or, 'I've finally come to like women.' There's always the sense that at one time they didn't like women and now they do. There's hostility, and it has to do with our relationship to the power structure. How we handle power. Or don't. How we share it or don't. How we manipulate it. A lot of that unresolvable stuff went into that play.

AG: MY PROBLEM WITH A PLAY ABOUT CASANOVA, AS WITH

MANY STORIES ABOUT WOMANIZERS, IS THAT THE TALE BECOMES ONE SEDUCTION AFTER ANOTHER, BECAUSE THESE MEN DIDN'T DO ANYTHING ELSE WITH THEIR TIME. IN *LIPS*, SEXUALITY HAS OTHER DIMENSIONS.

CC: In *Lips*, sexuality is more fluid, as it is in real life, particularly for women. In *Lips*, I had a strong event that I wanted to portray: what if a major female politician were gay or thought to be gay? Post–Bill Clinton scandal, what would people do?

AG: YOU MENTIONED ANGER. *CASANOVA*, *LIPS*, AND *DOG OPERA* SEEM MUCH ANGRIER THAN *FORMICANS* AND OTHER EARLIER PLAYS.

CC: In *Formicans* the anger is mixed in with many other things, but *Lips* is absolutely angry. There's no doubt about it. And *Dog Opera* is deeply angry with an anger that is probably never going to go away. Some day, when we get further from the days when AIDS first struck, maybe people will understand how extremely angry we were. There was so much pain. A whole generation wiped away. I'm constantly coming up against the absence of people. The loss of so many colleagues and friends who were supposed to be here throughout my life. Purely selfishly, I'm angry that they're not here. I want them to see my work, I want them to be in my work. I need them as friends. And where the hell are they? Part of my context went away. Yet again. That happened in my childhood and it happened in the eighties. The anger of *Dog Opera* is almost wrathful.

AG: IS THE CENTRAL CHARACTER, PETER, BASED ON A PARTICULAR PERSON?

CC: He's a conglomerate, but mostly Greg Leaming. Greg is completely healthy, but as the circle got smaller, I got more and more freaked out. This was me contemplating something I can't even imagine, which is that something would happen to him.

AG: THE PLAY BEGINS WITH A MEMORIAL SERVICE, WHICH FORESHADOWS LATER EVENTS. BUT THE PLAY FEELS LIKE A LOVE STORY RATHER THAN A TALE OF DEATH.

CC: That's why I ended up printing Shakespeare's sonnet, 'Let me not to the marriage of true minds/Admit impediments,' at the beginning of the published version. The play is about taking love to the edge of doom. I was also writing about the eternalness of friendship, how it outlives romantic relationships.

AG: IN YOUR PLAYS, IS HOMOSEXUALITY A METAPHOR FOR SOMETHING THAT IS GOING ON IN AMERICA?

CC: No. But portraying characters who are homosexual allows for a deeper truth. It's clear to me that homosexuality is a natural variation. It's always been a part of us and will continue to be. When other things get muddy and complicated politically, a person's stand on gay rights is what I latch onto. That becomes a litmus test for separating the good guys from the bad.

I love the character of Jackie, the young male hustler, which just burst out of me. I still am amazed when I read him. I think, 'Where in the hell did this come from?' There are times when I'm writing and I really do feel possessed. In a good way. I'm given a gift of a character that is kind of coming through me. There's nothing mystical about it; it is pure creation that comes from the brain and the emotions.

AG: WHEN YOU WRITE A PLAY, DO YOU GIVE YOURSELF EXERCISES? WOULD YOU TRY TO WRITE A SCENE IN DIFFERENT WAYS, FOR INSTANCE?

CC: No. To me, writing a play feels like painting. I'm not a good painter, but I have done some. You become absorbed in what is on the canvas, not in what is in your brain. You keep making the painting more and more of itself, until this thing appears. It's different than drawing from a still life. I'm not doing that. I'm not checking with the apple on the table. I'm looking at what's on the canvas or on the page. The play comes to me through language. The characters become clearer and start to tell me things about themselves.

AG: IN YOUR PLAY *A CONVERSATION WITH GEORGIA O'KE-EFFE* (1987), THERE'S A LINE ABOUT HER DOING A PAINT-ING A DAY.

CC: In her class with the American impressionist painter William Merritt Chase, O'Keeffe would do a painting a day. He kept his students keyed up. I apply that at Amherst and started applying it to myself when I thought I was running down. I would say, 'All right, I'm writing for an hour and not stopping. In an hour I'll stop if I don't want to do this anymore.' I would make my mind concentrate and take me where it was going to take me. O'Keeffe made me believe in my conviction about working quickly and moving on.

AG: DO YOU WRITE MANY DRAFTS?

CC: I will continue to work on a play until someone takes it away from me and it's time to publish it. Even when a play is published, if there's a production, and I have a chance to work on the play, I will work on it. Sometimes I'll make changes for a specific production that I may not end up instituting.

AG: WHAT INSPIRED *THE AUTOMATA PIETA*?

CC: A friend of mine told me that, when she was a girl, she and her sister were riding in a car to Mexico or Arizona, and they were having an argument over a Barbie doll. Their father got so furious that he said, 'If you don't stop arguing, I'm going to throw that Barbie doll out the window.' They didn't stop arguing and he threw the doll out the window, and I got this vision of a Barbie doll in the desert. And I decided that the doll would be real.

AG: THE PLAY HAS A FANTASTICAL NATURE BUT IT IS GROUNDED IN AMERICAN CULTURE. IT BRINGS TOGETHER BOTH THOSE REALMS.

CC: Arizona is the key. If my friend had told me that the Barbie doll was thrown out the window in Connecticut, I don't think the image would have grabbed me the same way. But Arizona and New Mexico are another world, and I have deep feelings about that area of the country. That got me started. Then I focused on the two girls and what, in fact, would really happen to them, knowing the childhood I'd had and also having two foster kids, whom I could never turn over to youth services. So even though the play has a comic sensibility, it has a dark story that is based in life.

AG: THERE ARE SEVERAL LAYERS OF FANTASY.

CC: The character of Time gets a giant cosmic whim and reverses everything. That struck me when I was writing: 'What if we could go back to the beginning, and the girls didn't argue? What if they behaved nicely that particular day? How would that change things?' I was very affected by complexity theory, which is the step beyond chaos theory and is about the effect of small things on entire systems.

I created the character of Time and thought, 'I'm calling him Time? Well, what the heck. The character of Rumour comes out at the beginning of *Henry IV, Part 2*.' So when I created Time, that allowed me to let rip a lot of the stuff that I was trying to write about through the other, more recognizably human characters.

As for Barbie — or Bambi in my play — I took her seriously and thought about why she would want to be human. It's the opposite of Pinocchio. Why would she want to be human? She's not wood. She's polyester. She's molded plastic. In some ways, it's a much better product.

AG: BUT THE STORY YOU TELL ISN'T SACCHARINE. MY EXPECTATION, WHEN BAMBI STARTS TO BEND AND SO FORTH, WAS THAT SHE WOULD BECOME COMPLETELY HUMAN AND ALSO HAVE A DIFFERENT PERSONALITY. SHE WOULD UN-BARBIE HERSELF. THAT DOESN'T HAPPEN.

CC: No. People still need to help her bend. She's still Barbie, she's still molded. Extremely plastic. I actually bought a Barbie doll and drilled a hole through the middle to see which parts were solid and which were hollow. The legs are solid, the arms are solid, the chest cavity is hollow.

AG: YOU ARE ONE OF THE FEW WOMEN IN THIS COLLECTION WHO WRITE FOR YOUNG AUDIENCES IN A CONCERTED WAY. DOES YOUR WRITING CHANGE ACCORDINGLY?

CC: I have more freedom. I don't need to worry about issues or explain the ingenuousness of the writing to collaborators. Not that that would hinder me; I think *Formicans* is ingenuous in a lot of ways. It was written with childlike enthusiasm. But take the happy ending of *Automata*: if the play didn't have young characters, it might have taken another turn. A lot has to do with people liking to see themselves onstage. An adult audience wants to see adults. Younger audiences want to see younger people. I'm always thinking about the audience, and there's an audience of one: me.

AG: ARE YOU THE PERSON YOU WRITE FOR?

CC: Yes. I'm all my ages at the same time. This is so difficult to talk about, and I don't really understand it, to tell the truth. I become different ages. I project different selves up there and in the audience as well.

AG: WHEN WRITING FOR A NON-ADULT AUDIENCE, DO YOU FEEL PRESSURE TO CONVEY A MORAL?

CC: No. If anything, younger audiences hate that more.

AG: WHY DO SO MANY PLAYS FOR CHILDREN MORALIZE?

CC: I don't know. Kids are fed up with that and they can see it coming a mile down the pike.

AG: THEATER FOR YOUNG AUDIENCES STILL HAS A MIXED REPUTATION IN THIS COUNTRY. MOST PLAYWRIGHTS WHO WRITE FOR ADULT AUDIENCES DISMISS IT.

CC: Because they haven't seen good theater. If they went to the Children's Theatre Company in Minneapolis, they wouldn't feel that way. They see bad children's theater or they don't see any. It's a shame, because I love it. We need more original work for kids.

AG: WHAT CAN WE DO TO ENSURE THAT MORE PLAYS BY WOMEN GET PRODUCED?

CC: We need to make sure they get produced. Not just developed. Audiences don't see our work, and our careers don't go forward. I don't know what the problem is. Maybe in the next generation our work will be considered not just the work of women but dramatic literature.

One of the problems I've come up against is that when I portray something, let's say a male-female relationship, it is always seen as a political statement, i.e., feminist or anti-feminist. I'm engaging feminism in some way. A man can write the same relationship and it's seen as life. It's seen as art. It's seen as universal. The male gets the universal, the female gets the particular. It's assumed that I have an ax to grind, when in fact I'm just writing.

AG: WHAT IF YOU DO HAVE AN AX TO GRIND? WHAT THEN?

CC: Then the play is seen as a political tract. Or as theoretical, or it's seen as something other than universal experience.

AG: BUT ISN'T A PLAY LIKE *LIPS* POLITICAL?

CC: In that particular case, yes. It's absolutely political. But it's still perceived in a different way, because it's written by a woman. That's the double standard. The object itself is seen in a different light. If I sat down tomorrow and wrote *Glengarry Glen Ross*, it would be seen as a woman's view of male competitiveness. Critics would say that Congdon is taking a stance against it. When Mamet writes it, the play becomes a universal statement about society's selfishness.

Casanova. If it had been written by a man, it would be seen as exploring male sexuality in an interesting way, with fresh sympathy toward the women's viewpoint. That kind of critical interpretation completely changes the way an audience comes in and looks at a play. Instead of getting pissed off, they go, 'Oh, wow. How nice of him to be able to see that. How interesting. How intriguing.' If you're female, there is a preconception that there's an agenda, and the audience doesn't trust the work.

AG: DO THE WOMEN IN YOUR PLAYWRITING CLASSES PRESENT THESE QUESTIONS?

CC: Yes. Students at that fairly young level write from their lives, and I have noticed that the male students have centuries of male characters to borrow from and bounce off of, and the women have fewer characters to bounce off of or recreate or be inspired by. As a result, the male characters that the students write are active, the female characters are reactive and internalized.

Without a lot of literary models, women are starting from scratch all the time. They use themselves and frequently end up with cerebral, sensitive females. So then there's the issue of 'write what you know,' which I struggled with, too, when I was their age. If my childhood friend Jim Davis were to write the scene where he broke with his parents, it would probably be about yelling, slamming of doors, almost a fistfight, maybe even a little throwing of furniture. My scene would be a look across the kitchen table at my stepmother, to let her know, and then her look: 'Oh, God, I'm never going to be able to control this child again.' Now which of those is the most 'dramatic'? Which could be seen from the back seats of the theater? Obviously, the chair throwing, door slamming, and screaming. The look across the table is a movie moment. One of the things that I love about Maria Irene Fornes is that she finds ways to externalize that kind of moment. She would have the window break. A sound. But giving that kind of theatrical language to young female playwrights and saying that they can still be just as true is hard. It takes exposure to a literature they haven't seen yet.

AG: IS THE CANON TO BLAME?

CC: The canon's not to blame, but if more women's work were taken seriously and done, and done well, more people would know about Irene Fornes. And they would be able to talk about Irene Fornes and her dramaturgy the way they talk about Sam Shepard. Who in my opinion is not as good as Fornes. That she's not known, and he is, comes from more than cowboy hats. There's something else at work there. Her dramaturgy is theatrical and wonderful, but she's seen as arcane, and I don't understand why.

AG: SHEPARD USES GENERALLY ACCEPTED, I.E., MALE AMERICAN MYTHS. THE MYTHS THAT POPULATE AMERICAN CULTURE ARE ONES THAT FEMINISM LARGELY REJECTS. SO

ALONG WITH YOUNG FEMALE WRITERS NOT HAVING CHAR-
ACTERS TO ACCESS, THE MYTHS AVAILABLE TO THEM ARE
MALE-GENERATED AND MALE-CENTERED.

CC: There's a lot of truth to that. And I do think that's shifting. I notice
in my female students' work that the characters are not just two young
women sitting across a table talking, one with a broken heart. And I
have also started to see the same broken heart embodied in larger-
than-life characters. That comes somewhat from movies, where there
are hard-ass women. Violent women. Women putting themselves into
monster characters. That is empowering and refreshing.

In our effort not to portray anything negative about women and
give ourselves good models, all we've done is taken June Cleaver and
put her in a pants suit. I'm interested in seeing June with a cleaver.
Women monsters and women giants. Young women need to present
that part of themselves in an uncensored way. Because they do censor themselves; they too often try to present good female role models. Well, any artist knows that is the death of art. You can't deal with
role models of any kind, good or bad. You have to let the truth come
out. If it's ugly, it's ugly.

AG: PERHAPS A TEARING DOWN HAS HAD TO HAPPEN FIRST,
AND FOR THAT REASON WOMEN HAVE SPENT A LOT OF
TIME DECONSTRUCTING MALE MODELS AND MYTHS. AND
WHEN WOMEN DO THAT — WHEN WE SHOW CASANOVA IN
HIS TRUE COLORS — THEN THE WORK SEEMS POLEMICAL.
AND IS.

CC: But what interested me about Casanova was his humanness. I
didn't set up to deconstruct him. I was trying to portray him. But because
I'm female, it's seen as deconstruction, when I'm really telling stories
from the journals that I read and interpreted.

AG: BUT YOUR PORTRAYAL ENDS UP BEING A DECON-
STRUCTION, BECAUSE WHAT YOU DRAMATIZE DIFFERS RAD-
ICALLY FROM THE MYTH OF CASANOVA AS GREAT LOVER.

CC: But you know what I'm saying. I was angry, but my intention
was not to deconstruct.

AG: YOU ARE SAYING THAT ANYTHING A WOMAN WRITES IS GOING TO BE PERCEIVED AS POLITICAL EVEN IF NOT INTENDED THAT WAY.

CC: That is the bind. But I do think all theater's political, because it portrays people behaving and speaking in the flesh. Theater is done in public, in our presence, and that is potent. We're in one big room together, and that can be horrifying for some people. During the workshop of *Dog Opera*, in a small community in Montana, people saw male homosexual foreplay happening in front of them. One woman said to me privately, 'Connie, you have to understand, I was watching this with people I went to high school with. I kept expecting my mother to come up the aisle and ask what I was doing there.' Language and behavior onstage drive people crazy; they feel complicit, because it's happening in front of them and there's an implicit dialogue between themselves and the play. Except that the audience's 'lines' can't be spoken out loud.

Maybe that dialogue is why women are not produced more. And the first dialogue happens when an artistic director reads the play, imagines it in his or her theater, and visualizes it as a dialogue with the audience. The dialogue is valued but threatening, because of the assumed political 'message' of the play.

AG: I WAS WONDERING WHAT YOU INTENDED AT THE END OF *LIPS*. YOU SEEM TO WANT US TO SEE THE PRESIDENT'S BRAVURA ANNOUNCEMENT OF HER LESBIANISM AS A GOOD THING. BUT SHE IS NOT A LESBIAN. HER PERFORMANCE IS A MANIPULATION OF POWER. ANOTHER PRESIDENT COULD MANIPULATE POWER FOR DIRE REASONS.

CC: Exactly. When the President gives that speech, you realize she is manipulating with eloquence and ingenuousness. Part of that came from my anger at the right-wing effort to bring Clinton down. Part of it came from my anger at Bill Clinton's stupidity and selfishness in doing something devastatingly harmful. In *Lips*, I gave the President's monologue at the gay rights march my best shot, in terms of writing political speech that sounds pro-democratic process. I totally believed it when I wrote it. Because that's what Bill Clinton does; he is completely present in the moment. But ultimately there's no back to him.

He's only the front. He's in a movie called 'Bill Clinton.' After the speech, the other two characters, Rachel and Andy, realize that they've been had again. I wanted that mixture.

AG: THE PLAY IS SATIRIC THEN.

CC: It's absolutely satirical. At the end, when Rachel is at home reading the kids' book, I knew what I was doing with that moment. During the worst of the Clinton mess I got out my novels that I loved as a child and started to read kid lit again, to shut it all out. It was so awful, to believe in a political figure again after so many years and then have my face rubbed in it.

AG: WE ARE MANY YEARS FROM THE 1960S.

CC: My son said the other night, 'You know, your generation's the most screwed up of them all. Half of you were over in the jungle, smoking dope, killing people, acting crazy. The other half were smoking dope on the streets, or dropped out, or on the streets trying to stop the war. And after it's over you're supposed to live together for the rest of your lives? Just no way.' And I thought, 'He's right.' Which is always encouraging, and humbling. But there's so much he doesn't understand about the sixties, and that is upsetting to me. And there's so much I haven't told him.

I wish a lot of the hope could come back. Of course, a lot of the sixties was before the Women's Movement, and I wouldn't want that back. But I'm just trying to fake hope now. I don't know what to do politically, except write checks and try to be informed. Grassroots theater I believe in, because that affects people's lives. I like very much being a part of that. I have hope for that. ▽

Kia
Corthron

Kia Corthron was born in Cumberland, Maryland. She graduated from the University of Maryland and also received an M.F.A. in playwriting from Columbia University.

Corthron's dramas are characterized by muscular, poetic language and by her dedication to illuminating social ills. Her many plays include *Wake Up Lou Riser* (1990), which involves members of an African-American family who infiltrate a local chapter of the Ku Klux Klan; *Come Down Burning* (1993), which focuses on an impoverished woman's attempts to take care of her sister and her sister's children; *Cage Rhythm* (1993), a dramatization of neediness, love, cruelty, and survival among a group of women in prison; and *Splash Hatch on the E Going Down* (1997), in which two teenage girls wrestle with pregnancy, motherhood, and their impotence in the face of a poisonous physical environment. Corthron's most recent play, *Breath, Boom*, concerns a woman who has made her life in a girls' gang.

Corthron is a member of New Dramatists. This interview took place on May 18, 1999, in New York City.

• • •

AG: WHERE IS CUMBERLAND, MARYLAND?

KC: Where I grew up is the skinny part of Maryland, where Maryland touches Pennsylvania. You could walk to West Virginia. It's a working-class town, probably ninety-seven percent white. I choose that figure because there were about three hundred students in my graduating high school class and ten were black. I think that in the entire four grades of high school there were three Asians.

My mother was born in Cumberland, but my father grew up on a farm in Virginia and moved there. He worked for the paper mill, a job he took when he got out of the army. When I was small, the town had the glass factory, the tire company, the textiles company. All of them went under except the paper mill, and my father felt really fortunate. But the reality is that he was miserable a lot of his life. He worked ten hours every day and sometimes went fourteen days without time off. He died from an aneurysm when he was fifty-one, suddenly, while at work.

I grew up in an atmosphere where everybody was concerned about there not being enough jobs; the unemployment rate was through the roof. I tried for years to get a job at the McDonald's and couldn't because it was so competitive, even though fast-food restaurants in Cumberland paid minimum wage. I remember when I was in my twenties, after college, I was working outside of D.C., and a young woman who lived in Keyser, West Virginia, about twenty miles from Cumberland, was killed in a car accident on an icy road, on her way to her job at the McDonald's. People talked about what a shame it was, because she was only twenty-three, but nobody talked about the irony and tragedy of dying while going to a job at McDonald's.

AG: WHAT KIND OF TOWN WAS CUMBERLAND FOR A YOUNG BLACK WOMAN?

KC: Most of the time I was the only black person in my classes. But all the black people knew each other, especially from my mom's generation, because they had all gone to school together and there were so few of them. My mother had been a junior when she went to the white high school; up until that time she'd gone to the black high school.

When I was a kid, there was all that fighting about busing kids to schools outside of their neighborhoods, and I remember my teacher saying how awful it was that kids had to be bused. I didn't understand the racial implications of it and I was very influenced by my teacher, and I went home and said how awful it was that those kids had to be bused. But my mother remembered when the black kids in Frostburg, which was way up in the mountains and got lots of snow, had to ride fifteen miles in cold buses because they couldn't go to the white school right around the corner. So she had no sympathy at all.

AG: DID YOU HAVE AN AWARENESS OF RACISM WHEN YOU WERE GROWING UP?

KC: I remember little experiences. One day when I was in high school, we were waiting for gym to start, and about fifteen girls were sitting on the steps between the floor of the gym and the balcony seats. One of them told a joke and whispered it into another girl's ear, and the other girl laughed and said, 'Oh, tell it, tell it.' Then *she* whispered it into another girl's ear, and they passed the joke along to every one of those girls. But they didn't even look at me because it was obviously a racist joke, and I was the only black person there.

But to some degree I suppressed my awareness of racism until I was a young adult, perhaps to survive it. I wasn't the type to call out to those girls and say, 'What's this joke about?' I knew what was going on, but I suppressed it. I was more outspoken within my extended family and more aware of sexism. I remember being six years old and telling my mother that I wanted to be a preacher when I grew up. We were Southern Baptists — we didn't go to church that often, but the Bible was there — and I thought it would please her that I wanted to do this. But her response was that women aren't preachers, and I remember how that struck me.

That was a long time ago, though. By the time I grew up, I don't think she would have discouraged me from anything as long as it made me happy. She was perfectly supportive of my interest in playwriting, despite my lack of any expendable income, long before I had any productions.

AG: IS THERE SOME OF YOU IN TRACE, THE POLITICALLY AWARE COLLEGE STUDENT IN *WAKE UP LOU RISER*?

KC: Yes, although I think there's some of me in all my characters. Because Trace goes away to college, as I did, she seems the closest to me in that play. But growing up, I was a lot like Cory — the loner, off reading her books. The nerdy kid.

My play *Digging Eleven*, which I began to write in 1994, is closest to the way I grew up, the closest I ever got to autobiography. A lot of the stories that Gram tells are my grandmother's stories, and I'm the little girl who takes clothespins and makes them into people. My sister Kim is fifteen months older than I am, and my mother said I began doing that after she started going to school and I had no one to play with. I would make the clothespin figures do their little stories and I didn't realize anyone was hearing me.

AG: WHAT WAS YOUR FIRST EXPERIENCE WITH THEATER?

KC: I remember doing small children's plays in school, although unfortunately, by about the time I got to third grade, the disgusting Board of Education cut the funding for that. I don't think there was another chance to act until the senior-year play, and I didn't participate in that. I mostly saw plays on campus when I was in college: *A Moon for the Misbegotten, Pippin*. I took a lot of English classes, so I read a lot of plays, and I was well-versed in the typical American classics: Miller and O'Neill and Williams.

I stumbled onto theater, really. I was interested in dramatic writing, I was interested in films, I was reading plays. But I only started writing plays when I took a playwriting class with a wonderful teacher named Jewell Rhodes, during my last semester in undergrad. I wrote a two-person play about the relationship between a Vietnam veteran and his sister, set on the day he comes home from the war; their father has died while he was away. I was a child during the Vietnam era, so I just remember being small and I remember a sense of chaos on television. With all that was going on with the war and the Civil Rights Movement, I had this sense of chaos whenever we turned on the news.

Anyway, in this writing course we would share what we wrote every week, and I'd gotten good comments. But it wasn't until the last class that we had to put our work up. I had two friends who were engineering students, and by the grace of God one had done some acting when he was younger, because I knew nothing about it. If he had been terrible, maybe I never would have written another play. And my other friend was okay. Jewell said the scenes had to be fifteen minutes, but none of us knew what that meant — these were our first plays. So everybody else's scene was about five minutes long, and mine went on for half an hour. Jewell had simulated a theater by turning off the florescent lights where we were sitting, and when the lights came up, there was quiet, except for one woman crying. She was a little older than the rest of us and had written a semiautobiographical play about having to work in a shoe store while everybody else was going to Woodstock, so she was from that era. And she kept saying, 'That's the way it was. That's the way it was.' Comments for everyone else's work had been verbose and intellectual, but for mine they were brief: 'poignant,' 'touching.' People were expressing how they had been *affected*, the first time I'd experienced that. It meant more than people just saying they liked it, as in my fiction classes. That's when I started writing plays.

AG: WHY WAS JEWELL RHODES SUCH A WONDERFUL TEACHER FOR YOU?

KC: She looked like one of us — petite and *very* young looking and black. (The latter made her look like *me*, actually; as I recall, I was the only black student in the class.) I remember the first day of class. There were something like twenty-five students. She seemed very stern and said she expected seventy pages a week. We gasped. One of the students raised his hand and said, '*Typewritten* pages?' She glared at him. 'Is there any other kind?' Then went on to say in a formal dialect that there were 'too many fucking students enrolled' and that she was going to leave and when she came back she hoped half of us were gone. She left, immediately followed by a mass exodus. I was ready to leave with them. The previous semester had been tough, and a girl who'd taken one of the more demanding classes with me that semester did leave. I decided that I'd at least stay 'til the end of the class but then would likely drop it. I couldn't take that kind of pressure along with all my other classes.

When she returned, along with about half the students who had exited (including the poor 'typewritten' pages soul), she smiled and said, 'What you've just witnessed is good acting!' The students who had come back, who had been the first and most gung ho to leave, were plants. She turned out to be *such* a joy as a teacher: sharp and encouraging and very enthusiastic about my work. After that final presentation, I remember her comment about my play: 'Fucking rich.' I actually get little pains in my stomach to think how close I came to leaving, and how that decision could have completely altered my future.

Something else. The semester before, I'd taken a screenwriting class. It wasn't very good. I now believe the teacher was a bitter, unsuccessful screenwriter himself. But at that time, he was the first black teacher — the first teacher of *any* color but white for that matter — that I'd had since my seventh grade black homeroom/home economics teacher. So despite that he was always discouraging, that, for the first time in my life, a writing teacher was *not* praising my work (interestingly, he wrote positive notes on my papers, but though he would say nice things about the white students' work, the only time he mentioned my name in front of the others was once to humiliate me for naming a male character 'Frances') — despite that all the other students hated him, I always felt compelled to defend him. And I was the one he was most unfair to. It wasn't until I had Jewell that I realized I had felt some loyalty to the jerk simply because he was black, and I was ashamed to go along with all the white kids criticizing the one and only black professor. Until Jewell. After her, I was able to see that guy for what he really was.

After graduation, when I was living and working in the D.C. area, I wrote a play about a mother and her two daughters that takes place on the first anniversary of the father's death, and all this stuff comes out about child abuse. Then I wrote a play about a man and a woman who were involved sexually, although the play was sort of asexual. The focal topic was breast cancer, because the woman had had a mastectomy. I don't have a copy of that play anymore, but I had been wanting to get back to the issue, starting from scratch but drawing from the original play. I finally did in a short play I recently wrote for Regina Taylor called *Safe Box*.

I got into Columbia with the original breast-cancer play. My first play *there* had to do with an old woman and a mentally ill young woman, and that also dealt with child abuse. I call those the 'ex-plays.' Those are plays that nobody knows, the plays that came before, when I was in a different place in my growth as a writer and a human being. The next play I wrote was *Wake Up Lou Riser*, and I started keeping them after that.

AG: WHAT LED YOU TO WRITE *LOU RISER?*

KC: *Lou Riser* started with a class exercise: my teacher, Howard Stein, wanted us to write something about a reversal. I had read a *Ms. Magazine* women-of-the-year issue from around 1980, and one of the women had sued the Ku Klux Klan for millions of dollars for murdering her nineteen-year-old son, and had bankrupted them. The story made me aware — and this is the part of me that is very much in Trace — of how much I thought that the Klan was dead and gone, despite the rumors that I heard when I was growing up. That article was on my mind when the teacher said to write about a reversal, and the initial scene that *Lou Riser* started with was this idea: what if there was a lynching, and the Klan was black, and the person about to be lynched was white?

AG: WERE THERE CROSS BURNINGS IN CUMBERLAND?

KC: Everybody talked about that sort of thing. I've never seen a cross burning. But it was well known that the Klan gathered at the old Super 51 drive-in, which had been closed down. We didn't know who the members were, but every so often they met in some general gathering of the Klan. The idea of the Klan rally in *Lou Riser* came from my high school fantasy of sneaking into a meeting just to see how they ran the place. Not infiltrating, the way the characters do in *Lou Riser*, but sneaking in and overhearing things.

AG: *COME DOWN BURNING* AND *CAGE RHYTHM* WERE INITIALLY PRODUCED TOGETHER. WERE THEY WRITTEN TO BE PRODUCED ON THE SAME BILL?

KC: *Come Down Burning* was written separately. That was the last play I wrote before I finished with Columbia, and Long Wharf Theatre decided to do it in their workshop series. When I wrote *Burning*, I was thinking a lot about *Roe v. Wade*, which was looking very fragile at the time. I wanted to address that, because I feel that wealthy women can always get abortions, but the poor have to go to dangerous means.

But *Burning* is short, so Long Wharf asked for a companion piece, and I had no idea that *Cage Rhythm* was going to become full length.

It was a difficult situation, because I literally found out a month before rehearsal that Long Wharf wanted another play, so I was writing it from the very seeds as we were rehearsing. I had no intention of writing that play at that time, but I was interested at some point in writing about women in prison, and because *Burning* only had women actors, and I had to use the same cast. I thought, 'Well, I guess it's time.' I had to write fast, and that propelled me to a new place in my writing, where I was very clipped and quick. *Cage Rhythm* became quick, short scenes that immediately went to the heart of the scene and then left it.

That was the first of three prison plays. *Life By Asphyxiation* takes place on death row and in *Breath, Boom* the central character is in and out of jail.

AG: ALTHOUGH YOU HEIGHTEN THE LANGUAGE IN *CAGE RHYTHM,* THERE IS AUTHENTICITY TO THE LANGUAGE AND THE CHARACTERS. DID YOU VISIT WOMEN IN PRISON?

KC: While I was at Long Wharf, a group of us connected with the production went to a women's prison. It was a pretty progressive place; not only did the prisoners receive work release, but a couple of the women were released to go to a community college. But it was overcrowded. There was a huge room that looked like a gym, with bunks stacked in threes, and we heard pure noise when we walked in. There were all these women talking, talking, talking. And *smoke.*

AG: WAS IT AT ALL SCARY?

KC: It didn't occur to me to be intimidated, and it surprised me that the actors and directors seemed to be. I was glad that I had read Jean Harris' book about being in prison, because I remember her writing that a lot of the women didn't like to talk about the reasons they were there. We visited a class that was mostly black and young, and I was having a good time talking to them. But I noticed that the actors were sitting back, not wanting to talk, and the first thing one of the actresses said was, 'So what are you in here for?' And this one young woman said, 'Drugs,' and then she completely shut up. Until that moment she had been gregarious, and we were having a great time talking. But saying 'drugs' brought this shame all over her and a separation from us, and she didn't say anything else.

The production was a difficult experience, because the play wasn't ready; I was developing it. And the actors had scripts in hand, so the play didn't feel fully produced to the audience. The theater fully produced *Come Down Burning* to some degree — the actors were off book. But because the production was a workshop, the theater pulled set pieces from storage, they didn't really have a set designer. Also, we're talking about a really upper-middle-class white audience. The theater handed out audience-response forms, and granted, only about twenty-five people out of two hundred to four hundred audience members, depending on the day, filled them out, and you figure they were the twenty-five who were most angry. But I remember somebody wrote, 'This isn't what black English sounds like. I know people who speak black English, it doesn't sound like this.' To me it was as though they were saying, 'If you play around with language and you're white, it's poetic; if you play around with language and you're black, it's inauthentic.' Somebody else wrote, 'I did not get a subscription to this theater to watch a play about inner city women.' There was blatant racism. I foolishly read the responses the first couple of days and then I stopped.

The best night was when twenty-five women from the prison came, and they were so *with* both plays. The theater asked me to talk to them when the production was over, and I did not want to, because I was scared that they were going to say, 'You don't know what you're talking about.' But they said *Cage Rhythm* showed prison the way it was. They were happy with it. Their only criticism was that the corrections officers could have been meaner, which was interesting, because most audiences had talked about how nasty the guards were.

AG: IN THE PUBLISHED SCRIPT YOU ARE NOT SPECIFIC ABOUT WHETHER THE CORRECTIONS OFFICERS ARE WOMEN OR MEN.

KC: We've always had all-women casts for *Cage Rhythm*. After the workshop at Long Wharf, I developed the play for Crossroads' Genesis Festival and expanded it so that I could have a bigger cast. That's how I was able to write the scene in which a lot of women line up to use the one pay phone. At Long Wharf, I could only have the three women and two children who were acting in *Come Down Burning*.

AG: IN *CAGE RHYTHM*, AVERY, THE WOMAN WHO MISSES HER CHILD DESPERATELY, PROJECTS HERSELF BEYOND THE WALLS OF THE PRISON, IN HER MIND. DID YOU TALK WITH WOMEN WHO HAD USED FANTASY TO GET OUTSIDE?

KC: No. The astral projection came from an event at the University of Maryland, where a fundamentalist Christian group held a seminar called 'Rock and Roll: Soul Control?' for two or three nights. It was like the Inquisition; they went through every pop singer and group and showed how they were evil for this reason or that. And they talked about the Bee Gees' album *Spirits Having Flown* and said that the title had come from astral projection, which I had never heard about before. A friend of mine who went with me was into occult book-shops, and he said there was a warning on one book that by reading it you could astral-project without thinking about it. And I said, 'I'm not leaving my body and letting someone take me over!' I never for-got that, and it struck me, when I started to write *Cage Rhythm*, that this was how these women could seek their freedom. But like I said, I was way too superstitious to research the thing properly. It's pretty much all my imagination.

AG: YOU MENTIONED EARLIER THAT THE SPEED WITH WHICH YOU HAD TO WRITE *CAGE RHYTHM* AFFECTED THE PLAY'S LANGUAGE. THE LANGUAGE IN YOUR PLAYS GEN-ERALLY IS RHYTHMIC AND LYRICAL. IN *SEEKING THE GEN-ESIS*, THE CONVERSATIONS BETWEEN C ANA AND THE TEACHER ARE A KIND OF RHYTHMIC SHORTHAND, WITH-OUT VERBS OR PREPOSITIONS.

KC: What is that experiment they do in science class, to show the dif-ference between noise and music? I think that even though our reg-ular conversation is noise, there is a little music to it in a general way that I make more extreme. There is a clipped, short rhythm to the con-versation of C Ana and the teacher, which I think is just a more lit-erary way of mirroring life. I'm meticulous with the exact words, but the dialogue still mirrors the rhythms of people speaking naturally.

Most of my favorite fiction writers write with some sort of music in their fiction: Annie Proulx, Toni Morrison, Maxine Hong Kingston.

But I especially feel that plays, like poems, are meant to be heard, and it's good to use that attention to what's going into your ear.

AG: DO YOU WRITE POETRY? YOU MENTIONED EARLIER WRITING FICTION IN COLLEGE.

KC: Recently I've been writing a bit of fiction, which I haven't done for years. I've never written poetry, although it's something that I would like to do, because I love to play around with language. I write poetic language but I've never written poems.

AG: WHY DO YOU LOVE TO PLAY AROUND WITH LANGUAGE?

KC: Plays are about the spoken word. The audience is gonna hear it, not just read it, as in a novel, so it may as well be exciting to hear. I fiddle around with naturalism: a line is *this* close to naturalistic — but not quite. So your ear and mind are ready for something, and it's not quite what you expect. Hopefully this keeps the audience alert and involved. Because it's not what you expect, you as an audience member are also a working participant in the process of this performance.

AG: CAN YOU TRACE THE CHANGES IN YOUR PLAYWRITING BY THE WAY YOU WORK WITH LANGUAGE?

KC: My early plays, the ex-plays, were much more realistic. In my earliest 'keeper' play I was working with language, but — the process being so new for me — I think I pushed the language *too* much, calling attention to it. As I developed as a writer, the odd language gradually melded with the odd world I'd created, enough that, though I've been told the words look strange on the page, with the right actors who get the rhythms, the words sound natural in this strange world.

AG: WOMEN AND WOMEN'S EXPERIENCE ARE VIVID IN YOUR PLAYS, AND THE WOMEN IN YOUR PLAYS OFTEN TAKE CARE OF EACH OTHER. DID YOU GROW UP AMONG A COMMUNITY OF STRONG WOMEN?

KC: Despite what my mom said about women not being preachers, I never felt that when women got together they only talked about men.

Kia Corthron 93

They were too busy working or raising kids. When I was little, my mom took classes to be a nurse's aide, and she did that for awhile and then stopped and was a homemaker. As I've gotten older, I've thought about that. Before she was married she worked in hotels as a maid, and I figured she probably thought, as a black woman at that time, that she had gone from cleaning toilets to cleaning bed pans and that there wasn't another kind of work she could get. But recently I spoke with her, and she said she had been interested in going for her nurse's degree, but it was because of some agreement she came to with my dad that she stayed home. She was the president of the PTA for a while, but she was terrified of speaking in front of people, so she stepped back from that.

AG: YOU TALKED ABOUT THE WHITE AUDIENCE'S RESPONSE TO *COME DOWN BURNING* AND *CAGE RHYTHM*. IS THAT A PROBLEM YOU OFTEN ENCOUNTER AT WHITE THEATERS?

KC: Yes. But that was the most extreme experience I've had, mainly because *Cage Rhythm* was so in process and because Long Wharf produced *Come Down Burning* in a big theater, and it needs an intimate space.

But in general, there is always the issue of how a largely white audience can connect with a black play. Center Stage in Baltimore produced *Splash Hatch on the E Going Down*, and since they always hold a luncheon for their subscribers before a play goes up, they asked me to talk about the script. I agreed, although I didn't know how we could talk about the play when audiences hadn't seen it yet. Most of the subscribers who came to the luncheon were middle-aged white persons, and they got the information that the central character was a very bright teenager and that she was pregnant, and they became threatened by the idea. They kept saying, 'Well, how could she be smart? A smart girl would not get pregnant.' They started talking disparagingly about girls having babies and their parents having to raise them. I was saying that the girl's parents are not going to throw her out in the street; they want her to go to college, and she is raising her own child. There was one black man at the luncheon, and he seemed supportive of the play and interested in the idea of it. So there was some sort of racism involved with this, but also something else: the subscribers were threatened by the possibility that I was advocating for unmarried girls to go out and have children.

After I thought about it for a few days, I realized that those audiences were used to the issue of teen pregnancy coming from outside the girls and to the idea of 'society' dealing with this problem. I was trying to write the play from the inside, trying to write what these girls go through and how difficult it is for them. For me, Shaneequa's speech about how painful it was for her to miss a math test, because she had to find a babysitter, is essential to the play. The subscribers and I were coming from two different points of view.

AG: WHAT WAS THE GENESIS OF *SPLASH HATCH*?

KC: I wrote *Splash Hatch* in 1996 at a writers' colony on Whidbey Island, north of Seattle. They take six writers at a time, all women, and you have your own, private, two-story cottage, completely free. I was the only playwright. I was a little freaked at night, because it was black out there, but I loved that place. I'd never been in the Pacific Northwest before, and to see how huge the sky was — I'd never seen the sky so big. I just never imagined it. Even in my small town, there were buildings and mountains that blocked the sky. Being in this space with wonderful writers, things started pouring out. I wrote the first draft in four weeks, the strongest first draft I had written up to that time. I can write in New York City, but I found that, with no distractions and inspired by the environment at the writers' colony, even only writing two or three hours a day was fruitful.

Anyway, for a while I had been wanting to address environmental racism, which has to do with the idea that environmental hazards are being placed in communities of color. From decades back, the classic case is nuclear testing on Native-American reservations. In the play, I refer to the actual park in Harlem that sits on a waste treatment plant, which is very near to where I live and is an example of environmental racism. It would have made more sense to put the treatment plant in the West Seventies, to cover the whole West Side. But it was moved uptown where people are more powerless politically. A lot of people argue that environmental injustice is about class rather than race, because there are instances involving poor white neighborhoods. But there are also instances of toxic plants being built in middle-class black neighborhoods.

Kia Corthron 95

With Thyme and Shaneequa, one of the facets of their lives that I was addressing — which also comes in that speech about the math test — is that Thyme knows about pregnancy and raising a baby from books, but Shaneequa is the one who's actually been through it. Thyme loves to go to the library and wants to do this and that with her life, and what Shaneequa's telling her, which Thyme cannot comprehend, is that when she has the baby she won't have time for herself. She can read everything she wants in books, but she's not going to know about being a mother until it happens.

AG: THE QUESTION OF BOOK KNOWLEDGE VERSUS LIFE KNOWLEDGE ALSO COMES FORTH IN THYME'S RELATIONSHIP TO HER BOYFRIEND, ERRY, ESPECIALLY WHEN HE BECOMES ILL.

KC: Yes. She knows everything about the environment, but she's missing the illness right in front of her, because she's afraid to deal with it. Again, it's great to read about environmental injustice, but when the problem becomes close, the reality is much scarier.

I always had the idea that my main character was going to be a pregnant teenager, but I thought originally that her father would get ill and that Erry would be a lesser character. But as I started writing, I quickly made Erry more important. Also, the women at the writer's retreat clutched on to Erry, and I came to like writing this non-cliché young black man who's gotten his girlfriend pregnant.

AG: YOU MENTIONED WANTING TO ADDRESS ENVIRONMENTAL RACISM IN *SPLASH HATCH*. IS THAT HOW PLAYS BEGIN IN YOU?

KC: It always starts with a political impetus. Always. I didn't know what I was going to write with *Splash Hatch*, but I knew before I started that I wanted to write about environmental racism, and I decided that the main character would be a pregnant teenager so that I could address teen pregnancy by virtue of that. With *Breath, Boom* — my newest play and I believe my strongest — I wanted to write about girl gangs, and in the early seeds of that, I also wanted to write about police brutality. But as soon as I started I realized that was too much material unto itself. The play I'm working on now deals with police brutality.

AG: YOUR BEST PLAYS SEAMLESSLY MINGLE POLITICAL ISSUES WITH THE EMOTIONAL LIVES OF YOUR CHARACTERS.

KC: I feel that way with *Breath, Boom* and also with *Light Raise the Roof*. In relation to *Light Raise the Roof*, I'd seen other theatrical pieces about homelessness, for a while with the homeless person talking to the audience. But I felt that often the work was *about* talking to the audience, about how we-the-homeless are not any different from you-who-are-watching. I wanted *Light Raise the Roof* to be about a community. Not that I wanted to excuse people who are not homeless from responsibility, but I didn't want to say, 'These people are just like you in the audience, therefore you should like them and help them.' I wanted to say, 'This is a community, and they're human beings — human beings like us and different from us.' It was important not to soften the picture in any way. I think what I want to say politically comes across by being as truthful as I can.

AG: WHY DO YOU THINK *BREATH, BOOM* IS YOUR STRONGEST PLAY?

KC: It's hard to say why I think that, but it's the one I'm most attached to. I went all the way with the main character, Prix, who's a leader of the gangs.

When I wrote *Life By Asphyxiation*, I deliberately wanted to challenge the death penalty, and I felt the death penalty was easy to challenge if the sentenced person was innocent, but harder if the person was guilty and had done something quite ugly, quite heinous. So I also challenged myself to make the audience have feelings for that character, without excusing what he did. With *Breath, Boom* even more so, because Prix is a mass murderer. She's killed a lot of people. Often when people write about those issues, either the central character is completely evil, and that's all there is to it, or an innocent person has gotten in over their head. I decided that Prix has done ugly things in her life, but that the play is not about judging her. In the course of the play, she grows as a human being. Actually, it's the only play of mine that takes place over many years. At the top of the play Prix is sixteen and by the end she's thirty, and you see what happens as she grows beyond the gang — is forced to grow beyond the gang, because she's too old to do it anymore.

Kia Corthron 97

Women are drawn to the idea of gangs, because in gangs women take things into their own hands, and there is only one man in the play — the one who raped Prix when she was a child. It has been suggested to me that the man is not necessary, and if you're talking about a basic plot, where this happens, this happens, and then that happens, he may not be. But I find him vital to what I'm trying to say. I did a week-long playwriting workshop with girls at Rosewood High School, which is the girls' school at Rikers Island, and from talking to them and reading about girl gangs and juvenile delinquency, I've learned that a lot of violence is done to these girls very early. A lot of these kids are abused. These girls are not suddenly out-of-the-blue violent at fifteen years old.

AG: DID YOU TALK WITH WOMEN IN GIRL GANGS?

KC: I read a book called *Eight Ball Chicks: A Year in the Violent World of Girl Gangsters*, by Gini Sikes. She lives in Brooklyn, but she did only a little research on girl gangs in New York City; she focused on L.A., San Antonio, and Milwaukee, because that's her hometown. Los Angeles is similar to New York City in terms of the women taking things to an incrediblly violent place. In terms of gory details, I didn't go there in my play; I didn't go as far as that reality. The play's quite ugly from some of the things that you hear about, and I wasn't going to be too graphic, because you wouldn't hear anything else in the play.

A lot of the girls at Rikers Island were Bloods, and I talked with some of them. I liked them a lot. Contrary to my expectations, the girl gangs in San Antonio and Milwaukee — especially the gangs that are auxiliary to boy gangs — take misogyny to the hundredth level, and I touch upon this a bit in the play. For example, a lot of the gangs in New York City have a thing called 'jump-ins,' an initiation where a girl will either have to be beaten up by everyone in the gang or be in there with the toughest one for two minutes. Well, in San Antonio, they have something called 'roll-ins,' and what they do is roll two dice, and the number that comes up is the number of boys that get to gang-rape a girl.

Sikes wrote about another instance where three girls had to have sex with a boy who told them he was H.I.V. positive. And the girls did it. To get into the gang. They went to doctors immediately afterwards and tested negative, so it could be that they were lied to about the whole thing and that he wasn't really H.I.V. positive. But they thought he was and they did it. It says so much about how they feel they need to belong.

The teacher at Rosewood High School asked the girls how they dealt with their friends, and all of them immediately said they didn't have friends, and a few of them said, 'We don't have friends inside *here*.' They were saying that we don't have friends, we have associates and sisters. And the teacher said, 'Well, how do you deal with your associates or sisters?' And one girl said, 'Well, the way I deal with my sister' — talking about one of her gang sisters — 'is I take her head and bang it against a concrete wall.' Then — it was quite funny — she paused and said, 'Maybe I should talk to the counselor about that.' It was almost like, 'Maybe I should get that carburetor fixed.' If I could just get that little thing fixed, then I could get out. She was a very high officer in the Bloods.

The sexism among the women in that school prison was interesting. There was one really pretty girl, I remember, and everything had to be just so for her. She was a total prissy butt. I knew that if she were outside, she'd have every bit of makeup and clothes — she was that type. She and another girl were having big fights for some reason, and when the first girl found out that the other girl was in for prostitution — this is something that I touch upon in the play, too — she went around telling everybody what a whore the other girl was. Now this first one had been charged with ten felonies —

AG: BUT SHE WASN'T A WHORE.

KC: The girl who was in for prostitution was very loud. She was the hothead of them all and she got very defensive and angry and was yelling. But it never occurred to her to say, 'Look what *you're* in for,' because she accepted that prostitution was the worst thing. She got defensive about it, but she accepted the same moral standard.

AG: WHEN YOU ARE IN A WORLD THAT IS SO DIFFERENT FROM YOUR OWN, DO YOU FIND YOURSELF REGARDING THE WOMEN AS 'OTHER'? AND IF SO, DO YOU TRY TO WORK AGAINST THAT?

KC: All I was really thinking about was getting them to do their plays. They did some incredible work, most of it somewhat autobiographical. One girl, who wrote about how she got into prison because of her boyfriend, could have been a film writer, because her play had very action-oriented scenes, and the structure led to this build of anxiety and tension. Another girl wrote about a guard being sleazy with her. I remember one who wrote about her boyfriend, and when we were doing improv work she kept getting mad, because nobody was doing it exactly the way it happened. At the final reading, two of the girls — the prostitute and one who wasn't chosen for the class — got in a huge verbal fight, because the second girl said something bad about the prostitute's play. And I said, 'Now you know she's just jealous of you,' and she said, 'Ah yeah.' They were all either completely badass women or little girls who would melt if you showed them the least affection or thought their plays were wonderful.

AG: AS AN ARTIST, WHAT DO YOU TAKE AWAY FROM A WORKSHOP LIKE THAT?

KC: Bits and pieces of things I've heard or that have struck me. On the day of that big fight — after we got the two calmed down — the girls were lined up to go into the lunchroom, and there was a woman cleaning the floor nearby, mopping or sweeping. No one was paying her any attention, but you could tell that she was probably younger than she looked. She had aged quicker than she should have and she was talking kind of crazy, off her head. I remember, in that moment, looking at her and looking at the girls and having this little tear in my eye, because I was thinking, 'I hope that's not where they're headed. Because right now they're still fresh and new.' Jaded to some degree, but they still had something of hope in them. Why were they in that workshop otherwise?

The next day, a Thursday, we were trying to stage the girls' plays, and they were whining and bitchy and impatient. Part of it was stage jitters. There had been a lockdown that day, which means that something has happened, the guards are looking for something, and the girls are in their cells. No one can move. Everything stops. We had about one hour to stage eight pieces. It was madness. But on Friday, the plays went off really well, just like in a Hollywood movie, and everybody was happy, everybody beaming. It was like a graduation.

AG: ONCE YOU HAVE THE POLITICAL IMPETUS FOR A PLAY, WHAT IS YOUR PROCESS OF DEVELOPING THE CHARACTERS AND THEIR STORIES?

KC: I don't have a story at the beginning by any means. That is the last thing I have. As I'm learning about the characters, as I'm writing, the story slowly comes. It's very rare that I even know how the play ends. *Life By Asphyxiation* was one of the few where I knew the outcome, because I knew it would end with the execution of the man. Technically the play ends with the speech of Katie, but the execution is the last action. I have an idea of how I want the audience to feel at the end. So I sort of get to know the characters. The more I develop the story, the more I write, the more I get to know them.

Story is my weak point. I can write forever. I can find characters, develop characters, do dialogue. I have a facility for that. But story's the hardest thing to come to me.

I have this perhaps sexist theory that men come to plays with story first, and women with character first. And for that reason, in some male writers' work you see an incredibly structured story but don't really understand the characters at all, whereas some female writers' work is episodic and there isn't really a story, but you understand the characters.

AG: YOUR CHARACTERS TEND TO COME FROM WORKING-CLASS WORLDS.

KC: I come from the working class, and that is most interesting to me, in whatever race. Sometimes I think of what I would write about if I were to write a play about bourgeois black society, but nothing comes to me, even though I think that is certainly an interesting subject.

AG: MANY OF THE CHARACTERS IN YOUR PLAYS ARE WOMEN WITHOUT MEN.

KC: I tend to write more often about women than men, for personal interest and to fill a gap. But when I do write about men — *Splash Hatch* really being the exception — it's also about men without women, so I actually tend to do singles in general. When we were preparing the reading of *Light Raise the Roof* at Manhattan Theatre Club, the actors were going on about whether Cole had a thing with Arnell — they were sort of making a joke. But many a truth is said in jest. I said that if they knew my work, they'd know it's generally asexual. Usually I do have people that are on their own, maybe because I am. I'm not going to let them have more fun than I am as the playwright. *Breath, Boom* is almost all women. There's an allusion to a couple of girls in prison having a relationship, but for the most part the main character is asexual.

AG: DO YOU WRITE MANY DRAFTS?

KC: That depends on the play. Some plays have gone through more drafts than others. Sometimes I need time — space — to be able to return to the play fresh. That's actually the best thing, because then the writing is not about fixing things but about seeing the play in a different way and making it clearer. But with *Light Raise the Roof*, even though I had just had a reading, I was able to attack it in a clear-headed way in order to rewrite. On the other hand, there's something about *Breath, Boom* that's very clean, and I didn't plan on a big rewrite because I felt that to change the play would ruin it. That rewriting was about fixing things that weren't working as opposed to looking at it from a completely different point of view.

Seeking the Genesis went through several rewrites, and I'm not sure that I've got it yet. But there's a side of me which thinks that's the way the play is and perhaps I should leave it alone. *Genesis* came out of the Violence Initiative. There used to be — I'm sure there still is — debate at the National Institute of Mental Health, and to some degree the Department of Justice was involved, about whether there is a violence gene, and about whether certain communities — which means black and Latino communities — have that gene, thus allowing the government, through teachers, to intervene and use drugs with black and Latino children.

AG: DO YOU KEEP A NOTEBOOK?

KC: I always write my dialogue in a notebook and type it in later. I write a whole draft in longhand first. With *Breath, Boom* I wrote a very, very skeletal draft in a week. *Breath, Boom* went through a skeletal draft, then a real draft, and then a final little rewrite. The first draft that I actually showed to people I wrote quite quickly.

AG: DO YOU EVER SPEAK DIALOGUE OUT LOUD WHILE YOU ARE WRITING?

KC: The only time I would probably talk out loud would be to get a sense of the characters talking at once, to get that rhythm. But I usually hear dialogue in my head.

AG: DO YOU SEE YOURSELF AS PART OF A CONTINUUM OF AFRICAN-AMERICAN WOMEN WHO WRITE PLAYS, WOMEN LIKE ZORA NEALE HURSTON, ALICE CHILDRESS, AND ADRIENNE KENNEDY, TO NAME THREE OF MANY?

KC: I take pride in being part of that history, but I don't feel myself in a continuum, because that thought would intimidate me. It would almost stifle my writing, because I would suddenly feel that I had to compare myself to them. If I compare, I compare the play I write now to the play I wrote last year.

AG: WE HAVEN'T TALKED ABOUT WRITERLY INFLUENCES AT ALL.

KC: I can name my favorite playwrights, but the influence question is always hard, because I feel I've been influenced by every single thing I've read, even if I hated it. I read Adrienne Kennedy relatively late — wasn't introduced to her until graduate school — but I'm really drawn to her language and where she's coming from politically, because it changes. *Wedding Band*, by Alice Childress, had an impact on me. I saw a dramatization of that on TV when I was a kid and I remember the mother of the son, in the face of her potential black daughter-in-law, screaming, 'Nigger whore.' Being a black child and seeing that on TV really disturbed me.

AG: YOUR PLAY *ANCHOR ARIA* REMINDS ME OF ADRIENNE KENNEDY'S WRITING, PERHAPS BECAUSE YOU USE PHYSICAL OBJECTS IN A SURREAL WAY AND BECAUSE CONTEMPORARY FIGURES APPEAR TO AGNES IN A DREAMLIKE WAY THAT EVOKES *FUNNYHOUSE OF A NEGRO*.

KC: That play came out of the Square Project, which the playwright Chay Yew ran at Mark Taper Forum. He does a lot of Asian-American projects there, and he asked sixteen writers, eight of whom were Asian, eight of whom were non-Asian, to write about the Asian experience in the U.S. He assigned each playwright a number of characters — I was assigned one; a year: 1920; and a theme: chaos. At first, when I opened up my assignment and saw 'one,' I was thinking, 'Oh, my gosh, I do not want to do a one-person show.' And even before I read 'chaos,' I knew it would be chaotic, because I would have other characters that would be objects — I knew I was not going to have somebody stand there talking. But it was good for me. I thought at the time about calling Chay and saying, 'Can I have two? Please?' But I decided to challenge myself. Chay told me that I was the only person who actually researched and found events that happened in their year.

AG: IT IS ONE OF THE MOST NON-REALISTIC PLAYS OF YOURS THAT I'VE READ.

KC: Because I only had one person. I said, 'Let me just give her a little consumption so I can do whatever I want.' A little fever.

Some people have described my plays as heightened realism, and there is something that I find exciting — and also really hard — about taking these characters that are in a specific world and throwing the audience into that. It's really hard when you go into production, because every actor has to be on the same wavelength as I am, or the play doesn't work. I have only found a handful of actors over the years who can really do my plays.

AG: COMING BACK TO POLITICAL IMPETUS, MARGARET B. WILKERSON WROTE IN HER INTRODUCTION TO *NINE PLAYS BY BLACK WOMEN* (1986) THAT 'SOCIAL, ECONOMIC AND POLITICAL FORCES HAVE LONG DEMEANED AND DISTORTED THE LIFE OF THE BLACK WOMAN, BEGINNING

WITH HER ENSLAVEMENT IN AMERICA.' DO YOU HAVE ANY THOUGHTS ABOUT THAT AS WE MOVE INTO THE TWENTY-FIRST CENTURY?

KC: I think the reason I wasn't so aware of race issues while I was growing up, even though I would feel painful things every once in a while, may have been because those painful moments seemed so trivial compared to the experiences of my mother, who couldn't go to the white school, who couldn't swim in the white swimming pool. In some ways, being really the first generation post-Jim Crow, my generation probably took the brunt of growing up with hidden racism, which was there but which no one was talking about as much. I don't disagree with what Wilkerson said at all, but the writers in that collection came a bit before me, and I think things are a little different now. Which is not necessarily to say better or worse; I have had lots of discussions about subtle racism.

AG: YOU SAID EARLIER THAT WHEN YOU BEGIN TO WRITE A PLAY YOU KNOW HOW YOU WANT THE AUDIENCE TO FEEL AT THE END. SINCE YOU START WITH A POLITICAL IMPULSE, HOW WOULD YOU DESCRIBE THE PURPOSE OF YOUR ART?

KC: I hope that someone leaves the theater thinking a little differently than they did when they came in. If someone leaves *Life By Asphyxiation* thinking it was terrible that Jojo murdered Katie, but that we are equally animals if we execute him — if someone thinks that at least to a degree — I feel I've been successful. But whether or not you think the way I do after seeing one of my plays, I want you to know where I'm coming from. I don't put out the issues and then sit on the fence, ever. There's some place I'm coming from, and whether you agree or disagree, you have to hear it or I wasn't successful in what I was saying. Not to belittle agitprop, which can be immediate and theatrical, but I think that what I'm doing affects an audience more emotionally. But my plays cause maybe a gradual change. Maybe down the line, when it comes to voting about the death penalty, you will think differently than you did before. Maybe down the line you will think in a new way about pregnant teenagers or environmental racism or girl gangs. Maybe you will see an issue differently. ▽

Migdalia Cruz

Migdalia Cruz was born in New York City, in the South Bronx. She briefly attended Queens College and subsequently received a B.F.A. in playwriting from Lake Erie College in Ohio and an M.F.A. in playwriting from Columbia University.

Cruz has written more than thirty-five plays in a range of styles, notably *The Have-Little* (1987), a drama of two friends whose lives take frighteningly opposite paths; *Miriam's Flowers* (1988), a dark, wrenching story of a girl's despair in the aftermath of her brother's accidental death; *Fur* (1991), a startling love triangle; and *Another Part of the House* (1995), based on *The House of Bernarda Alba* by Federico García Lorca. *Salt* (1998) is a contemporary tale of redemption inspired by John Ford's seventeenth-century tragedy, *'Tis Pity She's a Whore*. Her recent play, *Yellow Eyes* (1999), is a reminiscence of her grandfather. Cruz is an alumna of New Dramatists.

Cruz lives in Connecticut with her husband, James M. Kent, and their daughter, Antonia. This interview took place at their home on August 15, 1999.

• • •

AG: WHERE IS THE SOUTH BRONX?

MC: The South Bronx begins at Hunts Point and runs North — the 130s, 140s, 150s, 160s — those streets are probably the South Bronx. Our family lived in the 170s, so we were on the edge geographically. But economically we were part of it. It was a very poor neighborhood. When you played, you went into the deeper South, rather than going into the better neighborhoods.

AG: WHAT IS YOUR FIRST MEMORY OF GROWING UP THERE?

MC: I remember the day my sister got sick. My sister Nancy had lead poisoning when she was two and I was one. This could be totally wrong, but I have this memory of us being in white dresses on the floor, and my dad painting the house. My dad scraping off paint, because he was going to repaint. I remember that as my youngest memory. Because then everything in my life changed. My sister got very sick. We both ate leaded paint chips and we both began to convulse, so my mom had to take us to the hospital, not knowing what was happening and not speaking any English really. I guess Nancy was more advanced in eating, so she ate more and she was the one who got sick. They were able to pump my stomach in time — I was only in the hospital a short while. But Nancy stayed almost a year. At the same time, my sister Gloria, who's nine years older, was in the hospital. She had gotten trichinosis. My mom, at the age of thirty, and my dad, at the age of thirty-four, had three children in three different hospitals. I always think of them as my picture of bravery. It's amazing what my parents have endured — and not speaking the language, which must be so horrifying. So that's my first memory, which is a horrible one. But I think most people remember those traumatic things. The house was empty, because my sisters were in the hospital, and when I came home there was this quiet house, and people were sad. Adults were sad around me.

AG: WHAT HAPPENED TO NANCY?

MC: She was left severely retarded from the lead poisoning. She still lives at home with mom and dad in the Bronx.

AG: YOUR PARENTS HAD EMIGRATED FROM PUERTO RICO,

AND YOU SAID THEY DID NOT SPEAK ENGLISH. DID YOU
SPEAK SPANISH BEFORE YOU SPOKE ENGLISH?

MC: Yes, that was my first language. When I started school I immediately switched to English, almost entirely. My Spanish is like the
Spanish of a five-year-old, unfortunately. I keep trying to improve it.
I meant to study, to go to school this year, before the baby was born,
so that I could teach it to her, but I haven't. I managed to learn how
to drive, though, which was a great accomplishment after forty years.

AG: WHEN DID YOU REALIZE YOU WERE A WRITER?

MC: I realized I wanted to be a writer in college. Freshman year, I
was at Queens College — I was a math major and a history minor —
and I took a course in Beckett. I thought it was going to be about
Thomas à Becket and it turned out to be about Samuel Beckett. I had
read plays in high school, but I had never thought about playwriting,
and when I started to read Samuel Beckett, I thought that this would
be what I wanted to do — explore human emotional experience —
that that could be the highest personal achievement for me. It just
seemed like such an amazing thing, to be able to give that back to the
world. I didn't know if I was going to be able to do it, but I thought,
'That's something I really want to try.' I wrote a really terrible play
in that class. It was this weird, absurd play about clocks that melted,
sort of based on Dali's painting. I didn't learn how to write a real play
until I studied with Maria Irene Fornes in 1984, almost ten years later.
I had this idea that writing plays was about writing things that weren't
anything to do with you. To be a writer was to write science fiction
or remove yourself as far as possible from the subject, because, you
know, I couldn't possibly be that interesting first of all. I also had an
idea that people wouldn't be interested in where I came from.

AG: HOW DID THAT CHANGE?

MC: When I met Irene, she browbeat me out of it. Embarrassed me
out of it, really. She's a strong woman, and in her classes, if she doesn't
like what you're doing, she'll tell you right off that it stinks. The word
she used for my work was 'glib.' And when I heard that, I thought,
'Oh, my God, this is what I don't want to be. I can be many other

things — I can be evil — but I don't want to be glib.' It just sounded really horrible, and a waste of my life. And a waste of other people's time. So I started to write these personal essays in her class.

AG: ARE THESE THE ESSAYS CALLED *TELLING TALES*?

MC: Yes. I started writing *Telling Tales* there, and part of *The Have-Little*. That was the first time she said, 'You're finally telling the truth.' She was the one who made me aware that I needed to pay attention to my past and respect it, that it was okay to be who I was and where I came from. And write about it. It's not that I consciously thought, 'Oh, it's not okay,' but I didn't know if people would be interested in me or my parents or where I came from. Poor people didn't really seem to be entitled to poetry. And I thought, 'That's something I want to change.' I started to write. And that's where I learned to begin to tell the truth.

AG: BOTH *THE HAVE-LITTLE* AND *MIRIAM'S FLOWERS*, TWO OF YOUR EARLIEST PLAYS, ARE WRITTEN IN SHORT SCENES. DID YOU DEVELOP THAT STYLE IN FORNES' WORKSHOP?

MC: That's something that naturally comes out of her workshops, because of the structure of the teaching. She gives you many different exercises at the same time. Each exercise has several parts, so in the course of three hours you might go through six or seven changes in a scene, and if you expand something, sometimes you come up with seven scenes, and they can be short scenes. But also, Beckett writes short scenes. So there was his inspiration, and my thinking, in my head, that's who I wanted to be like. Certainly, he being an inspiration and Irene being an inspiration made me think it was okay to write that way. And it kept my interest, changing from one thing to another quickly. For a long time, I found it hard to write long scenes. Not until recently did I write longer scenes, although Irene kept encouraging me, because she thought I was better at it.

AG: THE TREND IN MOST POSTMODERN PLAYWRITING IS TOWARD SHORT . . .

MC: Sound-bite writing. Which is about attention span, I think, more than artistic choice. One of the things Irene encouraged me to do was look at my narrative writing, and I find that by adding my narrative voice, like in *Cigarettes and Moby-Dick*, the plays get much longer and the scenes get much longer, and I feel more satisfied. *The Have-Little* was at first one hundred and eighty-five pages. That's a long play! It was more of a novel. When I look back on it, that version was much more satisfying to me, and I think, 'Why did I cut it down so much?' I feel like I conformed. The previous version took Lillian from age eight to forty. She was reunited with her son, there was all of this intrigue. I think that's really where my interest lies, in writing this kind of epic play.

AG: WHY DID FORNES WANT YOU TO USE A NARRATIVE APPROACH?

MC: I think she liked my essays better than my plays. I think she thought that I wrote better when I was able to write descriptively. But then she encouraged me to write long scenes, too, so that's a contradiction. But every time she encouraged me to do something, it did push me to try something more. My most recent plays are much longer, and I think I've gone full circle. I've gone back to that one hundred and eighty-page play that I really wanted to write. No one will produce it probably.

AG: ARE YOU TALKING ABOUT *SALT*?

MC: Yes. It feels so very close to me. I feel very proud of that play.

AG: WHY?

MC: For me, it really is a social play. It's about the state of the world and the ability to maintain hope in hopelessness, which is something I've always written about. I think with *Salt* I've written a play that's my vision of the world, and dark as it may be, I also think that *Salt* maintains a certain hope of the innocence of the children in that play. That they would still believe in a God, that they still could follow a God, even if it's to their death. And in death find rebirth, which is something I'm exploring a lot in my work lately. After children die, where do they go? And how do they get reborn? What is that hope that they bring back with them, and can they be reborn without that hope?

AG: CHILDREN ARE A RECURRING IMAGE IN YOUR PLAYS. WHY?

MC: I have this theory that everybody has one age at which he or she stops growing. There are some people that are perpetually twenty, some people who are perpetually eighty. I think I'm perpetually fourteen. That's the age where I felt I suffered the most emotionally, was the smartest I ever was, read the most books probably. Thought the most about the world. I feel like I sort of stopped then, and I keep re-exploring that age. That's the age I have to get through and work through — those horrible teen years were really traumatic for me. And I feel that's the age I relate to the most. If I look at it intellectually, it's probably because I think children are able to grow into adults who could make the world a better place. Of course, in my plays it doesn't always happen that way. But there is that hope that it might. That's true redemption, having that possibility. Because there isn't redemption in life, really. Yet.

I just heard two days ago that a twelve-year-old child had his throat slashed by two other children. Last week some kid in the Bronx shot another kid — one was eleven, the other was thirteen. All these school massacres. There's no safe place for children anymore. What do you do? How do you teach them to protect themselves? And can you protect yourself from this random violence? And how do you as a parent — which I'm thinking about a lot now, being a new parent — how do you let your children know that they need to protect themselves, but not make them so scared of the world that they don't leave the house and not give them so much freedom that they become psychotics?

AG: *THE HAVE-LITTLE* AND *MIRIAM'S FLOWERS* TAKE PLACE IN THE SOUTH BRONX, AND THE WORLDS OF THOSE PLAYS CONTAIN A LOT OF VIOLENCE.

MC: Sure, but I kept thinking it would get better. I wrote those plays, and people would say, 'Oh, you shouldn't write things about Puerto Ricans that are negative, because people will think negative things.' I thought, 'Well, I'm not writing something that's negative; I'm writing the truth of what I saw and experienced, and what I don't want to have happen. I want people to see that it gets stopped, that we learn from it, and then we move on and grow.' But it's not changing, and that's disturbing to me. It's still the truth. Unfortunately.

AG: DO YOU BELIEVE IN GOD AND IN REDEMPTION?

MC: I was brought up Catholic and went to church and I was baptized and communed and confirmed. I even played with wanting to be a nun for a while. I think all Catholic girls do at some point in their lives. But I was always someone who questioned things. I've always questioned the edicts of the Catholic Church. I'm a lapsed Catholic, although I continue to be inspired by the Church. I love the ritual. I love the idea that there is the possibility that you could die and go to Heaven. Then, dying isn't so horrible to think about. You're just starting a different life, a new journey. I don't know that I'll meet my maker when I die, but I'd like to.

AG: WHAT INSPIRED *THE HAVE-LITTLE*?

MC: *The Have-Little* came out of an essay I wrote called *Sand*. It was the first play I wrote in Irene's workshop and really my first play. Probably most writers' first plays are autobiographical and sentimental, and that's what I feel about *The Have-Little*. My most sentimental play. Definitely my most linear and straightforward. I think I was just figuring out for myself what a play was and paying respect to one particular memory, one particular friend at that time in my life.

AG: THE GIRL WHO BECAME THE CHARACTER LILLIAN?

MC: Yes. The real Lillian died when I was about fourteen. We were best friends since eight or nine. It was painful to write that play. I kept thinking about how unfair it was that she died, and it was painful just having to think about growing up the way we grew up, with so few opportunities and little chance of changing our destiny. For me it was different, because my parents were very religious, and they were together. That was unusual. Very loyal to each other and to us. Very hard-working. All of my sisters went to college, except of course my retarded sister. That was unusual, too, that there were three women in a family who went to college, all professionals. A lot of people around us weren't doing that. They were sucked into that horrible cycle of poverty and drugs and violence. A lot of my cousins who I was close to when I was young grew up not so lucky. That's why it was hard for me, thinking back about it. It was stuff I hadn't mined. Now it's a place I can go back to easily. Not that it's easy for me, but I can access it quickly. I can understand how amazingly resilient people were there. I was surrounded by amazing survivors. As a kid, you don't know that. You think, 'Oh, wow, I wish I had another quarter to get some more candy. Why can't I have that ice cream, why can't I get that dress?' You don't understand why you're poor, when everybody else seems to have so much. And now I know how much my parents did give me, and how lucky we were. *The Have-Little* — it surprises me, some people think that's my best play. I don't think so. But it is certainly a play that came from my heart. It feels too heavy in my heart; that's why I call it sentimental. There's a wistfulness to it that I don't think is in my other work.

AG: BUT THERE IS IRONY, TOO. AT TIMES THE PLAY SEEMS LIKE AN IRONIC RETELLING OF THE BIRTH OF CHRIST, WITH LILLIAN AN IMPOVERISHED, CONTEMPORARY MARY, HAVING HER BABY BY HERSELF AND TRYING TO KEEP IT ALIVE IN THAT ICY APARTMENT.

MC: Well, that is an interesting theory. That certainly wasn't conscious on my part. I don't know if I agree, but if you saw that, that's good. It is in a sense an immaculate birth, because Lillian is so innocent.

AG: IN *THE HAVE-LITTLE* YOU EMBARK ON THEMES THAT YOU PICK UP AGAIN IN LATER PLAYS: WHAT IT MEANS TO BE LATINA AND TO BE A WOMAN IN THIS UNITED STATES OF AMERICA.

MC: I think you're right, but I don't think consciously about what my themes are. That's where I'm from, so obviously I'm always going to go back there, to that place.

AG: THERE IS AN EXTRAORDINARY SCENE IN *THE HAVE-LITTLE* WHEN THIRTEEN-YEAR-OLD MICHI SUDDENLY BRINGS OUT A PAIR OF HER OLDER SISTER'S BLOOD-SOAKED

PANTIES AND DARES LILLIAN TO LICK THEM. WHAT DID THE SCENE COME OUT OF?

MC: It came from an experience I had with two girls who lived next door. The older one had started her period, and the younger had found her panties in the garbage and decided to shock me. I must have been about six or seven. I think what really happened is that she showed them to me and I screamed and ran. I don't think anything really deep happened, any mystical moment. But then in thinking about it, or redreaming it, it became a mystical moment for me in this passage for Lillian. She was about to become a mother in a few years and make that passage into womanhood far too early.

AG: YOU DON'T APPEAR TO CENSOR YOURSELF. ANOTHER WRITER MIGHT HAVE SAID, 'YEAH, THAT HAPPENED, BUT I'M NOT GOING TO USE IT.'

MC: That's one of the things I learned from Irene. You use everything. She said, 'Keep every scrap of paper you write on. Put down every idea. Every time you have a memory, write it down. Because you're going to use it in something.' It's true. You need to allow yourself access to yourself, if that makes sense. You have to be able to open yourself and not protect yourself. Censoring is something other people do to you — not something you should do to yourself.

AG: IN *THE HAVE-LITTLE*, *MIRIAM'S FLOWERS*, AND ESPE-CIALLY *FUR*, YOU EXPLORE ASPECTS OF BEING A WOMAN THAT SOME MEN AND SOME WOMEN CONSIDER UGLY: MENSTRUATION, A WOMAN'S SMELLS, HAIRINESS. ARE YOU CONSCIOUS OF THAT?

MC: I wasn't conscious that what I was dealing with was ugly. I was conscious in *Fur* that I was writing about despair, that I was maybe writing from the place in myself where I find myself most ugly, where I look in the mirror and say, 'I don't like what I see,' sometimes lit-erally, sometimes figuratively. I've never liked the way I've looked, but that's my own thing. I think most women have issues with their bod-ies and how they look. Unfortunately. It feels okay to write about it, it feels like it's important to explore that part of my psychology. I don't censor those ugly things. I'm pretty happy with who I am, but I remind myself of the times when it's not so easy to be who I am. Everyone has those moments; I just live there in my work, I don't know why. Again, I think it's the fourteen thing. All teenagers feel that way.

AG: WHERE DO PLAYS START IN YOU? WITH A VISUAL IMAGE, CHARACTER, A DREAM?

MC: They usually start with character. But I get inspired by smells sometimes. I find that smells evoke memory. I'm writing a play about my great-grandfather now — *Yellow Eyes* — and I keep thinking that I have to go out and get some chewing tobacco. I need to have that on my desk, I need to have the smell of tobacco. I need to be able to rip it in my hands and smell it and I think that will help me remember him. That will help me remember him better than looking at a picture. I need to get some cherry chewing tobacco and then I'll be able to finish writing that play.

Dreams come in later. Once I've found characters and start working on them, or somehow get an image of a character along with this memory, I'll start to also dream about and with the character. I remember with *Miriam's Flowers*, I had a dream about Delfina, Miriam's mother. It was before I finished the play, before I had her commit suicide, before I knew she was going to. She came to me in my dream, reached into her chest, pulled out her beating heart and presented it to me. She said, 'Well, if you're not going to write the real story, then you might as well eat my heart.' It was a very graphic dream. So I woke up and I thought, 'Boy, I want to finish that play soon.' She didn't tell me in her dream, 'I'm going to commit suicide' — I don't have anything that specific in my dreams. But that particular dream was guilt-provoking and was showing me the passion of the character. I don't usually take a dream and just put the dream into the play. The dreams spur me on to finish something or make me go through private things that I have to reinterpret in order to write.

AG: YOU ARE VERY SPECIFIC ABOUT THE MUSIC YOU INCLUDE IN YOUR PLAYS.

MC: I always think characters have signature songs or music. When I was working on *Another Part of the House*, I listened to Bach all the time. I think I read somewhere that Lorca listened to Bach. The music seemed to always put me in that place, the way smells do. *Miriam's Flowers* was the Jackson Five, not only because the characters liked that music, but for me, if I want to evoke 1975, it was the Jackson Five that we were listening to. Obviously my taste in music comes out in my plays. There's a lot of Latin music and soul music in my plays, and that's what my characters listen to. *Fur* was the Beatles. For me, the Beatles wrote the most beautiful love songs, and when I was looking for music for Citrona, I thought, 'She would learn the most romantic music, I know she would.' That's what she would gravitate toward, as opposed to what you'd think: 'She's a beast, so she'll sing *Sexual Healing*.' She makes a joke about that herself, that she doesn't know any Marvin Gaye songs. She is a romantic, and in her music you see that. I do always find music for my characters, because I need to have white noise and background noise.

AG: DO YOU PLAY THE MUSIC WHILE YOU WRITE?

MC: Yes. I listened to lullabyes for *Featherless Angels*, which is about the souls of seven children who have each experienced a different kind of war-generated violence and must learn to trust again in order to be reborn. For *Salt*, it was totally disco. It's funny to write to disco. Disco is such empty music in a lot of ways, it's like pure entertainment. To go through all these deep things in *Salt* with disco in the background, I felt as though I was in a constant state of irony.

AG: YOU SAID THAT DREAMS 'SPUR YOU ON TO FINISH SOMETHING.' DO YOU FEEL YOU EVER REALLY FINISH A PLAY?

MC: I think *Miriam's Flowers* is finished. *The Have-Little* is finished. *Fur* is finished. There are certain plays that I feel are finished.

AG: CAN THIS BE A LONG PROCESS?

MC: *Fur* took me seven years to write and that's only forty-four pages long.

AG: WHAT DOES FINISHED MEAN TO YOU?

MC: The condition of being finished would be to have the play go into a full production that I would participate in fully. I would have to be part of the rehearsal process, so that I can make changes all the way through and then see it done in the way that I think is my vision of it. Then I feel a certain closure. I don't see how people can just write a play and think it's finished without also going through a rehearsal process. I don't mean to workshop something to death — you get too much direction and too much encouragement, too many questions that just begin to dilute your vision. But to participate in a production is so important. I tell my playwriting students that they have to do that.

But the process of writing varies from play to play. *Fur* took seven years. *Dreams of Home* took three weeks. *Another Part of the House* took one year. *Salt* has taken . . . I'm still not finished with that. It's been around for three or four years. But also I juggle a lot of projects, so I could be working on three different things at the same time. I never did a workshop of *Fur*. I just wrote it and then got a production.

AG. WHAT INSPIRED *FUR*?

MC: I was attending the Padua Hills Playwriting Festival in California in 1990. I went there to visit a friend but also because Irene was teaching there, and for some reason I needed to see Irene. I needed to get a refresher course. I was feeling very depressed. I don't remember what was happening in my life — it wasn't about career, it was personal. The word is despair. So I went, to see if I could get inspired by Irene or something, pick myself up. But I felt myself getting even more depressed, and I wrote the first monologue in *Fur*, when Citrona, squatting in her cage, talks about touching herself between her legs in the dark and about the comforting warmth of her body fluids. That's why I set the play in the desert, in Northridge, California. It was like one hundred and fourteen degrees in that place. It was awful. I felt that if there was going to be an apocalypse, it would happen here. It was hot and horrible. The architecture was ugly, the university where they held the Festival was ugly — like concrete. The whole world just suddenly was ugly for me at that point, and it all ended up in the play.

At the end of the week, they gave a day for the students to read their work, and I wasn't really a student anymore — I'd had some professional productions — but I thought, 'Well, it wouldn't hurt.' So I was sitting next to Irene, and there were writers of note there, and a couple of scenes from my work were read. They were raw and unpolished, since I was just putting scenes and monologues together, not knowing what plays they were going to be. The writers tore the work apart. I have never been in a situation like that, that was so evil. These guys — and it was all guys — said, 'This is too graphic, no one could possibly want to see this. It's so ugly. So unbelievable — women don't talk about sex this way.' I was so raw, and I'm such a jerk, I go in there thinking, 'Oh, they'll be nice. They're teachers, and I'm strong. I'm a professional writer.' I burst into tears. I was feeling bad about the world anyway, so then I get attacked, too, by these arrogant idiots.

AG: DID IRENE COME TO YOUR DEFENSE?

MC: Oh, yeah. She was quiet through the whole thing, and then I started crying and she started nudging me, 'Why are you crying? What are you crying about?' She started screaming at them, 'Look at what you've done to this woman. I don't know why she's crying, but you've made her cry. What do you think you're doing? This is a good writer. How could you say these things? You don't even understand how women write. You don't understand anything about passion.' And they shut up. But it was a strange experience for me, because I'd just started my career, and I thought, 'Wow, I guess people aren't going to be nice ever again.' It was ugly. Competitive. These men needed to assert their authority by destroying another writer's confidence. Was it because I was a woman? Because women aren't supposed to talk about their sexuality, only men talk about their sexuality?

AG: DID THAT EXPERIENCE FIND ITS WAY INTO *FUR*?

MC: It certainly fueled Citrona's sense of despair, Michael's sense of loneliness and need to buy a wife, and Nena's loss of innocence.

AG: HOW DO AUDIENCES REACT TO *FUR*?

MC: For the most part, I've had good reactions, especially from young women who feel that I'm saying a lot of things about sexuality and beauty, self-image and the image of the body — things they have never allowed themselves to say out loud. Women of color in particular understand that Citrona embodies the exotic sexual object of desire, which is dehumanized by society. They appreciate seeing this represented. It feels good, that I've been able to explore this issue in the play.

AG: THE TWO WOMEN SEEM LIKE TWO SIDES OF ONE WOMAN. NENA, WHOM YOU DESCRIBE AS 'A WOMAN OTHER PEOPLE THINK IS PRETTY,' IS THE WOMAN WHO WANTS TO BE PERFECT ON THE OUTSIDE, AND CITRONA, WHOM YOU DESCRIBE AS 'A HIRSUTE YOUNG WOMAN' WITH 'A GREAT SENSE OF LONELINESS' IS A WOMAN'S WILD, SEXUAL INTERIOR.

MC: I really think all three characters in the play — Nena, Citrona, and Michael — are both beauty and beast. Citrona thinks that they're twins, she and Nena. She looks at Nena and says essentially, 'I could be you, if only I could shave. If only I didn't get this horrible rash when I shaved; if only I wasn't so ugly, I could look just like you.' Both of them together would perhaps make a perfect woman, whatever that is.

AG: THE MAN LIKES CITRONA, THE MORE SO-CALLED BESTIAL WOMAN.

MC: Well, he likes the one who has access to herself, he likes the one that is the most honest, he likes the inside out. Because he is also lost. He's never been with a woman, he doesn't understand how to talk to a woman or what a woman wants. He understands what an animal wants, so when he finds a woman whom other people treat as an animal, it's easier for him to idealize that woman as his perfect mate. But it's also because he admires her — he admires her ability to be so out.

AG: BY 'OUT' DO YOU MEAN EMOTIONALLY EXPOSED?

MC: Yes. And so much herself. Citrona knows exactly who she is — and who she is not.

AG: YOU SOUGHT OUT IRENE FOR A 'REFRESHER COURSE' AND YOU DESCRIBE HER AS SOMEONE WHO SUPPORTS OTHER WRITERS. BUT WHAT IS IT LIKE TO STUDY WITH

SOMEONE WHO IS A STRONG DRAMATIST IN HER OWN RIGHT?

MC: Irene is generally terrifying. I found her terrifying, anyway. I'm sure that other people have other takes on her. She's a great artist — that's what I think. While I was in her workshop, she wrote *The Conduct of Life*, and being with her while she was writing that, and going to the theater and seeing what she created and also that she directed it — she was such a great role model. Because she is so strong and she's relentless with her own work and relentless with her actors — really explores in minutest detail every aspect of a production and every aspect of her text. It's an amazing thing to watch. But it was scary. The first three months in her class, I was a bad writer anyway. I didn't know how to write a play, I didn't know what I wanted to write about, I didn't know who I was, I didn't know how to access memory. I didn't know how to do anything.

AG: IT TAKES A LONG TIME, DOESN'T IT, TO LEARN HOW TO WRITE A PLAY?

MC: Yes.

AG: NOBODY IS BORN A FULL-BLOWN ARTIST.

MC: Maybe Mozart, composing at six. I was writing at six, but I couldn't write then about things I know now. We all have ideas about what writers are supposed to be and what artists are supposed to be, and none of it is true when you actually try to do that and be that person.

AG: WHOM DO YOU WRITE FOR?

MC: I used to answer that question, 'myself.' But I don't think that's true. And I don't think I write for an audience. It feels to me like I'm sort of recording. Sometimes I feel more like I'm an historian than I am a playwright, that I have a need to record and record honestly. If something affects me, I need to figure out why, and that needs to be also part of what I record. If I say I'm writing for myself — that seems so small or self-congratulatory. But writing for the world seems awfully grand. I think of myself as someone who records history, and not any grand history necessarily. I don't feel like I need to stand up and say, 'Pay attention to me, this is important.' But I do feel that I write about a world which is important.

I think I write political plays. Even *The Have-Little* is political, because it's about poverty, it's about giving dignity to poor people. And I think giving dignity to people who are not usually given a voice is a very big political statement. Just the act of my being a writer — as a woman, as a Latina, as a Puerto Rican born in the South Bronx — is political. It's a political act that I write at all, because the fact that I have a voice in this country, and that anybody can hear it, is important. That I think I have something important to say is a political act. Although people might think I'm just writing about some little girls in the South Bronx and why is that important?

A producer of a big nonprofit theater went to see *Miriam's Flowers*, the workshop production in New York that Roberta Levitow directed. He was in front of me as he was leaving the theater and he turned to the guy next to him and said, 'Well, you know, she seems like she's a really good writer, but my audience isn't interested in Puerto Rican women.' And I thought, 'Wow, I didn't know that was all I was writing about.' The characters were women, and they were Puerto Rican, and they happened to be in the Bronx, but I thought I was writing about a human experience. That I could be so easily dismissed and categorized because of who I was and who I wrote about — it was an eye-opening experience and very sad to me. I knew then that I could never have a regional theater career if I continued to write about people who are important to me. It disillusioned me, too, but it didn't stop me. I think there's inherent racism and sexism, which I expose and combat with my plays. I take courage that if people want to silence me, then I must have something important to say.

AG: YOU SAID THAT YOU THINK OF YOUR PLAYWRITING AS RECORDING. WHAT DID YOU WANT TO RECORD IN *MIRIAM'S FLOWERS*?

MC: That was about mourning for me. That was about loss and about trying to maintain hope in a hopeless situation. The loss of Puli in that family was the loss of hope in that family. The boy who would be a baseball player. As a kid, I remember thinking that the only way you could become famous as a Puerto Rican in this country was to become a baseball player. We had Roberto Clemente, and then when Roberto Clemente died, it was like John F. Kennedy dying, he was such a hero. And when he died on a mercy mission, bringing food to Nicaragua, he became even more mythological. He died leaving his country in an airplane, he died in the sea. He was legendary in my neighborhood and probably in most Puerto Ricans' hearts. He was also a black Puerto Rican. He crossed so many borders. So in *Miriam's Flowers*, I think I was also recording that feeling of a community mourning Roberto Clemente's loss. That big baseball player in the sky is dead, and then this little baseball player in the Bronx is dead, and what does that mean to us? I also had a cousin who died that way and I wanted to pay respect to that family, and to the despair and confusion that family went through. I somehow wanted to record it. It seemed important.

AG: HOW DOES PULI'S DEATH INTERACT WITH MIRIAM'S SEXUALITY?

MC: She wants to hurt herself because she's in so much pain from the loss of her brother, and the only thing she has to give that she has any control over is her body. She martyrs her body in that play, the way a saint would martyr a body. And she's really obsessed with what saints do, so she picks up on this kind of suffering. She's mourning this loss of self-esteem, this loss of hope in her family. She's really confused, because she's the one left behind. There's the guilt of the survivor.

AG: COULD YOU TALK A LITTLE ABOUT FEMALE SEXUALITY IN THE CONTEXT OF THE COMMUNITY IN WHICH YOU WERE RAISED?

MC: I think there's a perception of Latinas being hot-blooded, passionate, tight-clothes-wearing. There's jokes about Puerto Rican fashion. You know, if you don't get into it lying down, then it's too loose. There are stereotypes about being Puerto Rican. It's a very Catholic community, so there's the good girl and the bad girl. I don't know if that's just Catholics or all families. There's the girl that gets pregnant before she gets married, and then there's the one who waits.

AG: THAT'S WHAT WHITE, MIDDLE-CLASS GIRLS AND BOYS WERE BROUGHT UP TO BELIEVE IN THE 1950S.

MC: I think it was really the same in the Puerto Rican community, except that what we also had to deal with was the perception that Puerto Rican girls were easy. The hottest ones. I don't know why Puerto Rican girls have that reputation, but we do. So you have to deal with that, deal with yourself as someone who only has your body as a commodity. You think you're supposed to be sexy — everybody says it. But you don't really understand sex and you're really young, and yet you're going to wear those tight pants and you're going to try to attract attention. But when you get it, you don't know what to do with it, 'cause you're really still a child. So sexuality is confusing. I think it's quite confusing for all young women, but for us there was also this idea of what a Latina was and particularly what a Puerto Rican girl was. We had to deal with that outer image on top of our already confused inner image. I think Puerto Rican women are beautiful and sexy and all those things, but that's not all we are.

AG: IN YOUR DEVELOPMENT AS A PLAYWRIGHT, WAS THERE A POINT WHEN YOU WANTED TO LEAVE THE TERRITORY OF THE SOUTH BRONX AND EXPLORE OTHER THEATRICAL LANDSCAPES?

MC: I don't think I made a conscious decision to leave the Bronx. But I left the Bronx physically in 1981, when I met my husband and moved to Connecticut. My world started to get bigger, and I wanted to explore the new things and new people I was experiencing.

AG: WERE YOU LIVING IN THE BRONX WHEN YOU TOOK IRENE'S CLASS?

MC: By that time I had already moved to Connecticut, but I was still close to that world. I was just learning how to access that world. Once I could access that, I thought, 'Okay, I know I can go back there, but I'm not including where I am now.' So I started to bring all the new stuff in. It wasn't that I was turning my back on where I'd come from or deciding it wasn't worthy of further exploration, it's just that other things began to interest me. My world began to open up.

AG: BUT EVEN IN YOUR EARLY PLAYS THERE'S ANOTHER SIDE TO YOUR WRITING, A KIND OF WILD SIDE. *WHEN GALAXY SIX AND THE BRONX COLLIDE* (1988) IS A MUSICAL THAT TAKES PLACE IN THE BRONX BUT ALSO IN OUTER SPACE.

MC: In *Galaxy Six* I just wanted to write something fun. I've always had an interest in science fiction, although I probably don't write it very well. I got this commission from Duo Theater to write a half-hour musical, and it had to take place in a bed. So I wanted to write about a salsa singer that was abducted by aliens. I thought, 'It's twenty-five minutes, I want to write it fast, I don't want to get too deep with it. I just want to have fun.' But that's relaxing writing. I wouldn't consider that serious writing.

AG: ADAPTING LORCA'S *THE HOUSE OF BERNARDA ALBA* WAS ALSO A CHANGE OF DIRECTION. DID YOU CHOOSE TO ADAPT IT?

MC: Yes.

AG: DO YOU CALL *ANOTHER PART OF THE HOUSE* AN ADAPTATION?

MC: I call it a re-imagining, because I've changed Lorca's play so much and yet it has the same characters and the same events. It feels like the process I went through was having to redream the characters, to put them back in that house and then say, 'I'm going to let them talk about things that Lorca may have wanted them to talk about, but wasn't allowed, because of censorship in Spain.' Under fascist rule he certainly couldn't write about homosexualitiy and he couldn't write about sexuality in general. So to give these women voices — visceral voices — to really investigate their private lives, in a way that Lorca wasn't able to — I gave myself permission to do that. I had to keep asking Lorca for forgiveness. I would pray every time I wrote and look at his picture and say, 'Okay, forgive me,' because it felt like I was invading his space. I know there are lots of writers that steal from other writers, but I never do it. I never do it consciously anyway. But I learned a lot about structure, working with him. That's his most well made play.

AG: WHY DID YOU SET *ANOTHER PART OF THE HOUSE* IN NINETEENTH-CENTURY CUBA?

MC: I wanted to bring it to the New World, so I set it during the Cuban Revolution. I needed there to be a revolution, and I wanted it to coincide with Martí's death, which is the death of poetry. Because when Lorca wrote his play, he finished it the same year he was murdered, also by fascists. So I wanted there to be this feeling of revolution, this feeling of a war going on somewhere. I also thought that Cuba had the right class system. Puerto Rico wasn't quite so classist at that point in history.

AG: WHAT DID YOU LEARN ABOUT STRUCTURE?

MC: I learned how to write plot. It was freeing to work with a play where I already knew how it was going to end. I knew Adela was going to die, and I just had to get her there and write things that hadn't already been written about it. To take all those moments in between the scenes — look at each scene and go, 'Okay, what happened between here and here, and what's happening in that other room, and where are all these women and what are they wearing? What are they thinking about? They're sleeping right here, so what are they dreaming about in this section?' That gave me a lot of room to play.

That play inspired *Salt* a lot, where it felt all right to understand the story first. I used to think, 'Oh, no, that's not being inspired, if you know what the story is and you know how it's going to end. Then you've cheated yourself out of the experience of the writing, because you're already second-guessing.' But when I sat down with *Salt*, I actually knew what the plot was. I knew the Messiah was going to come, I knew he was going to help the children. I plotted it out in my head. Not on paper — I didn't write an outline. Adaptations force you to think about structure, and that's something I've always been criticized for, not having enough structure in my work. I always thought that characters would make their own structure, and they do to a certain extent. But you do have to figure out what the story is eventually.

AG: AS YOU SAID EARLIER, THERE WERE THINGS LORCA COULDN'T WRITE ABOUT EXPLICITLY, BUT HE IMPLIES A

GREAT DEAL. WHEN YOUR WRITING IS AT ITS BEST, THERE'S AN INDIRECTNESS. YOU DON'T SPELL THINGS OUT.

MC: I'm conscious of not making choices for characters. In real life, we almost never say exactly what we're going to do. We just do it. And I think when you put that on a stage, each person watching is going to make a different choice for those characters, and that's what's exciting about theater, that the audience is making the choices and finishing the play. I hate plays that tell you exactly what to think, and you leave and go and have dinner and go to sleep and you never think about those people again, because they've left you with nothing. Nothing to think about, nothing to hope for, nothing to hate. Nothing to cry or laugh about. I think you have to have some ambiguity, some open space.

AG: CHARACTERS DON'T ANNOUNCE THEIR INTENTIONS OR ANNOUNCE THINGS ABOUT THEMSELVES IN YOUR PLAYS.

MC: I think that's me, too. I think I'm very understated as a person. That's the kind of theater I like to see, so that's why I write that way. I don't think I'm conscious of it when I'm doing it, but it seems to me the honest approach. For me.

AG: *THE HOUSE OF BERNARDA ALBA* SEEMS LIKE A NATURAL PLAY FOR YOU TO WORK ON, BECAUSE THE CONFLICT BETWEEN REPRESSION AND FREEDOM IS SO CENTRAL TO IT. IN MANY OF YOUR PLAYS, THE CHARACTERS STRUGGLE TO EXTRICATE THEMSELVES FROM A REPRESSIVE OR CLAUSTROPHOBIC WORLD.

MC: I think part of that is my feeling of not having a homeland. Of Puerto Rico being still a colony of the United States. The Puerto Ricans that are born here are not quite considered Puerto Rican when they go to Puerto Rico, and as a Puerto Rican in the United States you are not considered completely American. If you speak Spanish, then you're also the outsider.

That experience of not being accepted in either place, being in geographic limbo, makes me think about repression and freedom, because it often feels that in order to be free you have to have ownership of where you're from. And I've never felt that. I know I'm a Nuyorican, I know I'm from the South Bronx, I know my parents are from Puerto Rico. But I also know that if I go there, I'm not going to quite be accepted there, and I also know here I'm not quite accepted. So where do I fit in? Where's my comfort zone? When you don't have a comfort zone, you're constantly fighting for your self-esteem. For your sense of self in general. You're writing about freedom and writing about repression because you're always searching for a voice, and you're having to fight to have a voice. Nobody cares what Puerto Rican women say, according to the great artistic director. But I do. I have to fight to make that voice heard.

I also have to fight not to say what people want to hear. One of the things I've been criticized for is not still writing about the South Bronx, not writing more family plays. My newest play, *Yellow Eyes*, will be a Bronx play, but that's because I feel like writing that play now. You get criticized by your own community for exploring those darker sides. Writing plays about the Bronx earlier in my career, people wanted to be able to keep me there. They want to be able to categorize you: 'Oh, you write about that. Don't go to those other places, you don't have a place there. We don't want you writing about politics, we don't want you writing about the bigger worlds.'

AG: DO YOU THINK PEOPLE WHO RUN THEATERS SAY THAT?

MC: People who run theaters and critics.

AG: WHY DO YOU SUPPOSE THIS IS?

MC: I think it's easier to categorize you if you stay in one place. It's easier to infantilize you, if they can categorize you. 'Oh, well, she's a Puerto Rican writer, she writes about the Bronx, writes these little family plays.' So the plays are not important, again. We're back to that producer. They don't want you to go other places, and for me, that's like asking me not to grow and not to respond to what's happening around me. And that's not healthy. And it does mean that maybe your audience will change. I was talking to another Latino writer, and he was saying, 'It's so interesting that you have so many white people at your audiences.' And I said, 'I do? Then why don't I get done more at the big white theaters?' I always think of my work as having a lot of Latinos in the audience, but that I'm perceived as having crossed over — I don't feel I've done that.

AG: DO YOU WANT TO?

MC: I want to make money as a playwright, and that's the only way to do it. I'd like to play to as many theaters as possible. To be able to work in Latino and other theaters is ideal to me. Not to feel that I can't do it, that I'm not allowed to.

AG: DO YOU MAKE A LIVING FROM YOUR PLAYWRITING?

MC: You have to define what a living is. I've made as much money as I made as a bank teller. It's not a lot of money. If I lived in Manhattan and I wasn't married, and my husband didn't have a job, then I'd probably be living with six other people in a two-bedroom apartment, but I could make a living. I also augment that with teaching, when I can. I've made about the same amount of money for the last ten years.

MC: WHAT ADVICE WOULD YOU GIVE TO A YOUNG PERSON WHO WANTED TO START WRITING PLAYS? HOW SHOULD THEY GO ABOUT HAVING A CAREER?

MC: To start out being a playwright, they need to find their voice, and I think they shouldn't worry about a career until they have found that. I found when I taught at N.Y.U., in the Dramatic Writing Program, that many of those guys are just writing for their careers. And it's like, 'But you've only written one play. And you keep rewriting that same play. Why do you keep rewriting that same play? Is that the only idea you're ever going to have? Do you think you're just going to have a career on one play? Has that said everything you ever want to say, and you think that's going to make you a million bucks and you're going to be able to retire?' That's not being a playwright to me. They're not excited about the act of writing. They seem excited about the act of getting an agent. As opposed to, 'What is it you're writing about?' and, 'Do you feel what you're writing when you're writing it?' Who are you paying respect to when you're writing? What are your ideas? What are you thinking about?

I encourage them to go into developmental programs. Go to those places first. Don't try to find an agent or go to producers until you've had a workshop production. Until you have a play that you feel is exactly who you are, you're not going to benefit from that. You're just going to get disappointed and decide you'll never write a play again.

AG: YOU FOUND A THEATRICAL HOME AT LATINO CHICAGO, WHICH PRODUCED MANY OF YOUR PLAYS AND COMMISSIONED OTHERS.

MC: It was an incredible home. It burned down in December of 1997, and it took years to get the insurance money, so they're just rebuilding now. I'm not sure what my role will be there in the future, but I was Writer-in-Residence. It was a place where I was able to write big plays, where I could be unafraid to fail. And that's so important.

AG: DO THE CHICAGO CRITICS COVER LATINO CHICAGO?

MC: Of course. There's even a critic there who respected us enough to grow with the company in understanding the work. But there are others who don't have a clue. The best critics I've ever experienced were in Minneapolis. I only got produced there once, but they wrote so thoughtfully and were so literate, I was very impressed.

The whole issue of criticism is a sneaky one. I feel so often that critics discourage writers, and I think that's a disgusting thing, that a writer would discourage another writer. There are ways of giving criticism that are constructive. Understanding the whole cycle of someone's work as opposed to going to one play and saying, 'Oh, this play is awful, I don't know why they produced it.' Saying instead, 'Well, I saw their last play, and they seem to have grown, they've gone in this other direction.' Literary criticism, that's what I'd like to see in theatrical criticism. Instead it seems like entertainment criticism. Often critics don't understand that there are many different reasons why something might not work. It might not be the writing. It might be direction, it might be the acting. It might even be set design. It might be producing. It might be the kind of money that was put into the production. I just wish there was an atmosphere of encouragement for theater. I see it not flourishing. Movies are flourishing. Good writers are going to movies and TV, and then you lose them.

AG: DO YOU WANT TO DO THAT, TOO?

MC: I would love to have a bigger audience. I would love to write for TV because I would touch people who don't leave the house, and it's important to reach those people. I'd like to write a movie, but I think I write strange things for movies. Maybe one day, when I have time to concentrate on what my ideal screenplay would be. *Salt* would be a good screenplay.

AG: COULD WE TALK ABOUT *SALT*, WHICH STEPPENWOLF THEATRE COMPANY IN CHICAGO COMMISSIONED IN 1996?

MC: After *Fur*, which is set in California, *Salt* is the first play that I set outside of New York. Writing about Chicago was good for me. To move to a new location in my work and yet continue to find the humanity there and relate to the same kinds of themes that I've always related to: children, religion, and sexuality.

AG: IN WHAT WAY WAS *SALT* INSPIRED BY JOHN FORD'S JACOBEAN DRAMA, *'TIS PITY SHE'S A WHORE*?

MC: There are twins in both plays, and the twins are in love. I've always wanted to write a modern Jacobean drama, and I started to think about what it would mean to write that. In such a violent world, can you show that kind of violence onstage and have it not be comical? I've always thought that I had an affinity for Jacobean writers. They were literally blood and guts, and I was more metaphorically blood and guts. I liked that they weren't afraid to show viscera. *'Tis Pity* talks also about the Church — it's anti-Church — and *Salt* is also critical of the Church.

AG: DID ANYTHING ELSE INSPIRE THE PLAY?

MC: Someone told me a dream that they had had. Juan Ramirez, who was the artistic director of Latino Chicago, told me this story. I thought he was telling me about a news story he had read, but he actually was telling me a dream, and I didn't realize he was telling me a fiction. We were talking in general about what happens to children who disappear. I had gotten this commission from Steppenwolf, and I had gotten permission to continue to work on *Latins in La-La Land*, which I had started in 1994. But Juan was going to direct and he really wanted to do something new. So we were debating what this new play could be, and he said, 'Why don't you write a play set in Chicago?' And I said that would be good, but that I don't write that way. I don't just decide, 'I'm going to do this.' Then we started to talk about children, and he told me a story about how children who had disappeared were being brought to a nightclub where they performed sex acts for men, and then the men got to kill them.

I thought he was talking about a nightclub in Chicago, and I said, 'My God, where is this place? Why aren't the police doing something?' And he said, 'No, no. It's this dream I had.' But we started talking about why, when you hear it, it doesn't seem so unlikely, a story like that. What does happen to all these children who disappear? It's not far-fetched to think that we're in a society that is so violent and sexually aberrant that something like this would happen.

When he told me this story, I started to think about a real news story I had heard, that in New York City there was a family of boy prostitutes living in the salt mounds beside the East River Drive. They were living in trucks beside the salt mounds and bringing tricks there. But they had formed a tight family unit from living in this place. I asked Juan if there were any salt mounds in Chicago, and he said that there were incredible ones on the South Side. We took a long drive and we got to this place, and the place was so evocative, so beautiful and eerie . . . the salt really looked like mountains, like glaciers, and the tops were tinged with bluish stuff that looked like it was ice. They cover the salt with black plastic, and the dye had leaked off, so the tops of the mounds were dark blue.

I stood on a bridge and I looked at the salt mounds, and the two tallest buildings in either direction were two churches, and one was a Mexican church and one was a Slavic church — both Catholic. And suddenly I started to hear sounds and see people, and the characters started to come to me on that bridge. It was really amazing. That's how *Salt* came to me. And I went back and told Steppenwolf, 'Well, I'll write a new play.' I'm sure they were happy about it. I'm sure they didn't want me to be recycling stuff.

AG: WHAT LED YOU TO THE BIBLICAL SIDE OF THE PLAY? YOU PORTRAY A WORLD THAT IS A KIND OF SODOM AND

GOMORRAH, IN WHICH ADULTS SURVIVE OFF CHILDREN'S PROSTITUTION, AMONG OTHER THINGS.

MC: I began to do research on salt and what it means, and that research began with the Bible. Especially evocative was the story of Lot's wife. Why was she turned into a pillar of salt? Did salt make her closer to God or closer to the earth?

AG: THE HEBREW SCRIPTURES REFER TO 'A COVENANT OF SALT FOREVER,' AND OTHER RELIGIOUS WRITINGS CONNECT SALT WITH THE IDEA OF A BINDING RELATIONSHIP BETWEEN GOD AND HUMANS, OR AMONG HUMAN BEINGS THEMSELVES. THE ANCIENT WORLD CONSIDERED SALT PURE AND PRECIOUS.

MC: It absolutely was. Very precious. Salt has many meanings. Rubbing salt in the wounds. That's the thing that struck me about the image of these children, who are already hurt and lost souls, having to live in salt. How much more literal a picture of suffering can you get?

AG: THE CHARACTER OF THE FORMER PROSTITUTE AND MOTHER FIGURE, BELILAH . . .

MC: Which I read somewhere was the name of Lot's wife.

AG: SHE DOESN'T GET TO FOLLOW THE MESSIAH AND THE CHILDREN INTO THE WATER AT THE END. WHY NOT?

MC: She doesn't believe.

AG: IT'S SUCH AN INTERESTING ENDING, BECAUSE ON A LITERAL, REALISTIC LEVEL, DEATH IS THE ONLY OUTCOME POSSIBLE FOR THESE CHILDREN. BUT READING THE PLAY, I FELT THAT THEY WERE ACTUALLY SAVED.

MC: That's how I felt. For me it's a hopeful ending. People say, 'But you have five children die at the end of that play — how can you call it hopeful?' I see them being reborn almost immediately, because they have such innocence. And I believe that Rocket is the Messiah. I like that it is ambiguous in the play whether he is a Messiah or a serial killer. So often we don't know in this society who's who anyway. But for me he is a Messiah, and they're already so miserable, their lives are so bad, that if they have this one moment of hope, I think it's okay. Some people have no moments like that.

AG: WHAT MORE WORK DO YOU WANT TO DO ON *SALT*?

MC: I think the work I have to do now is something I have to figure out in production. I know there's editing to do, but editing for me is hard unless I'm working with actors. It's hard for me to start getting rid of stuff until I've heard the play and have it clearly in my mind. Ideally, I would have a production that would have a long enough rehearsal period so that I could participate and get the final edit. I worry about the Bishop character. Many people think he doesn't need to be there. I still think he needs to be there. I'm not sure why, though. I know he has a very short part, so maybe that's something I need to explore further, rather than cut. I hate when people say, when something starts not to work, 'Oh, you should just get rid of it.' That's not necessarily the best thing for the play if you haven't explored it fully.

AG: HOW WOULD YOU PICTURE YOUR DREAM PRODUCTION OF *SALT*?

MC: In my dream production, I would picture it outside. I would picture it in Chicago on these salt mounds. Because they are so beautiful.

AG: HOW TALL ARE THEY?

MC: They're fifty or a hundred feet high. I couldn't get right up to them, because they were fenced in. But I would love to have an environmental production of that, to have people sitting in it and around it and walking to that bridge, going to that church. That would be amazing. Or in a really big theater. Like Steppenwolf perhaps.

AG: AT THE AGE OF FORTY YOU BECAME A MOTHER. HAS THAT BEEN SCARY?

MC: What's scary is that I don't know how I'm going to separate myself from my daughter when I need to sit down and write. I'm worried about not getting ideas. That's my greatest fear about being a mother: that I'll be forever inarticulate. I feel like I've entered a cross between a zombie and a bliss state. I feel very happy and at the same time I feel very disconnected from a lot of things. It's probably purely hormonal.

I also feel that if I never write another play, or my writing gets really bad, maybe I'll just open a bookstore. I've always wanted to do that, too. I'm beginning to appreciate enjoying a simpler life, not feeling I need the constant stimulation of being an artist. I've written a lot of plays in a short period of time, and it might be okay for me to rest for a while. It might even be better for my writing. I know it's going to be difficult. You have this idea, 'Well, I'll be home anyway.' It doesn't work that way. Children are very demanding.

When I was younger — last year, before I was a mother — if I thought about going out, it was to go to bars and have drinks and stay out all night, listen to music, go nightclubbing. I can't even imagine doing that now. I want a nice dinner, go to bed early, listen to some music. Play with the baby. It's a different way of being satisfied. It's a way I never thought I would be satisfied. I created some kind of image of myself as this wild artist who had to boogie down all the time. There was a self-destructiveness that I decided I needed to have in order to be a writer. When I was in college, after I decided I wanted to be a playwright, I remember sitting there with a bottle of vodka and a pack of Nat Sherman cigarettes and thinking, 'Oh, yeah, this is being an artist.' And writing stupid stuff. Not really exploring any kind of human emotion, just being a kid and pretending to be a writer. I've kept that idea in my head, that writers are self-destructive — they have to drink themselves to death. But you can also take a step back and say, 'I can stay alive and still write.' And have a life and give life to someone else. ❖

Elizabeth Egloff

Elizabeth Egloff was born and raised in Farmington, Connecticut, a picturesque town that she wryly notes is known mostly as the gentrified site of Miss Porter's, an exclusive boarding school for girls. 'When I grew up there,' she recalls, 'Farmington was a small town with a lot of undeveloped land.' She comes from a family of doctors and psychoanalysts, but she herself became a poet and playwright, receiving an M.A. in poetry from Brown University and an M.F.A. in playwriting from Yale Drama School.

Several of her plays are adaptations of short stories and novels, including *The Sin of Akaki Akakiyevich* (1987), a one-act inspired by Gogol's *The Overcoat; The Nose* (1988), a one-act based on Gogol's story of the same name; *The Lover* (1995), inspired by Turgenev's novel *On the Eve,* about an upper-class Russian girl who falls in love with a Bulgarian revolutionary; and *The Devils* (1997), an adaptation of Dostoyevsky's gargantuan political novel. Other plays include *Phaedra* (1989); *Wolfman,* which was inspired by Freud's famous case study; and *The Swan* (1990).

Egloff received the 1994 Oppenheimer Award from *Newsday* for best New York City debut by an American playwright, for *The Swan,* and she was a finalist for the Susan Smith Blackburn Award for both *The Lover* (1996) and *The Devils* (1997). Other awards include the 1994 Weissberger Prize for *The Devils* and the Lila Wallace–Reader's Digest Writers Award (1993), which enables a writer to create and run a three-year program of their choice. Egloff created a workshop for chronically ill writers that ran at the Public Theater. She is an alumna of New Dramatists.

Egloff lives in a suburb of New York City with her husband, the scenic designer James Youmans, and their son. This interview took place on June 24, 1999, in New York City.

• • •

135

AG: YOU ONCE TAUGHT A COURSE AT YALE DRAMA SCHOOL CALLED 'RADICAL ADAPTATION.' WHAT IS A RADICAL ADAPTATION?

EE: Because I came out of poetry, everything I wrote was very small; it was always about the details. I needed to get out of myself, onto a larger plane of dialogue. Adaptation was a way of educating myself as a playwright. I needed master classes in plotting and dealing with many characters and political themes, in order to be bigger as a writer. Adapting the nineteenth-century Russian novelists helped me with that. For me, adaptation is taking someone else's painting and doing my own sketch. Working from the masters. It would be boring to tell their story, so I tell their story my way. Adaptation also enabled me to keep writing at a time when I couldn't be personal. I had this phase in my life when I could not be that personal, from around 1990, when I got the commission to write *The Devils*, until about 1995. A member of my family was ill during those years and eventually died. Adaptation enabled me to keep going technically and emotionally.

AG: DO YOU THINK OF POETRY AS PERSONAL AND ADAPTATION AS . . .

EE: More technical. Ultimately, though, adaptation is an enormously personal statement about somebody's work.

AG: IS IT DIFFERENT TO WORK WITH METAPHOR IN A PLAY THAN A POEM?

EE: Yes. Which is something that I'm still trying to get my mind around. Metaphor in a play seems to emerge from the conflict. In poetry you are following the metaphor. It leads you to the end of the poem. In plays, metaphor is secondary. I didn't feel mature enough as a poet to manipulate metaphor. I didn't feel I had a voice that way. I needed something more tangible: a table, real bodies, and real people watching. The ultimate metaphor in poetry is the inside of the poet's skull. That's where we are. And it's both a great place to be and a hard place to be. It is easier for me to be a playwright. The inside of a poet's skull — the parallel to that is the stage. That is the inside of the playwright's skull. But there are real people with you and it's a less lonely place.

AG: THERE SEEMS TO BE MORE THAN ONE SCHOOL OF THOUGHT IN THIS COUNTRY ABOUT HOW TO ADAPT NOVELS FOR THE STAGE. FOR INSTANCE, FRANK GALATI, WHO ADAPTED JOHN STEINBECK'S *THE GRAPES OF WRATH*, BELIEVES IN ADHERING CLOSELY TO THE ORIGINAL WORK. SOMEBODY ONCE DESCRIBED THAT APPROACH TO ME AS WATCHING THE PLAY WITH THE NOVEL THERE BESIDE YOU.

EE: That approach doesn't interest me. After all, what makes any art interesting is the author's voice. Is Galati speaking with Steinbeck's (or John Ford's) voice? Of course not. That's impossible. So he's reproducing some of Steinbeck's events on stage without the voice. It's not only more interesting, but more honest, to state up front that this is *your* version of the novelist's story. That way, nobody's pretending to be anybody.

For me, adaptation is about trying to catch all the sparks that are going on. 'I'm going to tell you this story spontaneously. this happened and this happened, but then that happened, and this is the really great scene here.' It's often a messy approach, but that's where I find the room to make my personal feelings about the material felt. I'm not interested in a mirror image of the text, and I'm not interested in simplifying the text. I'm interested in catching what makes that text quicken in the reader. Sometimes that's a character, sometimes that's one event. That's the core I cling to. Then everything else is up for grabs.

AG: SOME OF YOUR ADAPTATIONS ROAM AND EXPLORE MORE THAN OTHERS. WHICH ADAPTATION DID YOU TAKE FLIGHT WITH MOST?

EE: *The Devils*. Definitely. In the Gogol pieces I was fooling around a lot more, but I felt that emotionally they were much closer to Gogol. With *Phaedra*, because it was in verse, I was constrained by the medium's demands: meter, rhyme, metaphor. *The Devils* was where I had the most fun and felt most intellectually involved as well. But I need to stay away from adaptation for a while.

AG: WHY?

EE: Doing adaptations is addictive. You're playing with somebody else's fireworks. It's fun, and they go off in unexpected ways, but they're ultimately somebody else's. Also, I'm out of the crisis that I was in for those five years when I started *The Devils*.

AG: YOU COME FROM A FAMILY OF DOCTORS AND PSY-CHOANALYSTS?

EE: My dad's a shrink. His mother and stepfather were also.

AG: SHRINK PSYCHIATRIST OR SHRINK PSYCHOLOGIST?

EE: Shrink psychiatrist. So was my father's aunt. His grandmother was a doctor, and his grandfather was a marine biologist who started the Marine Biology Lab in Cape Cod with a few other men. The tradition of a scientific approach to nature was in my background and fostered in me a certain intellectualization of life. And introspection.

AG: WERE THEY JUNGIANS OR FREUDIANS?

EE: My paternal grandmother was a Jungian, but my great-aunt was very Freudian. And my grandfather did a lot of work with manic depression and medication.

AG: DID ANY OF THEM ACTUALLY STUDY WITH JUNG OR FREUD?

EE: My grandmother studied with Jung. She was ferociously interested in dreams, something that I connected with her about. Of all my relatives, I connected most with her.

AG: WAS SHE BORN IN AMERICA?

EE: Yes. She was the daughter of Midwestern industrialists.

AG: SOUNDS LIKE A RADICAL FAMILY.

EE: They were politically pretty radical. My grandmother's mother was involved with labor strikes in Chicago, then went and got her

M.D. It was back when you could afford to be rarified and radical at the same time.

AG: WERE YOU BROUGHT UP WITH ANY PARTICULAR ATTITUDES ABOUT HOW WOMEN SHOULD OR SHOULD NOT BEHAVE?

EE: Not much. I was something of a tomboy. However, although I never said it aloud to myself, I thought of playwriting as something men did, because you have these characters onstage and you tell them what to do, where to go. You decide what's going to be there and how it's going to come out. That is frightening to some part of me that I've decided is female. It was very hard for me to leave poetry, which I think of as a more female form, and go into playwriting. I was blocked about making that transition. I spent five or six years in my twenties writing very little, feeling like everything I'd stood for was gone. I'd always considered myself a poet; that was everything. That was everything I read — I never read fiction, so even today, I'm woefully under-read. To leave poetry was crisis inducing.

AG: SEVERAL OF THE WOMEN IN YOUR PLAYS — ELENA IN *THE LOVER*, DORA IN *THE SWAN*, PHAEDRA — WANT ESCAPE OR RELEASE.

EE: The women in my work do tend to feel closeted to an almost fatal degree. Women seem to feel repression more intensely than men, and I think the Russians feel it as intensely as most women, which is why I connect so much with that literature. Women are the weather vanes of society. They're the barometers. The antennae. And that is definitely me.

AG: HOW WERE YOU FINALLY ABLE TO MOVE FROM POETRY TO PLAYWRITING?

EE: George Bass, a playwright and a theater professor at Brown. He had this rarified approach to playwriting. He always talked about it in poetic ways — maybe too poetic. Anyway, the first play that I wrote was a miserable exercise called *The Hired Man*. But George made me feel, 'Here's a guy who's really literary, and very feminine, and he's doing it.' So I think he was kind of the feminine who opened the door for me into that field.

AG: HOW DID YOU MEET HIM?

EE: I don't know. I bet somebody from the poetry program referred me to him. I was shy. I never got involved with productions at Brown. I had an independent study with George, and we would sit in his office and talk. I never even took drama courses.

AG: WHAT IS YOUR PROCESS WHEN YOU ADAPT?

EE: The way I pick the book often depends on things as superficial as jacket copy and the picture on the cover. That was how I picked *The Devils* (not really). I came up with a list of around ten books and talked about them with the director, Robert Woodruff, and we decided that *The Devils* was the most interesting. Mark Taper Forum had commissioned the adaptation, but the production never materialized, and Robert Woodruff and I ended up doing a workshop production at Tisch School of the Arts in New York City.

After I select the book, I read it rather quickly, noting what excites me, but not writing anything down — looking for the character or event that makes the book come alive for me. Then I read it a second time, very slowly, and take a ton of notes. I outline every thought, I footnote heavily. After that, I don't go back to the book. I follow what's on my pages. I combine characters, create characters, create plot, change lots of things. I'll go back to the book if and when the play is published, to make sure I'm not taking anything literally from it.

AG: SO THE LANGUAGE IN YOUR ADAPTATIONS IS YOURS?

EE: At times I'm paraphrasing, and at other times the language is completely mine. Once I start writing, I often do one draft and throw it out. Then I do another draft, because then I seem to find my feet. Adapting *On the Eve* went very quickly. It was a commission, and I wasn't interested enough in the Turgenev to live with the material for a long time. I wanted to do something fast. With *The Devils*, I wrote a whole draft, completely scrapped it, and started again.

AG: IT'S A PANORAMIC NOVEL.

EE: It was a lesson in panorama. A lesson that I'd been trying to learn since graduate school: how to deal with a palette that big.

AG: THE SATIRIC PARTS OF *THE DEVILS* EVOKE GOGOL'S PLAY *THE GOVERNMENT INSPECTOR*.

EE: It's the thing that I love about the Russians: that bitter, bitter, bitter, but funny . . . I'll cut my hand off, ha, ha, isn't that funny?

AG: IN YOUR ADAPTATION OF *THE DEVILS*, THE GOVERN-MENT FIGURES, THE REVOLUTIONARIES, THE INTELLEC-TUALS, THE GOVERNOR'S BOURGEOIS WIFE — THEY ARE ALL FOOLS IN ONE WAY OR ANOTHER.

EE: This is consistent with the novel. The only character Dostoyevsky took seriously was Nicholas Stavrogin, and so did I. But I changed one thing — I took his antagonist, Peter Verkhovensky, seriously. Peter is scary. He's a bit of a psychopath. In his final speech he talks about murdering one's society in order to start afresh — there is some part of me that agrees with him. Better to destroy your own two children than twenty of your grandchildren's children. But I also identify with Dasha, who is a pacifist, but utterly abandoned in the end. She leaves Russia and is alone, lost, forced to speak a foreign language. But at least she's alive.

AG: IN CONTRAST TO THE NOVEL, YOU BEGIN THE PLAY WITH PART OF THE EPISODE INVOLVING STAVROGIN'S RAPE OF THE YOUNG GIRL, MATRYOSHA.

EE: In the end, she comes back, and we see the complete episode. Then Peter comes in, making his political speech at the podium. Then Dasha comes in, writing a letter from her new country. I could never figure out how to make anything other than three endings. One of the things that was fascinating when I read the novel in English was that the editors had taken out Nicholas' confession of rape, just as Dostoyevsky's editors did when the novel was first serialized in Russia. The confession was published as an Appendix. You go through the whole novel and you suddenly encounter this story. I thought that was the most fascinating thing about the novel, that somebody had felt the need to come in and censor this. The act of censorship really frames the whole play. Everybody censors themselves, except for Peter. Peter is the only one who is able to vocalize and pursue what he wants. And people are terrified.

AG: IN 1993, YOU WROTE AN ESSAY CALLED 'THE NEW CENSORS,' WHICH WAS PUBLISHED IN *THE AUDREY SKIRBALL THEATRE NEWSLETTER*. WHAT WAS THE ESSAY ABOUT?

EE: It was about theater artists. It was talking about political correctness, but I didn't want to put the blame on playwrights or producers or directors. Censorship always seems an effort to preserve the sensibilities of the audience or the people perceived as victims in the play. But we are really censoring ourselves, to avoid talking about the important subjects facing our country. Partly that is because Americans are afraid of being perceived as pretentious or intellectual. But really, we're afraid of the explosiveness of the material. And theater has never been a radical art form.

AG: IN THIS COUNTRY?

EE: Yes. We've made huge strides in every other art since the industrial revolution, but it seems as if American theater is closer to melodrama now than at the turn of the nineteenth century.

AG: WHAT ISSUES IS AMERICAN THEATER AFRAID TO TALK ABOUT?

EE: Racism, for one. I'm talking about the plays I see and the plays I write. We still prefer to talk about racism in conventional ways, rather than challenge our own, white, liberal smugness.

I remember talking in graduate school about how I wanted to write a play about the pursuit of a black man that would turn the audience into bloodthirsty hounds. And the teacher said, 'You can't write that play.' He said, 'You as a white person cannot write a play about a black person.' He was trying to be practical. He was saying that nobody would put it on, and even if it were produced, it would provoke only rejection or outrage. That for a white person to write about *any* person of color would be rubbing salt in the wound. Well, that's a very disingenuous way of shutting down all discussion.

AG: HOW COULD WOMEN USE THE THEATER BETTER?

EE: To talk about subjects that are considered male subjects. Politics, violence. As women, we tend to restrict our subjects to things sexual. But too often we're dishonest about sexism. We judge other cultures and periods by our own.

What was brilliant about the movie *Howard's End* was that it talked about sexism at the turn of the nineteenth century in an honest way. Nobody was braver than their period. Nobody was a hero about sexism. That's an honesty that I almost never see in plays, movies, or TV. We don't let ourselves look at sexism in a calm, dispassionate way. Instead of setting sexism in a morally outraged context, we should be almost scientific about it. That would be truly inflammatory. The play that I'm working on now, *Folly*, is about marriage, disappointment, cynicism. What does it take to survive spiritually in marriage? It's hard not to make moral judgments about it.

One of the things I liked about Richard Nelson's play *Goodnight Children Everywhere*, was that he looked at incest as a continuing part of that family's life. To write about a family in which such crimes are committed, yet everybody continues to lead a somewhat happy family life — that's interesting. A businessman who commits murder, gets a promotion, and continues to get promoted — that's interesting. That is the kind of dialogue the theater should be having about our culture.

AG: SPEAKING OF INCEST, PERHAPS NOW WOULD BE A GOOD TIME TO TALK ABOUT YOUR *PHAEDRA*. YOU ORIGINALLY CALLED THE PLAY *PHAEDRA AND HIPPOLYTUS*, BUT WHEN YALE REPERTORY THEATRE PRODUCED IT IN 1989, THE TITLE WAS *PHAEDRA*.

EE: I realized it was Phaedra's story. It was not even about the love affair so much as about her.

AG: DID THE VINEYARD THEATRE'S PRODUCTION IN 1995 USE ESSENTIALLY THE SAME SCRIPT?

EE: Yes.

AG: WHY DO YOU THINK THE STORY OF PHAEDRA APPEALS TO SO MANY DRAMATISTS?

EE: Like any classic, it periodically becomes important again. I'm not as interested now that I've written it, but it's one of the great embarrassing subjects, and embarrassment functions very importantly for me in writing. If a subject is good, it should be really embarrassing.

AG: WHAT DO YOU MEAN BY EMBARRASSING?

EE: I mean, it reveals something about ourselves personally or as a culture that we'd rather not discuss, or would prefer to keep secret. And it speaks in a way that is so honest, it can't be denied.

AG: WHY DID YOU WRITE *PHAEDRA* IN VERSE?

EE: Phaedra needs to live in the individual skull, like poetry. She does so little; she does almost nothing. I'm interested in paralysis as dramatic metaphor. I'm interested in stillness, because that is an almost violent act onstage. Women are particularly paralyzed. Paralysis drives people crazy — it drives the chorus crazy when Phaedra won't say or do anything. She just sits there. In that sense, she's revolutionary. She forces people to deal with her by being still.

AG: HER STILLNESS IS POSITIVE?

EE: It's anarchic. Her refusal to speak is a radical act. She's forced into it; I don't think she does it in a premeditated way. But she finds herself cornered and refuses to get out of the corner. Just stays there. Forcing people to look at you is a radical act. Which is the great thing about theater, if we would only do it. To force people to look. If we were good enough writers and mature enough artists, we could force them to look at society.

AG: IN THE INTRODUCTION TO THE PUBLISHED VERSION OF *PHAEDRA AND HIPPOLYTUS* IN *THEATER* [YALE, SUMMER 1989], THE ESSAYIST CALLS PHAEDRA THE MOST 'IMPLODED' OF HEROINES. 'PHAEDRA IS DENIED THE CONSOLATION OF CONTEXT. SHE MUST POSTPONE HER OWN PASSIONS, BE HER OWN ORACLE, AND CAN ONLY RAGE AGAINST HERSELF, ISOLATED.'

EE: Yes. And any individual in this society, male or female, can identify with that.

AG: ONE OF THE THINGS I LIKE ABOUT YOUR *PHAEDRA* IS THAT THE CHORUS CAN'T STAND HER.

EE: They can't stand her, I know. She is the Stalin of that town.

AG: RIGHT. HERE SHE IS, WONDERING WHETHER OR NOT SHE SHOULD CONFESS HER ILLICIT LOVE, AND THEY ARE SAYING THAT THEY ARE NOT EVEN ALLOWED AN ILLICIT THOUGHT.

EE: What a luxury. Their children will be burned by her husband's soldiers. They are always the ones who pay.

AG: THE NARRATOR SEEMS TO BE PHAEDRA'S ALTER EGO.

EE: The narrator has always been played by a man; I wrote it for a male friend of mine who was a student at Yale at the time. He *is* her alter ego. And he is a damaged person, who, as witness to her act and the violence that's done to her, has been emotionally castrated. I have tremendous sympathy for that character. He's the witness. He can't act. All he can do is watch. Which is why he is damned. He's the counterpart of the writer.

AG: WHAT DO YOU MEAN?

EE: That the writer is condemned to watch. That's why I think I have impossibly high standards for writers. If all we can do, as writers, is watch, then we'd better be damned good watchers. But we're only human. We're so blind to the real thing. That's the futility of writing and why I keep writing. There's an idealist in me that thinks we can change society through writing and through theater.

AG: WHAT DID YOU LEARN FROM THE YALE PRODUCTION?

EE: The actress playing Phaedra was too beautiful and too young. It made the play too much of a romance. And the guy who played Hippolytus was too sexy. It tends to emphasize the older woman in love with the younger man, which is not, for me, what the story is about. To me, he *happens* to be younger. I don't think she perceives him as being younger and therefore attractive. What Phaedra finds attractive in Hippolytus is his isolation, that he's so close to nature and even more vulnerable than she. That's the nature of her sexual exploitation.

AG: YOU GIVE HIPPOLYTUS A FIERCELY MISOGYNISTIC SPEECH.

EE: And you thought he was going to be so nice. He really is as nice as he seems, but he's trying to save himself, and bile comes out of his mouth. I feel sorry for Hippolytus, because that's not who he is. Phaedra, however, understands this; she understands that he's destroying himself and that, in a sense, she has caused it. She can't save *him*, either. They can't save each other. People in that play seem doomed to witness each other's self-crucifixion. It's a sad and dark play.

One critic viewed it as a radical deconstruction, which it's not. It's a poem. It's a poem about Phaedra and it has a very strong emotional core. I don't think of deconstruction as being so emotional.

AG: IN YOUR SCRIPT, YOU CALL FOR A GIGANTIC ROBIN ON THE SET. ALSO, AT ONE POINT PHAEDRA DEMANDS THAT A GRAND PIANO BE RAISED INTO THE TREES. WHAT INSPIRED THOSE IMAGES?

EE: Phaedra started out as a painting in my head. A lot of times my plays start out as paintings. This was a painting of the Annunciation: Northern Renaissance, seventeenth century. Of course, later on I found out that the painting doesn't exist the way I envisioned it. This painting was of the Virgin sitting within a bombed-out abbey, with the Angel kneeling in front of her. The feel of the painting is cruel, cruel. Very two-dimensional and analytical. I think it was the bombed-out nature of the architectural structure that I was responding to.

As to the piano, I briefly dated a Chilean man, who told me a story about his grandfather, who was crazy and had the servants lift his grand piano into a tree. Everybody asked why, and he said, 'So I can play it.' That image stuck with me.

AG: WHAT INSPIRED *THE SWAN*?

EE: I woke up with it from a dream and went straight to the computer. A swan crashing into a woman's picture window. She brings it inside, and the next morning it becomes a naked man, crawling around her living room.

That play came almost entirely from a place of embarrassment, a lonely place where I wanted not just to fall in love but to be swept up by love and be taken away. It came almost as a piece. That's probably why the play worked, because I was able to let myself write from that embarrassed place. Which I wish I could do more often.

I managed to get through the whole first draft without realizing that I had written another version of Leda and the swan. Then I thought, 'Well, almost any time you have a woman and a swan in the same room, you're going to have Leda and the swan.' But Leda and the Swan was fundamentally a story about Zeus and primogeniture. *The Swan* is about the education of a human being, and the woman who unwittingly creates him, destroys him, and is overcome by him.

AG: CREATES AND DESTROYS?

EE: In a sense Dora creates him, because it's her window. She is the one who takes him in. She socializes him to the extent that he can be socialized. But then he wants too much. He wants love. So she destroys him. At the end, that they make it out together is improbable. But always, from the first draft, they ended up together, while everything implodes around them. I don't see that as an optimistic or positive ending. They do escape, they do end up together, but they are destroying themselves at the same time.

It's interesting to watch how directors handle the ending. Some think it's suicidal. Others think it's Disney. It is neither. It's a mix.

AG: THERE IS A FAIRY-TALE QUALITY TO THE PLAY, AND WE'RE ACCUSTOMED TO HAPPY ENDINGS IN FAIRY TALES.

E: Americans like happy endings. The Germans and Norwegians have dark fairy tales. In our American culture, or whatever this culture is that we're in, everyone's either the good guy or the bad guy. We seem incapable of tolerating complexity.

AG: I CONFESS THAT MY READING OF THE PLAY WAS POSITIVE, TO A DEGREE. SHE TRANSFORMS HIM, AND HE TRANSFORMS HER.

EE: Yes.

AG: HE GIVES HER SOME OF HIS SWANNESS. HE'S IN TOUCH WITH NATURE AND INSTINCT, WHICH SHE WANTS, BUT CAN'T REACH BY HERSELF.

EE: She's in a doomed place at the beginning and she gets out of the corner that she's in. That is positive. But part of me says, 'Yeah, but where do they go? This is not a relationship. It has no shelf life.' What I find sad about the play is that the escape is all. I would like to think there was more than escaping.

AG: STILL, AT THE END, WHO IS MORE TRAPPED? DORA OR HER LESS IMAGINATIVE BOYFRIEND, KEVIN?

EE: Oh, poor Kevin. Kevin is the most trapped of all. He's the one who's in the hard place at the end, because he's just seen a metaphysical transformation that he'll never be able to tell anyone about. Kevin, at the end, is where Dora was at the beginning. He has given up everything. But he doesn't have a swan. So he is really screwed. Except now that he's seen this transformation, who knows? Now that he's really screwed himself, he might get a real imagination. Kevin at the end of the play is standing on the threshold of his personal revolution.

AG: IT IS HARD TO UNDERSTAND WHY HE DOESN'T WALK OUT AND LEAVE HER.

EE: Why he comes back again and again. He has so much love and anger, and no place to put it.

AG: BUT YES, THERE IS A SAD ASPECT TO HER ESCAPE.

EE: The trick is to find both the release and the sadness. I don't think I've ever seen the perfect production of that play.

AG: IT IS THE MOST PRODUCED OF YOUR PLAYS.

EE: It continues to play a lot in Scandinavia. There was an Italian production that was Felliniesque. The Swan was in a white sailor suit. Everybody was in white.

AG: I READ TURGENEV'S NOVEL *ON THE EVE* IN CONJUNCTION WITH YOUR ADAPTATION, WHICH YOU CALL *THE LOVER*. YOUR CHARACTERIZATION OF THE HEROINE, ELENA, IS DIFFERENT FROM TURGENEV'S. YOUR ELENA IS MORE SPOILED AND CHILDISH.

EE: That is definitely how I saw her. Yet she creates herself during the course of the play. She has a formidable will. I can't really remember what the original character is like.

AG: IN THE NOVEL SHE IS DESCRIBED AS A WOMAN WHO CARES FOR THE WOUNDED AND THE MAIMED, WHETHER PEOPLE OR ANIMALS.

EE: I saw no place for that. Even her relationship to her white rat . . .

AG: THE PET WHITE RAT THAT YOU GIVE HER IS ALSO NOT IN THE NOVEL.

EE: I know. I don't know how that came in. Kali Rocha played that role at Center Stage in Baltimore and she had this enormous white rat.

AG: A LIVE RAT?

EE: Yes. It would freak out the audience when she came onstage with this white rat and proceeded to play with it while she was talking. What came across was this spoiled bourgeois. The rat is so erotic, frightening, and ugly, and it brings out an ugliness in Elena's character. The more I think about it the more I remember: I wanted to do something onstage with a small, horrible animal. The white rat is always itself onstage, and everything looks artificial around it.

AG: YOU SAID EARLIER THAT YOU WROTE THIS ADAPTATION FAIRLY QUICKLY.

EE: It was easier to do that with *On the Eve*, because it was essentially a small story, not like the Dostoyevsky, which was big and crazy. That was what I loved about working on the Dostoyevsky, that it would always get away from me.

AG: BUT DESPITE THE SIZE OF *THE DEVILS*, AND DESPITE YOUR REARRANGING, IT SEEMS TO ME THAT YOU COME BACK TO DOSTOYEVSKY'S INTENTION. HE LOOKS DUBIOUSLY ON THESE DESTRUCTIVE PEOPLE, AND SO DO YOU.

EE: I'm not a Dostoyevsky scholar, but I remember reading that what had fueled the writing of the novel was the murder of a man by the members of his own political cell: the Student Revolutionaries. The incident horrified Russia, because nobody thought the students were that radicalized. According to my limited research, Dostoyevsky was assigned the task of fictionalizing the event for a magazine. He came out with a few installments and was relieved of his duties, but he continued on his own with the material. I was fascinated that in some way Dostoyevsky was adapting this newspaper account for his own purposes. That became one of the dynamics of my play: how people use rumor and innuendo to gain control over uncontrollable circumstances.

AG: WHY DID YOU DECIDE TO WRITE IN FREE VERSE?

EE: From the beginning it was in free verse. It's not even really free verse, but by-the-breath verse. That enabled me to take the story out of its time, to create a world around it. To put it in my own skull and create a psychological environment for the piece. I had no interest in being historically accurate. Statements like that make some people crazy, but I'm really uninterested in the actual period of anything, because I don't think that anybody can get back there.

AG: STILL, THE LANGUAGE DOES NOT SOUND CONTEMPORARY TO THE LATE-TWENTIETH CENTURY.

EE: The language fluctuates. I was interested in using language to set context and then explode context.

AG: THE PRODUCTION AT NEW YORK THEATER WORKSHOP, WHICH WAS DIRECTED BY THE LATE GARLAND WRIGHT, HAD AN ENORMOUS, ELABORATE SET. ON NYTW'S PROSCENIUM STAGE, THE SET LOOKED LIKE A WARREN OF ROOMS. ACTORS HAD TO RUN UP AND DOWN VISIBLE STAIRS TO GET FROM SCENE TO SCENE.

EE: Which I liked. I liked that by sheer running the actors were kept a little off balance. But I've heard it said that the sets for all my work should be far simpler, that directors can get trapped by the set. It's probably true. The set usually needs to go away, so the language can come out.

Chris Coleman directed a production of *The Devils* at Actor's Express in Atlanta. They had no money and a tiny space — and got incredible reviews. There are many possible reasons for that, but one might have been that the production was not intimidating. Part of the problem with doing Dostoyevsky is that all the wolves come out of the forest. Everyone wants to make this their biggest work.

AG: YOU MENTIONED THAT *THE DEVILS* WAS ORIGINALLY COMMISSIONED BY MARK TAPER FORUM. DO YOU LIKE COMMISSIONS?

EE: You're always happy when someone asks you to dance. And getting a commission means you have no excuse not to write the play.

But I find it difficult to get the specific producer and the specific audience out of my head. Also, silly questions like, 'Will the literary manager like it?' If they take the play, you're damned, because it's the first production and far better that you should be able to place a new play in a low-profile theater. If they don't take it, then you start whining. It's hard for me to get away from the do-you-like-me, Sally-Field kind of response.

AG: IS THERE SUCH A THING AS AN IDENTIFIABLE WOMAN'S VOICE?

EE: I think there is, and I think it's a quality that is perceived after the fact. Much of the time I can tell if the voice is a woman's voice. I'm not sure if it's an emotional syntax, or if it's the choice of material. I don't see it as a good or bad thing. There's a certain kind of — I was going to say vulnerability. Women can certainly be as ruthless as anybody else. But most of the time, I can tell when the piece is written by a woman. Can I tell that because I'm a woman? Maybe men can't tell women's writing. For me, as a woman, women's writing exists. But it's an almost underground category of writing. What interests me about Russian literature is that the culture and its ideas are so repressed — literally — that the literature has developed a rich underground imagery. And women — this is what I'm going for — women have an extensive underground vocabulary, emotional vocabulary, and you can sense that in the writing. We tend to have an understanding of pretense and illusion, and we tend to be interested in . . . oh, gosh, I don't know if I can say this. Even as I'm about to say this, I'm saying, 'No, that's not true.'

AG: WELL, IT'S WORTH WRESTLING WITH.

EE: It is. It is. Everything that I say I will argue with a week from now. I think women can get into a miasma of looking at material so closely that they are very influenced by pressures upon them — from other writers, audiences, the circumstances of their own lives. Now I'm arguing myself into a state of paralysis about it.

AG: DO YOU FEEL UNCOMFORTABLE BEING INCLUDED IN THE CATEGORY 'WOMAN WRITER'?

EE: Part of me is uncomfortable with it. The paranoid part that suspects theaters of picking plays to fill slots. 'Let's see, we have the black slot, and the woman's slot . . . ' It's ghettoizing. Trivializing. But I think that it's important to analyze the body of work. It's important to try. Ultimately ninety percent of what women are going to do lies ahead of us; we've done so little. On the other hand, there are times when I think I should put a man's name on my plays and submit them to theaters that way.

AG: HAS BEING A WOMAN HINDERED YOUR CAREER?

EE: In part, yes. Certainly. Let's be honest — most women would say it has hindered them. Because unfortunately the theater establishment is still run by men for male aesthetics.

AG: WOMEN HAVE DIRECTED A NUMBER OF YOUR PLAYS. EVAN YIANOULIS STAGED *PHAEDRA* AT THE VINEYARD THEATRE, IN NEW YORK.

EE: Lisa Peterson did *The Swan* at La Jolla. Evan Yianoulis directed *Wolfman* in one of its manifestations.

AG: YOU SEEM TO BE DOING QUITE A BIT OF SCREEN-WRITING. DOES YOUR GENDER HAMPER YOU IN THAT ARENA?

EE: It's easier in TV and film, partly because you legally don't carry as much clout, so people are less threatened. It's the director's movie. Though people are still scared about giving a female screenwriter a big budget. Not that I want to write an action film, but we tend to be restricted to domestic subjects and films about women. But I don't have such high expectations for that field. I'm much more laissez-faire. I don't think film can come close to theater or novels or poetry as a medium.

AG: DO YOU STILL WRITE POETRY?

EE: No. The only poetry I write is inside a play. And that's not poetry; it's poetic writing. I don't really have much desire to write poetry anymore.

I have a desire to write fiction. I always used to be scared of fiction. I thought I'd go inside my head and never come out. I'd get lost. But now I'm getting braver. Now, sometimes I think that is really where I'd like to go. To be able to write on many levels at the same time: historical, social, plot levels. That said, *Folly*, the play I am writing now, is the tiniest play ever. After *The Devils*, I had to write something small. It's only five characters.

AG: IS IT AN ADAPTATION?

EE: No. But it has literary and painting sources. One source is *A Midsummer Night's Dream*. Another is Édouard Manet's painting *Le Déjeuner sur l'herbe*: two couples sitting on the grass having a picnic, the men fully dressed and the women naked. Of course, you can't start a play like that, can you? But maybe if I was really brave, I would. ▽

Eve Ensler

My dream of a good play is that you're laughing, you're hysterical, and then you're suddenly in the middle of hell and you don't know how you got there. That's why I like the Greeks so much. Those plays are not comedies, but you get pulled in despite yourself, and then before you know it, your heart and soul have been ripped open. To me, that's why we're in theater. It's the only place left where people can feel. Because they're not feeling anyplace else.

Writer, teacher, and political activist Eve Ensler found her voice in 1998. While she is the author of over a dozen plays and screenplays, including *The Depot* (1987), *The Ladies* (1988), *Reef and Particle* (1992), *Lemonade* (1993), *Extraordinary Measures* (1994), *Floating Rhoda and the Glue Man* (1995), *Necessary Targets* (1997), and *Conviction* (1999), nothing has brought Ensler more satisfaction than her Obie Award–winning soliloquies, *The Vagina Monologues*, which she first performed in New York and has performed in Zagreb, London, Jerusalem, and across the United States, most recently in a commercial venue off Broadway. *The Vagina Monologues* has also been performed by the likes of Glenn Close, Whoopie Goldberg, and Lily Tomlin, for a fund-raising event called V-Day, held on Valentine's Day 1998 in Manhattan's Hammerstein Ballroom. Subsequent V-Days have occurred around the world, and another major V-Day celebration took place at New York City's Madison Square Garden in 2001. The following interview is culled from two conversations that took place in New York City, in 1998 and 1999.

• • •

EE: I was born in New York City and grew up in a wealthy community outside of the city. I have a brother and a sister. I had a terrible childhood in every respect, except that we weren't poor. It was violent. It was abusive. It was very insane making. I grew up in a beautiful community where on the outside everyone had everything, whereas on the inside I was confined and condemned by a cruel, sexually abusive father, who raped me from the time I was five until the time I was ten. And then he brutalized me on a regular basis until I left home at sixteen. I left my body then, too. I wasn't sane by the time I left, and it's taken me most of my life to recover and re-enter my body.

But I'm not in a place of sadness anymore. I'm not in a place where it controls my life anymore. I've spent a lot of years working on this stuff in therapy and in recovery programs — I've gotten through most of it and I don't feel it controls my moods, my spirit, and my way of being in the world. And I write. Writing has been profoundly cathartic for me.

AG: WHEN DID YOU START TO WRITE?

EE: I started to write when I was very young — probably seven — as a way of recording the part of me that was trying to survive. I think I wrote to exist. Not to sound too cliché, but I think I instinctively knew that if I existed in words, I would somehow exist in matter. I felt profoundly invisible, because I was being so objectified. My being the subject of my own life had been eradicated so early, that writing let me be a subject, an 'I,' a being. I wrote so I wouldn't go crazy. I felt terribly isolated and guilty. I felt I was betraying my mother and I was filled with self-hatred. Other than writing, there was no place to express that.

AG: YOU WERE WRITING A DIARY?

EE: I wrote poems. Tragic little poems.

AG: SO YOU CAME TO WRITING BY YOURSELF?

EE: Yes.

AG: WHEN DID YOU FIRST GET INVOLVED WITH THEATER?

EE: I was in college. I did this production of *The Bacchae*, in which I played Agauë. I remember sliding onstage in the blood. I loved it. And then I acted in a Sam Shepard play called *Chicago* — the whole thing took place in a bathtub. I was wild by that point. Let me qualify that: I was wildly alcoholic, a hippie.

And then the head of the Drama Department was doing a production of Thornton Wilder's *Our Town*, with an interlude from Jean Genet's *The Balcony* (kind of like the subtext of *Our Town*), and for some reason, probably because I asked, I got to be the assistant director on this project. I learned a tremendous amount about theater from him. He had ideals, he was political, he had a sense of morality and a sense of ethics. He got theater in this very engaging way. And after that I got caught.

I know this sounds pathetic, but my only other theater influence happened when my mother took me to see the musical *Oliver!* and I identified so much with the poor children — the little orphan children — that I sobbed all the way through it. My mother didn't know what to do with me, but I remember thinking how amazing it was that on a stage you could say things, sing songs, and move people.

AG: WERE YOU A THEATER MAJOR AT COLLEGE?

EE: Oh, no. Actually, it was only after the production of *Our Town* that I focused on theater. I was hooked. I loved it. It was the first place that I ever felt safe, a community — I guess it's the first time I felt like part of a real family. I still feel that way.

And then after college I got lost. Without the structure of school, I had no money and no support. I went off on a bad spell for quite some time. I became an alcoholic and drug addict. I was in a bad place, literally and emotionally, and almost died. And when I finally made my way back to some sort of sanity, I wanted to start a theater company.

I came to New York, and in the back of my mind, despite the fact that my life had caved in, I had this fantasy that I would direct. Well, I couldn't find anything to direct, but I was writing. I was always writing. I wrote a play in verse — my first play — I don't even know where it is. It was about madness and suicide, and I'm sure it was dreadful. But people were encouraging.

Then I got sober, and for a few years I really couldn't do anything but survive — and write poems. I worked at the Lion's Head as a waitress, and I met a wonderful writer named Joe Flaherty. One night I got up my courage and asked him if he would consider reading my poetry. I waited for weeks. I was dying. And he finally called me and said, 'You're a writer. You're definitely a writer. Now you've got to do the work.' He would make these little red comments throughout the poems: 'You're hand-holding, don't walk with them through the poems, let them go through the poems themselves.'

Then I wrote *When I Call My Voices*, a one-woman show about a woman who has nine voices and is trying to integrate them, which was where I was emotionally at the time — trying to get a life. It was produced at a loft downtown, and then it moved to Ensemble Studio Theatre. It wasn't very good, but I realized that I wanted to write for the theater. And then I wrote *Coming from Nothing*.

AG: THIS IS ABOUT A WOMAN WHO, IN A SENSE, REGRESSES PSYCHOLOGICALLY; SHE BECOMES TEMPORARILY CHILD-LIKE AND REVISITS A HORRIBLE CHILDHOOD EXPERIENCE.

EE: And I couldn't finish it. Because I didn't really have my memories of what happened in my childhood until 1990. So the whole play was about a woman who experienced this horrific event that I could never get to. But the play attracted a lot of attention. And it was a great experience for me, because I learned how to write and rewrite and suffer. Boy did I suffer. I spent three years trying to get that play up. I didn't know from, 'Well, go write another play.' It was my baby, it was my life; I couldn't focus on something else. The play never got done.

But then my son, Dylan McDermott, whom I adopted, was in Joanne Woodward's acting class at Sandy Meisner's school, so Dylan brought her a copy of *Coming from Nothing*.

I was very active then in the Nuclear Disarmament Movement, spending most of my time on the street, handing out leaflets, tying myself to fences, to stop nuclear war. I was quite driven. This is where I was putting all my new sober energy. And Joanne was also very active in the Nuclear Disarmament Movement. And when I first met her, I had a moment of chutzpah — I don't know where it came from — when I said, 'I should write you a play.' I said, 'I really want to do a play on women's peace camps, so, what if I wrote you a play that a woman would perform at a woman's peace camp?' And she said, 'Write it.' (Then it became a moment of absolute terror.)

At the time, I was doing protests at peace camps in the parks in New York City and I started interviewing people. And from this came *The Depot*. I brought her the first draft, and she said, 'I want you to know that the play is good. But I want it funny.'

That was a turning point in my life, because it never occurred to me that you could make politics funny. I was so serious, so righteous. I was young — twenty-seven or something. So I went back and rewrote the play. It turned out to be quite funny.

We worked on it for a year and a half. And then, after some extraordinary nurturing and mentoring from Joanne and others, Joanne felt the play was ready. She decided she was going to direct it and we asked Shirley Knight to perform in it. It was very much the nuclear disarmament days: we went to boys' military schools, the Nevada test site, and to the Kennedy Center, to perform it for Congress. And in that period, I began to learn how to be a playwright.

AG: WHERE DOES THIS BEGINNING PERIOD OF PLAYWRITING GO UP TO?

EE: Through *Ladies*. Between *The Depot* and *Ladies* comes *Scooncat*, which is this crazy, high-tech, experimental piece that did well despite the fact that the critics hated it. It had a kind of cult following. But Clive Barnes hated it so much. He wrote, '*Scooncat* is a dog.' I will never forget it. My father died the night the review came out. It was one of these epic, 'Of course, what else would happen?' things. But everyone should get a terrible review — it's the best thing that can happen to you.

AG: WHY?

EE: Because if you can survive it, then you're writing for the right reasons. You're writing because you have something to say. It was such a horrible blow to be that badly reviewed, it was either die or become a writer.

AG: IN *LADIES*, EACH CHARACTER HAS WHAT SEEMS LIKE

A DREAM OR FANTASY. DID YOU WANT THE PLAY TO OPER-
ATE LIKE A FANTASY?

EE: I had been working in a homeless shelter, volunteering, and I said
I wanted to do a piece about homeless women. I met the Music Theatre
Group's artistic director, Lyn Austin, and was commissioned to write
a play. While this was certainly nothing that Music Theatre Group
had ever done before, Lyn gave me a chance to do it.

So I wrote *Ladies*. But I still didn't have the ability structurally
to write a play, because I wanted to live in my unconscious. I didn't
want to have to develop that other side of my brain. I believed in living in the poetic, unconscious places where things attach and find their
way together. I was violently opposed to structure because it represented the whole capitalist system for me. As a result, the play became
one long poem. It had a profound impact on people; we did that play
for years, and I raised over one hundred thousand dollars for homeless women using that play.

But the play never completely worked for me. I wanted to write
a play about six different characters, with a story that came together.
And I didn't know how to do it and was too defiant to surrender to
structure. Structure was my father — I somehow associated the two.
To structure things would be to bring his voice to my work, to live
with it. I was going to remain in my world, the world of accidental
dimensions. His world was about control.

AG: DID YOU INTERVIEW THE HOMELESS WOMEN YOU
WERE WORKING WITH?

EE: Yes, I spent three years interviewing them.

AG: ARE THE MONOLOGUES TRANSCRIPTIONS?

EE: Well, this is where I learned to develop the way I write. First I
interview and then I take those interviews, I read them, I let them filter through me, and from this process, I pick out a couple of lines
here and there that speak to me.

AG: DO YOU TAPE THE INTERVIEWS?

EE: No, I never tape. I only write, because I find that, after sitting in a room with the women, I'll write the lines that matter to me. And then when it comes to the monologue, I'll take, let's say, a sentence, and that will be the catalyst to the monologue. So the woman's being is in it, her essence is there, but her words may not be. There may be a couple of phrases. With *Ladies* I really developed the method that I've used for a lot of plays since then, including *The Vagina Monologues*, *Necessary Targets*, a couple of movies, and a prison piece that I'm writing right now.

And I formed relationships when I interviewed the women at the shelter. I became involved and I'm still involved ten years later. It brought me into a whole other world.

AG: ANOTHER COMMUNITY.

EE: Exactly. The same with the Bosnia piece, *Necessary Targets*. In Bosnia, the women are so happy you're there to begin with — that anyone who has come from America to see them is a miracle. I made a decision when I went to the Center for Women War Victims there, that I would stay on the couch for two weeks. I stayed for a month. I was going to live there and be there, and they got that. So it depends to what degree you're willing to come to people. It may seem that I pay a price for that, but I really don't. Because when you feel reality, you get to truly live your life. I'm not living my life in fear. The only thing I'm afraid of is airplanes. I cry all the time, I grieve, I live around enormous atrocity, and the lesson I've learned is that if you're willing to live with it, go through it, it doesn't own you. It's when you fear and resist and keep reality away that it begins to own you.

AG: YOU SEEM TO ENJOY WORKING WITH THE MONO-LOGUE FORM.

EE: I love monologues. I feel that they are a way of looking at the story of one's life. My whole childhood was a monologue. I lived in a world where people never connected, never interacted, and never dealt with anything that was going on with anybody around them. In a way I feel that monologues are the truest form. Most people are in monologues anyway — they're in their own realities. I mean, I'd like to believe that we're in a dialogue, but I don't think we're there yet.

I think people connect through monologues. Rilke wrote that, 'We are guardians of each other's solitude.' I don't think we're supposed to merge in dialogue. What interests me is how we are all in monologue together. Diversity interests me in the same way: how we are black and white together, not how we are blackwhite. How we coexist, not how we merge. The attraction I have to monologues is to keep looking at how we keep our separateness in the midst of each other and still love each other, as opposed to the ridiculous notion we are fed as children, that the way you love is to give up your identity and yourself.

AG: YOUR WRITING IS VERY WORD ORIENTED, AS OPPOSED TO BEING ORIENTED TOWARD THE MISE-EN-SCÈNE.

EE: Thats all that matters, right? Does anything else matter but words? Words saved my life. How you put words together so that they're dramatic, theatrical, emotional, so that they express the heart or the cunt or whatever — nothing excites me more. I'm not a visual person. I'm a person who doesn't trust what I see. There are so many illusions, and my whole life was about illusions. I had the most handsome father, a stunning mother, a gorgeous house, and a beautiful community, and all that was a lie.

AG: WHEN DID THE SECOND STAGE OF YOUR PLAYWRITING BEGIN?

EE: I think *Reef and Particle, Lemonade*, and *Floating Rhoda and the Glue Man* were a whole new phase. They were not based on interviews. They were attempts at plays. I began to find a way to put two people — even if they were both in their own monologues — in the same room. And I was writing about stuff that mattered to me: dark sex and abuse.

Lemonade was a great breakthrough because I found a voice that was a little wicked and minimal, which is in me and comes up every few years. Who knows where that voice comes from? I also loved writing *Lemonade* because I learned a lot about structure. It was the first time I surrendered and consciously structured a play.

AG: THEY SEEM TO BE ATTEMPTS AT STYLISTIC EXPERI-
MENTS. *LEMONADE* IS A LITTLE ABSURDIST.

EE: Exactly.

AG: WHAT INSPIRED IT?

EE: It was based on a guy from Westchester who killed his family and
disappeared. Nineteen years later they discovered that he was, in fact,
a murderer. In the time that he was missing, he had remarried and
had created a beautiful life. His new wife said she didn't believe it.
She said that if it was true, 'He must have been stressed out.'

Lemonade operated on two levels for me. Personally, it was a deeper
look at my family. It reflected my childhood — there's very little memory of it — nobody remembers where anybody was or what anybody
was doing. I'm obsessed with memory as an idea. People being remembered, people remembering what's happened to them, people remembering what they've done, and people knowing where they are as a
result of this memory.

And, on another level, I felt I was maturing as a writer. Some piece
had begun to drop that was a little more sophisticated. I was conscious
of the story. I had never thought story before — beginning, middle,
and end. In *Lemonade*, I was able to bring a story — this murder —
and a concept — memory — together.

And *Floating Rhoda* was a big jump for me, because it was A Play.
A friend of mine had said to me, 'Why don't you write a love play.'
And I said, 'I can't write a love play.' It seemed too happy, too hope-
ful. But the challenge excited me.

AG: *PARTICLE* IS A LOVE PLAY IN ITS WAY, TOO, AND IT HAS
A ROMANTIC ENDING. HE CHANGES.

EE: Well, he doesn't really change. He changes for that moment. It's
not a change you can depend on. When I wrote *Particle*, I wasn't very
hopeful. I didn't think people could change — I didn't see people breaking patterns. Now I believe people can break out. But to get out of
an addictive relationship like Reef and Particle's is a big struggle.

AG: IN A 1989 INTERVIEW WITH WILLIAM HARRIS FOR *THE NEW YORK TIMES,* YOU SAID, 'MY LIFE HAS BEEN DIVIDED BETWEEN BEING A WRITER AND BEING AN ACTIVIST AND TRYING TO FIND A WAY TO PUT THOSE TWO WORLDS TOGETHER.' WHERE DID THE ACTIVIST SIDE COME FROM? I WAS WONDERING ABOUT THIS WHEN READING *LEMON-ADE,* WHERE THE DAUGHTER, SAYS, 'MY MOTHER DIDN'T CARE ABOUT ANYTHING, SO I HAVE HAD TO CARE.' IS THAT YOU?

EE: Definitely. Every writer has a theme, and every writer has a character that crops up in every work. Part of the job of the writer is to become conscious of not only where these things live in your writing, but also where they are in you. I think that I always seem to be writing on one level or another about my mother. I've liberated her, sent her to peace camps, given her a political life, and I've saved her because she did not save me. I have been driven to make the world more just, less cruel.

The torture was trying to find the balance in me between my activism and this pull to write. Just time-wise it was torture. Writing *Depot* was the beginning: I was able to write a play about a political issue and then use it as a way of raising consciousness. With *Ladies* I began to see how to bring the two together. When *Ladies* began touring, it raised money and consciousness for and about the homeless. The two forces began to integrate in me. *The Vagina Monologues* has been the epitome of that. Because the monologues were based on actual women's stories, they were able to reflect politics without being preachy. As I perform them, I am able to create a platform for dialogue among women. I am able to stimulate outrage and unity, which comes from breaking women's isolation. I am able to link the intention and the art.

AG: IT DOES SEEM TO ME THAT MORE THAN MOST AMERICAN PLAYWRIGHTS, WOMEN OR MEN, YOU WRITE WITH A MISSION.

EE: I used to be embarrassed by that. I would meet playwrights who said, 'Art is objective.' That's not the way I am. I do write with a mission. I look at Tennessee Williams, Beckett, Caryl Churchill, and think, 'Do they have a mission?' Of course they do.

AG: SOME MISSIONS ARE MORE POLITICAL THAN OTHERS.

EE: Right. My mission is consciousness. I'm a woman, and I feel that as I write, I write myself into consciousness about the world. To go to Bosnia, to sit in a homeless shelter or in a maximum security prison for women, I see what's there: the atrocities, the injustices, the outrageous, the mysterious, the anger, the oppression. So the trick then is, how do you write that without beating people over the head with it or being didactic? In a way, my problem is working against the mission. I have to find a way to create. A lot of my early work was moralizing — at least more so than it is now. There were pieces of *Floating Rhoda* where I was shocked that I let the characters be as sympathetic as they are. I just finished a filmscript about two men, which was the hardest thing I've ever had to write. It took me eight years to do a screenplay about two guys, to give men that much space and attention, to make them both likeable.

AG: *EXTRAORDINARY MEASURES* CENTERS AROUND A MAN — PAUL WALKER, A NEW YORK DIRECTOR AND ACTING TEACHER WHO DIED OF COMPLICATIONS FROM AIDS. YOU BROKE A PATTERN THERE.

EE: That play really is a departure. It's about death, which has haunted and obsessed me throughout most of my life and exists in a lot of my plays. *Extraordinary Measures* was the first time I dealt with it head on.

AG: HAD YOU STUDIED WITH HIM?

EE: No, no. We had been very close friends, and he had directed *Ladies* and was supposed to direct *Lemonade*. He actually lived with me for a period of time when he first got sick.

AG: ARE YOU A PARTICULAR CHARACTER IN THE PLAY?

EE: Probably all of them.

AG: WAS IT ALWAYS YOUR INTENTION TO HAVE ONE ACTOR PLAY ALL THE ROLES?

EE: Yes. I wrote it for James Lescene. He's a spectacular performer. I had just directed his one-person show, *Word of Mouth*, and wanted to do something else with him.

AG: DO YOU LIKE TO DIRECT?

EE: I do. But it's tricky when you direct your own work. For instance, I don't want to direct *Necessary Targets*. I want someone to come in and take hold. I'm too close to it; it's too dear to me. I might sentimentalize it. I need someone who's going to tough-it-up a little bit.

AG: DO YOU LIKE TO REWRITE?

EE: I love to rewrite. Toni Morrison talks about the joy of rewriting and getting it right. I relate to that. It's a great stage — you have the blueprint, the house, and then you get to redecorate. The house is the hard part. Rewriting is the decoration.

AG: IN *EXTRAORDINARY MEASURES* YOU WRITE THAT PAUL TAUGHT, 'ART IS SPECIFICITY,' WHICH SOUNDS LIKE A TRUISM, BUT PERHAPS AN IMPORTANT ONE. ANY THOUGHTS THERE?

EE: Well, you know it's funny; the older you get, the more specific you allow yourself to be. I do this exercise at the beginning of a writing course I teach, where I have each student write the autobiography of their screenplay. They write down why they are writing a screenplay, based on their personal, psychological childhood. What do they have to say? And it's always fascinating to see who gets specific and who doesn't. The more specific a person gets, the greater their screenplay is going to be, because they've already opened up a world that's going to be a resource for them.

Two things occur to me more and more: that everything's about specificity and ultimately everything's really simple. What do you have to say, what is this piece really about?

I used to make everything so much bigger because I couldn't bear the truth of reality. I couldn't bear the pain that exists in simple reality, so I used to make everything very complicated, elaborate, and grand.

But writing is about stripping away, getting closer to what's really going on in you. And a lot of it's embarrassing.

AG: WERE *THE VAGINA MONOLOGUES* AND *NECESSARY TARGETS* WRITTEN AROUND THE SAME TIME?

EE: I had just finished the first draft of *The Vagina Monologues* when I started writing *Necessary Targets*. I started *The Vagina Monologues*, and then I went to Bosnia in 1994.

AG: WHY DID YOU GO TO BOSNIA?

EE: I went to Bosnia because I was going to do a film. I was going to do this utopian film, which I actually wrote.

AG: A UTOPIAN FILM?

EE: Yeah. A feminist utopian film. And in the course of writing that, I discovered the play. The Public Theater commissioned me to do it.

AG: *THE VAGINA MONOLOGUES* AND *NECESSARY TARGETS* ARE DIFFERENT FROM YOUR PREVIOUS WORK. YOU LEAVE THE MALE-FEMALE THEME AND DEAL WITH HOW WOMEN RESPOND TO THEMSELVES.

EE: I'm not a victim anymore. I'm not living in reaction to what happened to me as a child. This period of my life has been about finding out what's in me and realizing how to use my voice purposefully. And one of the things I've found is that I want to push women's relationships with their bodies forward. I was out of my body for most of my life, and now that I'm in it, and I'm aware of my breasts and vagina, among other things, I want to talk about them. People come up to me and say, 'Vagina Monologues is so exclusive.' It's not exclusive. It's about women. I've seen a thousand plays about men, and no one ever says they're exclusive. They say they're about men. So why can't there be a play that's just about women?

AG: MEN ARE THERE IN *THE VAGINA MONOLOGUES*; THEY'RE IN THE BACKGROUND.

Eve Ensler 167

EE: Oh, yeah, they have lots of interesting roles. Recently I wrote a new monologue, *Because He Liked to Look at It*, about a woman who gets involved with a man who is a vagina connoisseur, and as a result she comes to love her vagina. I couldn't write this piece until I actually heard it in an interview.

AG: COULD YOU CLARIFY WHAT YOU HAVE ADDED TO *THE VAGINA MONOLOGUES* SINCE YOU FIRST PERFORMED IT AT THE CORNELIA STREET CAFÉ IN 1996 AND THEN AT HERE IN 1997? WHEN DID YOU ADD THE MONOLOGUE ABOUT BIRTH, *I WAS THERE IN THE ROOM*?

EE: While I was still doing the *Monologues* at HERE.

AG: AND THE MONOLOGUE ABOUT THE VAGINA-FRIENDLY MAN?

EE: I wrote it for V-Day 1998.

AG: YOU ALSO ADDED *MY ANGRY VAGINA* FOR V-DAY 1998. AND IN THE PUBLISHED VERSION THERE IS A MONOLOGUE ABOUT MENSTRUATION.

EE: But I'm not performing it.

AG: HOW DOES IT FEEL TO HAVE OTHERS PERFORM THE MONOLOGUES?

EE: It's thrilling. After I leave the show, they're rotating in three women every two weeks, and I've reconstructed the script so they can do it without a narrator — with the narration clipped on to each piece. They split up the opening — 'I was worried about vaginas' — among three performers.

I also did a workshop with a hundred students that were flown into New York, to Columbia University. They were directing the piece at their colleges, so I did a day of training and worked with them on their fears.

AG: WHAT ARE THEIR FEARS?

EE: They range from threats that administrations will cut off women's programs to worries about not doing the material well. But you can't believe the things that students are doing on these campuses. They draw pictures of the vagina and identify the parts, and that is the card they give out to invite audiences. There have been student productions with shelters for battered women. There's nothing I will ever do in my life that compares with this. To see young women of fifteen to twenty-one coming into their sexuality. . .

AG: WHY DO YOU THINK THERE IS SUCH POSITIVE RESPONSE TO *THE VAGINA MONOLOGUES*? SUPPOSEDLY WE ARE IN THIS POSTFEMINIST ERA?

EE: Because we're not really in a postfeminist era. It's a big lie. Women are hungry to feel liberation at this moment in time. Women sit in that theater every night and they are ready to go. We need to stop talking about postfeminism. We need to get rid of that term. Women are struggling with the same issues they have always struggled with and they hunger for liberation as deeply as ever. I have no idea why *The Vagina Monologues* has been a catalyst, except that it's based on real women's stories, and women see themselves and respond. They don't feel judged. They feel there's a place for them in the spectrum of women. Who has ever talked about vaginas? And yet it's your life. It's your motor.

AG: IT IS INTERESTING THAT *THE VAGINA MONOLOGUES* BECAME A COMMERCIAL PRODUCTION OFF BROADWAY. A MAINSTREAM THEATER ISN'T THE USUAL VENUE FOR THIS KIND OF FARE.

EE: The function of capitalist theater is to calm the masses and quiet the masses. It isn't to inspire and outrage the masses. How we survive as artists who are trying to do radical things in this culture is really a dilemma.

AG: THERE'S NONPROFIT THEATER; IT'S NOT SUPPOSED TO BE CAPITALIST THEATER.

EE: But it's become that, and let's not pretend it hasn't. They buy all the same rules, feed into all the same systems. I've been deeply supported, but by and large, where is there a real source for people who are trying to question and engage? We don't have a theater of struggle in America. We don't have a theater of engagement. We don't have a theater that is evaluating society. Now you can slip things in, if you find the right little makeup of getting this star and that star, and that's what those of us who do this work have learned how to do. That's not what we should be doing. We should have people who want to do this kind of work. Now, if you get a great actress to do your play, people will tolerate the issue.

When I was a young activist, you went out into the streets, you handed out leaflets, you gathered crowds. People came because of the issues. Then around the late 1970s, early 1980s, everything changed. Nobody came anymore. Unless you had celebrities. That was the great turn in the culture. Theater changed then, politics changed. We've got to turn it back. We've got to get back to what people are struggling for, because as long as this remains a celebrity culture, people will remain disassociated from their own lives.

AG: ARE YOU WORKING ON A NEW PROJECT?

EE: Beginning in April 2000, I'm traveling around the world for four months, interviewing women about the parts of their bodies that they have systematically mutilated, hidden, transformed, in order to fit into their particular cultures. I started thinking about what women around the world are doing with their bodies, and how deeply distracted women are from the real work of life, which is running the world, leading, coming up with new ideas and policies. Like with *Vagina Monologues*, people are telling me stories. The project is called *Points of Reentry*.

I think women are at the peak of self-mutilation and self-hatred, that probably more women dislike their bodies, hurt their bodies, starve themselves, in the world today than ever in history. We say it's in the name of beauty, but I think it's in the name of distraction. We're terrified of taking responsibility for the world and being targets. It's so much easier to obsess about how flat your stomach is than to take a stand. You dis-em-body yourself.

AG: THIS DISTRACTION KEEPS WOMEN FROM TAKING POWER?

EE: Absolutely. The disembodiment of women is manifest everywhere. Why is skinny what people want to be? It's about literally giving away your power. You're no longer bodied, you're not inhabiting anything. You're gone. There's going to come a point where women reenter, where we come back into our bodies. And everyone will find their point of reentry. That's my vision.

AG: IN *NECESSARY TARGETS* THERE'S A COMMUNITY OF BOSNIAN WOMEN, AND FOR A TIME, THE VISITING AMER-ICANS — MELISSA, WHO IS AN ACADEMIC, AND JS, THE PSY-CHIATRIST — BECOME A PART OF THAT COMMUNITY. BUT THEY RETURN TO AMERICA, AND WE SEE JS SITTING IN HER PARK AVENUE LIVING ROOM, WEARING THE CLOTHES SHE WORE IN BOSNIA. WHAT IS YOUR FEELING ABOUT JS; IS SHE STILL PART OF THAT COMMUNITY?

EE: Yes. I think JS's life is completely different when she comes back. I think that an understanding of community is in her now, and the hunger to make that community in America is in her. I'd like to think that she stops being a Park Avenue psychiatrist and goes and works in a prison. That's my little fantasy about JS.

AG: THERE ARE NO RESOLUTIONS IN THE PLAY, NEITHER FOR THE BOSNIAN WOMEN NOR FOR THE TWO AMERI-CANS.

EE: I want the audience to draw their own conclusions about these characters — and themselves. The ending asks, 'What happens when you're affected by people?' Do you change or do you just hold that inside you? And is holding it inside you a change?

AG: WHY DO YOU THINK WOMEN ALL OVER THE WORLD TALK WITH YOU SO READILY?

EE: Because I identify with them. Because I'm not coming to them as an outsider. Most of the situations I've been in involve people, like me, who have been abused. I didn't suffer the atrocities in a war, but I was almost murdered by my father, I was raped by my father, I was destroyed on a certain level. So I'm not scared when I go into those worlds with them. It's actually very familiar. People sense when you are scared or judgmental. Actually, homeless shelters, to me, are the safest places I ever go. The same with prisons. I know that sounds bizarre, but when I first walked into a homeless shelter, it was the first time I felt at home. I don't have to pretend. I've always felt like an orphan, a nomad, an outsider. And there's such a deep level of honesty in a shelter, and such community, that you don't have to pretend.

AG: YOU CROSS BOUNDARIES.

EE: I hope so. I feel I'm just beginning. Just recently, I've felt like I've begun to get it. Now I could write a play — I'm beginning to get a hint of what that means. For so much of my life I've been catching up. I always have this feeling that I should be much further ahead than I am. But I feel more confidence — particularly with the form. *The Vagina Monologues* has given me the courage to venture into other areas with humor, because it broke through something and because it was able to hold that material and not frighten people. Humor's the key.

So much of my life has been weighed down by the desperate need to be approved of, to be recognized and acknowledged. To be loved. I'm now in a place where I feel okay. I exist. I feel I have the right to exist. This realization has freed up a deeper creative self, which just wants to explore without worrying about approval or validation. This feels very exciting. I feel free. I gave my father the first forty-some years of my life, and the next forty are mine. ▽

The Five Lesbian Brothers

The Five Lesbian Brothers are a New York City–based collective of writers and performers. Maureen Irini Angelos, A.K.A. Moe, was born and raised in Washington, D.C.; Dominique Dibbell hails from New Haven, Connecticut; Barbara Joan Davy, A.K.A. Babs, grew up in Minneapolis; Lisa Kron is from Lansing, Michigan; and Peg Healey was born on Long Island, where she also grew up.

Their plays and productions include *Voyage to Lesbos* (1990), wherein a group of women save one of their own from a fate worse than death (heterosexual marriage); *Brave Smiles . . . Another Lesbian Tragedy* (1992), a satire on an earlier generation's films about orphaned girls who go bad; *The Secretaries* (1994), which involves a female cabal at a lumbermill; and *Brides of the Moon* (1997), in which female astronauts are stranded in space, en route to service horny male astronauts. They have also authored *The Five Lesbian Brothers' Guide to Life,* subtitled *A Collection of Helpful Hints and Fabricated Facts for Today's Gay Girl* (Simon and Schuster, 1997). Currently, the Brothers are working on a project called *Scary Love,* which Dominique describes as 'a multiculti-age-sexuality piece about trying to find love in a perverted city (New York).'

An interview with Moe, Babs, Lisa, and Peg took place on October 27, 1999, at Lisa and Peg's apartment in New York City. Dominique subsequently wrote her responses to their edited interview.

• • •

AG: HOW DID EACH OF YOU BECOME INVOLVED WITH THEATER?

MOE: I was a child prodigy. No. I began doing plays when I was a very young child, at my mother's encouragement. We went to the theater a lot when I was a kid. The bus-and-truck companies of whatever was rolling through D.C. Big Broadway musicals. Then in high school I really became enamored and decided that that was what I wanted to pursue for a profession. I moved to New York and studied theater at New York University. My parents actually endorsed that idea, after some disappointment that I wasn't going to medical school.

BABS: You still could, you know. Go to medical school.

MOE: My father, 'til the day he died said, 'Well, when you go to medical school . . . '

AG: WHAT KIND OF ROLE DID YOU PLAY?

MOE: We tended to do things like *Arsenic and Old Lace*. School plays.

BABS: Did you play Cary Grant, Moe? That would be a perfect part in *Arsenic and Old Lace*.

MOE: It would be a good part. Actually, I wasn't in *Arsenic and Old Lace*. I did *You're a Good Man, Charlie Brown* and I was in *The Sound of Music* in a dinner theater in Washington. I played the Young Postulant. That's a whole other story.

PEG: I started doing theater at a very young age also, because [*THE-ATRICAL INTONATION*] I come from a theatrical family. My father was an elementary school music teacher and he used to put on these incredible productions. He wrote them, and he wrote the music, and he'd have the sixth grade orchestra play. My favorite thing was going backstage and seeing that everything was two-dimensional. I wrote my first play in fourth grade and performed it for all the 'little kids' — the second graders. My first cross-dressing role was Bernardo in *West Side Story* in sixth grade, where we all sang to the cast album and performed dances choreographed by Mrs. Greenblatt, our gym teacher. Then in high school I was a techie and just fell in love with everybody who was onstage. When I got to college, in Oneonta, New York, I started performing, mostly in contemporary plays: Lanford Wilson, Brecht — I did Grusha in *Caucasian Chalk Circle* — Tennessee Williams. I played Maxine in *The Night of the Iguana*. I was always playing the bitch. I never got to do any classical stuff, which made me kind of mad. I still want to do Shakespeare, the Greeks. I took this great contemporary theater class with one professor whom I loved, Richard Siegfried, and he brought us down to New York. We saw Mabou Mines and Wooster Group and Squat Theatre, and I just wanted to come down here and do all that. This was the early 1980s.

AG: DID YOU WANT TO ACT?

PEG: Yeah. Although I always wrote, too. Both those things.

DOMINIQUE: I was born into it. My mother was an actress, then later a performance artist, director, and teacher. My first acting experience was in nursery school — a Christmas pageant or something. I was a cat. I hated theater when I got to high school, because I felt I would never get cast. I had really small breasts and I felt uncomfortable being sexy or romantic with men. Then I saw performance art and it was like, 'Okay, now we're talking.'

LISA: I never saw a play until I was in junior high school. When I was a kid, I was in a Lansing Young Adult Players production of *The Hobbitt*, a musical! I played Willum, the Troll. Cross-dressing, one could say. It's interesting, looking back, how easily cross-dressing came to me. I was always making up plays with my cousins, and in my Hebrew school we did these very elaborate Purim plays. It never occurred to me not to play a male role.

PEG: I don't think it occurs to most kids. They can be whoever they want.

LISA: Then in high school, I didn't do plays. I hated my high school. I didn't do anything except sulk. But I was dramatic. I was very concerned with figuring out how to hold an audience in a conversation and how to be funny. That was a pretty conscious study that I undertook for myself.

AG: DO YOU REMEMBER WHY?

LISA: Well, I was extremely shy. In elementary school I remember thinking about how people talked — I was always listening for an interesting inflection. I wanted to make the way that I talked interesting and unusual. I had this dramatic, funny way of speaking that I developed with a great amount of concentration. I have no idea now what it sounded like, but for a long time it was a very conscious thought that I wanted people to say, 'She's the funniest girl I know.' So I made a very deliberate study of how to be funny but not be obnoxious. Once I became a teenager, it became clear to me that I was going to just disappear if I wasn't funny, that I wasn't going to get attention for being a girl. If I wanted not to completely fade I had to figure out how to be funny.

AG: MUCH OF THE BROTHERS' WORK IS VIRULENTLY COMIC. DO YOU THINK THAT WOMEN CAN SAY MORE THROUGH COMEDY THAN OTHER GENRES?

PEG: I'd say that applies to everyone. I think when you want to challenge someone with new ideas you have to sweeten the deal a little bit with humor. That's the way human nature works. If you're going to talk about something really dark, it has to contain something light, or no one is going to let it in.

LISA: This is also a moment in history that's suspicious of earnestness of any kind. It's a very ironic time, so earnestness is looked on as being kind of naïve. In the 1970s there was a lot of didactic, kind of self-important theater, and I think the backlash against that has continued.

MOE: But there was also a lot of interesting experimentation that doesn't happen anymore. People trying to challenge form.

LISA: I guess that's what I'm trying to say. That endeavor to say something political — people look askance at that. So that's why humor is a necessary tool at this moment. I think it's also true that any good work contains humor, because that's a critical element of human nature.

But I don't know if things always have to funny to be effective; I think at this moment in history it's helpful.

BABS: I think that if you're a woman and a lesbian it's really an advantage to have humor. If you're in the minority or saying unpopular things, it helps to use humor to get your message across.

AG: IS THE WHITE, MALE, HETEROSEXUAL AMERICAN CULTURE LESS AFRAID OF WOMEN IF THERE IS HUMOR?

MOE: I would say they listen more. I don't know if it's a fear thing. Like in *The Secretaries,* we said things in a humorous way that I don't think we could have said in a straightforward way. We talk about women's body issues, our self-images, images of ourselves that we construct because of our environments. I think to talk in a straightforward manner about how really poisonous and toxic those images and environments can be — already, that sentence that just came out of my mouth, nobody was listening. But if I say all that in a humorous way . . . the message has a sugar coating, but it's still pungent.

LISA: I think that's true. The rule is: men are universal, women are specific; so those issues that are particularly true for women . . .

AG: WHAT RULE? WHERE IS THIS RULE COMING FROM?

MOE: The Lisa Kron rule book.

LISA: I think that's the way audiences receive things . . .

PEG: Yes.

LISA: . . . that the male protagonist is a stand-in for the universal, that male problems are universal problems. That's why males are conceived of as suffering, and women are thought of as whining.

BABS: And could never write *Death of a Salesman.*

LISA: Right. Our stories are not about the human condition, but about . . .

PEG: . . . the specific person.

LISA: With *The Secretaries*, one of the main themes was the way women are enforcers of sexism, the way women torment other women. They're sort of agents of the patriarchy themselves. But once you start to say words like *misogyny, patriarchy,* then you tap into a whole negative thing. Because, you know, the backlash against the Feminist Movement worked very well. And even I start to think, 'God, it's so didactic and heavy-handed.' So, I think Moe's right that you wrap it in this delicious package of humor and arresting images.

But *The Secretaries* was talking about issues that have so seldom been talked about that they were not recognizable to men. Men saw the cartoony violence that went on, which had to do with these secretaries hacking up a man with his own chain saw every thirty days. But the more affecting violence, the more realistic violence, the emotional violence between these women — it didn't even register with the men because they had never seen it before. The humor and the theatricality let the play run on two tracks. So it could be interesting and entertaining to people who weren't getting that message, but for many women, and I'm sure some men as well, there was also this other layer that they recognized fully. And that was more exciting because they hadn't seen it before.

PEG: I think you reach more people with humor.

DOMINIQUE: We often take great pains to explain that *The Secretaries* isn't a revenge fantasy, that it's not a man-hating play. But I think at its heart is a good deal of rage. The rage of all women condensed to a point (as lesbianism was once described). Only we aren't on the streets, arms raised and fists clenched. The times have changed. Our expression is more implosion that explosion. One might say it is a feminine reaction to anger, to turn it within. We swallowed those horrible images (the panty hose as well as the blood) and regurgitated them. There is no getting around the cathartic fantasy element of the final killing scene. We walked a very clever line so that nobody could dismiss us as man-hating lesbian freaks, but there is an element of that.

AG: WHOM DO YOU WRITE FOR THEN?

PEG: Ourselves. And Holly Hughes of course.

AG: IT SOUNDS, LISA, AS THOUGH YOU ARE TRYING TO WRITE FOR A WIDE-RANGING, MAINSTREAM AUDIENCE.

LISA: I want to feel that the work has resonance beyond the people in the room. That's what makes the work interesting. You can't control how it's received, but I want it to be about something human.

AG: BUT DOES A MAINSTREAM AUDIENCE ERASE YOUR WORK'S LESBIAN AND FEMINIST CONTENT?

LISA: The way your audience receives a play controls what the play is about to a certain extent. And that's the art of it. For a play to work well, you provide sixty percent, seventy-five percent, and your audience interacts with it. That's true of any work of art. That's what makes it art, where the viewer and the presenter intersect. I remember doing stand-up comedy and realizing it was funnier if I didn't complete a sentence but let the audience do it. If I had a punch line and then led the audience to fill it in. That interaction is the most exciting thing that can happen in a theater. It's true, there could be a very upsetting, revolting thing that happened if we did *The Secretaries* for an audience that saw it in a conventional, misogynist way. It would be really upsetting.

BABS: *The Secretaries* was done up in Wellfleet, Massachusetts, by this company that was straight women, and Peggy and Lisa saw it and they thought it was really great fun. But the actors totally missed the whole dark part of the play, so that in the end, things didn't really add up the way they should have.

AG: BABS, HOW DID YOU GET INTO THEATER?

BABS: I don't know. When Peggy was talking, I remembered that I wrote a play when I was in the third grade and got to perform it for the other third grade classes. All I remember is that it had a wagon in it and involved my friend — I don't remember what her name was. My sister, Kate, was the actress. She went to drama classes, and we went to see her in plays. When I got to New York, I was hanging out at the WOW Café because I was coming out as a lesbian, so I was ushering and stuff like that and I got sucked in, onto the stage. Which is what I wanted secretly, but it terrified me. I used to go and sit in the audience and get nervous just thinking about, 'What if that was me up there?' and get myself into a whole big lather. And I'd have to remind myself that it was intermission now, and I was just in the audience, I didn't have to worry. It's been a wild ride.

AG: HOW DID YOU ALL MEET?

BABS: At the WOW Café [Women's One World Café], in the mid-1980s.

MOE: Babs, Peg, and I had been in a couple of shows of Lisa's — *Paradykes Alley* and *Paradykes Lost*. Dominique was our stage manager for *Paradykes Lost*. She had just come to WOW. We shared a sensibility. We were friends. Lisa and I had talked about having a company, because the way things worked at WOW, you did one show with this group of people and the next show with another group of people, and there was no real carryover. People were creating shows all the time — and this is still going on at WOW — but there was no carryover of skills. Like, how do you make a play? The shows just disappeared, and we never saw them again, and some of them were pretty great. So Lisa and I had talked about starting a company for the purpose of developing our own vocabulary about how to write work and for purposes of touring. Because we thought we could *get rich!* off the theater. [*LOTS OF LAUGHTER*]

MOE: Yeah, it was totally a fairy tale. No, we didn't really think that, but we thought we could tour. We thought a small unit would be tourable.

LISA: Because I asked Peggy Shaw — Shaw and Lois Weaver had formed the Split Britches Company with Deb Margolin — and Peggy said, 'Oh, yeah, you can tour. Yeah, just get on a plane and go to London.' I said, 'Really? With no bookings?' 'Naah, you'll meet people while you're there. You'll figure it out.' And I said, 'You can make enough money to live?' And she said, 'Oh, yeah. You'll be great.' 'And you can buy your food and everything?' 'Oh, you steal your food.' And she wasn't kidding. That's what they did.

MOE: We kind of shared a humor, and we were friends.

AG: HOW DID YOU COME UP WITH YOUR NAME?

DOMINIQUE: It was during our first or maybe our second production of *Voyage to Lesbos*. I was working at a law firm on the graveyard shift and I would get pretty loopy around 4 A.M. I was writing in our idea notebooks, which we would pass around, and I doodled this sketch of all of us and titled it The Five Lesbian Brothers. We'd been fooling around and acting like a silly familial circus troupe or something, and it captured the sense of bonding we were starting to feel. We were falling in love with each other. Anyway, we decided to put the sketch in our programs for the show, and the name took.

AG: HOW DID THE BROTHERS' STYLE EVOLVE? WAS THIS A STYLE THAT WAS ALSO AT WOW?

BABS: When I came to WOW, Lois Weaver and Peggy Shaw were still in and out of WOW. Holly Hughes was still there. Nobody had any money, so that really contributed to the aesthetic. The shows had to come up and down really quick. There was an ironic, New York sense of humor, and some people just didn't have it, and we did.

PEG: I think we had sort of a model from WOW, which was this pure collaboration. Like nobody's in charge. Lisa has said often, 'Oh, well, I imagined the Brothers would get together and I'd be the head of it.' [*LAUGHTER*] And I think it took her a little time to get over that notion. But we have really bought a hundred percent into this total collaboration thing, to the point where our first production, *Voyage to Lesbos*, didn't have a director — we directed it ourselves. And, you know, you learn from mistakes like that. We decided pretty much we always needed a director. In *Voyage to Lesbos*, we wrote our own characters, and we found that did not serve the piece.

AG: WHY NOT?

PEG: What happens is that certain people have different strengths. Certain people talk more, certain people will be more aggressive or more exhibitionist. So you get sort of an imbalance. What we did for *Brave Smiles* — the play after *Voyage to Lesbos* — is decide, 'All right, we're all writing these characters, and everybody can write on every character and in fact should.' And we didn't cast it until the end. And we kept that process, because it worked so well. Everybody's writing for the project, everybody's writing with the script in mind, and you're not as affected by ego and, like, how much stage time will I have. Because we're not just writers, we're performers, too. It's less every woman for herself and keeps bringing the project around to the strength of us, which is our strength as a whole. The best example of that is *The Secretaries*, which was a true collaboration down to the very last minute.

AG: COULD YOU WALK ME THROUGH THE PROCESS? HOW DO YOU BEGIN TO CREATE A PROJECT?

BABS: I was just looking through stuff in my closet and I came across the big piece of butcher paper for *Brides of the Moon*, and some of the stuff on that was really funny, that never got into the play, like, 'Bridget takes blood from Dai Dai.'

We get together, chat a good deal, gossip. In the early days we watched a fair amount of television. Sometimes half our time is spent with feelings — what's going on with us internally. Then we start free-writing. We just keep the pen moving for a certain amount of time.

AG: ALL OF YOU TOGETHER?

BABS: We're sitting in a circle. We have a timer, we set it for ten minutes, we all write for ten minutes then we read what we wrote. We listen to that, then write again for ten minutes, then we all read again. And pretty soon images from each other's writing tend to cross . . . pollinate. We also do improvs. A wide variety — without sound at all, or with certain limitations physically. And then we start gradually adding the ideas from the writings, ideas about character, location, objects. We sort of just play. And we have this big piece of paper that Lois Weaver taught us about, to keep track of all the images and any songs that we think of.

AG: EVEN IF YOU DON'T KNOW YET WHERE YOU'RE GOING TO USE THEM.

BABS: Right. Anything that has some resonance, that strikes us as worth keeping.

LISA: It's sort of a funny, backwards way of writing a play. There's a group consciousness that develops, which is not anything that any one person can control. It's not like we come in and say, 'We're going to write a play about X.' In the very beginning, people might have a newspaper article that's interesting. In *Voyage to Lesbos*, the main inspiration was a book Moe had that was a 1950s psychoanalytic study called *Voyage from Lesbos*. With *The Secretaries*, we were obsessed with the Lorena Bobbitt case, which was going on at the time. Also with the television series *Twin Peaks*. That obsession started with *Voyage to Lesbos*, but it lingered. We kept getting kicked out of rehearsal spaces and ending back at Babs' tiny little apartment watching *Twin Peaks*.

AG: WHY WERE YOU OBSESSED WITH *TWIN PEAKS*, AND HOW DID THAT EMERGE IN THE FINAL SCRIPT?

MOE: My obsession with *Twin Peaks* had a lot to do with the fact that it was clearly *not* rehearsal. In other words, procrastination. I enjoyed slipping into the creepy world of the Northwestern lumber town and I think that is the element that lingered into *The Secretaries* — the scary isolation of the beautiful woods.

BABS: And we watched the film *Seven Brides for Seven Brothers*.

LISA: Right. Because at first we wanted to call the play *Seven Brides for Five Brothers*, but then we didn't like that title.
But anyway, we do this thing of writing and reading, writing and reading, and there are arresting images that start to stick with us, and a world eventually lifts up out of this process. Places and characters and images and dramatic actions mostly. So we've got all these elements, and we have to figure out — what's this play going to be about? What is the story, and why is the story worth telling? And that, I think, is the second part of the process. We start to write scenes. We'll have an exercise where we say, 'Okay, everybody write ten actions that happen

in the course of this play.' Or, 'You've got twenty minutes, write the plot of this play.' And we just do free-writing on the plot of the play, and then we'll say, 'Ooh, I like that, I like that, let's try to put that together.' And then we get horribly stuck and have what we call 'The Worst Moment So Far,' where we feel like we're never going to get a play out of this. But by keeping at it, we have a play.

It goes from the specific to the broad. It's backwards compared to what an individual playwright would do, which would be to come in with a concept and then add details. We start with tons of details and then we figure out what is the play and why the play. Not just the plot but the theme, which makes itself clear ultimately but is something that is discovered very late in the process.

BABS: *The Secretaries* is a prime example, because we were entranced with the *Seven Brides for Seven Brothers* idea, and we rented the tape of the musical and were horrified that it's basically a rape musical, and the women are oh-so-glad it's happened. That was sort of in the back of our heads. And we kept plugging away with the lumberjacks, and it was going to be about the lumberjacks and their mail-order brides, and we just had the most fruitless improvs until Lisa kept saying, 'Well, what about the secretaries at the lumbermill?' (We decided that the lumberjacks were at a lumbermill somewhere along the line.) We all knew about secretaries pretty much, because of working in temp jobs and offices and stuff. And Dom had been reading about these motorcycle gangs, girl gangs that catch guys and drag them behind their cycles and torture them for the hell of it.

AG: WERE YOU INTO CHAIN SAW MOVIES?

MOE: No. But you don't have to be. Everyone knows the structure of that kind of slaughtery movie, so we really didn't have to watch them. The convention is already there.

BABS: Everybody assumes we were watching chain saw movies when really we were watching *Seven Brides for Seven Brothers*, and that's what took us there.

PEG: The way we work together, we don't consciously try to go someplace. You can see that in our plays. We let our subconscious dictate what it is we care about, and so when one person writes something out of her subconscious, and everyone else sits up and pays attention, those are the things that end up being in our plays. If it feels like it's going to resonate for the five of us, hopefully it will resonate for the hundreds of people who end up coming to see it.

LISA: The other element that I think good writers always have is to write from what's going on with them. With *The Secretaries*, I initially thought I wasn't going to be able to do the play. What happens if you have a tight group and one person leaves? What kind of resentment is there? We have these 'check-ins,' and if there's tension, we say, 'Okay, let's have a check-in,' and we go around and everybody gets to say how they're doing, with no talk-back, no cross-discussion about it. Those feelings are a part of our process, and we put them into the work. So we initially thought that, 'Okay, this is really a source of great tension in the group. Why don't we figure out how those emotional currents can be used in the work?' And what happened was, instead of writing about a closed group where somebody leaves, the play was about a closed group where somebody new comes in.

AG: WHAT HAPPENS IF YOU DISAGREE?

LISA: Fist fight.

MOE: War of attrition.

AG: WHILE YOU'RE SITTING AROUND TALKING, DO YOU GET UP AND WORK OUT A PHYSICAL PIECE OF BUSINESS?

PEG: I think we are all very physical performers. We use improvs in all areas of the development of our work and will start out with improvs that are just physical, that have no text. We like to find movement, or to find things through the body, before we rationalize and verbalize. We'll start very early on with just movement improvisation, but later we might say, 'All right, this is a scene where Patty and Susan are together after work,' and everybody will take a crack at getting up and improvising those characters. One very fruitful improv that I remember doing for *The Secretaries* was Susan Curtis in court. We did this trial: 'What's your name?' 'My name's Susan Curtis.' 'Where were you on this night?' You can get a lot of information about a character from that kind of improv. In *Voyage to Lesbos* I remember we each sang a song from our character. That totally informed my character of Bonnie. We taped them and transcribed them.

AG: WHEN DO YOU CAST?

BABS: Sometimes it's been about two weeks before we open a show. We always open them at WOW.

LISA: We've written always with a production already scheduled, so we're writing until we go into rehearsal.

MOE: We do the casting ourselves, without the director. Before she comes. We say, 'All right, what does everyone want to play?' We make our list, give our preferences, and then we negotiate it among ourselves. A couple of times, Kate Stafford, who has worked with us as a director most of the time, has given us suggestions for changing the casting, which we've taken.

PEG: It has become frustrating to me, after ten years, that this is our stable of five actors. What happened with *The Secretaries* is that certain relationships which had been in previous productions seemed to be recreated, and we wanted to do different things. So we try to switch them around, so that we're stretching ourselves as actors or not recreating similar relationships that people have seen us in onstage before. That's where Kate really comes in, because she's able to see those things more clearly.

AG: YOU COULD RECAST THEM NOW.

LISA: It's interesting that you say that. Once they're cast, you can't imagine it. I would look at any of the roles the Brothers have played and completely identify that Brother with that role. In the writing of a play — as we're writing and reading, writing and reading — we switch roles all the time, and there are certain delightful things about the way this one reads this character and that one reads that character. But after we're performing them, that character belongs to that actor.

PEG: We did a reading at the Public Theater of *Scary Love*, which was at the stage where we had all the writing but were nowhere near having a play. So that night we all played all the characters, and people came up to me afterwards and said, 'Wow, it was so exciting to see you all do this one character.' That would be a fun thing to try.

BABS: Yeah, people told us we should think of producing a show where we all play all the characters, because you would be able to see different facets of the same character and different facets of the same person. But I think it would raise hell with our egos.

PEG: That was my idea: that the five of us would write a one-woman show and we all would play her.

MOE: I have often thought about recasting the shows. Sometimes in rehearsal I'd become enamored of a character that doesn't end up being the one I play and I think, 'You know, I would really love to do that.' I would hope some day we could, but I don't think we will.

BABS: I feel about those plays that they're all really one play and that in every play we have a wedding, in every play we deal with heterosexuality, in every play we deal with brutalizing men. We sat here and read through the plays out loud prior to publication, so we could edit them, and I was struck by all the similarities.

AG: DO YOU IMPROVISE ONSTAGE?

MOE: No. Sometimes there's a little bit of it, like the part in *Brides of the Moon* where Slotya has sex with the monkey. In the script, it just says, 'Slotya has sex with the monkey,' but in performance Lisa and Peg did a funny thing that's more elaborate than that.

LISA: We were trying to remember what we did for the book, but we couldn't. It was very physical, and there were two versions of it.

MOE: It wasn't the same every night.

BABS: It changed a little bit.

LISA: Do I do that more than other Brothers? As we were going through the plays, I thought, 'Oh, I've got a bunch of places where I just make it up as I go along.'

MOE: Yeah, you do.

BABS: As we were sitting down to edit the plays, we realized that we've got stage directions which have become warm and fuzzy friends, but they don't bear any resemblance to what we actually did onstage.

AG: THE CRITIC JOHN BELL CAME DOWN ON *BRAVE SMILES* BECAUSE HE THOUGHT THAT THE LESBIANS CAME TO AN UNFORTUNATE END, JUST AS THEY DO IN THE MOVIES THAT YOU ARE PARODYING. WHAT'S YOUR RESPONSE TO THAT?

PEG: I have a good response to that. It's being performed by five totally out lesbians who are happy and healthy and laughing, and normally there are a bunch of lesbians in the audience who are laughing along with us and saying, 'The things you're talking about, we can laugh at them now because it's a part of our history, and we love it and we honor it and we cherish it, but nobody faces this anymore.'

LISA: But when we first performed that play, in the early nineties, I think it's going a little bit far to say that it was over. Things have changed in eight years. It used to be, if you heard there was going to be a lesbian kiss on *L.A. Law*, all the lesbians would stay home to watch. There weren't a lot of lesbian images. One of the things we talked about when we were writing *Brave Smiles* was how there's a love-hate relationship with all those lesbian stories with tragic endings: Radclyffe Hall's novel, *The Well of Loneliness*; Jane Chambers' play, *Last Summer at Bluefish Cove*. On the one hand, the ending of the story was always horrible. On the other hand, it was a way of learning that there were other lesbians in the world. So there's an affection for those stories as well.

But I think Peg's right. There is a triumph in exposing the ridiculousness that to be a lesbian is to meet a tragic end. And what exposes that in *Brave Smiles* is partly the overblown nature of the demise of these five orphans, but also that five happy-go-lucky lesbians are making and producing this play.

MOE: There's a wink in it.

LISA: And there is a sadness in the play, which I really love. That's what makes the play more interesting — that it is really funny and also there is a melancholy to it.

PEG: I think that's what separates us from Theatre of the Ridiculous, which people always associate us with. Thanks in part to our director, Kate Stafford, who makes us walk that line of never going all the way into parody but keeping the real center of these people whom we portray.

AG: HOW WOULD YOU DESCRIBE YOUR STYLE?

PEG: I don't think it is camp. It's ironic: but the more serious we are, the funnier we are. I feel we have what camp doesn't necessarily have: sincerity and truth. Although camp has truth in it. What we do feels to me like a different style than just plain camp. I hope that's true.

DOMINIQUE: Very deadpan. Parody. I would say parody is the essence of our style. One of the issues I had with *Brides of the Moon* was that I didn't know what, if anything, we were parodying. Without that, I was lost. *Voyage* was pulp, *Brave Smiles* was straightforward satire. *Secretaries* was satire of slasher movies. Of course, it's parody with a heart. Just when you think all we are about is making vicious fun of people who hate us, we throw in a heartfelt moment.

MOE: It's satirical definitely. And sometimes I think it's very campy. But sometimes the plays are really dramas, and I don't know if that opposes camp or is in the same camp as camp. There's some slight difference that I don't think I can put my finger on.

LISA: I don't think camp allows for pain, really. It doesn't take anything seriously, and we do have things that we take seriously.

BABS: Isn't camp about the visual? What's campy about *The Secretaries* is that we're lesbians dressed up in drag as straight women. Any campy moments come from that more than the content.

LISA: One of the big aesthetic decisions in *The Secretaries* was not to have great big wigs, not to have parodies of secretaries' clothes. Those costumes were clothes you would see in any office. We had a potential person to work on the wigs, who had worked at the Ridiculous, and she was like, 'All right, I'm going to make big wigs and put a notepad and a pen in them.' And we said, 'No. That's not where we're at. It has to look really, really, really real. So there's something more grounded than camp.'

MOE: There's a certain level of fabulousness. In *Brides of the Moon*, we could go out one door and come in another and have a whole other costume on. But that's just basic, raw theatricality. Fabulous and fun.

AG: *THE SECRETARIES* IS FARCE, AND FARCE DOES START FROM A REAL PREMISE.

LISA: Why do you think *The Secretaries* is farce?

AG: IT HAS A FARCE RHYTHM. IT STARTS SEDATELY, AND THEN THINGS GO OUT OF CONTROL.

LISA: It feels more Greek to me. People compared it a lot to *The Bacchae*.

MOE: I think that's about content rather than pace.

AG: HOW DID THE IDEA FOR ROLLING CHAIRS COME ABOUT? AT NEW YORK THEATRE WORKSHOP, THEY IMME-DIATELY CONVEYED THE PIECE'S COMIC SENSIBILITY.

MOE: Part of that was just a necessary convention because we were touring the show, and how could we have five women sitting at their desks? Amy Shock, our set designer for the first version at WOW, had made a little piece of wood, a panel that sat in front of us which we could swing in and out, and which we tapped our hands on as though at a typewriter.

PEG: Like an airline tray or something.

LISA: Amy did that original design with the rolling chairs with the little attachments, and Jim Nicola, New York Theatre Workshop's artistic director, really liked that. He really pushed to keep that homemade sense, that imaginative thing where there really weren't any typewriter keyboards.

AG: WHAT DID THE SET FOR *BRIDES OF THE MOON* LOOK LIKE?

BABS: The traveling set was just a wardrobe rack to hang stuff on. It had a piece of canvas and a little window that signified outer space, and it had kind of a Bullwinkle drawing on it, of spaceship controls and a coffeemaker.

MOE: Well, that was for half of the tour. Then we had a painted traveler for the other half.

BABS: And lots of imagination needed. The set at NYTW had everything you could ever want and probably didn't serve the play as well.

PEG: I think the difference between the touring set and the Workshop set was that the touring set was movable — things could come on and off, so that center stage could be either the Powers household or space. Then when two things happened at once, they were able to coexist in the same area. The set at NYTW took up the whole stage. It was huge. Space was above, and Earth was down below. The set hardened the play in a way that ultimately didn't serve the script, because it drew such a clear line between those two places. In the play, you start off in space, you start off on Earth, and little by little you're back and forth, back and forth, until both places are the same place. But that was harder to do with the set at NYTW.

AG: DO YOU THINK YOUR WORK HAS BECOME MORE COMPLEX?

LISA: I would say we've become more concerned with form. I think we weren't at first concerned with form at all, and we've become more concerned with through line and plot.

MOE: We're better writers I think.

LISA: The playwright Sybille Pearson was our dramaturg on *The Secretaries,* and that was an incredible experience.

AG: AT WHAT POINT IN YOUR PROCESS DID SHE COME IN?

LISA: Generally we write a first draft and tour it, and we don't write while we're performing. Sometimes we keep a notebook of what we want to work on when we write again, but we don't feel like we can combine the writing and the performing, because then you start to rewrite out of panic and ego. Traditionally what we've done is do rewrites before we bring it back to New York. So *The Secretaries* had toured, and we knew there were certain problems with it, and we went into an intensive rewriting period. We really totally rewrote the second act of that play. Sybille was present in that period.

MOE: But you know, she was present and not present, because my memory is that she didn't spend a tremendous amount of time with us. She was extremely efficient in identifying what we needed to work on and asking us the right kind of questions to get us to do that. She was like a brilliant play therapist. She didn't tell us what to do. She just said, 'What are you trying to do, what are you trying to say? Whose story are you telling?' That's what she kept saying to us: 'Whose story is this?'

PEG: She'd say, 'This is what I see. Is that what you want me to see?'

LISA: It was so fabulous, because it was all about who we were and what we wanted to say, not about what she would have done if she were writing the play. Which of course is what you want in that role. So generous.

AG: DO YOU LIKE BEING MORE CONCERNED ABOUT FORM? LISA DOES. SHE'S NODDING.

BABS: Yes and no.

MOE: I don't. Moe doesn't.

BABS: The Brothers' work is about characters, and it doesn't necessarily matter if it doesn't all add up. Our whole process — and the product — end up being about five very different things. The product is something you would never come up with if you wrote it on your own, and to try to hammer a plot out is not the best thing for it. But maybe it is. I don't know. If we continue with *Scary Love*, maybe we can get that mixture more equal — the plot and the characters together — and not have to sacrifice one for the other.

AG: DO YOU HAVE A DREAM PROJECT?

MOE: Yes. I do. I have a dream project that someone comes to us, somebody like Tony Kushner, and says, 'I want to write a play for you girls.' And he does. A fabulous star vehicle for all of us that we don't have to write, we just get to be in.

PEG: I can second that. Are you listening, Tony?

MOE: Ton?

LISA: I'd like Paula Vogel to write us a play.

PEG: I want Dorothy Allison to write us a play. She wrote the novel *Bastard Out of Carolina*. She writes fiction and nonfiction and the best lesbian sex stuff I've ever heard.

MOE: One of the ideas that we had when we were working on *Brides of the Moon* was to do a classic, to return to the Greeks. We were looking at the Greek plays. If somebody doesn't want to write us a star vehicle, then if they would just put us in something. Because I would love to just act with all of you guys without having the pressure of having to write the play, not to mention producing it and doing everything else that we have to do to get it up. That would be fabulous.

PEG: I would like to do a movie of *The Secretaries*.

MOE: Actually, a movie of *Brides of the Moon* would probably work really well.

AG: HOW DO YOU DEAL WITH GOING OFF AND DOING YOUR OWN THINGS AND THEN COMING BACK?

MOE: Well, we could talk about the bitterness, yes. [*LAUGHTER*] The anger. I think that we manage it well. It's difficult sometimes. It's hard enough for the five of us to schedule a meeting together when we're not doing other projects, when we just have day jobs. And if all five of us at one time wanted to go do our own projects, there would be no Brothers. There's kind of a balancing act that happens.

BABS: You can't not do the individual work, so whether it's good for the process or not, it's got to happen. And ultimately it is good for the process, because people would not be happy if we couldn't make room for that. But it's getting harder as we get older. We've been at this for ten years. I'm at the older end of the spectrum and I ran through my money, I ran up some debt, and I'm facing the music now. I'm back to a full-time job, five days a week. So I think my dreams are more modest now. The Brothers are the best thing and the worst thing that's ever happened to me.

DOMINIQUE: We just have to communicate a lot and be as honest as we can. It's similar to a romantic relationship. Of course, sometimes you grow apart. We're not married. Sometimes I'm not sure we're committed, so the pull to transform into something that is not the Five Brothers is always there and always considered a valid choice. After *Brides*, when we were all pretty down, some of our dearest fans were telling us that we *had* to stay together. That we were needed. But art doesn't work that way. We answer to our muses, not our public.

AG: DO CRITICS GET YOU?

BABS: Naah.

LISA: With *The Secretaries*, most of them missed the point — especially the men critics. But they didn't review it badly. I think we were in the right place at the right time. We started to do really competent, interesting work at the very moment when the institutional theaters in New York were opening themselves up to theater by lesbians, not as an oddity in a festival but as a part of the main theatrical season.

We had opportunities that the Split Britches Company, who were certainly my primary inspiration, didn't. And their work is stellar. I think the Brothers have had an unprecedented amount of success for a lesbian theater company.

MOE: Or for a women's theater company or for a collaborative theater company.

PEG: I think our accomplishment is not so much do critics get you or not get you. I think our accomplishment has been that we get reviewed. Critics pay attention to us. They certainly come see us and they evaluate our work as if it were Tony Kushner's work or any playwright's work.

BABS: But it is overlooked usually that we write it. They talk about the performances.

LISA: I would agree with that. I think the quality of our writing hasn't been properly appreciated, especially with *The Secretaries*. Mostly the play was seen as a pale imitation of Charles Ludlam. I felt at the time that that was the kind of thing that was happening to women in reviews, that men were being credited with originality much more easily than women. That we were doing something highly original and weren't being given credit. But reviews are reviews. There were reviews in San Francisco for *Brides of the Moon* that said this is the finest, most polished work the Brothers have ever done, and I did not know my lines when I went onstage. I've seen bad reviews for work that's good, good reviews for work that wasn't that good. The thing you really ask for is that the critics pay attention.

AG: COULD YOU ELABORATE ON WHAT YOU OWE TO SPLIT BRITCHES AS ARTISTS?

MOE: For hacking through the underbush.

LISA: When I first saw Split Britches, I had been in the theater department in my college, thinking, 'I care so much about being in the theater, and I care about it because it feels like it makes a difference. But these plays . . .' I was in *Picnic*, where I played Mrs. Potts, the neighbor lady, where my big monologue was about 'everything was so empty and then a man came into town, and I had a reason to live.' And it was just like rocks in my mouth. And *The Robber Bridegroom*, which is like *Seven Brides for Seven Brothers*. It's like, 'Oooh, kidnap her and rape her, she'll be happy for the rest of her life.' I remember sitting in college on my little single bed, in my dorm room, and thinking, 'I don't know what to do. I want to work in the theater, but I can't — it's just so abhorrent.' So when I saw Split Britches, not only was the work amazing to me because it was nonlinear, but they made it themselves. It was like a beautiful jewel that you could turn over and over, and every side was different. And the fact that they made it themselves — maybe I could do that. That was just a revelation.

PEG: I knew I was a lesbian when I was a little girl, but I didn't come out until after college. And seeing Peggy Shaw knead that dough in *Split Britches* (their first play) brought me out a lot further. The thing about watching Peggy and Lois and Holly Hughes and Carmelita Tropicana was that they weren't these sad lesbians who were trying to explain that they were like everyone else. They were like, 'You know what? I'm fucking fabulous, and if you don't get it, then you're left behind.' And that was a huge leap forward in lesbian theater, this given: 'Hey, we're all this thing, and this is what is great about us.'

LISA: Except it goes beyond that. It was so given that they never even said that. They never had to say they were fabulous because they were fabulous. They never had to come out because they were out. And that was part of the unbelievable miracle of it.

PEG: WOW variety nights were so amazing. You can't imagine what a lesbo fest that was. I was learning in my contemporary theater class that theater is the bread of life, and then you see Tennessee Williams and like, 'That's not my bread of life.' And then you see these women and you go, 'Oh, okay, I get it. I get why people make theater.'

LISA: For me, being at WOW was a process of unlearning all these stuffy old theater rules and having this outpouring of really, really messy creativity.

DOMINIQUE: WOW was amazing. Fabulous. I'll always remember

my first WOW meeting (I came on in 1987). I'd just moved from San Francisco, where the performance scene was typified by the Dance Brigade: very political, very rough-hewn, organic, hippie feel, though queer and feminist. I didn't like the scene too much. So I get to WOW, and here's this roomful of like thirty women, and all of them have my sense of humor. It was a very rich, very educational, very horny time for me.

MOE: I think WOW was a product of the times, of the eighties, in this neighborhood. Of there being the explosion of — well, I'll say performance art, to just throw everything in one bag. Everything from stand-up comedy to jello wrestling. Every kind of wild entertainment form, that we all participated in. Things were very disposable. We would do a show at WOW at eight o'clock and then tramp over to Avenue C to Club Chandelier for the ten o'clock show, and then we'd go to King Tut's Wawa Hut for the midnight show. It was almost like the old model of actors being trained by coming into a company and doing little roles over and over until they graduated to the larger roles. We had a lot of practice doing these funky, ephemeral shows. And that was a very eighties phenomenon. We came together at the end of that, in 1989, but we had had that education of those years before, at WOW and in the neighborhood.

LISA: I think that's really crucial.

PEG: And going full circle, back to what Moe was talking about, starting the Brothers and what happened, we didn't set out to start the Brothers. There wasn't this idea, 'We're going to start this theater company, and it's going to last this many years and create this many plays.' We started by saying, 'We all think alike, and what would happen if we did this?' And it just kept snowballing. It had a momentum of its own. And now we're sort of in the place where we don't know what the momentum is. We went to the top of a hill and now we're going back down hill and maybe up a higher hill. The momentum changes.

AG: HAS THE SCENE CHANGED AROUND YOU?

ALL: Oh, yeah.

LISA: Young people come and ask me all the time. Young people . . .

PEG: [*SINGS*] 'The fool on the hill.'

LISA: And they say, 'I'm working on this piece, where can I do it in the East Village?' And I don't know what to say anymore. I mean there's stuff down on the Lower East Side, but those people are up too late for me. There used to be ten million clubs here, and galleries and cafés.

PEG: You could really feel the tide turning when we did *The Secretaries*. Every theater that we went to on that tour asked us to do a financial appeal after the show. They had no money. Half those places that we used to tour are gone. All of them were in dire financial straits, and you could really feel that theater on that guerrilla level was disappearing.

AG: REAL ESTATE IS A PROBLEM.

MOE: Real estate. And the incentive to make money in other arms of the entertainment industry, like film and TV, are too great.

AG: THE BROTHERS CREATED SOMETHING FOR HBO, DIDN'T YOU?

DOMINIQUE: We were hired to write these ten-minute bits that would go between longer films in a program of lesbian short films. Peg wrote a parody of the *Twilight Zone* episode where William Shatner sees a gremlin on the wing of a plane. The other bit HBO picked was a parody of *Rescue 911* that involved some lesbians having loud sex in their tent in a campground, and the sounds being mistaken for a bear attack. But then the whole thing fell apart when the point person at HBO left.

MOE: Two years ago I went to Outwrite, a gay and lesbian writers' conference in Boston, and I went to a theater panel, and there were these young, scrubbed, fresh-faced little homosexuals coming up to the microphone to ask questions like, 'I'm starting a gay and lesbian theater company on Long Island, and I was just wondering if you have any advice for me.' I was in the audience and I was thinking, 'What would I tell these people? What would I tell these optimistic children?' Move to a different city, do not try to do it in New York.

PEG: There are people who think we've made lots of money as The Five Lesbian Brothers. Not a lot of people, but some. They find out you're still doing a day job, and they're like, 'Really!' My advice is: 'Go do it.' Do it for the love of doing it, because you're not going to get anything else out of it. And find the cheap way of doing it. WOW was ingenious. Have your own space and then you can do whatever you want. But you can't get that space anymore for what it used to cost.

MOE: I was talking to a friend about going through the plays and working on them for publication, and she said, 'You know, Moe, that must feel really great.' I was complaining that we weren't making any money, that we still couldn't make a living. And she said, 'It must feel really good to look at that work and know that you did all that for love.' And I thought, 'Yeah. Yeah.' It took a while for that to set in. But that is why we did it. Because despite my joke earlier on, we knew we weren't going to be rich from the theater.

Collaboration is a very labor-intensive process that requires tremendous human hours and human fortitude. But there is something to me, and I know to all of us, that is deeply rewarding, because the magical product that we make in the end is much more magical than anything I could have thought of by myself. The fun, the delight, that I get by being in a room with my Brothers and talking about ideas. Like when we were talking earlier about our process, I was getting all excited, like, 'Oh, let's do that again. I can't wait to do that again.' It doesn't happen a lot in our lives, that kind of exchange. Maybe in marriages and close relationships, familial relationships. I mean we are brothers after all. We are family. We are exchanging something really essential about ourselves with someone else. And I feel very lucky and grateful to have found my Brothers, because I know it doesn't happen very easily at all. ◆

Beth Henley

Beth Henley was born in Jackson, Mississippi, where she also grew up. Although Henley has lived in Los Angeles since 1976, and has written her plays there, she has spent a good part of her career introducing theatergoers to the people of Mississippi, whom she dramatizes with an acute eye and ear for their eccentricities, furies, and vulnerabilities.

In 1979, Henley wrote *Crimes of the Heart,* a poignant comedy about the lives and loves of the three Magrath sisters in the small Mississippi town of Hazlehurst, and in 1981 she was awarded The Pulitzer Prize for Drama. Subsequent plays include *The Miss Firecracker Contest* (1980); *The Wake of Jamey Foster* (1982); *The Debutante Ball* (1985); *The Lucky Spot* (1987); *Abundance* (1990); *Signature* (1990); *Control Freaks* (1992); *Revelers* (1994); and *Impossible Marriage* (1998), a comic fantasy about unpredictable love. In addition to writing plays, Henley has written filmscripts, including *Crimes of the Heart* (1986), *Nobody's Fool* (1986), and *Miss Firecracker* (1989).

Henley lives in Los Angeles with her son. This interview took place in Los Angeles on July 15, 1999.

• • •

AG: IN 1995 YOU GAVE BIRTH TO A FIRST BABY. CONGRAT-
ULATIONS.

BH: Thank you.

AG: WHY DID YOU WANT TO HAVE A CHILD AT THIS POINT
IN YOUR LIFE?

BH: I pictured five or six lives. In one, I pictured myself with eight
kids, and cooking spaghetti with an apron on. Well, no. Just lots of
dogs and a husband who works and loves me. That was one version
of a life that I didn't have. I'd probably kill myself immediately after
ten minutes of it, but one fleeting image of it sounds good. To love
my son is so great. To be in love with somebody like I'm in love with
him. My heart soars. Just to be with somebody like that is so rare.
And that's how much I love him

AG: ARE YOU WRITING ABOUT THIS YET?

BH: No. No. That sounds too saccharine, to write that. But I probably will write about him someday in some coded version.

AG: ARE YOU RAISING HIM BY YOURSELF?

BH: I have a nanny, but my nanny doesn't live with me. She picks
him up from school or wherever.

AG: YOU ONCE TOLD AN INTERVIEWER THAT YOU WISHED
YOU WERE THE SORT OF WOMAN WHO WANTED CHIL-
DREN, BUT YOU WERE NOT.

BH: I didn't want children, that's true. I was totally terrified of children. I didn't want the responsibility. I didn't want the distraction. I
didn't want the domesticity. I really, really wanted to do my work.
And to be free, in the sense of guilt-free about being able to travel. If
you are in the theater, you really have to be a gypsy, unless you have
a home in New York and your plays are always done there. But there
are about three people in the world that applies to.

AG: IN *IMPOSSIBLE MARRIAGE*, YOUR HEROINE, FLORAL, IS ENORMOUSLY PREGNANT. WHICH CAME FIRST, YOUR PREGNANCY OR YOUR PLAY?

BH: The pregnancy. I got the play commission, and my mother said, 'Would you please write a happy play,' because I had been writing these dark plays. 'You're pregnant and you don't want to upset this baby.' So I wrote part of the play before the baby was born and finished it afterwards.

I had been at a wedding while I was pregnant. Actually, I had been the bridesmaid. It was such an odd notion, being a bridesmaid while pregnant, and there was the beauty of the wedding. The idea of impossible marriage — me having a child was the impossible marriage as far as I was concerned. I was dealing with how to live with polar opposites and not diminish either of them. I was also reading Oscar Wilde, and then I was looking at Aubrey Beardsley drawings and Chagall drawings, and I said, 'Those Chagall people ought to be inside these Beardsley people.' That's really what I tried to do.

AG: ARE IMPOSSIBLE MARRIAGES THE BEST KIND?

BH: I think they're the only kind.

AG: DO YOU THINK OF FLORAL AS IN TUNE WITH HER PREGNANCY?

BH: When she connects to it, she totally connects, as much as she might be denying it. The actress has to find where the connection between Floral and her baby is, at different moments in the play.

AG: I WAS THINKING ABOUT IMAGES OF PREGNANT WOMEN ON THE STAGE, AND FEW COME TO MIND. THE DUCHESS IN *THE DUCHESS OF MALFI*. IN *AUNTIE MAME*, UNMARRIED, LUMBERING AGNES GOOCH IS SUPPOSED TO BE FUNNY. THERE'S A PREGNANT WOMAN IN YOUR PLAY *THE LUCKY SPOT*. FLORAL IS SOMEWHAT AWKWARD, AS HOLLY HUNTER PLAYED HER. BUT SHE'S ALSO SENSUOUS.

BH: Yes. It was interesting — at the Roundabout, the costume designer was doing Floral's dress for Act Two, when everybody is dressed up, and I said, 'Show some shoulders. She has to be alluring. She is sexy. She's very sensual and appealing. Maybe particularly so, because she's so robustly pregnant.'

AG: SHE RESPONDS TO NATURE. THE CHARACTERS WHO RESPOND TO NATURE IN *MARRIAGE* SEEM TO HANDLE LIFE BETTER THAN THE OTHERS. FLORAL'S HUSBAND, JONSEY, DOESN'T SEEM TO KNOW WHAT LIFE IS ABOUT.

BH: I don't know which characters in that play know anything about life. I felt very bad for Jonsey at the end. The others I felt all right about, even good about some of them.

AG: DO YOU MEAN THEY ARE GOING TO BE OKAY?

BH: Well, no. They aren't. But, you know, I thought they would have a good day.

AG: WHEN DID YOU FIRST MEET HOLLY HUNTER?

BH: We were doing *The Wake of Jamey Foster* on Broadway, and she came to audition.

AG: SHE HAS BEEN IN MORE THAN SEVEN PRODUCTIONS OF YOUR PLAYS. THAT'S AN UNUSUAL COLLABORATION THESE DAYS IN THE AMERICAN THEATER.

BH: That's a shame really, because it's so great to work with actors that understand your voice.

AG: HAVE THE TWO OF YOU EVER DISCUSSED THIS AFFINITY?

BH: Not deliberately.

AG: UNDELIBERATELY?

BH: We just talk about the work. I think she's a great actress. I feel confident she can get a tone of truthfulness and oddness. She always has hope and energy. She'll see the humor, but she won't play the humor, and that's crucial to my plays. I've had very good actors come in to do readings, and they don't get the tone. Don't get the irony or the heart, and how they connect, and the frightfulness of it all. Holly does. But I do think that when you know people, and they see you in real life, it helps. If the actors in a production get to know me, they seem to be able to look into the material with a keener eye.

AG: BEFORE WRITING *IMPOSSIBLE MARRIAGE*, YOU HAD WRITTEN *SIGNATURE* AND *CONTROL FREAKS*, BOTH OF WHICH ARE SET IN LOS ANGELES. WHY DID YOU RETURN TO THE SOUTHERN LANDSCAPE FOR *MARRIAGE*?

BH: I wanted an environment where there were more boundaries, where marriage was an institution that was valued and would put Floral more on a pedestal than, say, Los Angeles. I wanted an environment where there's an organized society for the characters to bounce off of. A pregnancy from an out-of-wedlock affair would have more mileage in that environment.

AG: COULD WE TALK ABOUT THE MOTHER IN *IMPOSSIBLE MARRIAGE*? SHE INITIALLY APPEARS SHOCKED AND DISTURBED BY HER DAUGHTERS' GOINGS-ON. BUT ULTIMATELY SHE SUPPORTS THEIR LOVE AFFAIRS.

BH: I think she takes a bit of a journey in the play. And she's keeping a secret. They're all keeping secrets from each other, that they think the others can't deal with. She's keeping the secret that she's ill.

AG: AND THAT SHE HAD AN UNHAPPY MARRIAGE.

BH: And that she had an unhappy marriage. But when she sees that Floral has been keeping a secret from her — because Floral was afraid of losing her love — there is movement to the mother's character. There has to be movement to where, at the end, the mother is going to be eating raspberries and letting the juice drip, because, well, thank goodness there's a boundary so I can go outside it. Basically she's intuitive and intelligent. When Floral says, 'People can change . . . . I've seen it happen,' she means her mother. Her mother has changed from caring about public opinion to saying essentially, 'Oh, who gives a damn? We lived and touched real life and inevitably we had some scandal.'

AG: A NUMBER OF THE MOTHERS IN YOUR PLAYS ARE NOT SO SUPPORTIVE OR BALANCED, OR EVEN PRESENT.

BH: *The Debutante Ball* — now there's a mother.

AG: YES, THERE'S A MOTHER. WAS SHE MODELED ON SOMEONE IN PARTICULAR?

BH: Well, it's based on a true story, a murder that I heard about when I was growing up in Jackson. A woman murdered her husband — shot him — and the daughter was there, and there was the rumor that the daughter did it and the mother took the rap. And we knew it was the truth, since her daughter was friends with one of my sisters. The mother ended up getting out of jail on self-defense or something, but this society-woman-in-jail situation stuck in my mind. A mother taking the rap for the daughter and actually making things worse.

AG: JEN, THE MOTHER, IS OBSESSED WITH EXTERNALS, WITH HOW HER DAUGHTER, TEDDY, LOOKS AND BEHAVES. EVERY TIME TEDDY GOES INTO THE BATHROOM, SHE PUTS MORE MAKEUP ON. I HAVE THE IDEA THAT HER FACE IS A GROTESQUE MASK BY THE TIME SHE GOES TO THE BALL. CINDERELLA IN REVERSE.

BH: The more secrets you have the more façade you need. They think that nobody will have to know Teddy killed her father, and the family will be accepted again. If they have the right boy and the right dress and the right presentation, then they will be seen as the mask they put on. They can't be seen as they are, because it's too horrifying.

AG: SINCE YOU SET THIS STORY IN THE CONTEXT OF A DEBUTANTE BALL, WHICH IS *THE* WHITE-GLOVE FEMALE EXPERIENCE IN THE UNITED STATES, THE BALL FEELS LIKE A

METAPHOR FOR WHAT WOMEN DO TO THEMSELVES IN ORDER TO APPEAL TO MEN.

BH: The notion behind the debutante ball is historically frightening, if you think about these virgins being brought out on display at the time of their blossoming, in the white dresses, presented by their fathers to the young men of a certain financial or social status, to hopefully mate with one of them. It's a mating call. And it's done quite seriously.

AG: WERE YOU A DEBUTANTE?

BH: No. My older sister and my younger sisters were debutantes.

AG: HOW DID YOU ESCAPE?

BH: I just said I didn't want to do it. I can be really . . . stubborn. I become very unengaged.

AG: JEN, TOO, IS TRAPPED INSIDE HER BODY.

BH: Yes. Her literal body is decaying as much as her secrets have decayed her insides, because her insides are becoming harder to mask. Everything that has been internalized and hidden is now coming through.

AG: BUT AT THE END, MOTHER AND DAUGHTER COME TO AN UNDERSTANDING.

BH: Yes. They share an honest moment. They have a cigarette together. They've both been lying about smoking, too.

AG: A NUMBER OF PEOPLE LIE ABOUT SMOKING IN THE PLAY.

BH: Teddy admits she killed the father. That she's pregnant. I wanted the image to be a peeling off, a renewal, a washing off, an applying of ointment to the wounds. 'I'm going and I'm telling you I'm going, instead of sneaking away.'

AG: FRANCES, THE NIECE OF TEDDY'S STEPFATHER, IS DEAF. WAS THERE A PARTICULAR REASON YOU WANTED THAT CHARACTER TO BE DEAF?

BH: Actually, I wanted to work with the actress Phyllis Frelich. I had loved her in *Children of a Lesser God*. So she played Frances at South Coast Repertory. I also wanted to write a part for a deaf person that didn't have to be sweet and perfect. I wanted to write a real person. And there are so many images in that play of isolation, of people having the need for love and not being able to express it. Frances' mother is dying, she's out of place, she doesn't fit in, and she's fallen in love with a woman and didn't even know she was interested in women. Having Frances in the play sort of embodies people trying to communicate. How do we connect? How do we love? The struggle when somebody is deaf, or for you, if you're deaf. Something in you is cut off or not open. All of that is in there. My agent got a letter from some theater saying the character was an insult to deaf people. It's not my most politically correct play, but I didn't care.

AG: THE LOVE RELATIONSHIP BETWEEN FRANCES AND BLISS SEEMS TO BE THE ONLY ONE THAT WORKS.

BH: Well, it probably won't work out eventually, but it will be good for a while. They both need each other so desperately and they've both been cruel to other people. But I don't know how it will end.

AG: IN *THE DEBUTANTE BALL* AND OTHER PLAYS OF YOURS IT SOMETIMES SEEMS THAT THE DAUGHTERS HAVE TO SEPARATE FROM THE MOTHERS IN ORDER TO FIND THEMSELVES.

BH: That's definitely the theme of *The Debutante Ball*. Teddy is guilty over her mother going to jail for what she did. They're enmeshed psychically. All of that has to get bashed rather quickly for Teddy to go on. And for the mother to go on, so she can let go of that obsession of keeping Teddy perfect, keeping her safe.

AG: EVEN THE THREE SISTERS IN *CRIMES OF THE HEART* HAVE TO SEPARATE THEMSELVES FROM THEIR MOTHER'S SUICIDE, OR AT LEAST LEARN TO ACCEPT WHAT HAPPENED.

BH: I think that same thing about the suicide, but it's when Babe tries to kill herself that the sisters start to think, 'We can't do this anymore, it's getting to be a thing in our family, we have to let that option go.' Probably once your mother commits suicide, that is always an option. The door's always ajar in that way. I suppose I was trying to shut it. 'We have each other.'

AG: YOU OFTEN MENTION IN INTERVIEWS THAT YOUR MOTHER HAD A FORMATIVE IMPACT ON YOUR WRITING. IN WHAT WAY?

BH: Well, in that she was an actress and took me to the theater. She worked in theater, and I got to be backstage. Also, she would pick plays, and since this was the community theater in Jackson, they used a lot of Samuel French and Dramatists Play Service scripts, and I loved the dialogue. For a long time I didn't write descriptions; they would bore me. I didn't care about the trees and the smells. I preferred the people. It's really taken me quite a time to develop an appreciation for narrative. Plays are about people.

AG: WOULD YOU CALL YOUR MOTHER A FEMINIST?

BH: Oh, sure. Oh, definitely. There's no question she's a feminist. I don't know if she would call herself that. To say she's a feminist is to box her in, because she's much more than that. Sometimes she can be the opposite of feminist and be, you know, real and practical.

AG: I GET THE FEELING YOU DON'T HAVE A HIGH REGARD FOR BEING A FEMINIST.

BH: I do have a high regard for feminists. But you could never box my mother into any label she wouldn't shoot out of.

AG: DID YOU WANT TO BE LIKE YOUR MOTHER WHEN YOU WERE GROWING UP?

BH: She was such a goddess to me, it wasn't even a question. I just wanted to worship her, watch her put on her makeup. Talk to her. Adore her. And I still do.

AG: WHAT WAS YOUR FATHER LIKE?

BH: My father was very emotional, in an odd way for a man. He could get very angry or very moved, and be very demanding. He was not the type that would let you win at chess or tennis. 'Why do you let the kid win?' Which was sort of a relief when I was a child, because once I did beat him at chess and I felt great, because I knew I'd really won.

He was a lawyer and a politician — he was in the State Legislature. He loved history more than the law practice. He was a good lawyer, but he had dreams. I really regret not getting to know him longer as an adult. Part of him was terrified of children, and he had these four daughters. He had older brothers and not a clue as to how to deal with daughters. So he was always sort of shy and sad.

AG: YOU'VE SAID ON OCCASION THAT HE DID NOT SMILE ON YOUR WRITING.

BH: Well, he died before I wrote *Crimes of the Heart*, so you can understand it.

AG: *AM I BLUE*, WHICH YOU WROTE IN 1973, IS A GOOD PLAY BY A YOUNG PLAYWRIGHT.

BH: I guess he went to see that. There was another play on the bill — *Bridge Head* — written by my friend Frederick Bailey, a wonderful writer. It was an incredibly violent Vietnam play set in Cambodia, where they shoot a Cambodian spy in the head at the end, and it was followed by my little play set in the French Quarter, where two virgins get together and dance at the end. And my father of course loved the guy play. He'd been in World War II, he was fascinated by the dialogue. It was real quick, quick, male dialogue. So I got the distinct impression he preferred that play. But why wouldn't he? And then I wrote the book for a musical about World War II, about a 4F guy who has to stay home . . .

AG: *PARADE*?

BH: *Parade*. And he didn't get it. His brother was killed in World War II, and I think he found it upsetting that the musical was fanciful. And not researched enough. Not serious enough. Had he been alive when I won the Pulitzer Prize . . . He would have liked *Crimes of the Heart*.

AG: FROM THE MOMENT *CRIMES OF THE HEART* APPEARED, CRITICS BEGAN TO PLACE YOUR WORK IN THE TRADITION OF SOUTHERN GOTHIC WRITERS. DO YOU AGREE WITH THEM ABOUT THAT?

BH: I don't know what it means to agree with them or not agree with them. If they meant it kindly, I was grateful, if they mean it unkindly, I'm not. I don't particularly like to think in those big terms. I like to read something and glean from it what's personal and specific to me, and get a communion going between whoever is writing it and myself. To say, 'Oh, it's Southern Gothic,' it's like, 'We've got that settled. We don't really have to feel what she's feeling or think about what she's thinking about, because it's in that tradition.' I suppose that's useful to a degree, but I don't think, when I read Shakespeare, 'He's Shakespearean.' I think, 'That's beautiful. That just blew my head off.' You nab from different things that will help you tell a particular story. I don't say, 'Okay, I'm going to follow this style exactly,' unless that's going to help the story.

AG: WHEN YOU WERE GROWING UP, DID YOU READ THE SOUTHERN WRITERS, LIKE FAULKNER OR FLANNERY O'CONNOR?

BH: I didn't read them as much as you would think. I read Tennessee Williams, Eudora Welty. I guess they had more influence. Flannery O'Connor — I love her, but I didn't start reading her until after I wrote *Crimes of the Heart* and the reviews said, 'You write like Flannery O'Connor.' For some reason I totally missed O'Connor. But it would have been impossible to steal from her, because she's writes too intuitively. She wouldn't be possible to copy.

AG: IN TERMS OF STYLE, *SIGNATURE* AND *CONTROL FREAKS* FEEL DIFFERENT FROM ANYTHING YOU WROTE PREVIOUSLY.

BH: All my plays seemed to be set in the past. Even *Crimes of the Heart. The Lucky Spot* does go back in time. *Abundance* goes to another century. So I decided to catapult myself into this century by going to the future. *Signature* and *Control Freaks* take place in L.A. I was trying to write more about now than about my nostalgic past. That's kind of how that happened.

AG: WAS THERE A PARTICULAR INSPIRATION FOR *SIGNA-TURE*?

BH: Yes. I was walking down Melrose Avenue with a friend, and I was having a bad time, just depressed, and there was a graphologist on the street. He read my friend's handwriting, and it was 'great, creative, spontaneous, genius,' and mine was like, 'Oh, yours is a measly life, Wretched and tormented.' It hit me in a profound way. I knew it was not real, but in my reduced state I felt overwhelmed by this total stranger's version of me and my life. I started pondering the notion of signature. What is our signature, what do we leave that's important to us? Is it our work, our family, our life, our love? Is it the evil things we do? I pondered that notion. And L.A. seemed the perfect town where people are looking to leave a signature.

AG: YOU INVENTED A NEW LANGUAGE FOR *SIGNATURE*.

BH: I'd been doing a lot of research, particularly for *The Lucky Spot* and *Abundance*. I researched *Abundance* for five years — I became obsessed with the late-nineteenth century and the American West. And I loved the idea of not having to do research because — it hasn't happened. The notion of inventing language and new concepts was fun.

AG: YOU INVENT A WORLD IN GREAT DETAIL. THERE IS A EUTHANASIA HOTLINE, VIDEO DIVORCE, UP-AND-COMING OBITS.

BH: Yes, but sometimes it makes no sense whatsoever. But I feel, that'll do. That's the way that world is: the outfits they wear, the things they eat, their philosophies and art.

AG: SPEAKING OF WHICH, THE 'ART PHILOSOPHER,' BOSWELL T-THORP, IS A FUTURISTIC CRITIC WHO PROMOTES HIS 'BOX THEORY.' WHAT DOES 'BOXDOM' MEAN TO YOU?

BH: Boxdom means a reduced way of thinking, in which you can put a box around anything. If you make a box big enough, it will fit around anything. If you make this truism big enough, it's a fear of the unknown, a fear of the mysterious and the spontaneous — it is what Boswell has. That's what this philosophy connotes.

But despite the futuristic world, I thought of the characters as very human in their fear of not being loved, fear of professional failure. Boswell and his terror of dying. Not getting along with your family. The wife of Boswell's brother, Max, leaves him, and Max goes crazy. She gets successful and dumps him. That seems quite the standard.

AG: COULD YOU TALK ABOUT THE CHARACTER OF THE READER, THE GRAPHOLOGIST TO WHOM BOSWELL GOES FOR ADVICE?

BH: The Reader is a mysterious character. She's hard to pin down, because she is a lunatic and a poet. And a criminal. All of those things that make people creative, that they struggle with. She's definitely a scam artist, but she's also intuitive and brilliant; she's using fortune-telling as an art rather than a science. And she does have a gift for it. But also, she's literally crazy and ends up in the insane asylum. Who do you listen to? Boswell chooses to listen to her and at a price.

AG: THE PLAY IS WONDERFULLY CRAZY, SATIRIC, DARK. IN THIS UNIVERSE YOU INVENT, PEOPLE CAN'T LOOK AT THE SKY DIRECTLY; THEY SEE IT ON VIDEO. OUTSIDE THIS ENCLOSED WORLD IS A DESOLATE, THREATENING DOWN-TOWN, ROLLING IN GARBAGE. WHAT HAVE PRODUCTIONS LOOKED LIKE?

BH: The first production, in Poughkeepsie, was very spare, because it was a workshop. But it was wonderful in its sort of coarseness. There was just a little box on stage, and some of the interns would walk on and play the people on the TV screens. There weren't actual videos.

It was very simple and low key, and I liked that a lot. The costumes were spectacular. Until they ran out of money, and then a couple of people didn't get costumes.

It was much more elaborate when it was later produced in Charlotte, North Carolina. And it was done in Trenton, New Jersey, and there was a nod to the futuristic 1930s. The way people envisioned the future in the thirties? That was a great concept.

AG: WHY DID THAT WORK SO WELL?

BH: I don't know. I think that's the era I was meant to be in — the twenties or thirties. The production used odd funnel machines that looked like something people might have imagined in the thirties for the future. People came in and out of stalls that reminded you of bath houses in the 1920s.

AG: HOW DID YOU COME TO WRITE *CONTROL FREAKS*?

BH: I was working with a theater company in Los Angeles, Met Theater, and I was thinking of writing it for actors there. Two men and two women. Also, I was getting to a point where I was tired of literal props and things. I just wanted everything to be more stylized, and simpler. So I wanted to play around with the style of it. It was written for a simple space. Not a huge production necessary.

AG: DID MET THEATER PRODUCE IT?

BH: Yes. First I directed it at Center Theater Ensemble in Chicago, then I directed it at Met.

AG: WHAT PERFORMANCE STYLE WERE YOU LOOKING FOR?

BH: It was interesting, because I spent a lot of time paring things down when I was doing it in Chicago, but it still had a bend toward naturalism. When I directed it out here, there was this atmosphere of chaos that we created, and we really invented a style. The actors invented a way of walking. The sister and brother had a way of walking together that was almost like a two-headed dragon. The style was very organic, in the sense that it was from the characters and their inner worlds, but it was not at all naturalistic. I loved it.

AG: WHAT KIND OF TONE RESULTED FROM THAT APPROACH?

BH: There was a starkness to it that unraveled. It went from a totally controlled, severe beginning to a totally chaotic, colorful end, littered with blood, stabbing, and screaming.

AG: DID YOU FEEL AS THOUGH YOU HAD EXPLORED A NEW STYLISTIC REALM WITH *SIGNATURE* AND *CONTROL FREAKS*?

BH: It's certainly not a conscious progression. But I do think things get stale for me, so I try something different. A new play I've written — *L-PLAY* — is twelve different scenes in twelve different styles. It's totally out there. A nonlinear piece. I was exploring style. I get interested in something and start obsessing about it. *Family Week*, my newest play, takes place in the desert and is very stark. It's sort of lacking in poetry, as opposed to *Impossible Marriage*, which is more poetic and more of a return to a former style. I'm writing shorter plays. Which I like.

AG: IN *CONTROL FREAKS*, ONE OF THE CHARACTERS DEFE-CATES IN HIS BACKYARD. THIS IS SOMETHING I NEVER EXPECTED IN A BETH HENLEY PLAY. THERE HAS ALWAYS BEEN GROTESQUERIE, BUT THIS IS DRAWING THE CURTAIN BACK.

BH: Yeah, I know. It was great fun to write, but it was terrifying. Then sitting with my agent was horrifying, because he was befuddled. Actually, some of the grotesqueries in that play are more theatrical than literal. The idea of defecating behind a bush onstage can be much worse than seeing it. And then someone steps in it. It's just playing with the audience's senses.

AG: COMICAL.

BH: Well, there's a nod to whimsy.

AG: THERE'S CERTAINLY WHIMSY AT THE END, WHEN SIS-
TER FLIES OFF AFTER TAKING HER REVENGE ON CARL. IT
WOULD PROBABLY BE CLEAR IF I SAW A PRODUCTION, BUT
HOW MANY PEOPLE DOES THIS CHARACTER SPLIT INTO?

BH: She's a split personality into three different people: Sister, Spaghetti,
and Pinkie. Pinkie knows about Spaghetti, and Spaghetti knows about
Pinkie and Sister, but Sister doesn't know about any of them. Holly
Hunter did the part here, and she's so brilliant she came up with three
totally different characters. Completely and utterly transformed herself within moments. It was staggering to be present.

AG: WHAT PERSONALITY DID SHE PROJECT AS SISTER?

BH: Well, when Sister was talking about jury duty, she was proud,
sort of plain, and a good girl. Wanted to please. Everything was held
in but steaming underneath.

AG: AND SPAGHETTI?

BH: Spaghetti was very sexual and wry and Mae West. Precise and
cutting and cynical, and terrified of things.

AG: AND PINKIE?

BH: Pinkie was the person who was the most whimsical. Innocent and
flighty and always believing in the spirit.

AG: THE SPLIT PERSONALITIES FEEL LIKE A WOMAN'S
ATTEMPT TO BE NICE ON THE OUTSIDE, WHILE INSIDE
SAVAGERY REIGNS.

BH: The play definitely says something about women's and men's roles
in the world. About constantly trying to fill them and not being able
to. Carl trying to be the man who comes in with the tie and has his
breakfast and goes off with the briefcase. Betty, Carl's wife, trying to
be the little woman with the apron running around making breakfast
and going shopping and having pretty underwear. The grotesquerie
of trying to fill those roles.

Beth Henley 215

AG: WHAT IS IT LIKE TO LIVE IN LOS ANGELES AND BE IN THEATER?

BH: It works well for me, because I like the notion of doing a play in New York and then coming back and either licking my wounds or just going on. Living here makes me think more about the work than about trying to be in the scene. I love New York; it remains the most romantic city for me on the planet. But I can't work there. It's too much fun. I don't know how people get anything done in New York City. In L.A. you're more isolated. I need a break from that energy.

AG: WHAT AMOUNT OF ENERGY DO YOU DRAW ON TO WRITE PLAYS AND FILMS?

BH: It takes more energy to write a play, because you start from scratch. Unless you're writing an original screenplay, which I've only done once. It's much harder to create all the characters and the story. I've mostly done adaptations of my own scripts or other people's for movies.

AG: IS YOUR PROCESS AT ALL THE SAME WHEN YOU'RE WRITING A PLAY AND A FILMSCRIPT?

BH: In many ways, yes. But screenplays are in a lot of ways easier, because you're not dealing with time and space in the same way you are in the theater. You can go anywhere. You can have a thousand characters, you can show things visually. I used to have an aversion to descriptions, but now I love to tell things through images in a movie. It's easier than a play. There's something more restricting about a play, which makes writing a play harder but more interesting.

AG: WHEN YOU ADAPTED *CRIMES* AND *THE MISS FIRE-CRACKER CONTEST* FOR FILM, WERE THERE THINGS YOU FELT YOU GAINED OR LOST?

BH: The main thing to keep in mind is that the movie is not going to be the perfect production. It's going to be a version. Hopefully it will be a good version done as a movie. There is no ideal play version. A play is always transforming, and maybe the greatest production ever will be in a hundred years. Or it's already been in Japan, and I missed it.

It was fun filming *Miss Firecracker* because you could see the beauty contest. In the theater, it's theatrical to have that action offstage and have people come on to give accounts of it. But you wouldn't sit for that for a minute in a movie.

AG: IN *THE MISS FIRECRACKER CONTEST*, AS IN *THE DEBU-TANTE BALL*, A CHARACTER IS CONCERNED WITH BEAUTY, ALTHOUGH SHE GIVES UP THAT DREAM.

BH: She gives up her dream to win the contest. When she comes in fifth or whatever. She gets to that point of, 'What can we hope for? Not much, not too damn much, but there's always eternal grace.' A letting go of the answers to what's going to make her life better and make people love her, and make her respectable and not Miss Hot Tamale. It's sort of the theme that people think they know the answers and try to fulfill that vision. 'If I get to be Miss Firecracker, win the contest, I'll be loved.' Which isn't true. But that makes her need to do it so extreme. Because she's not really doing it to win; she's doing it to be loved and accepted.

AG: BUT AS WITH *THE DEBUTANTE BALL*, IT HAPPENS IN THE CONTEXT OF AN AMERICAN BEAUTY RITUAL: THE BEAUTY PAGEANT. EVERY AMERICAN GIRL'S DREAM.

BH: Well, I think everybody wants to be beautiful. I think we envy beauty. People get better seats in restaurants if they're beautiful. I'd love to be beautiful. I know it has its problems, but beauty is an asset. Just as intelligence is an asset. I've become more in awe of beauty the older I've gotten. I just love to look at somebody who's beautiful.

AG: DID YOU FEEL THIS WAY BEFORE YOU MOVED TO LOS ANGELES?

BH: Well, no. I just think human beauty is great. It's sad that people go to extremes, but frankly, your looks mean something. That's a hard thing for me to admit because I hate to think I believe that, but I think it's a primal thing. Looks and presence and smell and the way you hold your body — all that counts.

AG: A VERSION OF THAT ATTITUDE EXISTS IN *ABUNDANCE*. MACON HILL PREFERS SEXY, ABUSIVE JACK FLAN TO HER HUSBAND. JACK IS ONE OF THE MOST DISGUSTING CHARACTERS YOU HAVE EVER CREATED.

BH: I know. I really love him.

AG: WHY?

BH: Well, he's just so selfish. He represents that affliction women have with the wrong guy. Both women fall in love with him. You see it in life all the time. There's this wonderful guy who only has one eye whom nobody wants. And then there's this horrible guy. He's totally lazy, totally deranged, totally sexy, and everybody wants him. I've seen it over and over. 'You should go for the guy without the eye.' 'I know. But I want that other one.'

AG: THE WOMEN START OUT AS FRIENDS, BUT THEY BETRAY EACH OTHER.

BH: It is a cautionary tale. How not to live your life. But I was entranced by the idea of California during the gold rush, and going West, and seeking new life and new fortune, a new self even. In many ways, I guess we're always dealing with two parts of ourselves. A part that wants to be this great writer and totally independent, and a part that wants somebody to love and have them love us. For different reasons, each of the women in *Abundance* gives up her primary desire. Macon relinquishes her search for adventure, to get more land. Bess allows herself to be abused, as she struggles to be loved. It's almost insidious how we let our dreams go when we lose that energy to go on. It's frightening to me how we turn away from ourselves.

And another frightening element is how tangents just take some people. These people end up with things they didn't even want. They destroy their lives for things they don't want. I do feel sorry for human beings, because they start off wanting things simply and innocently and truthfully, and getting through life can be so treacherous.

AG: THE CHARACTERS IN *ABUNDANCE* TRY TO CONTROL EACH OTHER IN VARIOUS WAYS. COULD YOU TALK A BIT

ABOUT PEOPLE WHO HAVE POWER IN YOUR PLAYS AND PEO-
PLE WHO DON'T?

BH: I think nobody in my plays basically feels they're empowered. I
think they're all struggling with that issue and doing cruel things to
empower themselves, or get what they feel would be empowerment.
Macon just can't stop flirting with Bess's husband and making herself
into the powerful woman of the house. Not sharing the power or even
relenting, but 'You're under me and I'm over you, and that's how I'm
willing to keep it in every small thing I do and say.' The oh-so-small
ways that Bess can't really notice. Until she does. And then she uses
her power to destroy Macon by taking everything away from her.

AG: WHAT DOES EMPOWERMENT MEAN? ARE THERE DIF-
FERENT KINDS?

BH: I guess empowerment is acceptance of your own worth and value
and not the fear that you're invisible. The belief that you count. Which
is what so many of my characters want to feel. They want to shine,
they need to show. The idea of just *being* totally eludes all of them.

AG: ALL OF YOUR CHARACTERS?

BH: I'm not sure all of them. You do get somebody like William in
Signature who understands that she is a mother and that she wants
her children, and that gives her something very clear to be.
Something clear to do with her life that is worthwhile. She likes cleaning the animals. But she can't help but love Boswell, and Boswell manages to make her feel invisible and worthless. Still, I think as a person,
she has a clearer sense of self than many of the characters I write.

AG: THE WOMEN IN *CRIMES OF THE HEART* HAVE MORE
OF A SENSE OF THEIR WORTH AT THE END.

BH: Well, so many of their secrets have been revealed. Meg, that her
career failed, and although she doesn't reveal it to her sisters, she admits
to Doc about having a breakdown. Lenny reveals to Charlie about
her shrunken ovary, and she also reveals that granddaddy didn't think
she was worthy of him. Babe reveals the truth about having this affair,

her husband beating her. Letting themselves be seen for who they are to each other makes them closer, or a little more empowered to just be.

AG: THAT'S SORT OF WHAT HAPPENS AT THE END OF *DEBU-TANTE* AND THE END OF *THE MISS FIRECRACKER CONTEST*.

BH: The end of *The Wake of Jamey Foster*. Just letting go and sleeping. Just finding some peace in all the turmoil.

AG: AND *CONTROL FREAKS*?

BH: Well, at the end of *Control Freaks*, Sister is empowered because she can finally be one person. Pinkie finds out about Sister, and then Sister finds out about Pinkie and Spaghetti, and they can all be together again, or at least try to reunite in a certain broad way.

AG: WHOM DO YOU WRITE FOR?

BH: Gosh. Myself. Period. When I write plays. It's not true always for a film studio.

AG: HOW IS THAT DIFFERENT?

BH: I've only written screenplays with a director involved, but it's more of a collaborative thing than totally on my own. With a play, I own the copyright, so that's for me. That's not to say I won't change things if a director asks, but I don't sit down and say, 'I'm going to write this for young people, I'm going to write this for a New York audience' — because I don't really know what that is. Basically I'm writing something that I'm totally concerned with and interested in, and upset by. Generally I'm upset by something, or haunted and intrigued by something. So it's, in that sense, a selfish occupation.

I spend a lot of time with characters before I even start writing, but a lot of times I've got a situation. A debutante ball, a wake, the Miss Firecracker Contest. Some event. *Abundance* is kind of a circular play to me. Writing about two mail-order brides who come out West with hopes and dreams, and what happens. So a little bit of both. In *Impossible Marriage* there's a marriage. *Family Week* is about going to a treatment center. A week in a treatment center.

AG: WHAT KIND OF TREATMENT CENTER?

BH: Well, that's a good question. For people who can't handle the world.

AG: AND *L-PLAY*?

BH: *L-Play* is really about trying to connect, trying to make the box. It's about how we go about finding anything solid in this world, where it can be the Marquis de Sade's world, Disney's world, Woody Allen's world, Degas' world. So many different perspectives on this one world that we live in. A look at 'How can anybody have a clue as to what's happening in the world?' All the scenes start with an 'L': Lunatic, Loser, Learner, Lost.

AG: DO YOU MAKE DETAILED NOTES ABOUT CHARACTERS?

BH: I spend a lot of time filling whole pages of notebooks. Several, several notebooks. Then I work from the notebooks, and I'll figure out, 'Well, this applies to this character,' and put it under that character, 'and here's an image for that character, and here's a piece of dialogue that character might say.' I really work out of total chaos before I even start writing. I have a thing with images. What are the themes? I write those down without questioning anything. I write everything down without thinking about it. Some of it doesn't apply, but I don't censor. And style. I write possible style things, or books to read. But mainly on the characters. The characters' things are really extensive.

AG: PHYSICAL AS WELL AS INTERNAL THINGS ABOUT CHARACTERS?

BH: Yes. And dialogue. Even some scenes will come to me. I'll say, 'This thought, or this philosophy, would go to this character. This character I see doing this image.' I write in notebooks and then I write on my computer, and then I take it to a computer typist, who types it up neatly.

AG: WHEN DO YOU KNOW THAT YOU ARE READY TO SIT DOWN AND WRITE?

BH: It's a feeling of a certain deep amount of self-loathing that finally I can no longer ignore.

AG: HAVE YOU MADE A LIVING AS A PLAYWRIGHT?

BH: I've made a living as a writer. I haven't figured out if I would have made a living as a playwright. Early on, I sold *Crimes of the Heart* as a screenplay, for a considerable amount of money. So as a playwright, I probably could have made a living, but it would be very tight. This would not be my office, this would be my house. Because it's tough. You're lucky if you can sell a play to the screen and make some cash.

AG: HAS BEING A WOMAN HELPED YOUR CAREER, OR HURT IT, OR NOT FIGURED AT ALL?

BH: I think it has hurt and helped. It hurts in that the stories I write are from a woman's perspective and feature women primarily, although not in *Signature*. And there are just more men in charge of theaters and more men directors, more men actors, and they can't help themselves. Like my father. I see a movie about Vietnam soldiers where I want to see a movie about somebody going out on a date. I want to see a woman. My son likes to see shows about little children. If a play is totally great, by some genius writer, I don't care if it's about men or women. I saw *Art*, which I loved, which is about men. But if I'm just going to see a play — is there a woman in it? Oh, good, at least there's one woman in it.

On the other hand, being a playwright is such an obscure profession, and being a woman playwright is even more obscure. Nobody would have the guts to do a male playwrights book. They'd have to be more politically correct. Different races and at least two women, so we might have a chance to be one of the two women.

AG: DOES IT BOTHER YOU THAT THIS BOOK IS EXCLUSIVELY WOMEN?

BH: No. No, I'm relieved because I'm in it. Did you ever read Tillie Olsen's *Silences*? It's such a beautiful book. I do believe so many women have been silenced. I think it's great to give them a voice. Growing up with all these John Wayne things — not that I don't love John Wayne — but . . .

AG: WITH YOUR SON, YOU MAY HAVE A LOT OF THAT.

BH: I know. I'm falling in love with trucks for the first time. And machinery. He's transfixed with the beauty of machines. I've never noticed. I don't care what I drive as long as it goes. But he can look at trucks, their design, their beauty.

AG: A NUMBER OF THE WOMEN I'VE TALKED WITH HAVE COMPLAINED ABOUT HOW CRITICS SEE THEIR WORK.

BH: I only read *The New York Times* review of *Impossible Marriage*, because it came to my hotel and I couldn't resist. I didn't read any others. I know the play got mixed reviews, and that's all I can stand to know. That seems wimpy, but I've got to go back and write. Even when I get a good review, I'm of such weak character that it can obsess me in the wrong direction. I can start thinking that I'm just too wonderful to work.

AG: DID THAT HAPPEN AFTER *CRIMES OF THE HEART*?

BH: No, but I do recall reading quite a few more reviews for *Crimes of the Heart* than for *The Wake of Jamey Foster*. Actually I have a kind of contract with myself, to always have a new play started before I have a play done in New York. Because no matter how bad the reviews are, I don't want the critics to have the power to make that be my last play. I want to be into another play that I'll finish.

AG: IS THERE LIFE AFTER WINNING THE PULITZER? WAS IT HARD TO COME BACK FROM THAT?

BH: It was harder than I thought at the time, because I was really busy. There were repercussions from winning that I denied, and they came back to haunt me. But it's hard to be anything but unspeakably grateful for winning the Pulitzer Prize. It made me think of myself as a writer. It made my family excited. It gave me a life. I get to have a life as a writer. I was working in the TRW parts department, and not to have to waste my life doing day jobs was a total gift. And it was glamorous and ridiculous, and I was young enough not to take it that seriously. I remember thinking, 'I could win a Pulitzer Prize. It must not be that much at all.' I'm glad I'm forty-seven and not longing to win a Pulitzer Prize.

AG: DO YOU HAVE ADVICE FOR WOMEN WHO WANT TO WRITE PLAYS?

BH: I love them. I love them if they're going to write, period. And then if they want to write in the theater, I really love them. It's a great art form. It's very tough, but it's a life. Even if you fail at being a writer, it's worth the failure. Because things will be revealed to you that would not be revealed by doing something safe. I have many friends who are artists and actors, and maybe it's not working out and they need a day job, but I look at their lives compared to those of people who stay in one place and are safe and have insurance and big cars, and I'd take the artist's life. Maybe I'm saying that because I don't have to work a day job. But I think if you have a desire to do something, you're blessed. The worst thing I've experienced is having passion but not knowing what for. But to find something you want to do . . . And with writing you're particularly lucky, because you can just do it. It's not like wanting to be an actor or film director, which take some support. You're just so lucky if you want to be a writer. ▽

Tina Howe

Tina Howe grew up in New York City, where her father, Quincy Howe, was an eminent news commentator on CBS Radio. Her mother, Mary Post, was a painter.

Howe is the author of *The Nest* (1969), *Birth and After Birth* (1973), *Museum* (1976), *The Art of Dining* (1979), *Painting Churches* (1983), *Coastal Disturbances* (1986), *Approaching Zanzibar* (1989), *One Shoe Off* (1993), and *Pride's Crossing* (1997), whose central character, the feisty, elderly Mabel Tidings, once swam the English channel. Howe's most recent play is *Women in Flames*.

Her awards include an Obie for Distinguished Playwriting, an Outer Critics Circle Award, a Rockefeller, an Academy of Arts and Letters Award in Literature, an American Theatre Wing Award, the Sidney Kingsley Award, the New York Drama Critics Circle Award, and two honorary degrees. In 1987, she received a Tony nomination for best play (*Coastal Disturbances*).

Howe has been a visiting professor at Hunter College since 1990 and an adjunct professor at New York University since 1983. Howe is proud to have served on the Council of the Dramatists Guild since 1990. Her greatest hour in the theater was playing the maid in a Hunter College production of *The Bald Soprano*.

This interview took place on July 13, 1999, in New York City.

• • •

AG: WHEN WE WERE TALKING ABOUT MEETING FOR THIS INTERVIEW, YOU SAID, 'LET'S START FROM A CLEAN SLATE.' WHAT DOES THAT MEAN TO YOU?

TH: A different set of questions. Looking through millennium eyes at a new person. I get so tired of my history, I'm always tempted to alter it. When my husband and I meet people we don't know, I often say, 'Let's invent new personas for ourselves. You be a dentist and I'll be an anthropologist. No one will ever know the difference.' I guess it's a desire to escape the confines of who I am and go in other directions.

AG: CAN AN ARTIST EVER RETURN TO THE POINT WHERE THERE'S A CLEAN SLATE?

TH: When students ask me where my plays come from, I tell them, 'Each one is a response to the one that went before.' If I've just finished a big sprawling play, then I'll do a claustrophobic one, then a sprawling one and then a claustrophobic one again. I think writers establish a chain of work that is always responding to itself in some way. But of course, the greatest joy would be to break that chain and start from scratch. Begin with a piece that comes from nowhere . . . or everywhere. I know in my case I'm totally trapped in my own limitations and I can only do so much. But I long to blast beyond myself, to get in touch with new feelings, images, and language.

AG: WHAT MIGHT THOSE BE?

TH: After I finished my latest play, *Women in Flames,* which is a huge comedy with seven characters playing about twenty roles, and a very complicated set, I was thinking, 'Why do I make it so hard for myself and my producers?' I began musing about a two-character play, which I have never tried before. To put my penchant for excess and extravagance in that one relationship, not in the scenery or huge cast. I've been exploring a new piece that seems very profound to me, because it is so intimate, with only two people and one set. I'm thinking of writing one continuous act with ten or fifteen scenes. The time has come to throw a rock into the way I do things and see what happens.

AG: WHAT DOES THIS URGE TO BREAK THE RULES COME OUT OF AT THIS MOMENT?

TH: I don't see much that's daring. More than anything, I'm a mischief maker. That's my imperative. To shake things up. Theater is in a very conservative mode these days. Producers are into British imports, which are beautifully acted but never offer any great surprise in terms of event or moving to another level. My models have always been the absurdists — Ionesco, Genet, Pirandello, and Beckett, who threw reality up in the air and let it drift down to the ground in new configurations — the writers who showed us the familiar in completely novel ways. Whenever I wrote my more experimental pieces, however, I got clobbered. The critics were appalled. *Pride's Crossing* was a traditional, well made play that had a lovely run. I hoped that it might be done regionally and in Europe, but none of that seems to be happening, so once again I'm broke and struggling. It's probably time to try something completely different. It might be instructive.

AG: HOW LONG HAVE YOU BEEN WORKING ON *WOMEN IN FLAMES*?

TH: It was another play for a year and a half, with a completely different setting and cast of characters. It's taken me about three years.

AG: WHAT HAS IT BECOME?

TH: It's my Cyrano play. I think all writers love Cyrano because we identify with the homely poet wooing the beautiful one on the balcony. *We* could be the ones onstage if we weren't so awkward and shy, but we are consigned to be witnesses, because we're too tall, too short, too fat or too thin. There's something exhilarating about the poet finally getting the chance to emerge from the shadows to woo the beautiful one face-to-face. I've often thought, 'Why couldn't it be a *woman* wooing a man for a change?' I thought, 'Okay, Cyrano's deformity is his nose. What would a woman's deformity be? What deforms a woman more than anything?' Age. If I could somehow position things so I'd have an older woman wooing a much younger man . . . But how to *do* it? And then I thought, 'She could be a playwright who's written a love story and in the course of the production she would fall head over heels with the rather brainless, beautiful, young, leading man.'

One evening during the run of *Coastal Disturbances* at Second Stage, Rosemary Murphy took ill, and I got a call from Carole Rothman, the director, saying, 'Tina, you have got to go on for Rosemary.' And I said, 'I can't go on. I'm not an actress! I don't know the part! I'll be a laughing stock! It'll ruin the whole production. What will the actors think? You've lost your mind. I can't do it.' But she said, 'No, you'll take the script in hand. We will have somebody announce to the audience that one of the actors got sick and the playwright is going to take over. It will be a novelty act.'

So I did it. I went on. The power of being in your own play, saying your words to other people who are also saying your words, left an enormous impression. I thought, 'I will create a moment when the leading lady gets sick, and Isobel, the playwright, has to go on and do a love scene.' I make it clear from the very beginning that's she's fallen for her young leading man. The guy isn't aware of her feelings, however, because he's always chasing the hot young ingenue. The play builds to the point where Isobel is on stage. Initially she's very frightened, but then she starts to improvise. He's lost, but she tells him, 'Slow down, just be in the moment and listen. I'm going to tell you how a woman loves.' Then she launches into this huge speech that's very fraught and full of the beating of wings. It gets more and more sexual and glorious. In the middle of it, he realizes that she's talking to *him*. There's a clinch at the end, and then the curtain comes down. In the next scene, they're in the dressing room, still in each other's arms. Everyone's trying to pry them apart, and the young actor's saying, 'No, no, tell me more.' Because it's all about his ego. He's fallen in love with the image of himself that she's created.

Next, we see them together in his apartment after a night of love. He's wearing his pajama bottoms, and she's wearing the top. They're smoking cigarettes in a state of bliss. Then comes the awful reality of having to talk to each other. It's clear that they have nothing in common and that she's old enough to be his mother. She finally says, 'Look, I've got to go.' He begs her not to leave. Finally we have a play where an older woman walks out on younger guy.

AG: WHY IS IT *WOMEN IN FLAMES*?

TH: Isobel's play is about Miss Havisham, the fabulous mad woman from Dickens' *Great Expectations* who literally goes up in flames. But rather than meeting her at the end of her life, we encounter her as a young woman and see her fiancé stand her up at the altar. Because we participate in her betrayal, we understand the woman she becomes. To add to the fiery imagery, Isobel is menopausal and always having hot flashes. She keeps asking, 'Is it hot in here or what?' All the women in the play are in love with the wrong person. They're all in flames.

AG: WHO ARE THE OTHER WOMEN?

TH: There's an ingenue who's in love with herself, an aging leading lady who's in love with the ingenue, and a female stage manager who's in love with the director. When the leading man goes off with the playwright, the ingenue falls into the arms of the older leading lady. Everyone finally ends up with the right person. It was very complicated to write. I've never done anything that was so plot driven.

AG: YOU SAY THAT THE EQUIVALENT OF CYRANO'S DEFORMITY IN WOMEN WOULD BE AGE. HOW DID YOU COME TO THAT?

TH: Once actresses turn forty, it's over. They don't get work anymore unless they do quirky character roles. When women age, men don't whistle at them in the street anymore. The aging man blithely goes on to his second and third wives. On the Upper West Side I am always seeing white-haired men on the arms of young women, pushing babies in strollers. There is something in me that cries out, 'Hey, wait a second, this isn't fair.'

AG: YOUR PLAYS CORRESPOND TO THE CYCLES OF YOUR LIFE MORE THAN MANY WOMEN'S PLAYS DO.

TH: My heroines age as I age. My first play, *The Nest*, is about women in courtship, my second, *Birth and After Birth*, is about women having babies. *The Art of Dining* is about a young woman beginning her career as a writer. Because she keeps telling these lurid stories about what it was like growing up, in my next play, *Painting Churches*, I put her onstage with her parents and turned her into a painter.

Tina Howe 229

My heroines do get progressively older. *Pride's Crossing* was about my ninety-one-year-old Aunt Maddy, but the flame inside her was mine. Maddy never broke away from her mother and father. She never married. She never struck out on her own. She never had a moment of triumph. So I was determined to give her one. But I was also writing about my own rebellion. I swam the channel, so to speak. I married David Bloom and made it to the opposite shore.

My heroine in *Women in Flames* is in her middle fifties, and in my next play she'll be in her late sixties. I've always thought, the older you get, the more transparent you become. I've always had this feeling that if I make it into old age, that's when I'll take off. Because I'll be relaxed and transparent. People will be able to look right through me like a pane of glass.

AG: IN HER BOOK, *WRITING A WOMAN'S LIFE*, CAROLYN G. HEILBRUN NOTES THAT WOMEN IN THEIR FIFTIES FREQUENTLY DISCOVER NEW AND STRONG CREATIVE IMPULSES.

TH: When women turn forty, something extraordinary happens. We become really powerful. After our parents die, we step out of that chrysalis of being a child, we emerge, suddenly orphaned. We either grieve or go forth.

Turning sixty was very scary because sixty is so close to seventy . . . and then eighty. I wake up in the middle of the night and wonder how this happened, because I still feel that I'm seventeen. But I also feel this transparency that I talked about. One can live in several time zones at once and straddle a host of continents.

AG: DID YOUR PARENTS DIE BEFORE YOU WROTE *PAINTING CHURCHES*, WHICH IS ESSENTIALLY ABOUT YOU AND THEM?

TH: Before. I couldn't have written it when they were alive.

AG: DID YOU EXPERIENCE ANY CHANGE IN YOUR ARTISTRY OR PROCESS WHEN THEY WERE NO LONGER THERE?

TH: I didn't worry about them liking my plays or giving me approval, because I knew they could turn on a dime. The critics were appalled by my first play, *The Nest*, which was very in-your-face. The heroine took off her clothes and jumped into a wedding cake and then was licked clean by her husband to be. My parents and the audience had a blast, but the play closed in one night. After the reviews came out, my mother couldn't contain her embarrassment. 'Tina, we brought important *friends* to your play. How can we ever *face* them again?' My father meekly stood behind her and agreed. I felt completely betrayed and realized I was on my own as a writer.

They would have been appalled by *Painting Churches*, because New Englanders honor rationality above everything. They would have felt hurt and confused by the sight of Gardner so lost and bewildered. To see an eminent man of letters lose his wits was inconceivable.

AG: YOU FREED YOURSELF FROM THEM EARLY ON.

TH: Early on. I rarely thought of them as fans. I inherited my father's addiction to work. I'm very much a Howe in that regard. My mother gave me her eccentricity and outrageousness. In many ways the best of me comes from her. My ancestors were largely writers and statesmen, so the written word is exceedingly important. I'm very grateful for that. But I realized very fast that I had to get out. I left the New England fold. I married a Jew and broke with everything that I was supposed to hold sacred.

AG: IN 1998, YOU GAVE A TALK AT A CONFERENCE ABOUT WOMEN AND THEATER THAT WAS ORGANIZED BY WOMEN'S PROJECT AND PRODUCTIONS IN NEW YORK CITY. YOU SAID THAT, IN THE PAST WHEN YOU WERE ASKED, 'WHICH ARE YOU FIRST, A WOMAN OR A WRITER?' YOU WOULD ANSWER, 'A WRITER!' BUT IN THAT SPEECH, YOU SAID, 'I'M MOST DEFINITELY A *WOMAN* FIRST. MY GENDER DEFINES MY WORK AND ITS RECEPTION.' WHAT BROUGHT ABOUT THIS CHANGE?

TH: I realized that the wellspring of my creativity comes from my gender. All I write about is myself. It's so embarrassing. When you're a playwright, people come up to you and say, 'Do I have a story for you!' Then they tell you some long-winded tale, and I find myself saying,

THE OBJECTS PROLIFERATING IN MANY OF IONESCO'S PLAYS. WHAT INSPIRED *ONE SHOE OFF*?

TH: I wrote it at a time when we were getting a lot of English plays about adultery and I thought, 'Wouldn't it be interesting to write a play about *fidelity* for a change? A couple who actually stays together.' My desire to be perverse was kicking up again. Having just written *Approaching Zanzibar*, which was a sprawling road play that covered three thousand miles, I wanted to do something more claustrophobic. I wanted to set a play in a teacup. Part of it was a response to *Approaching Zanzibar*, and also wanting to look at the price of fidelity — how poignant and painful staying together can be.

In many ways, it's a continuation of *Birth and After Birth*. Dinah and Leonard are Sandy and Bill Apple thirty years later. Nicky, the Apples' petulant four-year-old, is now a grown woman living her own life two thousand miles away. My dream is to have the plays done back-to-back. *Imagine!*

AG: WHY DID YOU CHOOSE PAUL BERMAN TO DIRECT THE WORLD PREMIERE OF *BIRTH AND AFTER BIRTH* AT THE WILMA THEATER IN PHILADELPHIA IN 1995?

TH: Paul had done an extraordinary production of *The Art of Dining* at Barnard College. He didn't put a scrap of food on the set. All the cooking and eating were mimed. This freed the actors to focus on the nuances of hunger and sexuality and to really relate to each other. With the food absent, the rhythms of the play took over. I remember screaming when the lights went up as I realized the food Ellen and Cal were eating was pretend. Finally, someone had gone beyond the literal into a deeper truth. It was an astounding production that left me and the audience breathless. Who would have thought? And Joe Papp spent something like twelve thousand dollars a week on groceries. So Paul was the obvious choice to direct the world premiere of another play that tapped into my more savage side.

AG: WHAT WAS HIS CONCEPT FOR THE PRODUCTION OF *BIRTH AND AFTER BIRTH*?

TH: We had a realistic set, but the actors' performances were all larger than life, particularly Rob Roy's, a large, rotund, adult actor who played four-year-old Nicky doing magic tricks, quoting Shakespeare, and breaking our hearts at every turn.

Howard Shalwitz directed the play five months later at Woolly Mammoth, in Washington, D.C. His production was much more surreal, which I now realize is the way to do it. The top half of the set was painted blue, so the family huddling around their television set looked as if they were on a little boat marooned in the middle of the ocean. The perspective was all skewed, and the furniture was wildly out of scale. The audience immediately knew they were in a wonderland, where anything could happen.

AG: ONE OF THE HALLMARKS OF THE EUROPEAN ABSURDIST PLAYS ARE THEIR VISUAL METAPHORS, WHICH I FIND AT THE CORE OF YOUR PLAYS, TOO.

TH: I always begin with the visual. Always. Because I think theater is all about transforming everyday experience into haunting images. With *Pride's Crossing* it was that croquet party. I never imagined there would be a dive at the end; I just had Mabel Tidings wade into the ocean. But Cherry Jones was determined to jump . . . and jump from a height. She wanted to be caught in the other actors' arms. She and Jack O'Brian, the director, figured out a way of doing it. My mouth fell open with gratitude and awe. And there was another really important image: Mabel teaching Minty how to play croquet in the dark. I loved the idea of a ninety-year-old woman teaching a mere girl how to wield a croquet mallet at four in the morning without waking the entire household. The whispers, the sudden cracks, the giggling and sense of mischief — that's what theater is about.

In *The Art of Dining*, I knew the most poignant sight would be the lost, nearsighted writer crawling into the kitchen to confront the cook, who's sitting in the dark because she's pulled out all electric plugs and gone on strike. There was something about the image of these two women trying to see each other, one who is hopelessly nearsighted but has a way with words, the other who can cook like a doll but has chosen to turn out the lights, and the audience seeing they were really two sides of the same coin.

AG: IN *PRIDE'S CROSSING*, WHY WAS THE IMAGE OF MABEL PLAYING CROQUET WITH HER GREAT-GRANDDAUGHTER SO IMPORTANT FOR YOU?

TH: A number of years ago I was struck by how seldom children are used on the stage. There's something about a child's small body and voice that is so powerful. We rarely see children onstage because most of our plays are written by men. Once I used children in *Coastal Disturbances*, I wanted to create real interaction between the generations in my next piece. In the last scene of *Approaching Zanzibar,* there is a transforming scene between a terrified little girl and dying old lady. They literally exchange identities. The girl puts on the old lady's wig, and the old lady puts on the girl's glasses. With that gesture, both receive comfort and grace.

In *Pride's Crossing*, I knew that if I was going to write about a ninety-year-old, I had to have a child in there. This time, I wanted the exchange to be more lighthearted. What better ruse than to have Mabel teach her grandniece how to play croquet late at night, when the rest of the house is asleep? We rarely see this sort of extreme generational exchange onstage, but it's part of life, for God's sake.

AG: YOU DEMYSTIFY THE DEFORMITY OF OLD AGE IN BOTH *ZANZIBAR* AND *PRIDE'S CROSSING*, DON'T YOU THINK?

TH: Well, in *Zanzibar,* eighty-one-year-old Olivia ends up jumping on the bed. I wanted her to do somersaults, but realized it was asking a lot of the actress playing the role. At Second Stage, the bed was a real trampoline, and ten-year-old Angela Goethals, who was playing Pony, studied gymnastics. How she jumped and twirled, testing the limits of heaven. . .

AG: THERE IS SOMETHING OF THE FAIRY TALE ABOUT THE END OF *APPROACHING ZANZIBAR,* AS THOUGH PONY WALKS INTO THE WITCH'S HOUSE, BUT THE WITCH TURNS OUT TO BE A GOOD WITCH OR FAIRY GODMOTHER.

TH: Because I was writing about a family going to pay a last visit to a dying relative, I wanted the play to end with a trumpet voluntary. I am an optimist. I believe that it's more important to leave the audience with hope than in a pool of shattering despair. We go to the theater to find a respite, a moment of transcendence. That imperative is factored into every play I write.

AG: IN YOUR PLAYS THE WOMEN BRING ABOUT THIS TRANSCENDENCE WITH THEIR CREATIVITY AND ARTISTRY.

TH: Women are inevitably my main characters. But when they're victorious, I don't want it to be at the price of a man's failure. I see men as being sympathetic and joining in a woman's journey toward self-realization. I don't write about the battle of the sexes. I've never seen men as the villain. At the worst, they're critics. I had a very sweet father, who believed in me. My mother was the tough one, the piece of work. My women triumph at the end because they are the main characters and it takes much more stamina to win than lose.

AG: AS YOU SAY, THE MEN IN YOUR PLAYS ARE FREQUENTLY CRITICS. CAL, IN *THE ART OF DINING*, IS NOT SUPPORTIVE.

TH: Yes, he's a problem. He eats his wife's creations out from under her.

AG: IN *PRIDE'S CROSSING*, DAVID BLOOM ENCOURAGES MABEL, BUT HER FATHER AND HUSBAND DO NOT.

TH: I was writing about another time, another generation. When *Pride's Crossing* took place, fathers and husbands were completely unaware of women as independent thinkers. In *One Shoe Off*, Leonard and Dinah, for all their problems, are very close. The married couple in *Approaching Zanzibar* are also close. In my new play, the sixty-five-year-old couple have almost fused into the same person.

AG: YOUR WOMEN STRUGGLE TO EXPRESS THEMSELVES.

TH: Indeed they do. They tend to be artists — chefs, painters, photographers, weavers, costume designers, swimmers, playwrights. I see the artist as our last hero, because an artist will sacrifice everything for their work. You can't say this about many other professions. Politicians are hardly the people we admire anymore. Wall Street bounders have their limitations. But people who create something that's never existed before — they're the ones flying without a net. So that's who I write about — women who are struggling to find their wings.

AG: WHY DOES ART HAVE SUCH INTENSE SIGNIFICANCE FOR YOU?

TH: Because art attempts to find meaning in chaos. There's a randomness to life that needs to be organized. When an artist succeeds, they transform experience. It's like Virginia Woolf seizing the moment. You read her prose and you're transfixed. She stops time and makes it vivid. If an artist can do that for just a moment — well, that's it. Isn't it?

AG: HAVE THE OPPORTUNITIES FOR WOMEN WHO WRITE PLAYS CHANGED IN THE THIRTY YEARS SINCE YOU BEGAN TO WRITE?

TH: I think things got better in the 1980s. There was all this flurry about women playwrights. We were getting written up all the time, but were secretly pissed off that we were being ghettoized. Because the cost of putting on plays is skyrocketing, and the audience that can afford theater is getting older and older, it's difficult for anyone to carve out a career. The freshest young female voices are being pushed into performance art, because it's cheaper to mount a one-woman show than a traditional stage play with six or seven characters. I find it terribly upsetting that women aren't given an entire stage to fill with the bounty of their imagination. My sense is, the more radical work is being done by artists who wish they could have more tools to work with, more bodies to work with. Young women are enormously frustrated that there are so few venues for them. Unless work is politically correct, it's very hard for women to make a living. Once again we are becoming ghettoized. But I'm not the best person to ask about this, because I'm an anomaly.

Every year there's an international women's playwright festival in some exotic country. My friends are always begging me to come. No way! As a six-foot-tall waspy white 'oppressor,' I would be stoned to death. My work is perceived as mainstream, even though my techniques and sensibility upset the critics. I can just see myself taking the

podium in the outback to talk about the cadences of *Painting Churches*.
I would be cut up in little pieces, tossed in the pot, and then feasted
upon like a Dodo bird. It's a terrible comment on all of us, that I am
perceived as the enemy, but I know it's true.

AG: ARE THERE ANY CHARACTERS OF COLOR IN YOUR
PLAYS?

TH: The glamorous news reporter Charlayne Hunter-Gault lived in
our building for a while, we became friends, and I based the character of the newscaster in *Zanzibar* on her. After the run, I was invited
up to the State University of New York at Albany to speak to students who were studying women playwrights. There were some African-
American students in the class, and one of them got very upset and
accused me of being a racist because the character of the newscaster
kept complaining about her impossible hair. And the student said, 'Don't
you know that for black women their hair is a real issue and you're
making fun of something that is sensitive to us?' I told her that I disagreed. I think all women hate their hair. I always wanted curls, my
best friend wanted straight hair. But she was on a tear and repeated
that she found it extremely offensive and suggested I should only write
what I know about. I felt roundly humiliated. At which point an Asian
girl rose and said, 'What about the way *Asians* are represented in the
theater. We don't even exist.' Suddenly the whole classroom erupted
in cries of anguish. I was seen as this belittling white racist. It was so
harrowing, I decided I'd never write a character of color again.

It's a real issue for white writers. The last thing you want to do
is offend anyone, and to offend out of ignorance is just as bad as offend-
ing willfully. I'd love to have this discussion with a group of black
women. I think we are becoming increasingly segregated. It's a tragic
fact of life these days.

AG: HAVE YOU BEEN ABLE TO SUPPORT YOURSELF AS A PLAY-
WRIGHT?

TH: I teach, I write screenplays, and I toy with writing fake memoirs.
I take out loans. I have a terrible time. We all have a terrible time.

AG: WHAT IS YOUR DREAM PROCESS FOR DOING A PLAY?

TH: 1. Having a theater commit to me.

2. Maybe even give me a generous commission along the way.

3. Offering me a production far from the madding crowd, where I can hone the play to within an inch of its life.

4. Giving me leeway to write and rewrite, no matter what catastrophes befall.

5. Having that theater beg for my next play, regardless.

It's about having a home and the opportunity to write plays into my old age.

More and more, being a successful playwright is about knowing how to act in the trenches. Playwrights need courses in guerrilla tactics. It's one thing to work on honing a script, but the ultimate test is knowing how to protect your play during a production. How to talk to the director, the actors, and the producer. How to cut, compromise, rewrite, stand firm, throw a fit, shut up, and deal with 'helpful suggestions.' For so many playwrights the first couple of experiences are a disaster because we simply don't know any better.

AG: YOU SPOKE EARLIER ABOUT WANTING TO SHED COMPLEX SETTINGS AND SITUATIONS IN YOUR PLAYS AND FOCUS MORE ON WHAT OCCURS BETWEEN CHARACTERS. COULD YOU TALK ABOUT THAT A LITTLE MORE?

TH: I've always believed that theater is an arena for extravagance, that one surrenders to the form, in the hopes of encountering extravagant characters in extravagant settings who speak wonderful words. And so I went out of my way to look for settings and situations that were packed with excess and surprise. *Museum* had a cast of forty-four characters. *The Art of Dining* required a budget of thousands of dollars for the food that was served each night. *Coastal Disturbances* called for twenty thousand tons of sand. The set for *Approaching Zanzibar* was pulled off due to the muscle power of three burly stage hands, who pulled masses of material on complicated rope pulleys. In *One Shoe Off* we needed a house that had sunk into the ground. Trees and shrubbery had to be brought into the theater, to say nothing of broccoli, mushrooms, and working carrot patches. Because *Pride's Crossing* dealt with the memories of a ninety-year-old woman, I needed settings that straddled eight decades and two continents.

In the course of these productions, the producers' lament was always the same: 'Tina, why do you have to make it all so *expensive?*' I noticed that regional theaters were turned off by these rangy plays, because of the cost involved. The time has come to focus my love of extravagance into a self-contained two-character play. One set. Continuous action in time. No trained seals. What's interesting about this progression is that I began with operatic flights of fancy. Usually writers' first plays are about themselves. It takes them half a career to broaden their horizons. I seem to be doing it the other way around. Kicking and screaming, it's time to examine my heart of hearts. It's time for me to enter the abyss and face the terrors within. Since less is more, I want to tackle a two-character play — something on the order of *Waiting for Godot* and *The Chairs*, a play about a couple who have been together forever. A play about the price of abiding love. I see it as an extension of *One Shoe Off*, but going deeper. I worked on it for three months and got so scared, I had to hide it in a cast-iron box lined with moss. I think I may be getting ready to put on my asbestos gloves and peek under the lid again. The play examines the ways in which creativity and pathology intersect.

AG: CAN YOU SAY MORE?

TH: It's about a couple who have been married forever. He is an installation artist working on a replica of a Scottish burial mound, built with a million stones. She is a hoarder suffering from obsessive-compulsive disorder. She can't throw anything out, and their loft is piled to the ceiling with junk. The action of the play centers around the impending visit of an art dealer who wants to see the husband's drawings for his installation. But how will he get into the loft given the wife's barricade? Obviously my couple have been through this dilemma many, many times, but on this particular day, the stakes have never been higher. I'm fascinated with our infatuation with things. An artist can organize the multiplicity of objects into a vision, but someone who's ill, like the wife, doesn't have these gifts. The objects in her life bury her. Hence my question: in what ways do creativity and pathology intersect?

AG: THAT'S A CHANGE FOR YOU, TO MAKE THE MAN THE ARTIST.

TH: Well, I thought I should switch it around for once and make the wife crazy. I'm finding it scary, but it could be funny. Once again, I want to explore how art is made. I figure one set, two people, and probably the gallery owner will come in at the end, because you need that outsider presence to give perspective, like the way the Orator shows up in *The Chairs*.

AG: WHY DO YOU WANT TO WRITE ABOUT OBSESSION?

TH: First of all, artists are obsessed. I'm struck with the current fascination for installation art, which celebrates the multiplicity of objects. Stacks of bones, clothes, hand grenades, pennies, all kinds of unlikely things. Where are the boundaries for objects that are organized, and those that aren't? Accumulation seems to be the operative impulse these days. None of us can get enough.

I think it would be interesting to divide this mania into two characters, one who can organize his obsession and the other who can't. I'd like to explore how they get through the day together. I may go up in flames trying to do it. I'm going to have to invent a whole new vocabulary. In a sense I'm an installation artist just finding my materials.

AG: WE'VE BEEN TALKING ABOUT BEING A WOMAN AND WRITING PLAYS. HOW WOULD YOU DESCRIBE YOUR PARTICULAR BRAND OF FEMINISM?

TH: It comes from my own experience as a woman — as a wife and mother. I've never studied feminism . . . whatever that is. I don't know the rhetoric or literature. I'm completely out of it. I'm amazed to be included in this book, because I'm so politically unevolved. I create my own weird little world, filled with children, lovers, art installations, beached whales, and houses that are sinking into the ground. I'm not part of the sisterhood. Maybe nobody's part of the sisterhood. Maybe there isn't even a sisterhood. Maybe that's the real truth of the matter. We like to band together and think we're a sisterhood, but probably every feminist is basically alone.

I gave a talk at Columbia University, where I was invited to teach master classes. I gave the Lucille Lortel Lecture. It was called 'Woman as Scavenger, Cook and Main Course' and was all about how I use food in my plays, and how women create the food and then often end up being consumed. When I told the chairman of the theater department, he got very excited and said, 'Oh, Tina, this is so right. This is just where the feminists are. This is just what they're thinking about.' I was amazed, I had no idea what feminists were thinking about.

It was the best speech I ever gave. I read parts of my plays and wept. I read Mags' speech from *Painting Churches* about making her cake out of melted crayons and having her mother destroy it, thinking it was rotting food. I was so moved by her need for approval, I broke down and wept. The audience went wild. They thought I was acting, but it really got to me.

AG: HOW IS WOMAN SCAVENGER AND HOW IS SHE MAIN COURSE?

TH: For so long, a woman's creativity was defined by how good a cook she was. That was how the world assessed our worth. Again and again, I've used handling food as a metaphor for a woman's creative impulse. Sometimes she hunts for it, sometimes she cooks with it, and sometimes she becomes the dish that is served up. In *The Art of Dining*, Elizabeth talks about her mother's suicidal episodes, which reach the height of folly when she tries to gas herself in the oven. '"I bet I would have tasted damn good," she said, smacking her lips.' This was a clear case of woman as main course. I carry this image even further in *One Shoe Off*, when Dinah starts tossing her salad all over Parker Bliss. She and all the other guests at the table realize with a shudder that it's not greenery she's throwing around, but her own sexual desire. When things become derailed in a woman's life, her relationship to food is one of the first things that's affected.

I didn't know where my speech at Columbia was going to take me, but I knew it was something I had to confront: the way I use food, defining women in their relationships to their loved ones and to themselves. Writers never know what they're doing when they're in the middle of something. We're the last ones to get it. But in the course of the speech, I figured it out.

AG: HOW DO YOU WANT TO USE THE NEXT DECADE OF YOUR LIFE?

TH: I need to be reawakened. I'd like to try something new — a one-woman show, a fake memoir, a musical. Why won't anyone ask me to do the book of a musical? I'd be really good at that, because I'm good at structure. I'd love to do the book for a musical! Or an opera! Why doesn't anyone ask me to write a libretto for an opera? Hello out there! I want to find new forms of expression. Sometimes I think my two-character play is really a movie. Maybe I should be in it. That's it. I should become an *actress!* Maybe I'm writing it for myself to be in. Just for the record, I wouldn't mind being in another production of *The Bald Soprano*. If anybody is looking for a Mrs. Smith or a Fire Chief, I can play either one in French or English. I would love to do that before I die. I want to leap out of my mind and go somewhere else. I want to break out. ▽

Jake-ann Jones

Jake-ann Jones was born in Harlem, where she also grew up. Her father was a jazz pianist, and her mother was a school librarian. Jones has a B.F.A. in acting from the Davis Center for the Performing Arts at City College of New York and an M.F.A. in creative writing from Brown University, where she received the 1997 Weston Award for Playwriting.

Jones' fluid, strongly imagist plays include *Bad Aim* (1993), a memory play that unearths the trauma of being sexually abused; *Terminal Waiting* (1995), which explores the issues and emotions surrounding abortion; and *Portrait of the Artist as a Soul Man Dead* (1995), a dramatization of a young painter's rise and fall during his pursuit of success. *U(nder) F(rank) O(bservation)* (1996) follows the personal journey of a young reporter who becomes involved with a homeless drug addict and a cult leader who may or may not have extraterrestrial powers. *Death of a Ho: A Fairy Scarey Whorey Tale* (1999) is a morality play with a tough, yearning heroine at its center.

Jones has worked as an actress for most of her life, onstage and in film. She performed the lead in the award-winning independent film, *Naked Acts*. Also in the realm of film, she co-authored a screenplay called *Spook City*, which won the grand prize in HBO's 1998 Urbanworld Competition. She is currently working on her first novel.

This interview took place in New York City on September 27, 1999.

• • •

JAJ: This is the building I grew up in. About seven years ago, I moved back.

AG: HAS THE NEIGHBORHOOD CHANGED SINCE YOU WERE GROWING UP?

JAJ: It has. It seems much more populated, and this area has become largely Dominican. There was a point five or six years ago when the use and sale of crack had gotten quite bad around here. I was shot at walking down the street about ten years ago. I heard a noise, and then this thing hit my jacket — went right through my jacket — and I said, 'Oh, my God. I think I just got shot at.' It was random gunfire. It's not so bad anymore. I don't know if that is because the neighborhood is cleaning up or the crack heads are just dying out.

An older gentleman lived for many years in the apartment next door, and at some point his two nieces moved in, and they were both crack heads. *UFO* is based on that. One of the women had a baby, and I remember seeing her one day with the baby and then never seeing the baby again. And I was thinking, 'Where did that baby go?' The woman eventually died of AIDS. The second niece had several children and had a baby while she was here, all of whom were living with her mother, I guess. When the uncle died, the building forced her out, although since then she has cleaned up and is working. I see her once in a while, and we always hug and promise to get together. She does look good and is really in a different place. She's transformed.

Many of the families who moved into this building over thirty years ago, like my mom did, came when this was a working-class neighborhood and this was a new building, and they worked to save money to buy their apartments and they were hoping that their children would have a better time in life than they did. But some of them just got swallowed up by living in the city.

AG: BEFORE YOU BEGAN TO WRITE PLAYS, YOU BECAME AN ACTRESS. HOW DID YOU COME TO BE AN ACTRESS?

JAJ: Acting was something that I wanted to do from the time I was really young. My father was a jazz pianist, and I remember going to the theater when I was little, because a couple of his friends were in the theater. I was hooked by the time I was three or four. Finally, my parents let me take an acting class — I remember being four or five and taking a class at Harlem School of the Arts. Then I stopped going, and when I was nine or ten, my mother said, 'You have to do something — what do you want to do?' I started taking piano, and I just couldn't hang with that. My sister took piano, my other sister took violin, my brother took guitar. So I started at Harlem School of the Arts again, and a drama teacher there named Miranda McDermott, who was an actress, ran something called the Children's Improv Company with her husband, a visual artist named Franklin Engel. They also had a theater called New Media Studio on the East Side. They would get students from Harlem School of the Arts to perform in their children's company on the weekends, and later the young adults got to do small roles in the adult shows. It was very much a community theater, now that I look at it, but I really thank them, because I was performing from the time I was eleven until I was sixteen. I would go there during the week to take acting classes, and we would do art classes and design classes. It was an amazing background in theater.

By the time I was ready for high school, my mother did not want me to go to an art school. She really wanted me to get an academic background, and since both my sisters had gone to Bronx Science, that's where I ended up. But I also felt that I didn't need to go to a theater school, because I had so much information by that time, that I couldn't imagine what I could have learned. And I'm really glad now that I didn't go to a performing arts school, because a lot of folks I know who did cannot read or write their way out of a paper bag, and I probably never would have become a writer.

I was sort of over the academics by the time I got out of Science, because it has a heavy academic program. But I had no idea what I wanted to do. My father died when I was nine, so my mom raised all of us by herself, and what she could afford was City University. So that's where I went to college. I really didn't care; I had spent my last couple of years of high school clubbing and partying and being wild, so college for me was some place to spend some time. I just blew off the first two years. Then in that second year I took an acting class with a woman named Rhea Gaisner, and she said, 'If this is what you want to do, you should be in the B.F.A. program.' So I auditioned and got in, and that was how I got back into acting. But I also wrote my first play in that program. I realized I was not simply going to be an actor with my life; I felt like it would bore me and not give me enough.

AG: AT THE TIME YOU WROTE YOUR FIRST PLAY, HAD YOU STUDIED PLAYWRITING?

JAJ: I'd taken a class at City. But at New Media, I remember writing skits. And we read so many plays, and I was performing so many plays and doing scene study, that it was good training. I guess I was interested in the idea of writing plays all along, although my sense as a woman of color was that I would quickly run up against a wall. When I was at New Media we studied and performed the classics — they were really big on doing everything from melodrama to Molière. But it was a predominantly white group; there were no actors of color in the adult company. So I was kind of, 'This is really cool except, where are the black people?' When I got to City, I started meeting artists of color, and one of my teachers, David Willinger, was the first person to give me a play written by a black person: Bill Gunn's *Black Picture Show*. And that was it for me. That play is so out — formally, it's so experimental. I had never read anything like that and I was like, 'You can actually do this with plays?' That was when I thought I would try it.

AG: I DON'T KNOW IF *BAD AIM* WAS YOUR FIRST PLAY OR NOT —

JAJ: That was my first play.

AG: THE STYLE REMINDS ME OF ADRIENNE KENNEDY'S WORK.

JAJ: Adrienne Kennedy was the other playwright David gave me to read. *Funnyhouse of a Negro*. And later I directed Kennedy's *A Rat's Mass*. Definitely Adrienne Kennedy was an influence. And Aishah Rahman — I used one of her pieces for my auditions. They are all experimental writers, and because of them I really became interested in playwriting. I think it's important to be able to write a well made play — although I don't think I ever have — but I don't find them interesting. But that's what film and television do, and because I am trying to move into film, I'm forced by that form to think that way. Maybe those are my just desserts; after all these years of refusing to write well made plays in theater, I'm forced to do that now in film.

AG: IN *BAD AIM*, VAN, THE SUCCESSFUL WRITER, IS AN OUT-SIDER WHEN SHE RETURNS TO THE FAMILY THAT RAISED HER. THAT OUTSIDER FIGURE APPEARS IN OTHER PLAYS OF YOURS, OFTEN AS A WOMAN. THERE IS BOBBY, THE JOUR-NALIST IN *U(NDER) F(RANK) O(BSERVATION)*, AND THERE IS BELLE, THE WRITER IN *PORTRAIT OF THE ARTIST*. IS THAT YOU PUTTING YOU INTO YOUR PLAYS?

JAJ: I'm sure it's me putting me into my plays. I'm sure it's me trying to figure out what I've probably spent several years of my life trying to figure out, which is how do I make sense of the things that I see, things that are complex and compelling but disturbing at the same time. Teachers and mentors would always say, 'Your lead characters are very underwritten,' and I guess my female lead characters are underwrit-ten because they are me, and perhaps my teachers understood that. Maybe I understood it, too, but it didn't matter, because the story was what was interesting for me. It's about trying to figure out what hap-pens when you go into a situation and try to fix it. Those outsider characters to a certain extent are people who walk into a situation and try to see if they can make it better, and are unable to. Instead of being able to change what they find, they themselves are changed. That's the biggest lesson for somebody who has the hubris of trying to save the world.

AG: THAT IS CERTAINLY BOBBY'S JOURNEY IN *UFO*. HER SOLUTION TO SHELA'S DRUG ADDICTION FEELS LIKE AN OUTSIDER'S RATIONAL SOLUTION, WHILE BROTHER JERE-MIAH'S IDEA OF CHAINING SHELA TO HER BABY'S BASSINET, THOUGH SHOCKING AT FIRST, ULTIMATELY FEELS MORE COMPASSIONATE.

JAJ: That was what I felt. But I think that is why people haven't liked the play. People ask, 'Are you advocating for this choice, for what this man does?' And I say, 'Well, what I'm advocating for is that people make the choices that are right for them.' I was raised Methodist Episcopalian and went to church school until I was thirteen, so I was brought up with moralistic thinking — that there's good and bad and right and wrong. And it's taken me years to undo that. You really can't judge other people by what's right for you. That's what confuses people about the play and propels a moral dilemma, which is what I wanted. Life is complex. Nobody wants to see anybody chained, but Jeremiah does it to keep Shela from doing crack. I mean, this woman next door to me had a baby, you know what I'm saying? She was a crack head and she had a child. At least one. And then the child was gone, and she was still a crack head. The choice that she made was for her drug. So while Jeremiah's actions seem drastic, at the same time they are about the life of this baby. And he's maybe saying to Shela, 'If you can kick this, maybe you'll have a better life too.'

AG: HE'S AN INTRIGUING CHARACTER. YOU DON'T KNOW WHETHER HE'S GOOD OR EVIL.

JAJ: Right. You don't. And you don't know whether he is sane or insane, although he is certainly sane in his own mind.

AG: YOU SAID THAT THE YOUNG DRUG ADDICTS WHO LIVED NEXT DOOR TO YOU WERE ONE SOURCE FOR THE PLAY. WERE THERE OTHER SOURCES?

JAJ: When I was at Brown, I met this guy who was part of a cult founded by a man named Malachi York, who felt that he was Christ revisited. But from space. This young black guy in Providence gave me a book and talked to me about the religion, and I was like, 'So . . . you guys really think you're from outer space?' At the same time, I was working with a cabaret troupe here, and our musical director was a ufologist. I had never heard of that before. And I also didn't think that was the kind of thing black people did, quite frankly. I just never thought black people got into that kind of stuff. So to have these two on top of each other — that was amazing to me.

The character of A.Z., in *UFO*, is based on the guy who was the musical director. He had been a stockbroker. He had been making tons of money, and one day he just realized that he couldn't deal with it. He couldn't deal with the racism, he couldn't deal with the obsession about money, and he said that he remembers that he had been 'visited' since he was twelve. Now, this was a really good friend, and I didn't know what to think. He and I and a lot of other people did a meditation in a mutual friend's apartment, and I fell asleep on the floor. I think I was just blocking it out, because I couldn't believe I was doing this. He was playing on his synthesizer, chords that sounded like they were out of *E.T.* Then we went up to the roof and broke into groups, and I swear, after twenty-five minutes of staring at the sky, I saw things moving too. Designs and patterns. This was done as a synchronized, worldwide meditation. I mean, these UFO people are everywhere. I still don't know what to think, but it fascinates me.

AG: AS IT FASCINATES AND FRUSTRATES BOBBY. RELATED TO THE QUESTION OF BEING AN OUTSIDER IS THE QUESTION OF COMMUNITY. IN *PORTRAIT OF THE ARTIST* YOU DRA-MATIZE THE PROBLEMS OF DISCOVERING WHO AND WHERE COMMUNITY IS, AND WHAT HAPPENS WHEN A PER-SON DESERTS THEIR COMMUNITY.

JAJ: You are raised to think that the world is open to you, and that if you work hard enough and try hard enough, doors will open. Then you reach a certain age, and all of a sudden, all the things they don't tell you when you're really young, because they don't want you to be depressed, you learn anyway. For me, I was nineteen. A friend of mine named Michael Stewart was killed by transit police officers in 1983. That's where *Portrait* came from. It was a really big case here, one of those first, major, police brutality cases, which went on for months and was all over the media. They brought cops up on charges and let them all go.

Michael and I were very close for a time. We met when I was sev-enteen and hanging out in the clubs, but I hadn't seen him in about six months when it happened. He got killed by a bunch of white police officers, and one of the reports that I remember reading in *The Village Voice* said that these officers might have seen him leaving a club by the side of this young white lady that he was friendly with. They sup-posedly arrested him because he was writing on the subway trains, but how did he end up hogtied and strangled, with no weapon? He was in a coma for a while and then he died. That did something so major to my psyche, because I knew him and also because I had thought that there was at least one place where race didn't matter, and that was in the context of young people getting together and having a good time. There were white people, black people, Asian people, Latino peo-ple in our clubs, and everybody was having fun, dancing, doing drugs, being young in New York. Michael's death woke me up about race.

I remember also, when I was in high school, a woman who was supposedly one of my friends called a security guard a 'nigger' in the cafeteria at Bronx Science, and that had its own strange repercussions, because I had all my white friends coming up to me, saying, 'Oh, but she really didn't mean it.' Or, 'You shouldn't feel anything about it because you're not really black.' So I think over a period of two or three years I got it. My mother had always been really clear, 'You have to be as good as you can be, because you're a woman of color, and they are going to make it a challenge for you.' She was never one to fill us with fear about it; it was always, 'Do the best that you can.' But 'they' was very abstract for me. And 'they' became very unabstract in a period of two or three years.

Being in the theater, you run up against it. There's a dominant culture, and the dominant culture doesn't see itself in your story. We learn to see ourselves in the stories of the dominant culture, because we have to. We learn from the time that we're very young to find ourselves in the cartoons that we watch or the *Brady Bunch* or whatever. Even if we're not there, we learn to meld our existences with the dominant culture and pretend that we are part of it. Then there comes some time when we realize that we're not part of the dominant culture, and not only that, but the dominant culture doesn't really care about us and doesn't intend to give up much, because we are a very minor part of that culture. You come to work in the arts and you think, 'Oh, it's different,' and then you realize it really isn't. Part of that is because this is capitalism, and the dominant culture cannot afford to do anything but what's going to make money. If white folks don't want to go to the theater to see black art, then the white people programming it, no matter how much they may want to deal with inclusion, just can't afford to.

AG: I'VE HAD THE DISCUSSION WITH MANY PLAYWRIGHTS ABOUT HOW COMPARTMENTALIZED AMERICAN THEATER IS IN THIS RESPECT. ACTUALLY, I USED THE WORD 'SEGREGATED' IN ONE INTERVIEW AND GOT A LOOK . . .

JAJ: It's segregated. We live in a segregated society in a lot of ways. I don't think that people like to talk about that, but it's true. And I think in the theater it's especially painful for people to hear those kinds of things, because in the theater there are a lot of people who are really what they mean when they say 'liberals.' It's painful to have to deal with realities like racism and capitalism when you're dealing with art, but this is America, and everything is a business. And art is a business. *Portrait* is about that.

AG: IN *PORTRAIT*, ONE OF THE MEANINGS THAT I TAKE AWAY FROM SONNY'S CAREER IS THAT HE CHASES THE WRONG IMAGES. HE GOES TOWARD CAPITALISM AND IT KILLS HIM, SPIRITUALLY AND LITERALLY.

JAJ: The play is also based on Jean-Michel Basquiat, a twenty-seven year old African-American artist who died in 1988 of a heroin overdose. He was one of those darlings of the Lower East Side. He started out as a graffiti artist and was making really interesting art that European art critics 'discovered' as rooted in 'primitivism' or whatever. He was very much taken up and put in galleries and was like 'the first black artist to ever . . . ' In European terms, he was the first. There had never been another black artist, ever, in the history of man. Which of course is racism, because nobody looks at African art, or even at the art of black people here in America, at the amazing history of not just folk art but of art by people who studied traditional forms.

And then Jean-Michel became a heroin addict and ODed. But he got what most people think they want when they think they want to become famous: people looking at you, exposure, money. But he was completely alienated and died.

AG: IN THE PLAY, ARE YOU COMPARING THE STORY OF THE FATHER, WHO WAS A JAZZ MUSICIAN, WITH THAT OF THE SON, A PAINTER? IS WHAT THE SON TRIES TO DO AS AN ARTIST MORE IN THE WHITE EUROPEAN DIRECTION YOU JUST DESCRIBED THAN WHAT THE FATHER DID?

JAJ: Oh, I don't know. It's more that jazz has always had its place in the dominant culture, been condoned and supported and truly loved to an extent. But jazz is not a money-making art form anymore in America. If it had continued to be a money-making art form, the father might have gone the same way as Sonny. But like the father says, the clubs dried up.

AG: IS THE FATHER BEATEN UP BY BLACK MEN OR WHITE MEN?

JAJ: The guys who cut So'Man are black, yeah. That actually is a terminology, 'cut.' People say, 'Can you cut me?' meaning, 'Can you outbeat me on the instrument?' Because of his arrogance, and just because of who So'Man was, he got cut. That was a trick of fate more than anything. That was his bad luck for being a big mouth and getting cut. And that ruined his career.

AG: WHAT DO YOU WANT US TO SEE IN THE RELATIONSHIP BETWEEN FATHER AND SON? YOU HAVE BOTH MEN TRYING TO GO BEYOND THEMSELVES IN SOME WAY WITH THEIR ART.

JAJ: It is basically what the father said, that you're not going to be allowed to fly but so high. He was cut down in one way by his own hubris, and Sonny is cut down by becoming popular and losing himself. I'm not saying that this is solely an African-American predicament. Artists are caught in a bind, because art is not concrete. An artist has to get money, but how do you get paid to figure out your existential place in the universe in a creative context?

I was raised with so many issues about money, coming up in a religious home where 'The love of money is the root of all evil.' I was raised with the whole idea that artists shouldn't think about money. I really did buy into that. There are people who are clear that, 'I'm going to make my art and I want to get paid,' and I think those people are kind of lucky. But there are also the people who say, 'Whose ass do I have to kiss and what do I have to do?' And maybe you can get there, like Sonny, but at what price?

So I don't think that's a bind only of race, but race complicates everything. As does gender. When you're a person of color, your primary fight in the world is to get out of this sense of the prison of your history. But being a woman is pretty challenging in its own way. So it's a double bind. Or it doesn't have to be. You can also realize that you're so outside the constructs of the system, that you can make up your own rules. That's sort of what I've decided to do. If my place is outside the system, how do I get in and get out of the system when I need to? How do I move around the system? How do I do what I need to do and survive? Survive with as much of my spirit intact as possible? More and more, that's what's important for me. Ten years ago I would have done anything to have a successful career in the arts. I don't feel that way now. I certainly won't give up the peace of mind that it's taken me this long to get. Maintaining that is my priority.

AG: IF THE ENDINGS OF *UFO* AND *DEATH OF A HO* ARE ANY INDICATION, YOU'VE MOVED TO A MORE POSITIVE RESOLUTION OF THESE ISSUES.

JAJ: *Death of a Ho* is changing. Even as we speak. I'm rewriting the play.

AG: ARE YOU REWRITING FROM SCRATCH?

JAJ: From scratch.

AG: WHY?

JAJ: Because after two years, seven drafts, and what feels like ten workshops, including one recently at New York Theatre Workshop, I realized from talking with people that the play I had written was not communicating what I wanted to communicate. I think it is just too complex. I think the structure is so complex that all the little machinations disenable me from saying the important things that I want to say. Also, I feel differently about the issues of the play than I did two years ago. When I started writing this play, it was a personal play. It was about sort of feeling like a prostitute. And now that's changed to, 'Yeah, I understand that I'm going to have to be a prostitute, and that's okay if I can keep my spiritual center intact. And I'm going to make the decisions about when and how and what I choose to get paid for, if I have to be a hooker.' You work and you get paid, fine. Capitalism exists, and the part of me that has to deal within capitalism is maybe the part of me that will always feel like a ho. But the part of me that is about my spirit and my sense of what it is to be alive and be grateful for life is bigger than that. So that's the place that I'm operating from. Which wasn't the place that I was operating from when I was first writing this play.

I also feel the play needs to be more universal, in the sense that this is America, and we're all caught up in the absurdity of capitalism. If I root the play in this person Rae-Ann, then people ask questions about Rae-Ann's history and her back story, and stuff that I didn't create because I really was using her as a device to talk about these issues. But once you give audiences a name, and a character who has an existential crisis, they're going to hook onto them. Just because of the way that we look at plays, that's the person whose emotional arc and journey we're expecting to go through the play with, and that's where we're expecting to get the catharsis from. And I didn't want that. I wanted Rae-Ann to be an emblematic, symbolic Everyperson.

AG: IT'S A MORALITY PLAY.

JAJ: It's a morality play, but it wasn't a well-written morality play. It wasn't doing what I needed it to do. People were coming up with too many questions about the wrong things. And I thought, 'There are too many issues, or else the issues aren't being routed in a way that helps the audience get there.' Now, all the themes are there, but the play has a very different structure.

AG: IF I CAN ADVOCATE FOR THE SCRIPT I READ, YOU MASTERED WHAT YOU SEEM TO HAVE BEEN AIMING FOR FROM YOUR EARLY WORK, WHICH IS A FLUID INTERCUTTING OF IMAGES AND CHARACTERS, DREAM AND REALITY. ARE YOU CHANGING THAT STYLE?

JAJ: What I'm changing is that instead of being Rae-Ann's play, there is no Rae-Ann now. There's a character called the Girl, who actually is born in front of us. She does not exist before the lights come on. Now, the Geechee Fairy opens the story and shows us a tabula rasa, a cardboard form, that then we see is built into a woman who happens to be a dark brown woman. Then we watch this woman learn who she is in this culture and in the media, and who she's not, and decide, 'This is what I really want.' She goes along a road, where she meets other people.

What I do better in this version is guide the audience, so that they have the experience the Girl is having while she's having it. There's no question of this woman Rae-Ann in a hospital bed who has a life to get back to. There is no life outside of this play. It is a fairy tale.

The whole representational idea of the play is over. It's all presentational, in the moment, morality, fairy tale. Which is also opening up places for me to play with, so that stylistically the audience has no question about what the world of the play is. What was confusing people were large places of what felt like representational theater. I had scenes between Rae-Ann and Gloria and Brenda that felt naturalistic, and I think that was deluding the audience in a way. In some ways it was enjoyable for the audience, to be in moments where it felt like they were watching a naturalistic play and then have that snatched away from them. But finally I had set up things that were too difficult to finesse, like the dead ghouls coming back. In workshop after workshop, people said, 'They just keep coming back and they say the same thing.' And I felt that too. So I would have to erase them and erase them. The version you read is the best that the play can be in terms of what I originally set up, but I don't think it really works.

AG: AT ONE POINT, RAE-ANN AND BRENDA ARE TALKING AND TOUCHING, AND I GET THE SENSE THAT THEY ARE ONE WOMAN, THAT RAE-ANN IS THE BLACK WOMAN INSIDE THE WHITE WOMAN. IS THAT IMAGE GONE?

JAJ: No, because that's really important for me. I think I always knew this, but it's easy to forget it when you're in your teens or at a place where you're obsessed with what the media is telling you about your body — obsessed by standards that are certainly not culturally going to work for you. I remember listening to my white girlfriends complain about their bodies and their unhappiness with their lives in general, and these were some of the same issues that I had, and I was like, 'Wow, life isn't really any better for them.' I realized that some of the issues are to do with being women in a male-dominated society and consistently having to believe that you count. That feeling is not necessarily one that only black women have.

AG: DO YOU THINK THAT A FEMINIST WOMAN OF COLOR AND A FEMINIST WHITE WOMAN HAVE THE SAME ISSUES?

JAJ: 'Feminist' is not a term I use, because I don't think I know what that means. I would say that women are similarly oppressed in a male-dominated culture. But I think that women of color rarely have delusions about access, because they cannot assume that they have access based on men. Men of color, while they have more access than women of color, and in some cases more access than white women, often do not have access. White women have had the luxury of being deluded that they can get access based on being white. And sometimes they can, even though, historically, white men have not allowed white women the access they have allowed themselves. But there is no illusion that there is black power. And because of what has happened historically to black men in our society, black women have had to get up and fend for themselves in ways that are superhuman. On top of dealing with racism and sexism, the issues that black women have to deal with are just *huge*. Huger than issues that white women have to deal with. The veneer of safety and comfort allowed to white women is not allowed to black women at all. Those delusions and those fantasies have never been in play.

AG: ANOTHER STRONG IMAGE IN *DEATH OF A HO* OCCURS AT THE (OLD) BEGINNING, WHEN RAE-ANN LOOKS IN A MIRROR AND INSTEAD OF SEEING HERSELF, SEES OTHER PEOPLE POINTING AT HER AND LAUGHING (YOU CALL FOR THEM TO BE ON VIDEO AROUND AND BEHIND HER). IT'S A DISTURBING CONCEPT.

JAJ: Did you ever see the movie *Paris Burning*? If it's disturbing to think of a black woman doing that, imagine how disturbing it is to watch that movie and see these black men with pictures of Marlene Dietrich all over their walls, making themselves up with blond wigs. Do you know what I'm saying? That's amazing, that people would decide that not only is their skin color wrong, but that they would have more power taking on the attire of a white woman than they would that of a black man. I think that the media is awesome in it's ability to replace your sense of self. You can lose yourself in images.

I really had to think about how to make the video work in this version. A lot of it is much more intentional now, because the content is restructuring the form of the play. Before, I could get away with writing the story, but in this version I really had to think about the relationship between language and video: how do I tell the story so that the video is now a character? Before, the video was like a design element. But really it has to be a character, or — what we have found through the workshops — people will watch the television monitors. They will watch the media before they watch the live actors. In the last three workshops I've had — in the Bay area, in Cleveland and at New York Theatre Workshop — we have had video, and inadvertently audiences say they watched the television monitors. Which says to me, if we put the video on a big screen, we can forget what's happening onstage. I have had to keep that in mind and be specific about what I am creating.

AG: YOU CALL FOR VIDEOTAPE OR FILM FOOTAGE IN A NUMBER OF YOUR PLAYS.

JAJ: It's been risky. Theaters don't necessarily like electronic media. John Dias at the Public Theater said, 'I always find it fascinating. I always watch it when it's there. But I'm not convinced that I understand or know why it's there.' This time around I really had to ask myself why I was putting video in this play. The answer has changed the narrative. It's changed the way I tell the story.

AG: IN THE VERSION I READ, THE VIDEO SEEMS TO PROVIDE A BACKGROUND, AMONG OTHER THINGS.

JAJ: Now I don't want a background. That's the thing. Her being in the hospital room — I don't want that back story. That shouldn't even be there. The audience should be seeing everything as it happens. Now the video is doing what the video should, which is to supply information in the present. The audience is getting more information about what is happening in front of them. It's helping the audience to understand the mind of this woman, helping them understand what media images are doing to her. How they are mutating her. Because that's what media does to us. Now, I'm using electronic media in a play where media is working on people.

AG: DO PLAYS BEGIN IN YOU WITH AN IMAGE?

JAJ: Usually with some issue that's bothering me. Something I don't understand, or that I find fascinating or disturbing and feel that the conversation should happen around.

AG: WHAT WAS THE ISSUE AT THE ROOT OF *TERMINAL WAITING*?

JAJ: My multiple abortions. I knew that I had to write a piece about that, because I just did not understand where I had gotten such an irresponsible idea about getting pregnant, after being raised in a Christian home where the one thing my mother told us about sex was, 'Don't come home pregnant.'

AG: TRANSFORMING PERSONAL EXPERIENCE INTO ART SEEMS TO ME ONE OF THE HARDEST, IF ESSENTIAL, TASKS FOR A WRITER.

JAJ: It's funny about writing. You can actually go into something thinking, 'This is not a problem. I can do this.' Then somewhere in the process, you realize what it really means to go into it. That was the case with *Terminal Waiting*. The experience of writing that was unexpectedly brutal. I teach writing for solo performance, and when I talk to the students, I say, 'You've got to get some distance from your work, because you can't control it if you don't have distance.' I am a dramaturg's dream, because I'm into rewriting, I believe in workshops, I believe in being objective about my writing.

One of the great things that I did at Brown was to take my independent studies in the Women's Studies Program, and I read a lot of cultural criticism and theory. It empowered me to understand that my words are just words, not jewels. Words are what I do. I write, and people will judge my writing. They will retranslate, deconstruct, reconfigure, and then they will put something else out. And sometimes it's what I want them to put back out, but a lot of times it's not. My job is to try to write the clearest interpretation of what I'm trying to say that I can.

Realizing that took a lot of weight off of me as a writer. When you're in this realm of creator, it becomes so real to you, that everything you look at, you understand as being real. I had to find a way to get some distance from what I do, to understand that my sense of myself as a human being is not hooked into what other people think about my work. Otherwise I would stop writing. Laurie Carlos, one of my mentors, said, 'The minute you feel like you are going to stop, that's when they have succeeded in silencing you. By not producing your work, by putting you through workshops, by telling you that your work is like this person and not enough like that person — that's how they basically negate what you do. And if you allow that to stop you from writing, then they have silenced you.' So in order to continue to write, I have to find a way to get some distance from it.

AG: IS WRITING A LONG PROCESS FOR YOU?

JAJ: I believe writing a play takes a while. I try to give myself enough time between drafts so that I've pretty much forgotten what I loved about the draft that I just wrote, so I can go back into it with clean eyes and let it be a new experience when I rewrite. A good six months between drafts is good for me. I did the *Death of a Ho* workshop in May, so now it's maybe three months since I had the idea that I would rewrite. And then I was so sick of seeing that version, and the same problems kept coming up for me, that I was like, 'Jake, why don't you see what happens if you sit down and give yourself the freedom to do something completely different?'

AG: IT TAKES GUTS TO DO THAT.

JAJ: Yeah, it does. But I couldn't let that earlier version be produced, quite honestly.

AG: REALLY?

JAJ: There's no way to go back. Not even for production. So I'm really hoping everyone likes this one.

AG: IT TAKES A LONG TIME TO BECOME A PLAYWRIGHT.

JAJ: I do feel that my ideas about form and content and how they work together are just beginning to happen for me.

AG: IN *PORTRAIT*, SONNY HAS THE LINE, 'POST-CIVIL-RIGHTS CHILLIN'S BALL-OF-CONFUSION,' AND I WONDER IF YOU COULD EXPAND ON THAT.

JAJ: It's the same conversation that Bobby and A.Z. have. There was a time in the sixties when there was the possibility that things were going to change for people of color and African-American people. There was a feeling of power and of power to the people. And some things happened, but some things didn't. So you learn your history, and you learn about the revolutionary movement and King and X and Angela Davis and Assata Shakur. And then you look, and here it is 1980 and 1985 and 1990, and the sense of struggle, and the sense of making things better for your people or the world or America — the sense that America will become the place Martin Luther King spoke about when he said, 'I have a dream' — becomes the realization that life is hard, and you have to pay your bills, and you have to figure out, 'What's my career?' You start growing up. I think that realization is especially strong if you had parents like mine, who were very much about having their children be better off than they were and having them be citizens who contributed to the world. My brother and sisters do things that are about civic duty; I'm the one who decided that I was more concerned with figuring myself out, although I believe in community and the possibility of people making things better.

AG: LOOKING AT AMERICA TODAY, IT IS DIVIDED BETWEEN THOSE WHO DO AND THOSE WHO WANT TO THINK, AND THE CULTURE IS GEARED TOWARD THE DOERS RATHER THAN THE THINKERS AND ARTISTS. BUT ISN'T IT VALUABLE TO SHOW THAT SPLIT, AS YOU DO IN *UFO*, WHERE YOU HAVE BOBBY STRUGGLING WITH THAT CONFLICT?

JAJ: Do you think it's valuable? We're having this conversation about work that I have written, because you have taken the time to read my work. But most people out there in the world have not read it and will probably never see it. In the community that I live in, someone could say that if I was a practical person, I would open up a community theater. But that isn't who I am. Is that because I don't have the drive and determination to take what I believe in, which is the idea of art and its contribution to the spiritual and the intellectual in human beings? I believe in that, but I'm the person who is inclined to take my own stuff and make art out of it, as opposed to the person who says, 'I'm going to make a community event happen around it.'

The way I make up for that is by understanding the value that I have when I teach writing. Recently I was teaching a woman who was an ex-drug addict. I was reading her writing, and she was terrified, sitting at the computer. And at the end of it, I was able to say to her, 'This is an excellent paragraph.' It really was. She was terrified and she wrote in the passage about her terror of my reading it. The grammar and the punctuation were perfect. And I could see her visibly go, 'Wow.' You know? And I felt that was real, that moment. So I'm beginning to understand that maybe that's how I can make up for this sense that I haven't yet been able to make a contribution through my art.

AG: PERHAPS IT GOES BACK TO THE QUESTION OF COMMUNITY. YOU MENTIONED KING; HE WAS ADDRESSING AN ENORMOUS COMMUNITY. BUT THERE ARE DIFFERENT LEVELS OF COMMUNITY, INCLUDING YOU HELPING THIS WOMAN TO WRITE.

JAJ: Community in America is a very complex question. This country has not engaged in conversation about community for a really long time. It is not part of the national agenda to talk about the community of America, in its wide variety and continuing change. Two black people walking down the street together don't necessarily have community. They may have the same skin color and maybe culturally they did many of the same things, but in terms of their way of communicating or their value systems they may not actually have community without doing some serious work. Some serious conversation. There are many issues here.

AG: IN A WAY, ISN'T THAT RAE-ANN'S SEARCH IN *DEATH OF A HO*? ISN'T THAT WHY SHE CALLS UP THE GEECHEE FAIRY IN THE FIRST PLACE? BECAUSE SHE'S SEARCHING FOR HERSELF, AND FOR SOME KIND OF COMMUNITY OTHER THAN THE ONE SHE'S TRAPPED IN?

JAJ: It's not even an issue of being trapped. It's just that life has so much variety, why not try to taste it all? I may feel more comfortable, at the end of the day, coming back to Harlem, where I've lived all my life, where there are people who look like me and people who like the same kind of music that I've grown up on and people who have the same references that I do and use the language that I use when

I'm hanging out with black folks. That is where I feel at home. But that doesn't mean that's all I want for my life every day. That's not the way to become the most faceted person that you can be. I don't want that to impinge on my freedom. Ultimately, maybe that's why I choose to do art. I feel there's a space to carve out the freedom that I need. ▽

Wendy Kesselman

Wendy Kesselman was born and raised in New York City, where her mother was a concert pianist, lieder singer, and therapist, and her father practiced psychiatry. After graduating from college and studying art history and poetry in Paris, Kesselman began her career as a professional singer and songwriter. She became an author of such books for young people as *Franz Tovey and the Rare Animals* (1968), *Angelita* (1970), *Joey* (1972), and *Emma* (1980). *Becca* (1977), the story of a young girl whose brother treats her like a doll and orders her about, is Kesselman's first work for the theater and a musicalization of her children's book of the same name. Like a number of Kesselman's plays and music-theater pieces, Becca delves into the realm of the fairy tale.

Other theater works by Kesselman include *My Sister in This House* (1981, revised 1987), based on a notorious murder in Le Mans, France; *Maggie Magalita* (1980, revised 1987); *The Juniper Tree, A Tragic Household Tale/A Music-Theatre Piece* (1983, revised 2000); *I Love You, I Love You Not* (1988), which involves the close relationship between an adolescent and her grandmother; and the musical play *A Tale of Two Cities* (1992, revised 1998). *The Executioner's Daughter* (as *The Butcher's Daughter*, produced 1993, revised 1999) focuses on the rapaciousness of the French Revolution as experienced by two women: the daughter of the chief executioner of Paris, and the playwright Olympe de Gouges. For Broadway, Kesselman adapted Frances Goodrich and Albert Hackett's play *The Diary of Anne Frank* (1998, revised 2000). Kesselman has also written films and is presently adapting John Knowles' novel *A Separate Peace*.

Among Kesselman's numerous awards are the Susan Smith Blackburn Award for *My Sister in This House;* the Lecomte de Noüy Award for *The Executioner's Daughter*—also selected by the AT&T New Plays for the Nineties Project; and in 1997 the New England Theatre Conference Major Award for Outstanding Creative Achievement in the American Theatre.

Kesselman lives in Massachusetts. This interview took place on September 19, 1999, in New York City.

• • •

AG: WHEN GEORGE LUCAS MADE *STAR WARS* IN 1977, HE TOLD A REPORTER THAT HE INTENDED HIS FILM FOR A GENERATION GROWING UP WITHOUT FAIRY TALES. WOULD YOU AGREE THAT FAIRY TALES HAVE DISAPPEARED?

WK: I think that largely they have disappeared, but that people still have the same passion for fairy tales and fairy tale-like stories when they hear them. To be honest, I saw the first *Star Wars* and went right to sleep. But even *E.T.*, which I suppose in a way is a fairy tale, doesn't have the quality of the true fairy tale, that combination of beauty and terror.

Not only did I grow up with fairy tales, but I thought they were real. I thought they had happened in the eighteenth century. And I always would turn to them in moments of unhappiness, as a soothing thing. Bruno Bettelheim writes in *The Uses of Enchantment* that the child or central figure in a fairy tale goes through terrible terrors, but fights against the terrors and survives in the end. For me, fairy tales were always a comfort. People now say that children shouldn't read them, 'They're so frightening, they're so disturbing.' But for me, fairy tales were always a comfort.

AG: BETTELHEIM ALSO BELIEVES THAT FAIRY TALES STIMULATE A CHILD'S IMAGINATION.

WK: As they did mine. I remember the illustrations to fairy tales vividly. And visual images were always powerful in fairy tales. Although I'm so involved with language and words — and I'm a fiend about periods and commas — usually the first thing that comes to me is a visual image.

AG: DID YOU READ FAIRY TALES TO YOURSELF, OR WERE THEY READ OR TOLD TO YOU?

WK: I imagine my mother read them to me. *Peter Pan*, which is a very fairy tale-like story, was a huge part of my childhood, because I was named after Wendy. Actually, my parents were going to give me the entire name: Wendy Moira Angela Darling. I thoroughly believed that was who I was.

AG: IS A FAIRY TALE A CAUTIONARY TALE?

WK: I would never think of a fairy tale in that way. I've never thought of them as moral warnings: 'Don't do this or you'll be harmed or punished.' Fairy tales are almost like films to me. I think of them as passionate and romantic stories. The true cautionary tales — the German *Struwwelpeter* stories — were read to me by my grandmother. They were terrifying. She always read the story about the child who doesn't eat, and all that's left in the end are the shoes. I still have the book, and it's scratched, and the pages are torn out.

AG: WHAT IS THE RELATIONSHIP BETWEEN A FAIRY TALE AND A DREAM?

WK: The feeling of entering a fairy tale is similar, for me, to entering a dream. A fairy tale is a completely enclosed world, where everything can happen. Which is like a dream. There's an entire world in a dream, but it's closed.

AG: IN *BECCA*, DREAM AND FAIRY TALE FLOW INTO EACH OTHER.

WK: Right. But it all takes place in that house, in that room — that enclosed space. So does *My Sister in This House*. The house is in the title because it was as important as any of those characters. One of the things that pulled me to the story was that it happened in a single house in a specific town — Le Mans. That's a very shut-away town, and even though it's not far from Paris, you feel when you're there that you are not going to escape. Which is sometimes what you feel in a dream. Certainly in a nightmare. There is that sense of border, and so much happens within those borders in both dreams and fairy tales.

AG: THERE IS A KIND OF INVERTED CINDERELLA STORY WITHIN *MY SISTER IN THIS HOUSE*.

WK: That's true.

AG: THE SISTERS' EMPLOYERS ARE EVIL STEPMOTHERS IN A WAY. BUT THERE IS NO FAIRY GODMOTHER.

WK: No. Not a one. I'll tell you the story of *My Sister in This House*. I was reading Janet Flanner's marvelous book, *Paris Was Yesterday*, on a cold February day. I don't know if it was the date that the crime had taken place, but it was the month. The crime occurred on February 2 — Groundhog Day. Halfway through this little paperback, I came across an article called *The Murder in Le Mans*. I read it and became instantaneously obsessed. When I got to the end, it flickered through my mind that this possibly was the story on which Genet had based *The Maids*, but I didn't hesitate and rushed down to the public library, because I felt that I had to see what those sisters looked like. There wasn't much in the major French newspapers, but I thought that if one newspaper would pick up the story of these girls turning on their employers it would be *L'Humanité*, the paper of the French Communist Party. And sure enough. There they were. I was with a friend, and she told me I went dead white when I saw the photograph.

In *L'Humanité*, the sisters were heroines. Simone de Beauvoir and Sartre called the murders a revolutionary act, until they learned of the likelihood that the sisters were incestuously involved and somewhat retarded. The crime was a huge event. There were several other plays. Novels. It was possibly the only crime in history where a victim's eye was removed without the use of an instrument. I eventually understood why people at the time kept talking about the optic nerve being left intact: that could have happened only by reaching all the way back into the brain.

I was so drawn to the sisters initially that the two other characters —Madame and her daughter, Isabelle — were very hard for me. When I asked friends who lived in France, 'What would women like Madame and Isabelle have done with their time?' they said, 'Rien.' Very helpful. So I had to concoct that part of the play, and I put in the card game — which I played over and over by myself first, in order to figure out the hands. My friends said that was exactly the kind of thing these women would have done. But really, they did nothing.

AG: BOTH PAIRS OF WOMEN ARE OPPRESSED, BUT AT LEAST THE SISTERS . . .

WK: . . . have their life. Their passionate life. But what I loved, in terms of borders, was that the whole thing happened in that enclosed space.

Now I am working on something that is absolutely the opposite of *My Sister*: a film adaptation of James Fenimore Cooper's 1821 novel, *The Spy*. Not even the French Revolution; the American Revolution. I was relieved to learn that the story takes place in New York's Westchester County and that the time frame is the fall of 1780 into the winter. But it's still a huge and very open situation, which is the challenge for me. When a story has borders, then it can become a big thing in an enclosed space. In *The Spy* there are no borders. No physical borders in any case.

AG: GOING BACK TO *MY SISTER IN THIS HOUSE* FOR A MOMENT, WHICH PAIR OF WOMEN IS MORE IMPRISONED THAN THE OTHER?

WK: Probably Madame and Isabelle. The sisters choose their imprisonment. They never leave that room. They leave to do the shopping, but on their day off — and this is true — they are always in that room.

AG: BUT THEY DIDN'T CHOOSE TO BE SERVANTS. THAT WAS DETERMINED BY THEIR ECONOMIC AND SOCIAL PLACE.

WK: That's absolutely true. But one of the things which interested me was that after they committed the crime, they didn't even think about leaving. They could have left. They could have fled. Not only did they stay in the house, they stayed in their room. They cleaned the instruments they had used, to some extent, and they washed their hands. They cleaned themselves.

AG: WAS CHRISTINE IN ACTUALITY A MAGNIFICENT SEAMSTRESS, AS IN YOUR PLAY?

WK: That was true. And Lea was the more awkward sister. But in everything that I read about the two, Lea was described as the dominating one, and to me it was clear that Christine was more fragile. In the actual story, Christine was condemned to the guillotine but she was not executed — women were not being guillotined at the time — and she died four years after the trial of a complete breakdown of body and mind. Lea, the little one, survived. I desperately tried to find her, but I was told that she was dead. In fact, she was still alive when

I was writing, and I could have tracked her down — I would have tracked her down — but I didn't know.

AG: THE SISTERS FIND AN OUTLET FOR THEIR SEXUALITY; THE MOTHER AND DAUGHTER DO NOT.

WK: Yet I had the sense that, with their increasing involvement, things became so entangled that, in a way, the sexual relationship became the imprisonment. In the beginning maybe the sex was a release, but then ultimately too much, too enclosed. Flanner makes a reference to the French psychoanalyst Lacan, who wrote an article about how the murder was essentially committed by one person, because each thing one sister did was copied by the other.

The Flanner article was originally published in the 1930s in *Vanity Fair*, and you see this remarkable photograph of the sisters — the photograph I always call the wedding picture, taken by an expensive photographer in town — where their hair is curled and they wear identical white collars. The scene in my play where they pose for a photographer was written because of that photograph. But there are other famous photographs. When the police came, a photographer took two pictures of the girls in their robes, and the surrealists wrote about the contrast between the fresh farm faces of the wedding picture and these two shocking pictures taken soon after the murder. There's also a photograph of the sisters coming out of prison. After a long time looking at these few photographs, I realized that the sisters were dressed identically in each. They had merged completely.

AG: YOU TALK ABOUT BEING OBSESSED BY THE STORY OF THE SISTERS. DO YOU GO INTO A DREAM STATE WHEN YOU WRITE?

WK: I'm not aware of it, but now that you say it, I think that's probably true. Certainly nothing else seems to come in. It happened to me recently with the latest expansion of *Merry-Go-Round*. In fact, the characters themselves enter that dreamlike state. And the recurrent music — the Schubert and Scriabin and the *Merry-Go-Round* song Michael plays on the piano — is part of that dream.

AG: YOU COMPOSE MUSIC AND YOU USED TO SING PRO-FESSIONALLY. DID YOU FIND MUSIC BEFORE WRITING?

WK: Yes. My mother was a musician — a marvelous pianist — so music was a huge part of my life always. She also sang German lieder. I've realized recently that lieder also have a contained feeling. Each song has a brief format, but there's an entire world within that one song. Each song tells a whole story in a brief span of time. Children's books also have a compressed form. So does a play in a way. It's not as if a play runs twelve hours. To encompass an entire world in that two-hour or hour-and-a-half span is . . . I love that limitation. Very different than a novel.

AG: MORE LIKE A SHORT STORY.

WK: Absolutely. Chekhov.

AG: DID YOU PLAY INSTRUMENTS AS WELL AS SING?

WK: Primarily the guitar. Some piano. Now I rarely compose on the guitar. I do it in my head, I go to the piano, then maybe to the guitar.

AG: WHAT DID YOU WRITE BEFORE YOU BEGAN WRITING PLAYS?

WK: Primarily children's books, and before that, poetry. I was a passionate poetry lover. I became involved with playwriting through Margot Lewitin — at what was then called the Women's Interart Center. She had read *Angelita* and had heard some of my music. The New York State Council on the Arts had set up a Young Audiences Play Commission Program, the idea being to use writers who had never before created theater and would not look down on the child. Margot asked what I thought about writing a play, and I said, 'I love the idea, but I've never done one.' And she said, 'Why don't you take your most dramatic story, and we'll submit it?' I knew the most dramatic story was *Becca*, which hadn't been published yet — and never was — so we submitted that along with other books of mine, and a year later the grant came through. I wrote the play. It was almost entirely music, because I had never written a play before.

The children's story and the play were sent to Maurice Sendak, who was my idol. He said the story was the best he had read in five years and he loved the dramatization, but he said that the book would never be published because it was too controversial. I never thought that this would be the situation with the play, too, but he knew.

I still remember that at Interart, when Jonathan hugs Becca and orders her to say 'I love you,' then slaps her when she refuses and pushes her into the closet, children crowed with delight. When the play was produced, there were big discussions with school groups after performances, and one question was, 'Have any of you ever had this kind of situation with a sister?' Every hand was raised. And without a qualm the kids started talking about infinitely more disturbing things than what happens in the play. But the adults have always been split down the middle. There are people who adore the play and people who say children should not be allowed in the theater to see it. And yet, in a production of *The Juniper Tree* this year, no one objected to the song *Soup* — where the father devours the delicious soup made of his little boy, who has just been murdered by his stepmother. Everybody loved that.

AG: BETTELHEIM HAS A THEORY THAT FAIRY TALES ALLOW A CHILD BOTH TO GET RID OF ANGER AND TO FEEL THAT HE OR SHE IS NOT THE ONLY ONE IN AN AWFUL SITUATION.

WK: Not the only one in the world. Of course, the people *in* the fairy tale often feel they are alone. And the story often says, 'She was all alone in the world,' or, 'Now he was all alone in the world.' Then the heroine is helped or rescued, or rescues herself.

AG: HOW DID YOU LEARN TO TELL STORIES?

WK: That was there from a very young age. I was wild for children, first of all, maybe because of being an only child. I also spent a great deal of my favorite time — a lot of my life — with my grandmother, who was a great storyteller. She was my mother's mother and the only grandparent I knew. That's Nana in *I Love You, I Love You Not*. My grandmother was not a Holocaust survivor, like Nana, but she was Jewish. She came from a small town outside of Riga, as did my grandfather, whom I didn't know.

Nana lived outside of Peekskill in a place called Mohegan Colony, and I remember sitting outside the house with a group of children around me, making up stories. I don't know what they were. I'm sure they were fairy tales or elaborations on fairy tales. Or my own versions of them. And Mr. Gilman, who is mentioned in *I Love You, I Love You Not*, and appears in a new play, *The Notebook*, had this incredible used-book barn down the lane. A country lane. And Nana and I would go there. That was a fairy tale with Mr. Gilman. Once, years later, he took me into his house, which was next door to the barn. This used to be a scene in *I Love You, I Love You Not*, but I took it out. We went into the bedroom, and there was a little step down and a little low door, which he opened, and down in the basement, as far as you could see, were books. They went on for a block, it seemed.

Maybe my storytelling is from reading all the fairy tales, but it was also from Nana and her stories.

AG: THERE ARE STORIES WITHIN STORIES IN YOUR PLAYS. THAT IS PARTICULARLY INTERESTING TO ME BECAUSE THE AMERICAN THEATER INCREASINGLY PRODUCES DRAMATIZATIONS OF CLASSIC NOVELS. PERHAPS IN POSTMODERN THEATER WE HAVE LOST THE ART OF TELLING A STORY.

WK: This goes back to your first question about the fairy tale. I think people have a longing for stories, and we don't have many with this whole new technological world.

AG: BUT THERE ARE TONS OF STORIES AROUND. PEOPLE APPEAR ON TELEVISION — ON *OPRAH* OR SIMILAR TALK SHOWS — TO TELL THEIR STORIES.

WK: Yes, but those are not the same kinds of stories. I don't know what the difference is. I'm not saying the stories people tell on *Oprah* are gossip, but those are not stories that you hear and want to pour your soul into. You feel compassion and you feel connected, but you don't have the sense of 'and then and then . . . and then.' It's not that entering into an extraordinary world which has mystery. Everything is out, everything is known. I think that's why I was hesitant to see the new *Star Wars*, because I didn't feel any mystery before.

Wendy Kesselman 273

AG: HOW DOES THE STORYTELLING IN CHILDREN'S BOOKS DIFFER FROM THE STORYTELLING IN PLAYS? OR DOES IT?

WK: I think that the children's book writing was almost a preparation for writing plays. I've never taken a course in playwriting. What was fantastic when I started writing *Becca* was that I realized the world of the theater called on so much from me, which I was dying to give. There is music in theater. There is the visual element. In a children's book, image is crucial, even though I didn't make the images myself. There's the compression of the story. One of the most important things with a children's book is getting it down to the fewest words possible, especially in a picture book. I instinctively do that with the theater. *The Notebook* has long monologues, but still there is an economy, because there is the need to get a whole world into two hours.

Revising is part of that. I love to revise. *My Sister* had about thirty revisions. In the early versions, there were other women, other employers. *The Executioner's Daughter* has had sixty or sixty-two revisions. There were sixteen people in the cast originally; now there is a cast of six. With *The Juniper Tree*, which I've just revised, the play was originally produced with a cast of two — now there's a cast of twelve.

AG: IS YOUR REVISING USUALLY A WHITTLING AWAY?

WK: With *The Executioner's Daughter* the revising has been overwhelming. Not so much the story of Celeste, because that came right out of my head, nor the background involving the executioners, because a lot of that is historically true. There was an executioner who played the violin, but the cello is my favorite, so in the script he plays the cello.

But I kept revising the character of Olympe, because she was real. She was a playwright. I read her almost thirty plays, which were not so wonderful. What was extraordinary were her ideas about women's rights, which really were two hundred years ahead of her time. But it was hard to integrate those ideas without her sounding as if she were preaching. In the many early drafts, she had all these huge speeches. Then there was Olympe's lover, her son — all these characters.

AG: DID YOU CUT THE LOVER?

WK: The lover is gone. There were several versions with her little boy. He's gone. The big shift came when I saw that I wanted her to sing rather than speak her beliefs. The other huge change was to see Olympe through Celeste's eyes. Before, the women's stories were parallel. They're not anymore. Although Olympe is still a strong figure, the play has to be Celeste's story. That's why the title has changed. For a long time the title was *The Butcher's Daughter*, which referred to both of them, because Olympe's father was a butcher and Celeste's father, the executioner, was often called *le bourreau*. The revising is not a whittling. It's a transforming, I suppose.

AG: YOU HAVE MENTIONED RESEARCHING *MY SISTER* AND *THE EXECUTIONER'S DAUGHTER*. HOW DOES THE RESEARCH FEED YOUR WRITING?

WK: Years before I started to work on *Executioner's Daughter*, I'd wanted to do a play about the last executioner in France. Do you know when the last guillotining took place? In 1976. Somewhere I have notes for doing a play about the last executioner. I realized that being the executioner was a job somebody had and I learned that the job stayed in the same family. Again, borders or enclosure. Although, in the play, the French Revolution has no borders certainly, that family of executioners has an enclosed feeling.

The research creates the root. The base. Certainly with *The Executioner's Daughter* all the research is in there, but it's compressed. I adored doing that reading, and I remember [playwright] Peter Parnell saying, 'You have to stop reading, you're never going to start writing.' But I knew nothing about the French Revolution except for *A Tale of Two Cities*. And then to read about those amazing events: ten thousand women marching to the King to beg for bread; the King's flight from Versailles. I thought, 'How am I going to get these huge events onto the stage?' But because I put music into a play whenever I can, I thought I would create a street singer — Pierrot — who brings news of the bread march and the King's flight to Varennes. Later, as I was continuing to read quietly on the side, I found that a woman at Princeton had done her thesis on street singers and learned that at the time there were hundreds of them in France spreading the news, because half of France couldn't read.

But that's one of the things which is thrilling when you really plunge into the material. Research feeds you in ways you don't even know. It's very much what Bettelheim was saying about the child with the fairy tales: it loosens the imagination.

AG: THERE IS A FAIRY TALE TOLD WITHIN *THE EXECU-TIONER'S DAUGHTER: LITTLE RED RIDING HOOD.*

WK: The story that Nounou tells Olympe is the oldest version of *Little Red Riding Hood*, in which the wolf eats her and she doesn't get away. The Bzou of Nounou's tale was a real fear in the south of France, where Olympe came from. People believed a Bzou was a kind of werewolf. It all fit together: the wolf, the executioner, the revolution, Nounou, Celeste's grandmother.

AG: NOUNOU, AS THE BZOU, ASKS OLYMPE, WHO IS PLAY-ACTING LITTLE RED RIDING HOOD, WHETHER SHE WILL TAKE THE PATH OF THORNS OR THE PATH OF STONES THROUGH THE WOODS.

WK: That's a line from the fairy tale. They're almost Christ-like images.

AG: TWO OLD FRENCH VERSIONS HAVE LITTLE RED RIDING HOOD CHOOSING BETWEEN THE PATH OF PINS AND THE PATH OF NEEDLES AND MAKE IT CLEAR THAT SHE FOLLOWS THE PATH OF GREATER EASE (PINS) RATHER THAN THE PATH OF DUTY (NEEDLES). THE TALES EXPLAIN THAT IT IS EAS-IER TO FASTEN THINGS TOGETHER WITH PINS, HARDER TO SEW THINGS TOGETHER WITH NEEDLES.

WK: I always thought that Olympe wanted to take the harder path and did.

AG: THE COLOR RED IS IMPORTANT IN THE PLAY.

WK: Crucial. Red was an important color in the Revolution. Red is the color of the nosebleeds. The nosebleed was the germ of the play — the first image. Again, images seem to arrive first. There was the image of Celeste's nosebleed, and then the father coming in. The image grew, and somehow it led to the Little Red Riding Hood story. Then came the blood. There's a line in one song about blood rolling down the streets, and that was true. The blood literally did roll down the streets.

AG: EVEN THOUGH OLYMPE IS THE OVERTLY REVOLUTIONARY CHARACTER, CELESTE'S PRIVATE REVOLUTION, HER REBELLION AGAINST THAT HORRIBLE FAMILY . . .

WK: . . . is huge. But Olympe in a way gives her the courage. Olympe helps her.

AG: IN *THE EXECUTIONER'S DAUGHTER* YOU WRITE STRONG SEXUAL SCENES BETWEEN CELESTE AND ANGE, THE YOUNG EXECUTIONER SHE MUST MARRY. DO YOU THINK THAT WRITING EXPLICIT SEXUALITY IS A RELATIVELY NEW FREEDOM THAT WOMEN HAVE TAKEN OR GAINED?

WK: I don't know the answer to that. For me, Celeste's relationship with Ange could not have been any other way. That's her tragedy. She falls passionately in love with him. He awakens her sexually.

Earlier you asked about dreams. The scene with the miniature carriage did come to me in a dream — possibly a daydream — although the moment in which Celeste finds the hair in the carriage, which seems to be disturbing for so many, came later, and recently I've also written that she has the nosebleed again. There was always Celeste's gradual realization that Ange slept with all those women before guillotining them, but not that he saved their hair in that exquisite miniature carriage. That image does have a fairy tale aura, because there's the mixture of beauty and terror: Celeste alone on the stage, pulling locks of hair from the little coach.

AG: WE SEE THAT MINIATURE CARRIAGE AND THINK OF CINDERELLA, AND WE IMAGINE THAT BEAUTIFUL THINGS WILL EMERGE FROM THE COACH.

WK: And they are beautiful. Celeste thinks the locks of hair are lovely at first. Then she realizes where they come from.

AG: YOU ALSO GIVE OLYMPE A STRONGLY EROTIC SCENE.

WK: The famous powder scene. People said, 'You didn't cut out the powder scene, did you?' That was great fun to write. Those other scenes were not so much fun, or anyway, that's not the word I would use. But they were essential for Celeste. And for Ange, because that's how he lived. His life is between that blood and that sexuality. He's a very contemporary character. There are men very much like that.

When you're deep into any kind of writing, there's a great excitement. For me anyway. Especially when the scene is just — happening. Those scenes barely changed. They were sort of written in stone even before I wrote them.

AG: SHIFTING TO *THE BLACK MONK*, IN THE CHEKHOV STORY THE CENTRAL CHARACTER IS A PHILOSOPHER — A MAN OF IDEAS. YOU MADE HIM A PAINTER — AN ARTIST. WHY?

WK: I felt that visually it was important to make the change. The other would have become wordy and you couldn't have had a visual element. It was also important to me that he be an artist.

AG: IT DOES SEEM TO BE A PLAY ABOUT WHAT IT MEANS TO BE AN ARTIST.

WK: You're right, but I never think that way about a play. When Frank Rich gave *My Sister* that marvelous review, he said it was about repression. But if I had thought that I was setting out to write a play about repression, or about an artist in the case of *The Black Monk*, I wouldn't have been able to do it. That's where the storytelling comes in. I approach a play through the story, and then those big things emerge. It's what we first started talking about, with the enclosure or the border. I'd rather start with something that seems manageable. If I think, 'I'm going to write a play about an artist . . . '

AG: WHAT COMES THROUGH IS THAT AN ARTIST NEEDS PASSION — OFTEN UNREINED PASSION — IN ORDER TO CREATE.

WK: I felt an incredible pull between André's love for Tanya and need for the family, and the obsession with his art, which is connected with the Monk. The Monk couldn't care less whether André loves Tanya or not.

AG: IS THE MONK SUPPOSED TO BE A BENEFICENT FIGURE OR AN EVIL ONE?

WK: We recently had a reading, and some people thought he was the devil and others thought he was another side of André. I don't want the Monk to be a supernatural figure, although he comes from who knows where. He has to be human. He's human even in Chekhov's story. The Monk encourages André — supports him in his work — but also seduces him and brings him down. He's André's muse. He's all those things.

AG: HAVE YOU BEEN WRITING *THE BLACK MONK* AND *THE NOTEBOOK* AT THE SAME TIME?

WK: Pretty close.

AG: THEY BOTH INVOLVE CREATIVITY AND THE SOURCES OF CREATIVITY.

WK: Yes, they're very parallel, the two newest plays.

AG: LIKE ANDRÉ, JENNIE, THE YOUNG STUDENT IN *THE NOTEBOOK*, IS DEALING WITH WHAT HELPS OR STIFLES HER WRITING. SHE BLOSSOMS FOR A TIME IN HER RELATION-SHIP WITH HER TEACHER, BUT THE TEACHER IS ULTIMATELY DESTRUCTIVE.

WK: In a way, what Miss Thorne does for Jennie, the Monk does for André: he opens up the world.

AG: LET'S TALK ABOUT ANOTHER ARTIST: ANNE FRANK. WHO APPROACHED YOU TO ADAPT *THE DIARY OF ANNE FRANK* BY FRANCES GOODRICH AND ALBERT HACKETT?

WK: The director, Jim Lapine, whom I've known for years, wanted me to do it. Again, the image came first. The Goodrich-Hackett play begins with Otto Frank coming up the stairs of the Annex after the war is over; I told Jim that I saw the play starting with a shaft of light on the Jewish star. I had the image of the star opening up, and the audience seeing the huddled Frank family. On Broadway, the Frank family came up from the orchestra pit in the rain, because Jim had to get them onstage. But I think my image probably convinced Jim. That's my guess, knowing him.

Then David Stone, who was producing it with Amy Nederlander-Case, said, 'You know, Wendy, you're only going to be able to do a ten or fifteen percent revision on the Hackett script.' And I said, 'What? Well, maybe twenty.' 'No, no. Ten or fifteen percent.' But when we had the first read-through, Linda Lavin, who had not yet read the new adaptation, came to a speech I had written for Mrs. van Daan and cried, and Flora Roberts, who represented the Goodrich-Hackett script, leaned over to me and said, 'I've never seen her do that before.'

AG: THIS IS MRS. VAN DAAN'S SPEECH ABOUT FIRST MEETING HER HUSBAND ON THE FERRYBOAT?

WK: Yes. The speech where she tells her husband, who's stolen the families' bread in the middle of the night, 'If you're hungry, hold on to me.' Later, Flora told Jim that she was very happy and wanted me to write more, so in the end the script changed at least seventy percent.

AG: IT HAS ALSO CHANGED SINCE THE BROADWAY PRODUCTION.

WK: Yes. I was changing the script two days before we opened in New York. I wanted Natalie Portman, who was playing Anne, to say more aloud. When the production was in Boston, almost all of Anne's monologues were prerecorded. But for example, monologues such as 'Unless you write yourself, you can't know how wonderful it is' — her speech about her passion for writing — and her monologue about Jews being gassed — seem to me crucial to be said out loud, because of the greater immediacy with which we then feel them.

AG: COULD YOU TALK ABOUT HOW YOU BEGAN TO WORK ON THE PLAY?

WK: The first thing that happened was that James, myself, Amy, David, and Bob Fennell, the publicist, went to Amsterdam for five days. I wanted to take Anne's final journey and go to Westerbork, Auschwitz, and Bergen-Belsen. But there was no time — we only had five days. Jim, Amy, and David went to Switzerland to meet with Buddy Elias, Anne's first cousin — her only remaining cousin — and I went directly to Amsterdam. I was so obsessed at that point — later they let me be in the Annex alone, and this is weird, but it was not dissimilar from the house in Le Mans where the sisters lived. The wallpaper was similar. After all, the time periods were not so different.

Anyway, the first night I met with two extraordinary women, the historians Dienke Hondius and Dineke Stam. We talked until three in the morning, and I said I wanted more than anything to go to Westerbork. So they arranged for me to go the next day with Dienke and a woman who, at age nine, had been first at Westerbork and then at Bergen-Belsen.

Seeing Westerbork was really the base for writing the new adaptation. Only remnants are left. There's nothing really except a little museum. But there is the indication of where the train ran through the center of camp. On Monday nights, the list would be read of the thousand people who were to be sent to the death camps on Tuesday. The scenes that happened on those Monday nights: people torn from other people; families ripped apart and destroyed. Being there was overwhelming.

I was reading like a fiend, of course. A book by Jacob Presser, *Ashes in the Wind: The Destruction of Dutch Jewry*, became my bible, after the diary itself. I had always thought Amsterdam was 'good' during the war, but in terms of percentages, the largest number of Jews exterminated in Western Europe came from Amsterdam. That was a revelation. A shock. On some level, that went into the adaptation.

AG: HAD YOU READ MEYER LEVIN'S DRAMATIZATION OF ANNE'S DIARY?

WK: I met Meyer Levin years ago. He gave me a copy.

AG: ANNE COMES ACROSS MUCH MORE AS A WRITER IN YOUR VERSION THAN IN THE GOODRICH-HACKETT.

WK: I took the diary with me to Amsterdam and started reading it again. I had read it many times, but had never been so struck by what a writer Anne is. Was, is. Such a gift. Her dialogue — she would have been a great theater writer. Those family scenes, her timing, her precision. Remarkable. I have notes to Jim in which I say, 'I want to make her words sing. Those words have to shine.' I was dying to put in practically the whole diary, just as I wanted to put the whole French revolution into *The Executioner's Daughter*. Being able to work on this play was a gift.

AG: WHICH VERSION OF THE *DIARY* DID YOU USE THE MOST?

WK: I had *The Diary of Anne Frank: The Critical Edition*, which contains the three versions: the original published version; Anne's unedited draft; and her own revision. I went back and forth between those and *The Diary of Anne Frank (The Definitive Edition)*, which was edited by Otto Frank and Mirjam Pressler, and translated by Susan Massotty. I would look at each version of the specific diary entry in order to decide exactly the right words to use — sometimes even using fragments of each translation in a single sentence.

A big issue was whether or not to put in the diary entry where Anne writes about wanting to touch her friend Jopie's breasts. I met Jopie in Amsterdam and went right into the whole story. I don't remember who was in the car with me, but they kept saying, 'I can't believe you're doing this.' But I had to, because we had no time.

AG: DID JOPIE REMEMBER THE INCIDENT?

WK: She certainly did . . . and she'd worried that she had hurt Anne's feelings. She kept talking about Anne's intensity and that she realized, when Anne didn't come back, what a friend Anne had been.

AG: THE PLAY SEEMS NOW TO BE ABOUT ALL OF THE CHARACTERS IN THE ANNEX RATHER THAN ONLY ABOUT ANNE.

WK: That was very important to me.

AG: GOODRICH AND HACKETT STRESS THE ROMANCE BETWEEN ANNE AND PETER.

WK: We have to see Anne and Peter slowly discovering each other in the attic. In that isolated situation, they find each other, and their friendship deepens. I introduced a fairy tale dance in the midst of that terror, when she dances to the Chopin Nocturne. It's an awakening, a longing.

AG: YOU SAID EARLIER THAT YOU MADE UP MRS. VAN DAAN'S MEMORY OF THE FERRYBOAT RIDE WITH HER HUSBAND.

WK: And the lines about 'If you're hungry.' It's really the end of the bread-stealing scene. It completes it. The story about the ferryboat just came. I was lying in bed writing it.

AG: YOU ALSO INTRODUCE A SCENE WHERE ANNE AND PETER EAT STRAWBERRIES. DID THAT COME FROM THE DIARY?

WK: There's a scene in the diary, but it happens earlier. Miep brings them fresh strawberries, and it's an amazing, wonderful scene. It brings tears to my eyes when I think about it, because Anne talks about how she doesn't even feel that they're in hiding, because of the strawberries and the smell. Everything is so fresh and alive, and they're moving around the Annex and cooking those strawberries. It's as if they're free. I put the scene at the end of the play, because the freedom of eating the strawberries seemed an incredible contrast with the Nazis coming up the stairs. I made the Nazis' arrival silent, which it was. There wasn't a banging or a crashing down of the door. They came in silence. And it was a beautiful day.

AG: DID YOU MAKE ANY OTHER SIGNIFICANT CHANGES?

WK: The big question was what to do with Anne's last line in the Goodrich-Hackett script, when she says, 'In spite of everything, I still believe people are good at heart.' Anne says it in the diary, but the context in which she says it is profoundly pessimistic. Anne certainly was an optimist, not a pessimistic person like her mother (which was one of the things that was so hard for her), but she grasped so much about the dark side of humanity, and that's all in the diary paragraph. We couldn't end on that line. In the final revision, I juxtapose the line, 'I still believe, in spite of everything, that people are really good at heart,' with the terrible 'RAUS!' that the Nazi Officer screams when he enters the attic. A few seconds later, when the Nazis push everyone out, and one of them slaps the diary from Anne's hand, we hear her final words as a voice-over: ' . . . I hear the approaching thunder which will destroy us too, I feel the suffering of millions.' Without the scream and the voice-over, Anne's words about people being 'good at heart' would be what remains with us. But the scream reminds us that once Anne was in Auschwitz, she could not have said that anymore. Actually, I wanted to end the play with them being taken out by the Nazis, rather than with an epilogue, so that what confronts the audience is the empty Annex.

AG: YOU DIDN'T WANT MR. FRANK TO COME BACK INTO THE PLAY?

WK: I didn't want any epilogue. But Jim was very definite that he wanted something — maybe the people who survive: Miep and Mr. Frank, Mr. Kraler. I just couldn't do it. Finally there had to be something, and I thought, 'Well, maybe it could be Mr. Frank, even though that was not the way it happened.' Miep, not Mr. Frank, actually found the diary. That epilogue was one of the hardest things I've ever written, because I wrote pages and then I had to trim, trim, trim. I knew it had to be very compressed. Now, at the end of Mr. Frank's epilogue, he simply picks the diary off the floor and says, 'All that remains.'

AG: AS A PLAYWRIGHT APPROACHING THIS KIND OF MATERIAL, IS IT YOUR RESPONSIBILITY TO BE HISTORICALLY ACCURATE OR TO BE AN ARTIST?

WK: I think you have to be both. I don't think you should deliberately change history, but maybe heighten it, or use it in a certain way.

AG: IS ANNE'S DIARY HISTORICAL RECORD OR ART?

WK: Both. I definitely think it's both, because she's such a writer. It is also a historical document — one of the few that's left of the Holocaust. That's the extraordinary thing about it.

AG: SHE, TOO, REVISED.

WK: Oh, she totally revised, but I don't think she revised the historical facts. She revised her writing, she revised for publication. That was one of the things I couldn't get over: how determined she was under those circumstances to go back to the beginning and rewrite. She was also writing a novel and several stories. She must have spent a tremendous amount of time writing. But I think it may have been what allowed her to survive.

The poet John Berryman once wrote that Anne was 'intact.' I think he means that there was a wholeness about her, a definition about her, that was remarkable in one so young. And I think that's true. It may have been the diary that allowed her to be intact, because she was so in touch with herself. There's something very whole about her in all her suffering, and I mean not only the suffering of being an adolescent shut up in that Annex, but the suffering that Peter and Anne's father and mother and Margot endured. That she's able to express all this and then work on it as well must have taken a fierce determination. To work like that in a place where you don't know what's going to happen, under that kind of torment, is amazing. Berryman's word is incredible: 'intact.'

AG: DO YOU THINK THAT THE HOLOCAUST SHOULD BE THE SUBJECT OF ART?

WK: I think so, yes. Yes, because then you have works like Anne's diary and Presser's autobiographical history. Where would we be without those books? ❦

Emily Mann

Emily Mann was born in Boston, Massachusetts, the youngest daughter of Arthur and Sylvia Mann. Her father was a professor of American history, first at M.I.T., then at Smith College, and finally at the University of Chicago. Her mother is a reading specialist.

As a playwright, Mann has carved a reputation by writing documentary plays or what she calls 'theater of testimony,' beginning with *Annulla Allen: Autobiography of a Survivor* (1974), based on interviews she conducted with a woman who escaped a concentration camp during World War II. Subsequent plays include *Still Life* (1980), drawn from the testimonies of a Vietnam veteran and the two women in his life; *Execution of Justice* (1983), a response to the 1978 murders of Mayor George Moscone of San Francisco and City Supervisor Harvey Milk; *Having Our Say: The Delany Sisters' First 100 Years* (1995), which Mann adapted from Sarah L. Delany and Elizabeth A. Delany's memoir, *Having Our Say;* and *Greensboro (A Requiem)* (1996), based on the events surrounding a 1979 Ku Klux Klan assault on an anti-Klan rally in Greensboro, North Carolina. *Meshugah* (1999) is Mann's dramatization of a novel by Isaac Bashevis Singer. She has also adapted Strindberg's *Miss Julie* (1993), Federico García Lorca's *The House of Bernarda Alba* (1999), and Chekhov's *The Cherry Orchard* (2001).

In tandem with playwriting, Mann forged a career as a director, working at regional theaters around the country. In 1990 she was named Artistic Director of McCarter Theater in Princeton, New Jersey. This interview results from two meetings in Princeton, in 1997 and 1999.

• • •

AG: WHY DO YOU MAKE THEATER?

EM: Well, I guess a very simple answer is that, like most human beings, I need to hear stories. I need to tell stories, I need to make stories. By telling stories, I hear back from other people and get their responses.

AG: WHY MAKE THEATER AS OPPOSED TO FILM, FOR INSTANCE?

EM: It's live conversation. It's more dangerous, more volatile. In the kind of theater that I like to make, there's a conversation going on between the actors and the audience. And hopefully it shakes you up enough, or stimulates or moves you enough, so that when you walk out you are continuing the conversation. It leaves an indelible mark on your heart and soul. I don't know any other art form that has quite that power to change another human being.

I always use the quote from the scholar Cornel West, from the lecture he gave for the Madison Medal at Princeton University a couple of years ago. He said the most important question at the end of the twentieth century was, 'How to be fully human in America.' We have to start looking at those values that are not market-driven. We have to start looking at tenderness, love, intimacy.

Part of that task is finding ways to have public conversations. We must see in our country that we are part of each other, that we are all in the same ship, as he put it. We go up together or we go down together.

AG: RELATING THAT TO THEATER, I WOULD SAY THAT YOUR PLAYS ARE A COMBINATION OF THE PUBLIC AND THE PRIVATE.

EM: Very much so. Because in order to have a public conversation that matters, you have to have lived very intensely and have that private story to tell. Conversely, you must be able to glimpse that private world, to have a full understanding of what the public conversation is. Or isn't.

AG: *EXECUTION OF JUSTICE* AND *GREENSBORO (A REQUIEM)* ARE ATTEMPTS TO HOLD THAT CONVERSATION WHEN THE PUBLIC DIALOGUE HAS BEEN VIOLENT.

EM: *Having Our Say*. All of them. I mention *Having Our Say* because of what the Delany sisters went through. The truth in Bessie Delany's life is not at all sweet. At one point she talks about how she really hates white people, and then a nice white person comes along and she has to eat crow. There's nothing cute about that. Bessie was an angry woman. She knew the other side, you see. Now, she talks about it in a way that's screamingly funny, but if she was twenty years younger, you wouldn't find it so funny. When two old ladies over a hundred years old are recounting these stories, they suddenly become very undangerous.

But there is a history lesson there, for blacks as well as whites. Authentic history, *lived* history. It's taking the private into the public arena and saying, 'Yeah, have a great time, but talk about it, because it's the real thing.' No one, after seeing *Having Our Say*, can really be terribly smug.

AG: HOWEVER, THE SISTERS SEEM TO HAVE MADE A PEACE THAT IS NOT FOUND AT THE END OF *EXECUTION OF JUSTICE*, FOR INSTANCE.

EM: They found a way to die. And because they believe in the Almighty, they are somewhat at peace with that. Bessie has real hope that she'll go to heaven. Everyone knows Sadie will.

AG: WHAT IS THEATER'S FUNCTION FROM YOUR POINT OF VIEW?

EM: A lot of functions. Someone has said that theater's function is to entertain, to teach, and to inspire. Entertainment, education, inspiration. I would subscribe to all three. I'm a big believer in entertainment, by the way. I think the next step in South African theater may be humor and joy, that what people there really need to be able to do is laugh a lot.

AG: YOUR PLAYS ARE OFTEN SERIOUS IN TONE, BUT THERE IS A GREAT DEAL OF IRONY. *HAVING OUR SAY* SEEMS THE MOST OUTRIGHTLY COMEDIC.

EM: *Annulla* is funny too. I think that one of my signatures is finding the humor in tragedy. *The Three Sisters* that I directed at McCarter was hilarious. My *Hedda Gabler* was very funny. It's a way to share an experience on a deeper level with an audience. They relax, they connect. They see themselves onstage through laughter.

The only piece of mine that does not have enough humor, in my opinion, is *Greensboro*. I thought there would be a lot more — well, there is in the David Duke section; it makes you screech with laughter, because it's so appalling. There's a lot of humor in *Still Life*. They are very serious pieces of work, but there are laughs of recognition, of release, some of horror. And some plain, old-fashioned belly laughs at the absurdity of the conditions that people are living in.

AG: WHAT WAS IT LIKE GROWING UP IN YOUR FAMILY?

EM: I had a sister, a father, and a mother. My father was an American historian; he died in 1993.

AG: YOUR GRANDPARENTS WERE JEWISH?

EM: Yes. My mother's *mother*'s family came from Ostrolenka, in Poland. Her mother came over in her teens with her older sister; everyone else stayed in Poland and was killed during the Second World War. That's what *Annulla* is really about.

AG: DID THEY TALK TO YOU ABOUT THAT BACKGROUND?

EM: Both my grandfathers were dead by the time I was born, and my maternal grandmother wouldn't talk about the war. When I went to Poland, to see my grandmother's village, she kept saying, 'Why do you want to go there? They killed us there. What are you doing?' But I had to do it. My mother on the other hand would talk about what she knew, and my father always told me about what he knew.

Our family really was an extraordinary family to grow up in. My father believed in the education of women — he taught at Smith College for eleven years. He pushed me and my sister to formulate and articulate ideas. The dinner table was a place where big ideas were discussed from the time I was a very little girl, and we were expected to participate. It was almost like a daily seminar. My father taught by asking questions about what we thought, what we believed. He would tell us what happened in the news that day, and we would have to think through where we stood on these matters. On the one hand, it was the greatest education a child could have, on the other, it was rather tyrannical, and very hard to come up to his standards. But I'm grateful that he pushed us. His best friend was another American historian: John Hope Franklin. He was like a second father to me.

AG: YOU DEDICATE *HAVING OUR SAY* TO YOUR FATHER.

EM: I thought a lot about fathers while doing that play. The sisters talk so much about their father, what he taught them, what growing up on a college campus was like. I very much connected first of all with that story, because John Hope's first teaching job was at Saint Augustine's School, where the sisters' parents met, and he had taken me there and introduced me as his daughter. My father missed the play — he had just died. He would have loved this play.

AG: WHAT WOULD HE HAVE LIKED?

EM: He would have liked the gentleness. He would have loved the history lesson. In the portion where there's a Civil Rights slide montage, there's a picture of him and John Hope Franklin marching from Selma, Alabama, to Montgomery, Alabama, which was a big, big, big moment in my life as a child. I sat at home and was very worried about him. It was really his one political act. He did that out of his love for John Hope and his belief in human justice and freedom. He thought it was the moral thing to do. I admired him enormously for that.

AG: HOW OLD WERE YOU?

EM: What year was the Selma march? 1965? I was around thirteen.

AG: YOU HAVE SAID IN INTERVIEWS THAT THE VIETNAM WAR TORE YOUR FAMILY APART.

EM: My father, strangely enough, was for the war, and I was against the war. It caused a huge rift between us. He at one time said that, if

I had been a boy, he would have sent me to the war, because he was a believer in fighting for this country. Our people found freedom here, and it was my duty to protect it.

And I said, 'Sorry. If you sent your son to the Vietnam War, you would lose a son, because I wouldn't go. It's against everything I believe in.'

We had a real domestic battle over it for many years. Then, when I wrote *Still Life*, and he saw it in Chicago at the Goodman Theatre, he embraced me and said, 'I will never agree with you, but you have earned the right to your opinion, and I respect you for that.' That's how we resolved it.

AG: DID WRITING THAT PLAY HELP YOU SEE HIS SIDE?

EM: Oh, yeah. I've always seen his side. There was an incredible intelligence in my father, but also, in my opinion, a naïve and romantic idea of what America is. He enlisted for World War II; he thought he was fighting the bad guys, and he saved a lot of people — his own people. He was right about that, but he thought that Vietnam was cut from the same cloth. I understand that he felt that, but it saddened me that he didn't want to hear that this may not have been the case.

I think he felt, from the late 1960s on, that it was no longer his world. He didn't understand it, he didn't like it. In some ways he was prescient. He did see the future of the Civil Rights Movement in this country and was very depressed by it. He saw what separatism would do. He was concerned about the Black Muslim Movement, he saw that there was going to be a rift between blacks and Jews.

But I was a radical kid and didn't buy his concerns. I probably am closer to him politically now, and I bet that he would have moved more my way. We would have met in the middle. He was sort of moving that way when he died.

AG: SOMETIMES THE KIND OF THEATER YOU WRITE IS CALLED DOCUMENTARY THEATER, DOCUMENTARY DRAMA, DOCUDRAMA. IS THERE A TERM YOU PREFER?

EM: The late Barney Simon, who co-founded the Market Theatre of Johannesburg, dubbed the plays Theater of Testimony, because in South Africa, they come out of that tradition. And I would say that is true. I hate the term 'docudrama.' Docudrama means it's an amalgam of fiction and documentary. I'm very pure with the documentary form. I always have been.

AG: HOW DOES A DOCUMENTARY PLAY DIFFER FROM A HISTORY PLAY?

EM: A documentary often has people speaking in their own words.

AG: WHY DOES THE FORM APPEAL TO YOU SO MUCH?

EM: I love how real people talk. The impulse to start writing *Annulla*, for example, was simply that. In the early 1970s, I thought I'd leave the theater as a profession, because there weren't enough pieces I wanted to direct. As arrogant as this sounds, the people I had met were a whole lot more interesting than the people I saw portrayed onstage, especially in new work. So I went out to get new stories.

I went to Europe in the summer of 1973 with my tape recorder, and an itinerary to meet my college roommate's family and then go to my grandmother's village in Poland. We didn't know if the result would be a book, an article, or a series of edited transcripts, but we thought it would be something along those lines, either in journalistic or oral-history style.

Then as I began to work on Annulla's transcript, and looked at the year ahead and wondered what I wanted to do, and got accepted as the last Bush Fellow at the Guthrie Theatre in Minneapolis — I thought this transcript could be a play. I don't remember why I decided to take that fellowship. Part of it was because I didn't have a job. I remembered how much I loved the theater, I had this transcript, I thought it might be a new way to make a play. All of that brought me to the Guthrie. Then I met an actress, Barbara Bryne, and I made the play for her. And I haven't really looked back.

AG: WHAT PARTICULARLY ATTRACTS YOU ABOUT DOCUMENTING AND REPORTAGE?

EM: It's a product of my upbringing. It has to do with being an historian's daughter, I think. You have to have earned the right to make these assertions. For example, in *Still Life* I wanted to prove something to my father about the Vietnam War, and to a lot of people who were hawks on the war, a lot of people who believed in that war. A lot of them had been soldiers themselves, so I took it from the soldier's point of view. If I had simply written a fictional piece, if I had made up Mark and his wife, maybe his girlfriend, they could always say, 'Well, that's out of your imagination, those are the feverish imaginings of a young playwright.' I wanted to say: this leading character lived through it. You may or may not believe him, but this is what he told me. Just deal with what he says he lived through, and then let's talk. But don't tell me I made it up, because I didn't.

Now I chose, out of hundreds of hours of conversation, to show these particular stories, and I chose to give this particular point of view. There's no such thing as an objective documentary. It's got to be subjective. These are some of the most personal pieces I can imagine ever writing. But it's authentic speech. These are authentic, lived stories.

AG: PERSONAL IN WHAT WAY? WHERE ARE YOU IN *STILL LIFE*?

EM: I'm every character in *Still Life*. The whole piece comes out of me. I needed to answer particular people about Vietnam, and I put together a piece from real life and I shook a lot of people up because of that. I shook up the people I wanted to shake up.

AG: AND YOURSELF?

EM: That one was absolutely traumatic to write. To work on. When I gathered that material, I was so shattered by it I couldn't touch it for months. I was scared of knowing what I had learned, I was frightened of the responsibility I had. I was scared of what it did to me personally. It made me physically ill. Having gone through what I went through with them, and after Mark had confessed to me what he did in Vietnam, I was absolutely shattered. So going back to this material was painful, and it took a great deal out of me to begin to shape the piece. Perhaps that's why it has power. There's a lot of blood on the floor, from all three real-life participants and myself. I didn't ask them to go through more in the telling than I did in the writing.

AG: YOU SAY THAT PEOPLE COME TO YOU WITH PROJECTS.

WHAT KIND OF A CHORD DOES A PROJECT HAVE TO STRIKE FOR YOU TO TAKE IT UP?

EM: Each project takes so much out of me that it really has to go very, very deep for me. It's got to be a story or a set of characters that I cannot shake off, that I'll wake up thinking about or arguing with in my mind and heart.

AG: ONE OF THE THINGS I FIND REMARKABLE ABOUT YOUR WRITING IS THAT YOU DRAMATIZE SO MANY PERSPECTIVES AMONG THE VARIOUS CHARACTERS.

EM: How do I do that? Well, I guess when a huge public event happens, and it's traumatic, which is the basis of *Greensboro*, of *Execution*, there is a huge spectrum of response to it. I'm interested in that collision of different points of view. I'm always interested in getting lots of viewpoints, because by doing that, you might get close to what's really going on. If you're listening to the Klan talk about what happened at Greensboro on November 3, and you're also talking to the Communists and the lawyers, you might get a better idea of why and how the event occurred. There's usually not a simple answer to any of the questions I raise, and hopefully the questions raise more questions. You keep peeling the onion back until you begin to get to more and more of the heart of it. That's my hope.

AG: THE MULTIPLICITY OF PERSPECTIVES IS A SIGNATURE OF CONTEMPORARY LIFE, NOT TO MENTION POSTMODERN THEATER

EM: I like having a lot of images at once, having things overlap, things happening simultaneously. When I was in South Africa in 1997, people were on cell phones, people listened to the radio, there was a TV going, all while you were talking to somebody at lunch. That is the modern experience of things. I think we can take in a whole lot more onstage than just the single voice. Sometimes that's all you want, but there are times when you want a lot of information coming at you, a lot of emotion, a lot of different kinds of people. And you can take it all in.

It's a complicated event. Theater is based on time; you have a finite amount of time to get your story across. And if you take the complicated stories that I like to take, it's a question of how you can get the complexity that each one demands crammed into that amount of time.

AG: THE WAY TIME FUNCTIONS IN YOUR PLAYS. . . .

EM: It's a huge question in how I work.

AG: EVEN THOUGH THE EVENTS TAKE PLACE OVER MONTHS OR YEARS, THE VIEWER HAS THE SENSE OF IT ALL HAPPENING AT ONCE.

EM: That's right. There you go. It's really hard to do.

AG: WHAT IS THE PROCESS? DO YOU COLLECT INFORMATION FIRST? HOW DO YOU DECIDE WHOM TO TALK TO?

EM: *Execution* was a good example of that. *Execution* started out with the Eureka Theater, in San Francisco. Oscar Eustis, who was dramaturg at the Eureka at the time, set up interviews for me. I wanted to meet with the George Moscone people and the Harvey Milk people and the Dan White people. I started with those, and then somebody would put me on to Harvey's best friend ten years ago, who could tell me what Harvey was like when he was getting into office. A lot of that information informs the piece even though it isn't in the piece. The more I pared it down, the more I could tell the story of the trial. And I used the Cop and Sister Boom Boom as the two extreme viewpoints.

I went to a cop bar one night to meet with a man, who, somebody had told me, was a real homosexual hater. He's the one who says, 'The city is stinkin' with degenerates—.' At that point in my life, I was hugely pregnant. He was talking to a pregnant woman, so he felt it was his duty to tell me he was going to protect women, tell me what the problems were with homosexuals. I often hear very different stories told me than a man does. To walk through the Castro district very pregnant, I got a lot of very interesting stories from people:

gay men who wanted to meet me, who wanted to be me, who wanted to kill me, who were revolted looking at me. It was a very fertile time.

I also have 'the look.' I don't have it much anymore, but when I was younger I used to go on a train ride or a plane ride, and by the end of the trip, the person sitting next to me had told me his entire life story, without my asking — often without my wanting to hear.

AG: HOW DID YOU ARRIVE AT THAT ILLUSION OF SIMUL-TANEITY?

EM: I don't know. I hear lots of voices at once in my head, often. That's true in *Still Life*, too. They're answering each other even if they're not directly talking to each other. That happened in court in San Francisco, where these people who were not allowed into the court had to jump up and say, 'But but but but.' That's the Chorus of Uncalled Witnesses in *Execution of Justice*. So they had to speak. So you have real time and court time, and you have out-of-real-time, which is the Chorus. Now why? I don't know why. I just felt it had to be there. I heard them in my mind. I think that happens to people a lot more than they'll admit to. While we're talking now, there's probably stuff going through your head, things that you've heard I've said, things that I've said to you — you can be listening to me and other things can be going through your head. I do the same thing when I write. I write down what I say plus the interior monologues sometimes of what you're saying.

AG: I HAVE AN IMAGE OF YOU SURROUNDED BY PAPER.

EM: Oh, that's also true. Clippings, shards of paper. In the old days, I didn't write at a computer obviously, I was like an old-fashioned film editor. I'd paste up different lines and speeches on the walls; it was like being a collage artist or a filmmaker. I still think that way. Sometimes I even write that way. I'll cut and Scotch-tape and mold a piece. I like to handle it in my hands.

I'm very upset usually when I'm working, so there's an emotional side. Then there's the craft side to all of it, when I'm shaping and honing something, when I'm the play wright, w-r-i-g-h-t. You learn how a piece is constructed, and what time is in the theater, what you want a section to accomplish, both emotionally and in terms of furthering the plot or the story, or whatever you are working on shaping.

AG: ARE YOU A REWRITER?

EM: Oh, God, constantly. I rewrite until opening night. I think it's because I was a musician as well and I'm very aural. I have to hear a piece to know it's alive. It may look great on the page, but it may not come off the page. I can work like mad and think, 'Gosh, I think I've got it,' and I'll hear it, and huge pieces will lie inert for me. And not because the actors aren't doing their jobs. I can write very quickly. I can shift and change and edit very quickly, if I can hear what's needed. What I need are actors. I love actors. Me as a writer working with actors — I can really go far.

AG: HAVE YOU DIRECTED *GREENSBORO* ANYWHERE?

EM: No. And that's why I'm not sure the piece is finished. I'm quite sure it's not finished. I feel like I haven't got my hands on it the right way.

AG: WHAT DO YOU THINK IT NEEDS?

EM: I'm not sure whether to keep the Interviewer or not. I still like her, so I sort of want to. But I think she may need more of a payoff. I was not pleased with the production. I was pleased with it before it went upstairs to the main stage, before it was teched, but I thought that all of that technical design got in the way of the piece. So maybe it is finished. It really worked in the rehearsal room.

AG: WORKED IN WHAT SENSE?

EM: It got the story across, I understood everyone's point of view, and I got blown away and upset and was deeply moved. The strands all came together for me.

AG: THERE'S A LOT MORE EXPOSITION IN THAT PLAY THAN IN OTHERS YOU'VE WRITTEN.

EM: It's so complicated a story. I'm not sure the exposition works actually. I'm not sure how much is needed. In fact, everyone was really pushing me to put more exposition in, and that's what I did. I'm not positive they were right. And I think it shifted the balance of the interview, too.

I wrote the play differently than it was expressed on the stage. The first song, to me, was a hot spiritual and had a lot to do with bridging the audience and the stage, and being all part of this event that made us need to remember. In the production at McCarter, you got a rather alienated, cold look at those people while he's singing that song. Which was a choice, but wasn't what I had in mind. So then you had to get people engaged during the next beat. You know what I mean? I thought we were always a step behind where I had written. But then there were people who adored that production, so maybe I'm just being a persnickety playwright. Kids loved it. It was a very hip production for teenagers, a kick-ass kind of show.

AG: ARE YOU WRITING POLITICAL THEATER?

EM: No. The poets and playwrights I most admire — Athol Fugard, Henrik Ibsen — were all called political writers, and they each said, 'Well, you know, I write about the human heart and the human soul.' What do you mean political theater?

AG: POLITICAL THEATER IN ITS PUREST DEFINITION PROBABLY WANTS TO CHANGE PEOPLE'S POLITICAL ATTITUDES AND MOVE THEM TO POLITICAL ACTION.

EM: I want to give people stories they haven't heard before and information that they didn't know about before. I'd like to be challenging to a set of already held beliefs. A politically conservative friend of mine said that *Greensboro* was the most challenging theater, so intellectually stimulating that it made him want to come to the theater again. Watching the play gave him a real shudder, because he realized that people like Newt Gingrich and the right wing of his party, which is the Republican Party, were closer to a David Duke than he was comfortable with, and it scared him and made him question his affiliation. That's what I mean about challenging people's points of view.

AG: IN SOME SENSE *EXECUTION* AND *GREENSBORO* ARE MORE OUTRIGHTLY POLITICAL BECAUSE OF THE EVENTS THAT GENERATED THEM.

EM: You could say the same thing about *Still Life* and the Vietnam War. But what you've got is an intimate look at three people. Somebody might say, 'Well, that's not political because it's so personal.' You know? Well, why not? Does the balance of private-public have to be more public to be a political piece? That's why I can't answer the question. What fascinates me are people going through political events that have huge personal ramifications. The new piece, *Meshugah*, is about the survivors of the Nazi camps and the choices they had to make in order to survive. Are we allowed to judge what people do to survive in a wartime situation? What are the ethical and moral issues that the survivor has to deal with?

Now is that a political play? I know that it's a play with huge moral and ethical questions. I know it's a play that deals with the politics of fascism, and good and evil, and oppression. It's also a love story. I don't know the answer.

AG: THE SUBJECTS OF YOUR PLAYS ARE GROUPS OR CHARACTERS WHO ARE AMONG THE OPPRESSED ON OUR WORLD HORIZON: WOMEN, JEWS, AFRICAN AMERICANS, GAY MEN.

EM: Absolutely. No question about it. And all the plays are dealing with trauma of some kind, or some kind of traumatic event. Mostly I think my plays deal with the question, How does the human being, and how does this society, deal with traumatic events, whether war or assassination or rape or abuse? One of my friends, who studies the brain, says that *Still Life* is the model for trauma, that the piece actually works the way traumatic memory works. How the play is constructed is how the brain works when it deals with trauma — jumping, putting things together that don't want to go together. A putting together, but in the wrong order.

A lot of political plays are agitprop. I think there's a place for it, but I don't write it. I hope I don't write it.

AG: WHY?

EM: Because I'm not writing a piece as agitation propaganda, I'm not writing it to get people going on a certain event, like *Waiting for Lefty*'s strike. I'm not doing that. I'm actually asking a lot of hopefully complex questions about what it is to be alive now in this society.

AG: THE CRITIC DAVID SAVRAN ONCE STATED THAT YOU WRITE ABOUT RELATIONSHIPS BETWEEN PARENTS AND CHILDREN THE WAY ARTHUR MILLER WRITES ABOUT THE RELATIONSHIPS BETWEEN FATHERS AND SONS: YOU WRITE ABOUT WHAT ONE GENERATION HANDS DOWN TO ANOTHER.

EM: Did he really say that? That's what *Meshugah* is about. Totally. The Isaac Bashevis Singer character and the woman, Miriam, are just married, and she wants to know when they're going to have children, which he promised they would until he found out what she had done. And he says, 'No, there'll be no children,' and she says, 'Why?' And he says, 'Because what you know must not be passed down. We have to be like mules. The last of a generation.'

AG: THE PLAY IS CALLED *MESHUGAH*?

EM: Yiddish for 'crazy.' In the 1980s, Isaac Bashevis Singer wrote chapters of a novel that were serialized in the *Jewish Daily Forward*. He never had a chance to edit it before he died and make it a real book, so it's kind of a mess, and I've made it into a play and reshaped it. The play is an adaptation, it's not a documentary. The basis for Singer's fiction is the stories that were told to him. He used to go to lunch, and someone would tell him their story, and then he would write that as a short story. That's how he worked. The material is so raw, you can still see the seams, so in a lot of ways it's a continuation of a documentary work, because of that. But the raw material is a novel.

AG: YOUR PLAYS SEEM TO ME TO BE ABOUT PERSONAL MORAL CONSCIOUSNESS, WHICH BY EXTENSION BECOMES AMERICA'S OR SOCIETY'S MORAL CONSCIOUSNESS.

EM: That's absolutely accurate.

AG: BUT WHAT IS MORAL CONSCIOUSNESS?

EM: What's just and unjust. In *Meshugah*, Miriam survived by being a whore. The Singer character can kind of deal with that — it takes him a while, but he can get past that. She whored with Nazis. Not so easy to swallow, but that's how she lived. But by the end of the piece, he comes to Israel with her, and it's revealed to him by a survivor of the camp that she had been an accomplice. She had been chosen to walk around with a whip and move people to the gas chamber. She was a Kapo. He realizes he loves her. He realizes he didn't go through the camp — he won't judge her, he can't judge her. It's in the past, and he has to love her and go on. But he can't have children. He can't get past that.

My mother read this and was furious that he married her. I was really surprised. I said, 'What do you mean, Mom? She wanted to live.' My mother said, 'Better she should have died.' I was amazed. One of the rabbis that I talked with for help on the piece said he had a very hard time with the play. At a time when anti-Semitism is rising again in the United States, what with white supremacists, Jewish children being shot at, you don't show that there were Jewish women who were whores. He didn't like the licentiousness of the male character, he didn't like the loose and easy way of the Warsaw intelligentsia. They weren't God-fearing.

There have been a lot of wonderful reactions. What is right and what is wrong? What can you abide and what can you not abide? My mother's response blew my mind: 'Better she should have died.' That there's a line beyond which morally, ethically, you cannot go. Oh, yeah, I'm always dealing with questions of moral consciousness.

AG: HOW WOULD YOU RELATE *MESHUGAH* TO YOUR EARLIER PLAYS, THEN?

EM: It's like coming full circle. Because if you say that *Annulla* is my first play, this is the same territory. Jewish refugee, trying to live her life.

AG: AND AGAIN, A MORAL QUESTION AT ITS CENTER.

EM: They're the same question really. How did you survive? What did you do? Could I have done it? At what point is it better to be dead?

AG: DID YOU WRESTLE WITH HOW FAITHFUL YOU HAD TO BE TO THE NOVEL?

EM: Absolutely. But Singer is such a magnificent storyteller, that I strove to stay within the bounds of his storytelling and make that work theatrically. Which meant I might have to write or change things around, but stay true to his intention. That's hard, but it's a lot like my other works. I never distorted Mark in *Still Life*, I always helped the words and the language say what he wanted to say.

AG: IN THE NOVEL, THERE IS NO SCENE SHOWING MIRIAM IN THE CONCENTRATION CAMP. WOULD YOU HAVE CONSIDERED IT A BREACH OF HONESTY TO WRITE SUCH A SCENE FOR THE PLAY?

EM: No, but I cannot think of a Singer work where he does that. In any of his novels, with all those refugees, all those survivors of camps, you never see a camp scene. I have a gut feeling why: there's no way to dramatize it. He writes about how they drink their coffee *now*, how they eat their soup *now*. How they go on. He's very Chekhovian that way. He doesn't suddenly go off to past events and dramatize them. He stays in the present, with the tiny moments that reveal the infinite variety of the human soul. That's what I love about both Singer and Chekhov. That's what is both heartbreaking and humorous.

AG: IS EITHER SINGER OR CHEKHOV A MORALIST AS A PLAY-WRIGHT?

EM: No. They're both highly moral people. They have a sense of what's right and wrong. But I don't think either would begin to say they have the answer, or even an answer.

AG: SHOULD A PLAYWRIGHT BE A MORALIST?

EM: I don't think so, because then you're talking about propaganda. The great writers keep unearthing the questions. The more you know, the less you know. Both Singer and Chekhov were anti anyone who thought they had the answer. They were anti-fascist.

AG: VIOLENCE IN YOUR PLAYS SEEMS TO BE MALE.

EM: That's true.

AG: IT'S NOT THAT WOMEN ARE NOT STRONG.

EM: They are very strong. They are also capable of violence.

AG: BUT THE WOMEN ARE VICTIMS, EXCEPT PERHAPS FOR THE DELANY SISTERS, WHO, WHATEVER THEIR LIFE EXPERIENCE, NEVER BELIEVED THEY WERE VICTIMS.

EM: Right, although they knew that they had a lot of prejudice against them for being women, and black women, so they knew about the barriers.

AG: WHAT HAS IT MEANT TO BE A WOMAN WRITING IN THE THEATER?

EM: It's got so many facets to it. Are there fewer opportunities for women who have something to say? Yes. Are there fewer opportunities for anyone who has something to say? Yes. For women, more so. I don't know how to talk about it.

AG: DID BEING A WOMAN AND WANTING TO WRITE PLAYS IMPEDE YOUR CAREER, NOT FIGURE AT ALL, HELP YOU?

EM: From a career level, I certainly think it hurt. I once called a colleague at a major theater, a director, who said, 'Oh, Emily, it's so great to hear from you, your name comes up all the time.'

'Oh, really? For what?'

'Well, you know, whenever we bring up who are the major women directors in this country, your name is always number one.'

And I said, 'Oh, how sweet. Listen, when you're talking about *directors* and my name comes up, call me.'

I thought that was long over. But it's not long over. That's one of the reasons I had to take over my own theater, because I was just sick of the gender war. I don't write plays necessarily about boys and girls falling in love, and I don't write comedies, and I don't write plays that necessarily are about the state of male and female relationships. But because I bring up tough issues and problems, and deal with them hopefully on a rigorous intellectual level and on a level that isn't always fun to watch — and a lot of my plays are more on the instructional side than entertaining, though I try to get the entertainment there as well — I come under a lot of attack. My male colleagues who do similar plays come under less attack, because they're not as threatening.

AG: ARE YOU OBJECTING TO THE TERMS 'FEMALE DIRECTOR,' 'WOMAN DIRECTOR,' 'WOMAN PLAYWRIGHT'?

EM: Of course I am.

AG: WHY?

EM: Because I'm a director. I can direct anything that hits me on a gut level.

AG: THERE'S SOMETHING IRONIC HERE. AT ONE POINT WOMEN IN THE THEATER WERE ASKING TO BE RECOGNIZED BECAUSE WE WERE BEING LEFT OUT. NOW, HAVING BEEN RECOGNIZED AS WOMEN DIRECTORS AND WOMEN PLAYWRIGHTS, WE DON'T WANT THAT. THIS IS NOT A CONTRADICTION?

EM: No. At a certain point I want people to say, Emily Mann wrote the play, Emily Mann directed the play, Joanne Akalaitis directed the play. Of course I'm female. That's part of who I am. One would never deny any of this, in fact it's a very exciting, informing part of who one is — you bring your entire soul and personage to what you write and direct. As an artist, you bring your whole self, so of course I bring that I am a woman to the work. Can't leave it behind. Don't want to leave it behind. But what it means to be female for me isn't necessarily what it means to be female for anyone else. And at some point haven't we earned the right to be the unique artist that we are without the rubric first of female playwright, female director, black musician, black composer, black director? I think we've come to that point.

AG: WHAT DOES IT MEAN TO BE A WOMAN AND A DIREC-
TOR, A WOMAN AND A PLAYWRIGHT?

EM: As a woman and an artistic director, it has come to my attention that many of the plays on the McCarter stage are by or about
women, whether it's Marivaux or the Delany Sisters or *The Old Settler*
or *The Mai* or *The House of Bernarda Alba*. There are a lot of women.
I also hadn't noticed that most of the staff for the theater are female.
They were simply the best people for the job. And now I'm noticing it.

So I know that this has to do with my being a woman. One works
from the gut, and it's more than likely that plays by or about women
are going to affect me. Which is common sense. I write from my life
experience and I make decisions from that. I also find that when I direct,
there is a sensibility consistent throughout the plays, even though the
works may be two hundred years apart. I feel a great link to Lorca
and I feel a great link to Tennessee Williams.

I don't have a real answer for you. I have this set answer that I
give the press, and I'm not giving you that set answer. So I'm grop-
ing here a bit.

AG: ARE YOU A FEMINIST? IS THAT A BAD WORD NOW?

EM: These labels are so hard. Of course I am. My definition of feminism is that it is a form of humanism. It simply says that men and
women are equal. That's all it means to me, so how can a civilized
human being not be a feminist, male or female? So of course I'm a
feminist, and I don't think it's a dirty word, and I teach my students
at Princeton University that feminism is something to be proud of and
an important movement to be a part of. I wouldn't be sitting here without it.

There are radical feminists who say I am not a feminist. I am not
a politically correct person, that is for sure. I almost take it as a red
flag, that sort of political line. I will try to disrupt and challenge.

AG: ARE THERE WOMEN'S POINTS OF VIEW?

EM: I go back and forth on this. There are individual points of view,
and certainly women's experience in this society is almost by defini-

tion different than men's. So that will be reflected in honest writing and in honest creation of any kind onstage. On a certain level, I feel — and I can only speak for myself — that there are certain stories that haven't been heard, and often those are women's stories. And it interests me a lot to get them out. There are a lot of men who write brilliantly about women, so I don't think it takes a woman to write a woman's story. But I would say I feel often a need to get those stories out. But sometimes I simply have to write about the brutes, maybe because I know what it is to be brutalized on a certain level.

AG: HAS YOUR WRITING AS A WOMAN CHANGED?

EM: I think I've changed. I've grown, hopefully. I write a lot more out of love now than out of anger. I'm not trying to purge pain or trauma, but I have a real curiosity to understand myself and others.

There's no question in my mind that I am a feminist. I take for granted that one can do a feminist analysis of all my work. For instance, I think putting both *Annulla* and *Having Our Say* into the kitchen is obvious feminist aesthetics. To me, the kitchen, and watching older women cook food, are where and how I learned some of the most important truths of life. The kitchen is where most people, male and female, used to go and put their little elbows up on the formica table, smell all the food, and be in a very close and secure place and learn about the world. They might hear terrible things. They might hear about lynchings and concentration camps, and they might hear also about how to pick a good man — or learn about the family history or how to make chicken soup. Some of the most profound wisdom came from older women in my life in the kitchen. I find that you can talk about the horrors of life and that, in domestic situations, people will listen. Much more than if you put that in an austere setting where people put up their guard. People's guard comes right down in the kitchen. Putting those plays in a kitchen was a very conscious choice. Now you can look at that from a feminist perspective obviously.

But also, I can talk about politics. Why should that be the province of men? I'm going to ask questions about war. Women have to deal with war all the time. So what I write might deal not just with the warrior, but with what war does to our society, what it does to how we see men, how we've been programmed to think about the very sexy man in uniform, that that's what we're supposed to want — that man who protects us and kills for us. Women can also talk about the other side. What is war like for the gentle man, the man with the intellect and the soul and the music? All these questions are feminist questions.

It's a really aggressive act to say, 'I get to talk about war, I get to talk about the justice system, I get to talk about the Holocaust, I get to talk about whatever the hell I please. It is not a male province. It has to do with me. I'm part of the society, I'm part of what the justice system is about, I'm part of the decisions about war. I choose to take part in that discussion.' I think women have been kept out of a lot of things. And if you say that women playwrights should be writing domestic drama, and should be telling the truth and secrets only of the private, and only of the domestic, I don't think I can back that. That's one thing women might do really, really well; women have a way into the private, the domestic, that men might not have. But we also have a way into the sphere of the intellect and politics and the public issues that have often been decided by men.

AG: HOW DID YOU GET TO *HAVING OUR SAY*?

EM: It's a kind of nice story. My sister, Carol, is a literary agent, and she gave the book to me just before it was published and said, 'You are going to love this.' And I read it and loved it and I didn't think about it again.

Then my friend Judy James was staying at my house, and I gave the book to her and said, 'You're going to love this,' and she looked at it, looked at the cover, turned it over, looked at the blurbs on the back and said, 'We have to do this book.' And I said, 'Pardon me. Do this book? What does that mean?' And she said, 'You and Camille [Cosby] and I are going to do this book. I don't know if it's a movie or a play, I don't know if it's both. You're going to write it, maybe you'll direct it, I'm going to produce. This is it.'

She called my sister and within about four hours she found out how to get the rights. Called up Camille, who had just come home from Europe, who said, 'Judy, I just read this great book,' and Judy said, 'I bet it was *Having Our Say*. You and Emily and I have to do this.' And Camille said, 'Okay.'

AG: DID YOU WANT TO DO THE PLAY THE WAY THE BOOK WAS WRITTEN? THE TOLD-TO FORMAT?

EM: Well, I went through a lot of ideas on how to make this a play. First of all, I said, 'Look, I've got a theater, let's not go through the whole Hollywood thing; we don't want them to tell us what to do. Why don't we just have some control over this and do it our way, and I'll put it on.'

I thought I could craft an amazing piece out of this. Judy said it should be acted with an ensemble of ten, but the image came into my mind of a white man with a beard and a squirrel gun, and that filled me with dread. I thought it should be told and should be a tour-de-force performance piece for two mature black actors. And Camille went, 'Oh, yes.' And Judy said, 'Ooh, I don't know. How are you going to sustain that? This should be a Broadway play, and that can't be a Broadway play.' And I said, 'Well, I don't know if it is a Broadway play or not, but I really think this is the way it should go. We should go back to just plain, old-fashioned storytelling. That's one of the things I do well. Let me just try and see if it can sustain a full-length evening with these two women. I did it with one woman, in *Annulla*, I can do it better now.'

So that's how I started. Then Mary Alice and Gloria Foster read us bits and pieces of the book, read what could and couldn't translate into spoken speech, what was overwritten and underwritten, and I began to look at how to get these stories out there. I got the structure, and I thought, 'You know, shouldn't there be a relationship going with the audience? First it's rather formal, and they don't like us, and then they invite us in.'

Before I'd written it, we'd put it into the season at McCarter, and I realized our dress rehearsal would be on the sisters' father's birthday, which is the day they make the birthday meal. I thought: 'They're going to be cooking.' It just struck me, like it had done with *Annulla*, that they should go into the kitchen. They would invite the audience in, to be there while they were cooking the meal. So that was my little event. It's such great activity, cooking. It keeps things going. Because it takes a lot of energy to cook — a lot of movement, a lot of action. So I built it around how long it takes to cook.

AG: AND THEN YOU SELECTED THE PHOTOGRAPHS? FROM THE SISTERS' COLLECTION?

EM: Their collection, plus Wendall Harrington, the projections designer, did a lot of research and found a lot of other things, and then of course they put in the picture of my father and John Hope Franklin.

AG: IN 1995 YOU ANNOUNCED THAT YOU SUFFERED FROM MULTIPLE SCLEROSIS. DO YOU WANT TO TALK ABOUT THAT?

EM: Well, I'm feeling so good. I have this brilliant doctor, named René. Camille's greatest gift to me was getting me to this woman in L.A. She came to Utah — to Sundance — with me. When I arrived I needed help walking three steps, and when she left I was walking half a mile, unassisted. It's astounding. What can I say? I'm feeling blessed to have had her.

I've learned a lot. When I first met René, she said to me, 'Those who see disease as opportunity rather than a catastrophe get well.' I wanted to literally sock her in the mouth. Thanks a lot. Great opportunity. But by the end of my first two weeks of working with her, I totally understood what she meant. It's been an incredible journey. I've written more, directed more, accomplished more since I got ill, because I prioritize. What is important, what is not. I don't do what is not. Even if it's important, but not of primary importance, I do not do it.

AG: HAS ANY OF THAT SEEPED INTO YOUR WRITING?

EM: I think it has.

AG: WHY THE BASHEVIS SINGER PLAY?

EM: My son had a bar mitzvah in the summer of 1996, and I was the one parent, and there was no male there to help me. Talk about feminist issues. I got very hip to the fact that I was an illiterate in my own temple. I was very typical of my generation. I came in and talked to the cantor and actually burst into tears, because I didn't know how, I hadn't been taught. In fact I'd been taught not to pray, not to learn Hebrew. Here I was alone, my son wanted to have a bar mitzvah, and I had to learn a lot to help him do it. So I studied and then started to read my father's favorite author, who was I.B. Singer. All of the culture started to seep in. I've been very hungry for all of this. I was very ill the summer of 1996, and I just stacked up about eight novels and four books of short stories and read them all.

By the end, I realized I had to do something with this, and the first one I read, *Meshugah*, was the one that kept coming back to me. And I realized, 'Well, I'll just adapt the book, rather than write a piece from it. I love it too much. I'm going to use it as the basis.' And that's how I did it.

It just came out of me. It's awful to compare it to projectile vomiting, but that's what it was like. I wrote it in six weeks. I sat down at the typewriter and came out with a play. And structurally I haven't changed very much. It was just falling out of me. I never worked that fast. It was thrilling. It just had to come out.

It brought a lot of things together. I felt like I was home, you know? I feel incredible kinship with that man. One of my biggest regrets is that I didn't meet him. I had two opportunities and missed them.

AG: I ONCE READ A PROFILE OF SINGER IN *THE NEW YORKER*. THERE WAS AN UNPRETTY SIDE I HADN'T KNOWN ABOUT.

EM: Oh, yeah. He was a womanizer, he was really tough to deal with. Very selfish. But you know — impossible Jewish men — I know them, I like them. I'm very drawn to them. I think we would have gotten on. ▼

Cherríe
Moraga

Cherríe Moraga was born in Los Angeles and grew up on the outskirts of that city to become a poet, essayist, and playwright. Her earliest writing took the form of poems, short stories, and autobiographical essays, which have been published in a number of collections, including *This Bridge Called My Back: Writings By Radical Women of Color* (1981), which she co-edited with Gloria Anzaldua; *Loving in the War Years: Lo que nunca pasó por sus labios* (1983); *The Last Generation* (1993); and *Waiting in the Wings* (1997), a memoir prompted by the premature birth of her son.

Shortly after the publication of *Loving in the War Years*, Moraga began to write plays. *Giving Up the Ghost* (1984) is a poetic exploration of women's sexuality. *Shadow of a Man* (1990), which she developed while studying with Maria Irene Fornes in New York City, takes place within a Chicano family amid the politically tumultuous period of the 1960s; it won the 1990 Fund for New American Plays Award. Other plays by Moraga include *Heroes and Saints*, which won the 1992 PEN WEST Award for Drama, and *Watsonville: Some Place Not Here*, which won the 1996 Fund for New American Plays Award. Both focus on the spiritual faith and the trials of working people in the agricultural towns of California. *The Hungry Woman: A Mexican Medea* (1995) is Moraga's version of the Medea myth and her answer to the Mexican legend of La Llorona, the Weeping Woman, set 'in the near future of a fictional Chicano past.'

Moraga is presently artist-in-residence in the Department of Drama at Stanford University. She lives in Oakland, California. This interview took place in Oakland on October 1, 1999.

• • •

311

AG: WHAT IS THE HISTORY OF THE TERM 'CHICANO'?

CM: During the early Chicano Movement of the 1960s and 1970s, the same way 'Negroes' began to name themselves 'Blacks,' we took a term that had been considered derogatory by more assimilated Mexican Americans, and we reclaimed it for ourselves. As opposed to being hyphenated Americans, the Chicano Movement used the term 'Chicano' as an affirmation of our being indigenous to the Americas. Also, our identification would not be as an immigrant population, because we were Native people.

So 'Chicano' is a term that associates us with our Native roots. It's very distinct from the term 'Hispanic,' which associates us with our Spanish roots. For the most part, those of us that came of age in the sixties and seventies, and who are artists, continue to use 'Chicano,' even though we're still called Hispanic or Latino by the majority of the population. Certainly most of my contemporaries who are artists call themselves Chicanos, because as artists we retain that perspective of our relationship to the nation-state of America. It's a very politicized term.

AG: IN YOUR POEM, *NI FOR EL SALVADOR*, DATED FEBRUARY 1990, YOU WRITE, 'I AM A WOMAN NEARING 40 WITHOUT CHILDREN./ I AM AN ARTIST NEARING 40 WITHOUT COMMUNITY./ I AM A LESBIAN NEARING 40 WITHOUT PARTNER./ I AM A CHICANA NEARING 40 WITHOUT A COUNTRY...' IF YOU WERE TO WRITE TODAY ABOUT WHO YOU ARE, WHAT WOULD BE THE CHANGES, IF ANY?

CM: Well, I'm now well past forty and I not only have my own birth son, who's now six, but I'm also raising a ten-year-old girl, who's my partner's granddaughter. So I have children. What's the other one?

AG: AN ARTIST WITHOUT COMMUNITY.

CM: Yeah, I wrote that on one of those days when you feel that. And I often feel that. It was political movements that gave me the room to write: the Feminist Movement, the Chicano Movement, the Lesbian and Gay Movement. The act of writing is isolating anyway, which is fine with me. But that feeling that you're writing with common cause —

sharing a common cause with other artists — feels continually remote to me, except with some individuals. Particularly as a theater artist, I'm not sharing common cause as I would like to be. Sometimes I feel I'm a voice out there in the night in terms of my subject matter.

Less and less do I feel common cause with lesbian and gay writers. Among Chicanas, I sometimes feel that, as we become middle-aged and middle class, our earliest reasons for writing, which had to do with countering an American solipsism, are fading. Chicano literature may be more popular today, but is its popularity at the price of our politics?

So I feel that sense of isolation, except for a handful of intimates. I feel that some of our best writers and thinkers have been hijacked into the academy and are talking a language that I don't understand. Teaching a theory that I feel is increasingly remote from class-based concerns. So, yeah; I feel that way often. Good days I don't. And I have a lot of faith in youth. But as a forty-seven-year-old woman, I feel without community in that sense.

AG: WHY DON'T YOU MAKE COMMON CAUSE WITH GAYS AND LESBIANS?

CM: I've always felt that in terms of the Euro-American gay and lesbian communities. I felt early on that as a Chicana I had a very critical position as a lesbian; my lesbianism is so informed by my culture. How we make love, our notions of ourselves and our bodies are informed culturally, whether we're Mexican or Jewish or Italian or WASP or whatever. So I felt early on that if I was going to understand my lesbianism, I had to look to my people, my culture. Although there are certainly many places of juncture with white gays and lesbians in terms of our disenfranchisement, I feel that, particularly in the nineties, the goals and issues of lesbians and gays are primarily focused on domestic questions like the right to marry, and I really don't care about them. I feel those are assimilationist goals. I like being queer. I don't want to be oppressed of course, and it's hard to encounter a new set of problems about being 'out' within my child's school system. These are real concerns and very real struggles. But I always thought lesbianism and gayness had to do with creating alternate views, even for heterosexuals to see how to make family, how to make unions outside the nuclear family system. That's why I like being queer. And I find that much of the mainstream lesbian and gay movement is getting really middle class and conventional in their perspective.

AG: WITHOUT COUNTRY . . .

CM: Of all that list, that has changed the least. Many things are changeable on that list, but the country thing will be that way until I'm gone. My writing — everything — has always been about trying to create country, if only in the spirit of the play or the spirit of the poem. I'm moved and driven by the knowledge that this land is Native land. I feel that on a daily basis. I look around at the culture at large, and it's this huge monoculture. All of us are supposed to speak English. There's this national paranoia about not being English-speaking Anglo-Americans. So I don't feel I have a country in that sense.

A country is land and language and values, a shared ethic. I feel that all one does is try to make little pieces of a country for oneself.

AG: WHERE EXACTLY DID YOU GROW UP?

CM: We lived in L.A., then from the time I was nine, we lived in San Gabriel, which is about ten minutes from L.A. We lived about two blocks from the old Mission. So that's home I guess.

AG: WHAT DID HOME LOOK LIKE?

CM: It was a place that, even as a child, I wanted to get out of. San Gabriel is a suburb of L.A., and there are tracks that separate the Mexican side from the Anglo side, and my mom always made sure we lived on the so-called 'better side.' The schools I went to were Chicano, Italian, and Irish. Always went to Catholic schools. Working-class kids. Working-class families.

AG: WHAT DID HOME LOOK LIKE WHEN YOU STEPPED OUTSIDE?

CM: It was a big suburban street. Now the whole block has turned into apartments. Now it's all Mexican, because now that there are apartments, it's all young families with kids. So the neighborhood has completely changed in terms of the population. When we came in, there were old white people. We were the only kids on the block. It was a two-bedroom house, and a little half of a room that my brother slept in. Once I had gotten conscious, I knew it was a place I wanted to leave.

My mother always had a beautiful garden, so what I remember that's nice about the house is my mother's garden and how she cared for flowers. My grandmother lived next door, and my cousins lived with my grandmother, because when my mom moved to San Gabriel, my grandmother moved there, so everybody moved there. Our social world was that family. My cousins were my friends. They've stayed there; I'm one of the few who left.

AG: YOU WRITE ABOUT YOUR MOTHER SO MUCH IN YOUR ESSAYS AND POETRY, AND PERHAPS INDIRECTLY IN YOUR PLAYS. WOULD YOU TALK ABOUT HER? WHAT IS YOUR MOTHER'S NAME?

CM: Vera in English. Elvira in Spanish.

AG: WHAT DOES SHE LOOK LIKE?

CM: My mother's gorgeous. Stunning. Even at eighty-five, she's a very attractive woman. She always was very made up. She's a prideful, proud woman. She's about as short as me. Skinny. But as small as she is, she's very strong. A powerhouse. My dad's the opposite. He's a very quiet, very sweet man. Very withdrawn. They got old together. They've been together over fifty years.

AG: YOU'VE WRITTEN THAT YOUR MOTHER WAS A GOOD STORYTELLER, AND I WONDERED IF THERE WERE A CONNECTION IN YOUR MIND BETWEEN HER STORYTELLING AND YOUR WRITING.

CM: Absolutely. But not at the beginning. I started as a poet, and even the early essays were in the voice which is really the English-speaking voice, because it's the voice of separation from your family. As a child, trying to individuate yourself, you have this language at your disposal which is English. Later on I began to use Spanish in my poetry and started to use it more in my essays.

AG: WHEN DID YOU LEARN SPANISH?

CM: When I was a young child, I spoke it. I can remember speaking it. But since my father didn't speak Spanish, and my mother's bilingual, we started speaking English at home. It wasn't until I got out of college, really, that I put myself in Mexico and suffered to get the Spanish back. Went through great humiliation to get it back. And I still need a lot of work; I'll never have the fluency that I have in English. But I try to speak Spanish to my son.

The point of the storytelling was that when my tias (my aunts) came over, we sat at the table, and they spoke English and Spanish. They'd go on in Spanish and then say some English, and the bilinguality that you see in my plays, that's that language. To me as a child, because I didn't understand Spanish that well, it was music. I remember hearing the inflections, and I'd say, 'What does that mean, mom? What does that mean?' They'd drink beer and tell stories, and it was great for writing. There was great passion. They were very descriptive. Particularly my mom.

When I write essays now, since I do a lot of speaking engagements, I write them to be heard. And the poems are obviously the spoken word. I teach a lot of Latino students and I say, 'The best shot you got in your writing is your oral tradition. Read your butts off, but when you find your language, you're going to find it through the oral.' I think of it in terms of literacy. I was the first generation to have real literacy. But if I'm trying to copy people that have twenty generations of literacy behind them, I can't compete with them. All I have is that original voice. And it's a voice that, for the most part, schooling and workshopping and every immigrant program in this country will tell me not to use. That's why I love to teach, because I try to bring that original voice back in. I fell in love with playwriting because these voices that had been disregarded by my teachers, and by myself, suddenly became speakers. As a poet, too, you can combine English and Spanish to make language have a beautiful lyricism. It's like making love to these people that nobody gives a damn about. So definitely I consider my original literature storytelling. I get mad at theater all the time, because I'm convinced that there are other ways to tell stories onstage, ways that are not 'the play' and not 'performance art.' I keep banging my head against the stage door trying to figure out what they are. There's something in this kind of storytelling that can happen on the stage that doesn't look like a play.

AG: HAVE YOU EVER SEEN IT?

CM: I see little pieces of it. I see it in my students when they're really writing organically.

AG: HOW DID YOU GET TO THEATER?

CM: It was quite simple. I had published a book called *Loving in the War Years*, my first collection of poetry and essays. The book was really hard for me because it was like a coming-out text. There wasn't any book by a lesbian who was Chicana, and in terms of Chicano literature, nobody had put the two words 'Chicana' and 'lesbian' together except in a derogatory way. But this was a book that was filled with these words. I see it now as the work of a very young writer, written from great fear and anger.

AG: THERE'S ENORMOUS PASSION IN IT.

CM: Writing is like that when you're writing against something. If I can look at it as the work of one of my students, I would say, 'That person is trying to tell something that's not been said.' I feel that kind of energy in that book. And the weaknesses in it, in terms of technique, have a lot to do with that. But if a story has never been written — if you've never read it — how the hell are you supposed to write it? Right? That's how that book was written.

When that book was done, I left. I went to Mexico, I was so terrified of coming out. Was just terrified. I thought I'd die or something. I don't know; it was still so taboo to me. When I came back, I started writing in my journals, as I always did. But suddenly this character started talking to me, and it was the young girl, Corky, in *Giving Up the Ghost*. The kind of girl I would have liked to have been if I had had the guts. So this character, this kid, is talking to me, and I'm going, 'This really isn't me. This is somebody else.' I was used to writing autobiographical poetry and essays — that's all I did. I had tried to write character in college, but it was so homophobic (since I wasn't out to myself yet) that it was horrible. But this character's talking in my journal, and I got so excited, that I kept letting her talk. And I had this idea — because sometimes my work starts with a problem — that I was never going to be of any value as a writer for my own people unless I could understand heterosexual desire. Even as a lesbian, I had to understand what a woman felt for a man. So I decided I was going to explore it in character — a second character based on somebody I knew — and put into that character her desire for a man.

And that's when theater was born for me. My first play, *Giving Up the Ghost*, is in a way genre-confused, because I was transitioning from being a poet to writing theater. The poems became monologues. Basically the whole play is composed of monologues with some physical interaction.

AG: I THINK IT IS FLUID AND DREAMLIKE.

CM: Well, it may have been in the end. I wrote *Ghost* as a poet. And I still try to write that way; I'm always breaking the rules in theater. I'd never even seen a live piece of theater when I wrote that play. I came to theater very organically. And I have to keep remembering that, because to this day, when I write plays, the difficulty I have is that I'm seeing theater as a poet. I've learned a lot about structure, I've learned about action. I know how to do it, I teach the 'craft' of playwriting. But at the same time, I have certain wants that don't fit the form. How do you make that work on a stage? This keeps being my dilemma.

I used *Ghost* to get into Maria Irene Fornes' Hispanic playwrights' workshop, at INTAR in New York in 1985. I didn't even know who she was; I read a little blurb about this program. And I brought in the work, and we talked, and I was shocked that she loved it. I mean, she was really in love with the characters. I worked with her only one year, but if it hadn't been for starting with her, I never would have continued writing plays. Because she let me be a poet in the act of writing plays.

There were only three women out of ten in that workshop. The rest were guys. And all these guys had these great structural things happening. They all had the plot worked out ahead of time, the synopsis, etc. And she was completely unimpressed with all the control.

And with me she'd say, 'Oh, that's great. It's your little broken heart palpitating.' That's what she was interested in.

AG: YOU WROTE ONCE ABOUT THE IMPACT OF SEEING NTOZAKE SHANGE PERFORM.

CM: That was quite early on. I saw Ntozake read her poetry in the late seventies, and what blew me out was that she didn't compromise her voice to be a poet. It woke me up that I had been writing in translation. That there were voices in me that I had not validated, because nobody in the world was going to validate them. And I felt shame that I had bought this kind of white, middle-American literary thing. I'm going, 'Damn. I cheated myself.' I'm ever grateful for that moment.

AG: HOW INTIMATE THE RELATIONSHIP IS BETWEEN LANGUAGE – HOW WE SPEAK, HOW WE WRITE — AND CULTURE.

CM: Right now I'm teaching a creative writing class at Berkeley, and they're all kids of color — mostly Latino — and you can always find something beautiful, even in the worst piece of work. And I say to them, 'Okay, now you got to live up to *that* part.' And they look at me with fear and wonder. That's what I meant about not having a country. First, you realize what you've lost. That's what's so painful. Language is so tied to culture, that if you love language, when you begin to open that up, the first thing that comes is incredible sadness about what you've lost. And then rage, and then trying to acquire it, which requires rigor. Because what you're basically asking is to open yourself even more, to feel even more of what may have been lost or destroyed. Particularly if your relationship to language has something to do with people who are disenfranchised. You have to be willing to feel what it•brings up. But I love language for that reason.

AG: IN PLAY DEVELOPMENT WORKSHOPS, DRAMATURGS OFTEN SAY THAT A PLAYWRIGHT HAS A DISTINCTIVE VOICE. I'M SITTING HERE LISTENING TO YOU AND THINKING THAT IT IS HARD TO PROTECT THAT VOICE, WHICH CAN GET INFECTED BY MANY SURROUNDING LANGUAGES.

CM: I have students who come out of literary workshop programs and come into my playwriting classes, or other creative writing classes, and they come in with 'workshop' language. We have to spend a good two weeks undoing the workshop language so we can talk about the work simply and directly. I get really angry with academia, because it reveres abstract language. I'm with students going, 'Okay, fine that you have that language. But it's one language. I know you have five or six languages inside you. Which is the language that opens you? And which is the language that makes you feel you have boxes around you?' It's a very intuitive thing. But you're asking people to be artists. What's hard for me is that the language of commerce is where playwrights often have to be. That language of commerce — what sells, what's commercially viable — influences the playwriting and the development process. So it's difficult to trust people's intentions with your work. Good for business is what a 'good play' comes down to, and that language diminishes so many possibilities. But that's just my lament; when I've had a dramaturg or a director tell me things in the spirit of my play's real intentions, and I learn, I'm excited. But when you feel that the room's getting smaller with all the words, and it's because somebody's showing what they know, they've got the Ph.D. in dramaturgy or whatever. . . Obviously I don't like that system, or the business of how the work gets done there.

AG: HAVE YOU EVER THOUGHT OF STARTING YOU OWN THEATER?

CM: Of course I've thought of starting my own theater, and I'm trying to figure out how you do that, support a family, and do your art. At the same time that I say, 'Yes, I would like to start my own theater,' I'd also like to start a Chicano cultural school for kids on Saturdays, because there's not a damn piece of cultural affirmation in the whole city of Oakland for Latino students. So you tell me which one should I choose. And tell me how am I going to do either one? Also, I'm not dumb about what it requires to do a theater, and that's a business I'm not willing to build. But a grassroots theater company, with a black box for doing things pretty minimally — that might be viable in the next couple of years. If I get fed up enough.

For many years I was involved with Brava! For Women in the Arts, a theater company in San Francisco. There I had probably the most

access to seeing works realized in a way that was a beautiful compromise. Not a compromise in the sense of giving up something, but
of bringing supposedly opposing needs together. Getting grassroots,
working-class communities to the theater and at the same time having strong production values.

AG: THINKING ABOUT THE FIVE PLAYS OF YOURS THAT I
READ, YOU SEEM TO HAVE JOURNEYED FROM THE PRIVATE
TO THE PUBLIC SPHERE. *GIVING UP THE GHOST* IS ABOUT
A LOVE AFFAIR AND YOUR OWN IDENTITY. WITH *SHADOW
OF A MAN*, YOU EXPAND THE WORLD OF A PLAY TO
INCLUDE FAMILY. WITH *HEROES AND SAINTS* AND *WAT-
SONVILLE*, YOU ENLARGE THE WORLDS OF YOUR PLAYS TO
INCLUDE GRASSROOTS POLITICAL ACTIONS, LIKE WORKERS
STRIKING.

CM: I think that did happen. I also think it's going back again. *The
Hungry Woman: A Mexican Medea*, for all its bigness, is a very intimate play. There are huge subjects in the play, like the issue of country, but I feel that the play is tied to intimate issues like betrayal. It's
like any play: grand themes are enacted in intimate relationships, like
our lives are. I think *Medea* is more intimate because it's a play I really
wanted to write, because these are still my questions.

But what you say is true. The first play came because I needed
and wanted to write it. Then I wanted to write a family play, because
I was responding to the Chicano intellectual community's notion that
somehow lesbian and gay people weren't concerned with the family.
I thought, 'Well, where the hell did we grow up, if not in a family?'
Heroes and Saints was my challenge to write a play that my community
would consider to be 'social protest.' And it is in the sense that the
plot revolves around the social-political issue of environmental racism.
Different communities look at that play in different ways. This is the
first play the Chicano teatro arts community embraced. They really
loved the play. But they talk about it pretty much as a play about environmental racism, and I always think that's amusing, because it's as
much about sexual desire as anything else. It's about a woman's right
to her body and it's a critique of the Catholic Church. But I thought,
'This is really great. Let them see what they want to see. We'll do the
play.'

Watsonville was a commission from Brava! It is the only play I *started* within the context of a theater, before I had written a line. The play ended up being a sequel to *Heroes and Saints* in terms of returning characters, because I wasn't done with those people. I really liked them. *Watsonville* fundamentally has the same immigrant community of workers as *Heroes*. I feel that was a whole development process for me; there is a sequence in those plays.

AG: THERE'S A CHANGE IN STYLE AS WELL, FROM THAT DREAMLIKE EXPLORATION IN *GHOST*. *HEROES AND SAINTS* COMBINES REALISM AND VISIONS, AND IN *WATSONVILLE*, CHARACTERS GIVE POLITICAL SPEECHES AND TAKE OVERT POLITICAL STANDS.

CM: What you're seeing also is my process of accessing what it means to write theater and learn what's possible onstage. If you look at the ending of *Watsonville*, Sonora's prayer is absolutely in the poetic spirit of *Ghost*. I'm constantly trying to figure out how to get away with poetic moments and reflect an internal spiritual world in a play that's being moved by external action.

Watsonville to me is distinct. I don't consider it a docudrama, but it's closer to one than any of my other plays, because I talked to those workers — I have a stack of interviews — and they spoke to me in Spanish the whole time. I wrote lots of the play in Spanish before I changed things. But the language of the play and the stories are composites of what real people said. It was a way to do work that is both generated from outside of me and from within me. The play's in conversation with an outside source and myself as the internal source. Something like *Medea* is all my own preoccupations.

AG: YOU SAID EARLIER THAT YOUR WORK STARTS WITH A PROBLEM. IS THAT THE WAY MOST PLAYS START WITH YOU?

CM: I think usually they start with a problem. By that I mean, they start with something that I feel is not right. With *Shadow of a Man*, they said that gay people don't care about family, and I said, 'Well, gay people are made in families.' So I wrote Lupe. Lupe is the beginning of that play. She's an adolescent girl who will grow up to be a lesbian, very much shaped by the forces within her family. *Heroes and*

Saints came out of an image, but an image attached to a problem. That play began with seeing a kid on a United Farm Workers video who had been exposed to pesticides as a fetus and was born a stump of a body. At the same time, I had been reading a play by Luis Valdez called *The Shrunken Head of Pancho Villa*, where he had a head character with no body. But the *problem* in the play was: *women do not have a right to our bodies*. The *problem* was that injustice, as much as pesticide poisoning.

Medea comes from my questions about land and nationalism, memory of a land and having no right to a land. Why is it that women aren't allowed to care about country? Somehow, like Medea says, this has always been a male prerogative. Traditionally all these nationalist movements have been men's movements.

I started *Medea* before I ever had a child. It was a play I had been writing for a few years. And it was a problem for me, that question of nation, and it was a problem for me, this figure of La Llorona, the Mexican Weeping Woman who, like Medea, kills her children. Male writers have always interpreted this myth from a sexist perspective, I think, where the woman's motivation for killing her children is her man's unfaithfulness. Well, Toni Morrison's *Beloved* certainly showed us otherwise. That woman did it to save her children from slavery. Women are killing their kids all the time out here in the Bay area. Poor women. And I said, 'No. There's got to be another reason.' The question to me was, 'Why would a woman really kill her child?' And it remained a question to me in the writing of that play. I knew it had to be something about that sense of betrayal. But is it really about a man betraying her, or is it a more profound betrayal?

Sometimes I don't know if these investigations will become essays or plays. A lot of times I'm writing them simultaneously. I'm working out the problem on the page in an essay and trying to work it out through character in the play. But the problem always seems to be about a contradiction. Somebody's lying. The world is saying one thing, but you know intuitively that's not what's really going on. And for me, 'the world' might be the Chicano intellectual community in one moment or the mainstream in the next.

AG: *HEROES AND SAINTS* AND *WATSONVILLE* SEEM TO EXPRESS A FUNDAMENTAL POLITICAL OPTIMISM. THEN I READ YOUR *MEDEA*, WHICH TAKES PLACE IN A HORRIFIC

WORLD, AND I WONDERED WHAT HAD HAPPENED TO YOUR
VIEW OF WHAT CHICANOS AND WOMEN CAN ACCOMPLISH.
BUT YOU SAY THAT YOU WERE WORKING ON *MEDEA* EVEN
AS YOU WERE WRITING THE OTHER PLAYS.

CM: I always think *Medea* is a hopeful play, because her son comes
back at the end. He may not come back in the flesh; it may be that
she's just dreaming him. It's interesting — in earlier versions he never
came back. But after I had a kid, he came back, or his spirit did. I
couldn't bear him being dead. But, yes, the play is dark. I feel that
way when I talk about having no country. I look at someone like Medea
and it's like the line from Christa Wolfe's novel, *Medea: A Modern
Retelling*, which I use as an epigraph at the beginning of the play: 'Where
can I go?' Medea asks. 'Is it possible to imagine a world where I would
have a place?' And Wolfe goes on, 'There's no one I could ask. That's
the answer.' And that is the answer.

I do believe and I do feel — and I'm going to write it whether
anybody wants to see it or not — that for a woman of color in this
country who has memory — racial memory and consciousness of what
has brought her to this point in time in her world — she might as
well just pack it up. You survive by not remembering. You survive by
not seeing. But artists have to see, and I know numbers of women of
color — artists — who have such tenuous holds on their lives, because
there's no place to be. People say, 'Oh, your Medea is so horrible and
everything,' and I say, 'Yeah. She's egocentric, she's vain. But when
she talks about her land having been taken from her, that's the truth
that nobody wants to recognize, not in the play and not in fact.' I'm
a die-hard feminist, but because my feminism combines with concerns
about nation, concerns about race, people don't think it's feminism.
My question is, Is this woman of color allowed to be all that she is,
which is too big? She's too big for the world, so her 'bigness' gets perverted. Gets destroyed. And when that happens, you do perverted,
destroying acts. Like killing your child. I've seen it every day of my
life with women who have more brains, more talent. . . My feeling
was, at the end of the play there is no place for her. So when Chac-
Mool says, 'I'm taking you home, Mom,' obviously she has to die.
There is no place for her in this world. So she has to go.

AG: THE OTHER WOMEN REMAIN.

CM: Luna's going to stay in her little ghetto, you know, and have her life. But Luna isn't a Medea. It's not a positive or a negative thing, but Luna is basically an on-the-ground person. She is not a visionary. She's a good soul and pretty loyal ultimately.

I'm not saying that Medea is a positive or negative character either. It's not even about that. All the portrait is about is that she makes bad decisions in a bad world and in the end she dies because of it. But she's in prison anyway, so what's the difference? To me, it's a tragic portrait of being too much woman for this world.

AG: I RELATE THAT PORTRAIT TO YOUR OPENING IMAGE OF THE DECAPITATED COATLICUE, THE AZTEC GODDESS OF CREATION AND DESTRUCTION. MEDEA IS BOTH CREATIVE AND DESTRUCTIVE. SADLY, SHE CAN'T BE ALLOWED TO STAY IN A WORLD THAT BELIEVES IT WILL NOT GO FORWARD WITH WOMEN LIKE MEDEA.

CM: But the world goes forward with patriarchs, right? What I'm saying in the play is that somehow men, with all of their destructive power, have been allowed to flourish. So they've created a destructive world. A world of violence. Early feminist anthropologists describe how, when men first witnessed women's power to give birth, to create life, they were awed by the phenomenon and respected women's power. But later the awe turned to fear of their own vulnerability toward women. Fundamentally, misogyny is about fear of women's power. Medea doesn't get to live out her creative power, but instead of passively accepting that, she brings out the destructive Coatlicue aspect — she brings out that other side of her which men fear. In society's view, the most anti-female thing you can do is kill your child. Because if you're anything in this world, you are the female animal that exists to give birth.

AG: BUT THE PLAY ALSO SEEMS TO BE SAYING THAT WOMEN CANNOT ALLOW MEN TO GROW UP.

CM: Not if they're going to grow up to be killers. Medea is theoretically right, but she's not right to kill her child. Still, it is justified in her mind, and that's all that matters. The idea in her mind is that the son is going to grow up to betray the mother, and the way he betrays is to become part of the patriarchy, which fundamentally means he grows up to hate the mother. It's the misogynist idea that you have to reject the mother to become a man.

I don't know if *Medea* will ever get produced. The times when it has been read well, I've been excited about it. The story is devastating, but it's my belief that in the devastation there's hope. Chac-Mool holds Medea in death as she held him. Even though the final action is death, the final image is union.

I started writing that play in 1990, and it's still with me, because that's always the conversation I'm having. This is the world I want: I want men and women, gay people, heterosexual, together. But I feel that even small progressive endeavors are unable to happen because of people's ignorance and sexism and fear. I experience that on a daily basis. I'm talking about tiny moments of possible solidarity that people are unable to have because of their fears. The fear of women particularly. Fear of strong women of color. Even non-Chicana women of color that have seen the play have really responded to it. And as a woman of color, I see that that is why men think we're crazy. The minute we start being ourselves, we are considered crazy. So for the most part, it's like we're walking around speaking another language, so we can just get through the day. These are things I hold inside me and witness in my intimates. This was the play in which I decided I'd look at that problem.

AG: THE FIGURE OF MEDEA COMES INTO WHITE-EUROPEAN CULTURE AS A SYMBOL OF THE BETRAYING, MURDEROUS WOMAN, MUCH AS MALINCHE REPRESENTS THE WOMAN WHO DESTROYED THE AZTEC PEOPLE BY BEING THE MISTRESS OF HERNANDO CORTEZ, THE SPANISH CONQUEROR OF MEXICO.

CM: I remember reading Euripides' *Medea* and I identified with her. I saw her as a woman of color. I thought, 'Well, she's my ally.' I mean, I loved her. The only thing I couldn't understand was that she kills her children. This was a big blank to me. And I said, 'Oh. A man must have written this.' The motivation given for killing her children didn't make sense to me. Something got skipped.

The thing about Malinche is that from the time we came of age as feminists, Chicanas have critiqued her role in our history and mythology. She is our 'Mexican Eve.' She was a sixteen-year-old Aztec girl sold into slavery and given to Cortez as his courtesan. She had no say in the matter. One work on the subject that impacted me a lot was Rudolfo Anaya's interpretation of her life, because he combines Malinche with the story of La Llorona, our Mexican Medea. In his version, Malinche's motive for killing her children is to prevent them from going to Spain to live with their father, Cortez. She refuses to let Cortez make Spaniards out of them and would rather see them dead than gone from their Native land. And that struck me. I thought, 'That's the play. The play is land.'

AG: I FEEL THAT *MEDEA* IS YOUR MOST RADICAL PLAY. IT SEEMS TO SAY THAT WE NEED A WOMAN'S WORLD. ALL THE CHARACTERS, INCLUDING THE MALE CHARACTERS, ARE PLAYED BY WOMEN, EXCEPT FOR MEDEA'S SON.

CM: Well, that's because the *play* is a woman's world. They're all in exile. It's interesting that you think that, because I feel I'm fundamentally not a separatist. I never have been. That's why I keep having conversations like this play. The conversation is as much addressed to men as to anybody, but probably even more so to men. It's, 'Do you see yourself reflected? And if you see yourself reflected, look who you're losing. Look at us here, in exile.' The gesture of depicting this world where men have betrayed us is the effort to raise consciousness. Not that I think this play will do that. I'm not naïve. The times that I've had this play read, Chicano men get really quiet. They respect the politics of it, they respect the notion of Aztlán — the idea of having territory. But when you put this feminist view on it, that if you get to be all man and have your land, what about all woman? Why can't we be all woman in your land? That's hard for them.

AG: BUT WHAT ARE CHICANO MEN TO DO IF THEY BELIEVE THE MAINSTREAM CULTURE TAKES AWAY THEIR MANHOOD?

CM: They're supposed to take it from the women then? Why not take it from the boss? Why do they have to take if from us? Absolutely you can say that white patriarchal racism has affected men of color's notions of their manhood and, I think, perverted it. The superman stuff, sexism, machismo, can be a response to an emasculation that happens by white dominant culture. But that being the case, who's the real enemy there?

There's a whole movement of young men, gay and straight, who have been very affected by Chicana feminist writing from the generation that proceeds them. There's nothing separatist about it. But *Medea* is a hard play, and it can be interpreted to be about killing masculinity, which I have no interest in whatsoever. Medea does kill the boy. In her mind it's justified. But my world view is not that it's a woman's world, but that men will not allow us shared position. I just depicted where we're at.

As a lesbian, you become sort of symbolic of not needing men. So we're the greatest threat, because it's assumed we'd want a world without men. But I've never ever felt that way in my life. In fact, I wrote critiques of lesbian separatism in the early days of the Women's Movement, when that was a viable theme. It's not the world I live in, it's not the world that I would aspire to. It becomes increasingly clear to me that feminism has everything to do with improving men, but by throwing the responsibility of improvement back on them. When I teach young men, I want to say to them, 'Don't you realize we could save your lives?' There are ways in which their unhappiness is formed by the restrictions of their own roles. But of course, they have to give up power. That's always the little detail.

AG: HAS BEING A MOTHER AFFECTED WHAT YOU WANT TO WRITE ABOUT?

CM: What I want to write about, or my time? I want to talk here about how many women playwrights are mothers. How many women in *theater* are even mothers. We had a long conversation about that when I did a women playwrights festival in Seattle. I was the only one who had a kid in the whole bunch, and a bunch of them were talking about that phenomenon. They said that men can have families and be directors and artistic directors and playwrights, travel all over the world, and everything is fine. But somehow women, if they want to have kids, aren't going to be able to do all of that.

AG: FIFTEEN OF THE WOMEN IN THIS BOOK HAVE CHILDREN, AND SEVERAL HAD THEM WHEN IN THEIR FORTIES. AT LEAST TWO ARE RAISING CHILDREN BY THEMSELVES. IN

YOUR COLLECTION OF ESSAYS, *WAITING IN THE WINGS*, YOU WRITE THAT YOU WERE CONCERNED ABOUT BEING SELFISH IN RELATION TO YOUR CHILD.

CM: For wanting to go back and write? In *Waiting in the Wings* I remember talking about all that mythology which says that your creative urges are fulfilled by having children. In my opinion, they have no relation to each other whatsoever. And that 'urge'? I never thought about being a mother as an urge. What is creative in it, to me, is pure animal. It's just body. I experience it so physically, even to this day, even in relation to the physical animal that my son is. It's a profound thing to know, which I wouldn't have known, but it has no relationship to creativity. The urge to write is something totally different. And so I wonder who made up that? I guess it was an excuse to tell women, 'Have your babies and you don't have to do anything else, because it's creative.' I think because motherhood is so compelling and demanding, wanting to go back and write happened because I said, 'I am more than this.' Not that motherhood isn't sufficient for some people, but for me, I wanted to remember that part of myself, that voice in me which has given me sustenance my whole life. And it's very different.

AG: HAVING LIVED A NONTRADITIONAL LIFE, YOU HAVE DONE A TRADITIONAL THING — HAVING A CHILD — EVEN THOUGH UNDER NONTRADITIONAL CIRCUMSTANCES.

CM: But none of my actions in my life have been motivated by tradition, or lack thereof. Do you know what I'm saying? I never did anything in my life to be nontraditional. To the degree that I was able, I did what my conscience and desires dictated. I didn't become a lesbian because it was nontraditional. I became a lesbian because I had no choice. I'd either lose my mind or be a lesbian. By the same token, my choice to have a child, if I was able — and I didn't know if I'd be able — was long in coming. It came with the development of my desires and consciousness. If you look at my work, you can see that my preoccupations with family have been tremendous, and I credit *that* from my tradition; I was raised to honor family. But it took me a long time to arrive at the fact that as a lesbian, I had the *right* to have children. That's something I let myself have finally. And if I couldn't have had Rafael, I would have raised a child; it wasn't that I had to be a biological mother. But everything was showing me that I had that to give to some-body, I had that capacity to love that way. Which is very distinct from lover relationships, because you have to put children's needs before your own.

I guess that's why it's so hard to be an artist, because you have to be really selfish to be an artist, and I say that with respect for that selfishness. When I finally decided I wanted to have a child, I was in my mid-thirties and I was sure that I would always be an artist no matter what. At twenty-five I couldn't have said that. But at thirty-five, no one's going to stop me. Not even a child. But after you have a kid, you balance those things, because your work does preoccupy you. I remember when Rafael was three or so, at an age when he needed more of my constant attention, I'd be reading or writing, and he would literally grab my face and make me look at him. I had to figure out when and how to be present and when I needed not to be present. When to give myself the space not to be present, but also how to take the time to be present with my child.

AG: WHY, IN THE TWENTY-FIRST CENTURY, SHOULD BEING AN ARTIST AND A MOTHER STILL BE AN ISSUE?

CM: Because it's still distinct. Having a kid is distinct from fathering. I keep thinking about models of producing art. If the model for pro-ducing art is that it's a business, then on a certain level what's required is that you better not have children. Also, we know that the best artists take the time and the space to go into terrains that most of us walk-ing around don't have access to or the need to go to. Is it possible to have children and go to those places on a regular basis? The irony to me is that when I allow myself to go to those places, I'm much more present to my child when I come out. But there's no guarantee of that. It's why it's difficult even to have a relationship with an artist. If you have a relationship with an artist, you have to let that artist go, and she has to let you go. Is the artist going to come back or not? Who knows what's going to come up.

So when you imagine having children dependent on you, those are real issues. But I feel happy right now to be in that struggle. I sleep less now. I'm a real morning person — I don't write well at night — but I'm learning to. To me it all ends up being a writerly life. Having a child has made me so much more committed to a life well lived.

AG: WE HAVE BEEN TALKING GENERALLY ABOUT PEOPLE WHO ARE CONSIDERED 'OTHER.' IN *HEROES AND SAINTS*, CEREZITA, WHO DOESN'T HAVE A BODY, SEEMS TO BE THE ULTIMATE 'OTHER,' THE EPITOME OF WHAT THE WORLD TRIES TO ERASE.

CM: I don't see her very differently from Medea. Cerezita is a sixteen-year-old Chicana, fine mind, a visionary — and she's trapped. She literally doesn't have a body. But she could have one and still be in that position. She is the same person as Medea, in the sense that she can 'see.' But unlike Medea, she's all kindness and compassion. She is why I've always believed ideally in a woman-of-color feminism: that if you've walked the oppression, then you have great compassion. When she reads those books on the body, there's her insistence on the body she doesn't have. I love her because she insists. She gets the community kids to get her out in the public view in order to politically move people. 'If nobody ever sees me, how will I know how I look? How will I know if I scare them or . . . move them? If people could see me . . . things would change.' Her mother tells her, in effect, 'You are my sin.' Every Mexican Catholic girl has been told that. 'You're my sin.' It's a profound thing how many of us, if we were raised traditionally, have that hatred of our bodies. Girls in other cultures get it too, but in a world where mothers feel that they have to protect their daughters from desire and sex, you begin to believe your body is the enemy. Well, Cerezita doesn't have a body. So she wants to get one, and her mother still tells her she's dirty, because the desirous thoughts are in Cerezita's mind. The play is a critique of Catholicism, but also of Mexican women's complicity in female oppression.

But the play's positive, even though the people of the town get shot down. Cerezita moves the people. 'Put your hand inside my wound,' she says. 'Inside the valley of my wound, there is a people.' Like Jesus Christ. That symbolism wasn't intentional when I wrote it, but all of a sudden, 'Oh, that's Jesus Christ.' Your steps may be different from mine, but if you put your hand inside my wound, if you can have compassion, you will be changed. That's the play, to me.

Juan, the leftist priest, was a much harder character to write. He's the epitome of waste. A person who has this fine body and can't act. In his ambivalence, in that he's mixed blood, he represents a lot of the latent parts of me that I don't like. Everybody's yourself on some level in a play. I have no problem taking a piece of myself that I don't like and making a character out of it.

AG: CAN YOU DESCRIBE THE PRODUCTION OF *HEROES AND SAINTS* THAT YOU LIKED BEST?

CM: Brava! got vineyards from the valley and brought them onto the stage, so that the vineyards came into the living room of the house. I had really wanted to get a sense of the valley penetrating the family's intimate life, and that was beautifully done.

Cerezita was in a kind of box. Physically she was in one of those electric wheelchairs, which the actress was operating with her hand, but she was covered in this box up to her neck. What I really liked was that you heard her entrance before you saw her, because there was the buzzing sound of the battery-operated chair. She never had any privacy because of that. Everyone knew where she was at all times. I was pleased with that production.

AG: IN *HEROES AND SAINTS* AND *WATSONVILLE*, YOU CONVEY THAT THE CATHOLIC CHURCH IS FAKE, EVEN RIDICULOUS. THE PEOPLE OF THE TOWN HAVE MUCH MORE FAITH THAN THE REPRESENTATIVES OF THE CHURCH.

CM: Even as children, we knew that. There was a real distinction between one's Catholic faith and the Church. The priests were never to be trusted. Priests were gringos for the most part and favored the gringo families. Those people who invited them to dinners. But my mother was very clear, that was all hypocrisy. Faith was about your private relationship with God and how you treated people. When I interviewed the women in Watsonville, their Catholicism came right out of that same belief.

AG: THE WORKERS YOU SPOKE WITH WERE ON STRIKE?

CM: It was a two-year cannery workers strike. Then an earthquake happened, and the appearance of the apparition of the Virgin of Guadalupe. All three things happened within a short period of years, and I combined them. One criticism was that all this happens in the same play, and I'd say, 'Well, it happened in the same town and it happened to the same people.' The person who saw the Virgin of Guadalupe was a cannery worker who had been involved with the strike. And of course all of them suffered the earthquake. I said, 'That's the story of their lives.' Watsonville is remarkable that way. It's been the epicenter, literally, of many things.

AG: DO YOU LOOK FOR A BALANCE BETWEEN THEATER AND POLITICS IN YOUR PLAYS? DOES WHAT YOU SAY EVER BECOME MORE IMPORTANT THAN HOW YOU SAY IT?

CM: My desire to write well is everything. The difficulty for me is to make what's considered polemical by the world at large believable in the heart. Believable and intimate. That remains a challenge, and I try to do it better and better. I never try to do one at the expense of the other. I don't sit down to write a political play. The plays are as they are. But I always sit down to write as best I can. The art is everything to me.

I've sometimes felt encumbered by the breadth of what I take on, to try to make it work theatrically. As an artist, I'm always dealing with how to create structures for all that I want to write about. What encumbered me about *Watsonville* were the three events. The hardest task was to get those three events to happen. And I didn't want to give up one of them, because I thought they were all related. I don't see many models that work for me. I don't read or see a lot of plays that are doing the same kind of thing. So it's hard work. Playwriting is hard.

AG: ONE OF THE THINGS I LIKE ABOUT *SHADOW OF A MAN* IS THAT, BY PORTRAYING SEVERAL OPPRESSED PEOPLE WITHIN ONE FAMILY, THAT FAMILY COMES TO REPRESENT A BIGGER COMMUNITY.

CM: But I don't think *Shadow* is any less political than the others. It's just that in *Heroes and Saints* and *Watsonville* the action is outside the family as well as inside. I feel the plays are driven by the same impulses. How do you show community onstage? How do you show solidarity onstage?

AG: DOES THERE HAVE TO BE A FORMAL SPACE? THERE IS STREET THEATER.

CM: But when you do street theater, the writing is not that important. You can't even hear it, and I take a lot of care with my words. The thing that was beautiful about working with Brava! was that I had Equity actors and pretty solid production values, and diverse communities came to those plays. In the case of *Watsonville*, even workers from the town came.

AG: PERHAPS THIS IS WHERE SEDUCTION BY MAINSTREAM THEATER COMES IN. THE AUDIENCES YOU WRITE FOR ARE NOT NECESSARILY GOING TO ATTEND THE THEATERS THAT CAN AFFORD THE PRODUCTION VALUES YOU WANT.

CM: It remains a dilemma. If I ran the world, I would have all kinds of audiences see my work. Not at million-dollar budgets, but nice, maybe two-hundred-thousand-dollar budgets. And I could improve as an artist. I could improve because I would see my work realized, and I would not have to limit what I imagined on stage. Seduction. That's a very good word.

The great thing about being a successful mainstream writer is that you can keep imagining. When you have access, someone is saying to you, 'Go ahead and imagine, and we'll back you up. Imagine whatever you can imagine.' When that stops happening, you kind of go, 'Maybe I don't know how to imagine anymore.' That's why we become novelists.

AG: HOW DO YOU ENVISION *MEDEA*?

CM: I think of things being achieved by light and sound more than anything else. And just some damn good actors and an indigenous Mexican choreographer. It's not even like I'm asking for big sets. You can even do *Medea* with eight good actors. That's why I'm starting to get enamored with readings lately. Because I'm at least 'hearing' the work. Particularly for those of us who really look at the language of a play, it is literature. If nobody gets to see it, I'll publish it, and you can imagine it with me. I've put a lot of energy into publishing my plays. It's not the same thing as getting my work produced, but at least the ideas get read and they get read by my community.

I've started to get really good at stage directions. A lot of playwrights I know talk this way. We have started writing plays to be 'read' really well. Because more and more it's hard to see something realized in production. You have to be kind of a crazy person to be writing these huge plays, as I am. And then to combine that with subject matter that is considered radical even within the context of the people-of-color community — but these are the living contradictions of being an artist of color in this country.

AG: YOU ONCE WROTE THAT YOU DREAMED OF A UNIFIED THIRD WORLD FEMINIST MOVEMENT IN THIS COUNTRY. WHAT HAPPENED TO THAT DREAM?

CM: Well, it doesn't exist, right? I was young when I wrote that about Third World feminism. The only thing I can reckon with now in my life, the most we can hope for, are small acts of resistance. I don't think my life is going to be much more than that. There's a beautiful line that Chrystos, a Native-American lesbian poet, wrote, talking about the world being on the brink of a nuclear holocaust. This was in 1980, but it's still powerful today. She writes, 'I will be screaming no no no more destruction in that last blinding light.' That's what I feel about this global monoculture: all you can do is scream no no no against it. Recently, I've been working with a group of young women, Indigenous Chicanas. We're looking at feminist issues from the condition of Native people around the globe. These women want teachers. They're interested in their history. They're interested in their roots. They want cultural affirmation for what intuitively they know but do not see reflected in the world around them. So they come to the generation that's older, asking questions. Responding to those questions . . . to those women, that's a small act of resistance. ▽

Lynn Nottage

Lynn Nottage was born and raised in Brooklyn. She graduated from Brown University and received an M.F.A. in playwriting from Yale School of Drama.

While at Yale, Nottage wrote a number of plays and began *Las Meninas* (1989), which takes its title from the famous Velazquez painting and dramatizes a romantic relationship between two outcasts: Queen Marie-Thérèse, the unhappy wife of King Louis XIV of France, and an African dwarf named Nabo. In 1992, after four years spent working for Amnesty International, Nottage wrote a funny, affecting monologue entitled *Ida Mae Cole Takes a Stance*, for the musical revue *A. . . My Name is Still Alice*, and the one-act *Poof!* (1993), about how two women do away with their abusive husbands. She won the Heideman Award for *Poof!* at Actors Theatre of Louisville.

Subsequently, Nottage wrote *Crumbs from the Table of Joy* (1995), which takes place in Brooklyn during the 1950s and shows the coming-of-age of seventeen-year-old Ernestine Crump, who navigates the relationships among her father, her late mother's sister, and her father's European second wife. *Por'Knockers* (1995) satirizes a group of would-be revolutionaries, and *Mud, River, Stone* (1996) examines the excruciating events that befall two middle-class Americans in Africa. Currently she is adapting Henrik Ibsen's *An Enemy of the People* for Seattle's Intiman Theatre.

Nottage is a member of New Dramatists and is the recipient of an NEA/TCG Residency Grant at Freedom Theatre in Philadelphia. She lives in Brooklyn with her husband, the filmmaker Tony Gerber, and their daughter, Ruby. This interview took place in Nottage's home on January 21, 2000.

• • •

AG: COULD YOU TALK ABOUT YOUR FAMILY?

LN: My father was born in Harlem. My mother was born in Brooklyn. They were hard-core, old-time New Yorkers, which caused problems on holidays, because we would have no place to go. Everyone else left town and went somewhere wonderful. We went to Brooklyn, because it was home. We moved to this house in 1968, so I was pretty much raised on this block. I didn't leave here until I went to college.

AG: WHAT IS THIS SECTION OF BROOKLYN CALLED?

LN: When we first moved here, it was Gowanus, then it became South Brooklyn, and then at some point Boerum Hill.

AG: HAS THE NEIGHBORHOOD CHANGED SINCE YOU WERE A CHILD?

LN: This neighborhood has changed drastically, probably more than most of the neighborhoods in New York City. It's undergone a tremendous amount of gentrification in the last twenty years. When we moved here, it was a mixture of boarding houses and one-family homes, and it was very racially mixed. There were Latinos from Panama and Cuba and Puerto Rico. There were Irish families who'd been here since the turn of the century. There were some Native Americans who roomed at a boarding house, and some black families. A sprinkling of hippies. This neighborhood was also probably one of the first gay neighborhoods in Brooklyn. A lot of gay politicians lived on our block.

AG: HOW DID THE NEIGHBORHOOD CHANGE?

LN: The neighborhood probably began changing when this area was designated a landmark and dubbed Boerum Hill. (You think of Gowanus, you think of the Gowanus Canal, you think of the stench, and you don't want to live here.) Slowly that brought middle-class families, and now even middle-class families are being pushed out of the neighborhood as the prices for the brownstones continue to escalate.

There are aspects of this neighborhood that have been bettered because there are restaurants, but the community isn't what it was. When we were kids, we still played in the street — some of those old

Brooklyn street games. My daughter, she's going to grow up here and she's not going to play any of those games, because there is no one who will know them. There was a sense of continuity from one generation to another. The continuity is gone, with the exception of a few of us who still live on the block. When I left Brooklyn for college, I said I'd never come back. And here I am.

AG: *CRUMBS FROM THE TABLE OF JOY* TAKES PLACE IN BROOKLYN. IS IT AT ALL BIOGRAPHICAL?

LN: Not really. I drew on my grandmother's and my mother's experiences of living in Brooklyn in the 1950s, but the characters are not based on them. The situation in the play is very different from my family's. My family didn't come from the South to New York City during that great wave of migration in the 1940s and 1950s. My parents were both civil servants. My mother was a school teacher who later became a principal. In fact, she was the principal at the elementary school she and my grandmother had both attended. My father was a psychologist, who then worked in prison reform.

My parents were avid art lovers and knew a lot of the African-American artists whose work they collected. They'd throw elaborate parties, to which writers and painters and musicians would come, and the occasional actor. I don't remember any playwrights. I remember art as being part of my life and my upbringing.

AG: DID YOU WRITE WHEN YOU WERE A CHILD?

LN: I did write. I always wrote. I tried to keep a diary, but I was never very good at it. I have looked back at my diaries and, oh, my God, I had nothing to say. 'I took a walk down to the store and I bought a pack of gum. I came back. I chewed the gum.' Nothing about my feelings, because I was too afraid that my brother would read them. And I wrote short stories, which I've saved as well, because I'm a pack rat.

AG: WHEN DID YOU WRITE YOUR FIRST PLAY?

LN: I have to admit that I wrote my very first play when I was seven or eight. I found a little audiotape — I had gotten a tape recorder as a Christmas present — and I cast my brother as the Prince, and I was the Princess, and you can hear me on the tape feeding my brother lines. You can hear this little whisper: 'Now you say . . . ' So I imagine that was my very first play. The tape was an actual performance for my parents.

AG: WHERE DID YOU PUT THIS PLAY ON?

LN: Here. Downstairs in the living room.

AG: HOW DID YOU BECOME INVOLVED IN THEATER LATER ON?

LN: I went to the High School of Music and Art as a music student — I played piano — and I became interested in musical theater. Also, I was interested in drama and when I was a junior, I guess, I took an English class with a specialization in drama, and one of the highlights was going to see Broadway and off-Broadway productions. During my senior year, I wrote a musical with a group at the Dramatists Guild, organized through the Young Playwrights Festival. Four of us spent the year working on a new musical, which was about a group of high school students from the Middle West who come to New York for the Thanksgiving Day parade.

AG: DID YOU COMPOSE AT MUSIC AND ART?

LN: I dabbled. I composed, but I didn't do it well. One of the things I had to do in the workshop was write music, and some of the people were very talented, and I'd come in and sit at my piano, and I could see them smirking and laughing. But I did it with bravado. I really enjoyed doing it.

AG: I'M THINKING ABOUT YOUR USE OF MUSIC IN YOUR PLAYS. DAVID IN *MUD, RIVER, STONE* SINGS BITS OF MUSIC.

LN: Yes, he hears music. That's how he sees the world; everything has a backbeat. In *Crumbs from the Table of Joy*, both Lily and Gerte, who is the German bride, are intoxicated by the sounds of jazz. The freedom of the music symbolizes something special for both of them.

AG: I'VE HEARD PLAYWRIGHTS SAY THAT THERE IS LITER-
ALLY THE FIRST PLAY ONE WRITES AND THEN THERE'S THE
PLAY ABOUT WHICH ONE THINKS, 'THIS IS REALLY THE
FIRST.'

LN: That's definitely true. I certainly wrote a number of plays which
were performed but weren't quite plays yet. They were me discovering how to write a play in public, which in retrospect seems very brave.

AG: BUT HOW ELSE DOES A PLAYWRIGHT DO IT?

LN: You have to do it. College was my laboratory.

AG: DID YOU TAKE PLAYWRITING COURSES AT BROWN?

LN: My first playwriting course was with George Bass, who was a
wonderful, inspirational, wild, amazing man. He gave me a great gift,
which was that he was completely free. He never worried what anyone thought about him. He said what he felt, which is very important for a playwright to be free to do. In some ways, when you go to
graduate school, a lot of what you're learning is how to censor yourself. How to curtail those impulses. Once I got out of graduate school,
I had to free myself again and find who I was.
    I also studied with Paula Vogel, who came to Brown my senior
year. She was the first female playwright I knew who considered herself a playwright. That's how she identified herself. She was very open
and generous with us and certainly pushed me in ways she doesn't know.

AG: CAN PLAYWRITING BE TAUGHT?

LN: Honestly, I don't know whether I learned to write plays by taking playwriting. It's a question I can't answer, because I don't know
the answer.

AG: WHAT TURNED YOU ON ABOUT THEATER?

LN: I always enjoyed storytelling. I was a very shy person, but I liked
the collaborative spirit of the rehearsal process and taking something
on to production. It was the way this very private person could suddenly

become public. I could speak without having to be up there delivering a speech, and I could sit in the back. And sweat. No one would actually see how much I was sweating.

AG: HOW SOON AFTER GRADUATING FROM BROWN DID YOU GO TO YALE?

LN: Directly after.

AG: WHY?

LN: I didn't know what I needed to do and so I went to graduate school. In retrospect, it probably wasn't a very good idea. I wish I had plunged into the world and worked for a while and then gone. I felt outside of my element. There were all these serious theater students, and I was just getting to know theater. I didn't know any of their cultural references. I hadn't read any of the plays. The productions I had seen had either been at Negro Ensemble Company or were musicals on Broadway. That was the extent of my theater experience, which was very different from most of the people's at Yale, who knew about the angry British drama and Brecht and Chekhov. I had to discover all those things and play catch-up.

AG: HOW OLD WERE YOU WHEN YOU WENT TO YALE?

LN: I was twenty-one. It was a difficult experience. I was one of the few African-American students, one of the few women, younger than all of my classmates.

AG: WHAT DID YOU LEARN ABOUT PLAYWRITING?

LN: I learned a lot about playwriting, because so much of the focus was on taking the play from its inception to the stage. I learned how to get a play up, which is something a lot of playwrights don't learn until they get to New York. I saw a number of productions of my plays and I understood what works on the page and what works onstage, and how you often can't marry those two things. How sometimes you have to sacrifice the things you love most to make the production work, because of a production's emphasis.

AG: YOU WROTE A MONOLOGUE CALLED *IDA MAE COLE TAKES A STANCE*, FOR A MUSICAL REVUE CALLED *A . . . MY NAME IS STILL ALICE*, AND A ONE-ACT CALLED *POOF!* DID YOU WRITE THOSE AT YALE?

LN: They were written after Yale. They were written when I'd sort of given up writing and was a human rights activist.

AG: HOW DID THAT CHANGE COME ABOUT?

LN: When I graduated from Yale, because I believed I hadn't had any life experience, I was hungry to do something different. I was also feeling as though theater was decadent and not relevant to this culture that I was living in, and I got a job working at Amnesty International as a public relations person. Then after four years of doing that, I thought, 'You know, theater is relevant. And I have to find a way of making it so.' And I wrote the monologue for *A . . . My Name is Still Alice* and I wrote *Poof!*

AG: THEY SEEM TO BE PRELUDES TO *CRUMBS FROM THE TABLE OF JOY*, IN THE SENSE THAT THEY ARE IN A REALISTIC STYLE AND ARE CHARACTER-BASED.

LN: They are character-based, because they're short pieces, and you have to know who the characters are the minute they open their mouths. In a full-length play, a playwright has the luxury of developing a character over a period of time.

AG: WHAT MADE YOU SUDDENLY DECIDE THAT THEATER WAS RELEVANT?

LN: I think that came from my frustration with working so hard as a human rights activist and discovering that I often couldn't reach an audience. As a public relations person, that's what I spent my time doing: trying to find an audience for the organization's views. And I found that even for this huge problem, there wasn't an audience. The Cold War ended, and suddenly human rights became the language of the time. And once the federal government was using that language, it became more difficult for the organization to place stories in the media. Newspapers and television news programs would say, 'You know what? People know that the problem is out there. We just don't have the room to include these stories anymore.'

AG: DID YOU EVER PLACE STORIES ABOUT FEMALE GENITAL MUTILATION?

LN: When I was at Amnesty International, the organization was discussing whether female genital mutilation was something that they wanted to take up. At the time, the organization considered genital mutilation to be culturally based, not subject to laws imposed by government. If it's culturally based, who do you hold responsible? At the time I was leaving, that discussion was going on throughout the organization.

AG: WHAT ARE YOUR THOUGHTS ON THAT SCORE?

LN: I think genital mutilation is a human rights violation. I think it is a cultural practice that is permitted to happen by governments. If the governments chose to crack down on it, we would see it less and less.

That was also part of my problem with the organization. I felt that once the Cold War ended, Amnesty needed to expand its mandate to include more issues, particularly women's issues. Genital mutilation, bride burnings, sex trafficking, etc.

Anyway, I thought that if I could find just a small audience, who would be willing to listen to my thoughts, perhaps I would be doing more and reaching more people. I'd been attending a theater workshop, but I wasn't really pushing my career, because I had a twenty-four-hour-a-day job. But the opportunity came to write the monologue, and I thought, 'Well, it's short.' I had sold my computer, so I wrote it on a computer at Amnesty late one night and sent it in. The producers loved it, and based on that monologue, Carole Rothman commissioned me to write *Crumbs from the Table of Joy* for Second Stage.

AG: AT THE TIME, SECOND STAGE THEATRE HAD RECEIVED A GRANT FROM THE LILA WALLACE–READER'S DIGEST FUND.

LN: Right. There was a huge grant, which Second Stage parceled out to playwrights to create theater that was aimed at a multigenerational audience. My understanding was that the grant was awarded to create theater that had an appeal to teenagers, that wouldn't talk down to them, but that parents and the regular subscription audience could attend and not feel as though the play were speaking beneath them.

AG: GOING BACK TO MY EARLIER QUESTION ABOUT A PLAYWRIGHT'S FIRST PLAY . . .

LN: I think *Crumbs* is my first play. It's the first play that, when I let it go, I didn't feel those little tingly things that tell me, 'It's not ready, it's not ready.' Even though it wasn't ready when it was produced at Second Stage, and I subsequently went back to an earlier version and rewrote the play for South Coast Repertory.

AG: WHAT DID YOU CHANGE?

LN: There were huge changes. I shortened the play by about twenty minutes. There were elements that I felt I had been pressed either to leave in or take out at Second Stage, and later I went back to my initial impulses. Having had a production that ran two-and-a-half months at Second Stage, I had the luxury of seeing what worked and what didn't. And because it ran for that long, the audience went from being by and large a subscription audience, to a more mixed and, toward the end, a black audience, and I was able to see how the life of the play shifted. Things that were not getting laughs, that I might have changed, suddenly had a new life with a black audience and were working.

AG: WHAT INSPIRED THAT PARTICULAR STORY?

LN: The 1950s was a period I knew very little about. Most of what I saw was black and white. I mean that literally. My knowledge was from Civil Rights documentaries that I had seen on television. I hadn't read a tremendous amount of literature from the period, except for James Baldwin and Tennessee Williams, and they had specific takes on the world. For me it was a journey of discovery; I wanted to find out more about this age. And I used my narrator, Ernestine Crump, this innocent who is learning about the world, as my guide. She comes from the South to New York essentially a blank slate, and she allows everything to wash over her.

AG: THAT WAS ONE OF MY QUESTIONS, ACTUALLY: WHY DID YOU CHOOSE TO HAVE ERNESTINE NARRATE THE STORY?

LN: I was interested in having someone look back from their adulthood. I wanted this child to have a kind of worldliness, but at the same time the naïveté that allows her to move through this household without questioning what's going on. Hopefully, that's what you see.

AG: DO YOU SEE GODFREY, ERNESTINE'S FATHER, AND LILY, HER AUNT, AS OPPOSITES?

LN: I don't think that they are opposites. I think they are similar people who at some juncture take different paths. They both anesthetize themselves. Lily turns to alcohol, and he turns to religion. They're people in a great deal of pain, who don't feel that they can express themselves.

AG: I ASK BECAUSE OF THE 1950S AS THE PLAY'S CONTEXT, AND I WONDERED WHETHER YOU WERE SAYING SOMETHING ABOUT ASSIMILATIONIST ATTITUDES?

LN: When I was writing the play I was just trying to tell a story. I didn't want to specifically say, 'This is how I feel about. . .' But I think I chose characters who represent different ideas. You have Godfrey, who is an assimilationist. You have Lily, who is somewhat of a separatist. You have the girls, who are trapped in the middle. There's a tug of war for them. And what Ernestine discovers is that her path is right down the center. She chooses what's useful from Godfrey and what's useful from Lily, to become the person she becomes. I'm not saying that one way is right or wrong — and I hope that that's clear. But these are two, very different philosophies, which come out of the experiences these people have had. Lily, if she lived today, would perhaps be a successful corporate lawyer. But because of when she was born, she's marginalized. For being a woman, for being this bon-vivant African American in a small town. When she gets to New York, she discovers that even up here she can't be who she is.

AG: IS THE CHARACTER OF LILY A TYPE THAT APPEARS IN AFRICAN-AMERICAN CULTURE?

LN: I think she does appear in our culture. One of the things that I hear from actresses and from a lot of women when I do talk-backs at theaters is, 'You know what, I had an aunt who was just like that.' I think that Lily speaks to a very specific kind of African-American woman, who is full of life and ambition, but because of circumstance is not able to move forward and self-destructs. I certainly have several Lilys in my family.

AG: THERE'S A LOT OF POIGNANCY WHEN SHE ASKS GODFREY, 'THEN WHY AIN'T I THE ONE IN YOUR BED?' SHE WANTS TO KNOW WHY HE PREFERS WHITE GERTE TO A VIVACIOUS BLACK WOMAN.

LN: And he says, 'You trouble's guide,' and, 'We on different roads . . . ' That's essentially what people are saying to that kind of person. 'You are too dangerous. Your ideas are too dangerous. Let's wait. I'm just going to try this other path.'

AG: EXCEPT THAT, IRONICALLY, HE DOES SOMETHING . . .

LN: . . . that is more dangerous, but he doesn't know that. But that's why I said they're not opposites. They're very similar. If they were opposites, he would choose a traditional African-American woman, a traditional path. But he doesn't.

AG: NEAR THE END, GERTE AND LILY HAVE A FALLING-OUT, THEN THEY SORT OF MAKE UP, AND THERE'S A WONDERFUL MOMENT WHEN ERNESTINE FANTASIZES . . .

LN: . . . of the reconciliation . . .

AG: . . . AND GERTE AND LILY DANCE TOGETHER. WHAT DOES ERNESTINE'S FANTASY MEAN TO YOU?

LN: I think for Ernestine, it's that, in a perfect world, we'd all be able to get along. Which is the naïve part of Ernestine speaking and fantasizing. But in reality, she can love both of these people and know that they may not, at this point in history, come together. I deliberately shy away from moralizing and leave it open-ended.

AG: HOW DO YOU WANT US TO SEE GODFREY? A LOT OF THE THINGS HE DOES ARE NOT VERY . . .

LN: . . . attractive.

AG: ESPECIALLY THE WAY HE TREATS THE WOMEN. ALL THOSE WOMEN SHARE . . .

LN: What they share is that they're oppressed by this man, who in turn is paralyzed by his own oppression. I think that I was just addressing a specific time in American history that was pre-Civil Rights, pre-feminist revolution, in which women with ideas were confined and oppressed. And rendered, if I may say it, impotent. I think the play is an allegory in some ways of the African-American experience in the 1950s, of the issues that people were grappling with. It was a very volatile period.

AG: PERHAPS BECAUSE OF THE TIME PERIOD, SOME OF THE ELEMENTS REMIND ME OF *A RAISIN IN THE SUN*.

LN: It's grappling with similar issues. One critic called it a cross between *A Raisin in the Sun* and *The Glass Menagerie*. When I was writing the play I specifically wanted to use language that was evocative of the period and so I did look to playwrights from the 1950s and 1960s for inspiration. Langston Hughes' work, James Baldwin. Part of going back is searching for the voices. A lot of our plays did not get published.

AG: WHAT IS THE MEANING TO THE PLAY OF ERNESTINE'S AND HER SISTER'S FASCINATION WITH WHITE FEMALE FILM STARS?

LN: I think that the popular images of the time that teenagers had access to were on the silver screen, and for a lot of teenagers, freedom was going to the movie theater. So you have the symbolism that freedom is equated with the images of these white screen goddesses. I don't know whether there were many cinemas in Brooklyn that showed the race films that were manufactured for the African-American audience.

In *Crumbs*, the only white women the girls are familiar with are those whom they see on the screen, and then suddenly this German peasant enters their home, and she's very different. Decidedly unglamorous, versus Lily, who is very glamorous. Lily's their version of Bette Davis or Joan Crawford. I think back to my childhood, when there were maybe five channels on television, and the films that you saw were old movies. I must have seen *Mildred Pierce* a hundred times. I remember loving those stories and these women, these heroines that seemed so strong but feminine, but nevertheless remote from who I was.

AG: CAN YOU TALK A LITTLE ABOUT THE LOOKS AND STYLES OF THE PRODUCTIONS AT SECOND STAGE AND SOUTH COAST?

LN: The looks were very different. At Second Stage, the production was expressionistic. The space was tiny, and there were large set pieces. A staircase dominated the set. At South Coast, where Seret Scott directed the production, the set was simple. It allowed the play to breathe. The set pieces moved freely. There were no blackouts. The scenes blended into each other.

AG: LIKE A MEMORY PLAY?

LN: Like a memory play. It was a softer production. A lot of the choices in costume were less severe. The music was less severe as well. The playing area was not that much larger than Second Stage's, but it was three-quarter rather than proscenium.

AG: HOW WAS GODFREY PORTRAYED?

LN: He was far more sympathetic than at Second Stage, because you saw a man who was oppressing himself. It was not only a matter of having a heavy hand that he was using against these women; he became a victim of his own narrow way of thinking, and that was moving.

What was helpful at South Coast was that Dorian Harewood played Godfrey, and his wife, Nancy Harewood, played Gerte. So there was a chemistry which you can't manufacture. What came across was Gerte's love for this man, and you suddenly understood why they chose each other. These were two lost souls who were riding a subway literally to nowhere and ran into each other in a moment of need.

AG: HOW DID SERET SCOTT INTEGRATE ERNESTINE INTO THE STAGING?

LN: Ernestine wandered through the scenes. She became the link from scene to scene. The stage never completely went black, and even when there were scene changes, Ernestine was doing something. It was quite lovely.

AG: YOU'VE WORKED QUITE A BIT WITH SERET SCOTT.

LN: Yes. The first time we worked together was on *Poof!* at Actors Theatre of Louisville. We met only for a week, and she staged it very quickly, but I liked her energy. She was very open, and I was very comfortable in her presence. I didn't feel as though I needed to get to know her; I felt as though I knew her. When we began working on *Crumbs from the Table of Joy*, I found that, particularly in casting, we could sit in the room and look at each other and know what the other was thinking. We were very much in tune in terms of how we saw the characters.

AG: WAS THERE A PLAY BETWEEN *CRUMBS* AND *POR'KNOCKERS*?

LN: *Por'knockers* came after *Crumbs*. I wanted to write something that was very different. I get bored very easily. I love to explore, and in some ways that keeps me active and interested in my own creative life. I didn't think I could revisit that world of *Crumbs from the Table of Joy* immediately, but that's not to say I won't go back to it.

AG: HOW DID THE IDEA FOR *POR'KNOCKERS* DEVELOP?

LN: I was watching a documentary on television about a man who was going in search of the por'knocker, which has taken on a mythic connotation in Guyana. A por'knocker is a miner who usually goes off by himself in search of gold, and he can stay out in the jungle for months, if not years, until he finds his fortune. The por'knocker takes a barrel of salted meat with him into the jungle for sustenance and knocks the barrel to get the salt pork out when he's running low on provisions.

The image that I had from the television program was of this man in Jockey's that were worn thin and hanging off of him, the only scrap of clothing remaining because he'd been in the jungle so long, panning desperately through the mud for the gold. I became obsessed with the idea of this por'knocker. I'd go to sleep and think about this man. But I couldn't quite figure out how to make that into a play which would be interesting for me. One man in a jungle searching for gold is not inherently dramatic. I was thinking, 'Well, what is the modern equivalent?' And I began thinking about the state of African-American politics, and how, certainly in the 1980s, there hadn't been one leader or philosophy that generated tremendous excitement. Why were we, in a sense, still panning for our gold? Who are the modern-day por'knockers? And I threw these people together in a room. The play was a bunch of archetypes, if I may call them that — I don't like using that word — who represent aspects of the African-American activist community. There's an intellectual professor, Tamara, who's married to academia. There's Kwami, who is a Black Nationalist from the 1960s and can't let go of that rhetoric. James is the conspiracy theorist. He sees a conspiracy in everything, including the way money is organized, because the penny is the only brown currency and has Lincoln on it. Everything is a conspiracy to keep the black man down. And then there's Ahmed, the young, hip-hop activist who's flirting with the Nation of Islam. He sees his death as his one great contribution. He imagines this very elaborate death. And then there's Lewis, who is the one white, Jewish liberal who sympathizes with the African-American cause. And they're all thrown into this room.

When I initially wrote this play, it was a comedy. The first time that it was performed, at Dance Theatre Workshop in New York City, the audience was laughing, because it was so ridiculous. The premise is that they blow up a federal office building, although what happens, which is not funny, is that children are inadvertently killed. And based on that production, Vineyard Theatre wanted to produce it a year later.

But the political climate in the United States had changed significantly by then. The bombing of the Federal Building in Oklahoma

City had happened. The day after the bombing, Douglas Aibel, Vineyard's artistic director, called me up and said, 'What are we going to do? Can we still do this play? How can we do that?' Also, the Million Man March happened right before the production. So to an audience that a year before was generous with its laughter, the play became frightening.

AG: ORIGINALLY, HOW DID YOU WANT US TO SEE THESE PEOPLE?

LN: I wanted you to see people who are confused. Who are frustrated. Who are angry. Who are paranoid. Who are grappling within that room with the questions and answers, because they don't know who they are. That's why they keep trying to make a phone call. The phone call is about who's going to take responsibility. When are we going to take responsibility? Who do we say we are today, at this time? And they can't answer that question. You read statistics that say, 'This is what blacks are thinking. And this is how blacks are voting.' I think, 'Wait a minute. We are many different people. We're much more complicated than that.' My play is in response to that. We have many more voices than they give us credit for having, and I think it's in the interest of the establishment to keep us as The Blacks.

AG: IT'S INTERESTING THAT YOU DESCRIBE JAMES AS PARANOID, BECAUSE ONE OF THE MOST EFFECTIVE MOMENTS OF THE VINEYARD PRODUCTION WAS JAMES' STATEMENT THAT THE REALLY SUBVERSIVE THING WOULD BE TO COMMIT 'RANDOM ACTS OF GOOD WILL. CLEANING UP NEIGHBORHOODS OVERNIGHT, ERADICATING CORRUPTION . . . IMAGINE THE HORROR THAT WOULD SET IN, THE FRENZY OF THE POLITICOS STRUGGLING TO RESTORE THE STATUS QUO.' IT SEEMS A COGENT STATEMENT.

LN: You can be paranoid and every once in a while have a good idea. But you see, the characters were supposed to be sketched in broad strokes and be easily identified. Perhaps that's the weakness of the play, but it was very deliberate on my part. I did see it as a satire. The success of the DTW production was that we only had a week of rehearsal, and the way it was done was just . . . la, la, la, la. The actors didn't have time to even think that these characters were not saying anything. Which is true. They're saying nothing. Saying nothing with conviction. It's only a one-act play; it runs forty-five minutes. But it took much longer at the Vineyard because we over-invested in the rhetoric, much like the characters in the play.

AG: IN THE PRODUCTION AT THE VINEYARD, THE POR'-KNOCKER WAS SITUATED ON A KIND OF BRIDGE ABOVE THE STAGE, AND OCCASIONALLY THE LIGHTS WOULD COME UP ON HIM. COULD YOU TALK MORE ABOUT THE PARALLEL BETWEEN HIM AND THE PEOPLE IN THE ROOM?

LN: Well, he's romanticized by Kwami, who says that there's something pure about the por'knocker, that his goal was simple. The por'knocker knew what he was in the jungle to get and was not going to stop until he got it. And that's part of these people's problem. They don't know any longer what they want, and they don't all want the same thing. They've come together, but they've all moved in such different directions, that they can't go back to that point of the single nugget of gold waiting to reveal itself.

AG: DO YOU WANT US TO ROMANTICIZE THE POR'KNOCKER THE WAY KWAMI DOES?

LN: Do you mean, when I'm sitting down to write, do I want the audience to romanticize or empathize with this character? I hadn't honestly thought about that. I was just presenting him. When I first wrote the play, there were just brief glimpses of him. I expanded the character for the Vineyard production, which was somewhat of a mistake. I think he worked best when he was a little flash of what could have been.

AG: WHY IS THERE ONLY ONE WOMAN?

LN: Because to a certain extent the African-American power structure has marginalized women. Pushed women out. Not been entirely inclusive. In twenty years of African-American leaders who are spokespeople for us, who are the women?

AG: ANGELA DAVIS . . .

LN: Right. Angela Davis. There aren't many women who have been allowed to voice their opinions in the larger arena. When it comes to appointing or anointing a leader, it's very rarely an African-American woman.

AG: WATCHING THE PLAY, I HAD THE FEELING THAT THE CHARACTER WAS FIGHTING TO GET AIRTIME IN THAT ROOM.

LN: One of the things I tried to show is that the men are always talking over her. Every time she tries to speak, she's not permitted to finish her sentence or thought. Or she will have a thought, and someone else will incorporate that into what they're saying, and the thought will become theirs, and she won't be given credit for it.

AG: IT MUST BE FRUSTRATING TO SEE INTENTIONS GO AWRY.

LN: That's the beauty of having a play produced more than once, if you get the privilege. I remember going to see a production of *Crumbs from the Table of Joy* that ran four hours. When people were leaving, I wanted to say, 'I'm sorry. I did not write this play. This is not my play. I do not know who wrote it.' But I hadn't been there for rehearsals. I just came, saw it. My husband, at intermission, said, 'Let's go.' I said, 'I can't go. This is my play. How's that going to look, if the playwright gets up and leaves?' But a playwright does feel that sometimes.

AG: HOW DO PLAYS USUALLY START WITH YOU?

LN: It shifts from play to play. *Crumbs from the Table of Joy* started with an idea that then was accompanied by sort of a sound track. I imagined the mood and the tone and the texture of the period. Then from there I began filling in the characters. I listened to a lot of Thelonious Monk. That was *my* sound track. When I was stumped, blocked, I would throw him on and imagine the thing that he would do and where he would go. And it was always sort of unexpected.

In the case of *Mud, River, Stone* I read an article in *The New York Times* about a town in Mozambique where, for a period of time, everyone who passed through was taken hostage by soldiers. When United

Nations representatives came in to negotiate, they, too, were taken hostage. Tourists — everyone. The soldiers' demands were very simple: they wanted grain and a blanket. That resonated with me. I'm like, 'My God. These soldiers have been fighting a war for fifteen years, and they won, and at the end they don't know to ask for something larger. They want only the basics. To be warm and to be fed.'

AG: *MUD, RIVER, STONE* WAS DEVELOPED SOMEWHAT DIFFERENTLY THAN YOUR OTHER WORK.

LN: The Acting Company commissioned me to write a play, and since this was the idea that was living with me at the time, I adapted it to their needs: a certain number of cast members, somewhat multicultural, and I had to take age into consideration. That kind of commission can be a blessing, it also can be a curse. During the writing process characters expand, contract, or you discover that this character who's been at the forefront of your mind for months has no place in the play, and you want to remove them, but you can't, because you have a company of X number of people that has to be satisfied. So for me, writing this play was somewhat of a struggle, in that I started to resent that I had to adhere to certain requirements. I did cut one character out — the mistress of the hotel — a silent character who sat onstage and for me represented Mother Africa. It was probably a wise thing to cut her out.

AG: IN 1996, THE PLAY WAS PRODUCED AT STUDIO ARENA THEATER, IN BUFFALO, IN ASSOCIATION WITH THE ACTING COMPANY, AND THEN AT PLAYWRIGHTS HORIZONS IN NEW YORK CITY A LITTLE OVER A YEAR LATER. DID THE PLAY CHANGE IN THE INTERIM?

LN: It didn't change as significantly as it would have, had my life not been so complicated at the time. I gave birth to my child three weeks before we went into rehearsal at Playwrights Horizons, and my mother died in the middle of previews. I could not commit myself wholeheartedly to the kind of rewriting that I would have liked to do. Effectively I was a zombie.

AG: I CAN APPRECIATE THAT. THAT SOUNDS AWFUL . . . SERET SCOTT DIRECTED THE PRODUCTION AT STUDIO ARENA, AND ROGER REES DIRECTED AT PLAYWRIGHTS HORIZONS. WHAT DID THE PRODUCTIONS LOOK LIKE?

LN: Studio Arena has an immense, three-quarter thrust stage, which permitted us to have a grand staircase. It gave the hotel a kind of dated majesty that was appropriate to the play. What was interesting at Playwrights Horizons was that its small proscenium gave a kind of claustrophobic feel. You felt the characters getting frustrated in that space. You felt the heat. You felt the oppressiveness of the hotel in a way that you didn't at Studio Arena. There were wonderful things about both productions.

AG: IS THE PLAY ABOUT AFRICA OR AMERICA?

LN: I think it's about colonialism. You could probably set the play in Asia and it would still resonate. It's about war, it's about colonialism. It's about identity. That's one of the themes which runs throughout the play. Who is African? What does it mean to be African? All these characters are saying, 'I'm African, I'm African,' but forgetting the one person who's born and bred there, who's been fighting this war, who is the sole African onstage. And who's struggling to hang on to who he is.

But because I've never been to Africa, I imagine that as much as it is about Africa, it is about America. It's about the experience that comes from my imagination, and my imagination was nurtured here.

AG: I GUESS I ASK THAT QUESTION BECAUSE THE AMERICAN COUPLE ARE TELLING THE STORY OF THEIR TRIP.

LN: They're telling the story and making the journey, and they're the ones who have the greatest arc in the story. They enter that room as one thing and leave as something quite different.

AG: HOW DIFFERENT ARE THEY WHEN THEY LEAVE?

LN: They become witnesses and choose to tell this story. I think the couple they are at the beginning would not have chosen to tell this tale, but afterwards, they feel it's something they have to tell — like a confession — to keep the story alive. Fundamentally they're not changed as people — they're still going to be ambitious and they're going to nitpick at each other. But they will talk about Africa and have a kind of . . . awareness.

AG: DO THEY HAVE ANY GUILT?

LN: I think they have tremendous guilt when they leave. They gave the gun to Blake that permitted him to kill this African man. But that guilt speaks for how they have changed. They recognize that they are complicit in the destruction by ignoring it. And once they choose not to ignore it — which is the beginning of the play, the telling of the story — they've changed. They're giving voice to the struggle.

AG: I SEE WHAT YOU ARE SAYING. IN THE FIRST SCENE, DAVID SPEAKS A TELLING LINE TO THE AUDIENCE: 'I'D ALWAYS IMAGINED OUR TRIP ACCOMPANIED BY A SOUND TRACK. A PERFECT BLEND OF RHYTHMS BY AFRICA AND ORCHESTRATIONS BY EUROPE.'

LN: I think he's describing himself. He's an African man living in America, but he has a uniquely American sensibility.

AG: WHAT DOES 'AMERICAN' MEAN IN THIS CASE?

LN: The value system that's here. It's what we learn by watching television, reading books. He's educated to be a certain kind of person, which in some places represents colonial power, Western power. When he goes to Africa, he realizes that he is part of the problem. He is an oppressor. And that's something he does not want to recognize. There's part of him that wants to embrace that African side, but there's another part of him that does not want to let go of all the things that America gives him. The comfort. The wristwatch. The good job. The ability to travel. He does want to embrace his African side. But he discovers that the African side is more complicated than he had thought. He went to Africa expecting a kind of Alex Haley reunion, where you go to the village of your ancestors, people greet you with open arms and hug and kiss you. What he discovers is that people are starving and desperate, and wars are ravaging the culture.

But he's able to see the soft, beautiful side of Joaquim. He is able to see the innocent side of this man, who is holding them hostage only because he's been pushed to the edge. David is the only one who sees that vulnerability in Joaquim. Everyone else chooses to view him as a great threat.

AG: IN REALITY, JOAQUIM HAS NO POWER.

LN: He's completely powerless. Even with the gun, he's only powerful in this room, in this hotel.

I'm reading a book called *King Leopold's Ghost*, which is about the holocaust — there's no other word for it — that occurred at the turn of the nineteenth century, when the European powers were racing to carve up the African continent. King Leopold of Belgium got the Congo, decided he was going to exploit it for the rubber trade, and killed millions of Africans in the process. According to the book, two outspoken critics of the Belgians were African Americans who went to the Congo: George Washington Williams, a minister, lawyer, journalist, and historian, who coined the phrase 'crimes against humanity'; and the Reverend William H. Sheppard, a Presbyterian minister and missionary, and an explorer. That's how word about Leopold's atrocities reached the world, and the only reason we have voices of Africans from that period is because these two men interviewed folks. Otherwise you'd only have the colonial record, and that would become the history. I'm trying to say that African Americans have been going back to Africa since we were brought over here. The journey goes both ways.

AG: THAT SAID, ARE YOU ALSO SATIRIZING DAVID AND SARAH A BIT?

LN: A little bit. They are slightly extreme, but it's the theater, so . . . They're products of the American system. They're as brainwashed as anyone else would be. They've bought wholeheartedly into the American dream and everything that represents. In writing those characters, perhaps I was being critical of myself in the way in which I travel, the way in which I find myself falling easily into the language of the ugly American and have to check myself.

AG: IT'S THE AMERICAN MANNER. WE TAKE SO MUCH FOR GRANTED.

LN: It's how we perceive ourselves as a world power. And whether you're black or white, you carry that out into the world, and that's what David and Sarah are doing. Except that they have a specific mission. They're going to Africa to get in touch with their roots. They don't know what they'll discover when they get there, but they feel this is a journey they're supposed to take. And they end up getting more than they bargained for.

AG: THERE HAS BEEN A GREAT DEAL OF DISCUSSION IN RECENT YEARS ABOUT CROSSING CULTURAL BOUNDARIES, IN THE ARTS AND ELSEWHERE. CAN A WRITER WRITE ACROSS CULTURAL BOUNDARIES?

LN: I think that the work can reach across cultural boundaries. I think that the work can resonate. Take a work like *Poof!*, which I wrote very specifically about two African-American women. It's wildly successful in Asia. It's been translated into Chinese, into Japanese. Obviously the topic of spousal abuse resonates with these women. Was I a writer writing across cultural boundaries? Or did the play reach across cultural boundaries? I didn't write to cross cultural boundaries, but in something that I wrote, this universal seed sprouted across cultural boundaries.

AG: THAT TAKES THE DISCUSSION IN A DIFFERENT AND INTERESTING DIRECTION. I'M AFRAID MY QUESTION IS NARROWER. CAN OR SHOULD WRITERS DEPICT PEOPLE WHO ARE RADICALLY DIFFERENT FROM THEMSELVES RACIALLY OR ETHNICALLY?

LN: I think that the people I depict aren't radically different from myself. I'm going in and channeling little kernels of myself. Particularly in America, and as an African American, there are many different people who are inside of me. Can a writer cross cultural boundaries? I certainly hope that I am permitted to source the different aspects of myself. And those aspects may come across as a white male or an Asian woman or a Latina. When I'm writing these people, I don't censor myself. And I think that all writers should be permitted to take that journey. Whether that journey's successful or not is determined by the audience at the moment, and the experience that the audience has once they're in the theater. I don't believe in censoring any writer. I think that there's something valuable in seeing how another culture perceives things, even if you disagree with the point of view. It's the same question about casting. Should an African American be doing Shakespeare? Other than Othello? Should the Chinese not have been doing *Poof!*?

It seems absurd to me after a while, and I think if we project ourselves five hundred years into the future, some of these racial ways in which we define ourselves are going to shift so much, that it's going to seem absurd that we're even having these discussions. But perhaps the optimist in me is speaking. Our notion of selves is dynamic. It shifts from year to year. How I identify myself changes every decade. It changes depending on where I am in the room. If I'm in a room with a bunch of men, I'm an African-American woman. If I'm in a room with white women, I'm an African-American woman. If I'm in a room with a bunch of black folks who are from the projects, I'm a middle-class African-American woman. Am I not to write about the experience of African-Americans who come from the Caribbean? Am I not to write an African character? Am I not to write a biracial character? Because these are not experiences that are indigenous to my imagination? You're asking a very complicated question. I think that I should be permitted. I should be permitted and I may not always be successful, but I will do it. In *Mud, River, Stone* I wrote a white colonial man and hopefully with some success. My play *Las Meninas* is set in the court of Louis XIV, and I revisit events that took place during that period, reinterpreting history from the point of view of an African-American woman. I think that once, as artists, we begin censoring ourselves, then we'll see the collapse of American theater. I think that we have to continue to push the envelope. And cross those boundaries. Write about each other. I feel liberated that I can write about more than what I have experienced within my own four walls.

AG: WHO IS YOUR IDEAL AUDIENCE FOR *MUD, RIVER, STONE*?

LN: I actually imagined a broad audience, though I was particularly interested in having a middle-class African-American audience that might relate to some of the subtleties in the script that perhaps white audiences wouldn't.

AG: SUCH AS?

LN: Such as the experience of Sarah and David. It's a very specific experience that you have, if you're an educated African American. You can be culturally isolated and hovering between two worlds. I'm writing a play now that is a scathing look at a middle-class African-American woman who has it all and has become culturally isolated from her family and her friends. She has a crisis and finds that she has to go back home, and she's ill-equipped to deal in the world that she has escaped from.

AG: DO YOU FEEL PRESSURE TO WRITE OR NOT WRITE ABOUT THAT MIDDLE-CLASS EXPERIENCE?

LN: It's what I know, so I feel compelled to write about that. I think that it's an experience that hasn't found a lot of life on the American stage, perhaps because there's been a hunger to discuss issues. I think that *Colored Museum* liberated us, as African-American writers in the theater, from having to write 'race' plays. I say that in quotes: plays in which race was the central character. We could begin to write plays that were irreverent, that were critical. I do think that in *Mud, River, Stone* I'm somewhat critical of Sarah and David and perhaps that was not something that African Americans used to permit ourselves to do. We didn't permit ourselves to air the dirty laundry in public. But I think in the 1980s and 1990s we moved in a direction in which we could look at the wide range of African-American experience. When I was young and first started to write, I remember feeling frustrated, thinking, 'I'm not from the South. What am I going to write about?' I came from a happy home. In Brooklyn.

AG: IS THERE A CONNECTION BETWEEN *POR'KNOCKERS* AND *MUD, RIVER, STONE*?

LN: Oh, I think there is. The plays are extremely similar. I think that they were probably the same play. And I'll probably write it one more time. Characters in search of identity.

AG: EVEN THE WRITING STYLE.

LN: Yes, it's similar. I think that, because *Por'knockers* wasn't entirely successful, I tried to find another way of exploring similar themes. So I'll probably do it again, until I'm happy with it.

AG: WHAT DOES IT MEAN TO YOU, TO BE AN AFRICAN-AMERICAN WOMAN WRITING AT THE BEGINNING OF THE TWENTY-FIRST CENTURY? WHAT DO YOU WANT TO DO AS A PLAYWRIGHT?

LN: To respond as an African-American woman, I feel more optimistic today than I did ten years ago about my prospects as a writer. Ten years ago I was feeling frustrated that I wouldn't be able to find an audience. Slowly I'm beginning to chip away at the establishment. And also move into African-American theaters and help create a new audience. That's what I'm hoping, that I'm part of a movement to create a new theater audience.

Theresa Rebeck

Theresa Rebeck grew up in Cincinnati, Ohio, where her father worked as a metallurgical engineer and her mother raised Rebeck and her five brothers and sisters. After graduating from the University of Notre Dame, Rebeck went to Brandeis University, receiving a Ph.D. in nineteenth-century British literature and an M.F.A. in theater.

Rebeck's plays range across the comic spectrum and largely explore the interplay of power and gender. *Spike Heels* (1992) concentrates on love and possessiveness among urban couples, while *Loose Knit* (1993) looks at, among other things, the anger and frustration of women living in urban America in the 1990s. *Sunday on the Rocks* (1994) involves four women's shifting friendships as they deal with the men in their lives and with each other.

From 1990 to 1991, Rebeck lived in Los Angeles, where she wrote for a now-defunct situation comedy called *Brooklyn Bridge*. She turned this loathesome experience into a satire of Hollywood's television industry, *The Family of Mann* (1994). She has also aimed her barbs at American politics, writing *View of the Dome* (1996), which examines how an innocent can become a political shark. Recent plays by Rebeck include *Abstract Expression* (1999), about a painter who has been working in obscurity for many years, and *The Butterfly Collection,* which involves a woman who becomes assistant to a famous novelist. With the composer Kim D. Sherman and with John Sheehy, Rebeck's co-lyricist, she was written the book of a musical, *The Two Orphans* (1999), adapted from a nineteenth-century melodrama of the same title.

Rebeck writes for film and television, notably for the prime-time dramatic series, *NYPD Blue*. She lives with her husband and son in Brooklyn, where this interview took place on October 9, 1999.

• • •

AG: WHAT KIND OF A PLACE IS CINCINNATI TO GROW UP IN?

TR: It's got a small-town feel to it. I was raised Catholic, so there was patriarchal religion to deal with, which was difficult for me and I'm sure has informed my work. The instruction is overwhelmingly, 'You're a girl and you're supposed to do what you're told,' and anytime you move against that, you create a rage within the system. But I did go to an all-girls Catholic high school that was progressive and very liberating. There's that weird thing the Catholic Church does. The body of it is conservative and authoritarian, and then along the fringes are incredibly passionate people who care deeply about spirituality and social justice. If you land with those people, there's interesting stuff going around.

But Cincinnati's a conservative town. Very Republican. I got invited to my high school reunion, and everybody had become a housewife. I was a strange thing in the midst of it all.

AG: HOW DID YOU BECOME THIS STRANGE THING DO YOU THINK?

TR: I have no idea. I truly have no idea. I did tell my mother when I was sixteen that I wanted to be a playwright, and she was like, 'Oh, my dear God.' She was horrified and terrified and completely bewildered as to where I'd come up with something like that. But I took piano lessons when I was young and was taken to the theater when I was young. I am one of those people who remembers the first play I ever saw: *Tartuffe* at Cincinnati Playhouse in the Park and it was a riveting experience.

I had parents who were not dismissive of the arts by any means, but it was a very traditional family, and the overall expectation was that you would not choose this as a career. You would do something practical. But in those sorts of environments, when all your options are laid out before you, you can consider something like playwriting. I had acted in plays when I was quite young and it didn't seem unnatural to me to drift that way.

AG: CAN YOU TALK A LITTLE MORE ABOUT YOUR UPBRINGING?

TR: There was a lot that was fraught about my upbringing, because of who I turned out to be in the mix — I have five brothers and sisters. The role that I played was the problem child, because I talked back. I got used to being the voice of contention, but it was a difficult position. I would be articulating things for the entire body of kids, but at the same time they wanted me to shut up. People have different natures; some are natural mediators and some of us are truth-speakers.

I got into enormous trouble for that in Hollywood, as you can imagine. I finally said, 'You know, it's a gut reaction to the world.' It's not like I intend to be a gadfly, but my gut reaction is to say, 'Come on, guys, this is nuts.' I think that everybody else is going to go, 'She's right. It's nuts.' But people are thinking other things as well, and they're not excited that I'm saying it. So it finally occurred to me that, You know what? Most people aren't interested in the truth. Most people are more interested in lies and the way lies grease the world. My instinct is to peel things apart. It's one of those things that's particularly difficult for the culture to accept from a woman.

AG: YOU HAVE A PH.D. IN NINETEENTH-CENTURY BRITISH LITERATURE. WHAT DID YOU SPECIFICALLY STUDY?

TR: I was studying British Victorian novels in the English department, and then I started to write plays, so when I decided to finish the Ph.D., I did my dissertation on melodrama as a trope in Victorian literature. I wrote about theatrical melodramas and about melodramatic constructions in the novel — how the two forms informed each other.

AG: DID YOU ANALYZE PARTICULAR MELODRAMAS?

TR: *The Bells*, *The Two Orphans*, *Masks and Faces*, and *The Poor of London*.

AG: YOU ALSO HAVE AN M.F.A.

TR: I was kind of working on the two at the same time. I started in the English department, went over to the theater department, went back to the English department. I never thought I was good enough to be a writer. I knew it was what I wanted to do, but I was afraid to step out there and do it, and I was thinking, 'Well, I guess I should teach.' I was almost sliding around to being a journalist, but I could never drag myself away from theater. Then I realized that it was a matter of giving myself permission to embrace playwriting, that it wasn't something I had to earn by virtue of being good enough or smart enough (I think I got that from the Church). So I embraced it, and I was pretty sure after a couple of years in the theater department that I was never going to teach, but I'm somebody who doesn't feel comfortable with unfinished things. I was also afraid that any time my career wasn't going well, I would think that I should go back and finish the Ph.D. — I was afraid of having that hanging over my head. So the Ph.D. was this strange thing I did to avoid not having done it.

The thing that was most compelling about the dissertation was studying the theater at a time when theater was a powerful force in the culture. I find it curious that theater professionals and academics talk about the nineteenth century as a theatrical wasteland because of melodrama. Everybody went to the theater all the time and they all went together. Upper classes, lower classes, I wish I had been a playwright in the nineteenth century. Now, so many forces prey on theater. It's so difficult to maintain a career, get the plays out to a wider audience, get people to come, get people to feel that theater is relevant. Those were not issues in the nineteenth century. It was in many ways a golden age.

I became interested in why this flourishing period is disdained, and I think, to a certain extent, the reason is class politics. There's always been a battle in America between an elitist and a populist idea of what theater is. There's a critical contingent that believes theater should be art in the highest sense, and they have a real unease with populist theater. It's the mass culture thing: if a lot of people like something, it must not be very good. I believe theater is art, but I don't think it's exclusionary. I'm not interested in writing cheese-ball plays, but I'm also not interested in writing stuff that nobody understands but that thirty people in New York think are great. There's an intelligent middle that many great artists over time have hit. Charles Dickens. Charlie Chaplin. You can achieve something that does crack open the human experience and still make it fun.

AG: HAVE YOU EVER WRITTEN A NINETEENTH CENTURY–STYLE MELODRAMA?

TR: I'm working on an adaptation of *The Two Orphans* right now, and I'm thinking about adapting *The Bells*.

I do find myself stealing from those sources. I wrote *Spike Heels* shortly after I finished the dissertation, and I had spent a lot of time in the dissertation talking about hero-heroine-villain triangles, and that totally informed the writing of the play. In melodrama, the villain and the hero both want the body of the heroine. The villain wants to rape her, the hero wants to marry her — there's this whole social tension resting on that woman's body. We all know these tropes: you must pay the rent or you're out on the street; if you're out on the street, you're not in the home and you're vulnerable to me. That's the villain's power over the heroine: to kick her out of the home and make her vulnerable. The hero wants to keep her in the home. He wants to domesticate this female body. As far as the two men are concerned, it's not a relationship really. They're objectifying her.

So I started writing *Spike Heels*, and I was like, 'Andrew thinks he's going to tame Georgie and domesticate her, right? He's playing the part of the traditional hero and he thinks he's such a good guy. And we all think he's such a good guy.'

AG: FOR A WHILE.

TR: Well, that's what I kept thinking: 'I'm not so sure the good guy is any better.' I became interested that the villain, Edward, was at least in touch with the sexuality of this woman. And then I went from there. I flipped it over, I started spinning people around each other. But that central triangle came from thinking about Victorian melodramas. Of course no one ever notices that I'm doing these things . . .

AG: AT LEAST EDWARD IS UP-FRONT ABOUT HIS CYNICAL ATTITUDE TOWARD THE WORLD.

TR: Right. When I first started writing that play, I thought it was going to be a little one-act that pondered these things between Georgie and Andrew. And then I thought, 'Oh, I should make it longer.' And Edward showed up, and he was much more interesting than I thought he was going to be. He does tend to walk away with the play.

AG: IN MELODRAMAS THE VILLAIN IS USUALLY THE BEST ROLE.

TR: Yes. They're powerful, they know who they are, and they always have a sense of humor. Go back to the cartoon character Snidely Whiplash, with his evil 'yah hah hah' — they're always laughing. Which I also use with a character like Edward. Their embrace of life gives them great pleasure, as opposed to the hero, who's always fumbling within his own set of rules. I've moved on from that construction, but I was working with heroes who are always trying to hold together a social construct and have a place in the social construct.

AG: THERE ARE A VARIETY OF RULES IN VICTORIAN MELO-DRAMA, IN BOTH ITS FORM AND WITHIN THE WORLDS OF THE PLAYS.

TR: In terms of the rules of nineteenth-century melodramas, they express a terror of the culture flying apart. The melodramas start with very simple constructs — the underlying rules are straightforward and simple. Then there's enormous chaos in the middle of the melodramas, and then they get wrapped up really tight at the end. It was a response of the culture to the industrial revolution, to the class warfare that was erupting — to trying to contain serious trouble.

I think another reason melodrama is disdained as a form is that many of them center on the lower classes. The heroine is often a noble girl from the lower classes, and there is a lot of expression about what the working classes are going through. But those things didn't build to a big, 'We must revolt.' Huge messes and crazy things happen in those plays. A house catches fire, and somebody leaps off a balcony. There are chaotic spectacles. People jumping from three stories onto the stage, animals on the stage. And then they just wrap them up. I think there was a need to have that anarchy, and then to put it back tightly.

AG: WAS *SUNDAY ON THE ROCKS* ALSO AN EARLY PLAY?

TR: Yes. I wrote that as a one-act when I was in graduate school. It was an important play to me, frankly. I was pretty young and I was really depressed, and I thought I would write a piece of dialogue among three women to make myself feel better and because it was fun. So I put them in three chairs and gave them a bottle of scotch to lubricate them. I mean, *O'Neill* did it. People talk a lot easier when they've had three glasses of scotch in them, right? So I wrote that first scene, when Gayle, Elly, and Jen are on the porch, and people responded to it. I had written a lot of other, much more experimental things that never worked. When you're in graduate school and young and think, 'I'm going to be a playwright,' you say, 'I'm going to be Beckett. This is the shape of what an artist is.' I was trying to write stuff that I had no way of knowing how to do, and I went back and wrote this very simple thing.

I found out by writing *Sunday on the Rocks* that I was funny. I did not try to be funny — I was just writing the world as I saw it. But when that happened, I said, 'Oh, that's what they mean when they tell you to write what you know.' We all have a particular keyhole through which we see the world, and our job as writers is to keep the keyhole clean and report what we see. I see sexism more strongly than other people do. I learned from *Sunday on the Rocks* that you start with how you see the world and build on that.

AG: COMPARED TO THE REST OF YOUR WORK, *SUNDAY ON THE ROCKS* IS UNUSUALLY CLEAR ABOUT WHO IS RIGHT AND WHO IS WRONG. USUALLY THERE ISN'T A CLEAR DISTINCTION IN YOUR PLAYS.

TR: No, there isn't. I don't think anybody's right or wrong — I think we're all in the soup together. In *Sunday*, I spent so much time trying to make Jessica more likeable, and I finally said, 'We have so much fun without her. Those three women have so much fun without her. We're never going to like Jessica, because she's the mom figure and she kills the fun. You can get closer to understanding her, but you're never going to like her.' So I gave up.

AG: WHERE DO YOU THINK YOUR COMIC ABILITY STEMS FROM? ARE YOU A NATURALLY FUNNY WRITER?

TR: I never thought I was, but I am. I thought *Spike Heels* was the darkest, angriest play I had ever written. I was going to toss it. Then I heard a reading, and people laughed their heads off. I think partially it's that I come from a large family, where one of the survival tactics is comedy. Six kids, and life becomes a competition: who can be the funniest person in the room? For me, I think comedy comes from anger and depression. You can either kill yourself or you can start telling jokes about it.

AG: YOU SAID EARLIER THAT YOU ALWAYS WANTED TO BE A WRITER. WHEN DID YOU KNOW WHAT A WRITER IS?

TR: I don't think I know that. I don't. I know I don't. People ask me about my process, and I'm not sure I have a set process, my process changes so much. I spent an enormous amount of time feeling unworthy, feeling like an aspirant, and I still feel that way sometimes. In Hollywood, you get asked for rewrites, and I sit there in terror, because I think, 'I don't know if I can make the next draft good.'

I find that there's a huge well of self-loathing involved in the act of writing. It's not a secure way to live your life. So I think that's why I don't know what will come out next. And then on the other hand, I go, 'Well, you have technique and craft now.' My work has gotten stronger, and I'm much more in control of it. If the inspiration's not there, you have to be able to fall back on technique, and I do feel that I have the technique to support myself in those moments of self-loathing and terror. Does that answer the question? What is a writer?

AG: OH, YES.

TR: I do think that writers are witnesses. To the world. A lot of writers, I think, believe writing is purely expression, that you just need to put it out there and it's all about yourself. I don't feel like it's all about myself. There's active social responsibility involved. I've had a lot of women come up to me after seeing my plays and say, 'Thank God, someone's writing about our lives the way we live them.' I do feel the responsibility that someone's got to speak.

AG: SPEAKING OF WOMEN'S REACTIONS TO PLAYS, I WANT TO TALK ABOUT *LOOSE KNIT*. I SAW IT AT SECOND STAGE AND FELL HEADLONG INTO A TRAP. I DIDN'T LIKE THE FEMALE CHARACTERS ON THAT STAGE SO I BECAME FRUS-

TRATED WITH THE PLAY. YOU PRESENT WOMEN WHO MAKE A LOT OF MESSES, AND I GOT ANGRY.

TR: I always thought that we were allowed to do that. I was so naïve when I started, but I still believe that part of what feminism has to accomplish for us is give us permission to make the kinds of mistakes that men are allowed to make on the stage. Female characters should be allowed to be as big of a mess and have as big of a struggle as anybody. I think that feminism hasn't gotten us anywhere until we are given permission to find ourselves and make mistakes the way men can. That's where the power is. I'm also not interested in girls who are right.

AG: WHAT DO YOU MEAN?

TR: There is a train of thought that women are more civilized than men innately. We may or may not be, but we're on individual journeys, and I think it's dangerous to make generalizations. I remember that the reviews for my early plays reflected, 'Why aren't these women behaving better? That's women's job; they're supposed to be better than men.' And I thought, 'Oh? I didn't know that was our job.' Someone once told me that there was critical unease with my work because it was not ladylike. Girl playwrights are supposed to be more refined.

AG: WHAT DISTURBED ME ABOUT *LOOSE KNIT* WAS THAT ALMOST ALL THE WOMEN IN THAT PLAY ALLOW MILES TO TRAMPLE THEM. THIS MISOGYNIST INSULTS THEM LEFT AND RIGHT, AND THEY APOLOGIZE TO HIM WHILE HE'S DOING IT.

TR: I know women who do that. Who collude with the assholes. And sometimes I collude with the assholes. I find it sympathetic and sad and funny that we sit there saying, 'My God, I feel terrible. He's making me feel terrible. But do you like me?' There's something so weirdly female about that, it interests me. Maybe you're the person who's never done that.

AG: NO, I'VE DONE IT.

TR: I collude all the time. Maybe I don't just find it horrifying, I find it funny. I find it forgivable. Actually, of all the dates with Miles that take place, the one that people really respond to is Margie's, because she's so pathetic. She's so pathetic and so desperate to have a man. I'd been single for a long time, and no matter what you have in your life, you're still like, 'Oh, I have no boyfriend.' I tried to turn the play into being about the male as object of desire. There are so many novels and films and plays about the woman as object of desire — plays with a bunch of guys sitting around talking about one woman — what would it be like if a bunch of women sat around talking about one guy? What would the male object of desire be?

AG: PERHAPS THIS IS THE RIGHT TIME TO ASK WHAT FEM-INISM MEANS TO YOU, AND IF YOU THINK OF YOURSELF AS A FEMINIST.

TR: I do think of myself as a feminist. I was so sad that it became kind of a dirty word, because I don't think feminism is about anything other than women being as fully human as men. I thought the idea was to erase the bigotry that says we have certain roles to fill. I thought it was about teaching us to see each other as complicated human beings who have choices. That's what feminism has always been to me.

AG: WHERE DOES A PLAY BEGIN WITH YOU? WITH IDEA, IMAGE, CHARACTERS? IS IT ALWAYS DIFFERENT?

TR: It's always different. *The Family of Mann* was autobiographical, because when I started working in television, I was shell-shocked by it, like Belinda ultimately is. I mean, I went and spent a bunch of time in Egypt once and did not get culture shock the way I got it in Hollywood. One time I was driving around Hollywood in a state of panic, and I had a flash of insight that the place I was working was *King Lear*. I went, 'He's Lear, and I'm Kent, and this person is . . .' I was putting constructions together, and it made me understand Shakespeare and a world where Machiavellian power games are real. That's also when I thought, 'I know how to make a play about Hollywood.'

I think that's why people do write about Hollywood. You go out there and say, 'This is really weird. There's got to be something that can be written about how strange it is.' The other thing I found is that Hollywood is not just made up of psychos. There are people like you and me out there. There are decent people going out and getting drunk together and trying to make themselves feel better about the world. And there's a continuum between normal human behavior and the monstrosities that people become. That's what the story of the play is: how far do you go down that road and when do you turn off?

AG: WHY DOES CLARA, THE PRODUCTION ASSISTANT WITH WHOM BELINDA MAKES FRIENDS, SPROUT ANGELS' WINGS IN ACT TWO?

TR: I do think the power of the human imagination can take us to better places. With that kind of pressure on you, you've got to become a monster or an angel. Clara didn't take herself out of the situation, so she went to some place in her head that was more powerful. It's a hopeful thing that she sprouts wings.

AG: WHAT IS BELINDA'S ADJUSTMENT AT THE END?

TR: You can become a monster — and I do think Ed is a monster — or you can become enlightened and not let it touch your spirit. I believe you can stand in the world in these situations and protect yourself from them. I started reading Lao-Tzu's *Tao Te Ching* this year and I believe that enlightenment is a possibility. I don't know that I'll ever get myself there, but I don't believe that we are doomed just to struggle or become monsters. And I don't think the struggle is just about trying to stay out of the muck. I think that you can walk toward the stars. I believe that.

Idealists make the most God-awful cynics, because nothing ever lives up to their ideals. Ever, ever. But I think there are plenty of playwrights who have had these visions of humanity. Read Molière. I don't mean to compare myself to that . . .

AG: MOLIÈRE, TOO, WROTE MONSTERS. OBSESSIVE MONSTERS.

TR: I see the Eds and I go, 'That's what they're like.' They are. Part of what happens with those people is that no one else is allowed to be in the room. Their insecurity is so huge, that they fill the room with narcissism and then there's no space for anyone else. It's very king-like, and everybody else in the room is a subject. Obviously it's not a world that makes sense to me ultimately, because I split. I said, 'I can't live this way,' and I came back to New York.

AG: WHAT LED YOU TO GO TO LOS ANGELES IN THE FIRST PLACE?

TR: I first went out because we were so poor. I was making eleven dollars an hour temping at AT&T and I was writing at night. My hus-band is a stage manager, and he was working two shows at once. One time I came home, and he was collapsed on the couch. He couldn't even get up to say hello. And I thought, 'I have got to try and get work in Hollywood. I have to try, because we're going to die or we're going to quit.' It was what we had always wanted for our lives, to work in the theater. But it was too financially devastating.

So I got a job on a sitcom, but I didn't want to stay out there. I got fired — it was after about a year-and-a-half of this nonsense — and I said, 'This is nuts.' My husband had stayed in New York for most of the time — he'd fly back and forth between New York and L.A. It just didn't make sense. So I came back to New York and we lived here from like 1991 to 1995, and then I got offered *NYPD Blue*. I had just had a baby and I had occasionally been working on episodes of different shows and I was happy. But then they asked me to write an episode of *NYPD*, and the experience was pretty wonderful. They shot it the way I wrote it. Jimmy Smits was wonderful. It was like his third episode, and it was early in the second season, so everybody was watching the show, and I felt really jazzed by it. They offered me a job on staff, which meant moving back to L.A. And I was still not going to do it, because it had been such a disaster before, but my hus-band said, 'That's fine if that's really your decision, but that decision means you are never going to work in TV again. Because you are never going to get a better offer than this.' And I had had such a good expe-rience with *NYPD Blue*, and there's something about crime drama which my little heart responds to, so we decided it was worth it. But we kept our apartment and rented a furnished house out there. I stayed on that show for two years and it was time to move on. I'm proud of the work I did, the show won a ton of awards. I had a good time.

But again, it was a very macho environment. I was more prepared to deal with it, but there's still a shelf life.

AG: COULD YOU HAVE MADE A LIVING AS A PLAYWRIGHT?

TR: I haven't yet.

AG: HOW ARE WOMEN WHO WRITE PLAYS SUPPOSED TO MAKE A LIVING?

TR: In the theater you can fall through the cracks. Hollywood is sexist, but there's a demand for product, and if you're good, they finally just go, 'Okay, give it to me.' So you get to work.

AG: STILL, STATISTICAL STUDIES OF THE TELEVISION INDUSTRY SHOW THAT IT HIRES MORE MEN THAN WOMEN AS WRITERS.

TR: I get to work out there a lot more than I get to work in the theater, so maybe I'm only talking about my own experience. There's just such a demand for product out there.

AG: HOW DOES WRITING FOR THE THEATER AFFECT YOUR TELEVISION WRITING, AND HOW DOES WRITING FOR TV AFFECT YOUR PLAYWRITING?

TR: I got nailed in a couple reviews about, 'Oh, she's written for Hollywood, it must have ruined her.' I don't think so. It's my pet peeve, because I go, 'Look, John Patrick Shanley wrote *Congo*, and no one ever implies that having written crappy movies has an effect on his work as a playwright.' I think critics are always looking for ways to take women's authority as writers. There's a cultural unease with women having creative authority.

AG: BUT FROM AN ARTISTIC POINT OF VIEW, HOW DOES WRITING IN A SHORT FORM THAT DEALS WITH THE SAME CHARACTERS WEEK AFTER WEEK AFFECT YOUR PLAYWRITING, IF AT ALL?

TR: Because you have to work so fast, you become facile with language and also you pretty much write the way you hear people talk. On a certain level that's good, but on another level it stops the theatricality. I had to recommit to letting language take the stage more. In the television shows that I worked on, language was an expression of character. I found that I couldn't write for sitcoms anymore — I didn't do it for very long anyway — because I truly am not a joke writer, which is what sitcoms are. If I had stayed with sitcoms, I would have had to change the way I hear and write. People tend to think that is the right world for me, because my plays are comedies. But my plays are character comedies, and you don't have time to write that way in sitcoms.

There was one point when I thought I had learned good things in terms of writing plays, because on *NYPD Blue* the standard was so high. I had to move things forward on two levels all the time. I had to move the plot forward and the characters forward. I could have characters moving in different directions, but every scene had to move something forward. There wasn't a stillness to it. And I actually found that to be a powerful way of storytelling. It uses my interest in Dickens and colliding worlds, and arc storytelling. So that was useful, but finally the theater is not so single-mindedly reliant on momentum. There should always be forward movement, but you do in fact have more time, more leeway, to let language perform.

AG: WITH ALL THE WRITING YOU ARE DOING NOW, HOW HAVE YOU FOUND BEING BOTH AN ARTIST AND A MOTHER?

TR: I find it difficult. I am in a problematic position in that I'm an artist and the breadwinner and the mother, and that tends to be really exhausting and stressful. I'm lucky, because my husband decided to stop working when I went to L.A. to write for *NYPD Blue*, and he stayed at home during the day. So we stuck with that arrangement, because he really enjoys it. And he's better at it than I am or was or could be. He's a stage manager. I find it exhausting to make time for all three of those things. I have virtually no social life anymore. I never go to movies. I write movies, but I don't go to them. I also find that I get crazy if I go too long without working on a play.

AG: IS ONE OF THE DIFFERENCES BETWEEN WRITING FOR TV AND WRITING FOR THEATER THE DIFFERENCE BETWEEN WRITING FOR AN EXECUTIVE PRODUCER AND WRITING FOR YOURSELF?

TR: I found writing for television more and more debilitating because it was so disheartening to keep answering other people's notes. It's exhausting to write according to someone else's specifications in very short periods of time. With my own notes, I sit around thinking about things and going, 'Well, maybe I should do this.' But I have to say that when I started out as a playwright, people talked to me differently than they do now. It was much more directive at the beginning. Now I'm much more in control of how I respond, and the process is much more rewarding.

AG: YOU SAID EARLIER THAT YOU DO NOT IMPOSE THE JUDGMENTS 'RIGHT' AND 'WRONG' ON THE CHARACTERS IN YOUR PLAYS. BUT THERE FREQUENTLY ARE THOSE CHARACTERS WHO BEHAVE ETHICALLY AND THOSE WHO DO NOT, ALTHOUGH THEIR BEHAVIOR IS FLUID. I'M THINKING OF EMMA, THE HEROINE IN *VIEW OF THE DOME.*

TR: She's got an idealism that she's striving to hang onto, and it leads her . . . well, she doesn't behave very well.

AG: NO, BUT BECAUSE OF THAT, SHE'S AN INTERESTING CHARACTER. HOW DO YOU WANT US TO SEE HER? IS SHE NAÏVE? IS SHE CONFUSED?

TR: I thought when I was writing her that much of what she says is true. There is a yearning in us for the world to be better and to believe that we can make the world better, and that our leaders should be leading us to make the world better. It's an idealistic act to do what Emma does, to move into the political system with someone whom you believe can improve the world. But I feel it's difficult to change the world, in that our true journey through life is to take care of ourselves. My job is myself. So there are two responsibilities: you're responsible to the community and you're also responsible to yourself. Emma loses that distinction and becomes no better than the rest.

It was something that I was talking to myself about, because I really do get on a high horse about the mess of the world. But someone's got to say those things. What if people don't take those positions and fight the fight? You have to do that. But you also can't let the fight turn you into something that's just as bad as the thing you're fighting.

AG: THAT'S WHAT HAPPENS TO EMMA ESSENTIALLY?

TR: Yes.

AG: EXCEPT THAT AT THE END . . .

TR: She realizes what she's done. There's something about having a child that pulls her back from the brink.

AG: IN A NUMBER OF YOUR PLAYS, ONE WOMAN SPEAKS OUT NO MATTER WHAT: BELINDA IN *THE FAMILY OF MANN*; LIZ, THE LONE WOMAN WHO TALKS BACK TO MILES IN *LOOSE KNIT*; EMMA EVENTUALLY. THEN THERE ARE OTHER WOMEN WHO, FOR WANT OF A BETTER TERM, ARE WEAKER.

TR: They know how to get along. They know how not to put themselves out there. Sometimes I feel they know how to survive better. You don't survive by sticking yourself out there and taking a bullet. You don't survive by picking a fight with the patriarchy.

AG: RELATING THIS TO MELODRAMA, OFTEN THERE IS THE SO-CALLED BAD WOMAN, WHO IS MORE VIBRANT, MORE OUTSPOKEN. AND THEN THERE ARE THE GOOD, QUIET, SAFE WOMEN.

TR: That split is absolutely in my work, because I've had periods in my life where I did toe the line and periods when I didn't. Margie says to Gina in *Loose Knit*, 'You played by all the rules and got fucked.' I don't see why we're playing by the rules. I have to say, I've finally gotten to that position. We live in a deeply sexist culture. They are not going to let up on us. The Women's Movement was successful to a point, but now we've got to figure out what the second wave is going to be, because they have clamped down even more. There's been a huge retrenching, and it's absolutely present in the American theater. I think we really are in trouble.

But then sometimes I say, 'Oh, just shut up about that. Just shut up. Write your plays. You get produced. It's an enormous struggle to get produced, but you do get produced. You don't want them to know you're a troublemaker.' Then another part of me goes, 'Yeah, but playing by the rules doesn't get you anywhere either.'

AG: JUST OUT OF CURIOSITY, DO YOU THINK MEN WHO ARE TROUBLEMAKERS GET SHOT DOWN AS FREQUENTLY AS WOMEN?

TR: NO! I think it's admired. I mean David Mamet, Tony Kushner — these are guys who write enormously angry plays and they're praised for it. I swear to God, I had a producer this year say about one of my new plays, 'It makes you sound so angry.' And I said, 'Anger is a perfectly legitimate driving force for a piece of theater.' It's still not okay to be an angry woman. It is still not okay. And I say, 'I'm sorry, we've got a lot to be angry about. We have much more to be angry about than the boys do.'

Look, I describe the world. I have wonderful men in my life. I don't believe all men are sexist pigs and I don't believe that all women are not. But there's a global terror of seeing women as human beings. I don't think I'm inventing it.

AG: CERTAINLY THE WOMEN IN YOUR PLAYS RARELY HAVE POWER OVER WHAT THE DOMINANT CULTURE DISHES OUT. THE MOST THEY ATTAIN IS POWER OVER THEIR INDIVIDUAL . . .

TR: Over their hearts, yeah. Or over their little worlds. Emma actually gets more evolved than anybody I've written, except maybe for Clara.

AG: BUT THE WOMEN STRIKE BACK AT TIMES. THAT DEFINITELY HAPPENS.

TR: I guess I see the forces as weighed against us, that the best we can do is maintain a holding pattern. The victory of *Loose Knit* is that those women stick together. You don't know how long they're going to be able to stick together, because even though Miles is a bad guy, there is that siren song of money and power. But that's not a wacky construction, given our culture. Ronald Perelman, Donald Trump — these are not nice guys. These are not guys who are going to make a woman's life easy or happy. But these are the guys with the money and power, and there's a glamorization of it.

AG: SO GETTING BACK TO THE BUSINESS OF PLAYWRITING, HOW SHOULD WOMEN WHO WANT TO WRITE FOR THE THEATER APPROACH THIS BASTION OF MALE POWER?

TR: We must not give up. I don't think the answer is throwing in the towel and running off to make money in Hollywood. There is this assumption that if you could make money in Hollywood, why would you do theater, which I think is a bad assumption. But there are cultural forces that are going to have to change, for us to be heard. I think theater people and women in theater have to speak out more as a group. ACT UP did it and they were heard. The NAACP did it this year about the absence of people of color on network television, and they were heard, to some degree. We've got to stop being cowards. Thank God that Paula Vogel won the Pulitzer, because it gives her authority.

AG: BUT IN TERMS OF BEING ACTIVIST, A NUMBER OF WOMEN DON'T WANT TO BE IN THE CATEGORY 'WOMEN PLAYWRIGHTS.'

TR: That's because the power structure ghettoizes you that way. I was told at the beginning of my career to be careful not to get branded a woman playwright.

AG: 'BRANDED'?

TR: 'Branded' a woman playwright. And I'm going, 'But I am a woman playwright.' There is still this cultural assumption that the white male point of view is it. The white male point of view is agenda-less, and the rest of us have agendas. How do you change that? That's a much bigger question than the American theater.

AG: AS A WRITER, HOW DO YOU DEAL WITH IT? DO YOU LOOK OVER YOUR SHOULDER, 'OH, DEAR, NOW I'M WRITING FROM A WOMAN'S PERSPECTIVE. WILL I GET PRODUCED?'

TR: When I first started seeing Spike Lee's movies, I realized that what pisses white people off is that he's telling a story from the world he lives in. He's telling the story from over there, and we are not used to seeing stories from anywhere but here.

AG: BUT THEN THE CULTURE FOUND THAT THERE WAS A MARKET FOR HIS PERSPECTIVE.

TR: Right, so somehow we women have to convince people that there's a market. The other thing that we battle against is that they don't want us writing commercial stuff in the theater. They want us to write art.

AG: DO YOU WANT TO BE ON BROADWAY?

TR: Sure. You bet. I love big theaters. But I also would like there to be better stuff on Broadway. I feel a playwright can entertain and also say something about the culture and about human character. You can do all three. And I believe that women are ideally positioned to do it. I've read such good plays by women lately, that I think we're getting better and better. There's something about being excluded the way we've been that has made us dig in and say, 'I'm not going to stop.' At some point there's going to be an explosion. That is my fantasy anyway. The flip side is that there are plenty of male playwrights who are not being held to standards anywhere near as rigorous. A lot of the boys are being given a walk, and they're not pushing themselves.

AG: COULD YOU TALK ABOUT SOME OF YOUR MOST RECENT WORK, PARTICULARLY YOUR MUSICAL, *THE TWO ORPHANS*?

TR: *The Two Orphans* is based on a nineteenth-century melodrama that was originally set in France before the Revolution, and I moved it to New Orleans after the Civil War. As I said earlier, I have this theory that societies flying apart cling to rules ever more rigidly, and I think that's why many of these melodramas are set on the eve of, or right after, revolutions.

In the original, there were two girls — one beautiful, one blind and beautiful. I made them ex-slaves, and they come to New Orleans after the war, looking for family. The one that can see is abducted and taken to an orgy where she's almost raped. The blind girl is lost in the city and abducted by a troupe of beggars. She has a beautiful singing voice, which is why I wrote this as a musical.

What I find both interesting and a little frightening is that both girls become the objects of desire. There are two love triangles. Henriette is pursued by an evil guy and then saved by a burned-out Confederate soldier, who falls in love with her. A white guy in love with a black woman in the nineteenth century — it's a disaster. Louise, the blind girl, is pursued by one man who's a brute and protected by another who's crippled. This side of the play sings, the other does not. The two crippled people sing because they are trapped in their bodies and their souls have become huge. My co-lyricist, John Sheehy, and I use a traditional melodramatic structure, but every now and then someone will sing a song applicable to nothing, simply for entertainment, in Brechtian style. Melodrama is not something we go to easily anymore; you have to frame it for people and make them feel safe. You have to say, 'I'm telling a story. It's going to be big, come on in.' I also did a lot of work on the text to support the extremes of behavior psychologically.

But it was fun to do. There's a celebration in 'I'm going to tell a big story now and I'm not going to apologize.' The work was just dripping with pleasure at every moment.

AG: YOU'VE WRITTEN SEVERAL PLAYS WITH CHARACTERS OF COLOR.

TR: I started out saying, 'Write about what you know' and then I started knowing more people of color. I started writing about black people and white people together right when this whole discussion began in some theater circles about how we shouldn't be writing for each other's races. Of course that would be when I would start doing it. I started also when I began writing for *NYPD Blue*, because we were constantly writing for people of color, and I began listening to their stories.

AG: WERE THERE WRITERS OF COLOR ON STAFF?

TR: There was one guy. There were five writers: one woman and one black guy and three white guys.

AG: PEOPLE HAVE RECENTLY COME DOWN ON TELEVISION NETWORKS AND PRODUCERS FOR THE SMALL NUMBER OF CHARACTERS OF COLOR. BUT THE PLAYS PRODUCED IN MAINSTREAM THEATERS CONTAIN LARGELY WHITE CASTS.

TR: The hero of *Abstract Expression* is a black guy. *The Two Orphans* is about miscegenation in the deep South. My new play, *The Butterfly Collection*, is six over-privileged white people. And when I was writing it, I felt so stupid. Why am I going back to all these white people in a room? But there are things that really interested me — it's about an addiction to art, that art will save you the way God is supposed to save you, or the way alcohol will fill your terror. So I went ahead and wrote it. But we must write plays in which we inhabit each other's worlds. I find it a curious construction that black playwrights usually write only about black people, and white playwrights like me usually write only about white people. Because the world doesn't really look like that, now does it? We're all living it together.

AG: BUT MAYBE WE AREN'T REALLY?

TR: Yeah, maybe we aren't. But frankly, in my heart, I don't believe that. ▼

Carmen Rivera

Playwright, teacher, and actress Carmen Rivera lives in New York City with her husband, the playwright Candido Tirado, with whom she runs Latino Experimental Fantastic Theatre (L.E.F.T.) along with the director Gloria Zelaya. Rivera's plays include *To Catch the Lightning* (1990), a portrayal of a man who tyrannizes his family while the urban world beyond his locked doors grows increasingly violent; *La Gringa* (1996), about a young woman who visits Puerto Rico to reclaim the culture she believes she has lost; *La Proxima Parada—The Next Stop* (1999), which involves four people who meet on the subway and learn to hope for a better life; and *Julia de Burgos: Child of Water* (1999), a portrait of one of Puerto Rico's most renowned poets. Rivera has also written numerous one-acts, notably *ameRICAN, The Power of Words,* and *Betty's Garage,* which depicts the trauma experienced by women fleeing abusive men. Rivera received the Legacy Award for Achievement in Playwriting in 1997, and *La Gringa* was part of Repertorio Español's 1996 Obie Award–winning New Voices series.

In addition to writing plays, Rivera works with the City Lights Youth Theatre and the Lower East Side Tenement Museum, to help young people make theater, and she has taught writing in the New York City public schools. Currently she teaches playwriting at the City College of New York. This interview took place on September 15, 1999, in New York City.

• • •

AG: HOW DID LATINO EXPERIMENTAL FANTASTIC THEATRE COME INTO EXISTENCE?

CR: L.E.F.T. was founded in 1989 by Candido Tirado and Gloria Zelaya under the name Shaman Repertory Theatre. They started the company so that Latino writers, actors, directors, and designers would have a place to develop their craft; I was brought in as a young writer. The name 'Shaman' was selected to reflect the healing nature of theater. We felt that we should address the social ills plaguing our community.

I was only twenty-five, and it was an invaluable training ground in my development as a playwright. Not only did I workshop my plays, but I acted, stage-managed, painted the sets — cleaned the sets — wrote grants, and learned to produce. In 1994, we changed the name to Latino Experimental Fantastic Theatre, because many people came to our shows expecting actual shamanistic rituals. L.E.F.T. also properly describes the company's aesthetic, which tackles social themes in an experimental way. We produce on a shoestring budget — it is pure guerrilla theater. And pure joy. What I have learned about playwriting I learned at L.E.F.T. My growth as a writer happened in front of an audience. The plays I wrote for the company were produced, and I received immediate feedback. I learned how to write for production, to rewrite, and I learned to write within the collaborative process.

AG: IS THERE A NETWORK OF LATINO THEATERS IN THE UNITED STATES?

CR: There definitely is a network, but it's not united. The Latinos in L.A. focus more on Chicano work. People in New York focus more on the Caribbean experience. Chicago has both. There are a lot of Chicanos living in Chicago, and a lot of Puerto Ricans went to Chicago, so you have the Mexican-American experience along with the Puerto Rican. Miami's more the Cuban experience. Texas is definitely Chicano. The network is not disconnected, but it's made up of different visions.

AG: NOT ONE VOICE.

CR: Right. It's a voice that's very multicultural and multiracial.

AG: WERE YOU BORN IN PUERTO RICO?

CR: I was born and raised in New York City. My parents came here from Puerto Rico when they were eight years old, so they grew up completely American. Jimmy Hendrix music was played in the house, they both loved the Beatles. Only English was spoken in our home — we had Spanish music and food only during the holidays. That's where my play *La Gringa* comes from, because that's what I'm considered in Latin America.

AG: WHEN DID YOU FIRST GO TO PUERTO RICO?

CR: I was nine years old the first time I went, and I hated it. I didn't speak Spanish. I didn't even understand it. I was supposed to be there for two months, so I could learn Spanish and connect with my culture; I was there for three weeks. I couldn't connect with anybody. I didn't understand my cousins, so I couldn't play with them. There was a latrine in the back in addition to the bathroom, for when there were water shortages. I said, 'I'm not using that. I am not doing that.'

I grew up in the projects in New York City, but my projects were not the way they are considered now. In the 1960s and 1970s, they were great places to live. Completely integrated. There were Irish, African-American, Jewish, and Puerto Rican families there. I grew up with a lot of different races, so it was like a utopia. Everybody loved each other. All the older women would hang out on the benches in front. Everybody respected everybody's holidays. We had a Jewish neighbor who sent us Christmas gifts, and my mother knew when it was Hanukkah.

I returned from Puerto Rico and swore that I'd never go back. I said, 'I'm American, I speak English.' But when I was in high school, I started to study Spanish, and when I was sixteen, my mother decided to take a big tour of Puerto Rico. She took my brother, myself, and a friend, and we toured the whole island. And it was, 'Okay, I'm in love now.' My mother showed me this wonderful love for her island. We went to the town where she was born. She showed me a whole different place.

After that, I would go every other year. When I was twenty-one, I graduated from college with a degree in economics and Spanish, and I tried to get a job in an insurance company in Puerto Rico, like Maria does in *La Gringa*. But they told me, 'No,' because I wasn't Puerto Rican. That's when *The Universe* was born, the one-act that became *La Gringa*. It's a very short one-act: Maria and her uncle, Manolo, in a car, going to the job interview and coming back. I had spent one night talking with my uncle, who was also visiting Puerto Rico, and we had this amazing connection, the way Maria and Manolo do. He told me, 'You can't live your life the way I did. If you want to be a writer, you just got to forget everybody who's negative about it. Forget them.'

I came home and announced that I was going to write. My father and I have a very conflicted relationship, but he told me to stop living so safely, which surprised me. Anyway, people kept telling me to make *The Universe* full-length, but I didn't know how. Then my uncle passed away, and I felt that he was guiding me. It was as if he were saying, 'Okay, now you can write. I will help you write the full-length.' When he passed away, it opened the whole play up.

AG: HOW DID YOU GET INTO THEATER?

CR: My parents both loved the theater. They always knew what was going on in Central Park and at Lincoln Center, which used to have theater in the street for kids. My mother took my brother and me every summer and she also took me to the Puerto Rican Traveling Theater. When I turned twelve, in 1976, I begged my mother to take me to a Broadway show, so she took me to see *Grease*. And I fell in love. I told her, 'I don't ever want a birthday party again. Just take me to shows.'

When I was ten, my mother started attending Lehman College, where she studied English literature. She had to see lots of plays, and my father was working — he could never go — so I used to go. I got to see Shakespeare. I loved to see the musicals, because I danced. Theater was something that I always loved.

AG: DID YOU DANCE PROFESSIONALLY?

CR: No. I just studied it. I had a lot of injuries. My soul loves to dance, but my body is not strong enough. Actually, I wanted to audition for the High School of Performing Arts, because I was a very good tap dancer. But my mother said, 'Absolutely not. You're going to be a doctor.' I said, 'For thirteen years you tell me you love art, and Papi takes us to the museums' 'That's a hobby. That's what rich people do. You're going to be a doctor and you're going to have a hobby in the theater.' She wouldn't let me audition. That was a big bone of contention throughout my teenage years.

I went to New York University as a computer science major, which was a big mistake. When I changed my major to economics and Spanish, I had this professor of Spanish literature, who said, 'You're a writer. What you choose to do with it is your business.' So I started writing short stories. My favorite writers are from Latin America. There is one man from Uruguay — Horacio Quiroga — I love his work. I like all the darker writers: Julio Cortázar, Gabriel García Márquez, Pablo Neruda. There are also two wonderful playwrights from Argentina: Guillermo Gentile and Griselda Gambaro, who both write about violence and terror. Camus. Kafka. I think that's where *To Catch the Lightning* began, in Kafka's netherworld where you don't know who the enemy is. Or the enemy is somebody you love.

After graduation, I got a job in Philadelphia at an insurance company, and there I knew that I wanted to write plays. I returned to New York, saved money for three years, and joined the Puerto Rican Traveling Theater, where I worked with playwright Allen Davis III, their dramaturg. After about two years, I went back to N.Y.U. and got my Masters. I love working with kids — so I combined educational theater and playwriting and Latin American theater. I wrote a paper on the origins of Fantastic Realism and then I wrote *To Catch the Lightning*.

AG: WAS THAT YOUR FIRST FULL-LENGTH PLAY?

CR: Yes. It was my graduate thesis. I was studying violence in theater and I combined that with a theater development from Argentina. The Argentine playwright Guillermo Gentile worked with people in the 1960s, developing an artistic concept about how fantasies are the impetus for action, whether in photography, poetry, architecture, or novel writing. This was before García Márquez became famous. It wasn't a theatrical development per se; a group of artists studied different art forms from the beginning of Western civilization. They concluded that what's successful in art is the irrational: dreams, fantasies. Then what is called the 'Dirty War' happened in 1977, and most of the intellectuals were killed. Guillermo escaped to Spain and then went to New York.

AG: *TO CATCH THE LIGHTNING* SEEMS TO TAKE PLACE IN A FUTURISTIC, VIOLENT WORLD.

CR: The model was Latin American dictatorship.

AG: THE CENTRAL CHARACTER, ANTONIO, IS HORRIBLY CONTROLLING OF HIS FAMILY.

CR: Right, and he makes his eight-year-old daughter paint him. All dictators, not just South American, have pictures of themselves everywhere. Even Simón Bolívar, who is our God because he was the first liberator, had statues built to him. Pinochet, Somoza, Duvalier, Stalin, Hitler, Mussolini — they had pictures of themselves plastered all over. That's where the art kept coming into my play. I was fascinated by that and by why people are violent, why people kill. I was inspired by a lot of things that were happening in America: babies being thrown in garbage cans; homeless children. That play took eight years to write. It's still not done.

AG: IT'S QUITE DIFFERENT FROM *LA GRINGA*, WHICH IS LARGELY REALISTIC IN STYLE. GOING BACK TO *LA GRINGA*, WHEN MARIA ARRIVES IN PUERTO RICO, SHE WEARS CLOTHES EMBLAZONED WITH THE PUERTO RICAN FLAG. HOW DO YOU WANT US TO PERCEIVE MARIA AT THE BEGINNING?

CR: I want you to see immaturity and naïveté. And fear. And desperation. The next time you go to Puerto Rico, notice how people are dressed. New York or Chicago Puerto Ricans — Puerto Ricans outside of the island — will wear a hat with a Puerto Rican flag. A jacket with a flag. They will have the pants with the flag. A shirt that says 'I'm Proud to Be Puerto Rican.' There was one woman I saw that had buttons of the flag all the way down her front. I never went to Puerto Rico like that, but in creating the character of Maria, I figured, this is a desperation to feel like you belong to something. Or to find out who you are. So I gave her that. I think all humanity needs to belong somewhere, whether it's to a culture or religion or cults. The 'we' is composed of many 'I's.' But once identity becomes dogmatic, it's no good. I would never walk around with the Puerto Rican flag on my back.

AG: MARIA STAYS WITH HER AUNT, NORMA, WHO IS A VERY ANGRY WOMAN. WHY DID YOU MAKE THAT CHARACTER SO ANGRY?

CR: When you don't live your dream, when you have a passion and you don't fulfill it, it doesn't go away. It festers inside of you. My uncle wanted desperately to be an actor. But my family is very conservative and did not support him in that. So he started drinking. He wasn't an incapacitated alcoholic. He became a super. He fixed refrigerators and air conditioners. He could fix anything. Yet at his house he would have thousands of music tapes of Gershwin, different versions of *Rhapsody in Blue*, and he knew all of Shakespeare's plays. This was somebody who had a tremendous mind. But he didn't fulfill his dream.

Norma is somebody who would have loved to come to the United States and be a singer. Or would have loved to be a singer in Puerto Rico. That story is actually my grandmother's: my grandmother was asked to sing with a famous singer in Puerto Rico, and her mother — my great-grandmother — wouldn't let her. She said, 'Singers are prostitutes.' And my grandmother didn't do it. My grandmother's not negative like Norma, but I felt for the play I had to go all the way with that, so I could bring her back.

Norma feels that life has passed her by. She didn't get to go to New York, which, for the immigrants who came here, was an opportunity to change your life. In the play, her sister had a better life by coming here, and Norma had to stay and take care of everybody. Had to bury the parents. She got saddled with all the responsibility. That eats at you.

I tried to keep the character of her husband, Victor, as a soft but wise man, who says, 'Hey, if you're upset at your life, that means the life we made together, you don't like. You don't love the child that we made out of love. This beautiful house that we have, you don't love.' I wanted to show with Norma that if you are afraid to reach, then there's an emptiness in your spirit. She could have gone to America. When Victor and Manolo are talking to Maria in the second act, they say, 'We all told her to be a singer.' Victor would have loved her, would have still married her. But she was afraid, and when you're afraid, you get angry at yourself, and self-hatred builds up. In Norma I'm trying to encapsulate lost dreams.

AG: WE HAVEN'T TALKED MUCH ABOUT THE MALE CHARACTERS IN YOUR PLAYS.

CR: I try to show them dimensionally. Even in *To Catch the Lightning*, the despotic father wants to be loved. The actor who played him at Puerto Rican Traveling Theater had a hard time understanding that. He said, 'But he's beating everybody up.' And I said, 'But fascist dictators are babies.' When you are very afraid of something, you abuse it even more.

I enjoy writing about men. Actors usually love playing my men, so I take that as a good sign.

AG: THE MEN IN *LA GRINGA* ARE VERY APPEALING: MANOLO, VICTOR, AND ESPECIALLY MONCHI.

CR: Monchi, which is short for 'Ramon,' is based on Candido and is named after the great Puerto Rican Nationalist leader, Ramon Emeterio Betances. Monchi's wanting to go back to the land is a political statement about buying the land back. But more than that, it's about giving reverence to Mother Earth.

AG: MONCHI IS AN INTERESTING CONTRAST TO MARIA. HE WANTS TO TAKE THE LAND BACK, BUT HE KNOWS IT'S A SLOW, DIFFICULT PROCESS. MARIA WANTS EVERYTHING TO HAPPEN QUICKLY.

CR: That's Maria's immaturity. When they encounter each other in the first act, she's still living this, 'Oh, my God, I'm here in Puerto Rico, this is so great, I'm so Puerto Rican.' For the play, she needed to be like that, because in the second act she has to release her ego. I had read *The Cry for Myth* by Rollo May, and he talks about the different steps in acculturating oneself. Actually, I followed those steps in the second act. Maria has to release her ego — that's the first step. You have to release the ego of your own definition, let it go. So she throws her 'Puerto Ricanness' away and says in essence, 'I'm nothing. I'm Puerto Rican in the United States, I'm American here. That means I'm nobody from everywhere.' There's a libation — that's the second step. Then Manolo says he's going to take her to the cemetery: the worshipping of ancestors is the third step. The fourth is the baptism in the rain forest, and the fifth is the celebration, the parranda.

AG: WHAT IS A PARRANDA?

CR: Let's say we lived in a town with ten houses. During the holiday season, from Epiphany to January 6, you and I and my grandmother who sang, we would get together with instruments and go to each house. There would be a feast at each house, and we wouldn't leave until we were fed. When Monchi and Manolo are singing together, they sing, 'I'm not leaving until you feed me.' The song is very traditional. That's what a parranda is. Many people do them in East Harlem every year, but a lot of the older Puerto Ricans have moved out or died, and my generation doesn't really do them so much. I'm the corny one who wants to.

I try to show in the second act that what Maria is looking for is already inside her. When Manolo dies, he doesn't really have to pass the culture on, because he gives her insight and love.

AG: I EXPECTED THAT THERE WOULD BE MORE OF A ROMANCE BETWEEN MARIA AND MONCHI, BUT YOU AVOID THAT.

CR: Yes. There's an indication that they're soul mates and have a great love for each other. But I didn't want one of the last images to be that a man was going to make her okay; I wanted it just to be her. Also, I don't specify if she's actually going to stay in Puerto Rico, because I don't think it's that important. I'm assuming that she's going back to New York and will take care of what she needs to take care of.

AG: DO YOU CONSIDER YOURSELF AN AMERICAN PLAYWRIGHT? A PUERTO RICAN PLAYWRIGHT?

CR: I don't know. I've been thinking about that. I spoke at some colleges when La Gringa opened, and students asked me that. I feel that to say I'm an American playwright is not clear; it's not how the label is used here. And to say that I'm a Puerto Rican playwright, it's not how the label is used in Puerto Rico or here. I'm not considered American here; I'm considered Puerto Rican. I kind of don't care now. I felt for a long time I was a Puerto Rican who was born and raised in New York. But I feel more comfortable in New York City than any other place that I've been to. I feel like a New Yorker. I don't know.

AG: WHOM DO YOU WRITE FOR?

CR: I never thought about that. My husband and I have a theater company, so we always have to write in our grants who our audience is, and it's a mixed audience. I don't think I write only for Latinos. I don't think *La Gringa* is a Puerto Rican story, I think it's a very American story, because everybody is an immigrant here. I guess I write for American audiences. I would hope that anybody could connect to what I write.

AG: ONE OF THE REASONS I ASK IS THAT YOU SEEM TO INCORPORATE LESSONS IN YOUR PLAYS, AS THOUGH YOU WANT TO HELP YOUR AUDIENCES DISCOVER THEMSELVES. IN *THE NEXT STOP*, THE TWO WOMEN ON THE SUBWAY ENCOURAGE EACH OTHER TO FIND THEIR IDENTITIES. IN *THE POWER OF WORDS*, THE TEACHER URGES HER STUDENTS NOT TO BE AFRAID TO WRITE.

CR: When I was writing *The Next Stop*, I was thinking about the dignity that poor people have, and the genius they have to make a dollar stretch. This play is about dreaming, about feeling hope. Fatima does not want to feel hope; it's better if Mickey stays in jail. She knows where he is, instead of having to hope that he might come out. Then she has something to lose. I wanted to show that you could have hope in Bushwick, Brooklyn, or in the projects. I had a lot of hope. I sold Girl Scout cookies in my building with my Girl Scout uniform on. I would take the elevator to the fourteenth floor and make my way down. People invited me to their homes. I didn't even think that something bad could happen to me. It was a totally innocent time.

The Power of Words, too, is about hope and dreams, and not being afraid of dreams. With the teaching-artist residencies, I primarily got sent to Special Ed classrooms, which are devastating. Those students have such heart, and it's something I enjoy doing, but I burned out; it destroyed my spirit. But every so often you'll get a student who has a light in him, like Mike in *The Power of Words*.

AG: BOTH SCRIPTS HAVE 1995 AS THE FIRST COPYRIGHT DATE. THEY SHARE A GRITTY LANGUAGE.

CR: 1995. It was the last year that I taught the Special Ed workshops. Both plays were inspired by actual events, which I wrote about for the Latino Experimental Fantastic Theatre. My husband and I decided the theme for one of our productions would be fathers, so I wrote a play called *The Classroom* and a play called *The Subway,* and one became *The Power of Words* and one became *The Next Stop.* I had a poetry workshop with fourth graders — this was actually a gifted class — where a girl wrote about her father getting killed. The family was having dinner, and the father went out and got killed.

Then I had another experience with a student in Special Ed in high school. His name was Henry Rivera. This was total hard-core Special Ed — kids who had just gotten out of Rikers Island prison — and he was sitting with a hood over his head. And I went up to him and said, 'Oh, you're Rivera, what's up? You know, us Riveras, we're writers.' And he was like — no response. So I gave my lesson. He didn't come back to class. He had been arrested. For two months, he was in jail. Then he came back; he had written a play in jail. To this day, I say this all the time: 'The most brilliant piece of theater I've ever read.' Aeschylus, Shakespeare, Euripides, Beckett — this guy wrote the most amazing play. A drug dealer trying to hold onto his family. It was a series of phone calls from jail. That's all it was. I thought it was brilliant. He said, 'No, you're just saying that because you're my teacher, because you're Puerto Rican.' I said, 'No, I would never do that.' I brought it back to my company, and we performed it in the school library.

Well, he didn't want to go see it. Something had happened that morning: his cousin was stabbed in front of the school — the school was near the projects in Brooklyn. So I'm trying to keep him in the school. I'm saying, 'Your play's going to get read. You have to stay here.' Like he cares about his play at that moment. 'The actors are here. They rehearsed your play. You have to stay.' The cops were in the building. It was this chaotic day.

We do the show. His play gets a standing ovation, and he's there, like all playwrights, hiding in the back. The next day I go school, and they tell me I incited a riot — because all the kids were cutting class to go see theater. It would have been okay if they had cut class to go outside and fight. Then they said that the content of the play was too violent. I was shocked. I said, 'What do you want these kids to write? You should be angry that they have to live the kinds of lives they do.' As an educator, you should say, 'What can I do to make this world a better place?' I never saw Henry Rivera after that. I wasn't able to put his whole story in the play, although I want to. But he's the character, Mike, who comes out of jail and wants his poem back.

AG: DO YOU KEEP A NOTEBOOK?

CR: Yes, but when people talk to me or I watch things happen I try to memorize it, because I don't want them to think that I'm writing about them. But I always have paper with me, and when I am alone, I try to make notes.

AG: IS THAT HOW YOUR PLAYS USUALLY START?

CR: Usually, everything I've written has been inspired by something I've seen or experienced — a very specific experience. *La Gringa* was my story. *To Catch the Lightning* was a recurring dream.

AG: IT'S INTERESTING TO COMPARE *TO CATCH THE LIGHTNING*, WHICH YOU BEGAN TO WRITE IN 1989, WITH *JULIA DE BURGOS: CHILD OF WATER*, WHICH YOU WROTE IN 1998. BOTH PLAYS ARE ABOUT POLITICAL OPPRESSION, BUT THE WRITING IS MORE SUBTLE IN *JULIA*, PERHAPS BECAUSE YOU DRAMATIZE SEVERAL KINDS OF OPPRESSION AND INTERLACE THEM. JULIA IS OPPRESSED BY POVERTY, CLASS . . .

CR: Herself.

AG: SHE IS OPPRESSED BY MEN.

CR: Yes. Definitely. I don't know what kind of man Julia was attracted to, but she was attracted to one man, the great love of her life, who was very conventional, as much as he said he didn't want to be.

AG: THE CHARACTER OF THE DOMINICAN SOCIALIST JUAN GRULLON, IN YOUR PLAY?

CR: Yes.

AG: HOW DID YOU LEARN ABOUT JULIA?

CR: I knew about her when I was growing up. I always knew that there was this great Puerto Rican writer named Julia de Burgos. As I got older, I found a collection of her work in Spanish, and she just blew me away. Miriam Colon, the artistic director of Puerto Rican Traveling Theater, had been wanting to do a play about Julia for a while — a lot of Puerto Rican theater people have wanted to be involved with a production about her. Miriam loved *To Catch the Lightning* and produced it, and she asked me to write about Julia. For the first two months, I didn't return her calls, I was so intimidated. I felt, 'I can't write about Julia de Burgos. That's one of our gods.'

Julia lived in an incredibly tumultuous time in Puerto Rico. She was born in 1914, sixteen years after the United States invaded Puerto Rico during the Spanish-American War. She was living at the time when the U.S. Congress made Puerto Rico a territory of the United States, so the U.S. could send the Puerto Ricans to World War I. In the 1930s, the Nationalist Movement really started going, and that's when she started coming out as a writer.

It's interesting that after the production opened, people were telling me that Julia was never a Nationalist. But all my friends whom I interviewed for the play have flyers showing her attending functions at a place called El Ateneo, which is a significant cultural center in Puerto Rico for the general public and for the Nationalists.

AG: IS THERE A FACTION THAT DOESN'T WANT TO CLAIM HER AND ONE THAT DOES?

CR: There's a faction that wants to deny that she was a Nationalist and wants to say she was just a drunk and a whore.

AG: HOW DO YOU SEE *JULIA DE BURGOS* IN RELATION TO YOUR OTHER WORK?

CR: This play was so hard to write. I couldn't figure the play out for about a year. I wrote five drafts, and the first three were each one hundred and fifty pages. Thirty characters. I couldn't get the story; I was writing a documentary about her instead. Candido told me, 'You know what? You have to look inside yourself and write about yourself. Because you can't write about Julia. You don't know what she thought, you don't know what she felt.'

Then I started reading her poetry. There's a poem — 'Mi Alma' — 'My Soul' — where she talks about how her soul lives in disorder and 'in the silence/of the free thinker, who lives alone,/in quiet exile.' And one day it hit me: 'I'm living that too.' I had gone through a period where I was fighting with everybody. I didn't mean to fight, but I say what I feel, and everybody gets mad at me. Women want to say what they feel. It had just gotten really intense.

Candido, who was the play's dramaturg, said, 'Carmen, you went through so many things. Your family was poor, you're of mixed race, and you had to deal with being a woman and wanting to write.' So I threw all the drafts out and started from scratch. I started reading her poetry every day. 'Okay, Julia, somewhere you're here.'

It was difficult to write during this time. Miriam Colon said, 'Look, Carmen, if you need another year, we'll give you another year.' But I didn't want to see myself as a failure. So I had a deadline. December 22, 1998, was the deadline to see if this would go up for the spring season. Candido and I took that trip to Puerto Rico, and I interviewed professors who knew Julia's family. And through a crazy set of circumstances I found the spot where her house was. It was raining, and when we got to the top of the mountain, a rainbow came out. And I started crying. Even now, thinking about it, I cry. My husband looked at me and said, 'She's blessing us.'

I still didn't have it completely, but then I said, 'You know what? I'm going to write about her soul. Her soul struggling for life.' Because I understood that. When Miriam first commissioned me, I thought I was going to write about the little Julia, the twenty-year-old Julia, and the thirty-nine-year-old Julia. Candido goes, 'Remember that idea you had? The soul works.' I wrote it in two weeks. It just came out. I didn't sleep. I was, 'Okay, Julia, I have to sleep tonight. You have to let me sleep.' A professor whom I know in Puerto Rico told me, 'That's what happens when you work with Julia: her spirit is present in your life. That's her disorder, and you have to ride the wave.' On December 22, I brought the draft to Miriam.

I needed another two rewrites, but the play was where I wanted it to be. I grew so much as a writer. I was writing in the dark, and that had never happened to me before. Writing had always come easily to me. Here, I could not get a handle on what I wanted to say with the play, because it wasn't just about Julia, it was my interpretation of Julia. What did Carmen want to say with the play? I wanted to write about the triumph of her spirit. What did she go through as a writer? My God, it must have been impossible; that she lived to thirty-nine is a miracle. And that she had all this love inside of her, and hatred for the injustices of the world. She had such a clear understanding of what was going on in the world, that it was too painful for her. That kills you.

AG: HOW DID THE DIRECTOR STAGE THE RELATIONSHIP BETWEEN JULIA AND THE WOMAN, WHO IS IN EFFECT JULIA'S SOUL?

CR: As if they were two people who knew each other.

AG: TWO FRIENDS?

CR: Friends and enemies. I learned how to define their relationship, because I didn't ever want to say that the character of the Woman was Julia's soul. But in rehearsals and previews, nobody got it. So I started adding the word 'soul' to the script more and more. Now, the Soul is dealt with as though she is desperately trying to nurse Julia back to life, even though Julia is dead from the beginning of the play. The actresses touched. They didn't have the same movements. The actress who played the Soul was a good foot taller than the actress who played Julia. People said Julia was tall, so it worked well for the Soul to be that tall.

AG: THE CHARACTER OF THE POET PABLO NERUDA TELLS HER THAT ANGER DOESN'T BELONG IN ART, THAT ART SHOULD COME FROM LOVE NOT HATE. SHE DISAGREES.

CR: Yes. I found an interview between Julia de Burgos and a boyfriend when she was living in the United States. The boyfriend hated Neruda and said politics should not be in art; Julia says everything belongs in art. In the interview, Julia talks about memorizing Neruda's love poems. For the play, I felt that Neruda had to teach her something. I had read that Neruda felt love was everywhere, so when I was thinking about how to construct a scene between the two, I decided to give them the discussion about love and anger. Also, somebody told me that Julia was a very angry person. Combining love and anger — that's an argument I have with my husband.

There are people who deny that she met Neruda. But I read an interview with a Dominican writer named Juan Bosch, who is now in his nineties, and he claims they met at his house.

AG: THE POEMS BY JULIA THAT YOU INCLUDE IN YOUR PLAY ARE ANGRY.

CR: Some are angry. Neruda tries to tell her that she has to experience anger, transform it, and release it. I tried to use that scene as a foreshadowing of what eventually happened to her.

AG: DO YOU THINK ANGER BELONGS IN ART?

CR: I think it has to be transformed. From what I've learned about trying to get a good night's sleep, if you don't release the anger, it will eat you up. I think everything belongs in art, but if Julia didn't transform it, it was going to eat her alive. Neruda tells her in the play, 'You have to release the anger. Once it's in the poem, it's gone. You can't hold on to it.' She disagrees. 'I'm going to hold onto it,' she says, and she becomes bitter and throws her soul away.

AG: YOUR PLAYS HAVE BEEN PRODUCED PRIMARILY AT PUERTO RICAN TRAVELING THEATER, REPERTORIO ESPAÑOL, INTAR, AND YOUR OWN THEATER. DO YOU WANT YOUR PLAYS PRODUCED AT SO-CALLED MAINSTREAM THEATERS?

CR: I want them to be done anywhere they can be done. I send my plays everywhere. But the mainstream theaters allocate limited time for Latino work or 'other' work, whether it's black, gay, women, whatever.

I've been very fortunate that these theaters have been interested in me. All three artistic directors — Miriam Colon, René Buch, and Max Ferra — said, 'We want your vision onstage.' They did not interfere. They totally gave me love and support. That's so rare. And I'm young; I'm thirty-five. I'm just beginning my career.

I believe that having an agent has a lot to do with dealing with mainstream theaters. With Latino theaters, because the budgets are so small, I can call Miriam and find her; the secretary will put me through. With René Buch I can stop by, drop a play off. They work the way theaters work in Latin America.

AG: DO YOU MAKE YOUR LIVING AS A PLAYWRIGHT?

CR: I would say forty percent of my money comes from playwriting. Most of my money comes from teaching playwriting in schools, as a teaching artist. I have great teaching gigs. I work with several youth theaters where we guide students in writing their own plays. I have a summer gig at the Lower East Side Tenement Museum, in conjunction with City Lights Youth Theatre, where the kids write a play about immigrants. In 1999, we wrote a play about the Draft Riot of 1863. We had a black student play Lincoln, and the students studied slavery and the freed slaves coming up to New York. We worked with the students to formulate this play. I love to do projects like that.

AG: WHY?

CR: Because I love politics and I feel that the young voice wants to talk about oppression and injustice. Everybody says young people are shooting people up or doing drugs, but they're not all like that. They have a legitimate voice and they want to know what's going on in the world.

AG: HOW DID THEY FEEL ABOUT MAKING A PLAY?

CR: They loved it. I came in with the structure, because we had only four weeks to write the play and put it on. We couldn't just muse. The Draft Riot happened in four days, so we divided the story into day one, day two, day three, day four. Lincoln's speech about 'Right makes might' at Cooper Union happened three years before the riot, but we put it in. We combined a story of a German immigrant who disappears. We made Lincoln's speech and the immigrant's disappearance frame the riot, which we recreated, and one student decided he wanted a newsboy to be the narrator, so we had a narrator. I wrote up information for the students so they could think of ideas for scenes, and I divided everybody up: 'Your scene is going to be the husband and wife, you're leaving for work, your scene is . . . ' They also came up with their own scenes. For one week, we were like a little factory. They would give me their material, and we would read it as a group, and I tried to teach them to critique constructively. 'First, what did you like about the scene? How does it fit into the play? We never say, "I have a problem with . . . " I don't want to even hear that.' They were great. Regardless of what happens in my writing career, I will do that forever.

AG: YOU SAID THAT EVENTUALLY A DRAFT OF *JULIA DE BURGOS* POURED OUT OF YOU. USUALLY, HOW DO YOU KNOW WHEN YOU'RE READY TO SIT DOWN AND WRITE?

CR: When I start working on something, the first couple of days will be hard. I can only work for an hour or two, then I get tired and can't think. Once I get the groove, I'm okay. But if I have a problem, I won't write the play itself, I'll write a character breakdown. That's what I tried to do with Julia and the Soul, when I had problems with their relationship. I spent maybe two weeks writing the experience of the Soul's life. As a little girl, Julia ran away from home all the time. She cut school — she could never be contained. Her family didn't have money for school one semester, and she would sneak into school. She sneaked out of places, like out of the hospital. For me that was the Soul. So I wrote the Soul's character bio: 'I'm not going to stay in this place. Come on, Julia, let's go. What's the matter with you?' Not a real monologue, but like a diary entry.

AG: STREAM OF CONSCIOUSNESS?

CR: Right. For her. Then I would write a monologue for Julia's fear: 'Oh, my God, Mami's going to be so mad at us. I don't know why my Soul does this. She does this all the time to me.' That was a bit more problematic than the flashback scenes.

Lightning I always keep separate. Since it was a horror fantasy that I had in me for so long, I didn't have problems writing. For *La Gringa*, I couldn't get the second act until I read Rollo May. When I read that one section in Rollo May, I wrote the whole play out beat by beat. There's a great book called *The Structure of Action* by Sam Smiley, which my husband and I read all the time. Smiley recommends that you write a scenario first and then the character breakdown, so that's how I wrote *La Gringa*. He says that the scenario is the foundation of the play and the dialogue is the paint. So I wrote out the whole play in scenario and then added the dialogue, and that helped me a lot. When I was fixing *Julia de Burgos*, I would write a list of beats. I'd change it as I went along, but I had a plan. It takes me a while. I try to do something every day, whether writing or reading for an hour on something that I'm interested in, like domestic abuse.

I don't know. I can't stop. My husband and I talk about that, because we both are obsessive-compulsives about writing. Maybe we're too obsessive. We don't know what other writers do. But it's right for us, and I love writing.

AG: SO WHOM DO YOU WRITE FOR?

CR: I am not sure. Writing makes me very happy but I also want the audience to take a trip with me. I guess I write for both of us. ▽

Diana Son

Diana Son was born in Philadelphia, where her parents met in a Korean carpool. She grew up in Dover, Delaware, and at the age of nine she decided to become a writer. Later, as an undergraduate majoring in dramatic literature at New York University, Son began to write plays.

Son has written *Stealing Fire* (1992), a dramatization of the Greek legend surrounding Procne and her sister, Philomela; *2000 Miles* (1993), a one-act involving two friends trying to reconnect after the mother of one has a stroke; *R.A.W. ('Cause I'm a Woman)*, a one-act in which four women address sexual stereotypes (1993); and *BOY* (1996), which focuses on a girl who has been raised to believe she is a boy. *Fishes* (1998), involves an imaginative young girl's relationship with her mother, after the mother turns into a fish, and *Stop Kiss* (1998) dramatizes the unexpected attraction between two women, and the violent event that transforms their lives. The play received the 1999 Media Award from GLAAD (Gay and Lesbian Alliance Against Defamation) for Outstanding New York Theater Production On or Off Broadway.

Son is a member of New Dramatists and the Dramatists Guild. She is 2000–2001 NEA/TCG Playwright-in-Residence at the Mark Taper Forum.

This interview took place on September 4, 1999, in New York City.

• • •

404

AG: WHAT IS DOVER LIKE?

DS: Dover is a small town. Officially, it's the capital of Delaware, but Wilmington is better known and more urban. Dover is in what upstaters call 'slower Delaware.' The center of town has that colonial look, around that are sub-developments, and beyond those are farms. It's the kind of town where the Rustler is next to the Sizzler is next to the Ponderosa is next to the Bob Evans.

AG: WAS THERE A KOREAN COMMUNITY IN DOVER?

DS: No. I didn't know what a 'community' was until I came to New York. New York introduced me to the idea that there's tension between Koreans and blacks and that, in some people's minds, those communities are polarized. Honestly, that's something I had to learn after I came to New York, because where I grew up, that was not so. I lived in a neighborhood that was equally black and white, and race didn't matter to us as much as whose house had a Ping-Pong table.

AG: DO YOU CONSIDER YOURSELF AMERICAN OR KOREAN-AMERICAN?

DS: In my mind, I'm classic American. My parents were immigrants. I was born here. I was raised in a small American town.

AG: DID YOUR PARENTS SPEAK KOREAN AT HOME?

DS: They did to each other sometimes. Now they really don't, because my mother had a stroke fifteen years ago and has aphasia as a result, so she has a problem with language, period. After the stroke, she only wanted to relearn English. But even when I was growing up, the only time my parents spoke Korean to each other was when they were talking about my brother or me in front of us.

AG: WHAT WAS YOUR PARENTS' ATTITUDE TOWARD WOMEN WHILE YOU WERE GROWING UP?

DS: My mom is a feminine woman, but she was also a business owner; she and my father owned a drugstore in an even smaller, more rural town than Dover — Milford, Delaware. It was a mom-and-pop drug-store. So my mother was a boss. She was not the type of woman to stay at home and read ladies' magazines or fashion magazines. I feel grateful that I was not exposed to fashion magazines as a kid, because I realize now, although I'm not impervious to body image and fash-ion, that at the end of the day it's pretty low on the list. A lot of my peers talk about the pressure they feel to be thin or garner the atten-tion of men, even men they're not interested in. I'm married, but I know married women who still feel the need to be recognized in the street as attractive. I feel shattered out of my little bubble when that happens to me. I feel, 'What are we going to get out of this? You're walking down the street, I'm walking down the street, what is it going to mean to me that you think I'm attractive?'

I was a big tomboy, and by the time I was in high school, was really into the Clash, so I started dressing in army fatigues. Obviously the army fatigues caused my parents some pause, but I didn't feel that they thought, 'You should not do this because you are a girl, or you should look this other way because you're a girl.' They didn't apply those images to me. The only way I was really aware of my gender, growing up, was that I got less than my brother, Grant, who is older. But if you asked my parents, they'd categorically deny it.

AG: IN ONE SECTION OF *R.A.W.*, A WOMAN REMEMBERS HER ASIAN MOTHER WARNING HER NOT TO BRING HER WHITE-AMERICAN BOYFRIEND INTO THE HOUSE. 'IT STINKS, I'VE BEEN COOKING DADDY'S FOOD. IT SMELLS. IT SMELLS LIKE KIMCHEE.'

DS: That's completely autobiographical, that section right there. Absolutely true to life. My parents were very committed to being American. That was part of not teaching me how to speak Korean, not teaching me anything about Korea, not cultivating an apprecia-tion of the culture, or curiosity about it either. That line, 'Don't eat the kimchee. . . .You'll never have an American boyfriend,' that's straight from my life. The point being that they *wanted* me to have an American boyfriend, because we were American.

AG: DID YOU GROW UP WANTING TO KNOW MORE ABOUT YOUR KOREAN HERITAGE?

DS: As I've gotten older, I've gotten to the point where I've had to decide that either I'm going to have to learn a lot about Korea, really fast, and integrate it into my daily life, or I'm going to have to go forward. It's a choice about what to do with my time. Am I going to Korean class three times a week or am I going to a friend's play reading? And I've made the choice to keep going. It's the backbeat of everything I write.

AG: HAVE YOU EVER BEEN TO KOREA?

DS: I love going there. It's a fantastically beautiful country. I used to think it was *M.A.S.H.* — that's the only image I had. My parents didn't show me pictures — nothing. All they talked about was war. So I went there, and it was fall. Eighty percent of Korea is mountains, and the mountains are covered with trees, and in the fall the trees turn colors, so all around me were orange and red and green and brown. You've never seen anything like it in this country. The first moment I was there, I thought, 'I'm going to learn everything. I have to. I know nothing.' I was in my early twenties and I said, 'I want to spend a year. I want to learn Korean. I'll come back and incorporate Koreanness into my life.' But it doesn't come true. I mean, am I going to be an ESL teacher or am I going to be a playwright? The generation of playwrights who want to create some relationship with their history has well-represented that experience in the canon of American dramatic literature.

AG: ARE YOU THINKING OF ANYONE IN PARTICULAR?

DS: David Henry Hwang and Philip Kan Gotanda have written about this beautifully. So it's only natural that I then commit to representing my experience, which is to be caught irrevocably in the middle. I'm not going to tell back-to-my-grandmother's-village stories. You're not going to hear gongs, you're not going to hear about East vs. West culture clash in my plays. You're not going to see fights about white boyfriends. You're not going to hear a parental figure say, 'I walked twenty miles through the snow in order to get to school, and you have five pairs of Nikes.' Those aren't my stories. My stories start where my generation is now, where the history is a part of our lives in a way that we don't expect. Where the history is unconscious but identifiable. With the exception of *R.A.W.*, I haven't written about Asian-

American people. But it's clear that I come from the perspective of 'other.' I write from the perspective of 'other.' I write about themes that can be traced to being Korean American. There's even a certain aesthetic that I would say is flavored by being Korean American.

AG: CAN YOU BE MORE SPECIFIC?

DS: My writing is pared down. I chase the aesthetic of being efficient. I will read somebody else's work and think, 'I enjoyed the language here, but I understand the meaning in one of these sentences, and there are five.' Sifting out the chaff. It's my parents' aesthetic.

AG: IT'S INTERESTING THAT YOU SAY YOU WRITE FROM THE PERSPECTIVE OF 'OTHER.' YOUR PLAYS OFTEN DEAL WITH WOMEN AS 'OTHER.' BOY IS AN OUTSIDER TO HER FAMILY AND HER COMMUNITY. CALLIE AND SARA IN *STOP KISS* ARE VIEWED AS 'OTHER,' ESPECIALLY BY THE HOMOPHOBIC MAN WHO BEATS SARA UP ONE NIGHT IN GREENWICH VILLAGE. 'OTHER' IN YOUR PLAYS SEEMS SITUATED IN GENDER AND SEXUALITY, NOT IN RACE.

DS: A lot of that is unconscious for me. I would say in *BOY* and *Stop Kiss* and an earlier play, *Stealing Fire*, that basically everybody in the world is crazy except the two people who love each other. It's about that rather than women.

AG: IN YOUR INTRODUCTION TO THE PUBLISHED VERSION OF *R.A.W.*, IN *CONTEMPORARY PLAYS BY WOMEN OF COLOR*, YOU WRITE ABOUT SEEING ANNE BOGART'S UNCONVENTIONAL PRODUCTION OF *SOUTH PACIFIC* WHEN YOU WERE AN UNDERGRADUATE. SHE HAD STAGED THE MUSICAL AS A PRODUCTION BEING PERFORMED BY PATIENTS IN A VIETNAM VETERANS HOSPITAL. DID YOU STUDY WITH HER?

DS: About nine years later, around 1992, between her time at N.Y.U. and when she started the SITI Company. She was teaching classes at Playwrights Horizons, and we had her for four or five months, once a week for four hours.

AG: WHAT DID YOU ABSORB FROM THE CLASS?

DS: Oh, so much. The most important thing was an appetite for making theater. The class met once a week, but we would spend the rest of the time thinking, rehearsing, collecting props. I probably did something every day in preparation for that class. It whetted my appetite for that kind of engagement.

AG: SHE GAVE YOU PROJECTS TO WORK ON?

DS: She would say, 'Who wants to direct?' People would raise their hands, and she'd pick six. Then she'd say, 'Okay, the rest of you are actors: you go with this director, you go with that director. Okay, here's the story: boy meets girl, boy loses girl, boy gets girl back again. In this piece you should have twenty minutes of repetitive motion. You should have an unexpected source of music. You should have a lover, a scream, a passionate kiss, somebody running across the street, and a book. You have half an hour: go.' We'd run across the street to the parking lot, and in half an hour everybody would help create the piece. 'What if I have just seen a robbery and I'm really shaken up, and I'm walking down the street, and this guy passes me. He's just a normal guy, but I'm really scared . . . ' Then each group would present their piece. It was instant theater. And no joke, some of the best theater I've ever seen was created in that class.

AG: DID YOU WORK WITH HER BEFORE YOU WROTE *R.A.W.*?

DS: Yes.

AG: THE STYLE OF *R.A.W.* IS DIFFERENT FROM ANY OF YOUR OTHER WORK THAT I'VE READ OR SEEN. IT'S AN ANTI-REALISTIC ENSEMBLE PIECE; THE MEN'S STEREOTYPING SEXUAL COMMENTS APPEAR ON SLIDES, WHICH THE FOUR RAUNCHY ASIAN WOMEN RESPOND TO. WHAT FED THAT STYLE?

DS: Style is an allusive . . . cloud for me. I have different goals with every piece I write, and the style has to follow that. *R.A.W.* is the first piece in which I wanted to write things that were meat, all meat. The other thing about *R.A.W.* is that I wrote it in an Asian-American play-wrights group which was meeting at the Public Theater. My first time sitting around a table with people who were Asian American who were also playwrights. There was this weird negotiating, like, 'I'm different from you, even though a non-Asian would walk in this room and think we're all the same.' We had to write about culture, and I thought, 'How am I going to do this in a fresh way? In a way that's entertaining to me?' I felt stuck. And then something happened to me on the street — probably the typical, 'Hey, China doll,' or any of the myriad things that can be said to you walking down the street, but Asian-specific. I remember: I was walking down my street early in the morning, and there was a big, burly guy with a woman and another guy. There was a sneaker on the side of the street, and he was talking to his buddies and he just turned and said to me, 'Hey, is that your sneaker, Chingaling?'

First of all, I'm just coming out of my house, so I'm getting my Walkman headphones, I'm thinking about which train to take, and I was caught unaware. I stopped and thought, 'Hey, buddy, I'm a . . .' At the time I was still training — I'm a red belt in tae kwon do. And I thought, 'I could really hurt him, and he has no expectation of that. He has no expectation that I might respond in a way that is confrontational. He would never say this to somebody whom he thought might respond.'

In the workshop at the Public, I was thinking about that incident and about the times when I'm at my bank or whatever, and somebody will say something like that. Being a writer, I craft my response: 'This is what I should have said, this is what I want to say.' I thought, 'Why do I never respond?' It's fear of physical harm, but also the feeling that I'm not supposed to. I wrote *R.A.W.* in answer to the people who say stuff to me on the street.

AG: IT'S A VERY ANGRY PLAY.

DS: I remember showing it to my best friend, who is white, and she said, 'This is so angry. This is really funny, but it's so angry.' And I was shocked, because I found it delightful to write. I was laughing. I thought it was hilarious. She said, 'Where do you get this stuff?' And I said, 'What do you mean, where do I get this stuff? People say this to me all the time.' I realized that I don't tell her about this because it's embarrassing to me. Also, it only happens when I'm alone. It never happens when I'm with my husband. He never witnesses it. None of my friends witness it, unless they're Asian American. Then it's a two-for-one deal.

The whole scenario for *R.A.W.* came from this call and response thing. There's that one line, 'I've never been with an Oriental woman before.' People say things like that to you, and you go, 'What am I supposed to say?' And then you move to, 'This is what I want to say in anger' or, 'This is what I want to say out of a bigger spirit than that. This is how I can teach you.' You run the gamut. I wanted to catalogue those responses. It had to be a ten-minute piece, so I thought, 'Well, just make the piece all lines.' People were saying, 'Expand it.' But it is the heart; I don't need to construct a body around it. Just take this quivering muscle and that's it.

I hadn't found the story that felt authentic to me about being Korean American until recently. That is what my next play is about. Basically it comes from the line in *R.A.W.*, 'From a place where I was neither black nor white. Where I checked the box marked "other."' I've been thinking about how, when the discussion around me is about race, and in particular if it's catalyzed by a moment of conflict between blacks and whites, I am assumed into the white perspective. I'm made an honorary white. A group of people can be talking about the outspoken voices of the black community in a negative way — freely, without worrying if I might be offended. Then two sentences later, I can be looked at, the more conciliatory perspective starts coming out, and I get included. I am a chameleon to other people. I take on the color that they assign to me at the time.

AG: HOW DOES THAT MAKE YOU FEEL?

DS: It's an uncomfortable place to be in, because when I'm being assumed into a white perspective, I think, 'I'm not white. I don't want to be included in this.' On the other hand, I'm not black, so when the discussion is about white and black, I can't pretend to be black. I can't go over to the black camp and say, 'What happens to you, happens to me. Your history is my history.'

AG: GOING BACK TO BIOGRAPHY FOR A BIT. WHEN DID YOU WRITE YOUR FIRST PLAY?

AG: THE EX-PLAYS?

DS: Yes. Literally the first play I ever wrote and the couple of plays after that. I remember I did take one playwriting class . . .

AG: AT N.Y.U.?

DS: Yes. With Thomas Babe. And he told me that I wrote with this Chekhovian sense of detail. And I'm thinking, 'Chekhov? I want to be like Genet. I want to be Dürrenmatt. Peter Weiss.' I'm nineteen, twenty, and I don't want to be like Chekhov. Like it was an insult. I became quite deliberate, then, in style. I thought, 'Well, I don't write like any of the writers I admire. That seems like something I should rectify.' That's why *Stealing Fire* is a myth. I consciously went after that. I thought, 'Ooh, that will help me write in this more imaginary way.' After that, *BOY* became quite simple. It came out of my imagination, based on real-life things. My mom was one of six girls. Korea's not a Catholic country; why six children? Because they kept trying to have a son. Finally had to adopt a nephew. I was thinking about that one day when I was trying to write. I was mopping the floor and thought, 'What if they just named one of the daughters 'Boy'? Would that have worked?' I saw the real-life scenario, to keep having children, as quite fantastical.

I made a conscious effort to lead myself away from the style in which I most naturally write because I grew up on TV. When Ben Brantley wrote his review of *Stop Kiss* in *The New York Times* — and I really appreciated this — he never, ever identified me as Asian American, he identified me twice as American. And he wrote that, as an American, I probably grew up on a lot of TV. It's true — in the summertime, I watched six to eight hours of TV a day; the first dramatic script I wrote was to *The Love Boat*. You can track my journey away from and back to more recognizable worlds. Although *Fishes* is fantastical, it's less cartoonish than *BOY*. By the time I wrote *Stop Kiss*, I thought that there must be a way to bridge my naturalistic storytelling instincts with the more theatrical conventions that I learned.

AG: WHERE DOES *2,000 MILES* COME?

DS: Actually *Stealing Fire* brackets *2,000 Miles* and *R.A.W.*, because it took me six years to write. The thing that you talked about — that although *BOY* has this broad exterior, there's actually quite a detailed, emotionally naturalistic narrative going on — that became apparent to me as we were auditioning actors. Some of them would come in, and I would wonder, 'Do you think this is a children's play?' Other people would be so naturalistic, I would wonder, 'Do they think this is a TV show?' Michael Greif, who's a wonderful director, would respond to the actors who could embody a large spirit but be emotionally honest. When we put the play up, I realized that was the challenge of *BOY*, to reconcile those two narratives.

AG: HOW DID THE ACTRESS PLAY BOY? DID SHE TRY TO BE MASCULINE EXTERNALLY?

DS: The actress had to learn how to throw a football and a Frisbee, and we cut her hair and dressed her in boy's clothes. That helped the character be more androgynous than feminine. But the most important thing about Boy is that she's dead serious. About building houses, about all the things that are important to her.

AG: WITH *STOP KISS*, THEN, YOU HAVE RETURNED TO WHAT YOU DESCRIBE AS THE NATURALISTIC STYLE WHERE YOU BEGAN.

DS: Yes, but having accrued valuable instincts about theatricality. The language of *Stop Kiss* is naturalistic, the story is naturalistic, but still the play is theatrical. For example, the juxtaposition of the scenes. The way the emotionality changes so quickly is specific to the theater. Some of the reviews said that the juxtapositions were the quick cuts you expect in a film. And I thought, 'In a film, there's nothing remarkable about that. What is specific to the theater is that you're going to watch an actress wipe her face and go from being shattered to being giddy and drunk.'

The wheelchair scene is only brought to fruition in performance. You can only approximate what is happening in that scene by reading it on the page. This is a play and not a would-be movie because it's brought to potent fruition in the theater. The maximum emotional engagement is achieved by being physically close to the performers.

I remember rehearsing that wheelchair scene. It's a page and a half in the script and it takes seven minutes to perform, because Callie dresses Sara in real time, which is difficult. Sara can't get her arm through the sleeves, and Jessica Hecht and Sandra Oh made those heartbreaking, involuntary sounds and gestures that would fill the silence, because the silence was excruciating. Jessica would fill in the wheelchair scene, with this, 'Okay, okay, okay' and 'Oh, oh, oh, oh,' when something was not going right, and it was devastating. I would stand at the side of the house and watch people. They would lean forward, silent, water covering their faces. I would think, 'This is happening between the actors and the audience.' I felt like I had the least to do with that scene of anybody. And that can only happen in the theater.

The play facilitated Jessica's choice as an actress to include the audience in the story. She made eye contact — not one-on-one, but if she needed to get from one place to another, she would sweep her vision across the house. We never talked about this, but I loved that, because for me a virtue of theater is that the play needs the audience.

AG: WHAT INSPIRED *STOP KISS*?

DS: At different times I have had different answers. Consistent with my other work, it has to do with the difference between the unconscious understanding you have of yourself, and the collision with the moment when you become conscious of how other people see you. I can go hours before thinking about what my Korean identity has to do with grocery shopping or going to the K-Mart. It's only when somebody says, 'Hey, Chinita,' that I go, 'Oh, I guess I'm a Chinese person.' Then I get into, 'But I'm not Chinese,' and then, 'I'm not any of the things that you must think I am by saying that.'

That collision is in all my works. In *BOY*, the collision is, 'You're not a boy, you're a girl.' I wanted to find the most potent moment. Dürrenmatt writes about the worst possible turn of events — that has to be how drama is created, when something happens that is the worst thing that could happen at this moment. When you think of Callie's hesitation to express her attraction to Sara, and she finally does — and it's a simple kiss — the worst thing that could happen at that moment is that somebody decides he has to punish them for their audacity. That's the worst thing that could happen to such a tender, vulnerable moment. The victory is taken away. But in the course of the play, it also catalyzes Callie to be a more courageous, committed person than she thought she could be. In the end, love wins.

AG: WHERE DO PLAYS USUALLY BEGIN IN YOU? AS AN IMAGE, A CHARACTER? DOES IT DIFFER FROM PLAY TO PLAY?

DS: To have an image is to know who the people in the image are. I'm sure I saw the kiss, and I knew that in order for this to be a monumental moment — for this kiss, this image, to be at all interesting — there had to be a story that you cannot see. For one of the characters, this has to be an immense act of courage. An uncharacteristic act of courage. So I knew that about Callie first. Sara came later. In fact, a lot of my early drafts were about distinguishing the two of them.

AG: TALKING ABOUT THE PLAY REMINDS ME OF WHAT YOU SAID EARLIER ABOUT ANNE BOGART'S APPROACH, WHICH IS TO LOOK FOR SOMETHING COMING OUT OF THE UNEXPECTED.

DS: I don't write thrillers. I don't write suspensefully. But I still want people to be perched forward in their seats. How do you achieve that? You surprise them, and you also give them a role. You ask them to do something that the play is not doing for them. You juxtapose time periods, so that they have to go, 'Wait a second, Sara's in this scene, but Callie talks about Sara getting beaten up in the scene that just came; is this in the future?' Then there's the next scene, and the audience goes, 'I think it's in the past.' You leave them the opportunity to do the thinking that the play doesn't do for them. A play is not about chronicling the playwright's thought process. It's about providing a narrative that allows the audience to create their own narrative experience of the story.

AG: HOW DID YOU LEARN WHAT YOUR PROCESS AS A PLAYWRIGHT IS?

DS: I still am. Every time I start to write something, I look at the blank page and think, 'Did I ever write anything before?' Then I pull a play off the shelf, and go, 'Okay, there's writing on all these pages, and there's like a hundred pages here. How do I do it?' But then I think,

'I did it, I did it, I did it before. That means I know how to do it.' But every time it's starting from scratch. Every time.

My process. It took me six years to write *Stealing Fire*, and *R.A.W.* took a long time, too. *2,000 Miles* and *R.A.W.* — those were short, under ten pages — yet each took me maybe six months. I thought I was the kind of writer that, if I wrote half a page in a day, I'd take myself out for sushi. That was a great day. Then I wrote *BOY* during my one-semester stint at the Iowa Playwrights Workshop. I was so busy working on *R.A.W.*, because it was in rehearsal in New York, that I had written nothing new in Iowa. It was Thursday, I had a reading scheduled on Monday, and I had nothing? I had some idea of what I wanted to do in *BOY;* a friend of mine had been helpful in terms of talking it out with me. So I had enough knowledge of what the narrative was, that I sat down, and on the first day, Friday, I wrote seven pages. And I thought, 'Oh, my God. Seven pages in a day?' I had summited Mount Everest. But I knew I couldn't go in with seven pages. So the next day I wrote thirteen pages and the day after, about eighteen. By Monday I actually had Act One. That shattered my reliance on my identity as a slow writer.

But when I came back to New York and was back to temping and waitressing and writing, it took me another eight months to write Act Two. Act One in three days; Act Two in eight months. When the Public commissioned me to write a new play, I thought *Fishes* was formed enough in my mind, and I told them to give me three months, because obviously I respond to impending deadlines. Sure enough, I started it about ten days before it was due, because I also had a day job at the time, and I wrote something fast, and we did a reading.

When I got the commission from Playwrights Horizons, for what turned out to be *Stop Kiss*, I asked for a year and actually wrote the first draft in six weeks, and I wanted to keep the momentum going, so I wrote a new draft every week. By the third draft I was meeting with Jo Bonney, the director, and she stopped that manic process. Jo can go beat by beat dramaturgically. And what she did for me, which was new, was to say, 'Here's the genesis of the thought, and here's how the dialogue and the characters are tracking it. And here is where you splinter into three directions. You're talking about identity, then you're talking about New York City, then here you're talking about these characters. You've got one beat representing this, another beat representing that, and it's a fray at the end. Do you know which one of these you're actually pursuing?' And I'd say, 'Yeah. I want it to be about this.' And she'd say, 'Okay. This is the beat. This line right here is where you start to follow that thought, and this next beat is where you go somewhere else.' More than anybody she encouraged me to commit to one intention for a scene and follow it. Then other things could become attendant to that intention.

AG: THAT SOUNDS LIKE A VERY VALUABLE THING TO LEARN.

DS: Jo has helped me be a better writer. I can't unlearn the kind of thoroughness that she facilitated in me.

AG: IS THE NEW PLAY ALSO IN A REALISTIC MODE?

DS: I'm in that murky phase in my brain, because I haven't identified what makes the play purely theatrical, as I was able to do with *Stop Kiss*. The structure of *Stop Kiss* came to me immediately. The first scene I wrote was the scene where Callie and Sara first meet and get to know each other. No. Actually, the first scene I wrote was the scene where the Detective interrogates her. Until the second preview, and through every draft, the Detective scene was the first scene. It was only after the second preview that we changed the order.

AG: THE SCENE WHERE CALLIE IS UPSET AND TELLS THE DETECTIVE THAT SHE AND SARA WERE ATTACKED — THAT ORIGINALLY WAS FIRST?

DS: That's the first scene I wrote, because I thought that, if I want this relationship to be interesting — if I want the simple getting-to-know-you scene to be worth somebody's attention — we have to know that something has gone wrong. Then we can look at that getting-to-know-you scene and go, 'Where are the clues?' But I discovered in previews that the Detective scene was so alienating to people that it distanced them. They felt, 'Oh, something bad happened, this woman got beat up, she's very vulnerable,' and in the next scene, when I wanted the audience to laugh with Callie, they wouldn't go there. They felt she was too tender. They felt protective of her. People had to talk me into this, but I realized that the getting-to-know-you scene is compelling, even though it is the longest of the play. I was anxious that, with the getting-to-know-you scene first, the play would seem like some sit-comy, naturalistic play about New York. But the scene is watchable enough so that, when you cut to the Detective scene, the audience goes, 'Oh. Wait a second.' By the time we were into the run, I took guilty pleasure in watching people ride that opening scene like a comfortable car and then basically get sideswiped by Scene Two. I'd hear laughing, laughing, laughing, then I'd watch them get silent in the second scene.

But comedy juxtaposed with poignancy is consistent with my other plays. That made my previous work difficult for people, and *Stop Kiss* was a way to sort of train audiences, so that I can eventually integrate the two experiences. It was an attempt to help people to the kind of emotional experience that I like to write.

AG: WE TOUCHED ON THIS BRIEFLY BEFORE, BUT THERE ARE RELATIONSHIPS BETWEEN TWO WOMEN IN SEVERAL OF YOUR PLAYS. IN *STEALING FIRE,* YOU WRITE THE RELATIONSHIP BETWEEN THE TWO SISTERS, PROCNE AND PHILOMELA. IN *2,000 MILES* THERE'S A BOND BETWEEN THOSE TWO WOMEN WHO WERE CHILDHOOD FRIENDS. IN *BOY,* THE RELATIONSHIP BETWEEN BOY AND CHARLOTTE IS INTIMATE EMOTIONALLY, PERHAPS PHYSICALLY. AND THERE'S *STOP KISS.* RELATIONSHIPS BETWEEN WOMEN SEEM TO BE A THEME.

DS: I have not yet found the fresh way to portray a male-female romantic relationship.

AG: DO YOU WANT TO PORTRAY A MALE-FEMALE ROMANTIC RELATIONSHIP?

DS: I can't say I don't want to, but until I find the original, under-represented way of portraying it, I'm not going to. Nothing could feel less theatrical to me than writing a classic boy-meets-girl story. I also feel happy and proud to write plays in which women have the lead roles. The more I talk to actresses, I realize that there are few plays in which the lead characters are female and their interactions are with each other and not their boyfriends.

I have to confess that I understand the way women relate to other women better than the way women relate to men. I can portray it more complexly. My husband said a couple years ago that my portrayals of men are accurate, but not flattering. I'm learning how to portray men more complexly, and they will probably become more prominent in my work as I become better able to do that. George, Callie's friend in *Stop Kiss*, is a complex character, but it's a small role. Same with Peter, Sara's former boyfriend. I have a lot of compassion for both characters, but I couldn't keep them on the stage for a long time without feeling as though I had run out of interesting ways to use them.

AG: DID YOU TALK WITH JO BONNEY ABOUT CASTING GEORGE AS AFRICAN AMERICAN AND SARA AS ASIAN AMERICAN? WAS THAT YOUR IDEA?

DS: Yes. The first thing I talk about with a director is that the cast has to be racially mixed. That is one of the reasons why I'm attracted to writing fantastically. In *BOY*, you can cast an Asian-American actor as Boy and a Caucasian actor as her father and an African-American actress as her mother. That is a specific interest and an aesthetic of mine, putting different races on the same stage and saying, 'This is the world.'

AG: IN ANOTHER PRODUCTION OF *STOP KISS* . . .

DS: Anybody could be anything. At the Public, we didn't want to cast George as Asian American, because then we would have had a different story from the one we were trying to tell. Now that the play is out of my hands and being produced in regional theaters, I can only hope that they will make an attempt to cast actors of color. Ultimately, casting actors of color and getting the best actor for the role coincide. But you have to work harder for it. You have to do one more hour of auditions, make a few more phone calls, just to get the people in the room. But you can always find an actor of color who's going to be the best actor for that role.

AG: WHAT IS *STOP KISS* FINALLY ABOUT FOR YOU?

DS: It's about Callie doing something that she never thought she could. She begins the play as a paralyzingly self-conscious person, but by the end, she makes a commitment to Sara that requires a courage she doesn't have when we first meet her.

AG: IS SHE GAY?

DS: Because the play stops, we don't know what's going to happen, right? Is she a lesbian because she kissed a woman once? The last moment of the narrative is Callie saying, 'Make a commitment to me. Stay here. I will take care of you.' In the course of the play, Callie changes tremendously. But I stop where the play stops. The last words of the play are 'try again.' It's a beginning.

AG: WAS THERE ANY DISCUSSION AT N.Y.U. OR THE IOWA PLAYWRIGHTS WORKSHOP ABOUT HOW A PLAYWRIGHT MAKES A CAREER IN THE AMERICAN THEATER?

DS: Nope.

AG: WHAT HAVE YOU DISCOVERED SO FAR?

DS: That you can't. You always have to have a day job. I mean, Neil Simon and Wendy Wasserstein write screenplays. Probably the luckiest thing that can happen to a playwright is that your day job is other writing. *Stop Kiss* did great, right? It's getting all these productions and publications . . .

AG: OPTIONED TO BE A SCREENPLAY?

DS: Yes. But I have not made a dime off of *Stop Kiss* or as a playwright since the show closed six months ago. For six months I have had no income from my playwriting career. I don't have a rich husband. I don't come from money. You realize why a lot of people in the theater come from rich families; you can't afford it otherwise. You have to be subsidized or take other kinds of work. The day the reviews for *Stop Kiss* came out — wonderful reviews, right? I should be celebrating — and what am I doing? I'm writing *Star Trek* trivia questions for the Sci Fi Channel website. I had gotten so behind because of rehearsal, I was late with them. But you know what? Writing for the theater is the greatest job in the world. I love my job.

AG: ONE OF THE QUESTIONS I'VE BEEN ASKING PLAY-WRIGHTS IS WHETHER BEING A WOMAN IN THE AMERICAN THEATER HAS HELPED, HINDERED, OR NOT FIGURED AT ALL IN YOUR CAREER.

DS: I have to say, I don't know. At the Public, the season that *Stop Kiss* was done, at least two other plays were by female playwrights: Lisa Kron and Ellen McLaughlin. It wasn't as though I was the one female. The slots were already filled. I can only hope that people choose a play of mine because they think it's a good play.

They say in the theater that the playwright is king. But that's not the role I want to play: 'Please me.' The playwright is the initiator of a collaborative process. You are the source — there is no play without you writing the next word, so there's that sense of pressure and responsibility and desperation. But once you have the play, and people want to produce it, then you're powerful. At that point, also, you have a choice about who you're going to be in the process. After *BOY*, I would request a certain director or request to interview directors. Put myself in the position where I choose the director. And I realize when I'm choosing a director that I am also choosing somebody to be in charge over me.

My most successful relationship was with Jo Bonney, because she came in on the script early and guided me. By the time it came to pre-production, without my asking, she involved me in every aspect. I sat in on design meetings. But I wanted to be helpful. It wasn't, 'Oh, I'll just be a presence here,' and it also wasn't, 'I'll tell these people what to do.' I couldn't begin to tell designers what to do. I don't know what my plays look like — that's something I need so much from a direc-tor and a design team. But I can be useful, because someone will have an idea for a design, and I can say, 'Well, that helps, because three scenes later she's going to need the chair.'

I always sit at the casting table, because I have very strong responses to actors and will argue, argue, argue. I know that I am at least fifty percent of the decision about who gets cast, and if a director and I really need to go head-to-head, I go head-to-head. I don't go, 'Oh, you're the director, you should have it.'

AG: DO YOU ATTEND REHEARSALS?

DS: Every day, eight hours a day. I even love tech. I'm happy to step out if a director says to me, 'You know, we're doing work this afternoon that the actors would feel most free doing without you there.' Happy to leave. Again, at that point, it's not that I'm king, it's actually that I have the most responsibility. If what the director needs is for me to leave the room, so the actors can make choices that are not right, but that they have to go through to get to the emotional place where I want them to be, I leave the room.

I would say that my writing takes the character of the collaboration between the director and myself. That's why I like to work with directors early on. I like for them to participate in the shaping of the piece. But I think there are specific things a playwright can do to maximize the chance that you and the director will have a great collaboration, and they have to do with understanding who you are in the process, what your power is. Sometimes being the most powerful means facilitating everybody else. My favorite part of the process is not when I'm locked in a room writing. That's the part I endure so that I can get into a room with people who are making theater. Writing a play is my way into the room. ♥

Paula
Vogel

Paula Vogel was born in Washington, D.C., and raised in suburban Maryland. She graduated from Catholic University and attended the Doctoral Program in theater arts at Cornell University. *How I Learned to Drive,* Vogel's tender, disturbing play about the sexual and loving relationship between a young girl and her uncle, won the 1998 Pulitzer Prize for Drama, making Vogel the tenth woman to receive that honor.

Vogel's other plays include *Desdemona: A Play About a Handkerchief* (1977, 1992, produced 1993), her view of the woman whom Shakespeare's tragic hero, Othello, marries and then murders out of jealousy; *The Oldest Profession* (1981, produced 1988), a comic but poignant look at a group of elderly women who practice the world's oldest profession in order to survive; *The Baltimore Waltz* (1990), a dream play about love and death in the time of AIDS; and *The Mineola Twins* (1997), which, with *How I Learned to Drive,* makes up what Vogel calls *The Mammary Plays. Hot 'n' Throbbing* (1999) explores the realm of pornography and raises the terrifying specter of spousal abuse.

From 1984 to 1998, Vogel headed the M.F.A. Playwriting Program at Brown University in Providence, Rhode Island. This interview took place at the Paramount Hotel in New York City, on June 22, 1999.

• • •

425

AG: WHAT DOES IT MEAN TO YOU, AT THE BEGINNING OF THIS CENTURY, TO BE A WOMAN WHO WRITES PLAYS IN AMERICA?

PV: I don't think I have a single goal when writing. But I do have a desire to see an American identity forged by as many writers of as many ethnicities, races, women, and in terms of sexuality, gays and lesbians, as possible. I do have a desire to see identity forged outside of the mainstream, outside of the status quo. So that's one of my desires and one of my goals. I'd like to see women looking at and defining male identity as women writers. I'd like to see women looking at female desire and sexuality.

My fear is that before we embrace this rainbow coalition of writers and viewpoints, we will have a backlash. As a theater and entertainment industry, I think we will have a last gasp of exclusion. I am hoping that the twenty-first century is not a male world anymore. I'm hoping it's not a white world anymore. I'm hoping it's an inclusive world. But I fear a circling-the-wagons mentality. This is happening right now on Broadway.

AG: A BACKLASH ARISING FROM WHAT?

PV: Fear and the politics of fear. Time and again, the political Right in this country turns us back. I have been noticing with some pain, in terms of Broadway and the industry in New York, that American playwrights are being excluded from the notion not only of what is popular entertainment, but the notion of what is high culture. At this point in time, that we still have an internalized self-hatred and esteem problem — a cultural inferiority complex — is very depressing. I think the majority of American playwrights, my colleagues, have been dismayed and depressed in the last seasons by the definitions of what is commercial and what will appeal to audiences. England is not my mother country. I don't recognize it as my mother tongue or my motherland. I would rather have a mother tongue and a motherland forged by people like José Rivera, Philip Kan Gotanda, Suzan-Lori Parks, and Nilo Cruz. There is a notion of American identity that is coming in an exciting way not only from regional theater but also from off Broadway and off-off Broadway. That is the twenty-first century. How long, however, there will be resistance to it, I don't know. In a number of ways in the last ten years, American playwrights have been told that they don't count. We've been told this politically, by Congress, and we've been told this by our own industry.

AG: WHAT IS THE BEST WAY FOR WOMEN WHO WRITE TO USE THE THEATER?

PV: Fearlessly. Absolutely fearlessly. Historically, women are at a point where we don't need to apologize. We don't need to pull our punches. As women, we do not need even to have as our priorities writing and thinking about women. We're now in a generation of directors like Tina Landau and Anne Bogart, whose aesthetics are not concentrated on female subjectivity, women, or drama. There's a whole spectrum now of aesthetics that women possess in the theater. Which is fabulous. So women need to be fearless about writing plays. Do I think that there's still a bias of perception? Yes, I do. However, I don't think women should be stopping because of it. The great women pathblazers, maybe they think about it privately, but they don't think about it when they sit down to the page. I detect a fearlessness in Maria Irene Fornes' every word.

AG: IN YOUR OPINION, THEN, WOMEN HAVE COME A LONG WAY IN AMERICAN THEATER SINCE THE 1970S, WHEN WE ADVOCATED FOR SUPPORTIVE IMAGES OF WOMEN ON STAGE.

PV: I still think we have to advocate. But in that respect there's a difference between the artistic persona — what the artist's voice is — and the private individual. As a private individual, it's important to embrace feminism, to proselytize, to advocate for other women artists. It's particularly important to mention younger women artists. It's not, 'Hooray, we've won.' We haven't. The statistics are still extremely bad. But historically there's enough groundwork behind us, that every time I sit down to write a woman character, I don't think I should be worrying, 'Does this make women look positive? Am I speaking for all of the women in the audience? All of the women in the theater?' I'm not. We've gotten beyond that point. And I don't mean to put that point of view down; those steps in the 1960s and 1970s were understandable and critical. But we've moved beyond that as the focus of the artist's voice.

AG: DO WE STILL NEED TO REMEMBER THAT PLACE FROM WHICH YOUR GENERATION OF PLAYWRIGHTS AND SUBSEQUENT GENERATIONS HAVE EMERGED? AND HOW DO WOMEN REMEMBER THAT HISTORY?

PV: It's crucial to remember our history. It's extremely important to know the women who have written plays in America. It's important to know about Aphra Behn. She's a huge role model, in the same way that women novelists shouldn't be sitting down without lighting candles to Virginia Woolf or Jane Austen. We need to think about the earth-shattering plays that were done in the sixties. I'd like to see an Encore Series for American plays. We've forgotten the amazing work done by people like Corinne Jacker and Julie Bovasso. I'd love to see a series of readings of those ground-breaking plays. As a teacher, I'm very aware of what falls off the edge, and not just in terms of women. *Journey of the Fifth Horse* is an American classic. Younger artists should know the plays of Ronald Ribman as well as the plays of Irene Fornes. We need to remember Susan Glaspell. It wasn't Eugene O'Neill who made the Provincetown Players; it was Glaspell, who was cleaning everybody's diapers, washing the dishes, and writing Pulitzer Prize–winning plays. Wouldn't it be wonderful to do rediscovery projects of playwrights from the twenties, thirties, and forties who have gotten lost?

AG: MEMORY SEEMS TO BE A PROBLEM IN AMERICAN THEATER, AND THE PAST IS A PROBLEM IN AMERICA GENERALLY. AMERICANS ARE ALWAYS TRYING TO FIND THE NEW.

PV: Not to remember the artists who went before is a mentality that derives from studio filmmaking and has become contagious. The notion that writers are for hire, that they are not an integral part of the process. Film creates a sense that we are in the present moment always and never age, never get older, whereas theater is about death and decay and the ephemeral. This country has a hard time with that. It has a hard time talking about aging or loss or grief. Film tends to be eternally young, and that's what we as a country have embraced as our national art form. Theater is a national art form in other countries, which have always said, 'The King is dead. Long live the King,' as a way of knowing that there has to be the dying of the old order but that you have to keep remembering the old order. The notion of memory in other cultures is much different. Theater for that reason is important, because theater allows us to process memory and grief and loss and dying and aging, in the way that Shakespeare did. It's the two hours' strutting on the stage and then no more.

At the root of this is the difficulty we're having in determining our notion of popular culture and highbrow culture, and where, as Americans, we place theater. We've never figured out how to produce theater. We've never figured out how to subsidize it. We've never figured out who the audience should be for it. It's the perpetual foundling child among the art forms. The sooner we include more artists and expand the definition of what theater should be, the stronger theater will be. One of the things that always astounds me is people saying, 'Oh, that's not a good play.' And I say, 'Wait a moment. It's not a good play if you have an Aristotelian definition. But if your definition of a play is anything that happens in front of an audience, it's a very exciting play.' If we insist that a play has to have a well made structure, where are you going to put Irene Fornes, where are you going to put Ellen McLaughlin?

AG: WHAT IS IN YOUR PLAYWRIGHT MEMORY?

PV. I started in high school with pretty much good, high school fare. Things like *The Skin of Our Teeth*, Edward Albee's *The Sand Box* and *The American Dream*, *Our Town*, of course. *The Sound of Music*. I saw a lot of musicals as a teenager in suburban Maryland, at the Shady Grove Music Fair. I got hooked on theater at about fifteen and went to the *Cambridge Guide to Literature*, looked up the Americans, and put myself on a reading course. I read everything O'Neill wrote. Just inhaled it. Then I read Tennessee Williams. All of Shakespeare. Before I went to college. Once in college, I was a history major for a short time before I transferred to Catholic University, and then it was fill-in-the-Greeks, fill-in-the-history plays, and fill in all the British. In the sixties, seventies, and eighties, I read the British — period. All of Oscar Wilde. All of George Bernard Shaw.

Finally grad school. The very wonderful mentors, Marvin Carlson and Bert States, gave me a reading list and said, 'This is it.' It was an extraordinary three years of reading twenty hours a day in the library. By that time, I knew I was going to be a playwright. I became steeped in Brecht, in Artaud. It turned me upside down, because I started reading this stuff at age twenty-two. Up until that point, I'd completely attached to Sigmund Romberg. *The Desert Song* — I had memorized it. Part of the influences were in one direction: the graduate training. The other part was my upbringing in this Jewish-Catholic household: all the songs of Judy Garland; every Broadway musical; and a gay brother, who, when I was seventeen, took me to see John Waters. The discovery of camp. I think I'd seen *The Bad Seed* twenty-five times. Another one of those texts which I've memorized. I developed pop-culture icons that I attached myself to, while trying to assimilate plays like Wedekind's *Spring Awakening*. But if you look at it, something like Jarry's *Ubu Roi* is really forged by a sensibility that would love *Female Trouble*, that would love *Desert Song*, and would love *The Bad Seed*.

One of the problems I had because of this dual sensibility, was that very early on I was told that I wasn't writing the way a woman should write. I actually had heard for a long time that I write like a gay man and that I'm not a gay man and how dare I write like a gay man. I don't know what that meant, but in the graduate reading I devoured Susan Sontag's *Against Interpretation* and tried to figure out, 'What is this camp aesthetic? Who can play this game and who cannot? Who can use comedy as a tool and who cannot? Is this gender-based, the use of comedy?'

AG: AND DID YOU COME TO A CONCLUSION?

PV: Yes. I think comedy is very hard for women to do. Comedy traditionally is a critique of society, and we still have problems accepting critiques from prodigal daughters, as I call them. It's fine to be a prodigal son in that tradition — Molière, Christopher Durang, Nicky Silver. But we have difficulty fitting what we think should be a woman's sensibility with the notion of comedy and the social critique. One of the reasons for the dominance of women in performance art is that a woman is the sole creator of the work, her body is the stage, and we look at her story psychoanalytically. The woman who writes comedies is really commenting on society, commenting on something outside of herself.

AG: COMEDY IS THE AGGRESSIVE, ANGRY GENRE.

PV: So are we comfortable with women being funny and women being angry?

AG: WHEN YOU SAY 'WE,' DO YOU MEAN AMERICAN CULTURE?

PV: Yes. The culture. Another reason that I think women and lesbians and women of color rush into performance art is that there's control of identity. You don't have directors and actors saying, 'This is what I think a woman of color feels, or this is what I think a lesbian feels. . . ' You're it.

AG: YOUR WORK IS OFTEN PLAYFUL AND SATIRIC.

PV: I feel that I'm comic. But I feel that's not at a high premium. I feel there's a decorum for women artists, the same way there's a decorum for female characters. Female characters in drama are still judged according to the notions of decorum: this is what a good mother would do; this is what a good daughter should do; this is what a good wife should do. That's still part and parcel of how we receive plays. Whereas male characters have an individuality that has nothing to do with decorum, or they've wrested themselves out of that. I frequently make a Gertrude/Ophelia versus Hamlet analogy: an actor playing even the smallest male character in a play trails clouds of Hamlet when he steps onstage. He's trailing clouds of individuality. A notion of male subjectivity. When women walk onstage, at best they're trailing clouds of Hedda Gabler. It's a dramatic legacy, but it's really talking about women characters through the notion of how they perform inside the family in the domestic functions of daughters, wives, and mothers.

AG: WHAT DO YOU MEAN?

PV: Everybody comes to a play and looks at 'by' and then has preconceptions about what kind of drama that should or should not be. 'Is it okay for this to be said onstage? Who's the writer? What gender is the writer?' And whether it's okay or not, our comfort level is constantly there. 'Oh, it's okay for this to be said, because it's by a woman writer.' Or, 'It's not okay for this to be said, because it's by a woman writer.' Or, 'You know what? There are too many penis jokes in this play. I'd take it from a man, but this is a woman writer. Too many penis jokes. Can't have that many penis jokes.' Doesn't matter whether or not women in real life make penis jokes; who's writing it? Gender is thought to have its own decorum.

AG: CAN THAT CHANGE?

PV: I don't think there's a quick fix. It goes back to being absolutely fearless. Letting the logic of the play's world dictate, not pulling any punches. I think it's going to take a long time of advocating for primacy of theatrical art, and of writers writing about other writers. A playwright has an understanding of another playwright that nothing else quite equals. It really is going to take discussion at a high level that we haven't had for some time in the American theater. For instance, when women dramatists are rocking the boat, we need to have a dialogue. Fights are great. Raging is great. The discussions over *Oleanna* — fabulous. The discussions over *Fires in the Mirror* were stunning. The discussions over *Angels in America* were amazing. All of those plays in some way or another break decorum.

AG: THERE IS ALSO POLITICALLY CORRECT DECORUM AS IMPLEMENTED BY THE POLITICALLY CORRECT POLICE. I FALL INTO THAT TRAP. WHEN I WENT TO SEE *DESDEMONA* AT CIRCLE REPERTORY THEATRE, I THOUGHT, 'WELL, PAULA VOGEL IS DECONSTRUCTING SHAKESPEARE. BUT THEN WHERE IS SHE GOING WITH THAT?' YOU SEEMED TO BE TEARING DOWN LITERARY IMAGES, MADONNA IMAGES, SHAKESPEARE'S PRECONCEPTIONS OF WOMEN. BUT I COULDN'T UNDERSTAND WHAT YOU WERE SHOWING IN THEIR PLACE, BECAUSE OF THE PRECONCEPTIONS — THE NOTIONS OF POLITICALLY CORRECT DECORUM — I BROUGHT WITH ME. I WANTED YOU TO SHOW ME A FEMALE UTOPIA, AND YOU WERE NOT ABOUT TO DO THAT. *DES-DEMONA* IS NOT DOING THAT.

PV: No, it's not doing that. We have to toss into this discussion a little bit of 'negative empathy' — a term, I think, from the end of the nineteenth century — to describe what happens when we're watching a play and we resist identifying with the protagonist. When we're scared to identify, when a protagonist shows a side of ourselves that we don't want to acknowledge, when we're repulsed — that phenomenon is known as 'negative empathy.' Almost all of *Othello* is negative empathy. Most of the Greeks and a lot of Shakespeare evoke negative empathy. You don't want to identify with Oedipus and you don't want to identify with Medea or Hedda Gabler. But you understand them. You don't want to identify with Iago or Othello.

The interesting thing is that I was watching myself, as a woman, identifying and weeping over Othello being cuckolded. But I wasn't identifying with Desdemona getting killed. And I thought, 'Isn't that astonishing? I am weeping for this man who believes he has been cuckolded and I'm a woman.' In terms of mechanism, it seems to me that the theater — particularly classical theater — has a mechanism of negative empathy. And one of the things that's been happening in American drama is that we have been resisting negative empathy more and more. We're sentimental right now. We don't want to go there. I think this happens in different times in different cultures.

When I was writing *Desdemona*, I sat down and thought, 'What, in terms of women's behavior toward each other, causes resistance in me? Would it be promiscuity as a game? Would it be a use of the body? Someone who takes no responsibility for her action, who absolutely falls into the virgin-whore category without thought? A situation where there'd be no acknowledging one's own agency? What would Desdemona be like if I were to create the equivalent of Othello or Iago?'

So I put that into *Desdemona*. There's a line that must have struck me when I first read *Othello*. He says, 'I had been happy, if the general camp. . . had tasted her sweet body, So I had nothing known.' I thought, 'Well, what if she had slept with the entire camp? Did she still deserve to die? Would it still bother me? If I put onstage someone whom I would absolutely loathe, at some point in this evening, if there's a glimmer of recognition or connection with her, would I want to see the mechanism of *Othello* stopped?' That was my attempt. And that is where I perhaps failed, because I stacked the deck against myself. I think the play doesn't work, in that a lot of people don't say, 'Oh, God, don't go offstage,' knowing at the end of the play she's going to be strangled. I would like people to say that and to understand, if not identify, but I don't know how many people actually do. Maybe I'm the only one.

AG: MY EMPATHY CAME FROM YOUR SHOWING THAT MEN DO NOT KNOW WHAT WOMEN DO OUT OF THE SCENE, OFF-STAGE. THEY HAVEN'T A CLUE. THEY WRITE US (SHAKE-SPEARE), THEY MARRY US (IAGO AND OTHELLO) — BUT THEY HAVEN'T A CLUE. BUT PERHAPS THE RESISTANCE YOU SENSE COMES BECAUSE IT IS DIFFICULT TO TRAIN OURSELVES OUT OF CERTAIN NOTIONS OF FEMALE DECORUM.

PV: I think Shakespeare automatically gives us that notion of female decorum in all his plays.

AG: HE TRIES TO WORK AGAINST IT.

PV: Sometimes. Sometimes. But I think that just reifies it. Portia. *Taming of the Shrew*. Rosalind. I think it's always reified. What can you say? He was writing in the late 1500s. That's what the performance of femaleness was. But it's Shakespeare's concept of femaleness that we remember and is therefore useful, because he's the one playwright who gets done over and over.

I originally had thought of doing something with Ophelia, but I thought that Ophelia had two dimensions to her — she had the dimension of madness. The most one-dimensional, functional female character I could think of was Desdemona, which is why I chose her. But it's a problematic play.

Here's the other thing. I started that play in 1977, and I'm recognizing that as I get older, I get more empathic. Going back and rewriting *Desdemona* three times was very instructive. Now I'm at a point where I think, 'She's just so young. She's playing with this. She doesn't know the trouble she's putting herself into.' I've seen young women like that in my classes at Brown. Can I hate them? No. Do I want something bad to happen? No. Do I want them to wake up? Yes. My empathies change. Regardless that I'm a gay woman without children, my position now is of a mother. I'm now maternal. I find my own positionality changing, and I'm wrestling with that.

For me, and I think for a lot of writers, writing isn't some neat thing where you finish a play and go on. You go back and back and back. You put it aside, write something else, and return to it. It's a layered process. Desdemona was about sixteen years in the making.

AG: THE AMBIGUOUS CHARACTER IS HARD TO WRITE.

PV: In theater it is. In a similar way that women in the theater are becoming performance artists because of the notion of control and the notion of being freer to make a social critique, women have been novelists because it's the way that you develop a notion of female subjectivity through the interior, which you can't do onstage. The whole notion of thoughts and feelings and reflections and points of view comes through the narrative of a novel, not from the stage, where what we see is the surface. What we see is action, what we hear is dialogue. You can't develop that interior in the theater unless you use soliloquies, and theater hasn't used those in a while, although that's a useful technique. Obviously, direct audience address is another useful technique.

Women have gravitated historically to the novel for a number of reasons, and one is that we were supposed to stay in our houses and parlors. Women could write at their parlor desks and pretend to be writing letters. Writing a play is engaging in public speech. Aphra Behn was called a prostitute, because she was out in the public world. I don't think it's coincidental that she's the one who basically started the novel as a form. That we could write in the privacy of our homes and write about other women in the privacy of their homes, that we could create the interior space and the psychological interior — that's through the novel. In the theatrical form, getting the division of empathy, breaking through the notion of decorum, are tough. It's why I stick in theater, because at times the challenge feels almost impossible. I can't tell you how many conversations I've had with people who say, 'Can't we see Iago or Othello in Desdemona?' In The Oldest Profession, 'Can't we see the customers?' And I reply, 'That's kind of not the point.'

AG: BUT WE WILL SEE THE WOMEN'S CUSTOMERS IN THE MOVIE VERSION?

PV: In the movie, you will. It's great fun to have those customers. I'm enjoying writing that. But they absolutely don't belong in the play.

AG: LET'S TALK ABOUT BREASTS.

PV: I love this. [*TWO WOMEN AT THE PARAMOUNT*] 'Let's talk about breasts.'

AG: WHO OWNS THE BREAST?

PV: The individual woman owns the breast. But I don't think that's a cultural attitude. I grew up at a point in the sixties when the breast was absolutely the property of men. It was an accessory. It was constantly on display and remarked upon, and that was absolutely fine according to the times.

It seems to me we can go one of two ways in this culture: we can get to the point where the breast belongs to the woman, or we can get to a point where bodies of both sexes are public property. Either would be fine. They're up for grabs.

AG: IN *HOW I LEARNED TO DRIVE*, SHE DOES NOT OWN HER BREASTS.

PV: I agree. She does not own her breasts. They are disembodied. I'm very happy about the way that soliloquy came out, about the breasts having a life of their own, taking over the body and draining it of all nourishment. I spent a long time before sitting down to write, however, looking back at things like *Laugh-In*. Have you gone back and seen the old tapes of *Laugh-In*? It's like going to the club Hooters. It's Hooters with a sound track and a laugh track. I read about the changeover from the Vargas pinups of the 1940s to the Bettie Page pinups of the 1950s. I spent time looking at 1960s movies, reading about the history of *Playboy* magazine and what Hugh Hefner did in terms of women's bodies. A very interesting thing happened in the 1960s in terms of breasts. If I were to label that decade, I'd call it the decade of the breast.

So starting with that, when I wanted to create the character recipe of Little Bit, I thought first about the name 'Little Bit' versus the large breasts. The second I thought of that name, I went, 'That's it. Little Bit with these enormous breasts.' Things that I didn't do in the play but that I thought about — and am glad I didn't do — include creating a character that has breasts the way Cyrano de Bergerac has a nose.

AG: WHO DOES OWN LITTLE BIT'S BREASTS IN *HOW I LEARNED TO DRIVE?*

PV: Every member of the family thinks they own her breasts. I think every kid in her school owns Little Bit's breasts. . .

AG: INCLUDING THE GIRLS WHO GAWK AT HER IN THE SHOWER AT SCHOOL.

PV: Absolutely. Everyone thinks they own those breasts. But in my own scenario, when I think about trajectories at the ends of plays, I'd like to think that she at some point owns them.

AG: AT A PERIOD OF TIME BEYOND THE ACTION OF THE PLAY.

PV: That's right.

AG: SOME CRITICS HAVE FELT THAT WHEN SHE FLOORS THE GAS PEDAL AT THE END, THIS IS HER TRIUMPH. BUT IT LEAVES ME SAD. I FEEL SHE IS FREE ONLY FROM THE NECK UP, EXCEPT WHEN SHE IS IN THAT CAR. BUT THAT CAR. . .

PV: What a price. I wanted to be respectful, and I've had a lot of discussions with audience members about the damage the situation would cause. She's been damaged, and I think it's an individual thing for each actress who plays it, how much damage there is. I also think that's age dependent. One gets a different Little Bit from an actress in her forties than from one in her thirties. I always say to actors, that's a choice between you and the director. But there needs to be some damage to her, or people who've been abused and come see the play will think Paula Vogel's writing these tit jokes. It's not a laugh. These things hang on for years. It's a delicate balance.

I wrote this when I turned forty-five, and I thought, 'I've gotten to this point, I've spent a long, long time as a teacher — this is, again, writing from the mother perspective, as an older woman watching these kids struggling — and I want to give them a gift.' I wanted to say, 'You know, there's a forward trajectory. You can drive forward, you can put it in perspective, you can get on with your life, while still acknowledging, yes, there's terrific damage.' There has to be . . . grief. But being on a campus and watching kids in emotional pain, I didn't want them spinning wheels in a victim mentality. I wanted to give them some degree of empowerment. But the degree of empowerment versus the degree of trauma is a decision for the actress.

I don't have that attitude about, 'This is the definitive production, this is exactly the way I want it, you must do this.' To me, the fabulous thing is, 'Show me your way. Oh, I hadn't thought about that. Let's try it that way. The fun is in watching your way.' Particularly in the Peck–Li'l Bit relationship and in the notion of victim versus survivor, watching different actresses making different choices has been phenomenal for me. I get my kick from watching where other artists change the text. And they don't really change the text; they change the subtext. I don't have an overarching concept. That's not true. In this play I have one thing I insist on: as much as humanly possible, that the production try to make us in some way love Peck. That's the only thing I say is important to me.

AG: WHY?

PV: Because, for me, Peck is the object of female desire, and Li'l Bit is the desiring subject.

AG: LOOKED AT FROM A FREUDIAN PERSPECTIVE, THE MEANING OF PECK BRINGING LI'L BIT THE AUTOMOBILE AND TAKING HER BREASTS IS CLEAR.

PV: I did a lot of research on cars in the sixties, and the symbolism is so blatant. The car designs had long, humped headlights and huge tail fins. We laugh about the Edsel having the vagina grill. They designed the Edsel to have a vagina in the grill, and that was why it didn't sell. American men were repulsed by it. They didn't want to buy it. But it's not just the Edsel. Who do the breasts belong to? Detroit. Absolutely Detroit. Again, one of my difficulties as a woman playwright is to write a play which suggests that we are all Li'l Bits in some way, that the standard in this country is young girls and older men, that it's all a parental, incestuous taboo, in terms of what we think of as adult sexuality. It's in that arena that the play rests.

AG: IT'S HARD FOR ME AS A WOMAN TO LOOK AT THAT PLAY OR READ IT AND NOT THINK OF MYSELF GROWING UP.

PV: Yes.

AG: AMONG OTHER THINGS, THE PLAY IS ABOUT WHAT IT MEANS TO GROW UP AS A WOMAN IN THIS COUNTRY.

PV: That's right. As women in this country, we are getting messages in terms of our sexuality. I plunged into sixties stuff for writing this play, and it was everywhere. The pop songs: 'Come back when you grow up, girl'; 'This girl is a woman now.'

AG: WHY DID YOU INCLUDE THE SCENE WITH COUSIN BOBBY, THE LITTLE BOY WHOM PECK TAKES FISHING?

PV: There are two places in the play I didn't plan on. I didn't plan on the fishing scene and I didn't plan on Aunt Mary's speech. It's those points where I as a playwright say to myself, 'I don't know where these things belong in the play, but just listen to them.' I wrote almost as if the words were being dictated. Originally, in the first couple of previews, I left it very ambiguous that Peck actually might be reenacting his own abuse. But Mark Brokaw, the director, came to me and said, 'I think it's too ambiguous.' And I said, 'Okay, then it's Cousin Bobby.' I just chose it. But I had wanted to float the possibility that the scene might be a flashback. Which occasionally people feel anyway. And I thought by making the boy invisible to the audience, there'd be that kind of slippage.

I was very adamant about making it happen to a boy, because of research I had been doing about pedophilia. There are different syndromes, but there is the type of the pillar-of-the-community, whose love object is children, and the gender of the victim does not matter. I wanted to attach that to this play. This is a private thing, and I am occasionally polemical in this way: having watched a gay brother who loved children and was a children's librarian, and having known the homophobia he endured because of the myth that it's gay men who prey on little boys — when the truth is that pedophilia has nothing to do with homosexuality — I wanted at least to put that out there.

Paula Vogel 439

I thought that if the play became something that traveled around, it would hopefully balance one myth about gay men.

AG: YOU WROTE *THE MAMMARY PLAYS* A YEAR APART?

PV: Actually, together. I wrote the first act of *The Mineola Twins* before *How I Learned to Drive*, and then I wrote *How I Learned* and then I finished *Mineola Twins*. I was actually working on both of them at the same time and had thought of them kind of in tandem. As breasts, actually. And I knew the second I did this that I wanted to call them *The Mammary Plays*. It's a weird thing, but when we went back to do *The Mineola Twins*, I thought, 'Oh, my God, this is embarrassing. I've written the same play.' The lines that leap out of both plays.

AG: CARS?

PV: Cars. Blood and family. I thought, 'It's embarrassing, Vogel. It's really a little too close.' I do two things that I really recommend to younger writers. I write to sound tracks, which is why I have a separate writing area far, far from my partner, because no one could live with that. Blaring at times. I had Theresa Brewer playing over and over as I was working on the early scenes of *Mineola Twins*. Peggy Lee or Roy Orbison or The Mamas and the Papas for *How I Learned to Drive*.

AG: CHANNELING THEM IN A WAY.

PV: In a way I think it is channeling, because the music provides an unconscious zeitgeist about the gender. If I suddenly hear Janet Jackson's *Nasty Girl*, I'm in *Hot 'n' Throbbing*. If I hear Theresa Brewer, I'm definitely in *The Mineola Twins*, and all I have to do is hear *Dedicated to the One I Love* and I know exactly what play world I'm in. I train myself to do that, because I know I'm going to go back and forth between plays as I do rewrites. I also have different fonts in the manuscript, which never show up in publication. I'm sorry about that; one of the things I ask younger writers is, 'How does your play look on the page?' The way a play looks on the page can actually give messages to actors and directors: 'Stay away from Stanislavsky on this one'; or, 'This is funny.' The spacing on the page can convey humor, the way that poetry at times reads differently according to its format.

Every play has such a different format and font, that usually when the text comes up on the computer screen I do not let one script spill over to another. But with *The Mineola Twins* I know I was spilling over.

AG: WHY IS THAT BAD FOR YOU BUT OKAY FOR SHAKE-SPEARE? JUST A QUESTION. ARE *THE MAMMARY PLAYS* THE MEMORY PLAYS?

PV: Yes. Walk down memory lane. There were two titles I was thinking of. One was *Memory Plays*, the other was *Mammary Plays*. I'd always liked Robert Wilson's title, *The Knee Plays*.

AG: AGAIN, ABOUT GROWING UP AS A WOMAN IN AMER-ICA. IT SEEMS WE ARE NOT ALLOWED TO GROW BEYOND A CERTAIN POINT IN THIS CULTURE.

PV: Don't you sometimes yearn to be in a culture — I know this is a romanticizing of the French, who esteem actresses like Catherine Deneuve and Simone Signoret — but if we are to be sexualized, can't the culture also eroticize and appreciate aging females? We are perpetually girls. It's very disturbing.

AG: BUT WOMEN ARE COMPLICIT IN IT.

PV: Absolutely complicit in it. Who thought that the firebrand, radical feminist that I was would get to the point where I actually do, occasionally, enjoy and appreciate being called a girl? 'One of the girls.' There's a sense of irony and fun to that, that I would never, ever, in my earlier days, have embraced. But yes, we are complicit.

There was one other thought in the design of the two plays. I wanted the plays to travel the same time period, from the end of the 1950s into the 1980s. When I started describing *How I Learned to Drive*, 'Maryland, the early sixties,' were the fifties. You're carrying the baggage of the fifties through the eighties in that play. When I sat down with *The Mineola Twins*, I wanted that same time period. I was doing a lot of research for both plays simultaneously and what I wanted — I don't know how else to describe this — was for one play to be looking at the culture from the outside and one to be exploring how the culture feels on the inside. I wanted an outside-inside relationship between the two plays. Which I think I have. One play was going to be a cartoon, and that word as applied to it actually delights me. I did not want dimensional character analysis. I love the technique of plays like *The Madwoman of Chaillot*, where Giraudoux specifically does that kind of cartooning. One would have an exterior, pop sensibility, and the other would dramatize the interior.

This is why, knowing the relationship between the two plays, I had wanted *Mineola Twins* to come into New York first. There would have been that laugh-ha-ha-funny take, and then, 'This is what it feels like on the inside.' I would have liked that as a kind of strategic knife. And it got reversed, which I don't think helped.

AG: ONE DAY A THEATER WILL PRODUCE THE PLAYS BACK-TO-BACK.

PV: I wrote a good play and a great play. I wrote *Mineola Twins* as a kind of warm-up, knowing that it was going to be the exterior canvas, and that I was going to dig in on *How I Learned to Drive*.

AG: *MINEOLA TWINS* SEEMS LIKE WOMEN'S HISTORY SEEN THROUGH AMERICAN POLITICAL HISTORY.

PV: Right. History of white, middle-class femaleness.

AG: BUT AGAIN, AMBIGUOUS. AT THE END YOU MAKE FUN OF POLITICALLY CORRECT PRO-CHOICE LESBIANS AS WELL AS RIGHT-WING RADIO TALK-SHOW HOSTS.

PV: Obviously I can't be balanced. I'm a member of Planned Parenthood. There's no way I'm going to be balanced, and I assume that's known. There's a peril when I say this, but I don't actually think there is such a thing as heterosexuality or lesbianism. I think there's sexuality. For me, it's a political choice right now, but the truth of the matter is that I think there's human sexuality in the way that there's animal sexuality.

Having said that, and again, reading the play through the persona of the playwright, I think it's fairly well known that I'm out, and I have to say that one thing I felt was interesting to explore — and the one thing that unites everyone — is homophobia. Anyone in the audience is homophobic, as am I. It's something that's culturally learned. It's culturally learned to be frightened and repelled. The things that unify us as an audience, as Americans, are homophobia, racism, and misogyny. From my point of view — it's not universal — that is what it means to be an American at the start of the new millennium.

What is interesting about this is that I laughed along with the audience at *Mineola Twins*, but it was a different kind of laugh. And I watched other gay women laughing, because the play really did say, 'You know what? This is the way we talk about lesbians and this is the response.' It created an interesting tension for me. I don't know how else to describe it. I think it created an interesting tension for gay women in the audience. This comes back to who owns the breast. Well, who tells the breast jokes? The breast joke is a different thing when a woman comedian tells it than when a male comic tells it.

It was an interesting thing for me, as a writer, to get to this point. I knew that among the cast at the Roundabout there wasn't a homophobic bone in the body, other than what's under everybody's skin. To put that out in public is in some ways liberating. I didn't want *Mineola Twins* to be just about that, but it seemed to me that I did get to a point where the logical playwright said, 'This is the division. There it is: sexuality and abortion. Those are the trigger issues in terms of women at the end of the twentieth century.'

There is something else I am noticing, and I am just going to talk about this directly. As a writer, I think age changes my notion of sexuality in an interesting way. As I develop more and more friends among straight men who are aging, the notion of masculinity that I thought of as set has become incredibly fluid. I find men softer, emotional, nurturing. Starting with a very feminist agenda in my twenties, and getting to this point now at age forty-eight, I don't think the feminist movement has gone away, but my notion of gender has changed a great deal in terms of men and women.

AG: YOUR NOTION OF WHAT CONSTITUTES A MAN OR A WOMAN, AS OPPOSED TO WHAT CONSTITUTES THEIR SEXUALITY?

PV: That's right. As opposed to what constitutes their sexuality. I see a great deal more fluidity than I saw as a younger woman.

AG: THAT'S AN ACHIEVEMENT FOR THE CULTURE.

PV: Yes, it is an achievement for the culture.

AG: I DON'T KNOW HOW WIDESPREAD IT IS.

PV: I don't know how widespread it is either. That's the perspective of being in New York at the moment and teaching at Brown. I can remember in 1972 feeling sure that the Equal Rights Amendment was going to pass and that McGovern was going to win the presidency.

AG: THERE'S A GREAT DEAL OF SEXUALITY AND EROTICISM IN YOUR PLAYS. THAT CAME ACROSS IN *HOW I LEARNED TO DRIVE*.

PV: If the play is directed well, it comes across. Hopefully it does.

AG: EVEN THOUGH YOU SAY YOU WORKED ON *DRIVE* AND *MINEOLA* CONCURRENTLY, I FEEL THAT IN TERMS OF CONTENT AND ATTITUDE *DRIVE* IS MORE OF A SEQUEL TO *HOT 'N' THROBBING*.

PV: Which I am going back and rewriting for Arena Stage. I had a discussion with Molly Smith, Arena's artistic director, and I said, 'How I Learned to Drive taught me how to do the ending of Hot 'n' Throbbing.' I always knew that I'd blown it. I said, 'There's a reason there's no catharsis in Hot 'n' Throbbing, and How I Learned to Drive taught me how to write it.'

AG: *HOT 'N' THROBBING* SEEMS TO ME TO BE YOUR MOST RADICAL FEMINIST PLAY.

PV: It is. But I'm not going back into all the theory that I read when I wrote *Hot 'n' Throbbing*. I'm more interested in going inside, the way that I did with *How I Learned to Drive*. My feeling is that I have to go inside Charlene and inside Clyde and inside the children, make the play more flesh and less abstraction so that the characters have more of an inner journey.

But it's a play that scares the hell out of me. I was absolutely petrified when I wrote it. It was one of the most difficult things for me to write. Talking about negative empathy, I had just read *Beloved,* and I thought, 'Come on, Vogel; Toni Morrison spent years on that book, you can certainly spend — whatever — two months — on this play.' Well, it's been over ten years of work on this script. It was one of those plays where I knew where it was going. I had the image. It was very clear what it was about for me. But feeling the terror of Charlene every night when I was writing it. . . I would stay up all night to write. *How I Learned to Drive* taught me how to — I don't want to say 'soften it.' I don't want to be abusive to an audience — that is the trick. How do you talk about abuse without being abusive in the dramaturgy itself? This may sound strange, but *Hot 'n' Throbbing* is the play that I'm proudest of. It's the most difficult thing I've ever done.

AG: BECAUSE OF HAVING TO DEAL WITH AN EXPERIENCE OF BEING ABUSED?

PV: No. I'm very empathic. I've known some childhood friends whom it breaks my heart to think about, and that's been tormenting me for years. I don't think there's a woman who doesn't know this, if not firsthand, secondhand. I think writing is very akin to acting; you almost give your body over to the experience. I've had this discussion with actors in *How I Learned to Drive*, and they say that playing it is exhausting. You have to allow yourself to be abused every night. It's similar with writing *Hot 'n' Throbbing*; I have to walk into that room and be trapped and not get out of it. Personally. And it's terrifying.

AG: THERE ARE SO MANY ASPECTS OF ABUSIVE MALE POWER IN THAT PLAY, FROM LITERATURE ON UP TO THE ULTIMATE MURDER. YOU ESTABLISH A CONTINUUM.

PV: I establish a continuum. In this next go-round, I want to be a little more out there. I am a First Amendment feminist. I am pro-pornography.

AG: IS THERE A DIFFERENCE BETWEEN PORNOGRAPHY AND EROTICA IN YOUR MIND?

PV: No. I would say I'm pro-erotica. There are very disturbing aspects and images of the male pornography trade. But the difficulty is that the second you say 'no' to that, what gets stopped and censored is women's control of their erotic fantasies. That's what gets stopped.

I need to make clearer the original impulse, which is, 'What do we label obscene and what do I think is obscene? What is dangerous in terms of our culture? Where are we spending our energy?' It's interesting, since the murders at the high school in Littleton, Colorado, we haven't spent a great deal of our time talking about pornography. I think we're recognizing the implications of violence and that what children see in terms of violence is far more pernicious than whether or not they see R-rated movies. Personally, as a human being, I think children shouldn't see either. But I'm far less concerned that my nephews or my godchildren see an R-rated movie than *Terminator 2*. And again I'm a First Amendment feminist. Do we want to censor the entertainment business?

The difficulty with this play is that I have to get to a place where I can ask the questions that are bothering me. I don't think I can answer them; I've been grappling with it for a long time, and there's something in me that really doesn't understand how a man can kill the woman he's married, that has been his lover and borne his children. There's something in me at a human level, as a writer — no matter how much I go into that — I can't get there. That's why this is the most difficult thing I've ever done.

AG: IRONICALLY, WHILE THEATER HAS TROUBLE WITH AMBIGUITY, IT ALSO AT TIMES HAS DIFFICULTY WITH EXTREMES, NO MATTER HOW TRUTHFUL.

PV: In different ages it does. We are seeing that right now. The difficulty with domestic violence is that no attention is being paid because it's called 'domestic.' The language itself implies that the act is hidden. I started with this whole thing by thinking about the meaning of the word *obscene*. It means 'offstage.' What keeps domestic violence offstage, out of our sight? I was reading Aristotle's *Poetics*, about what makes a tragedy, and as I read it, I thought, 'Wait a moment. What he's really describing among kings is domestic violence.' If you look at the Greeks, their plays are about domestic violence. It's just that the violence happens in royal families, which makes it earth-shattering. The Greeks have *The Trojan Women* or *Medea* or *Antigone*, but it's all domestic violence.

So I'm grappling with this now. Like *Desdemona*, I did it three times over. I don't even know if this new rewrite will go through. Do you think it's a good time for me to go back, after *How I Learned to Drive?*

AG: IT'S A QUESTION OF DARING TO BE FEARLESS, AS YOU SAID AT THE BEGINNING OF THIS INTERVIEW.

PV: Domestic violence has gone through the roof.

AG: THE HUSBAND'S MURDER OF HIS WIFE IS PARTICULARLY HORRIFIC BECAUSE HE PLANS IT. IT DOES NOT COME OUT OF SUDDEN FURY OR PASSION.

PV: Phyllis Chesler, in *Women and Madness*, has a fabulous thesis: when women go insane they commit suicide; when men go insane they take everyone with them. It's not just who owns the breast. It's who owns the family. Thank God the kids were out of the house.

AG: WHAT DID THE PRODUCTION AT AMERICAN REPERTORY THEATRE LOOK LIKE?

PV: There was a fabulous set by Christine Jones, but the production was done in such a hurry that I would have said, 'Ooh, don't go there.' There was a kind of semicircle with mirrors.

AG: COULD THE AUDIENCE SEE ITSELF IN THE MIRRORS?

PV: Yes. And there was a dancing ramp all the way around. It was a living room within a dance hall. With glass booths. And after I saw that, I thought, 'Now I know: it's got to be a dance hall inside a living room.' The thing I want to redo is that it's not the erotic which is scary. It's not the erotic that's the danger. It's the living room that's the danger. The next time, I want to see if there's some way that the erotic can almost be a life force. If the voice-over can be a positive life force for Charlene.

AG: WHAT IS YOUR MOST PRECIOUS TOOL AS A PLAYWRIGHT?

PV: Probably that I'm so emotional. That I am so empathic as a person. I go down the road and I pass a scene or I look into an apartment and I feel what it feels like to live there. I think we all are empathic in the arts. That empathy never gets turned off. If I see something that's upsetting, I'm destroyed by it. I carry it around with me. If I see something wonderful . . . Whatever that emotional thing is which I think actors have and directors have, it's the strongest thing that I have in terms of theater. Emotional empathy. That identification.

AG: SINCE WINNING THE PULITZER PRIZE FOR *HOW I LEARNED TO DRIVE*, DO YOU FEEL PLEASURE OR PRESSURE?

PV: It's done some strange things. It wasn't helpful that people said, 'Okay, now you know how your obit's going to read.' The second they said that, I thought, 'I've reached this goal.' There's something about a Pulitzer that makes you think, 'I'm not a growing playwright, I'm a step closer to death.' You hear the clock ticking in a strange way.

On the good side, it's making me go, 'Yeah, I am a playwright. This is what I'm supposed to be doing. Put all your eggs in this basket, concentrate on your writing.' The bad part: I don't ever want to take myself seriously. I hope people don't take me seriously. I never meant for anyone to take me seriously, you know? It's really bizarre to have a Pulitzer be an indicator. 'Got to listen to what she says.' The great thing about teaching now is that I have students who go, 'How could you say that? I don't see how you can say that. That's baloney.' They battle with me and prove me wrong. It's that way in which one wants to be taken seriously. It's not, 'Oh, every word is golden.' It's very bizarre.

What's great is that a friend had a dinner for me in his home, and I lifted my glass and said, 'Here's to the eleventh woman. May it happen soon.' And we all toasted to that. And I have to tell you what it felt like when Margaret Edson won the following year. I had been dancing about *Wit* anyway, but when she got the Pulitzer, it felt so phenomenal. To have two in a row . . . was great. ◆

Naomi
Wallace

Naomi Wallace was born in Louisville,
Kentucky. She spent half of her youth
on a nearby beef-cattle farm that
belonged to her father, and half in
Amsterdam, Holland, where she
lived with her Dutch mother. She
received a B.A. from Hampshire
College in Amherst, Massachusetts, and an M.F.A. from the University of Iowa.

A poet first, Wallace is the author of the collection *To Dance a Stony
Field,* published in the United Kingdom in 1995. She has received the National
Poetry Competition Award, as well as grants from the Kentucky Foundation
for Women and the Kentucky Arts Council.

Since the early 1990s, however, Wallace has concentrated on writing for
the theater. Her plays include *The War Boys* (1993), which dramatizes violence and racism among vigilantes at the Mexican border; *In the Heart of
America* (1994), an examination of the relationship among war, racism, and
homophobia; and *Slaughter City* (1996), which parallels the deadly fire in
the Triangle Shirtwaist Factory early in the twentieth century, with the horrific working conditions in a meatpacking plant at the century's end. *One Flea
Spare* (1996) is an exploration of the effects of the black plague on seventeenth-
century English society, and *Birdy* (1997) is an adaptation of William Wharton's
novel about a gay love affair in wartime. In addition, Wallace wrote the screenplay for the film *Lawn Dogs* (1997).

In 1999, Wallace received a prestigious MacArthur Award. Previously she
received the 1995 Mobil Prize for *Slaughter City,* the 1995 Susan Smith Blackburn
Award for *One Flea Spare*, and a 1997 Obie Award for *One Flea Spare*.

Wallace lives in England with her partner, Bruce McLeod, and their three
daughters. This interview took place on June 10, 1999, in New York City,
while Wallace was in rehearsal for her play *The Trestle at Pope Lick Creek,*
at New York Theatre Workshop.

• • •

449

AG: YOUR CHILDHOOD WAS DIVIDED BETWEEN KENTUCKY AND HOLLAND. HOW DID KENTUCKY INFLUENCE YOU?

NW: A lot of my work comes out of my childhood there. We were a privileged family compared to most people, who were poor. Kentucky's one of the poorest states in the country. But I grew up with a mix of people. There was a working-class community, and I hung out with those kids. I think that's where I was inspired to write.

AG: WHAT KIND OF WORKING-CLASS COMMUNITY?

NW: People who had rural jobs. They were mechanics and carpenters. They had real small farms.

AG: WAS YOUR FATHER'S FAMILY FROM KENTUCKY?

NW: My father's family came from genteel Philadelphia and not-so-genteel Paducah, Kentucky. But my father's father was editor of the Louisville *Courier-Journal*. I didn't know him, because he died when I was very young. My father was born in Kentucky.

AG: AND YOUR MOTHER?

NW: My mother lives in Amsterdam. They met when my mother was hitchhiking in the north of Africa, and my father, a journalist, was there as a stringer for *Time-Life*. You see, my father's family was privileged, but my mother was from a working-class family. So I grew up with the influences of both.

AG: THERE IS A STRONG POLITICAL AWARENESS IN YOUR WRITING, AND I WONDERED IF YOU CAME TO THAT ON YOUR OWN OR IF SOME OF IT CAME FROM YOUR FAMILY.

NW: My mother's family has been honored for their political work. My grandmother resisted fascism when the Germans occupied Holland during the Second World War; she ran a safe house for hiding Jews and Communists. So my mother was always very political. She educated my father, at least that's how the family myth goes. They were active against the Vietnam War and during the U.S.-inspired coup in

Chile in 1973. My five siblings and I knew more about the Vietnam War than about any kids' show on television.

AG: DO YOU CONSIDER YOURSELF A POLITICAL POET, POLIT-ICAL PLAYWRIGHT?

NW: I consider myself a political writer. I think anybody who doesn't is masking their politics behind what is usually a mainstream view of the world. All theater and all art have to do with representations, and certainly with representations of power. From the moment you talk about who has, who doesn't, who's weak, who's strong, and what position they're in, you're talking about power, and therefore you're talking about politics. The whole thing about 'This person's not a political writer' — that means their politics are invisible because we accept their positions as normal. They're in the middle — they're 'normal.'

I'm called a political writer and I'm happy to be called that. I don't think there's anything more exciting to write about than history and society and negotiations of power. If people want a label, they can call me a socialist. I write about capitalism, because that is how our society is organized; and how we make our way or don't make our way economically affects all aspects of our lives. That is usually at the base of anything that I write.

AG: THAT IS CLEAREST TO ME IN *SLAUGHTER CITY*, WHERE THE CHARACTERS OF COD AND SAUSAGE MAN EMBODY THE WORKER AND THE EXPLOITATIVE OWNER.

NW: Yes, that play is more overtly political than *The Trestle at Pope Lick Creek*. I set myself to write *The Trestle* against what one might call the myth of the dysfunctional family onstage in America — the idea that what goes on in a family is divorced from class, or that it doesn't matter what class a family is in or what color, this story is just about Ma and Pa and how the kids get along with them. American drama is not only extremely sexist when it deals with the dysfunctional family — you'll always find the raging mother who has destroyed everyone's lives — but also there's no real look at why that mother became the way she did. Why she takes things out on her children, why she feels trapped. What, in society, contributed? I'm thinking about O'Neill's work particularly.

So when I wrote *The Trestle*, it was about a basically sound family that has been torn apart by pressures from the outside. That's the opposite of how you usually find American dramatists writing about families. If playwrights are writing about minority communities, there's more of an awareness of the problems that enter a family. But for white middle-class American drama, the dysfunctional family play is usually divorced from history and divorced from the class within which it takes place.

AG: WOULD YOU SAY THAT IS TRUE OF *DEATH OF A SALESMAN*?

NW: Well, no. That's an exceptional play and an attempt to challenge the American dream in a lot of ways. I always thought it was a great denunciation of the American dream. But most American plays about dysfunctional families don't come close to looking at the ideas in society that helped destroy the family.

AG: WHAT INSPIRED *THE TRESTLE*?

NW: A friend of mine in Kentucky told me that in the 1970s, a group of kids from a poor white neighborhood used to get drunk and hang out at the bottom of a trestle. They would go run this train, except that they didn't play chicken with it, they would wait for the train to come and run in front of it. But there were no sides on this trestle. There was just a pretty shallow creek bed. About three kids were killed up there.

    I started thinking about why people would do this. Because they were drunk? I could have been loaded on alcohol, but I wouldn't have done that when I was a teenager, and my friends wouldn't have either. What were their lives like that they were willing to risk them? It's easy to say, 'Oh, man, when you're young, you don't know mortality.' That's not enough for me. What were they seeking in their lives that they were willing to risk their futures?

    That's how I created the character of Pace. Why is it so important to her to learn how to run the trestle and make it across alive? What was society offering so that Pace wouldn't run that trestle? The story my friend told inspired me. Most of my work comes from listening to people talk. That's more interesting than anything I could think up. It's real. It's history.

AG: YOU SAY THAT *THE TRESTLE* IS LESS OVERTLY POLITI-CAL THAN OTHER PLAYS OF YOURS. DOES IT DIFFER IN OTHER WAYS?

NW: Every time I write a play I try not to let myself do what I know how to do pretty well. With *The Trestle*, I said that I was going to make the canvas a lot smaller, as opposed to *Slaughter City*. Of course, after *Slaughter City* I wrote *One Flea Spare* and I said, 'No ghosts. I don't get to use ghosts.' But they crept back in *The Trestle*. Also, in my plays I usually include a character who represents the more priv-ileged classes. After *Slaughter City*, I wanted to write about capital-ism and poverty, but I didn't want a representation of capitalism in terms of a person — like Baquin, the bad boss at the factory in *Slaughter City*. I wanted one of the characters in *The Trestle* to be the economic situation outside the family. I wanted to write one of those family plays I was talking about and make a little twist on it there.

The Trestle is also one of the most irresponsibly positive things I've written. I say this in my defense, having recently been accused of writing a 'hopeless and sad' play with *The Trestle*. In the end, the father, instead of killing himself, tells his wife that he will go with her to the factory. Workers are taking the factory over. The wife has decided that what matters is her choice, even more than this marriage. We talked in rehearsal about reversing the last two scenes of the play, because someone whom I respect a lot said that the scene with the father and mother is so powerful, the play should end on that note. But that might be too upbeat. I like the play ending with the last memory the boy, Dalton, has. The girl's gone, but Dalton is reunited with his father. And Chas, the jailer, has finally told what he did to his own son. He's come to some kind of — I don't know if you'd say 'peace' — but he's finally shared his story and in a way helped Dalton speak again. Like I said: irresponsibly optimistic.

AG: THERE'S A LARGE AMOUNT OF ANIMAL IMAGERY IN THIS PLAY.

NW: I worked with a dramaturg in Louisville who said that a lot of the things Chas imitates or refers to, to communicate with Dalton, were animals. And I changed that and put in an airplane and a boat and a weather vane, because I didn't want the play to be read as biological. Which it still leans toward, but that's because I grew up on a farm.

AG: WHEN DID YOU DISCOVER POETRY, EITHER AS READER OR WRITER?

NW: Oh, I was writing poetry since I was in second grade. I was solely a poet until I was about twenty-eight. About ten years ago.

AG: WHAT CHANGED?

NW: I don't know. A lot of my poetry is what they call 'persona poetry.' I take on different voices. I found poetry an isolating endeavor after a while. Nor was the American poetry circle very open to me. If there's one place where being a political poet puts you in a 'B' class, it's American poetry.

AG: WHY?

NW: The elite poets have the attitude that poetry is above politics. I think it's a way of saying that certain politics are accepted and certain aren't. But recently *The Massachusetts Review* accepted a long poem, *Death of a Wobbly in Montana, 1917*. It's the most overtly political and historical poem I've written, and they loved it. I haven't left poetry, but I haven't done as much of it, because I knew that after I started writing a certain way in theater, something would change in my poetry. I've changed as a writer — for anything I do.

Writing is a way for me to embrace my artistic impulse and my political vision, and I find that far easier in theater. Theater is a community endeavor. Poetry you write alone. As a poet, you don't see your audience. You don't engage with your public. Pablo Neruda used to stand on a bucket in the village and read to people, but that's not the way American poetry works.

I had this myth about myself, that I was this 'want-to-be-alone, don't-talk-to-me artist' who wrote poetry in her room. But I find that I like hanging with people and that my work is better when it comes in contact with other artists. In this production of *The Trestle*, Lisa Peterson, the director, has done things that make my play more than I made it, and I love that. *Slaughter City* is a better play because of

Ron Daniels' work on it at the Royal Shakespeare Company. He helped me restructure it. He bugged me and bugged me about it, 'You need a monologue here, and this person needs to have their moment and they don't.' Friends would work with me on poems, but there wasn't the kind of influence that someone I trust and respect can have on my plays.

AG: WHEN I WAS READING THE POEMS IN *TO DANCE A STONY FIELD* I WROTE DOWN MY REACTIONS: DENSE, INTENSE, SENSUAL, MASCULINE, NO FEAR OF THE UGLY IMAGE, METAPHORICAL RATHER THAN DESCRIPTIVE.

NW: Oh, I like that. Who's that writer? I would like to read her.

AG: A LOT OF THE POEMS INVOLVE BIBLICAL SUBJECTS, WHICH SURPRISED ME.

NW: Yes, I went through this stage where I dealt with a lot of Biblical subjects. I wrote a play, actually, called *Joseph and Barabbas*, which was about Biblical times and about betrayal. It's never been done. Probably every poet at some point deals with things like that. It's not something in my work anymore, but there was a time when I thought about Christianity and the Bible and the relationship Mary had to her son.

AG: WHAT WERE YOU RAISED AS?

NW: Atheist. Religion wasn't something that was tormenting me in any way. I was just reading stories on it, reading other poets engaging with things. Thinking about love and betrayal and dedication and faith; issues of love and betrayal are always encapsulated in those Biblical stories.

AG: ARE LOVE AND BETRAYAL A HUMAN BEING'S CORE OPERATING MECHANISMS?

NW: No, I wouldn't say that at all. I don't remember why I went through that period of thinking about characters in the Bible. I would have to remember what was going on in my life, although I choose subjects that don't necessarily have anything to do with me. Hey, maybe I was at the point where I was either about to go to religion or theater. I guess someone could argue that.

But no, not core things, although love is always a subject in my work. A love story pulls through *The Trestle*. But that play is about what happens to our love, our desire, our lives, because of the historical moment we're caught in. I would never be interested in writing an encapsulated story about love, because I don't think it can be done — unless you artificially say that this story takes place in a room and nothing is on the outside. Imposing that room and saying nothing is on the outside would be a political choice.

It's funny to be asked these things, because you see how material can be gotten hold of. 'Naomi's conversion: she almost became a nun and then she went into the theater.' I can't answer some of those questions, except to say that I was searching for subjects to write about and there are exciting stories in the Bible. The United States is still one of the most religious countries in the world. And me thinking about American culture, that might have had something to do with it.

AG: SOME OF THE POEMS SOUND LIKE SCENES IN YOUR PLAYS.

NW: Often, when I'm writing a play, I'll write a poem first. There's a poem called *The Trestle at Pope Lick Creek*, which I wrote before I wrote the play. When I wrote *In the Heart of America*, about the Gulf War, I wrote the poem *A Kentucky Soldier in the Saudi Desert on the Eve of War*. And when I wrote *Slaughter City*, I wrote the poem *Meat Strike* first. It seems to be a pattern.

AG: THE POEM *TOUCHING IN THE SWEAT SHOP* ALSO EVOKES THE MATERIAL IN *SLAUGHTER CITY*.

NW: Yes, that too. When I'm doing my research and feel like writing something, but not starting the play yet, I'll sometimes write a poem. Sometimes you'll see something similar from a poem in a play, but usually that gets cut out. My poems sometimes are like small monologues as well.

AG: HOW DOES A POET MOVE TO THE PLAY FORM?

NW: I've thought about that and I don't know if I did move from the poetry. I don't think it was a transfer from one to the other. I think that the playwriting sprung from another area. I dislike it when people call my theatrical work 'poetic,' and if I hear there's a 'poetic play' on, I'll run in the opposite direction. Because when language onstage becomes self-conscious, you've lost it. The actor in *Trestle* who plays the father throws my language away like he's saying, 'Get me a Coke up on the corner,' and that's great. That's how my plays work best, when there's no attention given to the language. I give the attention to the language. When language is working to sound pretty, that's bad poetry anyway.

AG: HOW DOES METAPHOR OPERATE IN A PLAY AS OPPOSED TO A POEM?

NW: I'd say it operates the same way. But you've got a bigger canvas, and actors. It's a whole different medium. But I don't see a difference. There are various metaphors in my poems and in my plays. The metaphor works or it doesn't. I pulled a bunch of stuff out of *The Trestle*. Images of change. It was actually the word, *change*. I realized I had 'change' in images and I didn't need to use the word. I went back and forth on taking the lines out where Dray, Dalton's father, says to his son, 'I don't want to live like this,' and Dalton says, 'How?' and he says, 'Unchanged.' We initially pulled that out because I felt it was so evident, but the actor liked it, and he is able to do the lines so they don't sound like, 'Here's what the play's about.'

AG: HOW DID YOU ACTUALLY GET INTO THEATER?

NW: I first thought, 'I wonder if I can do this' and I read a good play called *The Go-Back Land*, by a close friend, Lisa Schlesinger. I'd never even really been to the theater at that point. I was probably twenty-eight before I went to see any theater. Or thirty. And I read her play and thought, 'You know, I think I can do this.' It felt familiar to me. It felt like that world, which I didn't even know existed, was someplace I should have gone to a long time before. But I'm glad I didn't. I'm glad I wasn't writing plays when I was twenty, twenty-five.

AG: WHY?

NW: Sometimes you learn too much about what you can and can't do and lose your risk-taking ability. Some of the first plays I wrote, like *The War Boys*, I probably couldn't write again. I had a certain innocence or naïveté about playing with the form of the theater. I don't know; it just felt right that I came to playwriting later.

AG: WAS *BIRDY*, YOUR ADAPTATION OF WILLIAM WHAR-TON'S NOVEL, AN EARLY PLAY AS WELL?

NW: No, *Birdy* I adapted in 1995 or maybe 1994. People probably consider that one of my more mature plays. I hate to label my own work, but *Birdy* is more 'mainstream.' It was written for the West End.

AG: *BIRDY* FELT EARLY BECAUSE, LIKE *IN THE HEART OF AMERICA*, IT INVOLVES A GAY RELATIONSHIP DURING WARTIME. BUT *IN THE HEART OF AMERICA* IS MORE SOPHIS-TICATED FORMALLY.

NW: Oh, right. But I wanted to be faithful to William Wharton's novel. I've strayed from it more and more every time I've done a rewrite, but it's still pretty faithful to his work. I didn't want to do Naomi Wallace. I wanted to keep Wharton's vision.

AG: I WONDER IF WE CAN TALK ABOUT *IN THE HEART OF AMERICA*.

NW: I didn't write the play until two years after the Gulf War ended. I remember having a conversation with Tony Kushner, who said that he doesn't think anger writes good plays if you write in the moment of that anger. You have to wait. I think Tony is right; if you get angry, sometimes you get stuck in your own propaganda. Anger has to be channeled.

The play had a workshop in the United States, but it has never had a major production here. I figure we'll just recycle it, call it *In the Heart of Yugoslavia*.

AG: WHY DO YOU THINK IT HAS NOT HAD A MAJOR PRO-DUCTION HERE?

NW: I think the play deals with some really touchy issues for America about foreign policy and racism and even the Vietnam War, which culturally we've never dealt with. We can't count the Hollywood movies. We haven't even started to come to terms with Iraq and what that means for American history. As a matter of fact, we'll probably skip Iraq and move on to Yugoslavia, if we even want to deal with that, with how that affects us as a people.

AG: I LIKE *IN THE HEART OF AMERICA*'S MIXTURE OF PAST AND PRESENT, DREAM AND REALITY. THE SEVERAL PERSPECTIVES SUGGEST THAT WAR IS CONTINUOUS, THAT THE SUBJECT IS NOT ONLY THE GULF WAR BUT ALSO THE VIETNAM WAR AND THE WAR ON THE STREETS OF AMERICA'S CITIES.

NW: It's continuous certainly, because the U.S. economy thrives on war, but I would think my work has failed if it is read as war is hell and is always going to go on. For me, the play was about connecting places in American history and showing their links, often through language. The Vietnamese were called 'gooks' and then the Arabs were called 'gooks,' and I would not be surprised to read that the Serbs are called 'gooks' by American soldiers. I was trying to show how we use language to dehumanize people, whether at home or abroad, in order to be able to kill them with less guilt. Or in order to support an American foreign policy. I wanted to talk about the racism that links the wars. I wanted to show how we think that what happens at home doesn't affect our foreign policy, or that racism abroad doesn't come home to roost. During the Gulf War, if you were an Arab American you had to keep your head low. There were people getting beaten up on the streets for being Arab. I thought about what it must be like to be an Arab American fighting for the United States against Iraqis. What kinds of complications that would bring up and what kinds of links about who our enemy is: the Arab American who's beaten up on his own streets going to kill Iraqis. The irony in that.

AG: YOU MENTIONED THAT YOU DO RESEARCH FOR YOUR PLAYS, AND THERE IS A BIBLIOGRAPHY AT THE BACK OF PUBLISHED VERSIONS OF *IN THE HEART OF AMERICA* AND

SLAUGHTER CITY. WHAT DOES THE RESEARCH PROCESS ACCOMPLISH FOR YOU?

NW: Well, like most Americans, if you went through the American educational system, you know it's really a system to de-educate you. When I wrote *Slaughter City* I realized I knew very little about labor history, which should be our major history, because the majority of Americans are working Americans. I had to go back and educate myself. Read against what I'd been taught, against what we learn in high school.

I usually try to read up on the history before and after whatever period the play is in, so I can place the play's situation historically and see how influenced it was by the past and what its reverberations would be in the future. History is much more imaginative than my own imagination, and I love to read about the characters in history. What amazes me is that we are taught in this culture that there have always been the rich and the poor, and it will always be this way, that there has always been war, and it will always be this way. But when you study history, you see how much resistance there always was to poverty, to war, to injustice. How much resistance and how little of it was recorded, or recorded in the mainstream. Many people said 'no' to having their lives diminished. Said 'no' to oppression in all its forms. I find that very inspiring. But you have to go look for that.

AG: IS THERE A POINT WHERE YOU SAY, 'OKAY, I'VE DONE THE RESEARCH'?

NW: You want to talk about that boring inspiration part?

AG: SURE.

NW: It's not something I'm all that interested in talking about — how a writer writes. But I know a lot of people are. Usually I'll reread my research once I've done it all. I'll take the research in and then put it away, and for a few days I'll do other things. Think in a less intellectual way. One of the inspirations for *The Trestle* was a little potato I had sitting on my desk. I found it in the drawer. It had grown all these little feelers. So I had that sitting on my desk and I used to look at that when I was writing. I'll often look at pictures. I'll put up on my wall a lot of photographs, or photos of paintings or strange things that inspire me in a different way than research does. *The Trestle* used to have a potato in it as a character that came up out of the ground. It was a metaphor for change. Both my agents told me I was insane; I don't think it worked dramatically. But I needed the potato in order to get somewhere, and then it wasn't useful anymore. But it's going to reappear in one of my plays and it's going to stay.

AG: PACE TALKS TO DALTON ABOUT HOW A POTATO LEFT IN A DARK BOX GROWS ROOTS TO SURVIVE, ALTHOUGH ULTIMATELY IT CAN'T SURVIVE.

NW: Yes. I really don't mind talking about how I write, but I'm not interested in talking about myself personally. The mythology I dislike is the one which says: we don't write because of the society we grew up in or the historical moment we're in, we write because when we were three years old a pan fell off the stove and burned us.

In *One Flea Spare*, I was interested in the plague and read Daniel Defoe's *A Journal of the Plague Year*. What interested me was this disease and how people reacted to it. The central image is when Darcy puts her finger in the sailor's wound. The play was partly written around that image. But that moment is not about this older woman and this young guy. They are from two classes, and they experience life differently; she was damaged by an accident, he was damaged through resistance and labor. That influences the moment of touch, which cannot be isolated from who they are or were supposed to be. In that moment they are stepping across a class boundary.

AG: YOU TALK ABOUT SOCIAL CONTEXT, IMAGES, METAPHOR, BUT NOT CHARACTERS.

NW: It's true. It's not that I think characters don't have their own lives and all that cliché stuff, but there's this myth that, 'I just start writing, and the characters take me places.' That's a cultivated irresponsibility toward the political vision of the play. As though writers don't make choices. I find that almost laughable. It's not that something doesn't come out of our unconscious. I'm not trying to diminish whatever it is that makes up the artistic impulse or imagination. I just find it's often used as a camouflage and a mask.

I'm looking for an understanding that goes beyond mainstream notions of 'character.' Someone who hits their child, like Chas in *The Trestle* — that's inexcusable. But how does someone become that way? That's where I find the tragedy. Chas became the way he did not because he was a bad father, but because he didn't have anything to give his son. He felt inadequate in his world because he had no future to give in terms of labor. He says to Dalton, 'I didn't have anything to give him. A key to a cell, maybe. A broom to go with it. Is that what you give your child when he grows up?' That's all he had to give him.

The myth of the American dream is that you can pull yourself up by your bootstraps. Well, most people who are born in the working class aren't coming out of that class, and the tragedy of the American dream, which is also its brilliance, is to bring to adulthood generation after generation and teach them that this system works if you work *it*, that you can be anything that you want to be. The brilliance is that when the American dream doesn't happen for the majority of people, their anger and disappointment is not turned on a system that's failed them but on themselves.

Those are some of the issues that inspire me to write.

AG: DID YOU RESEARCH THE GREAT DEPRESSION OF THE 1930S FOR *THE TRESTLE*?

NW: I studied how the federal government dealt with the crisis. I read Howard Zinn, who writes about working people in American history. I read *The Scapegoat Generation: America's War on Adolescents*, by Mike A. Males, an interesting book comparing the 1930s to the 1990s. In some way I wrote *The Trestle* in reaction to what I see as our anti-youth culture. People say that kids today are violent and immoral, but if you study it, you realize that not only are critics using the same language as naysayers in the 1930s, but that young people commit the least amount of crime of any age group, the least violent crime of any age group, and are given three times tougher penalties than adults. That got me angry. I thought, 'I'm going to write a play in which two complicated young people are trying to find their way in a system that doesn't give them any choices.'

There are different reasons why I write things. Pace says to Dalton, 'I want you to watch me . . . .Cause one day I might come back here to find out who I was — and then you're going to tell me.' I once went back to friends who knew me as a teenager, to ask who I was then. I had an image of myself as a quiet, shy person when I was fifteen or sixteen. I was always afraid when I was younger — just growing up in the world. But these friends said, 'Are you kidding? You were a loudmouth. You were always talking about women's rights and racism.' I was quite pleased with that image of myself, but I didn't remember myself that way. And I thought, 'Is this not-remembering connected to the views we have of ourselves as women? That if we are loudmouthed and in-your-face, that's negative?' I wondered if, through the process of sexism, I had changed my perception of myself as a teenager. And I thought that if I — someone who has pretensions to awareness — could do that — how brilliantly the system must work. History is rewritten, and not just on a personal level. If it hadn't been for that community I went back to . . . They knew more of who I had been than I did, and there's something valuable in that. We can go to each other and get validation. When Pace says to Dalton, 'I need you to watch me,' it's because, 'I may lie to myself when I'm older. I may want to believe I was something else.' We have to say to each other, 'No, you were also this,' so that we remember the parts of ourselves that were clipped or squashed or strangled because they didn't fit in with the norm.

AG: HOW DOES THAT RELATE TO WHAT YOU EARLIER DESCRIBED AS IRRESPONSIBLE OPTIMISM?

NW: Dalton has lost Pace, but accepts that he's changed and that he has a different view of the world. He says, 'Tell them I'm ready to talk.' When he tells about Pace's death, he's basically talking to the jury. And he says something very important in the play: that the two of them didn't want to die.

What happens with my plays repeatedly is that I don't give a tight, closed ending. In *The Trestle*, you get a more gentle ending, where Pace blows out the candle and you just see Dalton's face. It's perhaps less 'dramatic.'

Slaughter City ends with the workers having taken over the factory. There's a fire, but Cod has decided to stay in one place and love Maggot and work in the present, where she is. And finally Cod says

'Fire!' and everybody sees it. All through the play there's a fire burning that no one realizes is going to kill them all. In the end the workers are going to die, but if the play is directed properly, it should be evident that when Cod says 'Fire!' the past and the present connect, and the workers have an awareness of the danger in order to fight it.

In the Heart of America is positive in that Craver, who has not been able to speak of the death of his lover, Remzi, is finally able to say, 'Talking about it might keep me alive.' Through his relationship with Remzi's sister, Craver says in those crucial lines at the end that he is going to speak about the murder of his friend. We're talking about awareness and activism here. It's very similar to the movement that Dalton makes. Through loving a person Craver has been changed. The last line of *In the Heart of America* is, 'Go!' Often in my work — certainly in *The Trestle* and *In the Heart of America* — the last scene we see is of the past. With *In the Heart of America*, the last scene is of a moment when there was happiness and connection between Remzi and Craver, when they are going to race again. It's this feeling, for me, of energy and forward power, and although we know Remzi has died, in that moment we see that anything was possible.

AG: DURING *IN THE HEART OF AMERICA*, CRAVER REPEATEDLY SPEAKS THE NAMES OF BOMBS AND WAR PLANES AND PLANE ENGINES. THERE'S AN ALLURING IF AWFUL SOUND TO IT.

NW: I was fascinated by the language of the Gulf War. These weapons that tear you to pieces in every way you can think of had names like Sad Eyes and Bouncing Betty. I mean, imagine . . .

There's such sensuality in the reciting of the bombs' names, that if you didn't look at the meanings of the words, you could be singing a love song. That difference between how words sound and what their meanings are became part of the play. Are words used to clarify or are they used to obscure? Are the beautiful names used to mask death and destruction? A love story in a way.

AG: CRAVER DESCRIBES LOVING TO TOUCH THE WEAPONS. TOUCHING THE PLANES AND THEN TOUCHING REMZI'S BODY.

NW: It's hard for us, because we're so far away from the actual fighting, to think about the steel and sleekness and power of these weapons. They have a sensuality that's kind of frightening. So here's a young guy whose most complicated language is weapons. He's reading the weapons manual, and he's fascinated by it and by the beauty of how the words sound. Onstage, you see a person trying to define himself through a language about B-52s and the Beehive, Floggers and Fulcrums, the AV-8B Harrier II. If this is your language, how do you love someone with it? The language we are given is the language with which we love each other. Can you turn this language around, and what's the cost of that? My impulse is to break up the language, or highlight it so that it works against the purposes it was invented to work for. In that play, a man connects with another through this language in a way that leaves one of them dead but one of them completely changed and willing to challenge the system.

AG: THERE IS ALSO THE STOMACH-CHURNING IMAGE OF THE MEN STEPPING OUT OF THE TANKS TO COLLECT PIECES OF BODIES.

NW: I wrote *In the Heart of America* because I was thinking about the body in war. We forget that these weapons are used to tear up as many *bodies* as possible. When they were dropping cluster bombs in the former Yugoslavia, that was to kill as many Serbian soldiers as possible. The body that kills is the same body that loves. How do you use your body as a war machine and also to make love? What happens to that body in the process?

AG: IN THE PLAYS OF YOURS THAT I'VE READ OR SEEN, THE BODY IS USED FOR WAR MORE THAN LOVE. IN *THE WAR BOYS*, THERE IS SO MUCH VIOLENCE AGAINST THE BODY.

NW: Yes, everyone's poked and burned and prodded. I noticed that. That's been pointed out to me before.

AG: THE BODY TAKES A LOT OF DESTRUCTION IN YOUR PLAYS.

NW: It does. That's always been a central thing I deal with. I'm trying to think about that in relation to *The Trestle* . . .

AG: WELL, THE BODY IS PUT AT RISK.

NW: Certainly the body is put at risk. And Dray feels his body is invisible because he no longer works. Spirits we may be, but it's our body that walks around.

War wreaks extreme damage to the body, either by putting it at risk or turning it into a killing machine. But how are our bodies damaged through sexism? How is our desire damaged through homophobia? I also wrote *The Trestle* because most of the love relationships in my plays have been between two men or two women. I remember thinking to myself, 'God, heterosexuality has gotten to be such a bore, but what can we do here? Is there a site within heterosexuality that can be used as a site of resistance?' I think it's important that heterosexuals realize their sexuality is intricately linked to gay and lesbian sexuality. Although gays and lesbians, bisexuals, transsexuals, the whole continuum, are openly oppressed for their sexuality, invisible norms have been imposed upon all of us, straight people as well. Invisible norms are imposed on what we're allowed and not allowed to do sexually, the places we are allowed to touch one another.

I like to think that we humans have a desire and sensuality that break through what's 'right' or what's 'wrong,' what's ladylike, what's malelike, what's first love and first sex and the sites of desire on the body. When Pace first kisses Dalton, she tries to find the part of his body, the part of him, that has not been trained to be a certain way. If you find that part within yourselves or each other, that is the place where it's possible to make a new vision of yourselves. Or a new vision of desire. I think that's what I'm trying to do with the boy and the girl in *The Trestle*. How do these two people connect sexually in a way that isn't already determined because one is a boy and one is a girl? If they can connect in a different way, something new could happen. That's why the last scene is important, because Dalton goes back in his memory and realizes that Pace was inside his body in a way that no one had ever been. And he is changed by that.

AG: YOU WRITE MEN WELL.

NW: I have no problem writing men. It's probably more challenging for me to write women. But I don't especially want to write positive roles for women. I want to write complicated roles; none of those boring stereotypes. Sometimes I'll challenge other writers, but it's not because a role is sexist; it's because a role is boring. You want to make the character a bitch and a murderer, that's fine with me. But make her interesting. That's what I try to do with my women characters. It's not about them being positive role models; it's about their being complicated agents.

AG: IN *SLAUGHTER CITY*, WHY DO YOU HAVE COD, THE WOMAN WHO HAS LIVED THROUGH SEVERAL HISTORICAL PERIODS, DRESS AS A MAN?

NW: I liked the idea of Maggot running after boys all the time, and that the man she finally falls in love with is a woman.

AG: IN THE STAGE DIRECTIONS, YOU REFER TO COD AS 'HE'; IS THE AUDIENCE SUPPOSED TO BE AS FOOLED AS MAGGOT IS?

NW: If the play hinges on that, I'm cooked. It's not going to work. I think you should be able to tell from the beginning that Cod is female, but we can go along with Maggot's surprise, because she doesn't know.

I was really interested in how men and women are constructed, and how a woman's desire is supposed to work a certain way. Cod, being the smart fellow she is, knows that she has to dress as a man in certain periods of history to be treated well. She says, 'Working like a man, I feel more like a gal.' Doing decent, dignified work made her feel more of a human being. More of a woman.

I always like to dress people in funny things. You've got Roach making Brandon put on a dress when she finds him in the women's changing room, and Brandon to my mind is the all-American boy. Usually you'll find them in my work. Even Dalton is a mild version of the good boy, although some people would read him in a sexist manner and say he's a mama's boy. Which he isn't. He and his mother just share some cool things.

AG: ACCORDING TO AN INTRODUCTION YOU WROTE FOR *SLAUGHTER CITY*, YOU TALKED WITH MEMBERS OF LOCAL 227 OF THE UNITED FOOD AND COMMERCIAL WORKERS BEFORE WRITING THE PLAY.

NW: There was a strike going on in Kentucky against the Fischer Packing Company. Strikers did go back to work under a new contract, but the company tried to punish a lot of the rebels. There's been a movement to break labor in the whole meatpacking, poultry industry, and there's also been great labor resistance.

I went to see union members speak one night last summer at a strike against Tyson. This was an impoverished community on the river in Indiana. They were ready to go for months: labor in that area was backing them and even put out videos about the strike. They won within six weeks. It was a great victory, because the companies like Tyson are trying union busting all through that industry. The companies don't need white, highly unionized labor like they used to have fifteen years ago — people earning fifteen-to-eighteen dollars an hour. They're using Asian and Latino labor now and dropping the wages down to six dollars an hour.

One of the most inspiring things I did in relation to *Slaughter City* was interview strikers. One of the people who was organizing the strike at Fischer's said to me on the phone, 'Yeah, you can come on down here.' And I knew what position I was in, this university-educated, let-me-write-a-story-about-you-folks person. I went down there with my tape recorder, and you know, they were half-smiling out of the corners of their mouths. But they were so generous to me. At some point there were about twelve men and women sitting around, and I said, 'Well, tell me, what do you all like about your jobs?' There was dead silence. This thing had never occurred to me. This one guy spoke up and said, 'We never liked the jobs. It was the money. We had a decent wage. And now that that is going, there's nothing left for us here.' It's hell working in that industry. The stink, the danger. It has surpassed coal mining as the most dangerous job in America. I asked if they'd been hurt on the job, and each one had a story. One raised his shirt and showed he'd been cut, a woman had her arm in a sling, another guy said that he can no longer cry tears. I used his story; that's what happened to Brandon in the play. All their bodies were damaged through their labor.

That's when I started thinking about how labor intimately affects our lives and relations and our desire. If you work twelve hours a day, and your hands are ruined and your back's ruined, are you going to have energy to make love to your closest person, whoever that is? If your hands hurt so much from working, can you play a puzzle game with your daughter when you get home from work? Bodies are used up and thrown aside. That's why the industry is so anti-union: companies want to use the labor, then — 'Out the back door and bring in the new.' I'd like to write a trilogy about American labor. *Slaughter City* is the first one. I thought *The Trestle* would be the second but I realized it wasn't.

I'm also very interested in the connection between race and class. Race is a major issue in this country, but class is often invisible, and I'm interested in the connections. Can you separate them, and what's the point of separating them if you're trying to develop resistance or awareness? I try to touch on that in *Slaughter City*, with the relationship between the two women, Maggot and Roach. And then, does the awareness mean we can't work together anymore? Can't be friends?

AG: WHAT DID THE LONDON PRODUCTION OF *SLAUGHTER CITY* LOOK LIKE?

NW: Bare, minimal. Which most of my work is. There's always a struggle over that. Some of the action in *Slaughter City* is obviously mimed, but in London, the actors used actual knives, because you had to have the feeling of the danger there. They did have meat turning in London, but there's a cloth that the industry has to use to cover the meat, so the carcasses were sort of masked — they almost looked like maidens, like draped people spinning on hooks. Of course, if a theater doesn't have money, you get into a problem putting together a paper-mâché slab of beef, which is horrible. But that's part of what the play is about — the realism and the not. You can do very different productions of that play, but if you go for total realism and try to build a meatpacking company, you're in trouble. But the London production looked beautiful and classical and very bare actually. They did use big metal tables, because they can slide in and out easily.

AG: YOUR STAGE DIRECTIONS AT THE BEGINNING OF SEVERAL PLAYS OFTEN SAY 'MINIMAL AND NOT "REALISTIC."'

NW: My warning is to try to get designers and others to forget kitchen-sink drama. You have the bodies and the language. The language of my plays may be pared to the bone, but there's a lot of it, so if you load a stage with 'things,' a production becomes cluttered. It can even become suffocating. The language needs all the space it can collect.

I'm influenced by Brecht and Brechtian theater. Pretending that something is real — what is the point? Realism stifles things. It eliminates the possibilities of what you can do.

AG: WHY DO YOU THINK YOUR PLAYS HAVE BEEN WEL-COMED STRONGLY IN ENGLAND AND LESS STRONGLY IN THE UNITED STATES?

NW: I don't know. If a play is about how we can have our fair shot at our American dream, that's acceptable. But if you start saying that maybe the American dream is a myth and a lie, and do we want that kind of dream — and is it even possible — you're getting into a whole different set of politics. Theater is largely a middle-class and upper-middle-class endeavor in terms of the audience in the United States. And audiences don't like to see the reasons that they are privileged being challenged.

The British have a longer tradition of political theater. When they read my work, the quality is more an issue than the politics. With playwrights like Trevor Griffiths and Edward Bond and Caryl Churchill, there's a bigger space for political theater in Britain. But the idea that my work is favored in the U.K. is changing. My last three productions were in the U.S. *The Trestle* is not scheduled for production in the U.K. until 2001, and then it will be done in Scotland. It has yet to receive a London premiere.

AG: IS THERE A WAY, WITHIN CAPITALISM, FOR SAUSAGE MAN AND COD TO RECONCILE, FOR OWNERS NO LONGER TO EXPLOIT LABOR?

NW: It's interesting that you say that, because I recently wrote a T-shirt play called *Manifesto* for Actors Theatre of Louisville. It was brief enough to be printed on the back of a T-shirt. I thought, 'Hell, I'm going to write about the Communist Manifesto.' You have the specter of Communism and the actual laborer, in the ruined body, arguing, and the laborer saying, 'Come back to earth. You've gone too far away. I'm the laboring body. I know about oppression.' Well, somebody read it and put out in the press that the play was about the coming together of two classes. And I thought, 'Oh, my God, do they have to search for this in my work?' Because it doesn't exist. The play is not about two classes negotiating, because I don't think that's possible.

Can capitalism take care of everybody? It cannot. I'm not going to say I know what would work, but I know that we can have a system in which education and health and the arts are priorities. We've had that at times in history. There are countries that take better care of people. I'm not utopian. I know we're never going to have a society where there's no injustice. But a society where a majority of people can't have decent healthcare? That's not democratic. A society with the highest incarceration rate in the world? If you want to talk about violence influencing young people's lives, talk about the violence of poverty. The violence of parents with no jobs. A truly democratic society is different from what we generally think of as democracy: a laissez-faire economy and the American dream.

In my work, I attack a system, never its people. You will never find 'evil' people in my plays, just evil systems. Even Boxler, the abusive, homophobic lieutenant in *In the Heart of America*, is not evil, although some people may not agree that he's a human being. My question is, How do people become corrupted? I try, with people who are caught up in an oppressive system, to find the moment when they changed, when they still could have become someone else. That's what excites me. ▽

black people did this.' And twenty years later, for me to be writing lines for André de Shields in *Play On!* — what a thrill. He doesn't know how much he changed my life.

Ntozake Shange came to Champaign to speak and perform her work, and I remember telling a friend, 'Oh, if I could ever do that.' I could never do what she does, but I was so enamored that somebody could have that much creativity and honesty, and that fury, and weave it into art. Those two experiences had such an impact on my life.

Anyway, I wrote *Getting Right Behind Something Like That*, a play about miscegenation, and showed it to somebody at Women's Studies, where I was working part-time, and she said, 'Oh, we should do this for the women's conference. Flesh it out some more and we'll do it. I'll direct it.' And I said, 'Oh, okay.' I went and really expanded it — I had no idea what worked onstage. Came time to do it, and the woman who had agreed to direct was too busy with the conference. So she said, 'You go and do it.' And I said, 'How do I do that?' And she says, 'Oh, here's a book' — something like *Directing 101*.

An actress named Crystal Laws Green, who had been working in L.A., had returned to Champaign to be with her mother, and everybody said that if I could get her, she would be great. And she said, 'I'll do it.' We got other actors from the community and put the play on. It ran about three hours. I can look at the piece now and think there were some compelling scenes, but whether it worked as a play? I don't think so. But it got reviewed. If people could hang in there, they got something out of it. It was a challenging experience in that I was doing the publicity, shopping for furniture for the set, painting the flats, selling the tickets, working the sound — I did everything. But it was the best training ground, because later I did *Before It Hits Home* and a couple of other plays that way. The same group of people would say, 'Oh, Cheryl's got a play, let's go do it.' The community college gave us space. That's how I got started.

AG: WOULD YOU ADVISE A YOUNG PLAYWRIGHT TO START THE SAME WAY?

CW: If you have a journey — something you want to do — you cannot wait for the establishment to give you permission. It is very difficult to get produced in regional theaters. If you have something to say, and you're knocking on that door and they're not answering, then you need to start at the community level. Because somebody in the community may get something from what you have to say, and you will learn. I learned so much and I was able to ignite others with the passion for what I was doing. Our group played about four years. At one point we were taking *Before It Hits Home* to East St. Louis and Iowa and other neighboring towns. We would rent trucks and put in the flats — too much stuff, because I had no idea you could do things simply. I would rent the trucks on my credit card, and we would do the shows and charge two dollars. We would get home at three in the morning, people had to be at jobs at seven in the morning. That's how *Before It Hits Home* developed.

AG: SINCE THEN, YOUR PLAYS HAVE BEEN PRODUCED IN MAJOR REGIONAL THEATERS. HOW DID YOU MAKE THAT LEAP?

CW: I sent *Before It Hits Home* to a contest at the Group Theatre's Multicultural Playwrights Festival in Seattle, and it won, and I went to Seattle for two weeks to workshop it. Tazewell Thompson, who at the time was artistic associate at Arena, was sent out there to look at the Festival's work. He loved what I was trying to say and told me that he was going to take my work back to Arena. Well, they weren't interested. There were people on Arena's staff who said that audiences would walk out because of the explicit language.

AG: DID YOU BELIEVE THAT WAS THE REASON?

CW: I believe that in the late 1980s and early 1990s black plays had to be a certain way for big regional theaters to embrace them. They had to have a certain level of artistry, they had to be palatable for the subscribers. I've heard often that women's work is so personal that subscribers won't turn out. White males' work is not personal, I guess. And when you add black onto personal, then the work becomes so specific that it won't attract an audience. That was the argument with *Before It Hits Home.*

I was pretty disheartened, but Tazewell hooked me up with his agent, who decided she would take me on. In the meantime, I wrote *Jar the Floor* and sent it to Kurt Beattie, who was running Empty Space

Theatre in Seattle at the time. He had come to the workshop of *Before It Hits Home* and he said, 'You have a great voice. If you ever have anything else, let me see it.' I sent *Jar* to him, and he said, 'We're going to produce this.' Also, Tazewell didn't give up. The year after that Festival, Zelda Fichandler at Arena asked him, 'What do you want to do?' and he said, 'I want to do *Before It Hits Home*,' and that's how my career took off. Tazewell was very connected with the regionals and championed my work at those theaters. Now, theaters probably produce me because I have a track record. People who were my champions early in my career still are. Beattie is now at Seattle Rep, and they're commissioning me to do a musical. But all artists know, it's an uphill climb.

AG: *PUDDIN 'N' PETE* AND *HOLIDAY HEART* HAD THEIR FIRST PRODUCTIONS AT MAINSTREAM REGIONAL THEATERS. DOES THAT AFFECT THE WORK AT ALL? ARE THERE THINGS THAT A LARGELY WHITE AUDIENCE MIGHT NOT GRASP?

CW: That can affect the play, although at Arena they really work when they have a black play to get a large black audience in there. When I started out, at the community level, I had a community network of people who would come in the beginning, when I was first working on something. The response would be clear and what I needed to hear as I worked on a piece.

I think it's always a struggle for writers. I've been produced at predominantly black theaters like Penumbra and Freedom Theatre, and my work can be controversial in that community as well.

AG: IN WHAT WAY?

CW: When I did *Before It Hits Home*, people thought that I shouldn't have 'AIDS' and 'black' in the same sentence. I got a lot of flack for that play when I first did it. You have to remember, that was more than ten years ago, and at that point people thought AIDS was a conspiracy against black people. Our journey with AIDS has mirrored the gay white community's in terms of denial: the idea that somebody has planted AIDS in the community. We're still struggling with that, and now AIDS is the leading cause of death among black women.

AG: HOW DO YOU RESPOND TO GETTING FLACK?

CW: I tend to let the work speak for itself. If you as an artist begin to filter how people should respond to your work, then you rob them of their total experience. I've never been so attacked that I felt I had to defend myself. I've worked with directors who took that on. I started writing to have people look at things differently, so if people get angry, then hopefully they're being challenged in some way. But if people think that I'm trying to denigrate my race by my work, that's hurtful. That's certainly not what I intend.

But you also have to understand that there are historical images of black people in this country which give us a right to be suspicious. And when we look at a theater's season, there's one play by a black person, so we expect that one play to do everything about our experience. If we had a play about a pimp, a priest, a pope — whatever — then we wouldn't expect that one Cheryl West play to cover the whole range of black experiences. As a writer, it is difficult to know that people draw conclusions about black life based on one play and that black people want that play to protect how people see us.

I've had black actors and actresses be very upset about *Jar the Floor*. Would not even read for it. With one production, an actress whom I really wanted said, 'I cannot as a black woman embrace this show and I feel insulted that you would even write something like this. I cannot be a part of it.' It was startling and hurtful, because I feel that *Jar the Floor* is a celebration of women. It attempts to be honest about different kinds of women and not apologize for them. The women in that play have their own poetry — the way Lola speaks is her own poetry. But one actress said the part was too 'colored' for her.

AG: WHAT DOES THAT MEAN?

CW: It means different things to different people. For many, it's the underside of being black. People tend to say 'colored' in the sense of 'those black people who we don't really want to see onstage.' Or they equate the work with so-called 'Chitlin' Circuit' kind of work. I think they must have missed what I was trying to do.

AG: WHOM DO YOU WRITE FOR?

CW: In the beginning of anything, I write for black people. When I became a writer I really wanted to write for my community, and so I start there. Someone told me once that the more specific you are, the more universal you are, and all races and genders enjoy my work. But I start with black people. First and foremost. Always.

AG: BUT IS THERE ONE BLACK COMMUNITY? THE STREET-WISE URBAN COMMUNITY THAT YOU DRAMATIZE IN *HOLIDAY HEART* IS DIFFERENT FROM THE COMMUNITY OF VARIED WOMEN IN *JAR THE FLOOR*, WHICH IS DIFFERENT FROM THE CONSERVATIVE FAMILY IN *BEFORE IT HITS HOME*.

CW: I try to be as inclusive as I can. I see the black community as made up of all kinds of people, so that's where I'm coming from. We are not a homogenized group. We are all kinds of classes, all kinds of interests, all kinds of images. You could write forever. There's so much richness in our history and in who we are today, trying to work and live in small towns and inner cities. I'm interested in the whole language of black experience.

AG: YOUR FOCUS, HOWEVER, SEEMS TO BE THE FAMILY.

CW: I'm always looking at how families continue to press on and stay intact. Often in my work I look at families that are built on shaky foundations, and then, when something hits that family, I look at how they grapple and come together. How something destroys the family, and how the family rebuilds.

AG: THE BAILEY FAMILY IN *BEFORE IT HITS HOME*.

CW: I love the Baileys. As complicated and flawed as they are.

AG: YOU GO AGAINST THE STEREOTYPICAL EXPECTATION OF A MOTHER'S BEHAVIOR. WE EXPECT THAT REBA, THE MOTHER, WILL BE THE ONE TO NURSE HER SON WHEN HE BECOMES ILL, AND THAT THE FATHER, WHO HAS BEEN SO CRITICAL OF HIS SON, WILL TURN HIS BACK.

CW: All along in that play the mother had stayed with her son. And one day I got this idea to change it. I said, 'I know what I'm going to do with that play; I'm going to make the father stay.' Some people had seen it the first way and were upset about that. Other people were, 'What a great thing that the father is the one who stays.'

At Arena, the audience was outraged, and the mother got hissed. The last monologue she has is, 'I hate what you've done to my house Wendal . . . . It's like somebody came in and smeared shit all over my walls . . . I'm scared to touch anything . . . ' And then she walks out. And the audience hissed her. I will never forget that. Yeah, the father stays behind. I so loved that, because he is the one we expect not to be able to do it. But he really loves that son. He just didn't know how in the beginning, but he learned.

A few people take issue with Lola in *Jar the Floor*, because she is occasionally profane and always oblivious to the wounds she inflicts on others. But she loves her family and does her best to take care of them. She cooks for them, she cleans, she buys them presents. She does everything but give them what they need. But she tries. That's what's beautiful and unique about families, and tragic: people are trying to give you the love that they have, but they don't always give you what you need. What's interesting artistically is how that plays out. In *Jar*, it plays itself out in several generations.

AG: YOU WROTE *JAR* AFTER *BEFORE IT HITS HOME* AND IT HAS QUITE A DIFFERENT TONE. MORE JUBILANT, PERHAPS.

CW: When *Jar* first came to me. It was like going to dinner with crazy people who were passionate in their craziness all the time and having a ball. I would sit down and think, 'What are you all going to do today?' Those women were so funny and full of life. I really wanted to write a play like *Jar*, so it came easily. Everything doesn't come like that, but *Jar* did.

AG: COULD YOU TALK A LITTLE MORE ABOUT HOW *JAR* BEGAN?

CW: *Before It Hits Home* was so hard to write and so about men that I thought, 'I'm going to do a play about some fun women.' That was basically it. I looked at the most interesting women that I could enjoy developing. I always say, 'I write the people I want to know. They have something to teach me.' Interestingly, both my great-grandmothers were still alive when I was writing *Jar*, although the one I was closest to died the first day of rehearsal for the first production. The play is dedicated to her.

AG: WHERE IS YOUR FAMILY FROM?

CW: My mother's mother is from Durant, Mississippi — West Mississippi — and my father's people are from Durant as well. My parents knew each other when they were kids and then met up again years later in Chicago, because everybody came to Chicago.

AG: DID YOU EVER VISIT YOUR GREAT-GRANDPARENTS IN MISSISSIPPI?

CW: Actually, the term 'jar the floor' came from there. I must have been fourteen or fifteen, and my mother and brother and I had gone down to visit. My great-grandparents thought they were upscale because they lived in town then. They had been sharecroppers and lived in the country with cows and chickens (they still had chickens, but they didn't have cows or a pig). They only had three rooms and a kitchen, and sometimes, when all of us would visit, twenty would sleep in this house. But it was fun, because it was all about family, and nobody ever said, 'Where's my room?' People would get lawn chairs and sleep on the porch.

Anyway, my mother and brother and I were sleeping on the pull-out couch, and my great-grandfather, my mother's grandfather, believed in getting up with the roosters and the hens. And we didn't get up. He came to the doorway and said, 'You all better get up now.' And we kept thinking, 'He must be kidding. We are from Chicago, we don't get up like this.' To us it was still dark. About the third time he came in, he said, 'You children better jar that floor.' I asked my mother, 'What's he mean by that?' And she said, 'He means he wants to hear the floorboards move.' That stuck with me. The image of your movement, your power, making the floor move. When I started writing *Jar the Floor*, I thought that when those women finally connected, the floor boards would actually move. It would be that powerful.

One time I was visiting there and I came to the table with shorts on, and my great-grandfather put his fork down and wouldn't eat. He said, 'You're not coming to this table with bloomers on.' I looked at my mother like, 'Oh, please. Can't you talk to him?' In the end, I had to go change clothes. Down there, I also had to serve my brother before myself. To this day, my grandmother serves her brothers before any woman gets served. It was assumed that when men came in from the fields, they would get the best of the food. It was enlightening being there, and I loved it, because it was where I came from. The woman I am today has a lot to do with those experiences, which traveled through all those generations to make me who I am.

AG: IT WAS CLEAR TO ME WHEN I SAW *JAR THE FLOOR* AT SECOND STAGE THAT A CHAIN OF HURT HAS BEEN PASSED ALONG THROUGH THOSE FOUR GENERATIONS. EACH MOTHER HAS REJECTED HER DAUGHTER, BEGINNING WITH MADEAR'S MOTHER — THE GREAT-GREAT-GRANDMOTHER — WHOM WE HEAR ABOUT BUT WHO IS DEAD BY THE TIME OF THE PLAY. EACH DAUGHTER FEELS REJECTED BY, OR IS ANGRY AT, HER MOTHER. AS A DAUGHTER, I HAVE BEEN THERE. BUT HAVING READ ESSAYS AND STORIES BY BELL HOOKS, ALICE WALKER, AND OTHER AFRICAN-AMERICAN WOMEN ABOUT THE REVERENCE THEY FEEL FOR THEIR MOTHERS, I WAS TAKEN ABACK.

CW: I wrote Lola for Crystal Laws Green, who did *Jar the Floor* all over the country. She recently died, at fifty-two. She used to say, 'Well, if you wrote that a black woman was losing her mind, they would really be mad at you, because black women never have breakdowns. We never commit suicide. We are the salt of the earth. We can do and take everything.' We used to laugh about that.

There is a perception that we revere our mothers. There used to be a line in *Jar the Floor* that I borrowed from Alice Walker, about how black women never get healed in therapy, because they revere their mothers so much they can never get angry enough at them. I'm one of those daughters who reveres her mother. My mother has been a beacon of courage and inspiration for me. But we are complicated women. It's a disservice to say that we are all powerful all of the time. Then if we're not, we feel so much worse, because we are supposed to be able to be strong and carry everybody.

I like to think that we are strong, but I also think that we travel a complicated road. *Jar* looks at that. These women in *Jar* think they have worked really hard and provided. It wasn't enough, but that family is going to go on, and they never stop trying to find ways to love each other.

AG: THERE DOES SEEM TO BE A CHAIN OF SCARRING. EACH MOTHER SCARS HER DAUGHTER A BIT.

CW: And then Raisa comes in wearing her scar on the outside, which makes all their inside scars start to jump. Here's somebody who's saying, 'I have this scar, and it's out here.' When we see somebody's scar on the outside, it makes what we're hiding inside jump a little more.

AG: DOES THAT CHAIN BREAK AT ANY POINT?

CW: When Vennie says, 'You're not going to stop me, Mother. I'm going. I'll find a way,' and MayDee says, 'I know whatever you decide, you'll survive,' in some way MayDee is releasing her. My idea with *Jar* is that until you know your mother's journey as a woman, you will never be able to understand her mistakes and forgive her. We tend to look at our mothers only as our mothers. If women were able to understand what our mothers' personal journeys were — what they had to give up, for instance — maybe we could have a different view of them. Vennie finally learning that her mother was a victim of sexual abuse gives her clarity about why her mother has been cold and controlling. But often we are not privy to that kind of information.

AG: MY MOTHER KEPT AN ENORMOUS AMOUNT HIDDEN. WHEN SHE DIED I FOUND DIARIES, LOVE LETTERS. I DISCOVERED A DIFFERENT PERSON.

CW: I think parents keep these things to themselves because they want you to have the image of them that they want. They have a fear of disclosure, especially of things that they want to forget. But I think that attitude does a disservice to the mother-daughter relationship once the daughter is a grown woman. Maybe we could forgive them things if we had that knowledge. That's what *Jar* is looking at: how do we forgive? Because if our parent has a wound and doesn't know how to deal with their own hurt, they're going to wound us. MaDear never really loved Lola, or if she did, Lola never knew it. So it was hard for Lola to be a parent to MayDee. How do you parent someone else — be loving and nurturing and present — if you never had that for yourself? Lola did the best she could. The women say that all through the play: I'm doing the best I can here.

Money's a real big deal in *Jar*. People buy for each other. That's the way they show love. They show love in other ways, but not in ways that the person needs. But they keep trying. That's the dignity in it to me, that they're still in there trying. Lola comes every day. MaDear will not say a kind word to her, but she still comes every day. MayDee is a cold fish to her own daughter, but she takes in MaDear, and every day MaDear makes her life miserable. But MaDear has a home.

AG: BUT MAYDEE DOESN'T ALLOW MADEAR TO HAVE A GARDEN.

CW: I know. She has to control something. And just at the moment that MayDee finally gets happiness, Vennie says that she came home in order to get money. When I wrote the play, I thought Vennie's attitude was cute. But now that I'm a mother, I sit in rehearsal and look at the daughter and say, 'I just would kill Vennie.' But I understand her. She's still punishing her mother.

AG: DOES THE PRODUCTION OF *JAR* AT SECOND STAGE DIFFER FROM THOSE THAT HAVE GONE BEFORE?

CW: I got much more involved in this one. I made a concerted effort this time to stand up for things.

I think it's a struggle women have sometimes when working with directors. We're so into making sure everybody's happy, and sometimes the work suffers as a result. There are times I have not wanted a certain actor to be cast and I caved in, because I thought that maybe the director knew better than I did. But this time I decided that I wasn't going to acquiesce if I didn't think something was right. That's a lesson for women working in the theater: to be assertive when you sometimes don't want to be. You can't be scared they're going to call you a bitch, because they're going to do that anyway. I used to be so scared of that. Now, I can't be scared of it, not at the expense of my work getting hurt. I want to be the kind of woman who is fair but tough.

AG: THERE SEEMS TO BE MORE OVERLAPPING OF DIALOGUE IN THE PRODUCTION AT SECOND STAGE THAN IN THE PUBLISHED VERSION OF THE PLAY.

CW: It is a thing I do in every play. There is always a place where conversation overlaps, because I think people do that in order not to hear each other. *Before It Hits Home* has a whole scene where two realities exist side by side. *Jar* always had that outdoor scene and the indoor scene happening as an overlap. But there are times in *Jar* now where it occurs more, because the women do not want to hear each other, and that's one of the tools they use. Some of it is in the script; a couple of places the actors have found.

AG: IN THE PUBLISHED SCRIPT, MAYDEE HAS A LINE TO HER MOTHER, LOLA, 'HOW MANY THIRTEEN-YEAR-OLDS START WETTING THE BED AGAIN. HUH?' IT OCCURS WHEN SHE CONFRONTS LOLA ABOUT BEING SEXUALLY MOLESTED BY ONE OF LOLA'S BOYFRIENDS.

CW: That's been cut. I took out a little section in that scene, and now the scene is clearer.

AG: YOU ADDED AN ACTUAL TELEPHONE CALL FROM A.H., MADEAR'S SON.

CW: Right. From the beginning, I've reworked and reworked that last scene, when MaDear relives the betrayal and loss of her husband. We used to have a huge picture of MaDear's mother that Lola had brought, and there was a whole beat of that. But I never really liked that, because it seemed to stop the play. So Marion McClinton — the director — and I came up with the idea that A.H. would trigger MaDear, because she's been waiting all day for his phone call, since it's her birthday. I realized that all the women are waiting on something to deliver them, and that all they have is each other.

AG: DO YOU LIKE TO REWRITE?

CW: Do I like to rewrite or do I rewrite? I rewrite a lot. *Jar* is ten years old, and I still rewrote during this rehearsal process. Rewriting *Holiday Heart* for the screen was fun, because the screenplay could do so much that I couldn't do onstage. But sometimes you're exhausted, and you're like, 'I'm through with this. I don't want to go back.' Writing is wonderful when you first sit down and it's just coming — that's the greatest high you could have. But when you go back and you know it's not working . . . I clean the house. I look at my kids. It's hard.

AG: HOW DID *HOLIDAY HEART* BEGIN?

CW: Usually I just get annoyed by something I've read, and stuff starts to cook. But I read where an elderly woman had shot her daughter, who was a crack addict, at close range. I was so moved: how could an older woman shoot her daughter? She shot her in the chest and she got off. And the reason she got off was that she said, 'I put my daughter out of her misery.' In my family, if you did something really bad, you might hear a mother or father say, 'I brought you into this world, I'll take you out.' And I remember saying to a friend that the story gave new meaning to that.

I kept thinking about what drugs were doing to people, and then I read where black children were going to have to go to an orphanage system, because there are many black kids in foster care as a result of drugs and AIDS. I thought, 'What about these kids who lose their parents and are going to be in foster care? Are people out there who would want to love them?' And I thought, 'I'm going to write a story about that.' And Holiday came to me, and I thought, 'He's going to be the best parent for her. I'm not going to make anybody the bad person, because it's all about loving, and it would be great if they could all parent her. That would be the ultimate.'

AG: YOU SAY THAT *HOLIDAY HEART* BEGAN WITH THE STORY IN THE NEWSPAPER. BUT YOU SEEM TO EMPHASIZE CHARACTER IN THAT PLAY AND IN YOUR OTHER PLAYS.

CW: I always start from character. That's why it's harder for me when I write for television and film, because those mediums are about plot points. I don't always know where I'm going to end up, but in television and film they want you to come in with an outline and know where you're going. That ruins the fun. For me, writing a play is about where a character's going to take me. I had no idea Holiday was that guy when I wrote it.

The essence of *Holiday Heart* was the wonderful love story between this drag queen and this little girl. And I thought it was interesting that here were all these people who love this little girl in their different ways and try to have a family. If you polled the audience for *Holiday Heart* before they walked in — 'Would you want a drag queen to raise a little girl?' — they would say, 'No.' But three-quarters of the way through, they're rooting for him. That's the great thing about art: you can have audiences go on a journey and switch attitudes when they don't even want to switch. In life, we don't see the heart of somebody like Holiday, because we are turned off by who he's supposed to be. We don't get to see that there may be a heart in a drug pusher, or that a mother who uses drugs may have her own journey. In life, we look at people, label them, and thus discount them. But they may have a child they love somewhere, and that child may be depending on them. In *Holiday Heart*, I wanted to show that.

AG: HOLIDAY HEART IS SUCH A LARGE CHARACTER.

CW: Holiday to me is a modern-day hero. Someone who is willing to live and die by the dictates of love. He loves Niki and Wanda so totally that he still loves them even after they hurt him terribly. The characters in *Holiday Heart* all struggle with what a family looks like and what a family is. A mom and pop and two kids is the image many of us grow up thinking the average family looks like, but what a family is are people who are joined not necessarily by blood but by a willingness to love each other through the darkest hours. Holiday knows what a family is. So many of us still struggle with what it is supposed to look like.

AG: STILL, *HOLIDAY HEART* HAS A BLEAK ENDING.

CW: Yeah, I didn't leave it with hope, because I feel so strongly about what's happened with children. I never think I have sweet endings to anything. They're unsentimental plays, because the truth is sometimes very hard. I want to leave an audience with something to ponder. They can bring their own ending if they need to. If they can go back to their families and make a different ending than what I put out there, then that's good. I want people to see there was love between these characters, but I don't see life tied up neatly.

In the movie, though, he doesn't die. The president of Showtime had one note: Holiday cannot die. He was obsessed about that. I rewrote it, but it still has a hard ending, so it still has integrity.

AG: *PUDDIN 'N' PETE: FABLE OF A MARRIAGE* DOES NOT HAVE A HARD ENDING, ALTHOUGH THERE IS NO CERTAINTY THAT PUDDIN AND PETE'S MARRIAGE WILL SURVIVE.

CW: That play is very different from the others. It had two versions, and the second was like a fable. At the Old Globe Theatre, in San Diego, we had a set that evoked the Garden of Eden. We had a dancer who was like a snake doing the narrative. The audience loved it, the critics hated it. I never will know the secret to making that play work.

It is about two people from different classes trying to make a marriage. The guy is a janitor, and she is in business. He is fun, but he is a simple man and doesn't know how to reach her. He thinks she is ashamed of him, and she is, in a way. She wants to dress him up and make him different. He tries. One of the funniest scenes I think I've ever written is their dinner party. Puddin's friends come, and they are all playing Scrabble, and he puts down three-letter words. Later, the two have a huge argument about it. Puddin's friends talk about sex, and Pete has never been in that kind of environment. He says, 'Have they all slept together?' The play is about class, but it is also about people trying to love each other across a ravine, trying to find a way to meet somewhere.

AG: CLASS IS AN UNTOUCHABLE SUBJECT IN AMERICA.

CW: We don't like to talk about that. He pushes broom at a school, and she wants more. She thinks, 'I'll just make him over.' But he doesn't want to be made over. He has a collection of hats — this collection is his prize possession — and he even buys her a hat. In a way he is always changing hats to figure out who he is. It's an interesting play.

AG: BECAUSE YOU USE A CHORUS OF CHARACTERS WHO COMMENT TO EACH OTHER ABOUT PUDDIN AND PETE'S

RELATIONSHIP, THE PLAY FEELS LIKE A FORMAL DEPARTURE FROM *BEFORE IT HITS HOME AND JAR THE FLOOR.*

CW: I'm experimenting with form even more now. I'm working on a piece that's looking at racism, and I'm playing with linear structure, going back and forth and having overlapping realities. It depends on what you're trying to do on a particular play. Some plays should be linear. Some lend themselves to experimentation.

AG: WHAT IS THE DIFFERENCE FOR YOU AS A PLAYWRIGHT, IN TERMS OF MONEY OR ANYTHING ELSE, BETWEEN HAVING YOUR PLAYS PRODUCED IN THE REGIONS AND HAVING THEM PRODUCED IN NEW YORK?

CW: Second Stage wanted to do *Jar* in 1991. Carole Rothman, the artistic director, had gone to see it at Arena. But after my experience with *Before It Hits Home*, I said, 'No. I cannot go near New York again. I can keep *Jar* out here in the regionals and not worry about New York.' *Jar* paid my mortgage for years. Kill it like *Holiday Heart*? People talked me into bringing *Holiday* in, because it had been done at regional theaters and was well received. People said, 'Don't worry, Cheryl, this will be the one. You can bring that in.' And we got slammed. And if a play fails in New York, that's it. I have not had one other regional production of *Holiday Heart* since, and up to that time, regionals wanted to do it. Came into New York, got slammed, and nobody even asked to read it again. Not even to read it.

When you're doing your career, you have to think about what will happen if you come to New York with a play and it's not received well. I have two kids. I want to feed them. Maybe if you're August Wilson or Wendy Wasserstein, Albee or John Guare, your work will continue even if the critics don't like it. Even when critics don't like those playwrights' work, they seem to be respectful. When they don't like my work, it's like I have no talent.

For a while I was probably the most produced African-American female playwright, but I was still labeled as an 'emerging writer.' I used to say that a white boy could come in here, have one hit, and never be called 'emerging' again. He may not have even done the regional theater struggle. But women are emerging for the longest time.

When do you get that kind of respect? Is it when you make it in New York? Is it when you win a certain prize? Is it if you write a play that is controversial? We could be doing this for fifteen years and still be called 'emerging.'

It takes a lot of courage to do theater, because you deal with critics, with the audience, with other artists, and every day you have to keep believing, 'I've got something to say that's unique.' It takes a lot to keep going, particularly if you do work that you believe in but nobody gets. Until *Jar the Floor* opened at Second Stage, I had never done well critically in New York.

AG: MANY OF THE WOMEN I'VE SPOKEN WITH HAVE COMPLAINED ABOUT CRITICS, ESPECIALLY THE NEW YORK CRITICS.

CW: Well, they're largely white males, and unless you're appealing to their interests, they don't have the background to discuss your work. If you're not August Wilson, who I think they think they understand, how do they measure what you have to say against what he's doing? An artistic director said one time, because I wanted director approval: 'Who does she think she is? August Wilson?' I'm telling you, it can be very insulting. August Wilson is an extraordinary playwright, but I don't believe he wants to be the yardstick against which every black writer is measured. Is there not room for all kinds of voices examining the black experience?

AG: IS THERE AN ANTIDOTE TO THAT KIND OF ATTITUDE?

CW: Integrate a theater's staff, so that your staff is bringing something to the table, and listen to them. If you don't know how to evaluate a play because it's far from your experience, then go out and learn about that experience. I don't think that everybody running a theater knows about the Holocaust, but they educate themselves to know that such a play has something to say. So why not do that for Asian plays, African-American plays? Get to know our experience. Our experience is not what you see on TV. If that's how you know who we are, then when you get a *Jar the Floor* or a *Holiday Heart*, you won't know what to do with it.

AG: WOULD YOU LIKE TO SEE CRITICS EDUCATE THEM-
SELVES?

CW: I would like to think critics are reading about who you are —
not so much as an artist, but the world you're trying to create. Coming
with an open mind. Critics have to see a lot of different work, just as
artists need to have a bunch of experiences to create. If critics are only
going to see mainstream twenty-eight-year-old plays, or plays by 'recognized' artists, then they won't know where to put our work. If they
never come out of whatever their community is, what kind of yardstick will they have to judge our work? I feel as though critics don't
know the world that I'm writing about. I also think that I'm compared to people they've accepted as the 'real' writers. And if that's their
narrow definition, then I'm always going to fall short.

AG: SOMETIMES IT SEEMS THAT THE AMERICAN THEATER
IS BECOMING INCREASINGLY COMPARTMENTALIZED AC-
CORDING TO ETHNICITY AND GENDER.

CW: Well, I'd hate to think that. I think art's goal is to heal, and if
we compartmentalize then we aren't healing. If I don't get to see *The
Joy Luck Club*, I may never see Asian people in the way that changed
me when I saw that piece of work. I saw how alike families are. If
that story was not available to me, because it was only for the author's
community, I may not have grown as a person. I don't think com-
partmentalizing is the answer.

AG: YOU NOW LIVE IN SEATTLE.

CW: Seattle Rep offered me an artistic home.

AG: WHAT DOES THAT MEAN?

CW: It means any work I have, I can workshop there. Use their
resources, go and watch other artists work. I'm working on a gospel,
hip-hop musical, something that I came to them with and they said,
'Let's do it.'

AG: DO YOU MAKE A LIVING WRITING FOR THE THEATER?

CW: I definitely have to do at least two projects a year that are television or film. No. I couldn't make it off of my plays, especially with two kids. I'm a single parent. There were a couple years, when *Jar* and *Holiday Heart* were being produced, that my royalties were nice, so I could have lived off of that. But you may take a year to write a play, and then you have to wait until it comes up in the season. And even that is so iffy. A theater can change its mind. A writer almost always has to write in other mediums in order to have enough money if they are supporting a family.

AG: HOW DO YOU DEAL WITH BEING AN ARTIST AND A MOTHER?

CW: It's hard. One time my two-year-old got on my computer and just started banging and saying, 'I'm working.' So I'm probably not dealing with it well.

What I had from my mother, and what I hope my kids get from me, is that work is important. Whatever work women choose to do, it should be important to them. When my kids are on the couch some day, talking with some therapist about their difficult lives, I hope they appreciate that I want them to find work they feel passionate about. They went to *Play On!* and they can sing a lot of the words to the songs because they listen to the CD, and they dance to it. So they were able to get what I do by going to it. Now, when I get ready to leave for rehearsal, they say, 'Mommy, you're going to work today?' But they don't have a real clear idea about *Jar*, and I know if I take them to see it, they'll say, 'Those women are angry.' They can't stand *Annie*, because they think Miss Hannigan is too angry.

I hope that when my children review my sins, they will realize that I feel my work is a mission. With strong families, we build strong communities, and with strong communities, we build a better world. Art teaches us, hopefully, where we fail, where we soar, and where the two mix together. So if by chance I create art that will last the test of time, I hope my children will be gracious about those times my art borrowed me away from them. Yes, I have to make compromises. I'm tired much of the time. They want mommy the first thing in the morning. I used to write first thing in the morning. Well, forget that now. I write until midnight and one in the morning and then get up at six in the morning and start all over again.

But you have to hope, like every mother hopes, that they'll forgive you and understand why you were who you were. My mother worked a lot. My mother had to work mostly for survival, but she also has passion about what she does, so I grew up honoring work and believing that a woman's outlet for creativity is important. And if I'm not happy as a woman, I'm not going to be a very happy mother. I make tons of mistakes. But I always wanted kids, so I would have a big hole if I hadn't become a mother.

But this production of *Jar* is the first time I've been doing a show and had my kids with me constantly, and that's been a learning experience. They've adjusted, but I feel badly. I went to work one day and felt, 'Here I'm writing a story about mothers and daughters and I'm not even being a mother.' I called my mother up and said, 'I'm not even being a mother.' And she said, 'I tell you what, Cheryl — they'll get over it.' And I said, 'But I feel so guilty, and they're getting behavior problems because they're only seeing me three hours a day.' It's great that I still have my mother, so I can call her and she can say, 'Trust me. It will be okay.'

AG: FAMILY AGAIN.

CW: Yes. You know, my family came up from the South in the 1940s. My grandmother was part of that big exodus to the North. My grandmother always says that in the forties, people had a sense of community. You knew almost everybody black in Chicago, and people helped each other out.

That whole sense of finding a home again, it started with coming from Africa. It's continuous in the history of black people: where do we find that home again? I see it in my work. We're trying to get back that sense of community and family. We can go and live anywhere now and so we've moved out of the community and assumed that is better in a lot of ways. But there has been a cost.

The key is to be free to find community, and that's an individual journey. Unfortunately, we're into limiting what people should do in this world. There's a hatred toward people, an intolerance, and it's frightening. When people talk about affirmative action now, it's become okay to hate affirmative action. 'Why don't black people just get over it?' I hear people say, 'Why don't Jewish people get over it?' And I'm thinking, scars heal but they don't go away. You asked about that in

Jar. Scars don't go away, and if we don't respect that, we're really headed for trouble, because the hurts are going to resurface. We're going to keep them full of new blisters.

It's amazing to me how people want to discount other people's journeys and history. I want the world to be better, but sometimes you think people are slipping. But as artists, you can't give up. You cannot get cynical. Your art cannot do that. You have to keep trudging ahead and thinking of a different way to look at the world. And hope that people will take that journey with you. ▽

Elizabeth Wong

Elizabeth Wong lives in Los Angeles, a city with the kind of visible and invisible cultural borders about which she writes in her plays. Before turning to theater and receiving an M.F.A. from New York University in 1991, she was working as a journalist: a field producer for KNXT-TV in Los Angeles, a reporter for *The San Diego Tribune*, and a reporter for *The Hartford Courant* in Connecticut. She still writes in a variety of media, believing that the only way to survive as a playwright in America. She has been an editorial columnist for *The Los Angeles Times,* a writing fellow at Disney studios, and a staff writer on the ABC Television situation comedy, *All-American Girl.*

Wong's plays include *Letters to a Student Revolutionary* (1989), which dramatizes the changing friendship between a rebellious American girl of Chinese descent and the politically sensitive Chinese girl she meets for a few moments during a trip to Beijing; *Kimchee and Chitlins* (1990), a play that is satirically titled after the 'trademark' dishes of Koreans and African Americans, and delves into the racism that roils a New York City community; *China Doll* (1995), based on the life of film star Anna May Wong; and a dream play called *Inside a Red Envelope* (1999).

Wong is an avid golfer; this interview took place on July 19, 1999, at the Los Feliz 3-Par Golf Course in Los Angeles.

• • •

AG: HOW DID YOU BECOME INTERESTED IN THEATER?

EW: My first brush with the theater was watching *Equus*, with Brian Bedford. He was in a production at the Huntington Hartford Theater here in Los Angeles, and I got to sit on the stage for five dollars, student rush. We were the jury, and Bedford, who played the psychiatrist, was pleading his case to us. It was a very involving, absorbing experience, and then to have Brian Bedford wink at me, and on top of it there was nudity! That was a seminal experience.

AG: HOW OLD WERE YOU?

EW: Eighteen or nineteen. I had led a sheltered life, and theater seemed daunting and frightening, so for a while I approached it as spectacle, as someone who liked to sit in the dark.

I was a journalist for ten years, but in 1988, I resigned and gave myself the gift of a year to explore. I moved to New Haven, and I happened to be walking down Chapel Street one day and saw a sign, 'Office Manager Wanted,' at a place called Performance Studio which produced Shakespeare outdoors. Although I had vowed to give myself a year free of encumbrances, I had not taken stock of my finances, so I took that job as a buffer.

At Performance Studio, I hooked up with Yale School of Drama, and I was encouraged to see plays and write, to participate as a stage manager and set painter — things in the background. My first actual job in theater was as a lighting board operator — that's what I consider my initiation. I didn't know a thing about it; I faked my way and, in fact, was found out. I thought that surely it cannot be hard to push the lever up and down and count one, two . . . but it was.

Dennis Scott hired me to do it. I had heard that Yale Drama needed people to work for the world premiere of a play about Australian aborigines, and I went in to volunteer my time, and Dennis, who is no longer with us, was the director and he made everyone audition. So I had to come up with something on the spot, never having auditioned in my entire life, and I thought up a scenario of a woman who's sane in an insane asylum, and I went bananas. I flung myself from wall to wall. I was rolling on the floor. I don't know what possessed me. Later on, I asked Dennis why he even asked me to be part of the project, and he said he liked my energy.

Those are the things that influenced my steps toward theater. But it always seemed that I was gravitating toward theater naturally, so I never wrote that short story or began that novel. From the moment I hit New Haven, got the job at Performance Studio, got associated with the folks at Yale — sneaking into classes, stealing an education — it made sense to me. I felt comfortable and knew theater was what I wanted to do. I wrote my first play: *The Aftermath of a Chinese Banquet*. It's my first dysfunctional-family drama, which I think every young playwright writes. It has never been produced, but it helped me get into graduate school.

AG: DO YOU MAKE A LIVING AS A PLAYWRIGHT?

EW: I've been making a living as a writer since I became a journalist. But the financial realities of being a playwright are pretty grim. One year I had three plays in production at the same time: I made nine thousand dollars that year. Very substantive productions, nine thousand dollars. Oh, my God. Cannot be done. So I look for other things. Not only working in Hollywood, but also teaching. I'd love to be a marshal on a golf course, but I don't have time for that.

As a playwright, you have to co-opt a phrase from the business world and 'diversify your portfolio.' I have been on staff for a Hollywood sitcom. I have written television episodes and films. Ironically, those projects always come because someone saw a play of mine. I got the job on *All-American Girl* because the executive producer came to see a reading of *Kimchee and Chitlins* at Mark Taper Forum. By staying on track and focusing on my work as a playwright, these other things come.

AG: WHAT DO YOU LIKE ABOUT THEATER?

EW: I love the theater because it's about the *immediate*. I love that theater has a sense of urgency. Theater is reflective of the way life is; it's just a concentrated dose of life. I also love the way people speak, and being able to have a verbal dialogue with audiences. It's my most direct form of communication, although I have also learned that some of the most exquisite communication onstage is nonverbal. I like the way theater provokes people and provides a place for robust debate.

I take delight in seeing my work done in places like Louisville,

Kentucky, or Cincinnati, Ohio. When my plays go to middle America, I feel that I'm doing my job. When I'm having a dialogue with people who might not have encountered my experience, I feel that maybe I'm enriching their lives, because they can access ideas and even a culture that they have never accessed before. Without sounding like I'm trying to be a politician, part of my job as a playwright is to try to change and improve things. My audience is anyone who wants to make things better. I think any writer who puts pen to paper — metaphorically, because now most of us work with computers — is an activist in some way. We're taking action. I hope that's taking action. I want it to be taking action. When I feel that playwriting is no longer causing robust debate, then maybe I'll do something else.

AG: IN HER PREFACE TO *LETTERS TO A STUDENT REVOLUTIONARY*, ROBERTA UNO WRITES ABOUT THE SIGNIFICANCE OF YOUR SEEING WAKAKO YAMAUCHI'S DRAMA *AND THE SOUL SHALL DANCE* ON TELEVISION.

EW: That was around the same time I saw *Equus*. It was the first time I saw people who looked like me having truthful emotional upheavals. Upheavals that I didn't completely relate to, because Nisei were not part of my experience, but I was relieved finally to see reflections of myself in popular culture. I felt, 'Oh, maybe I matter.' Subsequently, after David Henry Hwang's *M Butterfly* was a Broadway hit, I realized 'Oh, maybe *my stories* matter.' Prior to the arrival of people like Wakako and Velina Houston and Frank Chin and David — I didn't think my stories mattered.

AG: WHERE DID YOU GROW UP?

EW: I was born in a place called Southgate, which is in South Central L.A. After my father died, my family moved to Chinatown. Then after Chinatown we moved to a city on the outskirts of East Los Angeles. So I'm a ghetto girl from all the best ghettos.

AG: L.A. CHINATOWN SEEMS QUITE DIFFERENT FROM NEW YORK CHINATOWN.

EW: In what way is it different?

AG: TO ME, NEW YORK CHINATOWN LOOKS LIKE A NINETEENTH-CENTURY URBAN GHETTO: NARROW STREETS, TENEMENTS. L.A. CHINATOWN FEELS OPEN AND EXPANSIVE. POSSIBLY JUST A MATTER OF DIFFERING URBAN GEOGRAPHIES.

EW: I think of New York Chinatown, which I love, as a very lively place. It seems like part of the city, where the Chinese people happen to live. L.A. Chinatown always seems carnivalesque. It seems set up for tourism, an artificial place capitalizing on whatever stereotypes people have of Asian communities. You can find the wishing wells and the pagoda-style houses. It's mostly gift shops.

AG: IN AN INTRODUCTION TO AN EARLY VERSION OF *CHINA DOLL*, YOU WROTE THAT YOU LONGED TO LEAVE CHINATOWN.

EW: I always wanted to get away. I didn't like living in Chinatown, I couldn't relate to anything that was in Chinatown. It took the self-reflection that comes from being an artist to find my way back home. Now I feel comfortable with who I am, and the Chinese culture enriches me and enriches my work. I'm grateful that I have a foundation which I can operate from. It gives me an anchor, a sense of stability in a life that is often tempestuous, financially and emotionally.

AG: YOU MENTIONED FRANK CHIN. IN THE 1970S, IN A PREFACE TO *AIIEEEEE!*, HE WRITES THAT 'WE HAVE BEEN ENCOURAGED TO BELIEVE THAT WE HAVE NO CULTURAL INTEGRITY AS CHINESE- OR JAPANESE-AMERICANS, THAT WE ARE EITHER ASIAN (CHINESE OR JAPANESE) OR AMERICAN (WHITE), OR ARE MEASURABLY BOTH. THIS MYTH OF BEING EITHER/OR AND THE EQUALLY GOOFY CONCEPT OF THE DUAL PERSONALITY HAUNTED OUR LOBES WHILE OUR REJECTION BY BOTH ASIA AND WHITE AMERICA PROVED WE WERE NEITHER ONE NOR THE OTHER.'

EW: When you do not look like everyone else, you quickly discover that you are treated like a stranger in a strange land. I grew up with Humphrey Bogart and John Wayne, tacos and hamburgers. But I also grew up with Chinese food and dragon dances. I grew up with stories about my family's life in China. So I can see where Frank's coming from.

But I don't have that sense of otherness. Maybe I did as a youth, but now I don't. I have a sense that that's what being American is: we are an amalgam. Our country is an aggregate, and we should wake up to the fact. I am American. If anything, I abhor the hyphen that makes me 'Chinese-American,' because I am American. When I travel abroad, I'm keenly aware that I'm American, but in my own country I'm often perceived as foreign until proven otherwise. That happens even with innocent questions like, 'Where are you from?' If I say I'm from Los Angeles, California, I often get a second question saying, 'No, no. I mean where are you *from*? Where is your family from?' And I say, 'Well, my family is from mainland China.' I try to force a further conversation, because people get to know you better once they ask more questions.

AG: PERHAPS IN THE YEARS SINCE CHIN WROTE THAT, AMERICANS HAVE BECOME MORE ACCEPTING OF OUR MULTICULTURED CULTURE.

EW: Actually, from the artist's point of view, it might not be so, because you can look at the number of productions by people of color and make a comparison with the number of productions by white artists, and you'll probably not find much difference between then and now. If you look at popular culture on television, there have been strides in the black community, but the presence of Hispanics is almost non-existent and the Asian presence is rare. It's paradoxical. Americans are more advanced than we used to be in terms of race, yet just as backward. We're more sensitized and also complacent, because we think the problems of racism are solved. I disagree. Racism permeates every thing.

People often ask me, 'What is the solution to the race problem?' I do have an answer in *Kimchee and Chitlins*, but the answer is so difficult for people to hear that often they don't. In my view, you have to abandon your own pain to recognize another's. Abandon your pain and embrace that other person's, even if you loathe them and they say things that make your blood boil. You have to have what is akin to an altruistic brotherly love, a Godlike recognition that we're all one.

Elizabeth Wong 499

I don't mean to get mystical — that's not my intent — but that's an answer in *Kimchee and Chitlins* which people often ignore. That's my answer to myself.

AG: HAVE YOU ENCOUNTERED AUDIENCE RESISTANCE TO *KIMCHEE AND CHITLINS*?

EW: If there's resistance, it's primarily because the play is a satire, and often people feel that the subject of race should be dealt with seriously and that comedy isn't an appropriate vehicle. I disagree; I think comedy is the most powerful tool for dealing with complex problems. You'd be amazed how powerful that play can be once audiences allow themselves to laugh at how they perceive people. The scene in which blacks play Koreans and Koreans play blacks, in which they layer on each other's roles, can be horrifying initially. But eventually audiences embrace it because they see the stereotype layered on top but hear the language telling someone's truth. The physicality is comically dissonant, and that dissonance helps audiences loosen up and finally hear what causes people to misunderstand one another.

AG: IN BOTH *LETTERS* AND *KIMCHEE* YOU GRAPPLE WITH THE DIFFICULTIES OF RELATIONSHIPS AMONG PEOPLE FROM DIFFERENT CULTURES.

EW: My world is made up of different people, but I find that there is not a lot of discussion in popular culture about the relationships among varying cultures. In the first drafts of *Kimchee*, there was more Haitian language and many more dialects, so that when the audience looked at the black characters they would see many cultural differences. Similarly, when I was writing about Korean Americans in *Kimchee*, I was also watching how they might interact with Chinese Americans and Japanese Americans. They all have histories that inform how they interact, and although at first blush we may look alike, our different histories bear on whether we get along or don't get along. It is not always about relating to the so-called dominant white culture. That's not the only dynamic happening in America. That was something which interested me in *Kimchee and Chitlins*: the dialogues which I have with others who may look like me, but are from other cultures.

    I wish people would take more delight in their differences. A lot of times the work by people of color is perceived as angry and complaining, and on the one hand I feel that complaining is necessary — the history of Asian Americans complaining in America is brief and only now emerging. But I'm also interested in exploring how joyful and enriching inter-relationships can be.

AG: HOW DID *KIMCHEE AND CHITLINS* COME ABOUT?

EW: I was watching television and became incensed by the horrific way the news media were covering the tensions between blacks and Koreans in Brooklyn. For two weeks I never saw a Korean get a chance to explain their position. I knew something was amiss, because reporters usually have their hearts in the right place; they're not trying to do a bad job. What was happening to cause this skewing and escalation of the problem? My impulse was pure, sheer frustration. And an apologia for my own profession.

I thought I would approach *Kimchee and Chitlins* in a roundabout way, through a love story. So initially the play started with Mark Thompson, the news director, and Suzie Seeto, the television reporter, in a closed-door conversation, negotiating personal waters. But Spike Lee's film *Jungle Fever* had just come out, with its story of a black architect who falls in love with his white secretary, so I abandoned that idea. Fourteen drafts later, I found what I needed — that this is a woman in the workplace, thrown into a volatile situation with little preparation, as most reporters are, and figuring out how to negotiate that.

AG: DID YOU GO TO BROOKLYN AND TALK WITH THE BLACKS AND KOREANS INVOLVED IN THE CONTROVERSY?

EW: No. Friends in the news media in New York gave me videotapes of some of their reports. This is probably the most heavily researched play I've written; I have file folders five inches deep of news coverage. In fact, some of the ugly language and names that characters hurl at each other are borrowed from transcribed news reports. I took what I saw on the news coverage and tried to do what the journalist was doing, but in a theatrical way. Tried to have a play that is balanced but also looks at imbalance. What happens when events and issues are tilted in a certain direction? What are the reasons for that imbalance?

Layered on top of those questions is a central character who is Asian and who is dealing with personal issues.

The play is often done in college settings, because students are willing to tackle the subject matter and they understand humor as a way of combating social ills more than mainstream theater does, unfortunately. Theater needs to be braver. Our job as theater artists is to butt heads and to kick butt.

AG: IN *LETTERS* AND *KIMCHEE* YOU SPREAD YOUR SATIRE AROUND, TARGETING ALL CULTURES AND PARTICIPANTS. IN *LET THE BIG DOG EAT*, THE SATIRE IS DIRECTED SPECIFICALLY AND PUNGENTLY AGAINST THE FOUR WHITE MEN PLAYING GOLF.

EW: *Let the Big Dog Eat* was commissioned by Actors Theatre of Louisville in 1997. The parameters were four characters or less, and because I love golf, I picked a golf course as the setting, and because at the time Ted Turner was giving a million-dollar donation to the United Nations, and there was a lot of hoopla about that, he came to mind. Then I wondered who he might be playing with, so Bill Gates came to mind, and from Bill Gates, who's good friends with Warren Buffett, came Buffett, and then came Michael Eisner, because Ted Turner was trying to speak to them all through his donation. So I thought it would be fun if they could all respond — in my play — about this notion of high-stakes philanthropy, and about concepts of generosity and social responsibility, especially from people who have that kind of money. If you had a billion dollars, would it really solve hunger?

The production was beautiful. Michael Dixon, ATL's literary manager, thought of having the production open with music from the O'Jays, you heard cash registers, and a gentle green strobe lit hundred-dollar bills as they drifted from the fly space. Then the money settled down, and that became the golf course. That's the correct tone for the play.

It was fun to write, because I had not had a male protagonist before. I could also make a golf course have an important role and be a metaphor for the issues that I was grappling with. That was key. A golf course is perceived as a place where men go to make deals; they go to have a certain fraternity that opens the doors for other opportunities. I can tell you as a woman who golfs that men are often horrified when I come striding over to that first tee, to join them on their

foursome. I have overheard many conversations in which men negotiate and do business, and I know how subtle the interaction is. They
tell each other what they do for a living without saying it directly. They
are adept at helping one another. The golf course is the ultimate net-
working party.

AG: IS THERE A FEMALE EQUIVALENT?

EW: I don't believe so. I don't know of any. Women are still holding
on to upper management by our fingers. We have not had a chance
to look back and grab someone from behind and bring them up, as
men do.

AG: HAVE WOMEN HELPED YOUR PLAYWRITING CAREER?

EW: The work of a couple of playwrights has influenced my life.
Ntosake Shange's work struck me down and laid me flat when I first
saw it. She and women like Wakako Yamauchi have helped me by
doing their work; I've come to it and felt a kinship for it. But as far
as the kind of help that occurs on the golf course, no. I don't feel competitive; I think there's room for all of us. There's room for all kinds
of voices, and none of us has to feel threatened by the other.

AG: DID YOU HAVE A MENTOR AT NEW YORK UNIVERSITY?

EW: Hard to say. When I won my first playwriting contest, at
TheatreWorks in Colorado Springs, I asked Tina Howe, who was teaching at N.Y.U., 'What do I do? What do I wear?' She said, 'Look like
an artist and wear big jewelry.' That was important advice. Truman
Capote gave me some important advice.

AG: WHEN DID YOU MEET HIM?

EW: Shortly before his death. For my twenty-fifth birthday, I was introduced to Truman in Los Angeles, and he sang *Happy Birthday* to me.
He signed a first edition copy of *Breakfast at Tiffany's*, which is one
of my favorite stories, and he told me that the one thing every writer
should do was 'keep writing.' So simple, and really true. And then
we proceeded to gossip.

Elizabeth Wong 503

AG: YOU ARE ALWAYS EXPERIMENTING WITH FORM AND YOU APPARENTLY DO NOT FEEL COMPELLED TO WRITE AN IBSENESQUE WELL MADE PLAY.

EW: Yes, my brain refuses to be linear. Naturalism, to me, is unnatural! I admire Ibsen greatly though. I admire him for his social consciousness, because having read his work, I know that he had a social program and a notion of how society should be. I don't know if I agree with it, but I'm influenced by the idea that people can remake their society with theater.

A professor named Judith Royer, at Loyola University, approached me to publish my work in an anthology of plays that looks at how women in theater deal with form and have changed American theater through the styles and idioms in which they write. And that's heartening, because that means she will put my work in a context that's appropriate, which has never happened before. I've been included in collections where the focus is on Asian-American playwrights or on women, and that's appropriate, but Royer's focus is on the ways women use theatrical tools to tell our stories. For instance there's a link between Megan Terry's work and mine through our use of a chorus and through the transformational use of time and space. But going back even further, I've co-opted the chorus from the Greeks. The chorus is a Western tradition, but I redigest it for my own purposes. Communal speaking, and the community that a chorus represents, provides context. That's something that I don't get in my creative life — context and historical perspective — but a chorus can give that in my plays. The notion of the chorus representing a community that is observing action, pushing and spinning the action, commenting and providing context — that all seems key for me and is part of my style, my idiom.

AG: THE POLITICAL ATTITUDES AND FRACTURED STYLE OF SEVERAL OF YOUR PLAYS REMIND ME OF MEGAN TERRY'S PLAYS FROM THE 1960S.

EW: I love Megan Terry. She has been incredibly influential to me. She has been a mentor to me. She brought me out to work with her at Omaha Magic Theatre, and I had a chance to experience what the theater that she created in New York must have been like. At Omaha Magic they still do a lot of yogalike physical exercises during the creative process. Group exercises. Free associations in wordplay. Working there opened my process up.

AG: DID YOU WORK WITH HER AFTER YOU WROTE *KIM-CHEE AND CHITLINS*?

EW: Yes. In 1996, Omaha Magic was doing a project called Exploratori YUM, and they commissioned me to write a ten-minute piece. They brought in artists from other disciplines: a poet, a drummer, a puppeteer, a painter. I was creating *Punk Girls: On Divine Omnipotence and the Longstanding Nature of Evil*, and there was an artist in the corner of the theater painting his experience of that creative process. So I am doing *Punk Girls*, and someone's painting *Punk Girls*. Jo Ann Schmidman and Megan Terry — we were all having an interweaving, interconnecting, free-floating, interdisciplinary creative process, which had never happened to me before. I'm used to working alone, and if I'm influenced by art work, it's usually because I've been to the museum, come back, and gone to my computer. This was the first time I had an artist sitting in the corner. I had actors mewling and meowing and doing vocalizations on the floor of the rehearsal studio, and I was asked to participate. I'm not trained as an actor. I never perform unless coerced. My world was being rocked.

I like to experiment with form, but because I'm interested in imparting a social element, I don't want audiences to be floating in space, wondering what the heck I'm trying to do. I want to ground you in a reality and then catapult you from terra firma into the stratosphere. Megan Terry and Jo Ann Schmidman furthered my ability to do that. They put visceral mind/body techniques at my disposal that I had not considered before. So if there are mentors, I would say they are Wakako Yamauchi, from her work, and Megan Terry, because of the tools that she laid at my feet so generously. And Maria Irene Fornes, for her fearlessness and passion.

And there were countless people not related to theater who influenced me. Muhammad Ali influenced me, because when he said that black was beautiful, I took that to mean me as well. His willingness to have a political conviction and pay the consequences — that integrity — empowered me. Sometimes when I make sacrifices personally, the strength of character that I hope to have comes from having witnessed someone like Ali, even though he's a man and a black man and you wouldn't think I would have this connection

I have a lot of connection with works by African-American writers, because those were the writers of color whom I read first; I did not experience works by Asian-American writers until the 1980s. The writers of the Harlem Renaissance taught me how to lay my foundation for a political bent, because my family is not a political family. We were in survival mode, surrounded by the stresses of living in a ghettoized situation.

I had a chance to meet Mohammed Ali finally. He was at a book-signing here in Los Angeles. His face is now pretty much a mask, because of the disease that's overtaking him. But to be able to access his spirit from his eyes overwhelmed me. It was thrilling to shake his hand and have him hug me. He even sparred a little, and I challenged him to take me down. I take my cue from him; he continues to give back as much as he's given, if not more, and I hope that I give back in small ways where I can. I hope to keep generosity in deed and spirit in my own life.

AG: THAT'S DIFFICULT TO DO IN AMERICA. THIS CAN BE A SELFISH COUNTRY.

EW: We're a selfish culture. There's nothing wrong with that, but hopefully we grow up from it and see that the joy in life is to give things away. Recently I gave a talk at Pepperdine University to students who were studying *Letters* and *Kimchee,* and they asked what problems in America I would solve that I hadn't addressed in my plays. I said that there's a lack of civility. It may sound formal, and I'm certainly not a formal person, but I wish we could say 'please' and 'thank you,' or 'I appreciate you,' more than we do. I wish we gave people the benefit of the doubt. That paves the way for people to relax. We can only tackle the big questions by looking at the smaller answers.

AG: IN *KIMCHEE*, THE AFRICAN AMERICANS THINK THE KOREAN GROCER INSULTS THEM BECAUSE HE DOESN'T LOOK AT THEM DIRECTLY WHEN THEY PAY THEIR MONEY. IRONICALLY, THE KOREAN BELIEVES HE'S SHOWING RESPECT BY NOT LOOKING IN THEIR EYES.

EW: If both sides were able to give each other the benefit of the doubt and trust that each was honoring the other, there wouldn't be this misunderstanding. Unfortunately, people of color have been so beleaguered and ignored, that their first impulse is to think that they're being insulted, because that's par for the course. It's hard to participate when people don't let you. I think writing plays is my way of participating.

AG: SPEAKING OF HONORING OTHERS, COULD WE TALK ABOUT *CHINA DOLL*, YOUR PLAY ABOUT ANNA MAY WONG?

EW: *China Doll* is dear to me. It was born because a friend of mine gave me a postcard of an Asian woman wearing a tuxedo, and on the back of the card were the words 'American actress. Anna May Wong.' The card didn't say 'Chinese-American actress.' There was no hyphen there. It was just 'American.' Obviously this was a postcard made in Europe, and it struck me that they would identify her as an American actress. I had this card around for a long time. I put it on my bulletin board. That was the genesis.

   When I did research, I found articles in magazines and of course her filmography, but really I had to imagine her life, because nothing is documented. That got me on the track of salvaging and reclaiming a history that belongs to American cultural history.

AG: I HAVE A *PHOTOPLAY* FROM 1930, AND THERE IS A PICTURE OF HER, WITH THE BANGS.

EW: Yeah, the bangs. If you remember, in *Letters to a Student Revolutionary*, the character Bibi resists the bangs. Anna May is the lady who invented that haircut. The geometric, banged, bobbed haircut was Anna May's, and people followed her fashion — more than her films, in a way. She was thought of more as a model than an actress, because she was tall. She was a tall Asian woman.

AG: WITH THAT HAIRCUT SHE INADVERTENTLY CREATED WHAT BECAME A STEREOTYPE.

EW: But at the time it wasn't a stereotype. It was fashion. She was the height of popular Asian beauty.

AG: I READ A ONE-ACT VERSION OF THE PLAY.

EW: That ten-minute version is the template for the longer work, although I do preserve that one-act as a scene. During World War II, Asian-American actors were not cast in movies, but they were often asked to teach non-Asian actors to play 'exotics,' as they were called back then in Hollywood. They had to teach a weird lexicon of what it means to walk, talk, and look like an Asian. In the one-act, Anna May uses the coaching as a framework for talking about the frustrations of her career.

AG: WHAT IS THE FULL-LENGTH VERSION ABOUT?

EW: It's about the way I imagine life as an artist of color would be during the Hollywood studio system. Originally I was attempting to explore how artists of color responded to World War II and to the meetings of the House UnAmerican Activities Committee. But ultimately my interest was to follow the adventure and struggle of a creative person in that time who happens to look like me. A creative person who achieves a modicum of success in her world, but feels, in my imagined telling of her story, that she was not allowed to flower as an artist. If you see her in later roles, when she was older and played countless maids, you see in her eyes — in the dignity that she imbued in a maid — that she could have played richer parts.

AG: HOW OLD IS SHE IN THE PLAY?

EW: She zigzags from her teens, when she plays a slave girl in *The Thief of Bagdad*, with Douglas Fairbanks, until her fifties, when she dies. My research revealed that she had been an actor in silent pictures when she was three; she had been a source of income for her family. But she didn't consciously make the choice of a career until she was seventeen.

AG: DO THE CHARACTERS IN THE ONE-ACT ALSO APPEAR IN THE LONGER VERSION?

EW: Yes. The long version is peopled by Irving Thalberg and Gary Cooper, Douglas Fairbanks and Marlene Dietrich. I see the play looking like an Avedon photograph: all angles and black-and-white, with shafts of light.

AG: YOU NAME THE YOUNG WHITE ACTRESS WHOM ANNA MAY TUTORS 'MISS HARRINGTON,' LIKE THE RUTHLESS ACTRESS IN *ALL ABOUT EVE*. WAS THAT CONSCIOUS?

EW: That was conscious. I love that movie and I love Bette Davis in that movie. The films of that period were very influential to me, maybe because I was a geeky girl with glasses and was transported by the glamour. A glamour that I didn't experience in my everyday life.

AG: WHO DOES?

EW: No one, but I assumed that everyone did but me.

AG: THE CHINA DOLL IMAGE . . .

EW: Meek and mild, with a hand over her mouth to cover her smile and laughter. It's an image perpetuated by Hollywood.

AG: WHERE DID THAT IMAGE ORIGINATE?

EW: Maybe it was created by guys who went off to war and whose first experience with the 'other' were Asian prostitutes. *Miss Saigon* is an example of that stereotype. Then there was the image of the evil dragon lady. These are stereotypes that prevail even now. In *China Doll*, Anna May tries to combat them, but also she embodies them, because otherwise she wouldn't have been able to get work. She has to decide whether she can work within the system. Can she work without the system? What is the best mode of attack as a creative person? This happens to me all the time as a writer. I recall an agent saying to me, 'Elizabeth, I can't put you up for that television show; there are no Asian characters on that show,' as if that would be the only authority that I have as a writer, to write only characters that were Asian or women or Asian women.

I feel a real affinity for Anna May. She grew up in Chinatown and so did I. She had brushes with Hollywood and so have I. Her desire to find expression for her creativity in her time was not fully realized, and perhaps that's my fear, too, for my own creative life. Often, when you hit roadblocks, you think that you'll never be allowed to blossom into the artist that you know you have it in you to be.

We feel invisible because artists of color are not placed in a historical context. They're not taught in the core college curriculum. They're not credited in reviews of work by white artists who are influenced by artists of color. It's rare that critics will see the theatrical antecedents in my plays.

AG: HOW WOULD YOU DESCRIBE THE STYLE OF *CHINA DOLL*?

EW: I'm interested in *China Doll* in co-opting cinematic styles and finding theatrical ways to realize them. The play is episodic, and there's a sense of being both in the movie of her life and watching a movie being made of her life. I try to blur realities: is the action in her mind? Is it actually happening? I like this play because it deals directly with creative process, with how someone makes something. The play is dreamlike and yet percussive, because of the quick cuts.

There's also a chorus, and the actors transform from character to character before your eyes. There are times in the play when I break out of the action and make sure you know that you're in a theater and watching an actual actress, although hopefully that delights you rather than jars you.

AG: DO YOU ULTIMATELY SEE *CHINA DOLL* AS A FILM?

EW: I want it to be a play. I can see it as a film, but movie devices used as theatrical devices are not as fun in an actual movie. They are unconventional in a play. My heart tells me that *China Doll* must be a play first.

AG: YOU HAVE WRITTEN PLAYS CALLED *THE HAPPY PRINCE* AND *THE PLAY FORMERLY KNOWN AS THE HAPPY PRINCE*. WHAT IS THE DIFFERENCE?

EW: They're both adaptations of Oscar Wilde's short story *The Happy Prince*. The Kennedy Center commissioned an adaptation in 1996 and asked me to make it funny and do whatever I wanted. In the story, the central figure is the statue of a prince; I changed the statue to a car — a 1956 red Corvette convertible. The most stunning car. I was in Portland, Maine, in a bar, and above me was a chart of all these Corvettes. I looked up and saw this beautiful convertible and I thought . . . 'Ah ha!'

Once I picked that car, the play fell into place. I tried to capture the spirit and message of the Wilde story, which is that you must do generous work in this life, but you may not be rewarded — you may have to sacrifice yourself to preserve your integrity. It is a wonderful message, although difficult to impart, especially to kids. I knew my audience would range from elementary school children to high school kids, but because each age emphasizes things in different ways, it was difficult to know how to gear the play. I decided I would tell the story in a way that I wanted and do it simply, and see what happened. *The Play Formerly Known as the Happy Prince* was my comic take on a serious subject, a play written in a fairy tale tone but hopefully preserving the integrity of Wilde's story.

But when the Kennedy Center got it, I was told that it was very L.A., that it had a car, that it was very ethnic. They said it was very hip-hop, but I think that's because portions are written in rhymed couplets. Also, the main character, aside from the car, is a swallow whose name is Boyd. That comes from having been in New York, and if you're around New Yorkers, you know that some of them say 'boid' for bird.

To me it was an innocent, urban update, which I thought kids could relate to more. I could relate to it more. But the producers disagreed, so they asked me to write a version more classical in tone. So I wrote *The Happy Prince*, the straight version.

AG: WHICH VERSION DO YOU PREFER?

EW: I like both. They have different energies. The first one is like a little atom bomb. It's a nucleus vibrating with all this energy. The other is more dreamy and ethereal. This was my first time adapting anything, and I learned that you have to rethink the original completely, but find a way to preserve the original author's tone and intent.

AG: IS IT EASIER FOR MALE WRITERS TO CROSS CULTURAL BOUNDARIES?

EW: I think that men who cross cultural lines and happen to be people of color are more readily accepted, because their work is placed in historical context. When people study women's work, not just in Women's Studies but alongside men's work in the core college curriculum, we will see women's voices evaluated for the influences that they have had on all areas of life, and we will see that women are the ones who are doing powerful things. We just haven't gotten credit for it.

When I take Aeschylus' *Prometheus Bound* and reinvent the Prometheus myth to suit my purposes, that comes from an Asian-American woman's experience of it. Although my cultural history and gender may not be manifest in the words and actions on the stage, I'm the person making the creative decisions. *Prometheus*, which is about a man, is reflecting a woman's perspective. To me, Prometheus is the great mother who creates human beings out of mud. His crime is that he tries to protect these mewling mud sticks, as I call them. Part of my interpretation is to look at how a man can allow this maternal nurturing side. Since I am a woman, I can make that an underlying theme in a strong, muscular play about sacrifice. *Prometheus* is also about affecting the government of Zeus; his suffering is able to push Zeus to saying, 'I rethink my previous law. I will adjust it and free you.' Is that a woman's issue? I don't know. I am a woman, therefore this is my issue.

AG: DID YOU WANT A MAN OR A WOMAN TO PLAY PROMETHEUS?

EW: The director and I toyed with the idea of a woman, and she found an actress whom she thought could play the role. But I advocated against the idea, because I thought the maternal notions in the play would be more provocative and profound if a physically strong, muscular man wanted to protect the human race; we assume a woman would do it. Also, I didn't want to layer in political commentary that wasn't really part of the play, although I'd like to see a production with a woman to learn if that enhances what I intended.

My initial image for the play's opening was a man weeping. To see a Titan crying would make you wonder what was going on, and then to find out why he's weeping seemed a nice way into the play and different from Aeschylus' version. Aeschylus has a strong-armed god bringing in a struggling Prometheus and chaining him to the rock, which of course is a good way to start a play — plenty of action — but I wanted to emphasize other aspects of men, because I adore men and I think they get a bad rap. So the original concept was to see a big guy cry, but that got eliminated, because producers wanted a more 'story book' beginning. Then, to set the framework for the story, I had the idea of a big guy sleeping, and faces floating in space. But the play, which was commissioned in 1998 by Denver Center Theatre Academy, was traveling to school auditoriums that might not be able to create the production values of a theater, so we abandoned that idea. Now Prometheus is sleeping, because he's been on a long journey to Mt. Olympus to beg Zeus once again for fire for human beings. The play begins with the notion of a journey.

AG: DO YOU OFTEN START WITH AN IMAGE?

EW: Well, this play started with an image. Faces floating in space, the image of a man weeping. The plot of Aeschylus' *Prometheus Bound* is pretty spelled out, although I had the freedom to condense and remold.

AG: IS THE PLAY IN VERSE?

EW: No. I learned my lesson from *The Happy Prince*.

AG: WITH *INSIDE A RED ENVELOPE* YOU ACTUALLY DO UTILIZE ASPECTS OF ANCIENT CHINESE CULTURE.

EW: That play was a commission from playwright Michael Wright. It was going to be in a book about the writer's process. I was to write, preserve my drafts, and keep a journal. And because Michael Wright was also commissioning an Hispanic writer and a black writer, I knew that my role was to be the 'Asian' writer. I have a piece of jade statuary that I got in China of Kuan Yin, the Goddess of Mercy, and although I didn't know anything about her myth, culturally and ancestrally the myth belongs to me. So I tackled a subject that normally I wouldn't be interested in; I haven't written plays in which ancient Chinese mythological characters come to bear. But I researched the character and kept a diary of the twists and turns of how I came to finish the play.

AG: DID YOU IN FACT WRITE SEVERAL DRAFTS?

Elizabeth Wong 513

EW: I had trouble with the first two pages. I wrote them maybe five times. Finally I realized what I wanted to say and wrote it from beginning to end in one evening. At about that time I had become interested in physics; notions about quantum theory and about the space-time continuum were converging in my mind. The play's structure comes from the idea that all the choices before us are happening simultaneously. I wanted to look at a dream and make it be happening and yet not happening. I wanted all the characters to be having the same dream, to a purpose, with the dream as key to solving a problem.

AG: READING THE PLAY, I HAVE THE SENSE THAT YOU CONSCIOUSLY DO NOT WANT US TO KNOW WHERE THE BEGINNING IS, OR WHOSE DREAM IS WHOSE.

EW: All the characters are living in different time lines, but they are the same person. The man, the child, the woman — they're all the same. The writer. We meet in a dream.

That dreamy style is more what people expect of an Asian writer, and that's why I've avoided writing like that. But when I started the play, I found that the story, the dream, was part of my inner life, so I didn't want to reject it.

AG: THERE IS A STRIKING MOMENT IN *ENVELOPE*, WHEN JAMES REMEMBERS AS A YOUNG BOY THAT HIS FATHER INVITED HIM TO GO OUT FOR ICE CREAM; THE BOY DIDN'T GO, BUT THE FATHER WENT OUT, AND DIED.

EW: My father died when I was five. *Inside a Red Envelope* is probably the most personal of my plays, even though it is the shortest. But I found myself writing about something that must be sitting around in my psyche, which was that, when I was about five, my father asked us all to go out to get ice cream with him, and we said, "No"; we were having too much fun playing. We had guests over, and my mother was babysitting, so we were all having fun and we didn't take that walk with him to the corner store. That evening he died. Out he went on a gurney, and I never saw him again, except in a box at a funeral home. My life was fodder for this play, even though initially my impulse was not personal.

AG: CAN YOU TALK ABOUT YOUR VISIT TO CHINA?

EW: I went with my mom in the early 1980s. China was a strange and alien place to me. I certainly didn't fit in. It was very much like when my character Anna May goes to China. She thinks that, because she's getting such horrible roles in the United States, she'll be understood in China. But she finds she isn't accepted there either; she is vilified for promulgating inappropriate, immoral images of Asian women. I felt more American than ever as a result of my visit to the motherland.

AG: FROM THE POINT OF VIEW OF THE CHINATOWN COMMUNITY SHE LEFT, SHE HAD MADE IT.

EW: Right.

AG: BUT YOU ARE DESCRIBING AND WRITING A WOMAN WHO WAS OPPRESSED.

EW: Anna May was oppressed. I am oppressed. Whenever opportunity is denied you, you are oppressed.

AG: IS THE CREATIVE EXPRESSION FOR YOURSELF ALONE?

EW: I know there are artists who say, 'I just do it for myself. I write for myself, and that's sufficient.' I'm not one of those people. I need to reach out, tap you on the shoulder, and say, 'Would you be interested in looking at this? I have some questions for you. Hopefully you'll find them engaging.' My definition of entertainment may be different from other people's. I think it's entertaining to be provoked. I like, when I go to the theater, to have a fourteen-course meal emotionally and intellectually. I'm writing to instigate conversation. I need an audience.

Writing plays is my aggressive act. Getting a play produced is an aggressive maneuver waiting for the counter-maneuver of an energized and curious audience. I think American theater has been suffering severe anemia for years and is in dire need of a transfusion of vitality that comes from playwrights of color. All I can do is keep writing. Keep pressing the issues that concern me. Keep finding ways to express the amplitude of our common humanity. ▽

Wakako Yamauchi

My stories are about immigrants.
There have always been immigrants. We
were there in prehistory, travelers
from another place, another continent,
or just stragglers from a larger society.
We are a tribe of wanderers remembering a garden we'd left or looking for
an Eden that waits.

That is Wakako Yamauchi in the Preface to her collection of stories, plays, and memoir, *Songs My Mother Taught Me*. She was born in Westmorland, California, the daughter of a Japanese farmer and his wife, both of whom had immigrated to the United States. She spent her childhood in Imperial Valley, about three hundred miles from Los Angeles, close to the Mexican border. There her father leased one farm after another, for because of California's Alien Land Law, Japanese immigrants were not allowed to own land, nor could they lease the same land for more than three years.

Eventually her parents ran a boarding house in Oceanside, California, north of San Diego. But in 1942, the United States government evacuated her family to a concentration camp, the Poston Relocation Center in Arizona. Yamauchi remained there until 1944, when she signed a loyalty oath and was allowed to travel to Chicago, to work briefly in a candy factory; she returned to camp when her father died.

When World War II ended and she was released from camp, she moved to San Diego and then Los Angeles, where she worked in a factory, hand-painting plastic shower curtains. In her thirties, she began to write short stories and recollections, and at the age of fifty-three, to write plays. Her first play, *And the Soul Shall Dance* (1977), is an adaptation of her short story of the same title, about a first generation Japanese (Issei) woman named Emiko, who desperately wants to leave her abusive husband and return to Japan. The play was filmed for PBS. Other plays by Yamauchi include *The Music Lessons* (1980), which, like *Soul,* takes place in Imperial Valley during the 1930s; *12-1-A* (1982), which dramatizes the frictions and moral dilemmas of life in

516

camp; *The Chairman's Wife* (1990), about Chiang Ch'ing, the third wife of Mao Tse-Tung; and *Taj Mahal* (1997), an encounter between a homeless African-American man and a Japanese immigrant during the Depression.

In 1995, Yamauchi received the National Book Award for Literature, presented by the Association for Asian-American Studies, for *Songs My Mother Taught Me*, which was also selected by *The Hungry Mind Review* as one of the one hundred best books of the twentieth century. She has received grants and awards from the Rockefeller Foundation, the Brody Art Fund, and in 1998 was awarded a Certificate of Appreciation by the Japanese American Historical Society.

This interview took place in Yamauchi's home in Gardena, California, on July 17, 1999.

• • •

AG: YOU ONCE WROTE, 'THERE HAVE ALWAYS BEEN IMMI-
GRANTS . . . .WE ARE A TRIBE OF WANDERERS. . .' DO *YOU*
FEEL AS THOUGH YOU ARE AN IMMIGRANT?

WY: Because I'm not an immigrant, I don't feel like one. I do not have
a remembrance of another country nor the desire or longing to return
to one. I was born in the Southern California desert and stamped with
idealized remembrances of isolation, simplicity, and the purity of life
there. Maybe if I were to leave the United States, I would feel like an
immigrant. But it's true: I've always felt like an outsider. I think that
most creative people do. And I suppose I shall always feel that way.

AG: WAS THERE A PARTICULAR EVENT OR CATASTROPHE
THAT BROUGHT SO MANY JAPANESE TO THE WEST COAST
DURING THE FIRST TWO DECADES OF THE TWENTIETH CEN-
TURY?

WY: There was the draft into the Japanese army. And there was much
difficulty economically. Poor people were not getting enough to eat.
The immigrants were the ones that really couldn't make it in Japan.
The first-born son inherited everything, and the rest had to scrap for
themselves. I remember reading a book called *Silk and Straw*, a collection of oral interviews with the residents of Nagaya, and oh, God,
they had a hard time. The women were dying in childbirth because
they were malnourished and they hemorrhaged. My father was a first-
born son, but he left anyway.

AG: WHAT PART OF JAPAN DID YOUR FATHER COME FROM?

WY: My father came from Shimizu, and my mother came from
Shizuoka. I think Shizuoka is a prefecture, and Shimizu is a small area
of that. My father lived by the sea. My mother lived inland a bit more,
because her family were tea packers. Both families were merchants.
I know they didn't have the hard time that some of those farmers had.
Some farmers didn't have a sash to tie around their kimono, I tell you.

AG: WOULD YOU TALK A BIT ABOUT IMPERIAL VALLEY,
WHAT IT LOOKED LIKE, AND WHAT IT WAS LIKE TO LIVE
THERE?

WY: When I was living there it was desert. It still is. There are large expanses of sand and tumbleweed. It was dry. Hot in summer, cold in winter. My father would farm about forty acres — tomatoes, cantaloupes, summer squash — and you'd have to go two or three miles before you found another patch of land that had been tilled and cultivated.

AG: DID YOU WORK ON THE FARM?

WY: Anybody that could, did. The women did things like patching the cover. We used to have what they called brush cover. We would stick brush in the ground to protect these little plants and then we'd weave a big roll of paper, or use newspapers, to shelter them. When the rain came, it would tear up everything — rip the paper. And we'd have to patch it, if the weather was still cold. And we did thinning. There'd be too many plants in one spot, so we had to thin them out.

It wasn't that bad for girls. My brother had a really tough job. He was the only son. My father would rouse him out of bed at three in the morning, and say, 'We've got to burn the smudge pots.'

AG: WHAT ARE SMUDGE POTS?

WY: They're used to heat the atmosphere around the plants, so the plants won't die in the frost. Smudge pots are fed by kerosene, but we didn't have that kind of equipment, so we would gather brush together and burn it.

AG: DID YOU SPEAK JAPANESE AT HOME?

WY: Yes. My folks never spoke English to us. We always spoke Japanese to our parents.

AG: WHEN DID YOU LEARN ENGLISH?

WY: I have an older sister and brother — my sister's three years older, my brother's two years older — and they had some knowledge of English. I should have had some knowledge of English by the time I went to kindergarten, but I remember that the teacher drilled me on *R* and *L* sounds. I was a very forward kid, until I learned that life wasn't what I thought it was, and I volunteered for everything. The hands went up, and mine went up, and the teacher chose me one day to go to the principal's office, to hand her a note. So I went to the principal's classroom, because she was teaching, and she was standing on a platform pointing with a pointer to the blackboard, and I said, 'Note.' And she turned around and growled at me. I didn't know what she said. So I repeated, 'Note,' and she put down that pointer and was going after me. And I ran like hell back to my classroom. Then a couple of days later this Japanese girl came up to me and told me that the principal said, 'Next time you come over, you must whisper.' I said, 'What is that?' 'Do like I'm doing.' 'Ohhh.' So I learned a new word that day. And I learned not to volunteer.

AG: AT THE JAPANESE AMERICAN NATIONAL MUSEUM IN DOWNTOWN LOS ANGELES, ONE EXHIBIT SHOWS THAT A NUMBER OF CHILDREN WENT TO PUBLIC SCHOOL DURING THE DAY AND TO JAPANESE SCHOOL IN THE AFTERNOONS OR ON SATURDAYS.

WY: Our Japanese school met once a week. And every New Year's we got together and had a ceremony, and on the Emperor's birthday we had a little ceremony. We dutifully went, even though we didn't know what it was all about. You were not supposed to look up, not even to look at the Emperor's photograph. He was not to be seen by mortal eyes, I guess.

AG: YOU HAVE WRITTEN THAT YOUR MOTHER WAS DETAINED IN PRISON HER FIRST DAY IN THIS COUNTRY.

WY: I think it was at what they call Angel Island, near San Francisco. She didn't know where she was.

AG: WAS THAT THE WEST COAST EQUIVALENT OF ELLIS ISLAND?

WY: Yes. I think the Chinese had it much worse than the Japanese, but she said that they kept her there and examined her — they had to make sure that the immigrants didn't come with any diseases. That's all she told me. She never spoke about that. She did remember that she stayed about three days in the prison, and my father went to get her. And when he drove her to his house, my mother said that my father led her to two rocks set around an earthen hole — I suppose, like an outdoor cooking pit — and he said, 'Make rice.' So she put the pot over the rocks.

AG: SHE WASN'T EXPECTING ANYTHING QUITE THAT BASIC.

WY: Primitive. She said that in Japan they had a lot of servants, because they had apprentice tea packers — little boys. Child labor, I think they call it now, who lived in and did the work. And her family had cooks, because they had quite a group of workers to feed.

I was the last one to leave the house and I think my mother spoke to me more than to my brother and sister. Little by little she told me these stories, and I incorporated them into my stories.

AG: YOU MENTIONED IN ONE OF YOUR RECOLLECTIONS THAT WHEN YOUR MOTHER DIED YOU FOUND A DIARY SHE HAD KEPT.

WY: It was seldom written in. I do remember one entry. She said, 'Went to town and bought gloves.' This was after the Second World War, and she was living in San Diego and I was in Los Angeles. But that's all she said. It filled me with sorrow.

AG: IN THE COLLECTION OF YOUR WORK, *SONGS MY MOTHER TAUGHT ME*, THE EDITOR, GARRETT HONGO, DIVIDES YOUR STORIES INTO 'COUNTRY STORIES' AND 'CITY STORIES.' THE COUNTRY STORIES GENERALLY SEEM TO BE SET IN THE PERIOD BEFORE YOU MOVED TO OCEANSIDE AND BEFORE YOU WERE EVACUATED TO CAMP, AND THE CITY STORIES GENERALLY TAKE PLACE AFTER YOU WERE RELEASED FROM CAMP. DO YOU AGREE WITH THIS DIVISION?

WY: Yes, I think so.

AG: WOULD YOU DIVIDE YOUR PLAYS THE SAME WAY?

Wakako Yamauchi 521

WY: I guess they could be divided that way. First you write your child-hood stories and when you get through with that, you start writing your adolescent stories, and when you get to now, you just write about old people and our problems. Alzheimer's, the strokes.

AG: WHAT INSPIRED THE SHORT STORY *AND THE SOUL SHALL DANCE*?

WY: Well, I was over thirty and I was trying to write. Most of all I was trying to set these stories down so that I'd have something, when I go, that my daughter could read and know, 'This is what my mother's background was. This is how she was thinking.' That's when I started seriously writing. Before that I used to write sketches.

Part of the story comes from an incident in my childhood. I must have been about nine, and these people, their name was Nagaoka, lived not far from us. Their name means 'long hill,' but I cut it to 'hill' in the story. I was always walking over to their house — just like I said in the story. Mr. Nagaoka looked like a toad, and I really thought he was icky. But when I grew older, I thought, 'What made him and his wife like that? What made them able to endure that barren, loveless, existence?' Not even any kind of a love with each other. But who knows? I can't see everything, even as an adult. So I wrote the story, tried to find out, in my mind, what was keeping Mrs. Nagaoka alive. I made up the wife's long-ago romance in Japan. But Mr. Nagaoka's daughter did come to the United States, and I thought, 'Well, this is what kills Emiko. Nothing to fight against. The money's gone. Her husband doesn't care. Won't even fight with her anymore.'

AG: DO YOUR SHORT STORIES USUALLY EVOLVE FROM AN INCIDENT?

WY: Usually I start with an incident that somebody tells me or that I heard of, or I know to be true. I figure if it really happened, then at least no one can say this is contrived. Although they say that anyway. I start out with an incident and the characters. Why this incident hap-pened is because this character is this way. I find that almost every-thing in life is cause and effect, cause and effect.

AG: THE DESCRIPTIONS IN YOUR STORIES ARE QUITE RICH.

WY: Years after I started writing seriously, I read somewhere that the object of Haiku is to get the precise essence of a feeling. Like finding a perfect description of, say, a drop of dew on the underside of a leaf. And I thought, 'That's what I try to do.' I try to get exactly how I feel, to give it to you and see if you can feel that way too. I think most people have the same feelings. When I wrote *And the Soul Shall Dance*, the short story, I asked my ex-husband to read it, and he read a few pages. 'I can't read this,' he said. 'It hurts.'

AG: YOUR PLAYS *AND THE SOUL SHALL DANCE, THE MUSIC LESSONS,* AND *FOR WHAT?* BEGAN LIFE AS SHORT STORIES. ARE THERE ANY OTHER SHORT STORIES THAT YOU TRANS-FORMED INTO PLAYS?

WY: I have one called *Shirley Temple, Hotcha-Cha.* I was trying to write a play and I couldn't get it moving, so I decided, 'Well, I'm just going to go back to the short story and see if I can move it.' And I went back to writing a short story and got out of where I was blocked, and I finished the play.

AG: WHAT ARE THE CHALLENGES OF TURNING A SHORT STORY INTO A PLAY?

WY: Well, everything has to be done by dialogue and action in a play. In a short story you can say, 'Oh, he was really mad.' Or, 'I don't know what he was thinking, but this is what he did.' But you have to make that clear in a play, so that the audience can understand, let's say, that surreptitiously a character is stealing from the company. But you can't say it — you have to show it, without being too obvious. You insult the audience's intelligence if you're too obvious. That's the difficult part I think.

AG: YOUR SHORT STORIES ARE USUALLY WRITTEN IN THE FIRST PERSON.

WY: Yes.

AG: BUT IN A PLAY, THAT IS DIFFICULT TO DO.

WY: But you have a narrator in a play. You have an observer in a play. Usually.

AG: IN THE STORY *AND THE SOUL SHALL DANCE*, EMIKO DOES NOT TRY TO SELL HER KIMONOS, TO RAISE MONEY SO SHE CAN RETURN TO JAPAN. BUT IN THE PLAY SHE DOES. HOW DID THAT CHANGE COME ABOUT?

WY: Well, I had enrolled in a screenplay class, and this guy read my script for *The Music Lessons* — I was trying to write a screenplay for that — and he asked me if I had anything else, and I showed him the script for *And the Soul Shall Dance*. And he said, 'You've got to find something that's going to go *bing*.' So I devised that Emiko had brought all these things with her from Japan, and there was nowhere else for her to get money except to sell them, because the money that she had been stealing from her husband was gone. Which I added, too.

I didn't know a thing about playwriting. I bought a playwriting book and I didn't learn anything except where to indent, and to put the characters' names in the middle of the page and then start your dialogue. And I quit that, because one artistic director told me to leave the names at the side, so that we know who's talking immediately. But I didn't know what I was doing. I just had to wait for that thing to come and help me out. The muse. 'I'm in trouble.'

AG: MEMORY PLAYS A VITAL ROLE IN YOUR SHORT STORIES.

WY: I use memory because it is easier to see then and now, then and now, than if you go straight down the line. With memory, you see why a thing happened, or why it didn't, or why it should have.

AG: HOW DO YOU TRANSFER THAT TO A PLAY?

WY: When I started writing the play of *Soul*, first I had a narrator, a grown woman talking about her childhood. Then I took her out. Then I tried several ways to put in a narrator to say that this is an old story. Then Mako, the artistic director of East West Players, said, 'Don't worry about that. I'm going to do it with lights.' So that's what he did. I don't know if it was the lighting, but everybody who saw the production understood that this was a memory play.

AG: WHEN MAKO SAID, 'DON'T WORRY ABOUT THAT,' WHAT DID YOU DO?

WY: I threw out the narrators.

AG: WHY AND HOW DID THE JAPANESE WOMEN COME HERE?

WY: Well, the men came here because they were railroad workers, they were farmers — they were people who came to work. And they had to have women, so they sent for picture brides. They used pictures. They had a go-between usually. A lot of them were illiterate, so they had a guy who wrote the letters. And the lies. There were so many young men and women who had nowhere to go, there in Japan. There were women who could not find good husbands, because they were of a lower class or in different classes. They were being sold to geisha houses. So being a picture bride was just one of those steps or choices that women of that caliber had to make.

My father was a single man when he came here. He worked in dairies, he worked in laundries, he worked on farms. Then he went back to Japan. His was an arranged marriage, which was more normal in Japan. He brought my mother here.

AG: AN AIR OF ISOLATION SURROUNDS THE WOMEN IN YOUR PLAYS, ESPECIALLY IN *SOUL* AND *THE MUSIC LESSONS*.

WY: I think the women were living in isolation, especially on a farm. My mother had a little more education than the picture brides, so she taught Japanese school in the Buddhist church and she had some social contact, with the parents, with a women's club, and also with the kids she taught. But most of the women led very isolated lives. They just wore their husbands' pants and worked in the fields. Cooked their food and took care of their kids.

How did they survive so isolated? Well, I live isolated. I have my daughter and my grandkids, but I live isolated. I don't mind. I feel like I'm becoming a different person even as the years go by. I keep changing. I feel older. I'm beginning to feel like the poet, though I don't write poetry. I'm beginning to appreciate the sun on the wall. The leaf fluttering on a tree. Do you remember that Wordsworth poem? 'I wandered lonely as a cloud'? I begin to understand that. All at once your heart makes a leap with the sight of golden daffodils. I never thought of that when I read it as a kid.

AG: THE WOMEN IN YOUR PLAYS ARE ISOLATED BUT THEY DON'T SUPPORT EACH OTHER MUCH EMOTIONALLY. IN *SOUL* THERE IS A SORT OF FORMAL CLOSENESS BETWEEN ELEVEN-YEAR-OLD MASAKO AND HER MOTHER, HANA. BUT HANA'S REACTION TO EMIKO IS HARSH.

WY: But don't you find that women are more critical of women than we expect? You'd think there'd be more support, hunh? But I think that even now, even in the workplace, women with women bosses have a hard time.

AG: FEMINISM WAS SUPPOSED TO HELP CHANGE THAT.

WY: But I think it's like a form of racism. There are not enough crumbs filtering from the big table, and too many people scrambling for them. So we step on each other trying to get them.

AG: NOBODY REPRIMANDS MR. OKA FOR BEATING EMIKO.

WY: No. No. No. No, this is of a different era. I think that women were systematically beaten. The women that had the gall to step out of their place, they were beaten. I heard of many cases of it. My mother was a pretty independent woman, but she couldn't control everything, because my father was pretty obstinate too. There were arguments. But my father was a quiet man, so he just let it go.

AG: EMIKO IS CERTAINLY HER HUSBAND'S PROPERTY.

WY: As far as her husband is concerned, but not as far as Emiko is concerned. She keeps that part of herself standing and strong. I really tried hard not to make her a victim. As long as she has the dream of returning to Japan, she doesn't care what he does to her. In fact, his abuse keeps her alive. But when his daughter comes, there is no longer anything for Emiko to stand up against, because he can love the daughter, and she can return the love. He no longer has any use for his wife. For her tantrums.

AG: WHY DO YOU CREATE A SPIRITUAL CONNECTION BETWEEN MASAKO AND EMIKO?

WY: As you get older, you start thinking about the people whom you knew, and what pain they went through. You think, 'How could I have ignored them. Why didn't I help them?' But of course when you are young you don't have the knowledge or the empathy. Those are things that happened to me with that story.

AG: IN THE PLAY, DESPITE EMIKO'S SUICIDE, THERE IS A SENSE OF RENEWAL THAT COMES FROM MASAKO.

WY: You mean, a coming-of-age type of thing?

AG: YES. AT LEAST THIS YOUNG GIRL *SEES* EMIKO. NOBODY ELSE SEES THIS WOMAN. SHE IS INVISIBLE.

WY: That's because of the little girl's own feelings of romance or her own feelings of maybe getting away from there some day.

AG: GARRETT HONGO WRITES THAT YOUR OVERALL MODE AS A WRITER DERIVES FROM *SABI*, A JAPANESE WORD FOR THE SADNESS OF BEING, A MODE THAT INVOKES PITY AND COMPASSION. CAN YOU COMMENT ON THAT?

WY: Part of my sense of the world comes from my mother's stories about lovers. In Japan most marriages were arranged, and you know that there must have been millions of stories never told. Some lovers committed suicide rather than go through an arranged marriage. They were very strict about class, too. If you had a disease in your family, you could never get married. Families did research on the prospective bride or groom. Part of that has never left me. I do remember watching a movie called *Tsubaki Hime*, which means Princess of the Camellias. I think it was an adaptation of Dumas' *The Lady of the Camellias*. I was just a girl, and I would come home with this really achy-breaky feeling, and I wanted to do that to other people. I wanted to make them cry.

AG: SEVERAL OF THE ISSEI WOMEN IN YOUR PLAYS DENY THEMSELVES LOVE AND SEXUALITY, EVEN WHILE THEY YEARN FOR IT: EMIKO; CHIZUKO, THE MOTHER IN *THE MUSIC LESSONS*.

WY: Well, I can only say that you have to go back and figure out where they're coming from. A culture that's totally different from now. A culture that's totally different from ours in America. Even with the generation that I come from, there's sexual repression. If anybody had a child out of wedlock, it was a terrible shame. None of the guys wanted to marry the girls that got in trouble like that. That's the way the Japanese males thought in those days. They thought they were *it*. No matter what they did for a living. There was a girl in Oceanside who had a two-year-old son, and I remember one of the neighbors said, 'Oh, she had this affair with this guy that came to work at the house.' A beautiful girl and seemed very nice, but even these neighbors didn't want anything to do with her.

AG: THE MEN IN *SOUL* AND *THE MUSIC LESSONS* SEEM TO HAVE MORE COMMUNITY THAN THE WOMEN. THE MEN SIT AND DRINK AND TALK WITH EACH OTHER.

WY: Mako said during rehearsal, 'That was the only recreation the men had.' They didn't have male clubs. The men just sat around and drank and sang songs and talked about old times.

The Music Lessons was also based on people I knew. When I was a little girl, I met a boy in the first grade who did my arithmetic for me. His mother became widowed and she ran the farm. This was a sweet, gentle, Issei woman, driving trucks, and she had a five or six-year-old girl who died of pneumonia. I wondered what would have happened if the daughter had lived and grown up, and the mother was there without her husband, and if this handsome, untrained guy had come into their lives.

AG: THE VIOLINIST WITH WHOM THE DAUGHTER FALLS IN

LOVE SEEMS TO BELONG TO A SORT OF BACHELOR CUL-
TURE.

WY: Yes. After the Asian Exclusion Act of 1924, the law that halted
Asian immigration to the United States, Japanese men couldn't get married. When I was in Oceanside, my father used to hire some Japanese
transients — laborers — and some of them were very attractive, and
some were not. But most of them were carousers. They'd slick their
hair down with pomade, and when they were going out, they'd dress
up. Some of them were musically inclined, and they'd play their man-
dolins at night. They'd sing Japanese songs. It was sad sometimes,
because you'd think of them cut away from their families and living
this barren life, scrunched up in a strawberry field, picking ripe fruit
day after day, cutting heads of lettuce day after day. They had to make
a living, and they didn't have farms of their own, because they couldn't
own land.

AG: ONE REASON YOUR STORIES AND PLAYS ARE SO AFFECT-
ING IS THAT, IN ADDITION TO THE POIGNANCY OF THE
CHARACTERS AND SITUATIONS, YOU PROVIDE A CULTURAL
AND SOCIAL BACKGROUND.

WY: I think that unless you're writing science fiction or a fairy tale —
but even fairy tales have their backgrounds. The stories you write have
a lot to do with who you are, because you're coming from a certain
era, you're coming from a certain psychological background. If you're
coming now as a woman maybe you're more liberated than I was. I
still have the ways of the Japanese-American woman, what they call
Nisei woman. I'm reticent. I've got some self-restraint when it comes
to the public or other people. It all shows. It all comes out in how
the characters behave. Or how they think.
    But I never think really about social issues, except like the immi-
gration, or the camp experience, which figure largely in our lives.

AG: I WONDER IF WE COULD TALK ABOUT THE EVACUATION
TO CAMP. DID SOMEBODY COME TO THE BOARDING HOUSE
IN OCEANSIDE AND SAY, 'YOU HAVE TO LEAVE NOW'?

WY: See, the community got together. The Japanese and Japanese-American community. In our area — the Oceanside area — we were very young as Japanese Americans, as Nisei, and very naïve. So the older folks, those that were left, took care of everything with the government. The government had already taken the more important folks, but most of us were farmers. The evacuation had already started in Los Angeles — in Los Angeles they had older Nisei, who went ahead and opened the camps and arranged for food to be cooked for the evacuees. By the time the government told us to get out, we had gotten notices. Where to meet. What to carry.

AG: WERE THE NOTICES POSTED?

WY: I don't remember seeing them publicly in Oceanside. I don't even remember seeing them in the paper. But I do remember we were issued a number. My brother meticulously painted our number on everything that we carried.

AG: YOU WENT AS A FAMILY?

WY: Yes.

AG: DO YOU REMEMBER YOUR PARENTS' REACTIONS TO EVACUATION?

WY: Well, they were Japanese immigrants. They had seen a lot of hard times. And I guess they were used to obeying. In Japan, people are told to do something and they're supposed to obey, even as children. They have a philosophy which they call shikata ga nai, which means, 'There's nothing you can do about it.' So you make the best of it, right? I don't remember my parents complaining a lot about it, because we were invaded by the FBI every so often. I'd come home from school, and there would be stuff scattered all through the house. They looked through our books and photographs.

AG: HOW DID YOU FEEL WHEN YOU HAD TO PICK UP AND LEAVE?

WY: I didn't feel anything until I got there. Then I felt, 'This desolate place. This is wrong.' You know? But what could you do, with thousands of you in the same place?

AG: HOW DID THEY TRANSPORT YOU?

WY: In Oceanside we walked to the railroad station. The transient workers used to board when they came to Oceanside to pick strawberries, and my mother would cook for them and make their lunches. There was a guy who was an accountant, and he used to take the workers to different farms. So I think what happened was that they took the truck and took everybody's stuff to the railway station the day before, and then they brought the truck back and abandoned it at the boarding house. Because we never got anything out of there. There was a sedan. There was the truck. There was all this equipment — the beds and the kitchen utensils and the flatware and the dishes. And we just left it all there. And the day we were supposed to report to the depot in Oceanside, we walked there. I do remember that. We abandoned everything and left.

AG: HOW LONG DID IT TAKE TO GET TO POSTON?

WY: One day. We took a train to L.A. depot. I do remember that. There were lots of Japanese there with their suitcases by their sides, waiting. And then we took a train to Parker. And then we took a bus to Poston.

AG: IS PARKER IN CALIFORNIA?

WY: Arizona. It was a little tiny town, like Westmorland. One street running through it. And I think by the time we got to Poston it was late at night. It was dark, I do remember that. And walking off of that bus, you stepped calf-deep in dust. It was a river bottom. God. Then you went to this one barrack where they did what they called 'intake.' So you had to register there. And then they sent you — this is about ten-thirty at night — they sent you to a barrack, and there were cots, like the army cots. Some were iron, with springs, but not like what they have now. And they gave you bags, and your men folk went to a certain area and stuffed the bags with straw and brought them back, and you slept on the bags of straw.

AG: HOW MANY PEOPLE LIVED IN A BARRACK?

WY: There were six of us.

AG: I SAW PHOTOGRAPHS AT THE MUSEUM. THE BARRACKS WERE LONG WOODEN STRUCTURES.

WY: Yes. But they were divided into apartments A, B, C, and maybe D. We had one apartment. It was one bare room with six cots. It was like an army barrack. It was wood. There was no dry wall. You saw the raw boards and two-by-fours. We used them as shelves; we put our hairbrushes and stuff on them.

AG: WAS THERE A BATHROOM IN THE BARRACK?

WY: No, no. You walked to the bathroom. There was a mess hall in each block. And there was a laundry room, with about half a dozen tubs. And then there was a toilet for girls with maybe a dozen toilet seats. One after another. No stalls. And the showers were maybe half a dozen spouts on the wall.

AG: DID YOU FEEL ANGRY ABOUT BEING THERE?

WY: Well, later. Later. At first you're stunned. You have to take all these kinds of shots. You're stunned. And then you start to think, 'What is happening?' And then there seemed to be no way out, because first of all it's in the middle of the desert. You'd die out there if you tried to escape.

AG: THERE WAS BARBED WIRE IN SOME OF THE PHOTO-GRAPHS I SAW.

WY: Yes.

AG: WERE THERE GUARDS?

WY: In Poston I think the guards lived across the road. When *12-1-A* was produced, this woman came up to me — this white woman, who apparently was a teacher there — and she said, 'There were no guard towers.' Well, I know there was a fence, because they opened it when we went out, and they opened it when we came in. I don't know if it was barbed wire; I don't remember. But I remember that this woman said, 'There was no guard tower.' So I told that to my girlfriend, and she said, 'What does it matter whether there was a guard tower or not in Poston? There were guard towers and mounted guns in other camps. This is a story. This is a play about what we went through, and it's symbolic of what we went through.' So I just decided to forget the teacher.

AG: THE TITLE *12-1-A* REFERS TO THE BLOCK AND BARRACK AND APARTMENT NUMBERS THAT WERE STENCILED IN WHITE ON THE BARRACK DOOR. WAS THERE AN INCIDENT THAT INSPIRED THIS PLAY?

WY: Yes. There was a group called JACL — the Japanese American Citizens League — that advocated that we go quietly. They even advocated tattooing.

AG: WHAT KIND OF TATTOOING?

WY: Numbers. And when we went to camp, the JACL advocated ratting on your uncles, your father, your mother — anybody who might be espousing Japanese values or Japanese victories. They were naturally a much-hated group. I think there were one or two in our camp, and they got beaten up. And I believe two people were incarcerated for the assault. Rumors were going through camp like crazy, of sending them to Tucson and trying them there, and then the whole camp went on strike.

AG: HOW DID YOU STRIKE?

WY: There were firebreaks between the blocks, between the rows of barracks, and everybody occupied the firebreaks and had banners out, and all the block people would assemble there and build a fire and eat there, and then another shift would come in, and that's the way we protested. Eventually it came to be a protest against the camp conditions. I don't know how it was resolved. I think the prisoners were taken to another camp to be tried. And something was resolved about some of the complaints, and then they dissipated. In a way, it was like a picnic to us youngsters.

AG: HOW OLD WERE YOU?

WY: I was seventeen.

AG: THE AGE OF THE GIRL KOKO IN *12-1-A*.

WY: Yes. I know that isn't considered a youngster now, but we were pretty naïve. We didn't know what was going on. Lots of people had good times there, but I was very depressed. So what I tried to do was tell a story about how, even in camp, where all of us were Japanese, there were outcasts. I felt like an outcast. All the characters in the play are outcasts. Expendables of America and outcasts among the inmates.

AG: THIS SEEMS LIKE A MORE COMPLEX PLAY THAN SOME OF YOUR EARLIER ONES.

WY: I wanted to tell a story of what happened to a handful of people in a camp of ten thousand inmates. Although it felt like it, we did not live in a vacuum.

AG: IS THERE A MORAL DILEMMA AT THE CENTER OF THIS PLAY?

WY: The question was, how to reconcile the America that promised freedom and equality to all with the reality of our incarceration.

AG: DID YOU GROW AS A PLAYWRIGHT WITH THIS PLAY?

WY: Yes. I had to get into the hearts of all my characters and try to understand what led to the decisions and the final parting, even when my own decision was quite different.

AG: THERE IS A DIFFERENCE BETWEEN THE LANGUAGE OF YOUR EARLY PLAYS AND THE LANGUAGE IN THE PLAYS YOU HAVE WRITTEN SINCE THE 1980s. YOUR RECENT PLAYS TEND TO HAVE MORE SLANG, FOR ONE THING.

WY: Well, you know, styles of writing change. When we were kids, we never ended a sentence with a preposition. We never started with a *but* or *and*. So that's the way I wrote. At the beginning. Then I realized that it was stilted, and that you don't get the free feeling of somebody talking or trying to pull you into the story. So I started writing more like I speak and I found it liberating.

AG: THERE'S A DECOROUSNESS TO THE LANGUAGE OF *AND THE SOUL SHALL DANCE* AND *THE MUSIC LESSONS*, BUT I WOULDN'T CALL THE LANGUAGE STILTED.

WY: In both plays I tried to write about the lives of Japanese-speaking people, in English, and at the same time use the colloquial language of the Nisei in English.

AG: DO YOU REWRITE AND THROW THINGS OUT?

WY: You have to be merciless. So it takes me forever to write anything, because I put it aside, and then two months go by. 'Well, I better start working.' And I look at it, 'Ah, you have to throw that out, and you have to throw this out.' But I don't throw too much out. Maybe that's my problem. See, I don't change directions either. I hardly change direction once I get started on a play.

AG: WHAT DO YOU MEAN?

WY: I might add something to push the thrust, but I've decided that this is the statement I want to make and I try to make it. To me, first comes the statement.

I studied with an art teacher who said, 'You must make a statement in your painting.' It's the same thing with writing. You have to keep the idea of what you want to say first and foremost and not direct it elsewhere. That's why I'm such a slow writer. I have a friend who goes to McDonald's and has a cup of coffee and watches the people coming and going, and she starts writing her story. I can't do that. Someone tells me a story about something, and I think, 'Gee, that's interesting. Why? Why did it end up this way?' I try to keep the movement going and I try not to go off my direction too far.

AG: WHAT INSPIRED *TAJ MAJAL*?

WY: I wrote a short play, a one-act, and I had a white guy there, riding the rails. And I thought, 'Let me just see what would happen if he was a man in his fifties in the 1930s, and he's talking about his life and was it a waste, was it for naught.' I had a guy who said he'd like to direct it, and he said, 'Can't you make it a two-act?' And I said, 'Oh, I guess I can,' and I wrote it as a two-act. And of course he's an Asian director, so I had to put an Asian in there. So I decided to make the guy with whom the hobo talks Japanese. And then the director said, 'I have this black friend who's a good actor, why don't you make the first character into a black man?' And I said, 'Well, I have to change the whole dynamic, because a black man riding the rails, that's not too common — but they were there — and I have to include the prejudice he's been through and still goes through in the 1930s.' Now I can't get it produced.

AG: WHAT HAPPENED WITH THE DIRECTOR?

WY: We had a reading. But I can't get anybody to produce it.

AG: WHY DO YOU THINK THAT IS?

WY: I think the real reason is that producers think it's a racist play. I don't think it's a racist play. Do you?

AG: NO. IT'S *ABOUT* RACISM.

WY: And it's about lonely people. This particular black man is going to end his life without a friend, with his stories locked inside him, and he tries to make friends with the young Japanese guy, who is racist.

AG: HISTORICALLY, WHAT HAS THE JAPANESE ATTITUDE BEEN TOWARD BLACK PEOPLE??

WY: They are very racist. Japanese people are rather racist, because they come from an old island, all Japanese, and they've been taught, as most nationalists, that there's nobody better than the Japanese.

AG: AND THE BLACK MAN IN THE PLAY IS AN AMERICAN CITIZEN, BUT THE JAPANESE . . .

WY: The Japanese couldn't be a citizen at that time, no.

AG: THERE ARE SEVERAL IRONIES IN THE PLAY, ONE OF WHICH IS THAT THE AFRICAN AMERICAN, DESPITE BEING AN AMERICAN CITIZEN, WANDERS ABOUT THE COUNTRY, HOMELESS. ONLY THEN CAN HE BE FREE.

WY: And not put up with the things, the bigotry, that he'd usually have to put up with.

AG: THE CHINESE OWNER OF THE HOT DOG STAND GIVES THE JAPANESE FIFTY DOLLARS, TO COME WORK FOR HIM. IS THAT UNUSUAL, CHINESE HELPING JAPANESE?

WY: That is unusual. Because the Chinese as a rule just hate Japanese. Koreans hate Japanese even more, because they are suppressed by the Japanese in Japan. The Japanese think they're better than anybody. And the Chinese think they're better than everybody. The Chinese call their country the middle country, because they think everything started there.

AG: WHAT ARE YOU SAYING THROUGH THAT GESTURE OF THE CHINESE IMMIGRANT HELPING THE JAPANESE IMMIGRANT?

WY: In those days racism in America was rampant; even traditional enemies like the Chinese and Japanese trusted each other more than other races. I guess I'm saying that in the face of a larger enemy, we choose to stand together.

AG: IS THE AFRICAN-AMERICAN HOBO AN IMMIGRANT TOO?

WY: Actually, no. But in a sense he is, because he left his family, the mines, and sticky situations to avoid certain social stresses.

AG: WHAT IS THIS PLAY'S STATEMENT?

WY: There are moments in our lives that, in the scheme of things, last only an instant. Then they are gone and can never be relived, retrieved, or changed.

AG: HAVE YOU MADE A LIVING WRITING PLAYS?

WY: No. And I never made a living writing stories. I still don't. I bless Roosevelt every day for his Social Security. Every once in a while I have a windfall, but you can't live on a small windfall now and then. I think that maybe my style of writing is passé.

AG: IN WHAT WAY?

WY: Well, it's not what people do now. On television, you can hardly keep up with the commercials even. They go pop, pop, pop. And I don't write like that. I want people to stay still a while and feel and think.

It's not just a matter of how you write, you have to keep the theater alive and do things that please people, so that they come flocking to your play. And I don't think I'm that kind of a writer. This is what I would say: I don't have that many years left. I don't have that much time, and what is the money going to do for me? Nothing. It won't change my health. It won't change my life. I've got to produce things that I'm going to be proud of. So I write my own stories in my own way and hope for the best. That's all I can expect from myself. ▽

Appendix: Published Plays

Editor's Note: The following is a selected list of the most recent
or most available published plays.

ALVAREZ, LYNNE

Analiese. In *Women Playwrights: The Best Plays of 1997.* Lyme, New
Hampshire: Smith and Kraus, 1998.

Lynne Alvarez: Collected Plays Volume I. Lyme, New Hampshire:
Smith and Kraus, 1998.

CLEAGE, PEARL

Blues for an Alabama Sky. New York: Dramatists Play Service, 1999.

Chain. In *Playwriting Women: 7 Plays from the Women's Project.*
Portsmouth, New Hampshire: Heinemann, 1993.

Flyin' West and Other Plays. New York: Theatre Communications
Group, 1999.

Late Bus to Mecca. In *Playwriting Women: 7 Plays from the Women's
Project.* Portsmouth, New Hampshire: Heinemann, 1993.

CONGDON, CONSTANCE

Dog Opera. New York: Samuel French, 2001.

Lips. New York: Broadway Play Publishing, 2000.

Tales of the Lost Formicans and Other Plays. New York: Theatre
Communications Group, 1994.

CORTHRON, KIA

Cage Rhythm. In *Moonmarked and Touched by Sun: Plays by
African-American Women.* New York: Theatre Communications
Group, 1994.

Come Down Burning. In *Contemporary Plays by Women of Color.*
London and New York: Routledge, 1996.

CRUZ, MIGDALIA

Dreams of Home. In *The Best American Short Plays* 1991–1992. New
York: Applause Theatre Book Publishers, 1992.

Frida. In *Here to Stay: Five Plays from the Women's Project.* New
York: Applause Theatre Book Publishers, 1998.

Fur. In *Out on the Fringe.* New York: Theatre Communications
Group, 1999.

The Have-Little. In *Contemporary Plays by Women of Color.* London
and New York: Routledge, 1996.

Miriam's Flowers. In *Shattering the Myth: Plays by Hispanic Women*. Houston: Arte Público Press, 1992.
Telling Tales. In *Telling Tales: New One-Act Plays*. New York: Penguin Books, 1993.

EGLOFF, ELIZABETH

The Devils. New York: Dramatists Play Service, 1999.
Phaedra and Hippolytus. In *Theater*, Spring 1989.
The Swan. New York: Dramatists Play Service, 1994.

ENSLER, EVE

Floating Rhoda and the Glue Man. In *Women Playwrights: The Best Plays of 1993*. Newbury, Vermont: Smith and Kraus, 1993.
Necessary Targets: A Story of Women and War. New York: Random House, 2001.
The Vagina Monologues. New York: Dramatists Play Service, 2000.

THE FIVE LESBIAN BROTHERS

The Five Lesbian Brothers: Four Plays. New York: Theatre Communications Group, 1999.

HENLEY, BETH

Am I Blue. New York: Dramatists Play Service, 1995.
Beth Henley: Collected Plays Volume I. Lyme, New Hampshire: Smith and Kraus, 2000.
Beth Henley: Collected Plays Volume II. Lyme, New Hampshire, Smith and Kraus, 2000.

HOWE, TINA

Appearances. In *Plays for Actresses*. New York: Vintage Books, 1997.
Approaching Zanzibar and Other Plays. New York: Theatre Communications Group, 1995.
Coastal Disturbances: Four Plays by Tina Howe. New York: Theatre Communications Group, 1989.
Pride's Crossing. New York: Theatre Communications Group, 1998.

KESSELMAN, WENDY

Becca. New Orleans: Anchorage Press, 1988.
The Diary of Anne Frank. New York: Dramatists Play Service, 2000.
I Love You, I Love You Not. New York: Samuel French, 1988.
The Juniper Tree, A Tragic Household Tale. New York: Samuel French, 2001.
Maggie Magalita. New York: Samuel French, 1987.
My Sister in This House. New York: Samuel French, 1988.

MANN, EMILY
The Cherry Orchard (Mann, Trans.). New York: Dramatists Play Service, 2001.
Having Our Say. New York: Dramatists Play Service, 1996.
The House of Bernarda Alba (Mann, Trans.). New York: Dramatists Play Service, 1999.
Testimonies: Four Plays by Emily Mann. New York: Theatre Communications Group, 1997.

MORAGA, CHERRÍE
Heroes and Saints and Other Plays. New York: West End Press, 1994.
The Hungry Woman: A Mexican Medea and Heart of the Earth: A Popul Vuh Story. New York: West End Press, 2001.
Shadow of a Man. In *Shattering the Myth: Plays by Hispanic Women.* Houston: Arte Público Press, 1992.

NOTTAGE, LYNN
Crumbs from the Table of Joy. New York: Dramatists Play Service, 1998.
Ida Mae Cole Takes a Stance. In *A. . . My Name Is Still Alice.* New York: Samuel French, 1993.
Mud, River, Stone. New York: Dramatists Play Service, 1999.
Poof! In *Plays for Actresses.* New York: Vintage Books, 1997.

REBECK, THERESA
Theresa Rebeck: Collected Plays Volume I. Lyme, New Hampshire: Smith and Kraus, 1999.

RIVERA, CARMEN
Julia. In *Nuestro New York: An Anthology of Puerto Rican Plays.* New York: Dutton Signet, 1994.

SON, DIANA
R.A.W. ('Cause I'm a Woman). In *Contemporary Plays by Women of Color.* London and New York: Routledge, 1996.
Stop Kiss. New York: Dramatists Play Service, 2000.

VOGEL, PAULA
The Baltimore Waltz and Other Plays. New York: Theatre Communications Group, 1996.
Hot 'n' Throbbing. New York: Dramatists Play Service, 2000.
The Mammary Plays. New York: Theatre Communications Group, 1998.

WALLACE, NAOMI

The Girl Who Fell Through a Hole in Her Jumper (Wallace and Bruce McCleod). In *Young Blood: Five Plays for Young Performers*. New York: Theatre Communications Group, 1999.

In the Heart of America and Other Plays. New York: Theatre Communications Group, 2000.

One Flea Spare. New York: Broadway Play Publishing, 1997.

Plays by Naomi Wallace. New York: Broadway Play Publishing, 1997.

The Trestle at Pope Lick Creek. New York: Broadway Play Publishing, 2000.

WEST, CHERYL

Before It Hits Home. New York: Dramatists Play Service, 1999.

Jar the Floor. In *Women Playwrights: The Best Plays of 1992*. Lyme, New Hampshire: Smith and Kraus, 1992.

WONG, ELIZABETH

China Doll (One-Act). In *Contemporary Plays by Women of Color*. London and New York: Routledge, 1996.

Kimchee and Chitlins: A Serious Comedy About Getting Along. Woodstock, Illinois: The Dramatic Publishing Company, 1996.

Let the Big Dog Eat. In *Humana Festival '98: The Complete Plays*. Lyme, New Hampshire: Smith and Kraus, 1998.

Letters to a Student Revolutionary. Woodstock, Illinois: The Dramatic Publishing Company, 1996.

YAMAUCHI, WAKAKO

And the Soul Shall Dance. In *Between Worlds: Contemporary Asian-American Plays*. New York: Theatre Communications Group, 1990.

The Chairman's Wife. In *The Politics of Life: Four Plays by Asian American Women Playwrights*. Philadelphia: Temple University Press, 1993.

The Music Lessons. In *Unbroken Thread: An Anthology of Plays by Asian American Women*. Amherst: The University of Massachusetts Press, 1993.

Songs My Mother Taught Me: Stories, Plays and Memoir. New York: Feminist Press at City University of New York, 1994.

12-1-A. In *The Politics of Life: Four Plays by Asian American Women Playwrights*. Philadelphia: Temple University Press, 1993.

Photo Credits

Lynne Alvarez, courtesy of the playwright
Pearl Cleage by Barry Forbus
Constance Congdon, courtesy of the playwright
Kia Corthron by Gabriel Schkolnick
Migdalia Cruz by Diana Solis
Elizabeth Egloff by James Youmans
Eve Ensler by Susan Johann
The Five Lesbian Brothers by C.T. Wemple
Beth Henley, courtesy of the playwright
Tina Howe by Cori Wells Brown
Jake-ann Jones by Brad Calcaterra
Wendy Kesselman by Marbeth
Emily Mann by Joan Marcus
Cherríe Moraga by Hulleah Tsinhnahjinnie ©2000
Lynn Nottage by Tony Gerber
Theresa Rebeck by Eileen O'Meara
Carmen Rivera by Felix Arocho
Diana Son by Julie Myatt
Paula Vogel by Carol Rosegg
Naomi Wallace by Bruce McLeod
Cheryl West by Joan Marcus
Elizabeth Wong by Ruth Wong
Wakako Yamauchi, courtesy of the playwright

Alexis Greene is a theater critic, dramaturg, and teacher. Her criticism and articles have appeared in publications such as *American Theatre, The Village Voice, The New York Times, TheaterWeek, The Star-Ledger,* and *The Journal of Dramatic Theory and Criticism.* She is co-founder of Literary Managers and Dramaturgs of the Americas and has taught theater at Hunter College, Vassar College, and New York University. She collaborated with Julie Taymor on the book *The Lion King: Pride Rock on Broadway* and is the author of a biography of Lucille Lortel.